Praise for the Second Edition

"Every clinical social worker, nurse specialist, and physician should read this book. A landmark achievement—this is the first comprehensive book to examine domestic violence from a multicultural perspective. This brilliantly written and all-inclusive resource provides new clinical knowledge and practice wisdom to alleviate the emotional pain and trauma of battered women and their children. I have been searching for a book like this for years, especially when I was consultant to the U.S. Army Surgeon General."

—**Jesse J. Harris**, PhD, BCD, ACSW
Professor and Dean
School of Social Work
University of Maryland
Colonel Retired

"This volume provides the step-by-step answers and solutions on how to detect, assess, and treat battered women in trauma, acute crisis, and emergency situations. Professor Roberts's timely volume provides concrete solutions and a nonjudgmental approach to a major societal and public health problem. If you are planning to purchase only one book on interpersonal violence this year, this is the essential book to purchase."

—**Karil S. Klingbeil**, MSW, ACSW
Director, Department of Social Work
Harborview Medical Center, Clinical Associate Professor
University of Washington, School of Social Work

"As the former Chair of the National Research Council's Panel of Research on Violence Against Women, I applaud this second edition . . . . It includes valuable adult abuse protocols, treatment models, and techniques on how to intervene effectively with women and children in violent homes. . . . I am particularly impressed with the breadth and depth of the topics covered ranging from emergency department triage teams to primary care settings, to group therapy, to shelter for abused women and their at-risk children. This is the first book of major importance that emphasizes the growing alliance between clinical nurse specialists and clinical social workers. . . . This volume is extremely well written, insightful, and thoroughly up-to-date—a must read for all clinicians."

—From the Foreword by
Ann W. Burgess, RN, CS, DNSc, FAAN
van Ameringen Professor of Psychiatric–Mental Health Nursing
University of Pennsylvania
School of Nursing

Springer Series on Family Violence

Albert R. Roberts, PhD, Series Editor

Albert R. Roberts, DSW, PhD, BCETS, DACFE, is a Professor of Criminal Justice and Social Work, Faculty of Arts and Sciences, Livingston College Campus, Rutgers—the State University of New Jersey, New Brunswick and Piscataway, NJ.

Dr. Roberts has over 30 years of full-time university teaching experience at the undergraduate and graduate levels in both criminal justice and social work, and 18 years' administrative experience as department chairperson, program director, project director, and director of social work field placements. (He has been a tenured professor at Rutgers since 1989.) Dr. Roberts has over 225 publications to his credit, including 33 books and numerous peer-reviewed journal articles and book chapters. During the 1970s and 1980s, he taught at Indiana University School of Social Work, Seton Hall University, Brooklyn College of CUNY, the University of New Haven, and Coppin State College. He is a Diplomate with the American College of Forensic Examiners, and has been certified as an expert witness by the Illinois State Courts in Chicago. Dr. Roberts received a DSW in 1978; PhD in 1981 from the School of Social Work and Community Planning at the University of Maryland in Baltimore. He is the founding Editor-in-Chief of two peer-reviewed scholarly journals, the *Brief Treatment and Crisis Intervention* journal, as well as *Victims and Offenders: Journal of Evidence-Based Policies and Practices.* He currently serves on the editorial boards of 10 scholarly journals. Dr. Roberts is also the founder of the Crisis Intervention Network Web site (2001–present).

Dr. Roberts is the Series Editor for the Springer Social Work Series (1980 to present) as well as the Family Violence Series (1998–present). In 2002, Dr. Roberts was the recipient of The Richard W. Laity Academic Leadership Award of the Rutgers Council of AAUP (American Association of University Professors) chapters. In addition, Dr. Roberts was the recipient of the Teaching Excellence Award by Sigma Alpha Kappa chapter of the National Criminal Justice Honor Society in both 1997 and 1998. He is a charter member of the Gamma Epsilon chapter of Alpha Delta Mu National Social Work Honor Society at Indiana University (1985–present). He is a member of The Board of Scientific and Professional Advisors, a Diplomate in forensic traumatology as well as domestic violence, and a Board Certified Expert in Traumatic Stress for The American Academy of Experts in Traumatic Stress (AAETS). He serves as a member of the editorial advisory board for *Encyclopedia Americana* (2002–present).

Dr. Roberts can be reached at: *prof.albertroberts@comcast.net.*

Battered Women and Their Families

3rd Edition

Intervention Strategies and Treatment Programs

Albert R. Roberts, PhD
Editor

Barbara W. White, PhD
Foreword

SPRINGER PUBLISHING COMPANY

New York

Springer Publishing Company, LLC
11 West 42nd Street
New York, NY 10036
www.springerpub.com

Acquisitions Editor: Philip Laughlin
Production Editor: Shana Meyer
Cover design: Mimi Flow
Composition: Techbooks

07 08 09 10/5 4 3 2 1

ISBN: 978-0-8261-4592-5

Library of Congress Cataloging-in-Publication Data

Battered women and their families: intervention strategies and treatment programs/
[edited by] Albert R. Roberts. —3rd ed.
    p. cm.—(Springer series on family violence; v. 12)
   Includes bibliographical references and index.
   ISBN 0-8261-4592-2 (hardback)
1. Abused wives—Services for—United States. 2. Family violence—United States.
3. Social work with women—United States. I. Roberts, Albert R.

HV699.B37 2007
362.82'920973—dc22

2006034189

Printed in the United States of America by Bang Printing.

THIS 3RD EDITION IS DEDICATED TO ALL SURVIVORS AND THEIR FAMILIES, DOMESTIC VIOLENCE ADVOCATES AND CLINICIANS SPECIALIZING IN DOMESTIC VIOLENCE INTERVENTION.

This book is dedicated in loving memory to my parents, Harry and Evelyn, whose love, faith, unconditional acceptance, and family values instilled in me the fervent belief that all women and children should be cherished and treated with compassion. Since my adolescence I have been *inspired* by my mother's quiet fighting spirit, resilience, and altruistic nature as she survived 17 years after having been diagnosed with breast cancer. This is my 34th book; it could not have been completed without the compassion and perseverance my parents instilled in me.

To Beverly, my wife of 35 years, whose love, altruism, and intellectual stimulation provide me with balance and focus.

This book is also dedicated to the many nurses, social workers, and counselors who provide essential health care, social services, and clinical intervention to battered women and their vulnerable children. The lives of thousands of chronically battered women in life-threatening situations are saved each year, because of the commitment of these nurses and social workers.

Contents

Foreword

I am honored that I was invited to write the Foreword to the third edition of *Battered Women and Their Families*. As an educator with nearly 30 years experience and as the long-standing dean of the School of Social Work at the University of Texas at Austin, I am in a good position to recognize a classic textbook on family violence. My university and faculty members have received national acclaim for their leadership in the domestic violence field; the first National Domestic Violence Hotline was established in consult with the University of Texas at Austin in 1996 (this was a collaboration between the Texas Council on Family Violence and our School of Social Work, with an initial $1 million grant from the U.S. Dept. of Health and Human Services).*

Dr. Roberts has thoroughly revised and updated the third edition of *Battered Women and Their Families,* and the result is a comprehensive new work that retains revisions of the best chapters from the second edition while incorporating 12 new chapters. More than 60% of this edition contains new and valuable material.

This important book provides an exceptionally well-written, up-to-date, and informative text that will rapidly become indispensable to all social work and counseling students as well as to clinicians committed to helping battered women and their children. This volume explores the vital role of social workers, crisis counselors, nurses, and domestic violence advocates in promoting safety, survival skills, recovery, and social functioning to battered women and their children. It provides in-depth and up-to-date coverage of the frontiers, policy changes, innovative programs, treatment

---

*In the spring of 2006, Senator Joseph Biden Jr. (sponsor of the Violence Against Women Act) proudly announced that after 10 years in operation, the 24-hour National Domestic Violence Hotline had received 1.5 million calls for help.

modalities, and evidence-based practices related to battered women and their children.

Among social workers, nurses, public health officials, and physicians, there is increasing recognition of the prevalence of woman battering. A substantial proportion of women across social strata experience intimate partner abuse and violence. The lifetime prevalence of abuse against women is estimated at a shocking rate of one in every four women. Fortunately, during the past 3 decades, a continuum of individual, group, and family services for battered women has become a major priority among federal and state governmental agencies as well as nonprofit social service agencies. Over the years, we have learned that woman battering is a harmful and life-threatening social problem in all age groups, all races, all religions, and all socioeconomic groups.

- We have learned that some women are battered for a short time and are able to end the relationship before the violence escalates in frequency and intensity. Some women are battered intermittently for several years, and some women are chronically battered for many years.
- We have learned that most battered women are intelligent, articulate, and hardworking but are stuck with or addicted to (or both) hostile and abusive intimate partners.
- We have learned from clinical research that 25% to 60% of battered women meet the diagnostic criteria for depression, acute stress disorder, substance abuse, panic disorder, generalized anxiety disorder, posttraumatic stress disorder, or a comorbid combination of these disorders.
- We have learned that the children of battered women suffer acute crisis episodes and trauma but can be helped by play therapists, child and adolescent clinicians, and trauma-focused therapists.
- We have learned that problem solving, motivational interviewing, cognitive–behavioral, and crisis intervention counseling can facilitate crisis stabilization as well as recovery.
- We have learned that these entrapped women *can* permanently leave the batterer and recover from mental health and medical disorders with help from experienced clinicians.

These and many other challenges, problems, intervention strategies, assessment and treatment methods, and empowerment approaches are documented in this book by one of the most brilliant clinical researchers in North America today—Dr. Albert R. Roberts—together with the highly experienced chapter authors.

This book will help readers learn about the most effective policies, programs, and intervention strategies for helping battered women and their families escape an abusive relationship and improve their quality of life. This book provides the knowledge base, assessment and treatment guidelines, and evidence-based clinical protocols that are critically needed by every clinician and advocate working in the domestic violence field. Sadly, there are still many women who remain trapped in violent relationships, and for numerous reasons they are unable to seek help. Therefore, we must continue the necessary education and outreach—to both boys and girls, both men and women, beginning in childhood—to underscore the most basic principle that all forms of violence in personal relationships are prohibited. *This is the most practical, evidence-based, inspirational, and well-written book on family violence that I have read in the past 10 years. Every social worker, counselor, nurse, and domestic violence advocate should read this book.*

Barbara W. White
Dean and Centennial Professor in Leadership
School of Social Work
University of Texas at Austin
Former President, Council on Social Work Education
(CSWE), and
Former President, National Association of Social
Workers (NASW)

Preface

Intimate partner violence, also known as family violence, domestic violence, dating violence, and spouse abuse, is all too pervasive around the world. In fact, domestic violence continues to be one of the most life-threatening and traumatic family and public health problems in all societies. Recent estimates have indicated that a woman is battered by a current or former intimate partner every 9 seconds. Intimate partner violence has no geographic boundaries and is prevalent among all age groups, races, sex, and socioeconomic groups.

In November 2005, the World Health Organization in Geneva, Switzerland, completed the largest international study ever on domestic violence in 10 countries, including Bangladesh, Brazil, Ethiopia, Japan, Peru, Namibia, and Thailand. Approximately 24,000 participants were interviewed by phone, and the findings clearly indicate the huge number of domestic violence incidents and related injuries—especially head, neck, and face injuries and miscarriages—that occur as a direct result of woman-battering incidents. Also noted was the lack of routine domestic violence screening in hospital emergency rooms, maternity units, medical-surgery units, and trauma centers. These women need help from skilled professionals who understand the emotional and physical impact of battering and who can implement effective crisis assessment and time-limited intervention on a 24–7 basis through well-coordinated social service and medical delivery systems.

During the 9 years since the second edition of this book was written, significant changes have taken place. As a result, I have recruited 12 new chapters and thorough revisions of the other chapters. The most important changes at both the federal and state levels have been the enactment of specific legislation responsive to the legal, social service, and mental health needs of battered women, including vulnerable immigrant women. Legislation without a major appropriation of funds attached to it is usually doomed to fail. In sharp contrast, the federal Violence Against Women Act has provided the necessary funding to state and local domestic violence coalitions for such critically important services as training domestic violence advocates, police, and court staff, expanding emergency shelters for battered women, crisis intervention hotlines, clinical and mental health interventions for battered women, legal advocacy programs, transitional housing services, specialized technologically advanced domestic violence courts, electronic pendants and other security devices to aid battered women, and digital cameras for police and emergency room staff to document the extent of injuries.

In this book, my author team—28 nurses, social workers, and criminologists and I—has documented the latest trends, intervention strategies, and treatment programs for battered women and their children. We focus on the following:

- The various levels of woman battering and methods of permanently ending the battering relationship
- Lethality assessment, safety plans, and Roberts's Seven-Stage Crisis Intervention Model
- The national survey of the structure and functions of 107 shelters for battered women and their children
- The stress–crisis–trauma continuum with battered women
- Applying the stages of change model and motivational interviewing techniques
- Strengths perspective and solution-focused therapy
- Cognitive problem-solving treatment
- Trauma and crisis recovery for children in shelters
- Battered women in imminent danger and ecologically based crisis intervention
- The strengths as well as the dangers of conjoint couples therapy
- Emerging roles for the emergency room social worker and nurse in the United Kingdom and the United States
- Health care issues, policies, and treatment programs for battered women
- Overcoming the challenges of poverty combined with domestic violence

- Same-sex domestic violence myths, facts, correlates, and treatment strategies
- Global issues in elder abuse and mistreatment
- Substance abuse and domestic violence
- Use of the culturagram in understanding immigrant women affected by domestic violence
- Assessment, treatment, and empowerment strategies with Chinese and Latino battered women
- Legal advocacy and court-based justice centers

The primary emphasis of this book is on the nuclear family, and the violence found behind closed doors within that unit. This is a handbook about family violence from the perspective of intergenerational linkages—including traumatized and often abused children of battered women, adolescent abuse, woman battering, the intersection of child abuse and spouse abuse, and elder abuse. It also focuses on cross-cultural issues, patterns, and intervention programs with family violence. Unlike most books on domestic violence, this volume provides step-by-step guidelines and practical applications of crisis intervention and other time-limited treatment approaches with battered women and their children. Because we are in the 21st century with managed care cost cutting and major health insurance restrictions looming over our clients and patients, the time-limited clinical strategies and programs examined in this book are of paramount importance.

In 1994, President Bill Clinton signed the landmark Violence Against Women Act (VAWA I) into law. This resulted in the establishment of the first federal Violence Against Women office in Washington, D.C.; funding of major grant programs (e.g., STOP—Services, Training, Officers, and Prosecutors grants); and coordination of state and local services to battered women and their children throughout the United States. President Clinton stated that:

Domestic violence—the enemy from within—is a national tragedy that calls all of us to action. . . . Our homes should be places of solace and comfort, not violence and pain. The only place worse than being attacked in your own home is feeling trapped with nowhere to turn for help. That is why in February of 1996 we launched a 24-hour, seven day a week, toll-free hotline which is helping direct women to get the help they need, including counseling, shelters, and law enforcement.

President George W. Bush is also highly committed to reducing domestic violence, and by January 2006, he had signed the Violence Against Women Act III and increased the five-year appropriation to $3.9 billion for fiscal years 2005–2010. With VAWA III, the U.S. Congress has developed a single set of definitions and conditions for all grantees. Thus, most programs will now be required to serve "adult and youth victims" of domestic violence, date abuse, sexual assault, and stalking. The third iteration of VAWA creates new prevention and intervention programs for child witnesses of domestic violence; funding to conduct outreach and education programs to youths focusing on dating violence and stalking; funding to the nonabusing parent or caretaker in domestic violence homes; funding to facilitate cross-training and collaboration between the child welfare and domestic violence systems; changes in immigration law to protect battered immigrants' children from threats of deportation relating to abuse; hiring victim assistants by law enforcement agencies to ensure adequate triage of cases, especially for persons battered by partners who are law enforcement officers; improving housing opportunities for battered women and their children and providing culturally appropriate resources for battered Native American women from tribal nations; amending substantive laws to child custody, visitation, and support; and engaging men and youth in community-based domestic violence prevention programs.

As mentioned in the previous two editions of this book, most other books on family and domestic violence examine the plight of the battered woman as an entity separate from her family. The overriding purpose of this book is to focus on the need for therapeutic intervention for all members of the violent family. The wide range of social service delivery issues, treatment techniques, court-based interventions, and research findings discussed in this book go beyond monolithic approaches to understanding woman battering. Throughout this book, case illustrations, assessment protocols, programmatic issues, and effective intervention strategies are presented.

Albert R. Roberts

Contributors

Patrick Au, DIP, PSW, CQSW
Executive Director
Family Services
Toronto, Canada

Kimberly Bender, MSW
Doctoral Candidate and
  Instructor
School of Social Work
University of Texas at Austin
Austin, Texas

Mary E. Boes, PhD
Associate Professor
Department of Social Work
University of Northern Iowa
Cedar Falls, Iowa

Patricia Brownell, PhD
Associate Professor
Graduate School of Social
  Services
Fordham University at
  Lincoln Center
New York, NY
Former Director, Women's
  Division of the Human
  Resources Administration
  (HRA), New York, NY

Ann Wolbert Burgess, RN, CS,
  DNSc, FAAN
Professor of Psychiatric–Mental
  Health Nursing
Connell School of Nursing
Boston College
Boston, MA
Co-Chair, Committee on
  Research on Violence Against
  Women, Institute of
  Medicine (IOM) of the
  National Academy of
  Sciences

Sondra Burman, PhD
Associate Professor
School of Social Work
University of Oklahoma
Oklahoma City, OK

Elaine P. Congress, PhD, DSW
Professor and Associate Dean
Graduate School of Social
  Services
Fordham University at
  Lincoln Center
New York, NY

Diana Valle Ferrer, PhD, LCSW
Professor
Graduate School of Social Work
University of Puerto Rico
San Juan, PR

Colleen Friend, PhD
Assistant Professor
School of Social Work
UCLA
Los Angeles, CA

Mary Jo Garcia Biggs, PhD
Assistant Professor
School of Social Work
University of Central Florida
Orlando, FL

Janet A. Geller, EdD, LCSW
Clinical Social Worker in Private
    Practice
New York, NY

Diane L. Green, PhD
Associate Professor
Department of Social Work
Florida Atlantic University
Boca Raton, FL

Nicky Ali Jackson, PhD
Associate Professor of Criminal
    Justice
Purdue University at Calumet
Calumet, IN
Editor-in-Chief, *Encyclopedia
    of Domestic Violence*

June Keeling, RGN, RM
Nurse Midwife
England

Karen S. Knox, PhD
Associate Professor and Director
    of Field Placements
School of Social Work
Texas State University
San Marcos, TX

Shirley Lebovics, LCSW
Lecturer
School of Social Work
University of California
Private Practice
Beverly Hills, CA

Mo-Yee Lee, PhD
Professor
College of Social Work
Ohio State University
Columbus, OH
Honorary Professor
Department of Social Work and
Social Administration
Research Fellow
Center on Behavioral Health
University of Hong Kong, China

Peter Lehmann, PhD
Associate Professor
School of Social Work
University of Texas at Arlington
Arlington, TX

Cynthia Wilcox Lischick, PhD,
    DVS
Director of Training
New Jersey Coalition for
    Battered Women
Hamilton Square, NJ

Leone Murphy, RN, MS
Nurse Practitioner
Ambulatory Care Center
ARC of Monmouth County
Tinton Falls, NJ

Maura O'Keefe, PhD
Professor
School of Social Work
University of California
Los Angeles, CA

Nancy J. Razza, PhD
Clinical Psychologist
Ambulatory Care Center
ARC of Monmouth County
Tinton Falls, NJ

Gina Robertiello, PhD
Associate Professor and
    Director,
Criminal Justice Program
Department of Sociology &
    Criminology
Felician College
Lodi, NJ

Albert R. Roberts, PhD
Professor of Criminal Justice
Faculty of Arts and Sciences
Rutgers—the State University of
    New Jersey
New Brunswick and
    Piscataway, NJ
Editor-in-Chief, *Victims and
    Offenders Journal*
Editor-in-Chief, *Brief Treatment
    and Crisis Intervention*

Aron Shlonsky, PhD
Associate Professor and Director
Bell-Canada Child Welfare
    Research Center
School of Social Work
University of Toronto
Toronto, Canada

Emily Spence, PhD
Assistant Professor
School of Social Work
University of Texas at Arlington
Arlington, TX

Pamela V. Valentine, PhD
School of Social Work
Florida State University
Tallahassee, FL

Katherine S. van Wormer, PhD,
MSSW
Professor of Social Work
University of Northern Iowa
Cedar Falls, IA

Mary W. Viani, MSW
Research Associate
Department of Social Work
Florida Atlantic University
Boca Raton, FL

Acknowledgments

First and foremost I am grateful to all of the members of my esteemed author team, leaders in the field of domestic violence, for writing original chapters and meeting all deadlines in a timely fashion. The clarity of many of the chapters greatly benefited from the discussions I had with my intellectually gifted colleagues—Professors Ann Burgess, Pat Brownell, Sondra Burman, Bonnie Carlson, Diane Green, Lennox Hinds, Karen Knox, Peter Lehmann, Mo-Yee Lee, Cynthia Lischick, Murray Straus, Diane Valle, Katherine van Wormer, and Mieko Yoshihama.

Special thanks to Springer Publishing Company's CEO, Ted Nardin, and Senior Editor Phil Laughlin who strongly encouraged me to compile, edit, and thoroughly update this third edition. I also appreciate my production editor at TechBooks, Shana Meyer, for meeting the difficult challenge of keeping this book of multiple authors on schedule. My heartfelt appreciation goes to Beverly Jean Roberts, my wife, for being a critical and useful sounding board on the four chapters I authored or coauthored. I am forever indebted to Imogene, a former battered woman and social work student from Brooklyn, New York, who openly shared her painful battering history with me in 1979. Her experiences with police and social service staff inspired my early national research on shelters for battered women and the effectiveness of crisis intervention. My honor students in victimology and domestic violence whom I have taught every fall semester for the past 16 years at Rutgers University have provided a stimulating learning environment and the types of questions that broaden our insights. My thanks and deepest appreciation to all of you.

The National Coalition Against Domestic Violence (NCADV) is to be congratulated for their nationwide efforts to educate legislators and the general public about the critical survival and safety needs of battered women and their children. In addition, NCADV provides free two-page fact sheets on its Web site focusing on domestic violence issues and topics related to violence against women such as Human Trafficking Facts, Economic Abuse Facts, or Elder Abuse Facts. For further information on state and local domestic violence hotlines and services, contact the National Domestic Violence Hotline: (800) 799-SAFE (7233).

The Family Violence Department of the National Council of Juvenile and Family Court Judges Association is also to be congratulated for their important annual publications, which are extremely helpful to legislators, magistrates, attorneys, legal advocates, domestic violence advocates, and educators. For example, each year I have received a monograph titled *Family Violence Legislative Update*. These useful monographs are made possible through funding from the U.S. Department of Health and Human Services and the Conrad N. Hilton Foundation. Volume 11 was completed in the summer of 2006 and provides a state-by-state update of family violence-related statutes, including new additions, deletions, and amended statutes.

Overview, Stages of Change, Crisis Intervention, and Time-Limited Treatment

CHAPTER 1

Overview and New Directions for Intervening on Behalf of Battered Women

Albert R. Roberts

This chapter begins with a discussion of the experiences and dilemmas battered women encounter; the scope of this prevalent social and public health problem; the barriers to seeking help; the myths and realities about battering; medical, criminal justice, and human costs; and the 23 warning signs of a batterer. Then the key findings are provided of a study of 501 battered women, which led to a continuum of the five levels of woman battering. The concluding portions of this chapter focus on practice implications and applying each stage of Roberts's Seven-Stage Crisis Intervention Model (R-SSCIM).

Every 9 seconds a woman is battered by her current or former intimate partner somewhere in the United States. Each year, it is estimated that 8.7 million women are physically abused by a male partner, and about 2 million of these women are victims of severe violence (Roberts & Roberts, 2005). Social workers, nurses, and counselors must make assessments and treatment plans to help women to permanently leave the battering relationships. The overriding goal of all domestic violence advocates and clinicians is to reduce and stop the pain and suffering, severe and permanent injuries, as well as domestic violence-related homicides.

Domestic violence is a global public health and criminal justice problem that has enormous consequences for the health and well-being of millions of women and children throughout the world. On November 24, 2005, the World Health Organization (WHO) in Geneva, Switzerland, published the key findings of the largest international study of domestic violence ever completed. The study findings are based on interviews with over 24,000 women residing in urban and rural areas in 10 countries, including Brazil, Ethiopia, Japan, Peru, Samoa, Serbia, and Thailand. The study indicated that women are at a much greater risk from violence in their homes than on the street. One-quarter to one-half of all female victims of physical assault by their husbands and partners stated that they had sustained physical injuries as a result of the battering. More than 20% of the women who reported physical violence in this study said they had never told anyone about the abuse prior to the interview. Despite serious medical consequences of domestic violence, a very small percentage ever sought help from health care providers or the police. Instead, those who sought help only reached out to neighbors and extended family members. Also, significant was the finding in most countries studied that 4% to 12% of the pregnant women interviewed in the random sample said that they were beaten during pregnancy by the unborn child's father. One-half of them reported they had been punched or kicked in the abdomen. The conclusions of this landmark study are that domestic violence by husbands and other intimate partners is still largely hidden around the world, and it is critically important for policy makers and public health officials to address the health and human costs, and for each country to develop national plans, policies, and programs for the elimination and prevention of violence against women and children.

CASE SCENARIOS

Case 1: Cathy

Cathy was a 24-year-old college graduate whose childhood and adolescence had been quite normal. She grew up in a two-parent home, the oldest of three children. Upon entering high school, she had feelings of inadequacy that are not uncommon for adolescent girls. During her junior and senior years in high school, she had a couple of boyfriends, but the relationships were not serious. During her freshman year in college, when she was living in the dormitory, she met Bryan, a college junior, at a fraternity party, and there was an immediate mutual attraction. Bryan was one of the most popular guys in the fraternity, and, initially, Cathy felt lucky that he was attracted to her. In the spring, when they had been dating for several months, Cathy told Bryan she wanted to work for the summer at a beach resort that was located approximately 85 miles away from the college. Bryan needed to take summer school classes and continue his part-time job near the campus, and he did not want Cathy to be so far away. Their disagreement over this issue turned into a raging argument that ended when Bryan grabbed Cathy's shoulders, shook her very hard, and punched her in the face. Cathy then called the police. When they arrived, they took Bryan to another room to calm him down, and they called the paramedics because Cathy's nose was bleeding. The paramedics took her to the hospital, where she was treated for a broken nose. When the police asked Cathy if she wanted to press charges, she said no, because she didn't want Bryan to get into trouble. (Roberts and Roberts, 2005)

Case 2: Julia

Julia was married to Steve, and she put her career on hold to raise their two daughters. Julia and Steve were married for almost 2 years when he first began abusing her. They always fought about their financial difficulties, and at times, Steve would get so mad that he would punch and kick her. Occasionally, the fights were so severe that Julia would call the police. When they arrived at the scene, they took Steve into a separate room to interview him, while the paramedics treated Julia, who usually had minor cuts and bruises.

The police department received calls from Julia once or twice a month, and sometimes they would arrest Steve, but Julia never pressed any charges or sought a restraining order.

One day, after a check bounced, Julia came home to find Steve furious after receiving a letter from the bank. Steve pushed her down the stairs and beat her with a baseball bat. Julia suffered a broken leg, broken ribs, and a concussion. After a long and painful recovery, Julia filed for a divorce.

Case 3: Cynthia

Cynthia was married to Anthony the summer after they both graduated from a small college in Arizona. They were both 22 years of age. Cynthia was a third-grade teacher and her husband worked as a mechanic. After she graduated, she immediately got a job as a teacher with a starting salary of $40,000 a year. This was much more than her husband earned as a mechanic. Anthony first began hitting Cynthia a few months after they were married, when he went out with his buddies and got drunk. When Anthony lost his job 2 years after their marriage, he became even more violent, due to his increased drinking and difficulty accepting Cynthia as the "breadwinner." After 2 1/2 years of marriage, Cynthia filed for divorce. Anthony began stalking Cynthia in order to get her back and he ignored the restraining order that Cynthia filed. When Anthony realized he was losing Cynthia to another man, his anger reached a new extreme. After leaving school one afternoon as Cynthia approached her car, Anthony pulled out a shotgun and murdered her. He then used the same gun to kill himself.

BARRIERS TO SEEKING HELP

Many women are ashamed of being abused and are not comfortable with the idea of others knowing about their abuse. Although some may seek emergency medical treatment after an abusive incident, because of embarrassment or fears of retaliation by their abusive partners, women may lie or avoid questioning from doctors and nurses who treat them. Many of these women may want to escape from their dangerous battering environments as soon as they feel it is safe to do so, and by not talking about it they seem to remove themselves from the situation for the moment even if it means reliving it at a later time. The following four cases from the author's research files describe what typically happens in emergency rooms through the voices of battered women.

Case 1

One night the battered woman in this case was accused of cheating on her spouse. He then started pushing her around; this led to her being pushed down the stairs after some verbal abuse. Her fall resulted in a broken leg and fractured nose. When she was brought to the hospital emergency room, to avoid questioning, she lied and said she fell down the stairs. In reflecting on the incident, she told an interviewer:

> Well, when my time came around to be seen by the doctor they called me into the room and asked me what happened. I told them that I fell. The nurse made a face like "yeah right" and they fixed my nose and leg and gave me crutches and aspirin and sent my ass home.

Case 2

In the evening when this woman's husband came home, he found that no dinner was prepared. This made him angry and he started verbally abusing his wife. He then picked up a frying pan and hit her face with it. She sustained a broken nose and cheekbone, and fractured jawbone from this incident of abuse. At the hospital where the woman required reconstructive surgery, the nurses and doctors kept asking questions, but she told them to just "fix me and send me home," and after that they did just that.

> All these stupid doctors and nurses came and asked me the same questions over and over again that really annoyed me. . . .

Case 3

In this case, the victim was confronted with a death threat by her husband, who was wielding a knife. The woman ran out of their house across the main street in their town, and her husband chased her down, threw her to the ground where he choked her, and subsequently slammed her head into the concrete. She had suffered a concussion and went to the emergency room (ER), where she was medically examined. She did not want to talk about her abuse because she did not like getting advice from strangers, so they sent her home without calling the police.

> [The doctors and nurses] examined me and gave me medication and they sent me home. I didn't really want to talk about [my abuse] so we didn't. They didn't give me any phone numbers or anything. I don't

like strangers giving me advice—who are they to tell me how to run my life—I'd rather talk to my friends about it.

Case 4

During this victim's pregnancy, the husband kicked and punched her in the stomach; it seemed like he was trying to kill the baby she was carrying. He was convinced the baby was not his. This woman almost suffered a miscarriage and went to the hospital to get it checked out. She felt the nurses were sweet but could not understand the situation she was in.

> When I was pregnant I thought that I was going to lose my daughter, but they were able to save her. A nurse told me that I shouldn't be with a man who would cause me and my baby such harm. She was sweet, but she didn't understand I had nowhere else to go.

Women from the author's chronically abused group are oftentimes sent to the hospital for different injuries ranging from bruises to broken bones. Many of these women choose not to report the battering to ER staff, consequently neglecting themselves of services. In their minds, they are avoiding retaliation and future abuse from their battering partner. To avoid being questioned on the topic of abuse, women may forget the sequence of events prior to the abuse, blame themselves, or outright lie to the health care provider. In some cases they shut down when confronted with the topic, and in other cases they altogether push the health care provider away from giving advice on abusive relationships.

Abused women may change their stories to keep professionals at a distance. Case 1 was about a victim who lied about her abuse. She merely claimed that she sustained the injury by falling down a flight of stairs because of her clumsiness. This type of lying pushes the doctor away. If the doctor still suspects abuse despite the woman's story, he or she may hesitate to help the victim because they perceive her as not receptive to advice about intimate abuse.

Many of these women feel that the nurses and doctors who confront them with the advice may not understand or do not really care about their situation. The victim in Case 4 did not feel as though the nurses and doctors could help her. She said that they could not relate and really understand her situation. This prevented her from getting advice on how to break the chain of violence that plagued her.

In some cases, especially when abuse is not as obvious, health care providers may be the ones who choose not to bring up the subject of abuse. Another woman in the study claimed that when she went to the hospital, nurses and doctors treated her injuries but asked no questions and sent her on her way. She felt the health care providers may have fixed her injuries but did very little to heal her.

Many women also experience shame for being abused and want to avoid the negative stigma that accompanies victims of intimate abuse. In these cases, victims are likely going to try to do whatever it takes to avoid situations that make them vulnerable to others knowing their pain. Some of these women may not even go to the hospital to avoid this situation. This was especially true for one woman who was a nurse and was adamant about treating her own injuries to avoid going to the emergency room. Regardless of the severity of the injury, many women are hesitant to let health care providers or outsiders see their vulnerable abused side. Unfortunately, their inability of letting others into this horrifying secret world often leads them to be quietly trapped in their abusive environments with no readily available means of escape.

MYTHS AND FACTS

1. **Myth:** Woman battering is a problem only in the lower socioeconomic class. **Fact:** Woman battering takes place in all social classes, religions, races, and ethnic groups. There is a large hidden group of battered women living in highly affluent suburbs throughout the United States. Neighbors rarely hear the violence because some of the battered women are living on 1-, 2-, and 3-acre estates. Although woman battering occurs in all socioeconomic classes, it is reported to be more visible and prevalent in the lowest socioeconomic groups.

2. **Myth:** Woman battering is not a significant problem because most incidents are in the form of a slap or a push that does not cause serious medical injuries. **Fact:** Woman battering is a very serious problem that places victims at risk of medical injuries as well as homicide. Many cases of domestic violence result in life-threatening injuries and/or lethal consequences. The most frequent site of

domestic violence injuries is the head, neck, or face of the battered women (Roberts & Kim, 2005).

3. **Myth:** The police never arrest the batterer because they view domestic violence calls as a private matter. **Fact:** As of 2001, all states have implemented "warrantless" arrest policies, and mandated domestic violence police training, specialized police domestic violence units, collaborative community police and prosecutor response teams, enhanced technology, and collaboration between victim advocates and police to enhance victim safety and offender accountability. The landmark U.S. Supreme Court case of the mid-1980s—Tracy Thurman vs. the city of Torrington, Connecticut—served notice to police departments nationwide to rapidly respond to domestic violence calls as any other crime in which the victim and perpetrator did not know each other. It was a catalyst for the development of mandatory arrest laws.

4. **Myth:** It is extremely rare for a battered woman to be homeless. **Fact:** Domestic violence is one of the primary causes of homelessness among women.

5. **Myth:** Temporary restraining orders and protective orders rarely are effective in stopping the battering. **Fact:** In recent years, family, criminal, and specialized domestic violence courts have instituted major institutional reforms including technology enhancement, automated case-tracking systems, and more victim protection of confidentiality rights. It has been documented that many thousands of women are being helped and having their legal rights protected by court orders. New innovations include around-the-clock methods of issuing temporary restraining orders and providing a pro bono attorney 24 hours a day, 7 days a week (Keilitz, 2002; Lutz, 2002).

6. **Myth:** All batterers are psychotic, and no treatment can change their violent habits. **Fact:** The majority of men who assault women can be helped. The main types of intervention are arrest, psychoeducational groups, and court-mandated group counseling. Research on over 1,200 batterers documented that mandatory arrest had a deterrent effect among abusers who were employed, White, and married. In Milwaukee, arrests for men who were minorities and unemployed led to an increase in battering (Roberts & Roberts, 2005).

7. **Myth:** Elder abuse is neither prevalent nor dangerous. **Fact:** More than 1.5 million older persons may be victims of abuse by their aging spouses as well as by their adult children. We can expect a sharp increase in elder abuse due to baby-boom children reaching retirement age and retiring within the next 5 years.

8. **Myth:** Children who have witnessed repeated acts of violence by their father against their mother do not need to participate in a specialized counseling program. **Fact:** Several studies have demonstrated that long-lasting harm and trauma to children result from exposure to violence between their parents. These child witnesses to their mothers being battered exhibit a range of adjustment and anxiety disorders. Boys who witness their mother being assaulted have a greater likelihood of becoming an abuser.

9. **Myth:** Although many battered women suffer severe beatings for years, only a handful experience symptoms of posttraumatic stress disorder (PTSD). **Fact:** Clinical studies of battered women revealed an association between extent and intensity of battering experiences and severity of PTSD (Robertiello, 2006).

10. **Myth:** Battered women who remain in a violent relationship do so because they are masochistic. **Fact:** Most battered women who stay in abusive relationships do so because of economic need, intermittent reinforcement and traumatic bonding, learned helplessness, the fear that the abuser will hunt them down and kill them if they leave, fear that leaving and moving will be a disruption for the children, and fear that they may lose custody permanently.

11. **Myth:** There are no marginalized and throwaway battered women or no women with serious mental health disorders, AIDS, PTSD, polydrug abuse, and/or developmental disabilities. **Fact:** Many thousands of battered women suffer from all of these. Recently, several model programs have been developed to provide them with legal advocacy and legal representation, medical or mental health treatment, and many community support systems.

12. **Myth:** Alcohol abuse and/or alcoholism causes men to assault their partners. **Fact:** The majority of batterers are not alcoholics, and the overwhelming majority of men classified as high-level or binge drinkers do not abuse their partners. Alcohol is used as an excuse, not a cause, for battering. Removing the alcohol does not cure the abusive personality.

The previously cited myths permeate the public's view of battered women. The false beliefs can be particularly detrimental when endorsed by women in abusive relationships whose belief in these myths may create excuses for the abuse or prevent them from taking steps to get out of abusive situations. Social workers and medical professionals should be cognizant that these myths are widely believed in our culture and should work to educate women and men of the actual facts.

23 WARNING SIGNS OF A POTENTIALLY ABUSIVE PARTNER

For professionals who are likely to come in contact with battered women and for women entering new relationships, it is helpful to be aware of common indicators of potentially abusive relationship dynamics. The next section identifies 23 warning signs or red flags (Roberts & Roberts, 2005) useful for all women and practitioners.

1. Abuser is extremely jealous and overly possessive of his date and has intense fear of being cheated on.
2. Abuser intimidates and instills fear in his date by raising a fist or kicking or mutilating a pet.
3. Abuser exhibits poor impulse control or explosive anger.
4. Most of abuser's desires need immediate response.
5. Abuser repeatedly violates his girlfriend's personal boundaries.
6. Abuser tries to dominate her by telling her what to wear.
7. Abuser uses extreme control tactics, such as monitoring the mileage on her car.
8. Abuser attacks the self-confidence of the partner (name-calling).
9. Abuser is emotionally dependent (wants her to spend her time just with him).
10. Abuser becomes hostile after binge drinking.
11. Abuser never takes responsibility for the role he played in the problem.
12. He cannot control his anger.
13. Abuser has poor communication skills.
14. Abuser has a history of having abused a previous girlfriend.
15. Abuser often was on college or high school sports team where violence was emphasized.
16. In a fit of anger sparked by jealousy or disagreement with his date, he threatens to hit, slap, or punch her.
17. He has a generational history of interpersonal violence among father or other familial male role models in which he was

beaten as a child or he observed his father/stepfather beating his mother.

18. He is demanding, overly aggressive, frequently rough, and/or
    sometimes sadistic during sexual activity.
19. He escalates intimidating and potentially assaultive behavioral
    patterns when his partner is pregnant.
20. He exerts coercive control by threatening and then attempting
    homicide or suicide when the woman attempts to leave the
    relationship.
21. He exhibits a narcissistic personality disorder.
22. He exhibits an avoidant depressive personality disorder.
23. He exhibits a borderline personality disorder and is highly im-
    pulsive, self-punitive, sexually abusive, moody, resentful, and
    tense.

PREVALENCE AND COSTS

Each year, approximately 8.7 million women are victims of intimate
partner violence (Roberts, 2002; Roberts & Roberts, 2005). Every 9
seconds somewhere in the United States, a woman is battered by her
current or former intimate partner. Violence among current and former intimate partners has been found to be highly prevalent in American society. Two national studies have provided methodologically
rigorous national estimates of the prevalence of women battering.
The Tjaden and Thoennes (2000) national violence against women
survey was based on a national representative sample of 8,000 women
and 8,000 men 18 years of age and older. The report from the National Violence Against Women (NVAW) survey indicated that almost
25% of the women surveyed and 7.6% of the men surveyed stated in
the telephone interviews that they were raped and/or physically battered by a spouse, cohabiting partner, or date during their lifetime;
and 1.5% of the women surveyed indicated that they were physically abused or raped by an intimate partner during the previous 12-
month period. These estimates are probably low because of the problem of underreporting. Many battered women do not make criminal
complaints and/or minimize the abuse or are in denial. Each year
for the past 20 years, approximately 1.5 million to 2 million women
have needed emergency medical attention as a result of domestic violence (Roberts, 1998; Straus, 1986). Annual estimates indicate that

approximately 2,000 battered women are killed by their abusive partners, and the majority of these homicides take place after the victim has tried to leave, separate from, or divorce their batterer. In addition, 1,250 chronically battered women have killed their mates each year as a result of explicit terroristic or death threats, PTSD, and/or recurring nightmares or intrusive thoughts of their own death at the hands of the batterer (Browne, 1987; Cascardi, O'Leary, and Lawrence, 1993; Federal Bureau of Investigation [FBI], 2003; Roberts, 2002; Walker, 1984).

The aftermath of domestic violence assaults has a destructive impact on the battered woman and her children. Carlson (1996) estimated that each year more than 10 million children witness woman battering in the privacy of their own homes. The impact of growing up in a violent home often results in an intergenerational cycle of violence. See chapter 9 in this book for detailed descriptions of treatment plans to help traumatized children of battered women.

Stark and Flitcraft (1988) have indicated that the impact of the battered women syndrome results in subsequent high rates of medical problems, mental disorders, miscarriages, abortions, alcohol and drug abuse, increased risks of rape, and suicide attempts. More recently, Hamberger and Phelan (2004) reviewed 14 studies to determine the prevalence of spousal abuse among patients presenting at family medicine and internal medicine clinics, and found that health-related problems from physical abuse ranged from 13% to 46% of patients.

It has been estimated that approximately $4.1 billion has been spent annually for medical care and mental health treatment, and almost $1.8 billion on lost productivity related to morbidity and premature mortality of battered women (NCIPC, 2003). This does not take into account the fact that hospital and physician fees are rising considerably every year. Any estimate of the costs of intimate partner violence should also include the intangible costs of pain and suffering to the battered women themselves and PTSD and other serious disorders of the children of chronically battered women. Any realistic estimate of overall domestic violence costs should also include advocacy and direct service costs of $3.3 billion that was allocated through the Violence Against Women Act-II for the years 2000 to 2005 as well as county and city criminal justice processing related costs including law enforcement, prosecution, and court costs. Therefore, an annual cost estimate of $10 billion for intimate partner violence in the United States may well be a very low estimate.

Because domestic violence frequently results in serious medical injuries, in addition to calculating criminal justice costs, it is important to include estimates of average and total hospital costs. Domestic violence is the number one cause of emergency room visits by women (Roberts and Roberts, 2005, p. 4). Estimating average hospital costs for a battered woman can be quite challenging and complex. Injuries can range from broken bones and bruises to mental illnesses. According to a national economic study conducted within the health sector, Max et al. (2004) estimated the prevalence and medical costs of domestic violence in terms of ER visits, outpatient visits, inpatient hospitalizations, physician visits, dental visits, ambulance/paramedic costs, and physical therapy visit costs. This economic analysis found that for intimate partner assault victims, the average cost per woman for medical care was $4,247.10 (Max et al., 2004).

Case 3, Cynthia, is an exception to the other two cases because it is a case of domestic violence that resulted in homicide. Therefore, not only should the total hospital costs be calculated, but also the largest cost estimates, those due to absenteeism and lost wages, should be computed. There is an assumption that most people work until the age of 66. If a batterer kills his 23-year-old wife or ex-wife, her salary must be multiplied by the number of years to age 66.

Cathy's short-term case is the least serious of the three. Her incident involved only one hospital visit, and no overnight admission was necessary. She suffered a broken nose, and the only fee charged was the standard emergency room fee of $760. An additional $195 was added to her total for cost of stitches. Her total hospital cost was approximately $955.

Julia's case involves more medical attention. Julia suffered a broken leg, a concussion, and broken ribs when her husband threw her down the stairs. She was admitted to the hospital for a total of 2 days and charged $760 for the emergency room fee, $2,320 for skull x-rays and an MRI due to possible head and traumatic brain injuries, $150 for the chest film and broken ribs, and $125 for sutures. She was also charged $500 per day for admission costs. Her total equaled $4,355.

Cynthia's case is the most complex and involves the calculation of additional costs not estimated for Cathy or Julia. Within a 2-year period, Cynthia visited the emergency room a total of eight times.

Each visit required an overnight stay and admission into the hospital. The initial emergency room fee for her eight visits totaled $4,880 for a 2-year period. Costs for x-rays, chest films, and sutures totaled $2,430. Admission costs totaled $5,100. Cynthia's total hospital costs for a 2-year period were estimated to be $12,410.

We also must compute Cynthia's costs due to lost wages. Cynthia died at the age of 23. At that time, she was earning an annual salary of $40,000. Individuals typically work until the age of 66, so Cynthia lost 43 years of wages. Forty-three years multiplied by her salary of $40,000 totals $1,720,000 ($1.72 million) in lost wages. If we factor in 32% in fringe benefits each year and a cost-of-living increase in annual salary each year of approximately 4.5%, then the lost productivity total is estimated at $4.25 million.

In addition, it is necessary to also calculate lost wages due to a lengthy recovery period. On average, if there are only 4 million domestic violence cases per year, and each case costs the victim on average about $6,000, the average number of sick days directly resulting from domestic violence is 28 days per year (4 million cases × $6,000 per case = $24 billion) per year in lost wages.

CONTINUUM OF THE DURATION AND SEVERITY OF WOMAN BATTERING BASED ON 501 CASES

The next section of this chapter summarizes the findings of a 7-year study of domestic violence that included over 500 in-depth interviews with battered women survivors. The author presents a qualitative analysis that compares chronically battered women with women who ended the battering relationship relatively quickly. A model for effective crisis intervention is proposed. It involves implications for police-based domestic violence units, 24-hour crisis hotlines, crisis intervention units at local mental health centers, and court-mandated batterers group treatment programs.

The continuum the author developed focuses on circumstances, situations, and the nature and extent of battering relationships. Interview points include checking onset, duration, and severity of injuries. Particular attention was paid to critical incidents and turning points where the victim either tried to leave the batterer or there was a lethal outcome; in the sample 105 women killed their partners. From the data collected, the author developed a classification schema based on duration and chronicity. It is based on the common themes extracted in a content analysis of the interviews.

The 501 women who participated in the study were comprised of four subsamples. These came from a state women's prison, two shelters for battered women, three suburban police departments, and a modified snowball sample. A 39-page standardized interview schedule was developed and pretested. The findings indicated a significant correlation among a low level of education, a chronic pattern of battering, PTSD, explicit death threats, and battered women who kill in self-defense.

The literature explaining the reluctance of women to leave their abusive husbands is inconclusive. There is no single characteristic that determines a woman's potential for leaving the batterer (Astin, Lawrence, & Foy, 1993; Roberts, 1996, 2002). Rather, it is a group or cluster of personal and situational characteristics taken together that can provide significant indicators of the battered woman staying in the relationship.

Methodology

Constructing the Sample: The study sample came from four sources:

1. Battered women who have killed their partners were found at a large state women's prison in the northeastern part of the United States ($N = 105$).
2. Three police departments ($N = 105$).
3. Three shelters for battered women ($N = 105$).
4. A convenience subsample of 186 formerly abused women was drawn by inviting 30 graduate students in two sections of the author's MSW Family Violence course, and 15 criminal justice honor students to locate and interview one to three friends, neighbors, or relatives who had been battered during the past 4 years. This type of convenience subsample is also known as a modified snowball sample (Roberts, 2002).

The final sample of 501 battered women consisting of the four waves of subsamples comes very close to the author's plan of sampling battered women from different educational, income levels, and racial backgrounds. The results of this exploratory and qualitative study indicate that the duration and severity of battering varies at different levels of chronicity.

Limitations.   The four subsamples of battered women all came from New Jersey. Thus, the findings are not general to all battered women. Although the study sample was carefully selected, there is always some small amount of sampling error.

All of the interviewers were college seniors or graduate students. Each interviewer received 30 hours of training on interviewing skills and qualitative research on women battering. The training included role-playing and practice interviews. The woman battering questionnaire was prepared, pretested, and modified. It consisted of a 39-page standardized interview schedule to guide the interviews.

Findings

The 501 battered women had three experiences in common: 1) They had experienced one or more incidents of physical battering by their partners; 2) jealous rages, insults, and emotional abuse; and 3) over one-fifth of the victims received terroristic or death threats from their abusive partner. Some of the women were hit a few times and got out of the abusive relationship quickly. These were primarily high school or college students that were not living with the abusive boyfriend. Others were assaulted intermittently over a period of several months to 2 years before leaving the batterer and filing for divorce. The largest group of the women endured chronic abuse for many years before permanently ending the relationship. The extent and degree of chronicity of battering is plotted on a five-level continuum (Figure 1.1).

Duration and Severity Level of Woman-Battering Continuum

As an outgrowth of the author's study, five categories of woman battering were identified based on the duration and severity of the abuse and demographic and psychosocial variables (see Figure 1.1).

1	2	3	4	5
Short-Term (N = 94)	**Intermediate** (N = 104)	**Intermittent Long-Term** (N = 38)	**Chronic and Predictable** (N = 160)	**Homicidal** (N = 105)
Less than 1 year (dating relationship for a few weeks or several months); mild to moderate intensity; usually high school or college students	Several months to 2 years (cohabiting or recently married); moderate to severe injuries	Severe and intense violent episode without warning; long periods without violence, then another violent episode; married with children	Severe repetitive incidents; frequent, predictable pattern; violence often precipitated by alcohol or polydrug abuse; married with children	Violence escalates to homicide, murder precipitated by explicit death threats and life-threatening injuries (cohabiting or married); weapons in home
1–3 incidents	3–15 incidents	4–30 incidents	Usually several hundred violent acts per woman	Numerous violent and severe acts per woman

Psycho-social variables and the 5-level women-battering continuum

1	2	3	4	5
Usually middle-class and steady dating relationship (severity; e.g., push, shove, and sometimes hit with large object; woman leaves after first, second, or third physically abusive act; caring support system, e.g., parents or police)	Usually middle-class and recently married or living together (severity; e.g., punch, kick, chokehold, or severe beating; woman leaves due to bruises or injury; caring support system, e.g., new boyfriend or parents)	Usually upper-middle or upper social class, staying together for children or status/prestige of wealthy husband (woman stays until children grow up and leave home; no alternative support system)	Usually lower socioeconomic or middle-class, often devout Catholic with school-age children at home (abuse continues until husband is arrested, is hospitalized, or dies; husband is blue-collar, skilled or semiskilled)	Usually lower socioeconomic class, high long-term unemployment, limited education; majority of battered women dropped out of high school; woman usually suffers from PTSD, traumatic bonding, or Battered Woman Syndrome

FIGURE 1.1 Duration and severity level of woman-battering continuum.

Source: Copyright © Albert R. Roberts (2002). Reprinted by permission.

Level 1. Short Term: Less than 1 year dating, one to three incidents, usually middle class, and steady dating relationship. Woman leaves after first or second physically abusive act, caring support system (parents).

Level 2. Intermediate: Several months to 2 years (cohabiting or married), moderate to severe injuries, 3–15 incidents. Usually middle class and recently married or living together.

Level 3. Intermittent Long-Term: Severe and intense violent episode without warning, long periods without violence, then another violent episode. Married with children. Four to 30 incidents. Usually upper middle class, staying together for sake of children and wealth and prestige of husband.

Level 4. Chronic and Predictable: Severe repetitive incidents, frequent predictable pattern, violence often precipitated by alcohol or polydrug abuse, married with children. Usually several hundred violent acts per woman. Usually lower class or middle class.

Level 4.5. Subset of Chronic With a Discernible Pattern: Mutual combat; 1–25 years.

Level 5. Homicidal: Violence escalates to murder/manslaughter precipitated by specific death threats, sleep disturbances, and life-threatening injuries. Numerous violent and severe acts per woman. Usually lower class, high long-term unemployment and low level of educational attainment.

Level 1+, Short-Term Victims.   The level and duration of abuse experienced by short-term abused women was determined from interviews with 94 battered women who reported experiencing one to three misdemeanor abusive incidents by their boyfriend or partner. Most of the victims were high school or college students in a steady dating relationship. The overwhelming majority of the women were not living with the abuser. The abusive acts could usually be classified in the mild to moderate range of severity, for example, pushing, slapping, and punching with no broken bones or permanent injuries. Most of these women were between 16 and 25 years of age, and ended the relationship with the help of a parent or older brother. Short-term victims generally seek help from their parents and sometimes call the police to obtain a temporary protective order. Most of the women in this level were middle class (Roberts & Roberts, 2005).

Level 2+, Intermediate.   The level and duration of women battering in this category ranged from 3 to 15 incidents over a period of several months to 2 years. The 104 battered women in this category were usually living with the abuser in either a cohabiting or a marital relationship. None of the women in this level had children. The women ended the relationship with the help of the police, a family member, or a friend after a severe battering incident. Many of the women had sustained severe injuries such as a broken jaw, stitches, and broken ribs, or a concussion. These women often obtained a restraining order and moved out to a safer residence. Most of the women in this level were middle class (Roberts, 2002).

Level 3+, Intermittent/Long-Term.   The intensity of each incident is usually severe, and the duration of battering is 5 to 40 years. Most women in this category are economically and socially dependent on their husbands. In addition, they are often religious and would not divorce for that reason. They are nurturing and caring mothers and want to keep the family together for the sake of the children. There may be no physical violence for several months, and then because of pressures (e.g., at his job), the husband vents his anger and frustration at his wife by beating her. Most of these 38 women are middle or upper class, and rarely go to the hospital. When they go to their family physician for treatment, they have an excuse for the causation of the injury (e.g., accident-prone).

Level 4+, Chronic and Severe With a Regular Pattern.   The duration of battering was 5 to 35 years, with the intensity of the violence increasing over the years. The 160 battered women who comprised this category all reported a discernible pattern of abuse during the recent past (e.g., every weekend, every other weekend, and/or every Friday night). Many of the batterers (68%) had serious drinking problems including binge drinking, drunkenness, and blackouts. However, about three-fourths battered their partners when they were sober. After many years, especially when the children are grown and out of the house, the battering becomes more extreme, more predictable and includes the use of weapons, forced anal and genital sex, and generalized death threats. The injuries for these victims are extensive and include sprains, fractures, broken bones, numerous stitches, and head injuries, that require treatment in the hospital emergency room (Roberts & Kim, 2005; Roberts & Roberts, 2005).

Level 4.5, Subset of Chronic With a Discernible Pattern-Mutual Combat.
Twenty-four (24) of the 160 *Level 4* cases fit the mutual combat category. This mutual combat and chronic category sometimes leads to
dual arrests, and at other times the police arrest the partner who
appears to have the lesser injuries. The level of violence was usually
severe, and the duration of woman battering in this category lasted
from 1 to 25 years. The study identified two types of mutual combat.
In the first type, the man was the primary aggressor and initiated
a violent act such as punching the woman, and she retaliated (e.g.,
slapping or punching him back). He then retaliated more violently
by beating her severely. In the second type of mutual combat, the
woman retaliates for physical or emotional abuse and uses a weapon
(typically a knife) to get back at him. The 10 battered women in this
category had either a chronic alcohol problem or a drug problem,
or a history of violent aggressive acts in adolescence (e.g., cutting another girl, boy, or adult with a knife). In 14 of the 24 cases, both the
abusive male and the female had a drug problem. Generally, there
are severe injuries to one or both parties. Most of the women in this
level were lower class. Many of these couples separate after a few
years.

Level 5+, Homicidal.   The duration of the battering relationship in
this category is generally 8 years or longer, although the range is
2 years to 35 years. The majority of these women are usually in a
common-law relationship (cohabiting for 7 years or longer), a marital relationship, or recently divorced. The overwhelming majority
(59.2%) of these women lacked a high school education and the skills
to earn a decent income on their own (Roberts, 2002). Almost half
(47.6%) of the homicidal battered women had been on public assistance for many years during the battering episodes (Roberts, 2002).
    The 105 women in this category began at Level 2, and usu-
ally escalated to either Level 4 or Level 5 for several years, after
which the death threats became more explicit and lethal. Also in
a number of cases, the victim had finally left the abuser and obtained a restraining order, which he violated. Many of the women
in this category suffered from PTSD, nightmares, and insomnia;
and some had attempted suicide. A smaller group of the homicidal women indicated that at the time they killed their batterer, they
were delusional or hallucinating due to heavy use of LSD, methamphetamines, cocaine, or other drugs. The most significant finding

related to the homicidal battered woman is that *the overwhelming majority (65.7%) of the women received specific lethal death threats in which the batterer specified the method, time, and/or location of their demise.*

PRACTICE IMPLICATIONS

Interventions and treatment plans should be geared to the type of abuse pattern detected. The short-term and intermediate patterns of abuse may be more amenable to crisis intervention, brief psychotherapy, support groups, and restraining orders. Crisis intervention can bolster the survivor's self-confidence, as well as suggest new coping and safety skills that can facilitate a permanent end to the battering relationship. The prognosis for the chronic/long-term category, whether it be intermittent or a weekly pattern of battering, is much more guarded. The chronic recidivist cases are frequently put into a life-threatening situation. However, when there are specific death threats and a loaded handgun in the house, even the short-term and intermediate battering cases can also escalate to a *code blue—life and death situation.*

In chronic cases, the human suffering, degradation, and emotional and physical pain sometimes end in permanent injuries to the victim, or in the death of the batterer or the battered woman. At other times, the chronically battered woman temporarily escapes to a shelter, a relative's home, or the police precinct. In many of the chronic cases, the victim returns to the batterer or is dragged back to the violent home. Finally, a small but growing number of chronically battered women leave the batterer and stay free of violence because they are empowered through a support group and counseling, legal advocacy, an out-of-state relative or friend who provides temporary housing, or the death of the batterer due to a drug overdose, cirrhosis of the liver, or other terminal illnesses. The final section of this chapter applies a structured and sequential crisis intervention model developed by the author.

ROBERTS'S SEVEN-STAGE CRISIS INTERVENTION MODEL

The Seven-Stage Crisis Intervention Model (Figure 1.2; Roberts, 2000, 2005; Roberts & Roberts, 2005) includes the following stages.

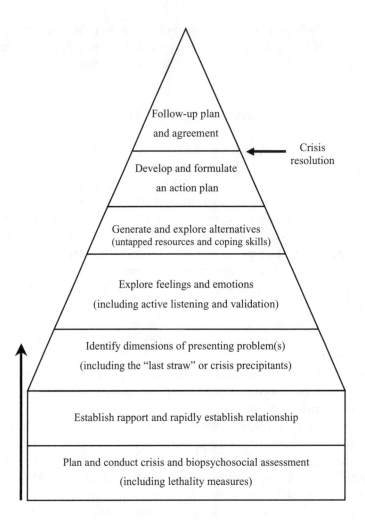

FIGURE 1.2   Roberts's Seven-Stage Crisis Intervention Model.

Source: Copyright © Albert R. Roberts, 1991. Reprinted by permission of the author.

It is important to note that Stages 1 and 2 need to take place simultaneously, immediately on making contact with the battered woman.

Stage 1. Assessing Lethality: Assess whether caller is in any current danger and consider future safety concerns in treatment planning and referral. Maintain active communication with the client.

Evaluating issues: severity of crisis, client's current emotional state, immediate psychosocial needs, and level of the client's current coping skills

Stage 2. Establishing Rapport and Communication: Active listening and empathic communication skills are essential in establishing rapport and engagement of the client.

Stage 3. Identifying the Major Problems: Crisis worker should help the client prioritize the most important problems or impacts by identifying these problems in terms of how they affect the survivor's current status. First priority of this stage is meeting the basic needs of emotional and physical health and safety.

Stage 4. Dealing With Feelings and Providing Support: Critical for crisis worker to show empathy and understanding. Validating and assurance.

Stage 5. Exploring Possible Alternatives: Crisis workers help clients recognize and explore a variety of alternatives such as situational supports, coping skills, and positive and rational thinking patterns.

Stage 6. Formulating an Action Plan: Crisis worker must help the client look at both the short-term and long-range impacts in planning intervention. Main goals are to help the client achieve an appropriate level of functioning and maintain adaptive coping skills and resources.

Stage 7. Follow-Up Measures: Help determine whether these results from the last stage have been maintained or if more work needs to be done. At this stage, four tasks of crisis resolution should have been addressed: physical safety and survival, venting and expressing feelings, cognitive mastery, and interpersonal adjustments.

The crisis intervention model will now be specifically applied to domestic violence.

Stage 1. Assessing Lethality: Assessment in this model is ongoing and critical to effective intervention at all stages, beginning with an assessment of the lethality and safety issues for the battered women. With victims of family violence, it is important to assess whether the caller is in any current danger and to consider future safety concerns in treatment planning and referral. In addition to determining lethality and the need for emergency intervention, it is crucial to maintain active communication with the client, either by phone or in person, while emergency procedures are being initiated.

To plan and conduct a comprehensive assessment, the crisis counselor needs to evaluate the following issues: (a) the severity of the crisis, (b) the client's current emotional state, (c) immediate psychosocial and safety needs, and (d) level of client's current coping skills and resources. In the initial contact, assessment of the client's past or pre-crisis level of functioning and coping skills is useful; however, past history should not be a focus of intake or crisis assessment, unless related directly to the immediate victimization or trauma. The goals of this stage are assessing and identifying critical areas of intervention, while also recognizing the duration and severity of violence and acknowledging what has happened.

Stage 2. Establishing Rapport and Communication: Survivors of acute crisis episodes and trauma may question their own safety and vulnerability, and trust may be difficult for them to establish at this time. Therefore, active listening and empathic communication skills are essential to establishing rapport and engagement of the client. Even though the need for rapid engagement is essential, the crisis worker should try to let the client set the pace of intervention. Many crisis victims feel out of control or powerless and should not be coerced or confronted into action, until they have stabilized and dealt with the initial crisis and trauma reactions (Roberts, 2005).

Stage 3. Identifying the Major Problems: The crisis counselor should focus on helping the battered women to prioritize the most important problems or impacts by identifying these problems in terms of how they affect the survivor's current status. Encouraging the client to ventilate about the precipitating event can lead to problem identification, and some clients have an overwhelming need to talk about the specifics of the battering situation. This process enables the client to figure out the sequence and context of the event(s), which can facilitate emotional ventilation, while providing information to assess and identify major problems to be worked on.

Stage 4. Dealing With Feelings and Providing Support: It is important for the crisis counselor to demonstrate empathy and an anchored understanding of the victim's experience, so that her symptoms and reactions are normalized and can be viewed as functional strategies for survival. Self-blame is a common reaction and many victims blame themselves, so it is important to help the client accept that being a victim is not one's fault. Validation and reassurance are especially useful in this stage because survivors may be experiencing confusing and conflicting feelings. Catharsis and ventilation are critical to healthy coping, and throughout this process, the crisis worker must recognize and support the client's courage in facing and dealing with these emotional reactions and issues (Roberts & Roberts, 2005).

Stage 5. Exploring Possible Alternatives: In this stage, effective crisis counselors help the client to recognize and explore a variety of alternatives, such as (1) situational supports, which are people or social work agencies that can be helpful to the client in meeting needs and resolving crisis related problems; (2) coping skills, which are behaviors or strategies that promote adaptive responses and help the client reach a precrisis level of functioning; and (3) positive and rational thinking patterns, which can lessen the client's levels of anxiety, stress, and crisis.

The crisis counselor can facilitate healthy coping skills by identifying client strengths and resources. Many crisis survivors feel they do not have a lot of choices, and the crisis worker needs to be familiar with both formal and informal community services to provide referrals. For example, working with a battered woman often requires relocation to a safe place for her and the children. The client may not have the personal resources or financial ability to move out of the home, and the crisis worker needs to be informed about the possible alternatives, which could include an emergency shelter program, a host home or safe home, a protective order, traveler's aid, or other emergency housing services (Roberts, 2005).

Stage 6. Formulating an Action Plan: In this stage, an active role must also be taken by the crisis worker; however, the success of any intervention plan depends on the client's level of involvement, participation, and commitment. The crisis worker must help the client look at both the short-term and long-range impacts in planning intervention. The main goals are to help the client achieve an appropriate level of functioning and maintain adaptive coping skills and resources. It is useful to have a manageable treatment plan with short attainable goals, so the client can follow through and be successful. Do not overwhelm the client with too many tasks or strategies, which can set the client up for failure. Clients must also feel a sense of ownership in the action plan, so that they can both increase the level of control and autonomy in their lives and ensure that they do not become dependent on other support persons or resources. Termination begins when the client has achieved the goals of the action plan, or has been referred. It is important to realize that many survivors may need longer term therapeutic help and referrals for individual, family, or group therapy should be considered at this stage (for further discussion of termination, see chapters 2 and 3 in this book).

Stage 7. Follow-Up Measures: The sixth stage should result in significant changes and resolution for the client in regard to his or her post-crisis level of functioning and coping. This last stage should help determine whether these results have been maintained, or if further work remains to be done. Typically, follow-up contacts should be done within 2 to 8 weeks after termination. At this stage, the four tasks of crisis resolution should have been addressed, which are (1) physical safety and survival, (2) ventilation and expression of feelings, (3) cognitive mastery, and (4) interpersonal adjustments and adapting to a new environment.

CONCLUSION

The hospital costs, judicial costs, and law enforcement costs that result from domestic violence cases are enormous. Although the vast majority of cases coming into the criminal justice system from intimate partner violence never go to trial and are partially remedied by family court judges or through plea bargaining, the costs still remain high. The amount of money paid in overtime to law enforcement officers for working extra hours on many cases alone constitutes significant costs. As Roberts and Roberts (2005) suggest, the police and courts can be used effectively to stop battering. The role of the police and the courts is to better protect victims of domestic violence. If state and county criminal justice agencies begin to have the same commitment with general revenue funds as the federal government has had through the federal Violence Against Women Act (VAWA II) and the $3.3 billion allocated for 2000 to 2005 for criminal justice and other domestic violence services, then the future holds much promise. With the passage of VAWA III on October 30, 2005, the 5-year allocation was increased to $3.9 billion for fiscal years 2005 to 2010. This is very promising in terms of the delivery of much-needed social services and criminal justice services to under-served groups of battered women throughout the nation.

The rapid assessment of the duration, intensity, and lethality of woman battering are among the most critical issues in forensic mental health and social work. This chapter provides a new evidence-based continuum for evaluating battered women and improving risk assessments of dangerousness. It should be used to determine the number and length of treatment sessions by behavioral health clinicians, family counselors, as well as other mental health clinicians. It can also facilitate court decisions on whether battered women are at low, moderate, or high risk of continued battering, life-threatening injuries, and/or homicide (Roberts & Roberts, 2005).

Biopsychosocial and lethality assessments should begin with an evaluation of the psychological harm and physical injury to the victim, duration and chronicity of abusive incidents, and the likelihood of the victim escaping and ending the battering cycle. The continuum presented in this chapter provides a classificatory schema by which forensic specialists and clinicians can make reasonably clear predictions of lethality and the repeat of the violence. It is important for all counseling, social work, public health, and criminal justice practitioners to document the duration and intensity of battering histories among clients in order to provide customized safety planning, risk assessments, crisis intervention, and effective services.

REFERENCES

Astin, M. C., Lawrence, K. J., & Foy, D. H. (1993). Risk and resiliency factors among battered women. *Violence and Victims, 8,* 17–28.

Browne, A. (1987). *When battered women kill.* New York: The Free Press.

Carlson, B. E. (1996). Children of battered women: Research, programs and services. In A. R. Roberts (Ed.), *Helping battered women: New perspectives and remedies* (pp. 172–187). New York: Oxford University Press.

Cascardi, M., O'Leary, K. D., Schlee, A., & Lawrence, E. (1993). *Prevalence and correlates of PTSD in abused women.* Paper presented at the 27th Annual Conference of the Association for the Advancement of Behavior Therapy (AABT), Atlanta, GA.

Federal Bureau of Investigation. (2003). *Crime in the U.S.: 2002.* Washington, DC: U.S. Government Printing Office.

Hamberger, L. K., & Phelan, M. B. (2004). *Domestic violence screening and intervention in medical and mental healthcare settings.* New York: Springer Publishing.

Keilitz, S. (2002). Improving judicial system responses to domestic violence: The promises and risks of integrated case management and technology solutions. In A. R. Roberts (Ed.), *Handbook of domestic violence intervention strategies* (pp. 147–171). New York: Oxford University Press.

Max, W., Rice, D. P., Finkelstein, E., Bardwell, R. A., & Leadbetter, S. (2004) The economic toll of intimate partner violence against women in the United States. *Violence and Victims, 19*(3), 259–272.

Robertiello, G. (2006). Common mental health correlates of domestic violence. *Brief Treatment and Crisis Intervention, 6*(2), 111–121.

Roberts, A. R. (1996). *Helping battered women: New perspectives and remedies.* New York: Oxford University Press.

Roberts, A. R. (1998). *Battered women and their families: Intervention strategies and treatment approaches* (2nd ed.). New York: Springer Publishing.

Roberts, A. R. (2000). An introduction and overview of crisis intervention. In A. R. Roberts (Ed.), *Crisis intervention handbook: Assessment, treatment and research* (2nd ed., pp. 3–30). New York: Oxford University Press.

Roberts, A. R. (2002). Duration and severity of woman battering: A conceptual model/continuum. In A. Roberts (Ed.), *Handbook of domestic violence intervention strategies* (pp. 64–79). New York: Oxford University Press.

Roberts, A. R. (2005). Bridging the past and present to the future of crisis intervention and crisis management. In A. R. Roberts (Ed.), *Crisis intervention handbook: Assessment, treatment and research* (3rd ed., pp. 3–35). New York: Oxford University Press.

Roberts, A. R., & Kim, J. (2005). Exploring the effects of head injuries among battered women: A qualitative study of chronic and severe woman battering. *Journal of Social Service Research, 32*(1), 33–47.

Roberts, A. R., & Roberts, B. S. (2005). *Ending intimate abuse: Practical guidance and survival strategies.* New York: Oxford University Press.

Stark, E., & Flitcraft, A. (1988). Violence among intimates: An epidemiological review. In V. B. Van Hasselt, R. L. Morrison, A. S. Bellack, & M. Hersen (Eds.), *Handbook of family violence* (pp. 293–317). New York: Plenum.

Straus, M. A. (1986). Medical care costs of intrafamily assault and homicide. *Bulletin of New York Academy of Medicine, 6*(5), 556–561.

Straus, M. A., & Gelles, R. J. (1991). How violent are American families: Estimates from the National Family Violence Resurvey and other studies. In M. Straus & R. Gelles (Eds.), *Physical violence in American families: Risk factors and adaptations in 8,145 families* (pp. 95–112). New Brunswick, NJ: Transaction Publishers.

Tjaden, P., & Thoennes, N. (2000). *Extent, nature, and consequences of intimate partner violence: Findings from the National Violence Against Women Survey.* Washington, DC: National Institute of Justice, U.S. Department of Justice.

Walker, L. E. (1984). *Battered women syndrome.* New York: Springer Publishing.

CHAPTER 2

Cognitive Problem-Solving Therapy and Stages of Change That Facilitate and Sustain Battered Women's Leaving

Sondra Burman

Intimate partner violence is one of the most dangerous, traumatic, and life-threatening social, public health, and criminal justice problems prevalent throughout the world. Intimate partner abuse, also known as woman battering, woman abuse, and wife beating, continues to be the single greatest health threat to American women between the ages of 15 and 50. "More women sustain injuries as a result of intimate partner abuse than from the combined total of muggings and accidents . . . every 9 seconds a woman is assaulted and battered, and domestic violence is the number one cause of emergency room visits by women . . ." (Roberts & Roberts, 2005, p. 4).

CASE SCENARIOS

Case 1

Sonia was battered twice by a former boyfriend during the Spring semester of her freshman year in college at NYU, but was able to end the relationship quickly with the help of her parents and the police, who quickly served Brad with a temporary restraining order.

Case 2

During her senior year at the University of Pennsylvania, Roberta met Jim, a marketing executive with an MBA degree. Shortly after her graduation, Roberta and Jim were married, had an enjoyable honeymoon in Hawaii, and within 6 months moved into a fashionable townhouse in Center City, Philadelphia. Roberta accidentally became pregnant during the second year of their marriage, and their baby was born with a developmental disability. Roberta quit her job as a high school English teacher because her son required frequent visits to doctors, and it was difficult to locate a day-care agency that would provide the attention his medical condition warranted. Soon after quitting her job, Jim started coming home drunk. She stayed with Jim for 5 years, and the more he drank, the more frequently he hit her. The intermittent violence increased gradually over the last 3 years of their marriage. The last straw was what Roberta called her "night of terror." It was Jim's birthday so her mother took their son, and Jim did not get home until after midnight. Even though Roberta had cooked a special dinner for him, he went out drinking with his buddies, and when he came home slapped, punched, beat, and dragged Roberta from room to room, and sexually assaulted her three times. This horrible episode lasted 9 hours.

Case 3

Naomi was a 34-year-old high school graduate with one child, and she had worked for the same company for 14 years as a customer service representative. In terms of intergenerational abuse, her father was an abuser and she was chronically abused by her husband for 7 years, mostly without any warning. She sustained serious injuries on three different occasions—broken nose, bruises all over body, eye swollen from punches, and broken eardrum and ear bleeding. In addition, she had been punched in the mouth, choked several times, and had faked passing out several times after being strangled in order to avoid being killed. Leaving her husband was initiated after a period of crisis following a severe episode where she was temporarily blind in one eye and deaf. This culminated 7 years of terror and incapacitating injuries. Naomi entered a shelter with her child, attended a battered women's support group, and received counseling that motivated her readiness to change. Roberts's Seven-Stage Crisis Intervention Model (Roberts, 1991, 2000, 2005) helped to identify recurring problems of violence and harassment that put her at great risk. It also assisted in contemplating options, developing new coping skills, and devising a viable action plan. The stages of change raised doubts about her husband's willingness and capabilities to alter his abusive behaviors and reinforced the need to sever emotional and physical ties that kept her captive in the relationship. After realistically weighing the costs and benefits of staying with her husband, Naomi became determined to take safety precautions and carried out her resolve to permanently leave the batterer and obtained a restraining order from the court with the help of her domestic violence advocate.

Whether a woman is battered several times or many times for several years, she will usually benefit from both crisis intervention and domestic violence advocacy services. However, if the duration and severity of battering episodes lasts from several months to several years, then the battered woman will likely benefit from intensive individual treatment as well as a support group, and legal advocacy. Generally speaking, problem-solving steps for Roberta and Naomi should include (a) a lethality, and mental health assessment; (b) problem identification and implications; (c) goal setting and contracting; (d) implementation of interventions; (e) termination, referrals, and follow-up when needed; and (f) an outcome evaluation of the effectiveness of interventions.

Consistent with both a crisis intervention and a cognitive problem-solving intervention protocol, the initial engagement of the client in a nonjudgmental, trusting, and rapport-building relationship is critical to establishing collaborative agreement and willingness to participate fully in treatment. This chapter fully applies the Naomi case study to the development and implementation of a specific treatment plan in order to monitor safety activities while facilitating the development of new problem-solving coping skills.

This chapter incorporates a cognitive problem-solving intervention model in a case report of a chronically abused woman from Roberts's continuum of the extent and chronicity level of woman battering. It depicts Prochaska and DiClemente's (1982) stages of change and Roberts's crisis intervention model in the progressive movement from living in a battering situation to leaving the relationship and becoming independent. By attempting to understand the nature of the battering experience and how women cope on a daily basis, insights can be illuminated into their survival skills and the strengths that are utilized to make the decision to leave, act on it, and sustain that goal. In addition, the application of the cognitive problem-solving intervention model to the battering experience of clients can assist practitioners in developing effective treatment assessments and strategies that intend to motivate their clients to move toward freedom of choice, disengagement, and empowerment.

As clinical researchers, we are always interested in learning about relevant advances in the knowledge base of vital topics related to our work. Since the Stages of Change paradigm was adapted to Naomi's case report demonstrating Roberts's duration and severity *continuum* of women's battering (Roberts, 2003), several articles have been published that focus on the stages of change and domestic violence. Most report on the application of stages (i.e., the transtheoretical model of behavior change) to the perpetrators of the violence (Babcock, Canady, Senior, & Eckhardt, 2005; Eckhardt, Babcock, & Homack, 2004; Scott, 2004; Scott & Wolfe, 2003). These studies convey batterers' movements through the stage processes in attempting to change their abusive behaviors. One published article specifically addresses women's efforts in ending intimate partner violence (Burke, Denison, Gielen, McDonnell, & O'Campo, 2004), which brings to mind Naomi's struggles in similar circumstances (Burman, 2003).

Analyses of Burke, Denison, Gielen, McDonnell, and O'Campo research data provide an understanding of subjective living experiences of abuse, accompanied by cognitive (e.g., consciousness raising; self-reevaluation) and behavioral processes (e.g., stimulus control; self-liberation) exhibited during movement through the change stages. The findings acknowledge the emergence of self-efficacy in elevating personal esteem that results directly from weighing the advantages and disadvantages of staying versus leaving, planning, and taking appropriate action to end the relationship.

Cognitive and behavioral processes assigned to respondents in the Burke study could also apply to Naomi's motivation in working through her doubts and formulating the escape route to freedom from fear and pain. Following her journey through the stages, we encounter the increasing awareness of her husband's inability to control his volatile behavior and her need to protect her children and herself from his wrath. An empowering stance is noted by her take-charge coping and survival skills in making a wise, thoughtful decision to leave, act on, and sustain that goal. This revelation of strengths emerged after many years of chaotic crises, terror, and incapacitating injuries.

Yet we also recognize that fear of being alone and raising the children; probable financial hardships; feeling trapped without supportive structures; expectations of escalating violence, stalking, or even death; and other underlying anxiety-producing concerns often maintain the status quo. These are among the obvious reasons women attempt to persevere in an emotionally and physically abusive relationship. What is not so apparent is the need to avoid the shattering of a dream. This is heard from voices who express the panic of losing what was once considered (or erroneously believed to be) loving and meaningful—a caring spouse and partner, the comfort and satisfaction of a "well-adjusted and happy" family, and as old and clichéd as it may sound, the belief in togetherness until "death do us part." Bonding and attachment issues can stifle the most motivated and goal-oriented individuals, as shown too often by women who depart shelters abruptly and return to their mates.

In the practice realm, these critical themes, among others, must be taken into account with the goal of helping clients gain safety, security, and manageable skills to persist in improving and moving on with their lives. Essential to this process is recognizing the degree of *readiness to change* that will either impede or facilitate change in a positive direction (Miller & Rollnick, 2002; Prochaska & DiClemente, 1982).

According to Scott and Wolfe (2003, p. 880), "An individuals' stage of change, or 'readiness to change,' likely reflects [among others]... motivation, efficacy, denial, and openness to seeking help." Consequently, increasing client motivation to problem-solve should be an important objective during treatment. This has been emphasized through the use of techniques of *motivational interviewing* that aim to assist clients in avoiding getting stuck in earlier stages (precontemplation and contemplation), while proceeding through more advanced stages of change (preparation, action, and maintenance).

In the succeeding chapter, Naomi's commitment to break the chains of dependency and despair is acknowledged. Reviewing her experience, it becomes evident that she ostensibly set in motion the process of change reminiscent of stages described in the transtheoretical model. However, she realized the fear of falling back (relapsing) was ever present. At times, she still felt vulnerable and helpless in detaching from the strong bonds and connections once held with her husband. The past seeped into the present when fond memories emerged, weakening her resolve to terminate the relationship.

Recognizing the powerful force of this menacing possibility, Naomi sought treatment to completely sever ties and, just as importantly, to gain coping skills and self-confidence that would prevent a recurrence of revisiting the life she struggled to leave behind in the guise of a new relationship. The cognitive problem-solving practice model assisted in this endeavor. Changing problematic and self-defeating behaviors has been shown to be an act of intentional self-change or accomplished in treatment (Prochaska, Norcross, & DiClemente, 1994).

Despite severe physical and emotional traumas inflicted by batterers, there continues to be a measure of suspicion and questions of culpability addressed to the target of the aggression. Queries like, "Why does she put up with that?" and "Why does she stay?" continue to haunt the battered woman and demonstrate a pervasive reversal of condemnation—from the perpetrator to the victim. The implication is "that the battered woman's behavior is problematic, rather than that of their abusive partners" (Ferraro, 1997, p. 124). This ego-deflating and incriminating element can serve to keep a woman trapped in a situation that she may view as being incapable of ending, and even one that is justified due to her own faults and imperfections. It is a classic incriminating spin of "blaming the victim" that women must defend against—one that serves to justify violence and the status quo in a violent-prone society.

Yet we know that women do attempt to end assaultive relationships and many do leave, often putting themselves at great risk. Roberts (2002) relates that no single characteristic defines the potential for leaving the batterer. However, staying in the relationship may be more likely when a group or cluster of personal and situational characteristics can be identified. Many are based on psychosocial variables, duration of the battering, and levels of violence against women.

By attempting to understand the nature of the battering and how women cope, we can also glean some insights into their survival skills and the strengths that are utilized to make the decision to leave, act upon, and sustain that goal.

With his prolific research and writings, Roberts has greatly contributed to the knowledge base of domestic violence. His formulation of a seven-stage crisis intervention model (Roberts, 2000) and different levels (a continuum) of the severity of battering that women endure through time (Roberts, 2002) can provide a therapeutic direction toward identifying coping skills needed to upset the status quo, thereby freeing these women from the torment they experience. In his study of 501 battered women who left their batterers, we not only can derive an indication of the extent and chronicity of the battering episodes, the demographic characteristics of these women, and the means of ending the relationships (Roberts & Roberts, 2005), but also can extrapolate varying stages of change (Prochaska & DiClemente, 1982; Prochaska & Prochaska, 2002) that eventually result in the leaving/escape phenomenon. By identifying these stages, practitioners can develop treatment assessments and strategies to be used at each phase of potential movement toward disengagement and empowerment.

The Stages of Change have been aptly described by Brown (1997) in her article on battered women, and by Petrocelli (2002) in his integration of the stages in the counseling process.

Expanding on their work, this chapter examines the stages' goals and tasks, Roberts's crisis intervention model and battering duration/severity continuum, and a cognitive problem-solving practice model that is detailed in a case report of the battering and leaving experience.

THE STAGES OF CHANGE

Prochaska, Norcross, and DiClemente (1994, pp. 13, 25) remarked, "... we can exert some power over the course of our own lives ... any activity that you initiate to help modify your thinking, feeling, or behavior is a change process." This empowering stance was introduced in the hallmark work of Prochaska and DiClemente (1982) that was heralded as a paradigm shift, confronting the staunchly held beliefs about the rigidity of maladaptive behaviors. Initially researched on smokers who quit on their own (without treatment), the Transtheoretical Change Model and its stages of change have been applied to drug cessation, weight reduction, and other problematic behaviors and conditions. From the data collections, themes of change were noted within six active stage categories entitled precontemplation, contemplation, determination/preparation, action, maintenance, and termination.

Precontemplation

During this period, the battered woman tends to minimize or deny the source, extent, and consequences of the problem, refraining from viewing her partner in a realistic light. She may be defensive if anyone suggests or suspects something is wrong, trying to hide or rationalize the remnants of bruises that others may see, much to their concern and dismay. She accommodates herself to the situation, constantly hoping that by pleasing her spouse/partner and improving her behavior, he will "change his ways." The excuses and promises that it will never happen again, and intermittent "honeymoon stages" provide a faulty sense of optimism that the abusive behaviors are under control and will not be repeated. At the same time, there is an invasive apprehensiveness in her daily routine—one that lies just beneath the surface and threatens the vulnerable state of stability and security.

Within the context of this stage, traumatic bonding becomes pronounced. Dutton (1992a) reported that this emotional connection is rooted during the early phase of the relationship, often before the abuse begins. Intermittent expressions of concern/reinforcement and violence intensify the attachment/traumatic bonding (Barnett, 2001; Saunders & Edelson, 1999). With increasing forced isolation, a dependency on the batterer grows, reducing the potential for constructive change and leaving the relationship. Concurrently, a demoralized and shattered sense of self-esteem and self-worth, accentuated by a feeling of responsibility and self-blame for the assaults, is noted. "If I had not spoken up and argued, if I had only done something differently, it never would have happened." Through the development of learned helplessness (Walker, 1994), the woman eventually accepts that the battering cannot be controlled no matter what she does, resulting in feelings of powerlessness, helplessness, and hopelessness.

Consequential emotional responses of depression and anxiety can be extremely debilitating. "Psychic numbing," an avoidance response that functions to deny or minimize an awareness of the traumatic experience and its aftermath, may occur (Dutton, 1992b).

Alternatives to living in this manner are cognitively unrecognized. Nevertheless, the seeds of change are being gradually sown. A primary treatment goal and task in this stage is to raise doubt about maintaining the current situation by providing information about the critical nature of abuse and increasing an awareness of the personal risks involved in continuing the relationship, if nothing changes.

Contemplation

Ambivalence marks this stage, that is, "simultaneously (or in rapid alternation) experienc[ing] reasons for concern and for unconcern, motivations to change and to continue unchanged" (Miller & Rollnick, 1991, p. 16). The cognitive dissonance between a loving and uncaring/abusive relationship begins to grow, accentuated by the batterer's inconsistent behaviors. As the abuse continues, denial and its adaptive mechanisms weaken. Escalation of the violence and its severity initiates a realization of the potential lethality and lack of personal safety. Ferraro (1997) related that during this stage of ambivalence, fighting back may be a defensive tactic, as self-protection becomes a vital need. However, it is generally not effective and often results in escalating the violence and resultant injuries. The first effort at leaving may be attempted, but is usually not permanent.

A goal in this stage is to reduce the ambivalence and cognitive dissonance through a reasoned evaluation of the battering relationship, leading to making a conscious decision to change. The decisive task that generally precedes the transition to the next stage of determination/preparation to creating a change is conducting a cost–benefit analysis (the weighing of the costs and benefits or pros and cons of remaining versus leaving—a treatment focus in the contemplation stage). The disadvantages of "going it alone" can be disarming and overwhelming, including economic insecurity and the possibility of not obtaining gainful employment to support herself and her children; lacking supports and other resources can also undermine an active move to the next stage of change. The batterer's terrorist

TABLE 2.1 Decisional Balance Chart

Disadvantages of Leaving	Advantages of Leaving
Fear of making it alone	Feelings of empowerment (self-efficacy, confidence, respect)
	Improved self-image
	Improved coping, decision-making, problem-solving skills
Financial insecurity	Greater opportunities for advancement
	Renewed hope for a better life
Fear of stalking/increasing abuse	Only survival/safety option left for my children and myself
	Breaking the intergenerational cycle of violence

tactics may immobilize the woman, placing her in a "no win" situation. If she stays, she is at risk; if she leaves, she can be stalked, harassed, and pursued with death threats. Harm to her children is also a reality of major concern. At this point of desperation, she may find that the choice of escaping may be the only viable option to survival. A *decisional balance chart* can illuminate positive aspects of leaving, which may hold aspects of risk, but compared to the alternative, holds more promise for safety and freedom from terror and bodily harm (see Table 2.1).

Determination/Preparation

The goal at this stage is to both determine the best course of action and prepare to carry it out. Ambivalence may still be evident, but this diminishes with each bout of terrorism and brutality. Awareness of these events, with no essential modification of the batterer's actions, reduces thoughts of staying and increases the commitment to change. A decision is made to leave, and strategies are formulated that are most suitable to personal needs and circumstances. Putting money away in a safe place to assist with the escape and getting started again in a different location; collecting phone numbers and addresses of supports and resources to contact at the crucial time of need; finding the location of a shelter for women (and their children, if needed); and checking into alternative housing, legal aid services, adequate transportation, and day care are some preparation tasks to consider. Women with greater amounts of resources, options, and supports are in a better position to leave, being able to utilize various sources of safety, protection, and independent living, while developing further plans to maintain the change.

Action

Taking action means confronting trepidation and fortifying efforts and goals of change. The prospect of leaving, with potentially dangerous repercussions, inevitably provokes fear and apprehensions, but the alternative at this stage can be more frightening and disabling. Having considered the options and made a rational decision to leave, energy is now directed toward the goal of carrying out strategies that will protect the woman (and her children) in the ultimate objective of safety and protection from continued assaults. Tasks/strategies can include going to a shelter, calling on relatives or friends for help, and obtaining a restraining order. Police intervention, which may have been required previously to counter attacks, can now be a means of keeping the batterer at bay. Unfortunately, even these efforts might not eliminate the danger, for an obsessed partner will return. His dependency needs and the desire for power and control are relentless and consuming. Yet once a woman takes action steps, personal strengths and survival skills are tapped, reinforcing the motivation to end the abuse and escape the battering relationship.

Drug use by either the perpetrator or the victim must always be a consideration when assessing the severity of battering. It can impede planning and taking action to leave the relationship when chemicals are used to self-medicate and cope with the stress, pain, and suffering. Dutton (1992) commented that this behavior "interfere[s] with the battered woman's attempts to gain control over her own life, may be dangerous to others (e.g., her children), or produce negative effects (e.g., drug or alcohol addiction, arrest, loss of children to social services)," (p. 126). To activate the tasks of rescue and leaving, cognitive processes must be clear of drugs that can impair and dull thinking, judgment, and coordination. The prospect of an addiction can add another entrapment that defies personal control and weakens the search and acquisition of a meaningful existence. For those women who have used drugs with their partners (and may have been introduced and supplied by them), the chances of escape and remaining independent are markedly reduced, as the compelling nature of the drug takes precedence over a way out of the relationship.

Maintenance

Understandably, Miller and Rollnick (1991, p. 17) explained, "Making a change, however, does not guarantee that the change will be maintained." That is precisely why the goal of this stage is to prevent a relapse to returning to the perpetrator of the horrific abuse. In the case of the battered woman, there are enormous obstacles to preventing this relapse, which in this context would lead to reestablishing the relationship. Ferraro (1997) reported that generally between five and seven attempts to leave are made before finally being successful. Many women return after departing from a shelter or other locations of escape. Various reasons have been given for this action, including ". . . fear, continuing emotional involvement, desire to keep the drugs that weakens fortitude, goal commitments, and resolve."

Also to be considered is the threat of impending death and incapacitating injuries if found. These fears become overpowering as time passes. No matter where the woman goes or hides, thoughts of being found create nightmares, intense trepidation, and emotional turmoil. Posttraumatic stress symptoms (e.g., anxiety-producing assault flashbacks and hypervigilance), as well as pervasive grief reactions over losses (e.g., reminders of positive aspects of the relationship; former economic security), exaggerate the vulnerability to goal commitment. These events make it difficult for some women to sustain a lasting change. Nevertheless, many women do indeed make and carry out strategies to maintain the separation, eventually moving toward the final stage of termination. The utilization of treatment resources and ongoing supportive structures can be crucial elements in alleviating troubling symptoms and coping with the marked changes this stage presents. With each step in this journey, a reaffirming of the self becomes more apparent.

Termination

If termination of the battering experience can be achieved, an empowering grasp of self-efficacy, self-confidence, and a positive self-image can emerge. Women come to believe that their actions/ behaviors have made a positive difference in their lives. The relief of being unburdened confirms the favorable aspects of change. Yet the aftermath of the harrowing experience may linger interminably, and despite its subtle effects, they may feel an attachment to the partner left behind. Even the perpetrator's death may not sever this bond. But a new life can be sought if needed resources and opportunities are available to counter this lingering emotional connection—for example, earning a satisfactory income, suitable housing and other basic necessities, legal assistance and protection, and enduring supports. Investing in trusting relationships and social networks takes time, patience, and effort, as with the seeking of satisfying goals and career choices.

ROBERTS'S SEVEN-STAGE CRISIS INTERVENTION MODEL AND BATTERING SEVERITY CONTINUUM

The Crisis Intervention Model (Roberts, 1991, 2000, 2005) provides pertinent guidelines to follow in the crucial period of early crisis resolution. Divided into seven stages, the model details hierarchal assessment and intervention activities that aim to subdue a crisis so that strength-oriented, empowering, cognitive, and independent functioning can be achieved.

Stage 1 details a risk assessment screening plan that examines imminent danger and potential lethality measures. Stage 2 initiates relationship building, based on trust and rapport, that will facilitate entry into the next phase (Stage 3). During this stage (problem identification and definition), the severity and duration of precipitating events that led to help-seeking are examined. Stage 4 employs therapeutic skills (e.g., active listening, empathy, reflecting, and summarizing disclosures) to explore clients' feelings and emotions. Stage 5 assesses previously developed coping mechanisms, both adaptive and maladaptive, that forged reactions to crisis events. From these data, alternative coping methods that tap into client strengths are introduced, laying the foundation for empowering cognitive problem-solving. Stage 6 formulates an action plan that involves incorporating rational cognitive functioning, goal setting, and taking steps to develop and implement problem solutions toward crisis resolution. The final phase, Stage 7, affords the opportunity to examine and reinforce

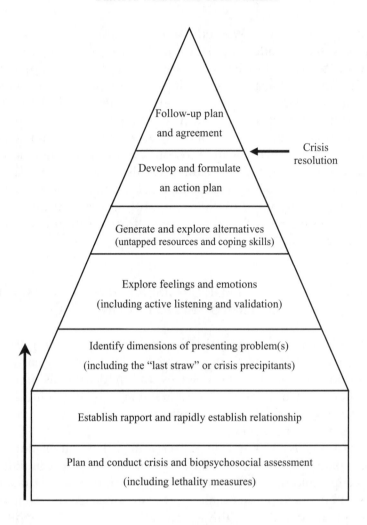

Crisis resolution

Follow-up plan and agreement

Develop and formulate an action plan

Generate and explore alternatives (untapped resources and coping skills)

Explore feelings and emotions (including active listening and validation)

Identify dimensions of presenting problem(s) (including the "last straw" or crisis precipitants)

Establish rapport and rapidly establish relationship

Plan and conduct crisis and biopsychosocial assessment (including lethality measures)

FIGURE 2.1   Roberts's Seven-Stage Crisis Intervention Model.

Source: Copyright © Albert R. Roberts, 1991. Reprinted by permission of the author.

progress made. Acknowledging the importance of maintaining these positive changes, follow-up sessions are mutually planned and agreed on (see Figure 2.1).

Five levels of duration and severity of battering (Roberts, 2002; Roberts & Roberts, 2005) have been developed from a statewide research study of 501 battered women in pertinent locations—"prisons, shelters, police departments, and the community" (p. 68). This continuum typology's usefulness, as a clinical diagnostic and risk indicator, is significant in identifying the level of subjective danger before more extensive injuries and even death might occur. With this vital information, mental health and criminal justice practitioners can intervene, with the aim of preventing further violence and harm, while empowering battered women to gain freedom from further pain and suffering.

From Level 1+ (short-term victims) to Level 5+ (homicidal), the battering experience is described from both duration and severity perspectives. Psychosocial variables of descriptive levels provide additional descriptive indicators for risk assessments. Figure 2.2 delineates the major significant points to consider in each level of the continuum.

THE COGNITIVE PROBLEM-SOLVING PRACTICE MODEL

Cognitive problem-solving treatment serves to reinforce and fortify the gains made through crisis intervention that provided a foundation for problem solving and empowerment. Yet we know that vulnerability remains; return to the nightmarish existence is not uncommon. Therefore, the client would benefit greatly with continued help in sustaining previous advances made, while reinforcing positive behavioral and emotional change. A continuity of supportive environmental resources should be recognized and tapped. This treatment approach is a natural progression to Roberts's crisis intervention model, complementing its cognitive problem-solving emphasis on positive change (see chapter 3 in this book by Professors Roberts and Burman for a more detailed discussion).

To demonstrate the usefulness of the practice model, this chapter concentrates on the case of Naomi, a severely battered woman whose traumatic experiences and efforts toward leaving her husband were previously cited in the *Handbook of Domestic Violence Intervention Strategies* (Roberts, 2002, pp. 74–76). The severity and duration of her abuse place her in Level 4+ of Roberts's continuum typology (i.e., a regular pattern of chronic and severe battering). The category includes the majority of women in the research study and therefore can be a focal point in illuminating pertinent strategic coping methods and problem-solving skills instigated toward terminating battering

1	2	3	4	5
Short-Term (N = 94)	**Intermediate** (N = 104)	**Intermittent Long-Term** (N = 38)	**Chronic and Predictable** (N = 160)	**Homicidal** (N = 105)
Less than 1 year (dating relationship for a few weeks or several months); mild to moderate intensity; usually high school or college students	Several months to 2 years (cohabiting or recently married); moderate to severe injuries	Severe and intense violent episode without warning; long periods without violence, then another violent episode; married with children	Severe repetitive incidents; frequent, predictable pattern; violence often precipitated by alcohol or polydrug abuse; married with children	Violence escalates to homicide, murder precipitated by explicit death threats and life-threatening injuries (cohabiting or married); weapons in home
1–3 incidents	3–15 incidents	4–30 incidents	Usually several hundred violent acts per woman	Numerous violent and severe acts per woman

Psycho-social variables and the 5-level women-battering continuum

1	2	3	4	5
Usually middle-class and steady dating relationship (severity; e.g., push, shove, and sometimes hit with large object; woman leaves after first, second, or third physically abusive act; caring support system, e.g., parents or police)	Usually middle-class and recently married or living together (severity; e.g., punch, kick, chokehold, or severe beating; woman leaves due to bruises or injury; caring support system, e.g., new boyfriend or parents)	Usually upper-middle or upper social class, staying together for children or status/prestige of wealthy husband (woman stays until children grow up and leave home; no alternative support system)	Usually lower socioeconomic or middle-class, often devout Catholic with school-age children at home (abuse continues until husband is arrested, is hospitalized, or dies; husband is blue-collar, skilled or semiskilled)	Usually lower socioeconomic class, high long-term unemployment, limited education; majority of battered women dropped out of high school; woman usually suffers from PTSD, traumatic bonding, or Battered Woman Syndrome

FIGURE 2.2 Duration and severity level of woman-battering continuum.

Source: Copyright © Albert R. Roberts (2002). Reprinted by permission.

relationships. Generally, unlike the short-term, intermediate, and intermittent long-term categories of battering, the violence directed at chronically battered women is predictably a discernible pattern and often precipitated by alcohol or polydrug abuse. Extent of the injuries may vary, but become more extreme and debilitating with the passage of time. Heightened consideration must be given to safety precautions, alleviating emotional distress, improving coping skills, developing and implementing action plans, and addressing other pressing concerns and issues that might arise during the treatment process.

NAOMI'S EXPERIENCE

Leaving her husband was initiated after a desperate period of crisis following a severe battering that culminated 7 years of terror and incapacitating injuries. Naomi entered a shelter with her child, attended a battered women's support group, and received counseling that motivated her readiness to change. Roberts's Seven-Stage Crisis Intervention Model (Roberts, 1991, 2000, 2005) helped to identify recurring problems of violence and harassment that put her at greater risk with the passage of time. It also assisted in contemplating options and devising a viable action plan. The stages of change raised doubts about her husband's willingness and capabilities to alter his abusive behaviors and reinforced the need to sever emotional and physical ties that kept her captive in the relationship. After realistically weighing the costs and benefits of staying with her husband, Naomi became determined to take safety precautions and carried out her course of action. Having accomplished these tasks, she shortly thereafter sought additional treatment to maintain the gains made. She realized that her current situation was precarious and was fearful of faltering in her resolve to terminate the relationship. This began the next phase of Naomi's journey toward empowerment and independence.

Treatment: A Cognitive, Problem-Solving Model

Consistent with intervention protocols, the initial engagement of the client in a trusting and rapport-building relationship is critical to establishing compliance and willingness to participate fully in treatment. Acknowledging Naomi's significant changes to date, the mutually agreed-on treatment plan was geared to preventing re-lapse, monitoring safety activities, and improving/developing new problem-solving coping skills geared to satisfying and healthy func-tioning. It was necessary to take a general history, type and severity of assaults and injuries experienced, and problems that emerged since leaving her husband, to design and implement the treatment plan.

Problem-solving steps included (a) a general, lethal, and mental health assessment; (b) problem identification and implications; (c) goal setting and contracting; (d) implementation of interventions; (e) termination and referrals; and (f) an evaluation of the effective-ness of interventions.

A General Background Assessment. The following data were derived from a preliminary interview with Naomi, placing her in the category of a chronically abused woman (Level 4):

Demographics: 34-year-old single parent, with one child; high school graduate; worked for the same company for 14 years as a customer service representative.

Abuse history: father was an abuser; chronically abused by her hus-band for 7 years (mostly without warning).

Abuse injuries: broken nose; bruises all over body; eye swollen from punches (three different occasions); punched in mouth; choked several times; faked passing out after being strangled (attempt to avoid being killed).

Seeking help: attended a shelter and support group for battered women, after which she made the decision to leave her husband; obtained a court restraining order.

A Lethality and Mental Health Assessment. The predictable nature of the repetitive cycle of abuse over a 7-year period and the mode and extent of the injuries acquired must alert to the potential for lethality. It can be surmised that if Naomi had not escaped from this situation, the abuse would have escalated to this magnitude. Yet the mental health assessment exhibits an overlying emotional attachment/grief over losses and emerging posttraumatic stress symp-toms, including emotional/psychic numbing, flashbacks, reexperi-encing the trauma, hypervigilance, insomnia, inability to concen-trate, anxiety, and depression. These symptoms are often debilitating and can readily deplete her energy and the positive changes made.

Problem Identification and Implications. From the assessments conducted, several problem areas should be targeted in treatment:

1. Recurrent emotional distress and symptoms of posttraumatic stress disorder (PTSD) that surface periodically.
2. Recurrent fears of the batterer's retribution/return (safety considerations).
3. Inability to maintain changes and potential relapse (return to the battering relationship).
4. Lack of a wide network of stable social supports and necessary community resources.

Interventions. Planned clinical procedures are designed to focus on the presenting problems, in order to produce meaningful behavioral and emotional changes to support treatment goals. A clearly defined, step-by-step format can follow this design:

Problem → Objective → Intervention → Goal

Problem #1: Recurrent emotional distress and symptoms of PTSD that surface periodically.
Objective #1: Client will utilize group and individual therapy to address the emotional distress.
Interventions: Homework assignment: Read checklist of cognitive distortions from *Feeling Good Handbook* (Burns, 1989, p. 96).
   a. Make a list of five recent times you experienced emotional distress.
   b. List cognitive distortions you experienced during these times of distress.
   c. Discuss this list during group therapy and individual therapy for feedback.
   d. Develop five rational responses (realistic thoughts) that will address these feelings of emotional distress.
Objective #2: Client's symptoms related to emotional distress and PTSD will be alleviated with the aid of medications (if medically indicated).
Interventions:
   a. Referrals will be made for testing of anxiety-related symptoms.
   b. Depending on test results, antidepressant and antianxiety medications may be prescribed.

Goals:
  a. To develop problem-solving and cognitive/behavioral coping skills through cognitive restructuring and other techniques to relieve the emotional distress and maintain the change process.
  b. To stabilize medically and relieve anxiety-related signs and symptoms.

Problem #2: Recurrent fears of the batterer's retribution/return (safety considerations).

Objective #1: Client will add new precautionary measures to the safety plan devised at the shelter with the assistance of therapy feedback and the book, *A Woman Like You: The Face of Domestic Violence.*

Objective #2: Client's fears will subside after safety plan has been updated, with reassurance from peers in the battered woman's group.

Interventions:
  a. Client will review her safety plan and discuss it in therapy sessions.
  b. Client will obtain 10 more safety measures from feedback and the assigned book, to combine with the original plan.

Goal: To empower the client to develop a safety plan that will have the effect of counteracting potential repetition of assaultive behaviors.

Problem #3: Inability to maintain changes and potential relapse (return to the battering relationship).

Objective: Client will utilize therapy groups and individual counseling to identify strategies that affirm the gains made by her decision to leave the battering relationship.

Interventions:
  a. Identify five danger signs that may provoke a potential relapse and return to the abusive relationship. Discuss these in treatment sessions.
  b. Detail five treatment strategies that will maintain positive changes accomplished and discuss the possible outcomes in treatment sessions to obtain constructive feedback.

Goal: To successfully complete the maintenance stage of change by improving coping skills; experiencing a sense of self-efficacy, self-confidence, and empowerment; and guarding against falling back to self-defeating behaviors and thought processes.

Problem #4: Lack of a wide network of stable social supports and necessary community resources.

Objective: Client will obtain lists of social supports and community resources from social service departments and personal/associate contacts to secure safety and will look into opportunities for advancement and healthy living.

Interventions:

    a. Identify suitable community resources from United Way and other agency resources.

    b. Note potential supports and resources from churches, schools, and media outlets.

    c. List five desirable goals and opportunities that will be of interest, will be manageable, and have potential for success.

Goal: To develop and maintain supportive structures and resources that can be tapped when needed in order to sustain efforts toward independent living arrangements.

Contract/Informal Agreement on the Number of Sessions

It is expected that the initial contract will specify 12 to 15 sessions, with more to be included if needed. An ongoing assessment and mutual agreement may alter the actual number of sessions and responsibilities/tasks.

IMPLEMENTATION OF THE COGNITIVE, PROBLEM-SOLVING MODEL

Naomi has thus far made courageous strides in escaping a potentially dangerous situation, but her resolve and actions remain uncertain. After leaving her husband, she and her child went to a shelter where they found safety, compassion, and vital services (e.g., counseling and community referral sources). They then moved in with a friend from work who was unknown to Naomi's husband. Realizing this was temporary, she had to formulate ideas and decisions about the future. During this period, fears of retribution from her husband and emotional reactions to past experiences created havoc in her daily routine. She considered moving away, but felt immobilized by having to make it on her own without the security of her long-held job. She began to have second thoughts about the decision to leave her spouse, as recurrent favorable memories were interspersed with the negative aspects of the relationship. The emotional attachment had not been severed, as she grieved the loss of the only man she had loved so intimately.

Therapy was sought to alleviate distressing symptoms and, as Naomi expressed, to "gain guidance before making a move that I might regret." She was obviously struggling against an impulsive action, attempting to control her emotions and behaviors by cognitively weighing the pros and cons of any decision she might make (as she had done in a previous stage of change).

Her inner strength had gotten her out of a hazardous relationship, but she was now feeling vulnerable. Due to the acute nature of posttraumatic symptoms and difficulty maintaining the changes she had made, treatment was to focus on these issues concurrently. In addition to reaffirming Naomi's positive changes, relapse prevention would be prominent in the plan to maintain her progress and help move ahead with her goals.

An assessment of her safety precautions, current emotional stability, and coping skills was conducted in order to ascertain an appropriate individualized treatment and action plan. Various scales were helpful in measuring the degree of symptom severity: the PTSD Diagnostic Stress Scale (Foa, Cashman, Jaycox, & Perry, 1997), the Beck Depression Inventory II (Beck, Steer, & Brown, 1996), and the Beck Hopelessness Scale (Beck, Weissman, Lester, & Trexler, 1974). The Response to Violence Inventory (Dutton, 1992a) assessed coping strategies in reaction to battering incidents; open-ended interviews enumerated safety precautions taken in the past and continued to the current time.

A contract was agreed on that Naomi would not return to her husband while in treatment (a period of 3 to 4 months), and if a personal decision were made to do so, she would discuss the advantages and disadvantages in a session. She realized the choice was hers to make, but rationally and not under duress. In the meantime, a therapeutic relationship was being established, based on mutual rapport and trust.

Cognitive Restructuring

It was important to point out, reaffirm, and have Naomi cognitively examine the reasons she left her husband, and the determination, strengths, and resourcefulness she exhibited while taking the necessary action steps to do so. Although many trepidations and other emotions were evident during this process, she willfully and forcefully set and followed through with her goal. Finding meaning in these actions was critical, to strengthen her commitment to change the status quo and take control of her life. Many problem-solving skills were in place, but she needed positive reinforcement to internalize the empowering gains already made by her own efforts.

Many factors, previously cited, jeopardize the maintenance stage of change. Among these are also intrusive, self-defeating thoughts (e.g., "I can't make it alone") that relate the feelings of hopelessness and powerlessness endemic in the battered woman's experience. Through reflective listening, reframing negativity, and reality testing, Naomi was coached to monitor, challenge, and modify these beliefs and thought patterns that created troublesome and unsettling emotions. Assertiveness training and positive self-talk in the form of affirmations added to her repertoire of coping skills. She was also reminded that her lengthy work record and advancement were evidence that she had the capability of surviving autonomously and independently, while making significant strides in protecting herself and her child.

The lingering attachment bonds posed another difficulty to overcome. She was challenged to provide indications that her needs and expectations were being met in the relationship. The betrayal of trust and dreams of a happy and secure marriage could not be justified; positive feelings that were developed earlier, before the advent of the abuse, had changed to fear and disillusionment. When reconstructing events, she concluded that what she had considered love was a developing unhealthy dependency. The caring and concern for her husband was not returned in kind; therefore, her self-esteem and self-worth diminished.

Naomi adamantly acknowledged that had she stayed, she might be dead by now. This was demonstrated by the last choking scene in which she felt compelled to "fake passing out" to stop the strangling resulting from her husband's rage. He had been drinking heavily during this episode and many others. Naomi had always blamed the alcohol or even her own provocation for these transgressions, but through recall and logic, was able to admit that "he beat me relentlessly, even when he was sober and no matter what I did or said." Exploring these events provided a new perspective to ponder.

Soon she realized that he was responsible for his behavior; the desire for control and power over her was the source of the aggression, and undoubtedly would continue if she returned.

Focus on Emotional Distress

Coping with debilitating memories of past abuses was facilitated by having Naomi recall accounts of the assaults in a manner in which the original anxiety and other debilitating emotions could now be controlled and subdued in a recognizably safe environment, without fears of being revictimized. Relaxation and stress management training preceded this endeavor so she could pace the emerging emotions to her level of tolerance. Homework assignments were constructed to practice these relaxation techniques, while simultaneously disqualifying the force of disabling fears that often erupted spontaneously. The aim of these activities was to decrease emotional reactions to trauma reminders by increasing her power and control over them.

It was important to have her understand the essence of posttraumatic symptoms as reflections of past painful and fear-evoking experiences that could be reduced and systematically desensitized when examining them in another context, under differing circumstances. Antidepressant medication (Prozac) was initially prescribed, while monitoring closely for mood stabilization and potential side effects. Similar to other treatment modalities, assertiveness training, positive self-talk, and affirmations had a positive effect in reducing the debilitating effects of emotional distress.

Grief work encompassed the many losses Naomi experienced—the relationship with her husband, her home and security, and her sense of self that she once valued. She had to come to terms with the reality of what the relationship had become in contrast to what she had hoped for, in order to let go of it. And she had to regain self-respect and confidence in herself as a vital, productive woman, unencumbered by self-blame and guilt. To accomplish these realms, the sense of loss and subsequent emotions had to be realized, accepted, and expressed, thereby acknowledging and comprehending the normality of the pain and confusion that accompanies grief. This also included the anger related to the unjustified abuses and betrayal that may or may not have been recognized. To establish a renewed identity, forged by improved self-esteem and acceptance of self, she was helped to make sense of her experiences—how they had a significant effect on her beliefs, values, attitudes, and actions; her subsequent choices and decisions; and the direction her life took. Passing through this process, as well as other tasks of rehabilitation, would enable her to grow and fully develop to move in another direction—toward self-actualization and empowerment in reinvesting herself in social ties and new goals.

Fears of retaliation by her husband required a realistic outlook of her safety options. Naomi soon recognized that she could not control her husband's impulsive behaviors and followed through with protective alternatives available—obtaining another restraining order and inquiring about an arrest, if the order was not honored; identifying people to call in case of an emergency; hiding money and a suitcase with necessary items in a secure place; and making sure transportation was readily available, if needed. She was aware that with the predictability and chronicity of the abuse, there was no guarantee that her husband would not attempt to find her and reenact the assaults and harassment.

Nevertheless, she was not ready to relocate, but knew that this (along with changing names) might be the only viable alternative available to safeguarding herself and her child. A positive aspect for her to consider was the ability to find suitable work and income, based on her many years of employment, responsibilities, and promotions.

Throughout treatment, efforts were made to activate supportive structures and increase social networks. In addition, continuous involvement in a battered woman's therapy and support group provided helpful feedback, reassurance, role modeling, and guidance.

Termination and Evaluation

Treatment was terminated with the agreement that follow-up contacts would be made, so that any problems and safety concerns could be immediately addressed. Naomi continued to show progress in stabilizing emotionally and maintaining her goals of independent living and securing social supports. Referrals for community resources were made available, as needed. In the event that she decided to move out of state, she was assured that assistance would be forthcoming in finding employment, housing, a school for her child, and financial, legal, therapeutic, and supportive aid.

Fortune (2002, p. 458) cites several criteria that would determine the ending of therapeutic services. Those of significance to Naomi's treatment experience include:

• Meeting goals set by the client or practitioner.
• Improved behavior and intrapsychic functioning for the client.
• The client expresses readiness to terminate.

CONCLUSION

Cognitive therapy methods and problem-solving are incorporated to enhance current coping capacities and decision making that can be generalized to many other problematic situations and interpersonal transactions. The development of functional behavioral, emotional, and environmental changes are paramount to its goals, utilizing various strategies that are formulated from assessing individual needs and resources. In working with a battered woman, a crisis intervention approach is inevitably a first-step in assuring safety with stabilization, initial problem-solving, and the exploration of alternative options that will culminate in meaningful action plans. Like the cognitive problem-solving model, crisis intervention necessitates a cognitive restructuring of perceptions, beliefs, and attitudes that empowers decision making toward change.

Prescribed and closely monitored psychiatric medications may be recommended, after evaluating the presenting symptoms. If the woman has been self-medicating with alcohol and other drugs, an assessment should be made to determine the amount, frequency, and duration of use. Substance abuse treatment may be necessary if abuse or dependency is suspected.

Cognitive problem-solving can be utilized in every stage of change. It exemplifies new modes of learning, with a reality/strength oriented focus that reinforces survival and actualization skills. Toward these objectives, self-defeating thoughts and beliefs that restrain rational decisions are challenged so that constructive problem-solving can be facilitated. Separating emotional choice-making from rational, cognitively planned actions can mean the difference between enduring victimization and potential death versus survival, a better quality of life, and breaking the generational cycle of violence. For many women, particularly those in the severely chronically battered group who experience years of escalating abuse, leaving the relationship on a permanent basis may be the only recourse. For as Ferraro (1997, p. 138) reminds us when considering survival and freedom from continued harassment and abuse: "the most realistic strategy... is for women to leave and begin new lives."

REFERENCES

Babcock, J. C., Canady, B. E., Senior, A., & Eckhardt, C. I. (2005). Applying the transtheoretical model to female and male perpetrators of intimate partner violence: Gender differences in stages and processes of change. *Violence and Victims, 2,* 235–250.

Barnett, O. W. (2001). Why battered women do not leave, Part 2: External inhibiting factors—Social support and internal inhibiting factors. *Trauma, Violence, &Abuse, 2,* 3–35.

Beck, A. T., Steer, R. A., & Brown, G. K. (1996). *The manual for the Beck Depression Inventory-II.* San Antonio: Psychological Corporation.

Beck, A. T., Weissman, A., Lester, D., & Trexler, L. (1974). The measurement of pessimism: The Hopelessness Scale. *Journal of Consulting and Clinical Psychology, 42,* 861–865.

Brown, J. (1997). Working toward freedom from violence: The process of change in battered women. *Violence Against Women, 3,* 5–26.

Burke, J. G., Denison, J. A., Gielen, A. C., McDonnell, K. A., & O'Campo, P. (2004). Ending intimate partner violence: An application of the transtheoretical model. *American Journal of Health Behavior, 28*(2), 122–133.

Burman, S. (2003). Battered women: Stages of change and other treatment models that instigate and sustain leaving. *Brief Treatment and Crisis Intervention, 3*(1), 83–98.

Burns, D. D. (1989). *The feeling good handbook.* New York: William Morrow.

Dutton, M. A. (1992a). *Empowering and healing the battered woman: A model for assessment and intervention.* New York: Springer Publishing.

Dutton, M. A. (1992b). Assessment and treatment of post-traumatic stress disorder among battered women. In D. Foy (Ed.), *Treating PTSD: Cognitive-behavioral strategies* (pp. 69–98). New York: Guilford.

Eckhardt, C. I., Babcock, J., & Homack, S. (2004). Partner assaultive men and the stages and processes of change. *Journal of Family Violence, 19*(2), 81–93.

Ferraro, K. J. (1997). Battered women: Strategies for survival. In A. P. Cardarelli (Ed.), *Violence between intimate partners: Patterns, causes, and effects* (pp. 124–140). Boston: Allyn and Bacon.

Foa, E. B., Cashman, L., Jaycox, L., & Perry, K. (1997). The validation of a self-report measure of posttraumatic stress disorder: The Posttraumatic Diagnostic Scale. *Psychological Assessment, 9*, 445–451.

Fortune, A. E. (2002). Terminating with clients. In A. R. Roberts (Ed.), *Social workers' desk reference* (pp. 458–463). New York: Oxford University Press.

Miller, W. R., & Rollnick, S. (1991). *Motivational interviewing.* New York: Guilford Press.

Miller, W. R., & Rollnick, S. (2002). *Motivational interviewing* (2nd ed.). New York: Guilford Press.

Petrocelli, J. V. (2002). Processes and stages of change: Counseling with the transtheoretical model of change. *Journal of Counseling & Development, 80*, 22–30.

Prochaska, J. O., & DiClemente, C. C. (1982). Transtheoretical therapy: Toward an integrative model of change. *Journal of Consulting and Clinical Psychology, 5*, 390–395.

Prochaska, J. O., Norcross, J. C., & DiClemente, C. C. (1994). *Changing for good.* New York: William Morrow.

Prochaska, J. M., & Prochaska, J. O. (2002). Transtheoretical model guidelines for families with child abuse and neglect. In A. R. Roberts (Ed.), *Social workers' desk reference* (pp. 379–384). New York: Oxford University Press.

Prochaska, J. O., & Velicer, W. F. (1997). The transtheoretical model of health behavior change. *American Journal of Health Promotion, 12*, 38–48.

Roberts, A. R. (Ed.). (1991). *Contemporary perspectives on crisis intervention and prevention.* Englewood Cliffs, NJ: Prentice-Hall.

Roberts, A. R. (Ed.). (2000). *Crisis intervention handbook: Assessment, treatment, and research* (2nd ed.). New York: Oxford University Press.

Roberts, A. R. (2002). Duration and severity of woman battering: A conceptual model/continuum. In A. R. Roberts (Ed.), *Handbook of domestic violence intervention strategies: Policies, programs, and legal remedies* (pp. 64–79). New York: Oxford University Press.

Roberts, A. R. (2005). Bridging the past and present to the future of crisis intervention and crisis management. In A. R. Roberts (Ed.), *Crisis intervention handbook: Assessment, treatment, and research* (3rd edition, pp. 3–34). New York: Oxford University Press.

Roberts, A. R., & Burman, S. (1998). Crisis intervention and cognitive problem-solving therapy with battered women: A national survey and practice model. In A. R. Roberts (Ed.), *Battered women and their families*, (2nd ed., pp. 3–28). New York: Springer Publishing.

Roberts, A. R., & Roberts, B. S. (2005). *Ending intimate abuse: Practical guidance and survival strategies.* New York: Oxford University Press.

Saunders, E. A., & Edelson, J. A. (1999). Attachment style, traumatic bonding, and developing relational capacities in a long-term trauma group for women. *International Journal of Group Psychotherapy, 49,* 465–485.

Scott, K. L. (2004). Stage of change as a predictor of attrition among men in a batterer treatment program. *Journal of Family Violence, 19,* 37–47.

Scott, K. L., & Wolfe, D. A. (2003). Readiness to change as a predictor of outcome in batterer treatment. *Journal of Consulting and Clinical Psychology, 71,* 879–889.

Walker, L. E. A. (1994). *Abused women and survivor therapy: A practical guide for the psychotherapist.* Washington, DC: American Psychological Association.

CHAPTER 3

National Survey on Empowerment Strategies, Crisis Intervention, and Cognitive Problem-Solving Therapy With Battered Women

Albert R. Roberts and Sondra Burman

Battering of women is one of the most pervasive and dangerous social problems in American society. Recent estimates indicate that 8.7 million women are victimized by partner abuse in their homes each year. Some of the women are assaulted by smacking or punching once or twice; others are repeatedly battered with increasing frequency and intensity for several months or years. As a result of being chronically abused, many battered women suffer from bipolar disorder, anxiety, posttraumatic stress disorder (PTSD), panic disorder, or suicide ideation (Petretic-Jackson & Jackson, 1996; Walker, 1985). Three clinical studies of abused women, living in shelters or attending support groups, have found PTSD rates ranging from 45% to 84% (Astin, Lawrence, Pincus, & Foy, 1990; Housekamp & Foy, 1991; Roberts, 1996). Descriptive and clinical studies have consistently found a high incidence of somatic problems and depressive symptomatology among battered women (Cascardi & O'Leary, 1992; Gelles & Harrop, 1989).

Crisis intervention units and emergency shelters for battered women have made great strides in the past 20 years. In 1975, for example, there were only a handful of such shelters, but by 1995 there were over 1,250 shelters for battered women and their children in the United States (Roberts, 1995; Roberts & Roberts, 1990). Respondents to Roche's (1996) national survey of 622 shelters indicated that the shelters' major function is to advocate for social change and the empowerment of battered women. The average shelter was approximately 9 years old, with an annual operating budget ranging from $135,000 to $160,000, employing 6 full-time and 4 part-time paid staff and 25 volunteers.

A scarcity of research documenting the types of counseling and treatment modalities or intervention approaches used at shelters for battered women was also evident. In addition, studies on the short and long-term adjustment of battered women receiving crisis intervention and cognitive therapy were minimal. Only four descriptive reports at local shelters have examined the types and components of shelter-based treatment. Dziegielewski, Resnick, and Krause (1996) illustrated the importance of crisis theory and crisis intervention in their work at a battered women's organization in Tennessee. The A-B-C model of crisis intervention was used at a shelter in Fort Myers, Florida (Roberts & Roberts, 1990). Webb (1992) examined the ways in which cognitive behavior techniques can be utilized to reeducate and change distorted belief systems among battered women at a North Carolina shelter. Geller and Wasserstrom (1984) conducted long-term psychotherapy and conjoint therapy with battered women and their partners at V.I.B.'s, a community outreach and residential program for battered women in Long Island, New York.

This chapter presents the findings of a national research study that was conducted to fill the knowledge gap in areas pertaining to clinical practice with battered women. A case study is presented, utilizing an innovative approach to treatment—the sequence of a dual, congruent practice model consisting of crisis intervention and cognitively oriented problem solving. Because of battered women's propensity to return to the abusive partner, it is being proposed that a longer, more intensive therapeutic experience is necessary than those now conducted by shelters and other agencies. This will reinforce ego strengths and empower battered women to make wise and appropriate decisions concerning their own welfare and that of their children.

A NATIONAL STUDY OF SHELTERS FOR BATTERED WOMEN

Until this national survey (Roberts, 1997) was conducted, there was very little information on the availability of clinical staff who provide crisis intervention, cognitive treatment, or other types of therapeutic interventions for traumatized and abused women. In this study with 176 respondents, 223 (24.4%) of the 907 staff members had an MSW or MA degree; 11 had PhDs. However, the overwhelming majority of the shelter staff had no graduate degree or clinical training. The data collected examine staffing patterns and the organizational structure of these battered women's shelters and units. Data were also collected concerning funding sources and different types of services provided by the shelters.

Due to the dearth of research on the nature and types of clinical practice models used by shelter staff, the aim of this study was also to learn the diversity of current models in use and how they are incorporated in interventions with battered women. The findings reported in this chapter will indicate the nature of three intervention formats utilized by shelters throughout the United States: intake assessments, practice models, and empowerment strategies. An illustration of these fundamental activities, the application of the proposed crisis intervention and cognitively oriented problem-solving practice model will be demonstrated through a case study of a battered woman. This will serve to illustrate the utility of this model in providing the battered woman with the tools to not only cope with current situations and resulting acute problems, but also to prevent more chronic dysfunction by learning strategies that will reinforce stabilization, healing, and growth. A wide variation of types of interventions that are likely to be used by shelter staff is examined, for example, peer counseling, support groups, advocacy, empowerment, generalist practice, crisis intervention, cognitive therapy, and the problem-solving method.

Methodology

The current study reported is part of a larger research project of 176 shelter directors. The sample is comprised of 87 subjects, or 49% of the respondents from the original study.

A mailing list was developed of 20% or 250 of the 1,250 battered women's shelters from the National Organization for Victim

Assistance (NOVA) directory and the Office for Victims of Crimes of the U.S. Department of Justice. Using a random digits table, a 20% sample was obtained. A four-page questionnaire was devised, pretested (with three administrators of shelters), revised, and mailed with a cover letter to 250 programs in early January 1994. One month after the initial mailing, a follow-up letter and another copy of the questionnaire were sent to the nonrespondents. By April 1994, 176 completed questionnaires were returned—a 70% response rate.

The study examined program objectives, staffing patterns, funding sources, types of services offered, approximate number of clients served by each program in 1993, self-reported strengths and weaknesses of the programs, and significant changes made in the past 2 years. This study was designed to be relevant to administrators and program development specialists. Unfortunately, hardly any information was provided on the nature and extent of clinical interventions by shelter staff. Therefore, a follow-up letter with a one-page questionnaire was sent to the 176 respondents in the first study. This questionnaire starts with a case scenario of a battered woman with medical injuries coming to a shelter in acute crisis, with her three children, in the middle of the night. Eighty-seven of the 176 shelters (almost 50%) responded to this survey.

The clinical survey collected data in three areas:

1. Intake forms and assessment protocols.
2. Types and components of crisis intervention and other clinical practice models.
3. Methods of empowering battered women.

Findings

There were 87 responses to the mailing of 176 clinical questionnaires—a 49% response rate. From the type and use of intake forms and assessment-protocols category, it was found that all of the respondents conduct a basic intake, ranging from a few questions to a seven-page form. The content of the intake forms includes medical injuries, safety needs, demographics, listings of the presenting problem, alcohol and drug use, current abusive incident, prior abusive incidents, prior use of services, and any abuse of children. The respondents indicated that an intake assessment can be delayed as long

TABLE 3.1 Practice Models and Techniques at Abused Women's Shelters

Technique	n
1. Provide support by reviewing options and choices and referring to a support group	28
2. Explore and validate feelings	19
3. Assess immediate needs of clients	15
4. Work with client to plan and formulate goals	14
5. Short-term crisis intervention	12
6. Active listening	9
7. Problem-solving method	8
8. Referral to community resources and private practitioner	8

as 24 hours, until the battered woman in acute crisis is stabilized. Surprisingly, only two of the clinical directors used standardized assessment scales to assess and measure suicide risk, depression, intrusive thoughts and fears, posttraumatic stress disorder, or other psychiatric disorders.

The second part of the survey examined the type and extent to which shelter staff are likely to use a clinical practice model to intervene with a severely battered woman. There were eight different patterns, which emerged in terms of the treatment strategy or practice model used by respondents:

- For the most part, the overwhelming majority of respondents did not answer the question that was asked. They do not seem to understand what constitutes a practice theory, practice model, or clinical/treatment strategy (Table 3.1) . We firmly believe it is important for clinicians to assure safety and stabilize the client, explore and validate feelings, listen actively and reflectively, examine coping skills, empower by exploring options together, and help the client to formulate an action plan. However, it is too simplistic and potentially harmful to assume that ventilation, active listening, and referral are solutions to severe and intense battering.

For the majority of battered women, permanently leaving the batterer, regaining their self-esteem, finding a safe place to live, and obtaining a steady, well-paying job are all needed. The ego-bolstering accomplished when a survivor returns to school or obtains a steady job is critical to recovery. However, in view of the large group of battered women with major depressive disorders, posttraumatic stress disorder, and generalized anxiety disorder, crisis intervention and cognitive and trauma therapy are necessary to prevent relapse. Battered women suffering from PTSD often find themselves in a state of high arousal and avoidance behaviors that cut off their attempts at establishing constructive interpersonal relationships. These survivors often have flashbacks, nightmares, and intrusive recollections of the traumatic battering events. The result of not resolving the trauma is a continued sense of danger and intense fears. Moderate to severe depression, accompanied by continued periods of loneliness, sadness, and crying, keeps them isolated and stuck. Through therapy, depressive and PTSD symptoms can be markedly reduced. Therapists need to help battered women identify their strengths and explore options, alternatives, and decision making (Walker, 1994).

To elicit a response to the methods of empowering-battered-women category, a question was asked in reference to the case of Sandra (described subsequently): "As a victim/survivor advocate, what suggestions would you have to help empower this client?" The responses can be grouped into seven categories (see Table 3.2).

Empowerment is critically important in order for battered women to recover, heal, and lead productive lives in nonviolent relationships. But many severely battered and traumatized women need both empowerment and therapy to survive and thrive. There are no quick fixes or easy solutions. Commitment to change and permanent escape from the battering relationship requires a trusting and empathic therapeutic relationship that bolsters ego strengths and reempowers the survivor through positive reinforcement of small changes as well as large ones.

The application of the dual practice model (crisis intervention and cognitively oriented problem solving) will coordinate each step of the process in the case study of Sandra. This case study portrays the tribulations of a battered woman as she struggles with her life of pain and fears that keep her trapped and unable to make constructive decisions that will alter the status quo. Through treatment, she began to realize that change was not only possible, but also within her reach. A higher level of functioning and self-fulfillment was achieved through her perseverance and courage.

TABLE 3.2 Types of Empowerment Methods Used to Help Battered Women

Empowerment methods	n
1. Examine options or choices, and refer to self-help/support group	38
2. Explore legal options and encourage client to file criminal charges	32
3. Educate about cycle of violence and power/control issues	24
4. Provide information about community resources, numerous referrals, and make first appointment for victim	24
5. Reassure client that abuse is not her fault, and correct victim-blaming	10
6. Initiate advocacy for welfare or housing	9
7. Accompany to court appearances and provide advocacy with judge	8

PRELIMINARY CASE REPORT

Sandra, a 28-year-old waitress with three children between the ages of 2 and 6 years, had just had an argument with her intoxicated husband, Luke. Although the argument started out small, it progressed and ended with Luke shoving Sandra and giving her a broken nose.

After Luke was asleep, Sandra decided she could not take the abuse any longer. She left the house with her three children. At 3:00 a.m., Sandra arrived at the center with a bruised face, no money, and fearful that she will be hurt again. She also revealed that this was not the first time Luke had abused her.

Initial Assessment

The information, taken by an intake worker, provided important data suggesting the physical harm and emotional turmoil Sandra had experienced in her relationship with Luke. A more detailed history was necessary to ascertain the most appropriate individualized treatment plan for her and her children. Nevertheless, from this brief report, it was hypothesized that Sandra had reached a turning point that was the catalyst for mobilizing her strengths and resources to not only seek safety and protection, but also some measure of positive change. This could provide a vital opportunity to help her gain the supports, knowledge, and skills that would prevent future occurrences of domestic violence.

THE PERSONAL IMPACT OF DOMESTIC VIOLENCE

As Sandra mentioned in the intake, this was not the first time she was abused in her marriage. A more in-depth, structured interview determined the extent and duration of the battering and the deleterious effects on her and the children. Over a 5-year period, she was intermittently brutalized and held captive by fear and the inability to control the inevitable recurrence of her husband's violent episodes.

Sandra was aware of Luke's dysfunctional upbringing as the only child of alcoholic parents. During the short courtship and early years of their marriage, Luke never displayed the kind of rage and bitterness that typified his parents' relationship. Sandra knew that he was never physically harmed at home, but the emotional impact of watching his father physically abuse his mother left wounds that he still felt.

Before the children were born, Sandra and Luke spent "good times" together, often socializing with friends at parties. She drank very little, compared to Luke, yet was always amazed (and somewhat pleased) at "how many he could put away" without showing signs of losing control and becoming "sloppy" drunk. She recalled, with sharp disapproval, how her own father would drink too much at times and become verbally abusive. With pride, she would point out that Luke could "hold his liquor," often becoming more amusing and affectionate. That this could change was not foreseen, and their early years together were described as "happy and without problems."

With the pressures of raising a family and increasing financial debts, conflicts arose in the marriage. Luke held a steady job as a construction worker, and with Sandra's income and tips as a waitress, they were able to pay their bills and even save a small amount each month. But this was short-lived, as Luke began to gamble heavily. He feared that his job was in jeopardy, as his drinking began to interfere with his performance. The escalating stresses particularly affected his relationship with Sandra, often climaxing in loud arguments that catapulted to torturous beatings.

Although he never physically hurt the children, Sandra often feared that he would someday. She also anticipated that witnessing their father severely injuring her could leave indelible emotional scars. The altercation and resultant bruises that actually triggered her leaving with the children was not as severe as past injuries in which a concussion and multiple fractures and bruises were inflicted. At those times, she fleetingly thought of escaping the pain of living, and occasionally considered taking the children and moving far away. But these fantasies vanished quickly, as she thought, "Where would I go?" "How can I support the children and myself?" "Will I be safe anywhere?" So she remained in a fearful, helpless, and untenable position, feeling more and more isolated within herself and incapacitated by the escalating depressive symptoms. She was unable to tell anyone about her fragile marriage and the battering. This was perceived as a failure on her part—one that provoked guilt and shame.

Yet there was a struggling part of Sandra that wished to deny the reality of her existence, hoping that Luke would change and become the man she once knew and loved. At times, there were signs that he cared, displaying regret that he hurt her and promising he would never do it again. However, this latest episode of violence, with no provocation, was the final straw—her perseverance was tested to the limit. She felt she had to do something before it was too late—for herself, for her children, and even for her husband. This led to the first stage of interventive guidance and support to help bring an end to the traumas she had been living through.

ROBERTS'S CRISIS INTERVENTION MODEL

Facing her fears and taking control was a self-empowering act that began the journey through and beyond the crisis Sandra was experiencing. An existence of pain and discomfort was being challenged by a shift toward hope and renewal. Assistance in this endeavor was forthcoming once the decision was made to seek help.

Utilizing Roberts's seven-stage model (for further details, see Roberts, 1991, 1995, and 2005), the goal is to assure immediate safety and stabilization, followed by problem solving and the exploration of alternative options that would culminate in a meaningful action plan. Implicit in this model is a cognitive restructuring of perceptions, attitudes, and beliefs that will confront irrational distortions, misconceptions, and contradictions. The identification of erroneous thought patterns ("I can't make it alone without him") and a redirection to empowering affirmations and beliefs ("If other women have made it, so can I") can enhance self-worth and self-reliance, while reinforcing constructive coping mechanisms. With support, guidance, and acceptance, meaningful solutions that were once unrecognized can become objectives to attain.

The use of standardized test measurements is highly recom-mended in making a comprehensive assessment. Several scales and checklists will provide pertinent information to add to the data collected. Among these are the Expanded Conflict Tactics Scales of Aggression—both verbal aggression and physical violence scales (Straus, 1990). Severe violence is defined as the occurrence of any of the following: beat up, choked, or strangled; threatened with a knife or gun; or use of a knife or gun. All clinical directors at shelters should use the Beck Depression Inventory (BDI; Beck, 1967), the Derogatis Symptom Checklist-90-Revised (SCL-90-R; Derogatis, 1977), and the Trauma Symptom Checklist-40 (Briere & Runtz, 1988, 1989; Elliott & Briere, 1992). These scales have been widely used in clinical prac-tice with battered women, and they give the clinician a normative standard of comparison. Because many battered women have multi-ple trauma histories, using all three scales seems most appropriate. The overlap of items will permit the multiple assessment of depres-sion, anxiety, sexual problems, dissociation, sleep disturbances, and postsexual abuse trauma.

Sandra's test results displayed low verbal aggression and physical violence scores (which concurred with her inability to defend herself against the abuse); a chronically depressed and anxious state, with intermittent suicidal ideations; and sleep disturbances. Her level of stabilization and immediate danger determination were also assessed through the use of the Stage I Crisis Assessment (Table 3.3). She appeared to be rational, but anxiety and agitation were high. Her safety needs posed a threat in returning to Luke, as the potential of physical violence remained. Other assessment items on this list were not evident, but the possibility existed that some of these might occur in the future.

After safety needs were established, rapport and trust were de-veloped in an effort to assist Sandra in identifying and prioritizing major problems. The worker encouraged her to express feelings and concerns about the events that prompted her to leave her husband and seek help. An assessment of her coping skills was prompted

TABLE 3.3 Stage I: Crisis Assessment (Including Lethality Measures)

1. First and foremost, patient/client needs to be stabilized.
   - Assess level of consciousness and orientation
   - Rationality
   - Anxiety
   - Agitation
2. Determine if client is in immediate danger.
   - Any guns or rifles in the home; threatened to use it on client
   - Any weapons used in prior battering incidents
   - Any threats with weapons
   - Any threats to kill client
   - Any criminal history of batterer
   - Client needed emergency medical attention
   - Threats or actually killing a pet
   - Threats of suicide by abuser
   - Batterer's fantasies about suicide or homicide
   - Marital rape or forced sex among cohabitants
   - Increased battering during pregnancy
   - Medical problems as result of pregnancy
   - Medical problems as result of rape (e.g., infections, sexually transmitted diseases, HIV infection, unwanted pregnancy, risk to fetus in a pregnant woman)
   - Psychological torture (e.g., degradation, forced drug use, isolation of victim, sleep or food deprivation, threats to family of victim)

by the question, "How did you handle those traumatic situations?" It was important to listen empathically and attentively and to acknowledge the intensity of her pain. The barriers and obstacles that undermined the ability to alter her life (e.g., lack of funds, perceived supports, or knowledge of available resources) were identified. From these data, possible solutions and their consequences were formulated.

Arriving at an action plan required the development of alternate options and solutions to resolve the crisis (e.g., a legal separation; a court-ordered restraining order). Sandra's progress through this intervention phase was supported and monitored closely. With her resolve and determination, she was able to reduce the distressful symptoms of the acute crisis and begin to act on the second stage—a plan to acquire the tools to move on with her life.

COGNITIVELY ORIENTED PROBLEM SOLVING

After ensuring the safety and survival issues of the battered woman, additional aid is often needed to continue stabilization while helping her resolve major issues and formulate important decisions that will affect her present and future functioning. Roberts's (1991, 1995) Seven-Stage Crisis Intervention Model has provided the guidelines for the crucial stage of early crisis resolution, using an integrated problem-solving approach. This critical phase is designed to assist the client in establishing adaptive and constructive coping skills that will reestablish the equilibrium necessary to pursue actions that can overcome obstacles to personal well-being.

Building on Roberts's crisis intervention model, which has developed the foundation for problem solving, positive change, and empowerment, the client is ready to move toward another stage in the healing and growth-producing process. This sequence can be likened to a progression from the resolution of an acute, debilitating crisis state to working with clients on sustaining previous advances made, while attending to new modes of learning that will reinforce the prolonged acquisition and internalization of survival and actualization skills. Toward this aim, a cognitively oriented, problem-solving approach will encompass the groundwork of cognitive therapy and problem solving that has been influential in behavioral and emotional change, as well as the needed alterations in environmental systems that block desired objectives.

We know that a battered woman's fears and problems are not completely allayed once the immediate crisis has dissipated. If she returns to her partner, the violence will probably reoccur (particularly if the perpetrator has not received help). If she leaves, the probability of battering and harassment, even death, becomes a constant risk. Proceeding successfully through the critical phase of crisis resolution can reestablish a sense of balance, rebuild self-esteem and a strong sense of self, and increase the determination to pattern a life free of turmoil and suffering. But the awareness of vulnerability, dependency, and helplessness may still remain within the realm of consciousness, provoking an unsettling indecisiveness as to the direction that should be taken. This is often magnified by any disconcerting emotional attachments that still linger. In the case of battered women, a traumatic bonding effect (Dutton, 1988) may be developed through the intermittent abusive behaviors and reinforcement of pleasant

conditions. This process sustains the dependency cycle, characterized by a power imbalance between the perpetrator and the subju-
gated female. Even after leaving the relationship, the unrecognized
attachment needs fulfilled by the partner can manifest itself, causing
the woman to impulsively return.

Given the enormity and depth of the problems encountered, battered women need a continuity of supportive networks and helping
services to transcend the horrifying situations they experienced (and
may continue to face, if no dramatic changes are made). Crisis intervention is often the critical starting point of a longer journey that will
not be culminated until safety is no longer threatened and emancipa-
tion and stability are finally achieved. Once the acute problems are
addressed, the more chronic difficulties and dilemmas that persist
must be assessed. Besides recurrent fears, dysfunctional symptoms
of PTSD and emotional difficulties may intrude into daily routines.
These problems must be dealt with, for the battered woman to regain
a sense of adequacy and normalcy.

A cognitively oriented, problem-solving approach is a natural supplement to Roberts's crisis intervention model. It adheres to the basic
format, concentrating on behavioral, emotional, and environmental
change through the incorporation of cognitive and problem-solving
strategies. The integrated principles will be identified, followed by
their application to the assessment and treatment phases of the case
previously cited.

Cognitive Therapy

Cognitive therapeutic methods have been developed from various
theories of learning, primarily operant conditioning (Skinner, 1938)
and social learning (Bandura, 1977). These theories espouse that
behavior is a learned process that occurs through transactions between individuals and their social environments. Through operant
conditioning, a response that is reinforcing (rewarded) will reoccur; and according to social learning theory, learning takes place by
modeling (observing and imitating others), as well as through self-
reinforcement and self-evaluations (Longres, 1995).

These theoretical frameworks have set the stage for the adoption
of many strategies, such as systematic desensitization to treat anxiety
and phobias; aversion therapy to eliminate an undesirable behavior;

shaping behaviors by rewarding successive approximations of the desired result; positive and negative reinforcement to increase or reduce targeted behaviors; and role modeling of adaptive behaviors (Longres, 1995). Cognitive restructuring, identifying dysfunctional core beliefs, role plays and rehearsals, relaxation and stress management training, self-monitored homework assignments, and problem solving are now widely in use to reinforce the goals of positive learning and change (Beck, Wright, Newman, & Liese, 1993).

Problem Solving

This approach has been a strategic mainstay of many professional disciplines. According to Hepworth and Larsen (1993), "[Problem solving skills are taught] not only to remedy immediate problems but also to enhance clients' future coping capacities . . . the principles can be readily transferred from one situation to another" (pp. 434–435). Through effective problem solving, a range of options can be generated that will enhance decision making, self-reliance, self-esteem, confidence, and self-efficacy; and tensions, anxiety, and depressive symptoms can be allayed.

The problem-solving model provides a step-by-step framework to intervention planning and implementation. An integral part of any therapeutic process is the initial engaging of the client in a relationship built on trust and rapport. Based on this foundation, the following tasks can be actuated by the mutual team effort of both practitioner and client:

1. Assessment developed from the data collected.
2. Problem identification and implications.
3. Goal-setting and contracting.
4. Implementation of interventions.
5. Termination and referrals.
6. Evaluation of effectiveness of interventions.

THE THERAPEUTIC EXPERIENCE

As the client progresses from the acute crisis resolution phase to a continuing stage of healing and growth, several alterations in functioning have developed. From a fearful, defenseless, and disempowered woman, resulting from numerous battering experiences, emerges a stronger, more self-assured individual who is ready to accept new challenges. This has not been an easy process, but one that has often been fraught with indecision and trepidation of great magnitude. If she does not succumb to old, familiar patterns that entice her to return to an unchanged partner (or a similar substitute), with persistent support and monitoring from practitioners and paraprofessionals, a major hurdle has been overcome. Her self-esteem has improved; her attitude toward life is fortified; and the obstacles that once seemed insurmountable now appear less formidable.

Yet the precarious journey ahead remains potentially unsteady, with sharp turns and sudden upheavals. The motivation to move forward and not fall back must constantly be reinforced. Relating to the case previously presented, the therapeutic means (a cognitively oriented problem-solving model) of achieving this goal will be explored.

The Assessment

Sandra's anguished experience mirrors many commonalities with other battered women. Avni's (1991) questionnaire findings of abused women expressed a lengthy range of battering, from 2 to 30 years, with the earliest reported during the first month of marriage. Of Sandra's 7 years with Luke, 5 of these were characterized as abusive. Hamberger and Holtzworth-Munroe (1994) state that victims of battering live in constant terror and stress, resulting in depression, anxiety, and somatic complaints. Yet there is a period in which concern, apologies, and assurances of ending the violence are offered that tend to restabilize the emotional bonds (Walker, 1994). This dubious and precarious reality typified Sandra and Luke's relationship.

A variety of stresses can increase the potential for violence (Stith & Rosen, 1990). The birth of children (Watkins & Bradbard, 1982), losing a job (or fear of job loss), and the concomitant financial instability that has a negative impact on an individual's self-esteem (Stith & Rosen) can all exacerbate the risk of abuse. Add to this the excessive use of alcohol or other drugs, and the frequency and severity of battering (and possible death) are heightened (Walker, 1989). Reviewing Sandra's experience, we can readily identify these factors that might have created the perilous exposure to physical and emotional harm.

This reign of terror can be endured indefinitely. What actually motivates women to escape these abusive relationships has been the subject of Davis and Srinivasan's (1995) research. Conducting focus groups as a means of learning their subjects' personal experiences, they found several rationales for leaving and seeking help (pp. 57–58):

1. Overcoming fear (by finding a way out, that is, a change in attitudes/policies that are more supportive of battered women).
2. Children as major catalysts (to protect their children from psychological harm).
3. Getting older and wiser through time (and the experience and wisdom that follows).

In Sandra's situation, the children definitely influenced her decision, and, perhaps, with no evidence of concrete changes in Luke's behavior, we can also attribute her subsequent move to the passage of time. These significant operative forces, coupled with Sandra's vulnerable position, the continued threat of severe violence and possible death, and the recognition of her own potential for retaliation substantiated the necessity for taking action.

Nevertheless, it took many years before Sandra could fortify herself and make the decision to leave. She had become more and more isolated and depressed, unable to reach out for help. As Fiene (1995) points out, "[B]attered women are reluctant to disclose their victimization even to close family members. . . . This reticence increases their isolation, and thus they forgo the potential social support available" (p. 179). Sandra's "secret" was kept well hidden, as the failing marriage was perceived as a personal failure. With her diminishing self-confidence and pervading emotional attachments to Luke, she began to accept much of the blame for the occurrences that followed. Many battered women feel impotent for their lack of control and influence over these events, thereby viewing themselves negatively. A belief of helplessness often expresses itself in passivity and submission that is continually being reinforced by their victimization (Walker, 1979). This learned helplessness reflected Sandra's growing image of herself—one that was so different from her earlier persona and relationship with Luke.

Additionally, Sandra's fear of being unable to manage on her own and take care of the children, and of Luke's finding her and the possible consequences this could entail, kept her immobilized. Her job training was in waitressing, an occupation that usually provides limited salaries and benefits. Without therapy and anger management skills, Luke may very well have bent his frustrations on Sandra for leaving. So this was certainly a realistic outlook on her part. Similar factors have affected many battered women's resistance to searching for safety through constructive channels (Walker, 1994).

The role that alcohol abuse played in the battering must also be taken into account. According to Bennett (1995), violence may be aggravated by substance use in some men, but it cannot be concluded that eliminating substances will stop the violence. The power–aggression relationship may be more applicable: " [A]ny quantity of alcohol for problem drinkers increases their sense of personal power over others. A man concerned with personal power and control is also more likely to drink heavily and more likely to be aggressive" (Bennett, 1995, p. 761). Violence as a learned behavior can be demonstrated by the high probability of reenactments in later years when children observe spousal abuse in the home (Burman & Allen-Meares, 1994). These concepts afford a likely explanation for Luke's assaultive behaviors. His father was overtly abusive to his mother, and Luke internalized these unsettling memories. But Luke's assaultive acts toward Sandra could most likely be expressed as a consequence of feeling a lack of control in other areas of his life (e.g., increasing financial pressures; possible loss of employment due to heavy drinking). The power and control he desired was transferred to his perceived domination of Sandra by the continuous acts of physical and emotional abuse.

When viewing learning theories (operant conditioning; social learning), it can be surmised that in her early years at home with her parents, although she was disturbed by her father's verbal abuse after heavy drinking, she observed her mother being targeted with no active recourse displayed. Sandra commented, "My mother almost expected it and geared herself for the torment." Sandra's marriage was somewhat reminiscent of her mother's. Her role as victim re-created her mother's role. With her low self-esteem and feelings of powerlessness and helplessness, Sandra's submissiveness increased, and Luke learned that he could control her through the use of verbal and physical assaults. When Sandra finally left, her help-seeking actions were rewarded by the immediate attention to her safety and emotional needs—a sharp contrast from her experience with Luke. Although still vulnerable and uncertain as to which direction to take, she became more amenable to partaking of the guidance offered by its reinforcing elements.

Problem Identification and Implications

The primary problem, identified by Sandra in the first stage of crisis resolution, was the continuous battering experiences she had endured over a 5-year period with no assurance of its stopping. She also realized that her children could be severely damaged by witnessing the battering. Associated with this were fears of continued violence and harassment if she would leave Luke and not being able to provide for the children and herself without his assistance. Despite the traumas, there existed an underlying attachment to him, which made her ambivalent about ending the relationship. Her lack of self-confidence and low self-esteem and self-worth were also prominent. Through the initial therapeutic process, the immediate crisis was allayed, but lingering trepidations and ambivalence remained that could diminish the gains already made. Without additional treatment, anticipatory problems were expected to arise, especially if she were to return to Luke and the violence that would invariably continue.

Goal-Setting and Contracting

Preliminary goals were aimed to fortify some of the previous goals made during the crisis resolution phase: (a) continuing to strengthen Sandra's emotional stability, self-esteem, and resolve; and (b) empowering her to make desirable, self-assured decisions based on what would promote optimal safety and a better quality of life for her and the children. This would entail helping her to challenge self-defeating thoughts and beliefs that restrain rational decisions; to explore the options and alternatives available; and to recognize and tap into her strengths that would facilitate problem solving. As therapy continued with Sandra, the assessment and goals were expected to expand, depending on the circumstances experienced. Contracting comprised a verbal agreement to work together on the proposed goals for a period of 20 sessions, after which progress would be evaluated. The need for additional meetings would be assessed at that time.

Implementation of Interventions

After a brief, but intensive, crisis-intervention foundation, Sandra was stabilized and acquired the tools to improve her coping and decision-making abilities. Nevertheless, self-doubts and fears still existed that needed qualifying and assuaging. Without sustaining, cognitive explorations of these elements and a dramatic change in emotional and belief manifestations, the depressive and anxiety reactions that were previously noted could result in more debilitating symptoms similar to PTSD. These imagery disturbances are evidenced by incapacitating flashbacks, intrusive thoughts, and nightmares that created profound emotional and cognitive upsets (McCann & Pearlman, 1990). To allay the possibility of regression and additional problems, the second stage of rehabilitation immediately followed. This allowed Sandra needed time to recover from past traumas and to develop new coping strategies to empower her to problem solve effectively.

Instrumental in working with Sandra was the development of a relationship based on rapport, trust, and empathy. When a woman experiences the extent and duration of violations against her (as is the case in battering), efforts must be taken to relay indelible support and guidance. Trust, hopes, and dreams have been previously shattered; vulnerability has been exploited. To rebuild a maligned ego and a self-concept weakened from years of abuse, feelings should be explored and validated, and options and solutions should be forthrightly presented that are personally meaningful and recognizably workable. In addition, the belief system should be modified to alter distressing and self-defeating thoughts that undermine progress toward positive change. Teaching Sandra to monitor and correct these thoughts proved to be an important step toward self-preservation and fulfillment of her goals.

Sandra began to realize that returning to Luke would be an error in judgment that she would forever regret—the promises to end the battering would continue, but the injuries and subjugation would not cease. Yet her ambivalence about leaving him was influenced by the fears of being autonomous and independent, coupled with an uneasy emotional attachment that lingered. Nevertheless, she did agree on the action plan to try a separation, moving with her children into an apartment that she could afford and obtaining a restraining order for added protection. In the interim, therapy continued to help her adjust to her new status and setting. This experience served to fortify her decision to make a fresh start, based on rational considerations of past events and present and future possibilities, options, and alternatives. An important part of the plan was to bolster her ego strengths and coping skills in order to overcome any difficulties that might occur, while providing supportive structures and resources as needed.

An essential element in the process was the initial turning point that initiated the help-seeking. This was seen as self-empowerment that had to be reinforced and supported continuously. Her depression and anxiety were treated with medication until they were markedly reduced. Acknowledging that maladaptive emotional reactions and subsequent behaviors are manifested through distorted thoughts and beliefs, cognitive strategies (Beck, Wright, Newman, & Liese, 1993) were implemented to help her challenge and interrupt these perceptions through reality testing and logic.

It was important for Sandra to recognize how her belief system had been keeping her trapped and immobilized, unable to seek help until years after the abuse had begun. And even more specifically, those intrusive thoughts could reappear to undermine the progress she had already made. Through reflective listening and feedback, she was taught to monitor and modify thought patterns that created unsettling emotions. By reciting these beliefs aloud (e.g., "I'll never be able to make it on my own") and confronting the message ("I haven't tried, so how can I know?"), a more positive attitude emerged. Finding meaning in her actions ("I stayed so long, not because of love for Luke, but because I was afraid of being independent") also helped to strengthen her commitment to change the status quo.

A cost–benefit analysis, citing the advantages and disadvantages of living with Luke, was heavily tipped in favor of a permanent separation. To desensitize her fears of being alone, an imagery technique was conducted, encouraging her to visualize this situation after being in a relaxed state. She was able to imagine the possibilities and alternatives open to her, such as the increased freedom of making her own decisions and returning to school and advancing her employment potential. She admitted that her waitress job was too limiting, and that in the past, she had wanted to improve her potential, but Luke had dissuaded her from advancing. His demeaning comments had discouraged her and shattered her self-confidence. The fear that Luke would retaliate when left without her was still credible, but Sandra knew that staying could be just as emotionally and physically injurious as leaving, and she was developing supports to call on for protection.

To reinforce her capabilities and talents, she was taught the "as if" strategy. In fearsome or problematic situations, she acted as if she could handle it (even visualizing it beforehand by approximating each step closer to the goal). This reinforced her confidence and prompted her to attempt difficult tasks. Role-plays of stressful events provided practice in overcoming ineffective responses to adverse conditions. And each day, she incorporated positive affirmations into her routine, thereby counteracting trepidation and negative thoughts.

Early fond memories of Luke kept disrupting the horror of what their relationship had become. These held together a weakened, yet enduring, attachment to him. By emphatically reframing the positive recollections to the disillusionment she felt and recognized in succeeding years, Sandra was able to displace the fragile bonds to other supports and to take pride in her own ability to decipher latent emotional dependency from the reality that her needs and expectations were not being met. Her former persona of normalcy, stability, and security had been essentially destroyed in the marriage. When this awareness solidified, she became angry and began opening up to new experiences. She had blamed herself for the failing marriage; now she realized that Luke's abusive behaviors and controlling nature were inexcusable and caused most of the friction between them. He had placed her in a defenseless and precarious position—one that provoked fears, isolation, shame, and guilt.

She was prompted to participate in a therapy group of abused women who gained strength from one another in their quest to break the destructive bonds they endured. She also joined a self-help support group that included women who left their abusive partners and were managing their lives quite satisfactorily. Many of these women formed special relationships that sustained them in moments of apprehension and indecisiveness.

Termination and Referrals

Primary treatment was completed when Sandra stabilized enough to pursue her own goals of independent living with appropriate supports and resources. Referrals were made for legal and financial assistance, and educational guidance was provided by a local academic institution. Follow-up was agreed to, with monthly contacts to determine her current functioning and needs. In addition, it was stressed that any problems and safety concerns would be addressed immediately. It was imperative to clarify this policy so that she would understand that provisions would be available promptly, when necessary.

Evaluation of Effectiveness of Interventions

It should be emphasized that the evaluation of interventions conducted should be an ongoing process. As work with the client continues, issues might arise that were unforeseen previously, and the action plan must be flexible enough to adjust accordingly. In summarizing Sandra's progress in treatment, problem solving entailed all the knowledge and skills she had learned from crisis intervention and cognitive therapy. She was able to critically ponder each problem, while weighing the consequences of her actions. Without the extended therapeutic experience, she might not have been ready to combat detrimental, impulsive responses that would have prevented necessary changes. She was amazed at her own strengths, which were unrecognized before, to make decisions that could finally end a disastrous relationship and save herself and her children from future turmoil.

DISCUSSION

This chapter integrates the findings of a research study and a practice model, demonstrating the strategies used by shelters for battered women and a more comprehensive strategic model that is designed to address the many inherent problems of domestic violence. It is suggested that limitations are placed on the helping process by not affording a more intensive, intervention-action plan, utilizing both crisis intervention and cognitively oriented problem solving. The dangers involved in battering can be so emotionally and physically devastating that extreme measures must be taken to ensure safety and increase the awareness of the dangers involved in remaining in an abusive relationship, while teaching and developing coping skills to resist any repetition of assaults in the future. The critical analysis and consequences of a battered woman's decisions should not be treated lightly. If she decides to return to the perpetrator, death or severe and prolonged injuries can occur. Therefore, every effort should be made to help her make an informed decision based on logic, not emotion.

The proposed model can be effectively utilized by generalist practitioners, specialists, and professionals in agencies and shelters. A multidisciplinary team can assume various responsibilities and tasks in carrying out the rehabilitative stages, from the acute crisis to the more chronic condition with related problems. The goal is to follow the client through the healing and growth phases, empowering her to protect herself and look after her best interests, while tapping and building ego strengths to prevent recurrent psychological and behavioral incapacitation. It is a present and future-oriented approach to security, healthy functioning, and self-sufficiency. With continual support and reality-oriented feedback, a battered woman who previously had lost hope can once again perceive life with optimism and a renewed sense of determination and the capability to strive toward independence and self-fulfillment.

REFERENCES

Astin, M. C., Lawrence, K., Pincus, G., & Foy, D. W. (1990, October). *Moderator variables for PTSD among battered women*. Paper presented at the convention of the International Society for Traumatic Stress Studies, New Orleans, LA.

Avni, N. (1991). Battered wives: The home as a total institution. *Violence and Victims, 2*, 137–149.

Bandura, A. (1977). *Social learning theory*. Englewood Cliffs, NJ: Prentice-Hall.

Beck, A. (1967). *Depression: Clinical, experimental and theoretical aspects*. New York: Harper & Row.

Beck, A. T., Wright, F. D., Newman, C. F., & Liese, B. S. (1993). *Cognitive therapy of substance abuse*. New York: Guilford.

Bennett, L. W. (1995). Substance abuse and the domestic assault of women. *Social Work, 40*, 760–771.

Briere, J., & Runtz, M. (1988). Multivariate correlates of childhood and physical maltreatment among university women. *Child Abuse and Neglect, 12*, 331–341.

Briere, J., & Runtz, M. (1989). The Trauma Symptom Checklist (TSC-33): Early data on a new scale. *Journal of Interpersonal Violence, 4,* 151–163.

Burman, S., & Allen-Meares, P. (1994). Neglected victims of murder: Children's witness to parental homicide. *Social Work, 39,* 28–34.

Cascardi, M., & O'Leary, K. D. (1992). Depressive symptomatology, self-esteem, and self-blame in battered women. *Journal of Family Violence, 7,* 249–259.

Davis, L. V., & Srinivasan, M. (1995). Listening to the voices of battered women: What helps them escape violence. *Affilia, 10,* 49–69.

Derogatis, L. (1977). *SCL-90R Manual-L.* Towson, MD: Clinical Psychometric Research.

Dutton, D. G. (1988). *The domestic assault of women: Psychological and criminal justice perspectives.* Boston: Allyn & Bacon.

Dziegielewski, S., Resnick, C., & Krause, N. (1996). Shelter-based crisis intervention with battered women. In A. R. Roberts (Ed.), *Helping battered women: New perspectives and remedies* (pp. 159–171). New York: Oxford University Press.

Elliot, D. M., & Briere, J. (1992). Sexual abuse trauma among professional women: Validating the Trauma Symptom Checklist-40 (TSC-40). *Child Abuse and Neglect, 16,* 391–398.

Fiene, J. I. (1995). Battered women: Keeping the secret. *Affilia, 10,* 179–193.

Geller, J., & Wasserstrom, J. (1984). Conjoint therapy for the treatment of domestic violence. In A. R. Roberts (Ed.), *Battered women and their families: Intervention strategies and treatment programs* (pp. 33–48). New York: Springer Publishing.

Gelles, R. J., & Harrop, J. W. (1989). Violence, battering, and psychological distress among women. *Journal of Interpersonal Violence, 4,* 400–411.

Hamberger, L. K., & Holtzworth-Munroe, A. (1994). Partner violence. In F. M. Dattilio & A. Freeman (Eds.), *Cognitive-behavioral strategies in crisis intervention* (pp. 302–324). New York: Guilford.

Hepworth, D. H., & Larsen, J. A. (1993). *Direct social work practice: Theory and skills* (4th ed.). Pacific Grove, CA: Brooks/Cole.

Housekamp, B. M., & Foy, D. W. (1991). The assessment of posttraumatic stress disorder in battered women. *Journal of Interpersonal Violence, 6,* 367–375.

Longres, J. F. (1995). *Human behavior in the social environment* (2nd ed.). Itasca, IL: F.E. Peacock.

McCann, L., & Pearlman, L. A. (1990). Constructivist self-development theory as a framework for assessing and treating victims of family violence. In S. M. Stith, M. B. Williams, & K. Rosen (Eds.), *Violence hits home: Comprehensive treatment approaches to domestic violence* (pp. 305–329). New York: Springer Publishing.

Petretic-Jackson, P., & Jackson, T. (1996). Mental health interventions with battered women. In A. R. Roberts (Ed.), *Helping battered women: New perspectives and remedies* (pp. 188–221). New York: Oxford University Press.

Roberts, A. R. (Ed.). (1991). *Contemporary perspectives on crisis intervention and prevention.* Englewood Cliffs, NJ: Prentice-Hall.

Roberts, A. R. (Ed.). (1995). *Crisis intervention and time-limited cognitive treatment.* Thousand Oaks, CA: Sage.

Roberts, A. R. (Ed.). (1996). *Crisis management and brief treatment: Theory, technique, and applications.* Chicago: Nelson-Hall.

Roberts, A. R. (1997). The organizational structure and functions of 177 shelters for battered women. *American Journal of Community Psychology, 32,* 400–418.

Roberts, A. R. (2005). Bridging the past and present to the future of crisis intervention and crisis management. In A. R. Roberts (Ed.), *Crisis intervention handbook: Assessment, treatment and research* (3rd ed., pp. 3–34). New York: Oxford University Press.

Roberts, A. R., & Roberts, B. J. (1990). A comprehensive model for crisis intervention with battered women and their children. In A. R. Roberts (Ed.), *Crisis intervention handbook: Assessment, treatment, and research* (pp. 105–123). Belmont, CA: Wadsworth.

Roche, S. E. (1996). Social action for battered women. In A. R. Roberts (Ed.), *Helping battered women: New perspectives and remedies* (pp. 13–30). New York: Oxford University Press.

Skinner, B. F. (1938). *The behavior of organisms: An experimental analysis.* New York: Appleton-Century-Crofts.

Stith, S. M., & Rosen, K. H. (1990). Overview of domestic violence. In S. M. Stith, M. B. Williams, & K. Rosen (Eds.), *Violence hits home: Comprehensive treatment approaches to domestic violence* (pp. 1–21). New York: Springer Publishing.

Straus, M. A. (1990). The Conflict Tactics Scales and its critics: An evaluation and new data on validity and reliability. In M. A. Straus & R. J. Gelles (Eds.), *Physical violence in American families: Risk factors and adaptations to violence in 8,145 families* (pp. 49–71). New Brunswick, NJ: Transaction.

Walker, L. E. (1979). *The battered woman.* New York: Harper & Row.

Walker, L. E. (1985). Psychological impact of the criminalization of domestic violence on victims. *Victimology: An International Journal, 10,* 281–300.

Walker, L. E. (1989). *Terrifying love: Why battered women kill and how society responds.* New York: Harper & Row.

Walker, L. E. A. (1994). *Abused women and survivor therapy: A practical guide for the psychotherapist.* Washington, DC: American Psychological Association.

Watkins, H., & Bradbard, M. (1982). Child maltreatment: An overview with suggestions for intervention and research. *Family Relations, 31,* 323–333.

Webb, W. (1992). Treatment issues and cognitive behavior techniques with battered women. *Journal of Family Violence, 7,* 205–217.

CHAPTER 4

Discovering Strengths and Competencies in Female Domestic Violence Victims:
An Application of Roberts's Continuum of the Duration and Severity of Woman Battering

Mo-Yee Lee

B ased on the data from a carefully designed study of 501 battered women, Dr. Roberts developed the Continuum of the Duration and Chronicity of Woman Battering. The Continuum provides therapists with a useful tool for identifying and assessing lethality issues in treating battered women. See chapter 1 for a detailed description of the five levels of the woman-battering continuum. Such a relatively new classificatory scheme also echoes the concern of some helping professionals who recognize battered women as a heterogeneous group with diverse experiences unique to their own individual and social context (e.g., Dutton, 1996). Treatment based on one predominant vision of battered women's experience and what is best for them runs the danger of decontextualization, thereby reducing the effectiveness and appropriateness of treatment to the individual woman.

The Continuum implies a diversity of battered women's experience and their life situations. Such recognition has important implications for assessment, treatment, and research with this population. Besides assisting helping professionals to focus their attention on those women who are at a high risk for severe abuse so that appropriate services can be provided, such a Continuum also captures the experience of those women who appear to be at the beginning trajectory of an abusive cycle (Roberts & Roberts, 2005). An understanding of their experience will have useful implications for early detection as well as early prevention. In other words, what may be helpful to protect a woman from an abusive cycle at its beginning stage will have useful implications for early detection and prevention so that the battering can be ended without being exacerbated both in its severity and chronicity.

In this application chapter, I describe a solution-focused approach for treating female domestic violence victims before discussing the implication of the Continuum to therapists and researchers working within a solution-focused frame. Solution-focused therapy is based on building on each person's hidden strengths and competencies, rather than using a deficit or pathology model. In individual and group treatment settings, I focus on what clients can do rather than on what they cannot do. The focus is on clients' successes in dealing with their domestic violence problems, and how to notice and build on small, attainable goals. The important first step to optimize the success of solution-focused treatment is based on the practitioner's ability to recognize and respect clients' strengths, sometimes more than clients respect themselves. This approach has been supported by numerous clinical observations on how clients discover partial and complete solutions more quickly if the focus is on their strengths, abilities, and accomplishments (Berg & Dolan, 2001). A solution-focused approach for the treatment of domestic violence is a relatively new approach developed in the late 1980s. Such an approach has been used for individual treatment for victims (Dolan, 1994), crisis intervention (Greene, Lee, Trask, & Rheinscheld, 2005), couple treatment (Johnson & Goldman, 1996; Lipchik, 1991; Lipchik & Kubicki, 1996), and group treatment for domestic violence offenders (Lee, Sebold, & Uken, 2003; Uken & Sebold, 1996) with encouraging outcomes.

PREDOMINANT TREATMENT FOR FEMALE DOMESTIC VIOLENCE VICTIMS

The predominant treatment approaches for female victims owe largely to the contribution of feminist activists, scholars, and practitioners who have been the force behind the Battered Women's Movement in the United States. These feminist activists, scholars, and practitioners have significantly contributed to our understanding of the suffering of female victims as well as their treatment (Petretic-Jackson & Jackson, 1996). Feminist social critics of domestic violence focus on how cultural beliefs about sex roles and the resulting institutional arrangements contribute to and maintain gender inequality and the oppression of women by men (Gondolf & Fisher, 1988; Martin, 1976; Warrior, 1976). Feminist psychologists further examine the psychological vicious cycle in which many female victims find themselves entangled. Lenore Walker (1984, 1994) employs the concept of "learned helplessness" (Seligman, 1975) and the "cycle of violence" to explain the battered woman syndrome. Mary Ann Dutton elaborates on the psychological mechanism of traumatic bonding that maintains the plight of female victims (Dutton & Painter, 1993). Based on a feminist analysis of the social and psychological roots maintaining the cycle of domestic violence, the current predominant paradigm of treatment is to separate the spouses; remove the woman from the abusive union and empower her through therapy, education, and advocacy; and legally punish the abusers and resocialize them through psychoeducational groups.

A SOLUTION-FOCUSED APPROACH FOR TREATING FEMALE DOMESTIC VIOLENCE VICTIMS

Solution-focused therapy was originally developed at the Brief Family Therapy Center in Milwaukee, Wisconsin, by Insoo Kim Berg, Steve de Shazer, and their associates. "Doing what works" is the basic tenet that guides the practice of solving problems and finding solutions (Berg & DeJong, 1996). Consistent with the widely accepted goals in the treatment of female victims as proposed by feminist therapists Lenore Walker (1994) and Mary Ann Dutton (1992), the overall goals of a solution-focused approach in the treatment of female victims are stopping violence, establishing safety, empowerment, and healing.

A solution-focused approach, however, adopts different assumptions and methods in assisting female victims to achieve these ends. Instead of building the treatment strategies on an understanding of the problem of violence, a solution-focused approach suggests an alternative view—that positive change in clients can occur by focusing on solutions, strengths, and competencies instead of focusing on problems, deficits, and pathology (Berg & DeJong, 1996; Greene, Lee, Trask, & Rheinscheld, 2005; Lee, 1997).

In interviewing clients, solution-focused therapists emphasize engaging in solution-talk over problem-talk. The focus on solution-talk to achieve change is based on a systems perspective (Bateson, 1979); and social constructivism and a belief in the resources, potentials, and capacities inherent in human beings (de Shazer, 1988). Social systems are constantly changing; no system is totally static with no fluctuations and movement. Even though it is well documented that many female victims demonstrate "learned helplessness" (Walker, 1994), have negative distorted beliefs about their self-worth, ability to survive on their own, and responsibility for the abuse (Webb, 1992), there must be times, however brief, when a female victim feels a little bit better about herself or better able to resist, avoid, and fight against violence. The task for the therapist is to first assist the female victim to be curious about fluctuations in her life, and then to notice, identify, amplify, sustain, and reinforce these exceptions to the violent times regardless of how small or infrequent they may be. Once clients are engaged in exception behaviors, they are on the way to realizing a more satisfying life that excludes violence in intimate relationships.

Influenced by *social constructivism*, solution-focused therapy further assumes that solutions are a result of how an individual has developed his or her views, beliefs, and assumptions about reality (worldview). One's construction of reality affects his or her future behaviors (Greene, Lee, Trask, & Rheinscheld, 2005). A major emphasis in solution-focused therapy is a future orientation. "The future exists in our anticipation of how it will be" (Cade & O'Hanlon, 1993, p. 109). The future orientation of solution-focused therapy is particularly relevant for female victims who, all too often, are stuck in an abusive relationship. Overwhelmed by the fear of violence accompanied by feelings of powerlessness and helplessness, many of them become paralyzed and withdrawn. By therapeutically moving clients away from the past mishappenings, encouraging clients to visualize a future without violence in intimate relationships, directing their attention to helpful things that they are doing in realizing the desired change, and emphasizing their strengths and resourcefulness no matter how small or insignificant they seem to be, solution-focused therapy becomes a validating process that helps clients to co-construct a violence-free reality and rediscover the resources they have to achieve that end. Such a violence-free reality may involve staying in and changing the relationship with her partner or leaving the relationship permanently, something that heretofore she has not been able to do.

Following such a view is also the belief that the client is the only "knower" and the "expert" of her or his unique experiences, realities, and aspirations (Cantwell & Holmes, 1994). Because individual experiences and realities are unique, there is no one "optimal" solution for female victims or one "best" treatment approach to this inherently heterogeneous population. Consequently, from a solution-focused perspective, clients define the goals for their treatment and they fully "own" the work for a more satisfactory life.

The collaborative orientation of a solution-focused approach is particularly appropriate for female victims because of the emphasis on self-motivation. Oftentimes, it is not uncommon for shelter workers to spend hours educating women about their rights and helping them obtain needed resources only to find them returning to their abusive partners for reasons ranging from being coerced, financial dependency, and/or still loving their partners (Johnson, 1992). The solution-focused approach does not make any assumptions about what is best for clients, nor does it educate them as to what is the right way. Echoing the concerns of other therapists who argue for a contextualized or phenomenological approach in treatment (Dutton, 1996; Eisikovits & Buchbinder, 1996), solution-focused therapists believe in the uniqueness of each client's experience. Solution is an individual's construction and has to come from within.

From such a perspective, therapy becomes a validating and collaborative process in which female victims are continuously facilitated in discovering, connecting with, and amplifying life goals appropriate to their unique life context as well as their own resourcefulness for achieving their goals. Through the empowering process that fosters an internal locus of control and a positive sense of self in female victims, we believe that clients will become more aware of their needs and resources. Consequently, there is a higher likelihood for them to develop a viable solution that is appropriate to their needs and life context. From this perspective, the client's self-determination is supported. The woman may decide to stay with or leave her partner. In case she wants to stay in the relationship, the therapist will advocate for a violence-free relationship. Couple therapy becomes a viable choice of treatment if the client desires and the couple meets the safety criteria for couple treatment (see Lipchik & Kubicki, 1996, p. 70, for details of the criteria).

Solution-Focused Interventions

Solution-focused therapy views language as the medium through which personal meanings are expressed and constructed. By its symbolic quality, language enables people to not only describe and organize their experience but also to relabel and reframe their experience in a way that creates an alternative, more beneficial reality (Eisikovits & Buchbinder, 1996). Solution-focused intervention, therefore, is a dialogue between the therapist and the client in which the therapist asks questions that help the client to think differently about her situation and engage in a solution-building process (de Shazer, 1994). In the treatment of female victims, the therapist uses different questions to assist clients to construct solution patterns that do not subject them to violence and abuse in intimate relationships.

Exception questions inquire about times when the problem is either absent, less intense, or dealt with in a manner that is acceptable to the client (de Shazer, 1985). In treating female victims, exception questions can focus on the times when the client is better able to protect herself, to resist, avoid, escape, and fight against violence. "When was the last time that Bill might have hit you but you managed to protect yourself?" "How did you decide to call the police instead of letting him continue to hit you?" When the client desires to leave the relationship but is ambivalent about it, exception questions can be used to support the client's decision: "When was the last time that you might have gone back to Bill but you didn't?" "How were you able to do that?" "What has been helpful to remind you not to go back to that relationship again?" "When have there been times in the past that you were able to get out of and stay out of a bad relationship? How were you able to do that?"

Solution-focused therapy is goal-oriented and clients define their goals. *Outcome questions* are commonly used to assist clients in establishing goals for themselves (Greene, Lee, Trask, & Rheinscheld,

2005). Outcome questions ask clients to state goals in the positive rather than the negative; that is, the presence of something rather than the absence of something. A widely used format is the "miracle question":

> Suppose that after our meeting today you go home and go to bed. While you are sleeping a miracle happens and your problem is suddenly solved, like magic. The problem is gone. Because you were sleeping, you don't know that a miracle happened, but when you wake up tomorrow morning, you will be different. How will you know a miracle happened? What will be the first small sign that tells you that a miracle has happened and the problem is resolved? (Berg & Miller, 1992, p. 359)

The important task is to assist clients to think in terms of small, observable, and concrete behaviors so they can notice any small positive changes that make a difference in their situation (de Shazer, 1985). To expand the miracle picture, the therapist can ask questions such as: "What do you think has to be different for a small part of the miracle to start happening?" "Suppose there are times when a small part of it has already happened, what is different?" "When are there times when the miracle happens just a little bit?" "What will have to happen for that to happen more often?" Other examples of outcome questions are: "If I run into you a year later and by that time you are no longer in an abusive relationship, how will I know that you are different? What will you be like then?" "Six months down the road, what do you want yourself (and your children) to be like?"

Coping questions help clients to recognize their resources in times of turmoil. Coping questions ask clients to talk about how they manage to survive and cope with the problems. Examples are: "What keeps you going despite the terrible situation?" "Looking at your situation, I'm amazed why things aren't worse. What are you doing (or other family members doing) to keep it from getting worse? How has that been helpful? What else will be helpful?" In counseling female victims, therapists have to be careful about focusing questions on how the women cope with the abuse because those questions may potentially collude with and, therefore, run the danger of reinforcing the abuse. Coping questions, however, are extremely useful to support a client's decision to have an independent life. "Life in a shelter is never easy. How do you (and your children) cope with the changes?" "How do you cope with ... (changes) and still hold on to your decision to leave Bill and be on your own?"

The *scaling question* asks clients to rank their situation and/or goal on a 1 to 10 scale (Berg, 1994). Usually, 1 represents the worst scenario that could possibly be and 10 is the most desirable outcome. Scaling questions provide a simple tool for clients to quantify and evaluate their situation and progress so that they establish clear indicators of change for themselves (Berg, 1994; Greene, 1989). Scaling questions are found to be useful in helping clients rate the intensity of the problems, their goals, their confidence of and motivation to change, and clients' progress.

Relationship questions ask clients how their significant others are reacting to their problem situation and solution-finding progress (Berg, 1994). The establishment of multiple indicators of change facilitates clients in developing a clear vision of a desired future appropriate to their real-life context. Examples are: "What will your child (friend, therapist, etc.) notice that is different about you when you are no longer in an abusive relationship (or Bill is no longer violent)?" "On a 1 to 10 scale, how would your child (friend, therapist, etc.) rank your ability to say 'no' to Bill's attempts to get you back?"

The solution-focused approach also uses *task assignments* (de Shazer & Molnar, 1984; Kral & Kowalski, 1989) to help clients identify exception behaviors to the problem for which they are encouraged to "do more of what works." For clients who focus on the perceived stability of their problematic pattern and fail to identify any exceptions, an *observation task* is given instead: "Between now and next time we meet, we (I) want you to observe, so that you can tell us (me) next time, what happens in your (life, marriage, family, or relationship) that you want to continue to have happen" (de Shazer & Molnar, 1984, p. 298). Again, the focus is on the presence of desired changes, not on the absence of undesirable behaviors. In sum, solution-focused techniques encourage clients to be curious about their behaviors and potentials and identify, expand, amplify, and reinforce solution-oriented behaviors.

Assessing Lethality and Mental Health Status

Despite a treatment focus on strengths, resources, and solutions and a deliberate deemphasis on "problem-talk," solution-focused therapists have made theoretical adjustments in terms of assessing lethality and mental health status when treating female victims. Therapists taking a solution-focused approach do not abdicate responsibility for keeping the victim safe and attending to signals that may contribute to the possibility of further abuse (Lipchik & Kubicki, 1996). The therapist, therefore, pursues information about the extent of violence as perceived by the clients—what causes the violence, how frequent and intense it is, where the responsibility lies for the conflict, and so forth (Lipchik, 1991). She or he also assesses symptoms indicating drug and alcohol abuse or psychiatric problems—issues that may be associated with the occurrence of abuse and complicate the help-seeking efforts of the women.

In assessing lethality, we especially pay attention to the safety of the women and suicidal risk for them. Because of the trauma that has happened to the victims, one-half of all battered women have considered suicide, and one-fourth of all suicide attempts are directly related to abuse (Geffner & Pagelow, 1990). Solution-focused therapists, however, take a solution-oriented approach in assessing lethality. We avoid asking clients problem-oriented questions such as, "Have you considered killing yourself?" or "How likely is it that Bill will beat you again?" Instead, we focus the conversation on how the client will know that she is safe and has a good life.

The "safety scale"—a variation of the scaling question—is an extremely useful and simple technique in assessing lethality (Johnson & Goldman, 1996). The safety scale asks the woman and other family members how safe they feel in their household, with a 10 meaning completely safe and a 1 representing a complete lack of safety. The safety scale quickly helps the client and the therapist realize the extent of safety as experienced by the client. The therapist continues to ask the client to think about "What needs to happen for you to know that you (and your children) are safe?" or "What can you (or her partner, shelter workers) do differently so that by *tomorrow* you can move from a 3 to a 4 on the safety scale?" The focus on a brief time dimension helps the client develop concrete, specific ideas relevant to the immediacy of the situation. "On a scale of 1 to 10, how confident (motivated) are you that you can keep doing . . . (behaviors suggested by the client) so that you and your children can be safe?"

The dialogue around the safety scale gives the therapist some ideas about how actively the client plans to do things to resist, avoid, escape, and fight against the violence. Such information also has an implication for the client's desire to live. If the client cannot respond to those questions, has no plan for tomorrow, and is obviously depressed, emotional and overwhelmed, the therapist has to pursue more intensely a mental status examination of depression and suicidal risk (Roberts & Dziegielewski, 1995).

In sum, a solution-focused therapist begins the therapeutic process by understanding the client's unique experience of her life situation and battering experience. She or he orients the client to a solution-focused frame by letting her know that the focus of therapy is to assist her to find solutions for her concerns. In understanding a client's construction of her situation, the therapist at the same time asks solution-oriented questions to assess lethality and mental health status of the client. Using outcome questions, the therapist assists the client to establish concrete, observable, specific goals that are stated as desirable behaviors. Through the therapeutic dialogue, the therapist continuously asks exception, outcome, coping, relationship, and scaling questions to assist the client to construct an alternative reality that does not contain violence in intimate relationships. The therapist compliments the client on any of her positive, beneficial behaviors and suggestions that are conducive to her self-defined goals. The ultimate goal of the therapy is to empower the client by helping her rediscover her own resourcefulness in resisting, avoiding, escaping, and fighting against the abuse; develop a vision of a life free of violence; and empower a woman who has been experiencing "learned helplessness" to reconnect with her potential to achieve a more satisfying life for herself or her children.

IMPLICATIONS OF ROBERTS'S CONTINUUM OF DURATION AND CHRONICITY OF WOMAN BATTERING FOR TREATMENT USING A SOLUTION-FOCUSED APPROACH

Roberts's idea of using a Continuum for assessing the duration and chronicity of a woman's battering experience is very helpful because often these clinical situations are complex and multifaceted. Because the duration and chronicity of battering experiences strongly influence a woman's strategic responses to the abuse and her environment, they may indicate different therapeutic challenges and issues in the assessment and treatment of female victims (Roberts & Roberts, 2005). Hence, the Continuum can provide a useful reference for the therapist to fine-tune the therapeutic dialogue in joining with the client and providing appropriate treatment relevant to the client's unique situation.

Using the Continuum in a manner consistent with a solution-focused approach, however, requires some modification. The idea of using a Continuum is consistent with the solution-focused technique of the scaling question that assists clients to gauge their problems, goals, and other dimensions of their experience. In addition, the focus on duration and chronicity as two important dimensions of the battering experience provides useful guidelines for a solution-focused therapist to assist clients in gauging their current situation. On the other hand, a solution-focused therapist believes that any classification of a client's situation has to be *self-anchored*. Because both problems and solutions are a client's construction, any presupposed understanding of clients' situations or categorizing clients may run the risk of overriding the clients' perception of their situation.

A solution-focused therapist will use the Continuum in the following modified manner: Instead of classifying clients' battering experience, the therapist integrates the ideas underlying the Continuum and presents them as a scaling question. Besides gauging the duration and chronicity of the battering experience, such a scale can be used to assist clients in establishing desired outcome goals. To assess the duration of the battering experience, the therapist asks the female victim, "On a 1 to 10 scale, with a 1 meaning that the battering seems to be forever and a 10 meaning that there is no battering, where will you put yourself on the scale?" (duration of battering) "Where would you like to be?" (outcome goal) Likewise, to assess the chronicity of the battering experience, the therapist asks the female victim, "On a 1 to 10 scale, with a 1 meaning that the battering is at its worst, and a 10 meaning that the battering is almost non-existing, where will you put yourself on the scale?" "Where would you like to be?" Although still using the idea of a Continuum and the dimensions of duration and chronicity of the battering experience, the present scale is self-anchored based on the client's description and uses a 1 to 10 scale. Such characteristics are consistent with the scaling question as used in a solution-focused approach.

Case Application

Using the case scenarios provided by Dr. Roberts, the following discussion focuses on how solution-focused therapy might be modified for women who differentially rate themselves on a self-anchored scale of the duration and chronicity of battering experience.

The Case of Josephine (Intermediate Abuse).   In response to the modified self-anchored scale, Josephine may represent those clients who give a 7 or 8 for both the duration and chronicity of the abuse. Based on the description, Josephine is well educated, generally resourceful, financially independent, but stays in the abusive relationship because of "love" (Roberts & Roberts, 2005). Because of her general resourcefulness, she may have a higher likelihood to discover *exception* behavior that will make a difference in her life. It may be easier for Josephine to come up with a vision of life without violence and reconnect with resources that she has to make the "miracle" happen. In terms of constructing homework assignments, it is also more likely that she can identify exception behaviors to the problem for which she is encouraged to "do more of what works." Hence, for women like Josephine, the use of exception questions, outcome questions, and action-oriented homework assignments will be especially appropriate to their situation and potentials.

The Case of Arlene (Intermittent/Long-Term Abuse).   In response to the modified self-anchored scale, Arlene may represent those clients who give themselves a 5 or 6 for the chronicity of the abuse and a 2 or 3 for the length of the abuse. Using the case of Arlene as an example, she is educated although highly dependent on and bonded to the abuser as a result of economic, emotional, or religious reasons. The long-term nature of the abuse and the fact that she still stays in the relationship may implicate a stronger sense of helplessness and passivity in her. Because a sense of helplessness is also associated with depression, there may be a higher likelihood for Arlene to be depressed as well. With such an understanding of the client's situation, a solution-focused therapist will be alerted to several clinical issues.

In terms of assessing lethality and mental health status, the therapist may pursue more intensely signals that may implicate the presence of depression and its influence on the client's life. Referral for psychiatric treatment may be appropriate for some clients.

Because of the long-term nature of the abuse, Arlene is likely to feel helpless and passive in the face of violence. She might also develop "distorted" negative beliefs on how to cope with the situation

(Roberts & Roberts, 2005). One common clinical trap for many therapists treating clients like Arlene is to first take a rescuing stance and overfunction for them to save them from the abuse. The rescuing effort may include educating them about their rights, persuading them to leave the abusive situation, and providing the required tangible support for her to end the abuse. As a result of unsuccessful attempts to convince the client to leave the relationship, many therapists may feel frustrated and give up on or blame the client (Petretic-Jackson & Jackson, 1996). Neither the rescuing stance nor the giving up stance is helpful because the dynamics involved exactly reinforce the feelings of helplessness, passivity, and failure in these women—stances that cannot empower the already powerless clients.

One major therapeutic challenge in such circumstances is how to join with the client without either overfunctioning for her or giving up on her. The therapist adhering to a solution-focused perspective understands clearly that any viable solution for the client has to come from within in order for the client to feel empowered and develop an internal locus of control. Therefore, the therapist does not give in to the urge to quickly find a normative solution for the client. The therapist stays focused on assisting the client to rediscover her own resources no matter how small or meager they seem to be. The process may be slow and tedious although the therapist is persistent and patient with the client in the process of co-constructing a solution-picture that excludes violence in an intimate relationship. Instead of rushing to ask exception questions, the therapist may need to take more time to listen to the client's story. Coping questions may be more appropriate at the beginning of the therapy in view of the negativity of these clients. The client may need more time and probing to establish goals that are appropriate to her needs and situation. Because the abuse is long-term, the client may develop a rigid perspective toward the permanency of the situation. As such, it is important to assist the client to first be *curious* about any small improvement in her situation before helping her to identify exceptions. The observation task (de Shazer & Molnar, 1984), therefore, may be more appropriate than action-oriented homework assignments to direct the client's attention to desirable behaviors and changes in her life.

Finally, if the client verbalizes her desire to stay in the relationship, the solution-focused therapist will want to assess the appropriateness of couple treatment for her situation.

The Case of Naomi (Chronic and Severe Abuse With a Regular Pattern). In response to the modified self-anchored scale, Naomi may represent those clients who give themselves a 2 or 3 for both the duration and chronicity of the abuse. Using the case of Naomi as an example, she suffers severe and regular abuse, comes from a low socioeconomic class, has low self-esteem, and is struggling with addiction problems (Roberts & Roberts, 2005). As such, Naomi might find her partner's violence as only one of the oppressors in her life (Davidson & Jenkins, 1989). Such characteristics present another clinical issue, namely, how to stay focused on solutions and not be overwhelmed by the multiplicity of problems.

The keys in handling such a challenge may be for the therapist to firmly believe in the potentials of human beings; to demonstrate curiosity about the client's ability so that she may begin to be curious about her own ability and resources to live a more satisfying life without violence; to stay focused on goal-oriented behaviors no matter how small they may be; to lavishly compliment the client on any successes and positive behaviors; to respect the client's pace in achieving her goals; and to provide appropriate assistance (e.g., tangible assistance, information) on the client's request. Because of the social disadvantages experienced by women like Naomi, they probably need more tangible assistance to end the violence and/or to start a violence-free life. However, it is important for the therapist "to lead from a step behind" (Cantwell & Holmes, 1994), that is, to act as a facilitator and let the client discover and decide for herself her goals and needs. If the client decides to leave the abusive situation, the therapeutic dialogue can focus on how she refrains from returning to the abuser, and how she successfully copes with the major changes in her life.

In terms of assessment, the therapist may pursue more intensely the extent of violence and the issue of safety both in terms of homicidal and suicidal risk. It is also important to understand the effects of alcohol or drug addiction on the pattern of abuse and the help-seeking effort of the woman. Such an understanding should be followed up with appropriate assistance as requested by the client. It is, however, imperative that the assessment be conducted within a solution-oriented frame.

Although solution-focused therapy does not rely on any diagnostic instruments in its treatment process, the concepts underlying the development of the Continuum are embedded in the scaling question that can be used to obtain relevant information for treatment. Still adhering to fundamental solution-focused techniques, the tone of the therapeutic process can be fine-tuned to adjust to the unique battering experience of the client.

IMPLICATIONS OF ROBERTS'S CONTINUUM OF DURATION AND CHRONICITY OF WOMAN BATTERING FOR RESEARCH FROM A SOLUTION-FOCUSED FRAME

As suggested by Petretic-Jackson and Jackson (1996), an empirically based understanding of assessment and treatment issues related to battered women is relatively meager. Further, because of the tendency to define battered women primarily by their battering experience, variation among battered women as a group and their differential responses to different treatment approaches have not been carefully investigated. The Continuum provides a useful typology to study the effectiveness and appropriateness of different treatment approaches with women experiencing different intensities of battering. Likewise, it can be used to examine the differential responses of women's partners to different strategies for ending violence such as the arresting policy, restraining order, and mandated treatment for male batterers.

Specific to a solution-focused approach, the Continuum has implications for several research questions. Currently, because of the emphasis on accountability and treatment effectiveness in a managed care context, it is imperative for therapists to establish outcome effectiveness of the approach. It is useful to examine the effectiveness of specific solution-focused intervention techniques with women at different levels of the Continuum. In other words, do all intervention techniques work equally well with women across all levels? If not, what specific techniques work better with women at which level? Such information helps therapists to refine their skills and increase treatment effectiveness.

Other questions examine the theoretical assumptions of solution-focused therapy. Solution-focused therapy assumes a solution is an individual's construction that does not necessarily correspond to the presenting problems (de Shazer, 1985). Further, because change is constant in any system, a person will discover exception behaviors (clues for solution) regardless of the severity of the problems. Hence, such an approach should be effective across different problems and different client populations. In addition, more severe problems do not necessarily require longer or more complex treatment. By examining the outcome effectiveness and the duration of solution-focused therapy with women situated at different levels of the Continuum, this classificatory scheme can be used to examine the validity of such theoretical claims of its effectiveness regardless of problems.

The Continuum also has important implications for investigating the use of couple treatment in solution-focused therapy. Different from feminist perspectives that largely exclude couple therapy in the treatment of female victims, a solution-focused approach views couple therapy as a viable solution (Johnson & Goldman, 1996; Lipchik, 1991; Lipchik & Kubicki, 1996). However, such a decision about therapy choice has to be carefully made due to the woman's safety and well-being in the potentially abusive relationship. A useful research question is to examine the effectiveness of couple therapy with women situated at different levels of the Continuum. In other words, will women at a certain level of the Continuum benefit from couple treatment more than women at some other levels? Will the partners of women who suffer long-term, severe battering (e.g., Level 3 and up) be less likely to take responsibility for violence and less cooperative with couple treatment? Together with research findings about typologies of batterers, the findings of such an inquiry will make the decision about appropriateness for couple's treatment much easier and safer (Lipchik & Kubicki, 1996).

The Continuum will also be useful for comparative studies of the effectiveness between a solution-focused approach and other approaches such as crisis intervention models (Dziegielewski, Resnick & Krause, 1996; Greene, Lee, Trask, & Rheinscheld, 2005; Roberts & Dziegielewski, 1995), cognitive-behavioral approaches (Dutton, 1992), and survivor therapy (Walker, 1994) for women at different levels on the Continuum.

The previous discussion focuses on the implication of the Continuum in its present form to do research from a solution-focused frame. Going beyond the premise of the Continuum that is problem-oriented, a "Solution Identification Scale" for female victims can be developed. Consistent with the philosophy of a solution-focused approach, such a scale will consist of items that ask respondents to self-report their strengths, competencies, and solutions regarding their efforts to attain a violence-free life. Instead of focusing on the problem and assessing lethality issues, the "Solution Identification Scale" will assess the ability of the female victim to say "no" to violence and to say "yes" to a more satisfying life. By asking clients to self-discover and identify their potentials, such an instrument can be a useful intervention in itself. The "Solution Identification Scale," therefore, uses the language of "solutions and strengths" in both its formulation and its approach to conduct research.

CONCLUSION

Significant progress has been made regarding treatment for female victims since the inception of the Battered Women's Movement in the 1970s. Although people increasingly recognize the heterogeneity of female victims who live in diverse social and individual contexts, the current treatment paradigm is still very much dominated by the perception that defines battered women only by their experience of battering and a singular—often a helpless and passive—response to it. The development of the Continuum provides a useful reference for us to refine our assessment and treatment strategies based on an understanding of clients' unique battering experiences and their life contexts. In the age of accountability, the Continuum also provides a useful scheme for researchers to examine the interactive effects between the intensity of battering experience and treatment responses. Such inquiries will be helpful for mental health professionals to increase and establish outcome effectiveness of any treatment approaches for treating female domestic violence victims.

A solution-focused approach for treating female victims is part of the pluralistic, societal effort to develop pragmatic solutions to empower women against male violence in intimate relationships. Although a solution-focused approach uses the language and symbols of "solutions and strengths" while the Continuum is more problem-focused, the Continuum has direct implications for investigating some important research questions specific to a solution-focused approach. In addition, the ideas underlying the development of Roberts's Continuum have indirect implications both for treatment and the development of a "Solution-Identification Scale" for female victims.

REFERENCES

Bateson, G. (1979). *Mind and nature.* New York: E.P. Dutton.

Berg, I. K. (1994). *Family-based services: A solution-focused approach.* New York: Norton.

Berg, I. K., & De Jong, P. (1996). Solution-building conversations—Co-constructing a sense of competence with clients. *Families in Societies, 77,* 376–391.

Berg, I. K., & Dolan, Y. M. (2001). *Tales of solutions: A collection of hope-inspiring stories.* New York: Norton.

Berg, I. K., & Miller, S. (1992). *Working with the problem drinker: A solution-focused approach.* New York: Norton.

Cade, B., & O'Hanlon, W. H. (1993). *A brief guide to brief therapy.* New York: Norton.

Cantwell, P., & Holmes, S. (1994). Social construction: A paradigm shift for systemic therapy and training. *The Australian and New Zealand Journal of Family Therapy, 15,* 17–26.

de Shazer, S. (1985). *Keys to solutions in brief therapy.* New York: Norton.

de Shazer, S. (1988). *Clues: Investigating solutions in brief therapy.* New York: Norton.

de Shazer, S. (1994). *Words were originally magic.* New York: Norton.

de Shazer, S., & Molnar, A. (1984). Four useful interventions in brief family therapy. *Journal of Marital and Family Therapy, 10,* 297–304.

Davidson, B. P., & Jenkins, P. J. (1989). Class diversity in shelter life. *Social Work, 34,* 491–495.

Dziegielewski, S. F., Resnick, C., & Krause, N. B. (1996). Shelter-based crisis intervention with battered women. In A. R. Roberts (Ed.), *Helping battered women: New perspectives and remedies* (pp. 159–171). New York: Oxford University Press.

Dolan, Y. (1994). Solution-focused therapy with a case of severe abuse. In M. F. Hoyt (Ed.), *Constructive therapies* (pp. 276–294). New York: Guilford Press.

Dutton, D. G., & Painter, S. (1993). Battered women syndrome: Effects of severity and intermittency of abuse. *American Journal of Orthopsychiatry, 63,* 614–627.

Dutton, M. A. (1992). *Empowering and healing the battered woman: A model for assessment and intervention.* New York: Springer Publishing.

Dutton, M. A. (1996). Battered women strategic response to violence: The role of context. In J. Edleson & Z. C. Eisikovits (Eds.), *Future interventions with battered women and their families* (pp. 105–124). Thousand Oaks, CA: Sage.

Eisikovits, Z. C., & Buchbinder, E. (1996). Toward a phenomenological intervention with violence in intimate relationship. In J. L. Edleson & Z. C.

Eisikovits (Eds.), *Future interventions with battered women and their families* (pp. 186–200). Thousand Oaks, CA: Sage.

Geffner, R., & Pagelow, M. (1990). Victims of spouse abuse. In R. Ammerman & M. Hersen (Eds.), *Treatment of family violence: A source book* (pp. 113–135). New York: Wiley.

Gondolf, E., & Fisher, E. (1988). *Battered women as survivors.* Lexington, MA: Lexington Books.

Greene, G. J. (1989). Using the written contract for evaluating and enhancing practice effectiveness. *Journal of Independent Social Work, 4,* 135–155.

Greene, G. J., Lee, M. Y., Trask, R., & Rheinscheld, J. (2005). How to work with clients' strengths in crisis intervention: A solution-focused approach. In A. R. Roberts (Ed.), *Crisis intervention handbook: Assessment, treatment, and research* (3rd ed., pp. 64–89). New York: Oxford University Press.

Johnson, C. E., & Goldman, J. (1996). Taking safety home: A solution-focused approach with domestic violence. In M. Hoyt (Ed.), *Constructive therapies* (Vol. 2, pp. 184–196). New York: Guilford Press.

Johnson, I. M. (1992). Economic, situational, and psychological correlates of the decision-making process of battered women. *Families in Society: The Journal of Contemporary Human Services, 73,* 168–176.

Kral, R., & Kowalski, K. (1989). After the miracle: The second stage in solution-focused brief therapy. *Journal of Strategic and Systemic Therapies, 8,* 73–76.

Lee, M. Y. (1997). A study of solution-focused brief family therapy: Outcomes and issues. *American Journal of Family Therapy, 25,* 3–17.

Lee, M. Y., Sebold, J., & Uken, A. (2003). *Solution-focused treatment of domestic violence offenders: Accountability for change.* New York: Oxford University Press.

Lipchik, E. (1991). Spouse abuse: Challenging the party line. *Networker, May/June,* 59–63.

Lipchik, E., & Kubicki, A. D. (1996). Solution-focused domestic violence views: Bridges toward a new reality in couples therapy. In S. D. Miller, M. A. Hubble, & B. L. Duncan (Eds.), *Handbook of solution-focused brief therapy* (pp. 65–98). San Francisco: Jossey-Bass.

Martin, D. (1976). *Battered wives.* San Francisco: Glide.

Petretic-Jackson, P., & Jackson, T. (1996). Mental health interventions with battered women. In A. R. Roberts (Ed.), *Helping battered women, new perspectives and remedies* (pp. 188–221). New York: Oxford University Press.

Roberts, A. R., & Dziegielewski, S. F. (1995). Foundation skills and applications of crisis intervention and cognitive therapy. In A. R. Roberts (Ed.), *Crisis intervention and time-limited cognitive treatment* (pp. 3–27). Thousand Oaks, CA: Sage.

Roberts, A. R., & Roberts, B. (2005). *Ending intimate abuse: Practical guidance and survival strategies.* New York: Oxford University Press.

Seligman, M. (1975). *Helplessness: On depression, development and death.* New York: Wiley.

Uken, A., & Sebold, J. (1996). The Plumas Project: A solution-focused goal directed domestic violence diversion program. *Journal of Collaborative Therapies, 4,* 10–17.

Walker, L. (1984). *The battered woman syndrome.* New York: Springer Publishing.

Walker, L. (1994). *Abused women and survivor therapy: A practical guide for the psychotherapist.* Washington, DC: American Psychological Association.

Warrior, B. (1976). *Wifebeating.* Somerville, MA: New England Free Press.

Webb, W. (1992). Treatment issues and cognitive behavior techniques with battered women. *Journal of Family Violence, 7,* 205–217.

CHAPTER 5

National Survey of 107 Shelters for Battered Women and Their Children

Albert R. Roberts, Gina Robertiello, and Kimberly Bender

Woman battering is harmful, dangerous, and sometimes lethal. Recent estimates indicate that approximately 8.7 million women are battered by their current or former intimate partners each year (Roberts, 1998; Roberts & Roberts, 2005). For some of these victims the abuse consists of one incident, but for many women the abuse increases in frequency and severity over several months or years.

The effects of partner violence, especially chronic abuse, on the health and mental health of abuse survivors can be severe. Three separate studies of women living in shelters or attending support groups yielded posttraumatic stress disorder (PTSD) rates ranging from as low as 45% to as high as 84% (Roberts, 1996; Saunders, 1994; Robertiello, 2006). Many of the short-term cases break off the abusive relationship quickly with the help of the police and judges who expedite a temporary or permanent protective order. Others are helped by close friends or relatives. However, some chronically battered women stay with their partners for decades, and the battering relationship only ends because one of the partners dies of cancer, cirrhosis of the liver, or homicide. Many chronically abused women successfully leave the abusive relationship by seeking safety in a domestic violence shelter or joining a support group.

In response to the large number of chronically battered women needing a safe place to escape to, emergency shelters began to be established in the mid-1970s. By the mid-1990s, many shelters had gone beyond providing emergency shelter, and had begun to provide counseling, legal advocacy and job placement for the women, and counseling for the children. To a large extent, shelter staffing and management has changed from a grassroots movement of paraprofessionals and former abused women to the hiring of trained professional social workers and counselors, many of whom have bachelor's and/or master's degrees (Roche & Sadoski, 1996).

Permanently breaking the cycle of violence and leaving one's abusive partner is dangerous, difficult, and challenging. One of the most difficult challenges is finding a safe place for the battered woman and her children to stay temporarily when transitioning to more stable housing, obtaining crisis-oriented services, securing a divorce and custody of the children, and finding a career and caring support system. Emergency shelters for battered women and their children usually provide these much-needed shelter, crisis-oriented, and legal advocacy services to battered women and their children.

Shelters across the United States currently operate independently from one another and consequently vary in the services they provide, funding sources, and organizational structures. This variation speaks to the varying needs of domestic violence victims. Examining existing differences and similarities among programs helps us to assess what is currently being done, on a national level, to provide services to domestic violence victims and to further assess strengths and limitations across shelter organizations. The purpose of this chapter is to summarize the latest findings of a national survey of 107 emergency and short-term shelters in terms of their objectives, types of services offered, staffing patterns, funding sources, approximate number of clients served, underserved victim groups, and self-reported strengths and limitations of programs.

BRIEF HISTORY OF SHELTERS: BRIDGING THE
PAST TO THE PRESENT

Over the past 25 years, the resources available to shelters have improved significantly. In the late 1970s and early 1980s, shelters were attempting to survive on shoestring budgets (Roberts, 1981). With very few shelters able to employ full-time professional social workers, the majority of shelters relied on staff comprised of student interns, volunteers, formerly battered women, paraprofessionals, and CETA (Federal Comprehensive Employment and Training Act) workers. The 1980s brought great progress as the federal Victims of Crime Act (VOCA) was signed into law in 1984 with an appropriation of $69 million from federal criminal penalties into the crime victim funds that emphasized the funding of domestic violence and sexual assault intervention programs. In addition, many populated states passed legislation that resulted in appropriations of several million dollars per state to domestic violence shelters. By the mid-1990s, both funding and employment of professional staff had improved in most shelters. Typical staffing patterns in the 1990s included 6 to 10 full-time professional staff as well as several part-time and volunteer staff. The vast majority of shelter directors (94.8%) had a bachelor's degree or above (Roberts & Lewis, 2000).

In recent years, the trend toward increased public funding support for shelters has continued. Over 50% of the domestic violence revenue received from state agencies originates at the federal level. As recently as 2006, President Bush signed the reauthorization of the Violence Against Women Act (VAWA III). This act not only reauthorized currently funded programs aimed at serving victims of domestic violence but also expanded funding for programs working with underserved populations such as disabled, elderly, legal immigrant, ethnic minority victims, and victims residing in rural areas (VAWA, 2005). Another resource, the Victims of Crime Act uses fines and penalties collected from criminal offenders to assist 4 million victims (many of which are victims of domestic violence), in 4,400 agencies across the United States (NCADV, 2006). Although current legislation continues to improve domestic violence shelter services, many shelters still continue to rely on creative ways to survive financially. Even those shelters with funding recognize the temporary nature of public funding and consistently invest time and effort in advocating for these services. The following survey of 107 currently operating domestic violence shelters sheds light on the funding, service delivery, and staffing issues faced by today's shelters.

METHODOLOGY

A nationwide cross-sectional organizational study of 107 shelters for battered women was conducted with the goals of understanding (a) who is being served, (b) what services are being provided, and (c) what resources are being utilized to provide services. Specifically, the questionnaire queried each organization's: location, year started, number of women served, services for underserved populations, types of services provided, crisis intervention procedures, auspices, budget, funding sources, staffing patterns, and self-reported strengths and weaknesses.

The study sample was derived from a 15% random sample of the 1,500 ($N = 225$) battered women's shelters listed in the National Organization for Victim Assistance (NOVA) directory, and the Office for Victims of Crimes (OVC) of the U.S. Department of Justice mailing list. A four-page questionnaire was developed, pretested (with three executive directors of shelters), revised, and mailed with a cover letter to 225 programs in late January 2005. Within 4 weeks after the initial mailing, 48 letters were returned unopened by the post office and stamped either moved with no forwarding address, forwarding address expired, or undeliverable. Thus, we were sampling from a valid list of 177 shelters. One month after the initial mailing, a follow-up letter and another copy of the questionnaire were sent to the nonrespondents. By May 1, 2005, we had received a total of 107 completed questionnaires from 38 states—a 60.45% response rate.

FINDINGS

In each section of the following findings, first aggregate results across shelter responses are reported. For example, the frequencies of answers given, as well as the average responses (mean) and most frequently reported responses (mode), are given. Second, examples of specific shelters are used to illustrate both typical organizations and those that lie on extreme ends of the spectrum.

Shelter Characteristics

Location. The respondents were from shelters in all parts of the United States and represented a cross-section of urban, suburban, and rural shelters. Thirty-eight states from all major regions of the United States were represented. Those states with the largest number of responding programs were Texas (9), Minnesota (8), Wisconsin (6), Missouri (6), and New York (6). The following states were un-represented, having no respondents: Arkansas, Delaware, District of Columbia, Hawaii, Idaho, Iowa, Louisiana, North Dakota, Nebraska, Rhode Island, South Carolina, West Virginia, and Wyoming. Further-more, the responding programs were geographically distributed in all 10 Federal regions of the United States, with the most representative region being Region V with 29 shelters responding. Table 5.1 displays the number of shelters distributed across 10 Federal regions.

Year Started. Shelters vary in age from those that started in the dawn of the shelter movement of the 1970s to those with very recent inception. Programs, when asked about the year their program started, responded with ranges from 1971 to 1999. The majority of shelter programs had opened in the 1970s and early part of the 1980s. From 1990 on, 14 shelter programs began. The median year was 1982, with a mean year of 1983. The mode was 1979 (with 11 shelters reporting a start-up year at this time period).

Curiously, historical research on shelters has determined that the first shelter for battered women in the world began in England in 1971, and a few years later shelters were opened in Fresno, California; St. Paul, Minnesota; and New York City (Roberts, 1981). However, it is interesting to note that two of the respondents stated that their shelters began in the United States in 1971. There could be several plausible explanations for this phenomenon: (a) These two shelters actually started as a host home network, or a woman's advocate sheltering a few battered women in her own large house; or (b) these shelter directors were estimating the year and were off by 3 or 4 years.

Neither respondent gave permission to be named in this report, but both gave permission for their information to be shared. One shelter was in Illinois, offered most services, had a budget of almost $1.6 million, and claimed its strength was "longevity." The other shelter, located in Indiana, also offered most services, had a budget of

TABLE 5.1 Regional Representation of Battered Women's Shelters

Region I		Region II		Region III		Region IV		Region V	
Connecticut	1	New Jersey	2	Delaware	0	Alabama	1	Illinois	4
Maine	2	New York	6	District of Columbia	0	Florida	3	Indiana	4
Mass	2	Total	8	Maryland	2	Georgia	1	Michigan	4
New Hampshire	1			Pennsylvania	4	Kentucky	1	Minnesota	8
Rhode Island	0			Virginia	5	Mississippi	1	Ohio	3
Vermont	1			West Virginia	0	North Carolina	2	Wisconsin	6
Total	7			Total	11	South Carolina	0	Total	29
						Tennessee	3		
						Total	12		

Region VI		Region VII		Region VIII		Region IX		Region X	
Arkansas	2	Iowa	0	Colorado	2	Arizona	2	Alaska	0
Louisiana	0	Kansas	2	Montana	4	California	2	Idaho	0
New Mexico	3	Missouri	6	North Dakota	0	Hawaii	0	Oregon	1
Oklahoma	1	Nebraska	0	South Dakota	1	Nevada	1	Washington	3
Texas	9	Total	8	Utah	1	Total	5	Total	4
Total	15			Wyoming	0				
				Total	8				

$2.1 million, and claimed its strength was "empowerment." They served and provided shelter to 701 and 304 women, respectively, and served 2,250 and 604 women via hotline, respectively, in 2004. Both were nonprofit agencies. Interestingly, the Indiana shelter also had the largest number of interns (50) and the most part-time employees with BA degrees (12 of 12).

The newest shelter surveyed started in 1999 in Virginia. It is a nonprofit agency serving 82 battered women and 374 via the hotline per year. Its budget is $322,000 (with no specifics on the distribution of funding). The shelter has 8 full-time employees, 1 part-time employee, and 35 volunteers. The self-reported strengths of this program included "direct personal service, very secure (on a military base), clients have their own room, we offer transportation, and we are one of the largest shelters on the East Coast."

Who Are Shelters Serving?

Number of Women Being Served.   Shelters can vary greatly in the number of women they aim to serve. This number can be influenced by several factors including urban versus rural location and financial resources. Shelters in this survey ranged from serving as few as 28 women (in Arkansas) and 50 women (in Ohio) to as many as 35,814 women (in Nevada). On average, shelters served 1,593 women per year. The median number of women served was 485.5, and there were two modes (150 and 188), each with three shelters stating this number of women were served in 2003.

The Arkansas shelter began in 1989 and is an independent nonprofit agency. It has a budget of $100,000 and offers most services (two full-time and two part-time positions as well as 40 volunteers). Its strengths include being a "safe shelter with good community backing, volunteers, contributes and networking." However, its weaknesses include "lack of public transportation, day care and affordable housing." Even though this shelter served the fewest number of women, and one of the fewest numbers of women via hotline (95), they had many of the same services, strengths, and weaknesses as the other shelters.

The other low was a tie between two Ohio shelters (both served only 50 women). The first Ohio shelters started in the late 1970s and offered most services, just to a very small population. One shelter started in 1986, currently has a budget of $180,000, and is an independent nonprofit agency. They claimed to have "geographic isolation and limited resources." The other Ohio shelter with only 50 women served is located in Ashtabula, Ohio, and is called Homesafe Shelter. It began in 1978 and is an independent nonprofit agency. Their budget is $401,594, and shelter director Heather McGuiness states that, "we are the largest County in Ohio and it is hard to reach those in outlying areas" as the reason for serving so few women.

The shelter serving the most women is located in Nevada and started in 1980. It has a budget of $1.7 million, 6 full-time and 3 part-time employees, as well as 15 volunteers. This shelter is an independent nonprofit and serves 35,814 women. It also serves the largest number of women through its hotline (33,402). See following section for information about women served via hotline.

Number of Women Served via Hotline Services.   Hotline services are frequently utilized by battered women whether in emergencies or seeking more information about their options in the future. Hotlines serve as an anonymous way for women to receive referral information, ask questions, and seek help. The number of women receiving hotline services ranged from as few as 53 women (in Wisconsin) to as many as 33,402 women (in Nevada). On average, shelters served 2,155 women via their hotline services. Table 5.2 compares the number of women receiving shelter services and those utilizing hotline services.

As mentioned previously, the Nevada shelter appears to serve the most women overall and via hotline of those that responded to the survey. Closer examination of the shelter serving the fewest number of women via hotline services reveals its very small staff yet wide range of services offered. It started in 1978 as an indepen-

TABLE 5.2   Number of Women Served During 1–Year Period

Number of women served in shelters		Number of women served via hotlines	
Range	(28–35,814)	Range	(53–33,402)
Mean	1,593	Mean	2,155
Median	485.5	Median	821
Mode	150,188	Mode	7,000

dent nonprofit shelter offering most services and has a budget of $147,805.85.

One concern of designing services to broadly address the varying needs of large numbers of battered women is that traditionally underrepresented groups may fall into gaps of service provision. It is common to find shelters, under the budgetary and staffing strains, that do not offer services specifically sensitive to the needs of these underrepresented groups. When shelters were asked what groups were underserved, 16 major groups were mentioned. Shelters most commonly noted a lack of services for non-English-speaking or undocumented women. Lack of bilingual staff makes it difficult to help this underserved group that often has few options for services. Shelters also commonly reported that women from rural areas, those with mental health problems, and the Gay/Lesbian/Bisexual/Transgender populations were underrepresented in their clientele. Specific age groups, such as the elderly, teens, and children, were underrepresented groups. Additionally, women with certain issues such as sexual assault, substance abuse, co-occurring disorders, and disabilities were also mentioned as underrepresented. Interestingly, both economic statuses were mentioned (some shelters felt the poor were underserved, whereas others felt that affluent women were underserved). Finally, male victims and uninsured victims were also mentioned. Table 5.3 shows the number of shelters mentioning each underrepresented group.

A typical example of the underserved population came from Battered Women Services and Shelter in Washington County in Burre, Vermont. They are an independent nonprofit agency started in 1991 that offered most services. They served 1,529 battered women and 3,416 via hotline with a budget of $371,600. According to Shelter Director Jernia Gentry, the underserved include "women and children living in extremely rural, isolated areas in Washington County, Vermont."

What Services Are Shelters Providing?

Types of Services Offered.   Because battered women can arrive at the shelter requiring help across several service domains, shelters are challenged with the task of offering a wide range of services. Our survey inquired about the various services offered by each shelter,

TABLE 5.3   Underserved Populations

Underserved population	Number of shelters citing this population
Non-English-speaking/undocumented	27
Rural	23
Mental health problems	18
Gay/lesbian/bisexual/transgender	13
Cultural/racial issues	13
Elderly	13
Children	10
Disabled	9
Poor	7
Male	6
Substance dependent	6
Sexual assault victims	6
Affluent	3
Teens	2
Those with co-occurring disorders	2
Uninsured	1
Missing	12

and the range of services was impressive. As can be seen from Table 5.4, services varied from those that helped women cope with the immediate crisis at hand to those that involved planning for future needs. These services involved health, mental health, legal, and educational domains. Most shelters offered Crisis Intervention (100), a 24-Hour Hotline (102), Assistance with the Court Process (98), Assistance with Completing Victim Compensation Forms (91), Court Advocacy (99), Referral to a Mental Health Agency (94), Transportation to Court (84), and Public Education (89). The majority also offered Legal Advocacy (77), and more than two-thirds offered Services for the Disabled. More than one-half offered Client Advocacy, one-fourth offered Childcare and Home Visits, and over one-third offered Bilingual Counselors. The following services were less likely to be offered: Play/Art Therapy, Batterer Intervention, Crime Scene Advocacy, Transitional Housing, and Domestic Violence Support. Very unlikely to be offered were: Training for Professionals, Employment/Financial Assistance, Parenting Assistance, Youth Mentor/Education/Tutoring, Project Reach, Case Management, Medical Advocacy, Child Case Management, and Elder Abuse Assistance. These infrequently

TABLE 5.4   Types of Services Offered

Services offered	Number of shelters offering this service	Crisis intervention procedures	Number of shelters utilizing procedure
24-hour hotline	102	Hotline	63
Crisis intervention	100	Safety plan	26
Court advocacy	99	Risk assessment	23
Assistance with court process	98	Referral to appropriate service	21
Referral to mental health agency	94	Shelter	20
Assist in completing victim comp forms	91	Set up services	19
Public education	89	Walk-in	13
Transportation to court	84	Referral by police	11
Legal advocacy	77	Intake interview	12
Services for the disabled	64	Needs assessment	9
Client advocacy	59	Empathetic/active listening	8
Bilingual counselors	42	Action plan	6
Home visits	29	Present options	5
Childcare	22	Support group	5
Domestic violence support	19	Crisis response team (referral by hospital)	3
Play/art therapy	16	Each situation is unique	1
Batterer intervention program	15		
Transitional housing	12		
Crime scene advocacy	11		
Youth mentor/ education/tutoring	8		
Child case manager	8		
Case management	6		
Medical advocacy	6		
Employment/financial assistance	5		
Parenting	5		
Rape/sexual assault prevention	3		
Training for professionals	3		
Elder abuse	2		
Drug/alcohol	2		
Visitation center	2		
Project Reach	1		
LPC	1		
Donated household item maintenance	1		
Anger management	1		
Intervention project	1		

offered services may reflect many shelters' needs to focus on more immediate services rather than having an ability to provide long-term training and assistance.

Crisis Intervention Procedures.   Many women seeking shelter services are in crisis. Whether women are in immediate danger or in crisis due to lack of shelter and security, crisis intervention procedures are an essential part of the shelter services provided to them. Several different procedures for crisis intervention exist, and shelters surveyed reported 15 different categories of crisis intervention services. A typical crisis intervention procedure reported by shelter respondents began with contact via the 24-hour hotline, conduction of a safety assessment, and ultimately resulted in a referral to the appropriate agency or service. Most contact began via the Hotline (63), but some women were Walk-Ins (13), some were Referred by the Police (11), and a few were referred from the hospital by a Crisis Response Team (3).

Once women made contact with the organization, shelters reported responding with assessment and planning services. Assessment procedures reported by shelters included conducting Intake Interviews (12), Needs Assessments (9), and Risk Assessments (23). Several shelters report working with women to create a plan of action and linking them with services; these shelters report creating Safety Plans (26), providing Action Plans (6), or Presenting Options (5) and then Referring Victims to a shelter (20), Referring Victims to the Appropriate Agency (21), and generally Setting Up Services (19). Shelters further report using Empathetic/Active Listening and Support Groups in crisis intervention procedures. Interestingly, one shelter responded by saying "each situation is unique" and could not respond, implying that crisis intervention was often an individualized service and general crisis intervention procedures were not dictated. Table 5.4 shows the frequency in shelters providing each service and crisis intervention procedure.

According to Catherine Olde, Director of Brighter Tomorrows in Grande Prairie, Texas, which is an independent nonprofit program, her shelter's Crisis Intervention Procedure is as follows: "Once a client contacts us, usually by referral or police, other service program or medical facility, needs are assessed and type of services needed is determined or safety plan is reviewed. If shelter is needed, then the client is directed to pick-up location." This is a solid, standard procedure, followed in many of the shelters surveyed. Brighter To-morrows served 555 battered women and 823 via its hotline in 2003. Their program began in 1990 and with a budget of $1,163,505 is able to provide a range of services to women in need, including Crisis Intervention, 24-Hour Hotline, Explaining the Court Process, Assisting with the Completion of Victim Compensation Forms, Court and Legal Advocacy, Shelter, Referral, Client Advocacy, Transportation, Public Education, and Services for the Disabled. A bonus with this shelter was Bilingual Services, Transitional Housing, and Parenting Classes. With a substantial budget, this shelter was capable of meeting a variety of needs.

What Resources Are Shelters Utilizing to Provide Services?

Auspices.   Almost all shelters are nonprofit agencies. Although reported under slightly different labels, including "Not for Profit"; "Independent private, nonprofit "; "Independent nonprofit"; "Private, nonprofit"; "Independent, not for profit" or simply "Nonprofit"; 100 shelters fit into this collapsed category entitled "Nonprofit." Only five other shelters considered their auspices to be something other than nonprofit. One was County run, one was part of the Department of Social Services, one was part of a Community Action group, one was State run, and one was run by Whole Health Outreach.

Sources of Funding.   Due to their nonprofit status, funding is of serious concern for organizations serving battered women. Often funding is pulled together from a number of sources and thus can be a complicated task and difficult to report. Several shelters described their funding sources with incomplete or missing information. These shelters checked off where they received funding from, but no monetary amount was given, and no percentage of the budget was given. In some "complete" surveys, the amount of funding from various sources only added up to 90% or 95%. Furthermore, some shelters may have had the information but had no staff member willing to calculate it. Others were unable to submit the information in such detail for unknown reasons. One respondent in particular (in Freeport, IL) claimed 100% of its funding came from grants only. Most shelters reported being funded by the state government (for 92 shelters) or Victims of Crime Act—VOCA (for 71 shelters), and a large number came from County General Revenue (for 56 shelters) or "other" sources, including Title XX, State Coalition, Violence Against Women Act (VAWA), Third Party, or Municipal Court.

State funding seems to be a major source of funding for many of the shelters. More specifically, funding from the State ranged from 2% to 88.78%. The mode was 50%, the median was 25%, and the mean was 27%. There were 87 shelters that utilized this source of funding. Funding from VOCA ranged from .5% to 70%, with 68 shelters reporting this type of funding. The mean was 19%, the median was 16%, and the mode was 12% and 20% (both cited four times each).

Funding from County General Revenue ranged from .5% to 44% with a median of 4%, a mean of 13%, and a mode of 3% (cited six times). There were 52 shelters utilizing this funding source. Funding from Private Sources ranged from 1% to 65.4% with a median of 8%, a mode of 5% (eight times), and a mean of 6.9%. There were 43 shelters that relied on this type of funding.

Funding from a Third Party ranged from 1% to 40%, with representation from only nine shelters. The mode was 3%, the median was 4.5%, and the mean was 9.8%. Funding from Title XX ranged from 1% to 10%, with only four shelters represented. There was no mode, the median was 3%, and the mean was 4.25%.

Funding from State Coalition ranged from 2% to 60%, with a mean of 19.4% and a median of 9%. There was no mode and only seven shelters represented here. Funding from VAWA ranged from 2% to 65%, with a median of 7.5%, a mean of 15.6%, and a mode of 4% and 10% (three times each). Twenty shelters were also represented here. Funding from Municipal Court ranged from 1.3% to 28.1%, with only three shelters represented. The mean was 16.46%, the median was 20%, and there was no mode.

Funding from "other" sources came from eight different subcategories. Most of these subcategories were combined, meaning they combined two sources together but did not specify the exact amount that came from either source. The highest number (count wise) was from State/Federal Grants, ranging from 1.5% to 100%. The median was 27%, the mean was 36.7%, and the mode was 18% and 24% (two times each). There were 24 shelters that used this source. Another "other" source was from a combination of Fundraising and Donations and ranged from 2% to 58% of a shelter's funding. The mode was 25% and 49% (two times each), the median was 17.5%, and the mean was 10.6%. There were 23 shelters that utilized this source of funding.

The United Way funded a portion of 20 shelters, ranging from 4% to 44%, with a mode of 10%, a median of 18.4%, and a mean of 34.1%. In addition, a combination of Fundraising and Federal Funding was utilized by eight shelters, with a range of 10% to 76.6%. There was a mode of 25%, a median of 28%, and a mean of 36.6%.

One shelter utilized the YWCA (14%) and one utilized the Homelessness Fund (13%). Two shelters relied on Gifts (34.6% and 43%), for a median and mean of 38.8% and no mode. Finally, nine shelters relied on "other" sources, but did not specify the actual source of their funding. These numbers ranged from 10% to 73.7%, with a median of 36.5% and a mean of 38.3%. Table 5.5 compares each funding source for the frequency it was reported across

TABLE 5.5   Sources of Funding

Type of funding	Count (number of shelters utilizing this source)	Mean percentage (average percentage)
State	92	29%
VOCA	73	21%
County general	52	13%
Private	43	8%
Combination funding: state/federal	24	36.7%
Combination funding: fundraising/ donations	23	36.6%
VAWA	20	15%
United Way	20	36.5%
Third party	9	9.8%
Other (not specified)	9	34.1%
Combination funding: fundraising and federal	8	10.6%
State coalition	7	9%
Title XX	4	4.25%
Municipal court	3	16.46%
Gifts	2	—
YWCA	1	—
Homelessness fund	1	—

shelters and the average percentage of funds attributed to each source.

A typical breakdown of funding sources was reported by Joelene Smith, Director of the Bolten Refuge House in Eau Claire, Wisconsin; her shelter's budget is as follows: VOCA, 13%; County, 20%; State, 38%; Third Party, 3%; Municipal Court, 20%; Private/Donation/United Way, 6%. This shelter is an independent nonprofit agency started in 1977 that offers all services plus day care and transitional housing. It serves 800 battered women and 2,000 via hotline. It has 12 full-time and 35 part-time employees, 2 interns, and 100 volunteers. Ms. Smith claims the strengths of her shelter include "longevity, first domestic violence program in state, first with licensed day care facility, first with legal advocacy in the courthouse, and first batterer treatment program."

Budgets.   Clearly the information described here indicates that shelters vary widely on what services they can provide and on the number of women they are able to serve; this variation is due in large part to differences in overall budgets. Shelter budgets varied greatly, ranging from a low of $40,000 in New Hampshire and $87,200 in Lewistown, Montana, to $3 million budgets in large, metropolitan areas of New Jersey and Petersburg, Florida. There was a mode of $500,000 and a median budget of $500,000. See Table 5.6 for a more detailed breakdown of the number of shelters in each budget category.

The New Hampshire shelter with a budget of $40,000 began in 1979 and is nonprofit. It offers most services, and serves 423 women and 207 via the hotline per year. There is one full-time employee, five volunteers, and no part-time employees or interns. Although its budget is low and its major limitation is funding, its strengths included "a core group of volunteers," so it is obvious this shelter is making the best of what resources it has.

The second lowest budget was found at Saves, Incorporated Shelter in Lewistown, Michigan, where 150 women were served, and 1,000 were served via the hotline. It too is a nonprofit agency that offers most services. It started in 1981, has two full-time and three part-time employees, as well as four volunteers. According to Director Naomi Summers, its limitations are, "Not enough money to provide needed services, but ability for quick response. Good working relationships with law enforcement and Child Protective Services."

TABLE 5.6   Budgets

Average budget (in $)	Number of shelters in this range
Up to 100,000	8
100,001–200,000	15
200,001–300,000	11
300,001–400,000	12
400,001–500,000	10
500,001–600,000	9
600,001–700,000	6
700,001–800,000	5
800,001–900,000	2
900,001–1 million	4
Over 1 million to 1.5 million	12
1.51 million to 2 million	7
Over 2 million to under 3 million	4
3 million	2

The largest budgets ($3 million each) were found in a shelter in New Jersey that asked not to be identified, and the Community Action Stops Abuse Shelter in St. Petersburg, Florida. In the New Jersey shelter, almost all services are offered; 1,200 women are served and 5,090 via the hotline. The shelter is a private nonprofit agency that started in 1976. The majority of its funding comes from "other" sources. They have 30 full-time, 45 part-time employees, 5 student interns, 120 volunteers, and offer a broad range of programs.

In St. Petersburg, Florida, the shelter serves 15,000 battered women and 7,000 via the hotline. It started in 1977 and is an independent nonprofit agency. It has 50 full-time employees (the second largest number of all surveyed shelters) and 25 part-time employees. It also has 2 interns and 1,000 volunteers (the second largest of all shelters surveyed). According to Linda A. Osmundson, the shelter Director, they provide a "full service center advocacy, with a social change emphasis." However, she further notes they "never have enough money to pay staff what they deserve."

Staffing Patterns.   Much like piecing together funding sources, shelters often rely on piecing together various types of staff in order to operate. Shelters are staffed by a combination of full-time staff, part-time staff, student interns, volunteers, and other specialty staff.

Employing full-time staff is often preferable yet expensive. Some shelters functioned with only 1 full-time employee, whereas larger shelters reported as many as 52 full-time employees. On average, shelters employed 10 full-time employees. Of full-time employees, 122 were reported to have a Bachelor's degree and 27 were reported to have Masters in Social Work (MSW) degrees.

Part-time employees are often utilized in shelters. Shelters employed from 1 to 52 part-time employees. On average, shelters employed about 6 part-time employees with shelters most frequently reporting employing 4 part-time employees. Of part-time employees, only 21 were reported to have their Bachelor's degrees; and 8, to have MSW degrees.

Student interns are another resource to shelters. By offering training and experience working with battered women, shelters can utilize student interns to provide certain services inexpensively. Shelters ranged from employing 1 student intern to as many as 50 student interns. On average, shelters employed approximately four interns. Interestingly, there was one reported intern who had earned a PhD.

Finally, several shelters rely greatly on volunteers to enable them to function on tight budgets. Shelters reported from 1 to 2,260 (Monroe, NC) volunteers per year. On average, shelters reported having 83 volunteers, emphasizing great reliance on this resource. Table 5.7 shows the staffing patterns for full-time employees, part-time employees, student interns, and volunteers.

The largest number of BA's from one agency was found in Pennsylvania. Although this shelter did not have the largest number of employees with 22 full-timers (52 was the highest), they had the largest number of full-time employees with their BA degrees (20). The other two full-timers had MSW degrees. This is a shelter started in 1974 with a budget of $1.74 million, five interns, and many services.

TABLE 5.7   Staffing Patterns in a Given Year

Employee type	Range	Mean	Median	Mode
Full-time	(1–52)	10	8	10
Part-time	(1–52)	6.18	4	4
Student interns	(1–50)	4.4	2	2
Volunteers	(1–2,260)	82	25	5

The largest number of volunteers came from a shelter in North Carolina that was nonprofit, but did not specify the year it started. It offers most services, serves 406 battered women, 333 via hotline, and has a budget of $613,720. There are 7 full-time employees, 8 part-time employees, 4 interns, and 2,260 volunteers. According to the shelter, they have "strong director leadership, a strong board, dedicated staff, volunteers, breadth of programs, are strong financially, have a base of support, facilities."

An example of a shelter with only one full-time employee (the lowest recorded) comes from an agency in Colorado that started in 1982. Its budget was $262,987; however, this shelter does offer most services, serves 491 battered women, and 236 via the hotline. It has one full-time employee, four part-time employees, and eight volunteers. It is located in a very rural area without bus service out of town and no in-town bus service—taxis only.

The largest number of full-time employees (52) comes from the Women's Shelter in Arlington, Texas, a nonprofit shelter started in 1978. According to Ronna Quimby, there are 10 part-time employees, 6 interns, and 300 volunteers. This shelter has an extremely large budget of $2.3 million, serves 3,203 women, and 16,644 via hotline.

A typically staffed shelter was found in Alabama, in an independent nonprofit shelter started in 1984. It serves 2,560 battered women, 829 via its hotline, and has a budget of almost $600,000. The shelter has 10 full-time employees and 6 part-time employees, one intern, and no volunteers. According to them, there is "not enough money for salaries or education needs."

"Other" Employees.   Beyond traditional types of employees, shelters mentioned several "Other" categories of employees. Many interesting job titles were mentioned, highlighting the diverse roles required in shelter services. Table 5.8 displays each "other" type of employee mentioned by shelter respondents.

What Are Shelter Strengths and Limitations?

Shelter respondents identified several strengths of their agencies. These components help make it possible for shelters to serve battered women and are identified as particularly important by shelter

TABLE 5.8   Number of Shelters Employing "Other" Types of Staff

Type of employees	Number of shelters employing this type of staff	Type of employees	Number of shelters employing this type of staff
Business employees	42	AmeriCorps	3
Contract	18	Full-time temporary	3
Advocates	11	Attorney	2
Relief staff	8	Experience works	1
Senior aides	7	Part-time data entry	1
Cooks	4	Full-time social worker with BS	1
Foster grandparents	3	Bookkeeping	1
Executive director	3	Psychologist	1

administrators. Twenty-eight different categories of strengths were identified by shelter respondents. Respondents especially valued their Knowledgeable, Dedicated, and/or Compassionate Staff (stated by 46 shelters). This is particularly salient considering the low pay for most employees working at nonprofit agencies and the heavy reliance on unpaid interns and volunteers. Several respondents also valued their ability to provide a Variety of Services, Programs, and Support Groups (38 shelters). Finally, the ability to Network and Collaborate with other community agencies was a commonly noted strength of shelter organizations (30 shelters). Several other strengths were mentioned by shelter respondents and they are described in Table 5.9.

Shelters identified several limitations that underscore the need for additional resources for battered women. Limitations reported were broken down into 24 categories of responses. Shelters commonly report Lack of Funds (46 shelters) and Lack of Staff (17 shelters) as clear limitations to their effectively serving battered women. A particularly challenging obstacle to shelters is Lack of Housing (17 shelters) for women as they attempt to transition from shelters to independent living. Finally, shelters noted Lack of Transportation (11 shelters) as a limitation, a key component that prevents access to many other valuable services. Table 5.9 shows limitation categories and frequencies.

A nonprofit Arizona shelter reports the typical strengths of a shelter program. Its strengths include "dedication of staff, combined

TABLE 5.9   Shelters' Self-Reported Strengths and Limitations

No. of Shelters mentioning this strength	Strength categories	No. of Shelters mentioning this limitation	Limitation categories
46	Knowledgeable/dedicated and compassionate staff	46	Lack funds
38	Programs/support groups and variety of services	17	Lack staff
30	Networking/collaboration with other agencies	17	Lack housing
22	Legal/court advocacy	11	Lack transportation
14	Community support	6	Lack bilingual
13	Safe shelter	5	Lack service to rural victims
8	Large coverage	4	Limited service
8	Children's programs	4	Lack follow-up
7	24-hour hotline	3	Lack child care
6	Financially stable	3	Lack legal representation
6	Volunteers	4	Lack job opportunities
6	Community education	3	Poor wages
5	Bilingual	3	Deteriorating facility
5	Housing	2	Too dependent on government funds
5	Open to all victims	2	Inadequate CJS/law enforcement agencies
4	Empowerment	1	Lack training of staff
2	Batterer treatment	1	Lack technology utilization
2	Client focused	1	No expense account for travel
2	Thrift shop	1	Inaccurate reporting
2	Employment	1	Lack of therapy for children
2	Referrals	1	Lack batterer treatment
1	Anger management	1	Lack medical care
1	Transportation	1	Government regulations
1	Forensic nurse examiners	1	Lack of care for advocates
1	Website		
1	Successful grant writing		
1	Walk-in office		
1	Teen program		

knowledge of staff and their diversification, excellent knowledge of available resources for residents and strong community and volunteer support."

CONCLUSION

Shelters across the United States are responsible for providing a variety of important services to battered women. To provide these services, shelters rely on piecing together various funding sources and types of staff support. This requires a high degree of flexibility on the part of the agency and dedication on the part of the employees and volunteers working at domestic violence shelters. Although shelters continue to struggle with ongoing funding and staff issues, they also report difficulty in connecting women to transitional housing and transportation that may be essential in securing a safe living environment after leaving an abusive situation. These are crucial services that require further attention by funding sources and policymakers. Promising in this regard is a recent extension of the VAWA to expand transitional housing options for victims of domestic violence (VAWA, 2005). Despite the challenges mentioned earlier, shelters credit their dedicated and knowledgeable staff, ability to network with other agencies, and flexible programming for their ability to aid battered women in making life-changing decisions.

The delivery of social services and advocacy in the community on behalf of battered women should not end with short-term shelters. Support groups, shelter outreach, legal aid, vocational rehabilitation, and aftercare services are essential complements to shelter services. Professors Leslie Tutty and Michael Rothery (2002) documented the fact that some shelters in Canada and the United States are frequently overcrowded and only offer time-limited services. They document the importance of weekly support groups, outreach counseling, and follow-up advocacy, especially because of the overcrowding in many urban shelters and the research documents that many chronically abused women try to leave the batterer several times before being able to permanently leave the battering relationship.

Planned social change and a large reduction in woman battering will continue to take place as long as (a) victim advocates, domestic violence advocates, legislators, social service administrators, prosecutors, police, and judges continue to be responsive to the life-threatening nature of domestic violence; and (b) large national organizations; the 51 statewide coalitions; and the National Coalition Against Domestic Violence (NCADV), the National Network to End Domestic Violence (NNEDV), and the National Organization for Victim Assistance (NOVA) continue their fervent collective action and legislative and agency advocacy (Roberts, 2002).

REFERENCES

NCADV. (2006, February 17). *National Coalition Against Domestic Violence Legislative Update.* Retrieved July 16, 2006, from http://www.ncadv.org/files/BudgetUpdate,Feb17.pdf.

Robertiello, G. (2006). Common mental health correlates of domestic violence. *Brief Treatment and Crisis Intervention, 6*(2), 111–121.

Roberts, A. R. (1981). *Sheltering battered women: A national survey and service guide.* New York: Springer Publishing.

Roberts, A. R. (1996). A comparative analysis of incarcerated battered women and a community sample of battered women. In A. R. Roberts (Ed.), *Helping battered women: New perspectives and remedies* (pp. 31–43). New York: Oxford University Press.

Roberts, A. R. (2002). Myths, facts, and realities regarding battered women and their children: An overview. In A. R. Roberts (Ed.), *Handbook of domestic violence intervention strategies* (pp. 3–22). New York: Oxford University Press.

Roberts, A. R., & Lewis, S. J. (2000). Giving them shelter: National organizational survey of shelters for battered women and their children. *Journal of Community Psychology, 28*(6), 669–681.

Roberts, A. R., & Roberts, B. (2005). *Ending intimate abuse: Practical guidance and survival strategies.* New York: Oxford University Press.

Roche, S. E., & Sadoski, P. J. (1996). Social action for battered women. In A. R. Roberts (Ed.), *Helping battered women: New perspectives and remedies* (pp. 13–30). New York: Oxford University Press.

Saunders, D. G. (1994). Postraumatic stress symptom profiles of battered women: A comparison of survivors in two settings. *Violence and Victims, 9,* 31–44.

Tutty, L., & Rothery, M. (2002). Beyond shelters: Support groups and community-based advocacy for abused women. In A. R. Roberts (Ed.),

Handbook of domestic violence intervention strategies (pp. 396–418). New York: Oxford University Press.

VAWA. (2005). Violence Against Women Act 2005 Reauthorization overview by the National Task Force to End Sexual and Domestic Violence Against Women. Retrieved July 16, 2006, from http://www.vawa2005.org/overview.pdf.

CHAPTER 6

The Stress-Crisis Continuum:
Its Application to Domestic Violence

Ann W. Burgess, Albert R. Roberts, and Pamela V. Valentine

Woman battering, occurring in 25% to 30% of families, is a pervasive, severe problem in society today (Roberts & Roberts, 1990). The depth of the problem in America is illustrated by the frequency of domestic violence incidents as well as by the severity and cost of physical injuries related to domestic violence. Each year, over 8 million American women are victims of domestic violence (see chapter 1 in this book for further details on the scope of the problem). Domestic violence causes more injuries to women victims than accidents, muggings, and cancer deaths combined (Nurius, Hilfrink, & Rifino, 1996). Almost 35% of emergency room visits are made by women seeking help for injuries related to abuse by a partner. The health care cost per year for medical services to battered women and children is $1,633 per person, or an annual total of $857.3 million (Lewin, 1997).

Not only does woman battering cost society in terms of medical bills, but also woman battering strains society by the disruption of families with which it is associated. Children who witness marital violence are found to be affected in at least three areas of functioning: internalizing behavior, such as depression and anxiety; externalizing behavior, such as aggression and uncooperativeness; and impaired social competence (Carlson, 1996; Malmquist, 1986). A report from the American Bar Association (1994) found that 75% of boys who were present when their mothers were beaten had behavior problems. Living in a home where their mothers were beaten was a factor in 20% to 40% of chronically violent teens. Additionally, 63% of males in the 11- to 20-year-old age category were incarcerated for having killed the man who battered their mothers (Roberts, 1996a). Not only does woman battering affect children who witness it, but its effects also are exacerbated when children are themselves victims of child battering (Carlson). Also, please see chapters 2, 5, 9, and 10.

Woman battering is a traumatic and multifaceted phenomenon. Often, woman battering presents itself as emotional, economic, or sexual abuse. Trauma disrupts cognitive functioning, resulting in feelings of worthlessness, helplessness, traumatic bonding, and phobic responses (Dziegielewski, Resnick, & Krause, 1996). Furthermore, the cognitive distortions often lead to intergenerational abuse. Finally, "one-fourth of all suicide attempts are directly related to abuse" (Dziegielewski et al., p. 164).

Although domestic violence has existed for centuries, America's focus on the problem has waxed and waned over time. Two manifestations of America's shifting responses to battered women are the degree of help offered to battered women and the frequency of articles published concerning domestic violence. In 1885, Chicago established the Chicago Protective Agency for Women and Children. This led to a widespread movement to establish protective agencies for women (Roberts, 1996b). Between 1885 and 1949, many women victims of domestic violence received shelter, personal assistance, legal aid, court advocacy, equitable property settlements, and protection through divorce or separation from their husbands. However, in the late 1940s, crime prevention bureaus replaced protective agencies for women, and male police administrators replaced female police social workers. Help for battered women became rare until the rise of the feminist movement in the 1970s.

In addition to the degree of help offered to battered women, society's attitude about woman battering is reflected in its journals. From 1939 until 1969, the literature on domestic violence replicated the pattern found in the protective agencies. During this period, no reference to domestic violence was made in the *Journal of Marriage and Family Therapy* (Schechter, 1982). Thereafter, 30 articles were published, 21 of which came after 1986.

Since the rise of the feminist movement in the 1970s, society began responding once more to woman battering. In 1990, more than 1,250 battered women's shelters had been opened in the United States and Canada. Trauma centers, hotlines, welfare and court advocacy, housing, employment, peer counseling, and parenting education are some of the services that are provided to victims of woman battering (Roberts, 1996a).

More recently, battering has been defined in a broader sense than acts of physical violence. Experts have begun to realize the psychological consequences of battering, noting that physical violence seldom happens in isolation (Petretic-Jackson & Jackson, 1996). Often emotional, economic, and sexual abuse accompanies physical abuse. Therefore, communities have begun to offer psychological counseling to battered women in addition to traditional services.

Psychological counseling has been impacted by the 1990s managed health care movement wherein American health insurance companies began to demand cost-efficient psychological interventions. Consequently, treatment providers started trying to demonstrate the veracity of the interventions given patients. Traditional scientific tools are the means for demonstrating effectiveness. These tools (theory, operationalization, replication, and prediction) serve to explain, specify, and predict. Scientific tools (a) explain which treatments work and why, (b) help specify the treatment procedures and the anticipated treatment results, and (c) help make predictions or prognoses about the length of treatment. As a result of applying scientific tools to psychotherapeutic interventions, brief (generally one to six sessions), goal-oriented, crisis-intervention, cognitive-behavioral, or group and family therapy has largely replaced longer, less defined, individual psychoanalytic therapy.

Specified, focused interventions can benefit clients, as well as managed care. Brief treatment often allows clients to participate in (a) prioritizing the most important problem to solve; (b) visualizing the desired behavioral results; and (3) recognizing the alleviation of the presenting problem(s) as it occurs.

Psychological interventions must start with therapists' recognition of woman battering. Two national studies have documented a serious problem in terms of therapists' ability to identify domestic violence.

Drs. Michelle Harway and Marsali Hansen (1993, 1994) conducted two studies on therapists' perceptions of family violence. These studies found that, when presented a case vignette and asked to "describe what was happening in the family, what interventions they would make and what outcomes they would expect from their intervention" (Harway & Hansen, 1994, pp. 6–7), many therapists lacked the needed skills and knowledge to both identify domestic violence and assess its lethality. In the first study, the clinical researchers sent a questionnaire that included a case vignette of a violent family to a random sample of members of the American Association of Marriage and Family Therapy (AAMFT; $n = 362$). Only 60% of the respondents recognized the issue of violence within the relationship. Yet even these respondents clearly minimized the extent of the problem, as evidenced by the finding that 91% considered the violence mild or moderate when, in reality, there was a good possibility of there being deadly consequences. Only 2.2% both recognized that the battering could become lethal and called for immediate intervention.

Because the researchers were so alarmed by the latter findings, they completed a second study. The case vignette was modified so that it clearly stated that domestic violence was involved and that it had a lethal outcome. Of 405 members of the American Psychological Association (APA), 71% of whom were men, 27% said that they lacked sufficient evidence to judge the seriousness of the case; they said that they would ask the client to return for another assessment appointment. We firmly believe that it is the therapist's ethical and legal responsibility to be able to recognize woman battering and to provide immediate intervention.

The tools required for effective intervention in the domain of woman battering are multiple. The tools, although similar to those required of mental health practitioners, are more complex, considering that victims of woman battering most often present in crises and that the stakes are high. In other words, there may be no second chance for the clinician or the client.

The tools for intervening with the victim of woman battering are the following: First, a clinician needs to be able to recognize the presenting circumstances as being those of woman battering. Next, the clinician must move in a determined way to secure safety for the client. Another essential step is the collection of accurate data. A thorough picture of the client's present and past life circumstances informs the clinician about appropriate treatment modalities.

Furthermore, a clinician either needs proficiency in various treatment modalities or an awareness of the need to link the client with a suitable treatment specialist who can address one or more of the various components in the client's profile. Because domestic violence is a crisis situation in which effective, timely intervention can make a life-and-death difference, it is important that a clinician have access to an assessment tool that will guide them along the steps as outlined earlier.

With the movement toward brief, empirical, psychotherapeutic interventions, *and* given the critical nature of woman battering, the Stress-Crisis Continuum (Burgess & Roberts, 1995) emerges as a timely instrument. It can aid the clinician in recognizing the severity of the crisis, linking appropriate treatment modalities with the level of crises, and grouping clients of similar internal conflicts and levels of chronicity. Based on an expansion and adaptation of Baldwin's (1978) crisis classification, the Stress-Crisis Continuum delineates seven levels of stress-crisis: (a) somatic, (b) transitional stress, (c) traumatic stress-crisis, (d) family crisis, (e) serious mental illness, (f) psychiatric emergencies, and (g) catastrophic or cumulative crisis. The levels progress as the nature and intensity of internal conflicts become more severe.

This chapter contains domestic violence case scenarios of each level of stress in the continuum. Following each given case scenario are the research and interventions associated with that level.

LEVEL 1: SOMATIC DISTRESS

Case Example

Ms. Abel, a 27-year-old occupational therapist, was a victim of emotional abuse. She sought counseling at a local mental health agency for relational problems associated with her live-in lesbian partner. Ms. Abel reported that she had not been struck by her partner, but viewed her partner as intimidating, controlling, and threatening. She said that her partner would stare at her for long periods of time, never saying a word. Her partner would also call her degrading names. Finally, her partner would periodically throw objects in the house and take a baseball bat to an outdoor tree to show her displeasure with Ms. Abel. Ms. Abel presented with depressive symptoms such as binge eating, crying, a lack of enthusiasm for work, and periodic absences from work due to migraine headaches. Ms. Abel took prescription medications for the headaches. She was also a victim of childhood sexual and emotional abuse.

Having addressed issues of safety, the therapist and Ms. Abel agreed that treatment should address Ms. Abel's passivity in her relationship with her lover. Believing that there was an association between Ms. Abel's childhood sexual abuse and her current passivity, the therapist engaged Ms. Able in an intense, brief, trauma treatment called Traumatic Incident Reduction (TIR; Gerbode, 1989). The intervention called for the repeated visualization of that particularly painful scene in which her parents had sexually abused her. After approximately 30 minutes of visualization, Ms. Abel reported that she had a migraine headache. Her counselor asked Ms. Abel if she wished to continue the treatment, and Ms. Abel said, "Yes." However, with another viewing of the childhood incident, Ms. Abel asked the counselor to stop the session, dim the lights, place a trash can before her in case of vomiting and call her primary physician requesting her prescription medication. The counselor did as Ms. Abel requested, and another staff member drove her to the emergency room to pick up the medication.

The following day Ms. Abel, sounding strong and chipper, called the counselor and requested an appointment. The counselor was surprised that Ms. Abel could be doing so well so quickly. That afternoon, the counselor met with Ms. Abel, who reported that she had never been so surprised in her life . . . that the following had never before occurred to her. Ms. Abel said that by the time she arrived at the emergency room, her headache symptoms were completely gone. She deducted that her body was cooperating in a convincing way to keep her from addressing the memory of the childhood sexual abuse. With this conviction, Ms. Abel completed the aborted session and found relief from the presenting symptoms. Additionally, Ms. Abel learned to seek intervention at the first sign of physical distress rather than waiting for either a headache or a crisis to develop.

Research

The word *somatic* refers to the body or to the physical. Distress is "(1) pain or suffering of mind or body; (2) severe psychological strain; or (3) the condition of being in need of immediate assistance"

(*American Heritage Concise Dictionary*, 1994, p. 249). Somatic stress is a physical manifestation of a biomedical or psychiatric difficulty. Somatic stresses come from stress that is either biomedical or psychological in origin. It is not always clear whether the stressor is biomedical or psychological in nature. For example, one who has cancer, lupus, diabetes, or other diseases that suppress the immune system experiences somatic stress. Depending on one's response to one of the aforementioned diseases, one may also experience minor psychiatric symptoms, such as anxiety or depressive symptoms. Breast cancer patients, for example, who express more distress about their illness have lower levels of a natural killer (NK) cell activity than other patients (Burgess & Roberts, 1995).

On the other hand, an underlying psychosocial difficulty might manifest itself in the physical. Barsky (1981) reports that between 40% and 60% of all visits to primary health providers such as physicians and nurses involve symptoms for which no biomedical disease can be detected. Mechanic (1994) postulates a close connection between the physical and mental domains and argues that physical and mental health care need to be integrated to address the coexistence of physical and mental disorders.

Somatic distress taxes the general medical sector, which provides approximately half of all mental health care (Burgess & Roberts, 1995). Studies show that the need for medical care increases when physical problems are accompanied by underlying psychosocial issues. Somatizers who are under stress overuse ambulatory medical services (Burgess & Roberts). Depressive symptoms, which occur in between 3% and 5% of the general population, are higher yet with disadvantaged populations.

Intervention

Patients with defined medical illnesses should be treated with appropriate medical protocols (Burgess & Roberts, 1995). For those patients with somatic symptoms but without a clear medical diagnosis, clinicians should conduct a thorough psychosocial history. In the interest of safety, the social history should include an assessment of the patient's current living conditions. The clinician should also inquire about prior occurrences of traumatic events to assess for residual effects of such events. Finally, the counselor needs to determine whether the symptomatology meets the criteria for the *Diagnostic and Statistical Manual of Mental Disorders* (4th ed., *DSM–IV*, 1994, APA, 1994) because early intervention has been shown to reduce symptoms and interrupt the progression toward major psychiatric disorders (Burgess & Roberts).

Engaging patients in the therapeutic process is the next intervention. It is an important part of treatment, for it facilitates the patient's feelings of ownership about his or her recovery. Engaging the patient also implies that recovery is the primary responsibility of the patient.

Several steps are involved for the patient to become involved in his or her recovery. First, the clinician should meet with the patient to share his or her clinical impressions of the patient's condition. If more than one presenting problem is identified (which is often the case), the therapist should then ask the patient to prioritize the problems to see which problem resolution matters most to the patient. Often, patients feel overwhelmed and are reluctant to try to prioritize their problems. Assisting the patient in prioritizing his or her problems can take the form of having him or her rank the level of distress he or she feels regarding each presenting problem. The therapist can list the problems, note the ranking assigned to each problem, and show the list to the patient. Another technique for promoting a patient to become engaged with problem resolution is to ask a question such as: "If you could only solve *one* problem, what would it be?" After prioritizing the problems, the clinician should ask the client to articulate what the solution to that problem would "look like." Here, one is aiming for an operationalized definition of the problem. It is important that the patient name the goal in terms of behavior acquisition rather than behavior disappearance. For example, rather than stating, "I'll know when the problem has gone away when I am no longer depressed," it is preferable that the patient visualizes something like the following: "I'll know that I am better when I have the energy to get out of bed and take a shower." Once the problems and goal have been prioritized and operationalized, the therapist engages the client by having both the client and the therapist sign a therapy contract, which lists the problem(s), the behaviors associated with problem resolution, the level of participation required of the patient, and the anticipated number of sessions required for treatment completion.

Reflecting respect for the patient and his or her perspectives is an integral part of the therapeutic process (Valentine, 1995).

Valentine interviewed clients who had been a recipient of a brief therapeutic intervention. She found that clients experienced respect by having therapists honor rather than dispute their accounts of incidents.

Intervention with Level 1 patients may take the form of education. Teaching patients about their illness(es) and available forms of treatment is a classical intervention. It is also safe and nonintrusive. However, if patients have been under medical care for some time, they may have already received the educational component. Proceeding to cognitive-behavioral therapy or trauma-related techniques, where appropriate, is in order.

LEVEL 2: TRANSITIONAL STRESS

Case Example

Ms. Stewart, age 49, said, "I'm sleeping these last few weeks, but it feels like I haven't. My mind is always racing because I think of the worst. I can hardly go to work cause I cry so much, and I don't want my co-workers to see me like this."

Ms. Stewart, a secretary, was married to a man who spent money wildly, denied her money for necessities, called her to verify that she was at work, yelled at her when she arrived home 1 minute later than what he believed the drive home required, and choked her on repeated occasions.

In therapy, Ms. Stewart minimized the domestic violence that occurred in her home by calling her husband's aggressive acts "idiosyncrasies." In fact, Ms. Stewart reported that she was accustomed to living with her husband's "idiosyncrasies," and felt no need to address the domestic abuse in therapy. Rather, she focused on her aged, widowed mother.

Ms. Stewart was recently tearful due to her mother's imprisonment. Ms. Stewart's mother, who was lonely after the death of her husband, had rented her two spare bedrooms to two young men. Having grown fond of the men, Ms. Stewart's mother was eager to please them, and she was arrested for transporting the men's drugs across the state line. Attorney costs were such that Ms. Stewart's mother needed to sell her home to pay legal fees. Ms. Stewart felt helpless and depressed over her mother's condition.

Research

The combination of an unanticipated event and a developmental challenge is called a transitional stress (Burgess & Roberts, 1995). A developmental challenge entails a life task common to many people at a given phase of development. Learning to crawl, toilet training, going to school, graduating from high school, attaining a job, marrying, parenting, launching children into adulthood, retiring, and caring for aged parents are examples of developmental events. An unanticipated event might interrupt a developmental challenge, making it a transitional stress. Birth injuries, a child's untimely separation from his or her primary caregiver(s), learning disabilities, accidents that mar one's appearance, disabilities, illnesses, adolescent pregnancies, infertility, imprisonment, and chronic illness are examples of unanticipated events that have the potential of interrupting or delaying the completion of a developmental task. One who experiences a transitional stress is likely to feel out of control and rigid (Burgess & Roberts). One frequently repeats acts that are counterproductive in an effort to regain control.

The case example of Ms. Stewart describes an unfortunate event in her mother's life. The event also represents an interruption in the developmental task of caring for aged parents. Ms. Stewart's wakefulness and tearfulness were due, in part, to her frustration at having had the developmental task interrupted. A psychosocial interview revealed that the symptoms were associated with the disruption of a strong intention or promise that Ms. Stewart had made as a child. Beginning at age 5, Ms. Stewart repeatedly witnessed her father battering her mother. When the abuse began, Ms. Stewart would run to her bed, close the door to muffle her mother's screams, pull the covers over her head and promise herself that when she grew bigger, she would protect her mother from harm. Her mother's imprisonment impeded Ms. Stewart's ability to protect her mother, thus thwarting a developmental task and a lifelong promise. This was her transitional stress.

Intervention

Interventions for transitional stress are several, consisting primarily of three approaches: (a) focused, individual educational sessions; (b) group sessions that both educate and offer support; and (c) when appropriate, brief trauma techniques that address prior incidents. Group sessions are particularly appropriate. Because a transitional stressor has a developmental challenge that is common to many people, clients may feel strengthened to hear other group members say that they are experiencing similar challenges and responses. The group setting normalizes the event, taking away a sense of isolation. A group setting can also aid in freeing clients of introspective concerns such as "What's wrong with me?" Clients are now able to absorb the educational component of the intervention. Some clients, however, do not appear receptive to or capable of applying the education presented in group *or* individual sessions. This may cue the therapist that a prior traumatic event is having a strong influence on current behavior, and prompt the therapist to introduce a brief trauma technique for altering cognitive distortions.

LEVEL 3: TRAUMATIC STRESS-CRISIS

Mrs. Baker, a victim of woman battering, arrived at the shelter with her two children, Danny (3) and Missy (9). Mrs. Baker had left her husband for battering her, sexually violating her daughter, and torturing the baby by placing a fork up the child's rectum to extract fecal material. Shortly after arriving at the shelter, Mrs. Baker enrolled her children in school, found a job, and began trying to rebuild her life.

One day, Mrs. Baker received a call from the sheriff's department, asking that she come to the station to make a deposition on her husband. The sheriff informed her that her husband had been charged with the murder of two men with whom Mr. Baker had suspected her of having an affair. A staff member drove Mrs. Baker to the sheriff's office, but had to stop the car various times to allow her to vomit. With her husband's incarceration, Mrs. Baker was now safe from his threats. However, instead of feeling relieved, she felt guilty. Rather than feeling as if she had been given back her life, she felt as if it had been taken away. Mrs. Baker experienced nightmares, despondency, and long crying spells.

Mrs. Baker's traumatic crisis was precipitated by a strong, externally imposed stressor. Trauma is distinguished from stress by severity and duration (Valentine, 1997). A traumatic event must be serious enough to challenge basic assumptions such as justice, fairness, safety, and predictability (Janoff-Bulman, 1992). One main effect of trauma is disorganization (Waites, 1993). One's cognitive schema is threatened, rules about how life works are shattered, and solace and hope evade the trauma victim. Trauma also elicits physiological responses to emergency situations. The victim's sense of "flight or fight" is increased. Responses are mediated by the autonomic nervous system (van der Kolk, 1987). Most alterations in microstructural neurochemistry will be temporary, but it is possible to have a traumatic event permanently alter structure.

Research

Posttraumatic stress disorder (PTSD), a phenomenon that was first associated with veterans of war, is a condition that some victims of traumatic events develop (Figley, 1989). Currently, PTSD is associated with precipitating events such as "abortion, burns, broken bones, surgery, overwhelming loss, animal attacks, drug overdoses, near drownings, bullying and intimidation," as well as criminal victimization (Moore, 1993, p. 116). The *DSM–IV* (APA, 1994, p. 424) states that PTSD may occur to those who either experience or witness an event that involves "death, injury, serious harm, or threat to the physical integrity of another person."

The three headings under which symptoms for PTSD fall are (a) intrusion, (b) avoidance, and (c) increased arousal (*DSM–IV*, APA, 1994). Intrusive symptoms mean that a person with PTSD will reexperience the event in the form of distressing dreams, memories, flashbacks, or a strong reaction to something that comes to symbolize the event. Avoidance manifests itself in one of the following ways: a strong tendency to avoid thinking or speaking about the event, a tendency to avoid activities that arouse recollection of the event, memory loss, a feeling of detachment, a restricted range of emotions (numbing), or a foreboding feeling about the future. The *DSM–IV* (APA, 1994) specifies that increased arousal refers to a level of arousal that the person did *not* experience before the traumatic event. Increased arousal could be manifested by difficulty falling or staying asleep, hypervigilance, difficulty concentrating, outbursts of anger, exaggerated startle response, or a physiologic reactivity to something that symbolizes or resembles the traumatic event. In short, PTSD begins with an "exaggerated reaction to the trauma and a subsequent preoccupation with it" (Waldinger, 1990, p. 217). The diagnosis of PTSD is made if a number of symptoms from each category continue beyond 4 weeks (Waldinger).

In addition to the three categories of PTSD symptoms found in the *DSM–IV* (APA, 1994), Moscarello (1991) speaks of four phases through which a victim of interpersonal violence passes: anticipatory, impact, recoil, and resolution. He links the three categories of PTSD symptoms with the impact phase and the recoil phase. The impact phase includes "rapid oscillation of intrusive and avoidance symptoms" (p. 240), while recoil is characterized by numbing. During the impact phase, one loses control, resulting in regression of the ego (Moscarello, 1991). During the recoil phase, one might have the outward appearance of adjustment, or alternatively fear, phobias, and depression. Other symptoms of PTSD include anxieties, insecurities, panic disorder, anger, rage, guilt complexes, mood anomalies, self-esteem problems, and compulsions (Dansky, Roth, & Kronenberger, 1990). PTSD can become worse as a person ages (Moscarello, 1991).

The notion that all survivors of traumatic incidents are dysfunctional is false (Everstine & Everstine, 1993). One's coping ability depends on several factors. Variables that exacerbate the immobilizing effects of a traumatic event include the following: if the traumatic event was at the hands of another person, if the action was intentional, if the perpetrator was known and trusted, the length of time since the incident (Everstine & Everstine, 1993), and a weak social support system. Additionally, how one's social support network explains the traumatic event (i.e., whether they blame the victim) has a large impact on the victim's psychological state and his or her self-esteem. Being blamed for the occurrence of the traumatic event increases one's subjective distress. Girelli, Resick, Mashoefer-Dvorak, and Hutter (1986) found that subjective distress is a better predictor of anxiety and fear than is observable violence. These multiple variables raise very complicated social–psychological issues.

Intervention

As for any victim of battering, the traumatized victim should first be assessed for safety issues. Once a safety net is in place, treatment can begin to address the emotional and cognitive processing of the event.

Effective assessment and treatment for the effects of traumatization is complex. Many theorists concur that the emotions, memory, and cognition are affected by the traumatic experience and that treatment, therefore, must address those three components. Foa, Rothbaum, and Steketee (1993) speculate that PTSD occurs because victims fail to *emotionally* process the traumatic event. They propose that therapy should be aimed at reducing symptoms associated with failed emotional processing. Symptoms associated with failed emotional processing are obsessions, nightmares, phobias, or inappropriate emotional processing. Other theorists posit that traumatic *memories* are central to manifestation of PTSD (Shapiro, 1989). These theories share the belief that reliving the painful memory allows the aborted emotional process to be completed, thus reducing PTSD symptoms. Roth and Newman (1991) argue that reexperiencing the painful memories allows the victim to understand the meaning of the event and to integrate the traumatic experience. This integration leads to a reduction of symptoms. Both Raimy (1975) and Gerbode and Moore (1994) emphasize the importance of *cognitive* restructuring along with emotional expression, because a physiological, cognitive, and affective component is involved in one's response to trauma.

Cathartic theory (Straton, 1990) incorporates emotions, memory, and cognition. The theory explains that the threatening incident strongly stirred the victim's emotions. Additionally, the mind was opened to new input by the heightened physiological response the victim experienced at the time of the incident. Typically, the victim finds it "impossible" to silence the survival messages received during the event. Messages given him or her when he or she is *not* experiencing a heightened physiological state do not impact the victim to the same extent as the message received during the crisis. Therefore, cathartic theory posits that it is necessary to "reexperience" the stressful event in order to change the victim's conditioned response(s). Reexperiencing the event via repeated visual imaging engages the client's memory, emotions, and finally cognition. The patient "tunes into" (recreates) the "frequency" (the heightened physiological state) that was present at the time of the incident to access the emotions, thinking, and decisions that occurred in crisis. When the patient understands the incident in a different light, after having reexperienced the incident, the insight is called a *re-decision* (Straton).

Several promising brief trauma techniques are based on a similar understanding of the etiology of traumatic responses. Among them are Eye Movement Desensitization and Reprocessing (EMDR)

(Shapiro, 1989), Calahan's Thought Field Therapy (TFT; 1987), and Gerbode's (1989) Traumatic Incident Reduction (TIR).

LEVEL 4: FAMILY CRISIS

Case Example

Monica, a mother of a 4-year-old boy, was introduced to Jose at a singles' club. Over the course of the evening, she grew to like him. The feeling was mutual. Soon Jose began sending Monica flowers and surprising her with romantic gifts; a sexual relationship developed. In the first few months of their relationship, Monica learned that Jose had previously been incarcerated in a federal corrections institute. She pondered why she was neither alarmed nor fearful about the safety of her son, toward whom she felt very protective.

Some months later, Monica lost interest in Jose and told him that she desired to "be just friends." Jose pleaded with Monica to change her mind, but to no avail. In the next weeks, his repeated phone calls, stalking, and veiled threats caused Monica much anxiety.

One night, after picking up her son from day care on her way home from work, Monica found that Jose had broken into her home and was waiting for her. Monica put her son to bed and asked Jose to leave the house. He refused. All night, Jose held her captive. He tore her clothes off her, raped her, threatened to kill her, and threatened to kill himself. Believing that he had succeeded in subduing her, Jose asked her to hand-cuff him to the bed and perform oral sex on him. She handcuffed him to the bed and fled the house with her child. At 2 o'clock in the morning, Monica and her son arrived at the shelter. Over the weeks, the shelter staff observed that Monica demonstrated watchfulness, hypervigilance, an exaggerated startle response, and depressive symptoms such as sobbing inconsolably.

The family crisis presented here dealt primarily with an interpersonal situation that developed within the family network. Other family crises might be "child abuse, the use of children in pornography, parental abductions, adolescent runaways, battering and rape, homelessness and domestic homicide" (Burgess & Roberts, 1995, p. 40).

Emotional crises involve an interaction of external stressors, internal stressors, and an unresolved developmental issue. An external stressor is an unanticipated forceful event. An internal stressor is vulnerability due to an unresolved developmental task. Frequently a developmental issue will involve "dependency, value conflict, sexual identity, emotional intimacy, power issues or attaining self-discipline" (Burgess & Roberts, 1995, p. 40). For Monica, the external stressors were Jose's stalking, invading her home, raping her, threatening, and endangering her child. The internal stressor was related to an unresolved issue with her father. The internal stressor manifested itself in that she was not alarmed upon learning of Jose's incarceration.

Research

Burgess and Roberts (1995) write that a shift occurs in Level 4. Although each level of stress in the Stress-Crisis Continuum (Burgess & Roberts) involves an interaction of an external stressor and a vulnerability of the individual, Level 4 transfers the weight of the balance toward preexisting psychopathology (Baldwin, 1978). Monica's unresolved issue with her father left her vulnerable to be raped; the sexual violence Monica experienced with Jose manifested her vulnerability.

Rape victims often fit the criteria of PTSD. In fact, Resnick, Kilpatrick, and Lipovsky (1991) found that 57% of rape victims met the lifetime diagnostic criteria for PTSD. The lifetime diagnostic criteria for PTSD are defined as having the symptoms 4 weeks after the event. Saunders, Arata, and Kilpatrick (1987) report that 16.5% of women who experienced PTSD at the time of their study had had it for an average duration of 17 years.

One distinguishing feature between the reaction to rape (often called the rape *trauma syndrome*) and PTSD is the traumatic event itself. That rape is the result of humans willfully acting to hurt another exacerbates the victim's reaction to the traumatic incident. The majority of rape victims are assaulted by acquaintances (Koss & Burkhart, 1989). When rape occurs with a known and trusted perpetrator such as a family member or a friend, it is called *confidence rape*. Confidence rape destroys trust and instills shame, making the reaction more severe and longer lasting than other traumatic events (APA, 1994).

When raped, a woman is treated as if she has no "rights, needs, or physical boundaries" (Koss & Burkhart, 1989). Physical injury is usually present (Everstine & Everstine, 1993). Rape often is concomitant with shame, self-blame, a sense of being powerless, fear of AIDS in stranger rape, hatred, paradoxical gratitude, defilement, sexual inhibition manifesting itself in loss of libido and a reduced capacity for intimacy, fear of being alone, broken will, re-victimization through the criminal justice system, and a downward shift in status. Women feel shame intensified when their autonomic nervous system loses control, resulting in vomiting, urination, defecation, or physiological sexual arousal (Moscarello, 1991).

Rape trauma syndrome is a common, persistent, and far-reaching problem among rape victims: "Only 25% of rape victims were free of significant symptoms on standard psychological test 1year after the assault" (Koss & Burkhart, 1989, p. 28). Burgess and Holmstrom (1974) report that 4 to 6 years later, 26% of victims still did not feel recovered. One to 16 years postassault, 31% to 48% of the victims sought psychotherapy (Koss & Burkhart). Rape produces a wider range of PTSD symptoms than do other traumatic events (Waites, 1993). Such symptoms are distorted patterns of attachment, pervasive problems of identity integration, and belief systems that rationalize the rape.

The rape trauma syndrome resembles the postabuse reaction characteristic of sexually victimized children (Burgess & Holmstrom, 1974). The victim is likely to become socially isolated and is more prone to drop out of counseling due to feeling unworthy. The victim is less sure that confidence rape *is* rape (Bowie, Silverman, Kalich, & Edbril, 1990; Koss & Burkhart, 1989). Kilpatrick, Veronen, and Best (1988) found that, of the women who met the legal definition of rape (force or threat of force, nonconsent, and involving the act of penetration), only 50% responded in the affirmative when asked if they had ever been victims of rape (Bowie, Silverman, Kalick, & Edbril, 1990).

Intervention

The treatment of a rape victim entails addressing safety issues, assessing for physical and psychological damage, creating a safe therapeutic environment, and allowing the client to tell her story repeatedly. Often, because traumatic events shatter assumptions of safety (Janoff-Bulman, 1992) or alter physiological chemistry in the brain (van der Kolk, 1987), traditional talk therapy fails to assuage fears or restore a client to her prior level of functioning.

Brief trauma-related interventions differ from talk therapy in several ways: (a) the sessions are focused on one particular troubling event; (b) the client is more active than the therapist; (c) the sessions often last longer than an hour; and (d) frequently, imaginal flooding is a component of brief therapies. Repeated visualization facilitates the client's becoming desensitized to the event. Open-ended sessions allow the client to become emotionally reengaged with the event, reach a heightened physiological state, grow desensitized to the event, and gain new insight about the event. TFT (Calahan, 1987) addresses anxiety and PTSD via stimulating particular meridians of the body to produce chemicals that help restore the body and brain to their pretrauma levels of functioning. Although research is inconclusive on EMDR and TIR, it appears that each of these brief interventions is appropriate for rape victims. Caution should be used, however, in that EMDR (Shapiro, 1989) and TIR (Gerbode, 1989) ought to be used only on verbal adults who are stable enough to focus on a troubling event for a sustained period of time.

LEVEL 5: SERIOUS MENTAL ILLNESS

Case Example

Nona (age 43) was an artist from a "well-to-do" family. She and her husband Rick had two little girls, ages 10 and 12. Never having found a career that suited him, Rick repeatedly borrowed money from Nona's father. Over the years, Rick grew ashamed and more frantic about his failure to support his family. His alcohol consumption increased.

One night when the children were at their grandparents' home, Nona came home to find Rick intoxicated, depressed, and acting out. Rick took a pistol from the drawer, placed it to Nona's head, and then to his own. In his rage, he stormed around the house making threats. At one point, he placed the gun in his mouth, walked toward Nona, and tripped on the coffee table. The gun fired, killing Rick.

Shortly after Rick's death, Nona entered therapy and was given an antidepressant. She felt depressed, lethargic, afraid to leave the home, unable to continue painting, and was nauseated at the thought of food. Nona began losing weight. Nona also began hallucinating, sure that she had a penis and that others could see it. Nona avoided going to the bathroom and undressing. An initial psychosocial history revealed no childhood incidents of abuse.

After 2 months of psychotherapy, Nona began to see "visions." The visions pertained to hands grabbing her as she urinated. Intense visualization techniques elicited more details. In time (without the therapist making reference to abuse), Nona realized that she was the victim of severe childhood sexual abuse. One memory revealed that her father had had coitus with the family dog, and then turned to Nona, demanding that she perform oral sex on him.

This crisis reflects serious mental illness as evidenced by Nona's depression and hallucinations. Her husband's violent death precipitated the crisis, but the preexisting abuse by her father was instrumental in her presenting symptoms. Her state was such that she was significantly impaired. Her usual coping mechanism had failed her.

Other examples of serious mental illness are psychosis, dementia, bipolar disorder, and schizophrenia. Seriously mentally ill patients experience disorganized thinking and behavior. The etiology of these symptoms is neurobiological in nature (Burgess & Roberts, 1995).

Research

The example of Nona is more complicated than the case scenarios that preceded it. Contained herein is a victim of domestic violence, a witness of an accidental suicide, and a victim of grotesque sexual abuse by her father. That Nona had suppressed the memory is not unusual. As a child, Nona had been the victim of "inescapable stress," that which results from being overpowered, helpless, and out of control (Waites, 1993). Memory loss is one form of symptom resulting from inescapable stress, and unfortunately can lead to accusations of being a malingerer. Identity confusion and lower self-esteem are concomitant with memory loss.

The symptoms of inescapable shock can present themselves in somatization, physical illness, substance abuse, or re-victimization (Waites, 1993). The specific effects of inescapable shock affect the following domains: learning and memory; addiction, immunity, and stress tolerance; identity formation and personality integration; and fantasy.

Intervention

Severe mental illness usually requires long-term treatment. One traditional intervention is pharmaceutical medications. Empirical research is insufficient to prove that any particular psychotherapeutic, nonpharmacological intervention is more effective in the treatment of hallucinations and depression than pharmacology alone. However, many believe that psychotherapy enhances treatment progress. Because pharmacology is beyond the scope of this chapter, the research referenced will pertain to psychotherapeutic interventions that address severe abuse, memory work, and self-concepts.

As in other case examples, the author presumes a treatment foundation of safety. Of central concern in Nona's case is her weight loss. Monitoring the weight loss and conferring with a nutritionist as well as an anorexia specialist is appropriate. A thorough history should be taken to see the multifaceted dimensions of the client's life. Family members should be brought in for collaboration and triangulation of data. Consents should be obtained to release information from other treatment providers. And, when possible, the case should be reviewed in the context of a treatment team. Once data are gathered, support systems are in place, specialists have been apprised of the case, and the threat of imminent danger is gone, one may proceed to address root causes of distress.

Treatment will have to accommodate individual coping responses (Lazarus & Folkman, 1984). Coping responses of victims of severe trauma vary. Variables identified by Everstine and Everstine (1993) that mediate the coping response are: whether the event altered one's vocation or role in life; whether the event occurred in what was considered a safe and nurturing place; whether surviving the incident was a source of pride or humiliation; and, whether the victim had a previous trauma or psychological condition that heightened the effect of the current trauma. Resick et al. (1988) noted that a history of incest, substance abuse, and personality disorders also complicate one's response to rape.

Because memory enhances one's sense of personal control (Waites, 1993), memory work may be called for in Nona's case. Recovery comes more slowly for incest victims who lose their memory (Maltz, 1987; Waites, 1993). The interventions that aid in memory restoration are similar to and encompass the brief trauma techniques mentioned in Level 3.

LEVEL 6: PSYCHIATRIC EMERGENCIES

Case Example

Mrs. Richards, age 32, had been blind since birth. She married a partially blind man. Within 2 years of their marriage, Mr. Richards began choking Mrs. Richards until she turned blue. Feeling depressed, Mrs. Richards sought counseling. She told the counselor that she felt desperate to leave Mr. Richards, but was also afraid to leave him, knowing that she depended on him for assistance in daily life skills.

One day, Mrs. Richards frantically phoned the counselor. She reported that she wanted to kill herself . . . that she had just learned that Mr. Richards was having an "e-mail affair." Her counselor immediately arranged to see Mrs. Richards. The counselor assessed the lethality of the suicide threat and determined that Mrs. Richards was not in imminent danger of harming herself. The counselor then arranged for both Mr. and Mrs. Richards to come to conjoint therapy.

Before the scheduled appointment, the counselor received a phone call informing her that Mrs. Richards had thrown herself in front of a moving automobile. The driver of the car stopped and called the police, who then transported Mrs. Richards to the hospital.

Research

Psychiatric emergencies involve situations in which the patient is a danger to herself or to others. Clearly Mrs. Richards was a danger to herself. Her judgment was impaired, and she was unable to exert control over feelings of betrayal and helplessness. Other examples of psychiatric emergencies include rape, homicide, drug overdose, and personal assault. Irrationality, rage, anxiety, and disorientation are symptoms that indicate the need for immediate intervention. Burgess and Roberts (1995) write that drug overdoses and suicide attempts reveal self-abusive behavior, while acts of aggression manifest a need for dominance and control. The case of Mrs. Richards involved self-abusive behavior. Therefore, the research presented here pertains to self-injurious behavior.

Self-injurious behavior has been explained by two variables: learned helplessness and escapable and inescapable shock (Waites, 1993). Mice who were previously defeated, for example, take a posture of defeat even before being attacked again. It is speculated that people who injure themselves have previously been abused by another human being; the experience of abuse was out of their control. Being in control raises one's self-appraisal; being out of control lessens the same. Therefore, victims of abuse may choose to injure themselves to exert a level of control.

Waites (1993) postulated that the desirability of escapable shock (e.g., slashing one's arms with a razor blade) over inescapable shock (e.g., incestuous molestation) could explain why traumatized individuals exhibit self-injurious behaviors. Those who harm themselves are replacing inescapable pain with escapable, controllable pain. In animals as well as humans, whether the traumatic event was escapable is a major predictor of the ultimate effect of the trauma on the victim (Waites).

Intervention

Psychiatric emergencies vary in nature, but each emergency has an element of out-of-control behavior. The first intervening step of the clinician is that of inquiry. The clinician should find out the location of the patient, what the patient has done, and who else is present. In the case of a suicide attempt, the clinician has to assess the lethality of the act. Published lethality scales can serve as an aid (Burgess & Roberts, 1995). Where medical or biological danger exists *or* where there is insufficient data for that determination, emergency medical attention is mandated. Naturally, police and rescue squads should handle immediately dangerous situations, providing rapid transportation to the hospital.

Confounding factors in psychiatric emergencies are multiple. The clinician may not be able to accurately assess the patient's condition due to incomplete or conflicting information. Disruptive behavior by the patient also makes psychiatric emergencies perhaps the most difficult of the crises to manage. Combatting these obstacles requires effective communication between therapists and other crisis care providers, as well as the ability to work calmly and effectively in a highly charged situation. After the patient is stabilized, the clinician should be careful to arrange for follow-up services to ensure continuity of treatment (Burgess & Roberts, 1995).

LEVEL 7: CATASTROPHIC OR CUMULATIVE CRISIS

Case Example

Susie (24), the fifth child in a family of 10, was reared on a farm. She was raped by her older brother (19) and his friends when she was 12. At age 15, her father committed suicide by hanging himself from a rafter in the barn. When Susie was 16, her widowed mother arranged for her to marry a 35-year-old man who beat Susie whenever he was intoxicated. The beatings grew more severe once her husband learned that Susie was infertile. Susie, too, felt distraught over the news, for she had hoped that a child would distract her from her dismal life and decrease the severity of the beatings. Susie became depressed; she ceased performing her ritual house cleaning and cooking, and she rarely left the house.

Concerned about not having seen Susie for a protracted period of time, Susie's neighbor came to the house to see if there was a problem. Finding the door ajar, the neighbor entered and discovered Susie sitting in a corner, disheveled and stuporous. Susie was covered in lacerations. The neighbor drove Susie to the hospital, where the staff learned that Susie was a victim of woman battering. The staff found safe temporary housing for Susie, treated her depression with medications, and discharged her.

Three months later, the hospital received a phone call from the resident manager at the temporary shelter. The manager reported that Susie had slashed her wrists and was catatonic. Immediately, Susie was hospitalized. After some time, Susie told a staff member why she had slashed her wrists: Susie had attended a Thanksgiving family reunion where Uncle Rob, Susie's father's brother, approached her and told her that she was the cause of her own father's suicide.

Level 7 is a complicated level of crisis. It "can occur in the aftermath of multiple traumatic crises and/or cumulative crises that were not resolved" (Burgess & Roberts, 1995, p. 45). Level 7 crises involve crises from Levels 4, 5, and 6. For example, in Susie's family, there were multiple family crises (Level 4; her rape, her father's suicide, her arranged marriage, and her uncle's accusation). Furthermore, Susie's prolonged depression hints of serious mental illness, a Level 5 crisis. Finally, Susie's attempted suicide constituted a psychiatric emergency, a Level 6 crisis. The preceding summary does not take into account the incompleted developmental tasks that must have happened in a family wrought with traumatic events such as Susie's. In other words, a Level 7 patient experiences trauma upon trauma. Treatment of Level 7 patients will require experienced practitioners who are familiar with crisis intervention, assessment, teamwork, and trauma work.

Interventions will vary according to the level of the crisis. Sometimes a crisis will resolve itself in a relatively short period of time. Other times, there is eminent danger associated with the crisis, and treatment is complex and lengthy (Burgess & Roberts, 1996).

Applying the Stress-Crisis Continuum (Burgess & Roberts, 1995) to victims of woman battering and classifying the victim into one of the levels of the continuum requires knowledge of the following: domestic violence, the continuum, the victim's past, and the victim's perceptions about her life events. Victims are grouped into levels according to the nature, duration, and intensity of the stressful event(s), as well as their perception of the life events (Burgess & Roberts, 1995). It is, therefore, crucial that practitioners access accurate information and respectfully listen to the victim.

To assure that the appropriate treatment is administered, it is important that practitioners continue making careful notes of client histories, previous treatments, and their results. Specificity and replication will call forth the most efficient treatments that will serve both battering victims and managed care.

REFERENCES

American Bar Association. (1994). *The impact of domestic violence on children.* Chicago: Author.

American Heritage Concise Dictionary (3rd ed.). (1994). Boston: Houghton Mifflin Company.

American Psychiatric Association. (1994). *Diagnostic and statistical manual of mental disorders* (4th ed.). Washington, DC: Author.

Baldwin, B. A. (1978). A paradigm for the classification of emotional crises: Implications for crisis intervention. *American Journal of Orthopsychiatry, 48,* 538–551.

Barsky, A. (1981). Hidden reasons some patients visit doctors. *Annals of Internal Medicine, 94,* 492.

Bowie, S. I., Silverman, D. C., Kalick, S. M., & Edbril, S. D. (1990). Blitz rape and confidence rape: Implications for clinical intervention. *American Journal of Psychotherapy, 44,* 180–188.

Burgess, A. W., & Holmstrom, L. L. (1974). *Rape: Victims of crisis.* Bowie, MD: Robert J. Bradley.

Burgess, A. W., & Roberts, A. R. (1995). Levels of stress and crisis precipitants: The stress-crisis continuum. *Crisis Intervention and Time-Limited Treatment, 2*(1), 31–47.

Calahan, R. (1987). *Successful treatment of phobia and anxiety by telephone and radio.* Unpublished manuscript.

Carlson, B. E. (1996). Children of battered women: Research, programs, and services. In A. Roberts (Ed.), *Helping battered women: New perspectives and remedies* (pp. 172–187). New York: Oxford University Press.

Corsilles, A. (1994). Note: No-drop policies in the prosecution of domestic violence cases: Guaranteed to action or dangerous solution. *Fordham Law Review, 63,* 853–881.

Council on Scientific Affairs, American Medical Association. (1992). Editorial. *Journal of the American Medical Association, 267,* 3184–3189.

Dansky, B. S., Roth, S., & Kronenberger, A. G. (1990). The trauma constellation identification scale: A measure of the psychological impact of a stress life event. *Journal of Traumatic Stress, 3,* 557–572.

Dziegielewski, S. F., Resnick, C., & Krause, N. B. (1996). Shelter-based crisis intervention with battered women. In A. Roberts (Ed.), *Helping battered women: New perspectives and remedies* (pp. 159–171). New York: Oxford University Press.

Everstine, D., & Everstine, L. (1993). *The trauma response: Treatment for emotional injury.* New York: W.W. Norton.

Figley, C. (1989). *Treating stress in families.* New York: Brunner/Mazel.

Foa, E., Rothbaum, B., Riggs, D., & Murdock, T. (1991). Treatment of posttraumatic stress disorder in rape victims: A comparison between cognitive-behavioral procedures and counseling. *Journal of Consulting and Clinical Psychology, 59,* 715–723.

Foa, E., Rothbaum, B., & Steketee, G. (1993). Treatment of rape victims. *Journal of Interpersonal Violence, 8,* 256–276.

French, G. D., & Gerbode, F. A. (1993). *The Traumatic Incident Reduction Workshop* (2nd ed.). Menlo Park, CA: IRM.

Gerbode, F. (1989). *Beyond psychology: An introduction to metapsychology.* Palo Alto, CA: IRM.

Gerbode, F., & Moore, R. (1994). Beliefs and intentions in RET. *Journal of Ration-Emotive & Cognitive-Behavior Therapy, 12,* 27–45.

Girelli, A. A., Resick, P. A., Marhoefer-Dvorak, S., & Hutter, C. K. (1986). Subjective distress and violence during rape: Their effects on long-term fear. *Victim Violence, 1,* 35–46.

Hansen, M., & Harway, M. (Eds.). (1993). *Battering and family therapy.* Newbury Park, CA: Sage.

Harway, M., & Hansen, M. (1994). *Spouse abuse: Assessing and treating battered women, batterers and their children.* Sarasota, FL: Professional Resource Exchange Monographs.

Janoff-Bulman, R. (1992). *Shattered assumptions.* New York: Free Press.

Kilpatrick, G., Veronen, A., & Best, G. (1988). *The psychological impact of crime: A study of randomly surveyed crime victims.* Charleston, SC: Crime Victims Research and Treatment Center, University of South Carolina.

Koss, M. P. (1987). *The rape victim: Clinical and community approaches to treatment.* Lexington, MA: Greene.

Koss, M., & Burkhart, B. (1989). A conceptual analysis of rape victimization: Long-term effects and implications for treatment. *Psychology of Women Quarterly, 13,* 27–40.

Lazarus, R. S., & Folkman, S. (1984). *Stress, appraisal, and coping.* New York: Springer.

Lewin, T. (June 22, 1997). Seeking a public health solution for a problem that starts at home. *The New York Times,* Section *14,* p. 19.

Malmquist, C. (1986). Children who witness parental murder: Posttraumatic aspects. *Journal of the American Academy of Child Psychiatry, 25,* 320–325.

Maltz, W. (1987). *Incest and sexuality: A guide to understanding and healing.* Lexington, MA: Lexington Books.

Mechanic, D. (1994). Integrating mental health into a general health care system. *Hospital and Community Psychiatry, 45,* 893–897.

Moore, R. H. (1993). Cognitive-emotive treatment of the posttraumatic stress disorder. In W. Dryden & L. Hill (Eds.), *Innovations in rational-emotive therapy* (pp. 176–195). Newbury Park, CA: Sage.

Moscarello, R. (1991). Posttraumatic stress disorder after sexual assault: Its psychodynamics and treatment. *Journal of the American Academy of Psychoanalysis, 19,* 235–253.

National Crime Survey. (1981). *National Sample, 1973-1979.* Ann Arbor, MI: Inter-University Consortium on Political and Social Research, University of Michigan.

Nurius, P., Hilfrink, M., & Rifino, R. (1996). The single greatest health threat to women: Their partners. In P. Raffoul & C. A. McNeece (Eds.), *Future issues for social work practice.* Boston: Allyn & Bacon.

Petretic-Jackson, P. A., & Jackson, T. (1996). Mental health interventions with battered women. In A. Roberts (Ed.), *Helping battered women: New perspectives and remedies* (pp. 188–221). New York: Oxford University Press.

Raimy, V. (1975). *Misunderstandings of the self.* San Francisco: Jossey-Bass.

Resick, P. (1983). The rape reaction: Research findings and implications for intervention. *The Behavior Therapist, 6,* 129–132.

Resick, P., Jordan, C., Girelli, S., Hutter, C., & Marhoefer-Dvorak, S. (1988). A comparative outcome study of behavioral group therapy for sexual assault victims. *Behavior Therapy, 19,* 385–401.

Resick, P., & Schnicke, M. (1992). Cognitive processing therapy for sexual assault victims. *Journal of Clinical Psychology, 60,* 748–756.

Resnick, H. S., Kilpatrick, D. G., & Lipovsky, J. A. (1991). Assessment of rape-related posttraumatic stress disorder: Stressor and symptom dimensions. *Psychological Assessment: A Journal of Consulting and Clinical Psychology, 3,* 561–572.

Roberts, A. (1996a). *Helping battered women: New perspectives and remedies.* New York: Oxford University Press.

Roberts, A. (1996b). Introduction: Myths and realities regarding battered women. In A. Roberts (Ed.), *Helping battered women: New perspectives and remedies* (pp. 3–30). New York: Oxford University Press.

Roberts, A., & Roberts, B. (1990). A comprehensive model for crisis intervention with battered women and their children. In A. Roberts (Ed.), *Crisis intervention handbook: Assessment* (pp. 105–123). Belmont, CA: Wadsworth.

Roth, S., Dye, E., & Lebowitz, L. (1988). Group therapy for sexual-assault victims. *Psychotherapy, 25,* 82–95.

Roth, S., & Newman, E. (1991). The process of coping with sexual trauma. *Journal of Traumatic Stress, 4,* 279–297.

Rothbaum, B. O., Dancu, C., Riggs, D. S., & Foa, E. (1990, September). *The PTSD Symptom Scale.* Paper presented at the European Association of Behavior Therapy Annual Conference, Paris, France.

Rothbaum, B., Foa, E., Riggs, D., Murdock, T., & Walsh, W. (1992). A prospective examination of post-traumatic stress disorder in rape victims. *Journal of Traumatic Stress, 5,* 455–475.

Schechter, S. (1982). *Women and male violence: The visions and struggles of the battered women's movement.* Boston: South End Press.

Shapiro, F. (1989). Efficacy of the eye movement desensitization procedure in the treatment of traumatic memories. *Journal of Traumatic Stress, 2,* 199–223.

Straton, D. (1990). Catharsis reconsidered. *Australian and New Zealand Journal of Psychiatry, 24,* 543–551.

Valentine, P. (1995). Traumatic incident reduction: A review of a new intervention. *Journal of Family Psychotherapy, 6*(2), 73–78.

Valentine, P. (1997). Traumatic incident reduction: Brief treatment of trauma-related symptoms in incarcerated females. *Dissertation Abstracts International, 54*(01), 534B, University Microfilms No. AAD93-15947.

Valentine, P. V., & Smith, T. E. (in press). A qualitative study of client perceptions of Traumatic Incident Reduction (TIR): A brief trauma treatment. *Crisis Intervention and Time-Limited Treatment.*

van der Kolk, B. (1987). *Psychological trauma.* Washington, DC: American Psychiatric Press.

van der Kolk, B., Blitz, R., Burr, W., Sherry, S., & Hartmann, E. (1984). Nightmares and trauma: A comparison of nightmares after combat with lifelong nightmares in veterans. *American Journal of Psychiatry, 141,* 187–190.

Waites, E. A. (1993). *Trauma and survival: Post-traumatic and dissociative disorders in women.* New York: Norton.

Waldinger, R. J. (1990). *Psychiatry for medical students* (2nd ed.). Washington, DC: American Psychiatric Press.

Wodarski, J. (1987). An examination of spouse abuse: Practice issues for the profession. *Clinical Social Work Journal, 15,* 172–179.

CHAPTER 7

Community Response Models for Battered Women:
From Crisis Intervention to Legal Advocacy and Court-Based Justice Centers

Karen S. Knox and Mary Jo Garcia Biggs

CASE SCENARIOS

Case 1

Angela is a 25-year-old woman who is 7 months pregnant and has a 3-year-old son; she also is the caregiver for her 6-year-old brother since her mother is in jail on drug charges. Angela is a survivor of childhood physical abuse by her mother, and sexual abuse by her mother's many boyfriends. Her boyfriend beat Angela last week, and the victim services crisis counselor with the police department referred her to the local domestic violence shelter.

Case 2

Estelle is a 78-year-old woman who is being cared for by her oldest son. He has been neglecting her physical and medical needs, and she has suspicious bruises all over her body when the Adult Protective Services investigator arrives after a referral from a neighbor. The APS investigator calls for EMS and police backup.

Case 3

Mary is a 45-year-old woman who has been married to her husband for 25 years. They have three children: Two are in college, and one is a senior in high school and will be graduating this year. Mary's husband has been physically and emotionally abusive to her since her last pregnancy, but she has stayed with him for the children's sake. Now that they are grown and leaving home, she worries about her future and whether she should divorce him.

Case 4

Lauren is a 19-year-old college sophomore who recently broke up with her boyfriend, as he was always accusing her of being attracted to other guys, and his anger and jealousy were escalating to the point where she was afraid of what he might do. On their last date, they were both drinking heavily and she passed out and doesn't remember what happened, but woke up the next morning in his apartment with her clothes in disarray. Yesterday, one of her friends mentioned seeing him hanging around the dorm. She is frightened about what happened on their last date, fearing that he may have raped her and that he may be stalking her now, but is unsure about calling the police to report it.

All of these women have experienced domestic/family violence and partner abuse, but each has a unique history and situation to deal with, which reflects the multiple needs and obstacles that battered women face. How have our communities responded to meet these needs? In the past 25 years, much progress has been made in developing community-based programs to make legal and social support services available to battered women and their families. However, domestic violence shelters still have waiting lists, courts are backlogged with family violence cases, and the complex problem of family violence requires innovative community responses to continue the progress the battered women's movement started two decades ago.

This chapter discusses key legal mandates, policy changes, and advocacy services that have made a difference in how our communities and systems respond to family violence. The intervention models that developed as a result of theses changes are presented, as well as the current initiative of community collaboration through Family Justice Centers. Case examples are provided to illustrate how these different models work with battered women and their families. The focus of this chapter is on how community partnerships can enhance services and assistance along the continuum of family violence, which includes child abuse, elder abuse, domestic violence/homicide, sexual assault, dating violence, and stalking.

TWENTY-FIVE YEARS OF PROGRESS: WHAT HAVE WE ACCOMPLISHED?

In the 1970s, the battered women's movement and feminist activists developed domestic violence shelters in a "grassroots" effort to provide supportive social services. However, it became obvious to those working with battered women and their families that domestic violence was too widespread and complex to be solved solely by the shelters (Goodman & Epstein, 2005). With more public awareness about family violence and domestic abuse, many victims and survivors spoke out and sought help from the few community programs available then. Advocacy groups lobbied for changes in legislation and in how the criminal justice system responded to domestic violence. Major shifts in societal values occurred during this time period, with the growing perception that domestic and family violence is unacceptable. The recognition of domestic violence as a serious, widespread problem involving multiple levels and systems was a major influence contributing to the progress made in the past 25 years (Mears & Visher, 2005).

National legislation and funding for victim services programs in law enforcement and the court systems improved criminal justice responses to domestic abuse and family violence. The crime victims' movement resulted in federal legislation and funding to establish victim assistance programs in all states through the Law Enforcement Assistance Administration (LEAA) and the Victims of Crime Act (VOCA) of 1984 (Knox & Roberts, 2002; Roberts & Fisher, 1997). These police and court-based victim services and advocacy programs resulted in significant improvements in how victims and survivors of family violence were treated in the criminal justice system.

Historically, police were often reluctant to intervene and arrest, preferring to mediate or separate spouses, and subscribing to sexist values/beliefs such as "a man's home is his castle" and "it's a family matter, not a police problem" (Roberts, 1996). The "criminalization" of family and domestic violence led to mandatory or pro-arrest policies that ensured legal sanctions for batterers and protected the rights of victims. Specialized police-training programs were implemented to educate law enforcement professionals on policy and arrest procedure changes, the dynamics and indicators of family violence, and how to respond in a sensitive and compassionate way when working with battered women (Roberts, 1996). In addition to changes in arrest policies, many law enforcement departments created specialized domestic violence units that worked in a coordinated effort with the courts and shelters in a proactive response to these cases (Roberts & Roberts, 2005). All law enforcement agencies are state-mandated to provide a victim services contact person to notify victims about Victim Compensation. Most police departments have social workers or counselors who provide crisis counseling, information and referral services, and follow-up contacts about the criminal case/process. A national survey by Knox and Roberts (2002) indicates that 74% of police departments ($N = 111$) provide 24-hour crisis intervention services, with 55% responding to requests by patrol officers on the scene and 70% providing on-call services.

In the past, if a domestic violence case got to the court system, the prosecutors and attorneys often minimized the dangers that battered women experienced and discouraged them from filing charges or proceeding with the prosecution (Roberts, 1996). It was not until 1988 that all 50 states took family violence laws seriously and passed legislation that created both civil and criminal remedies for battered women (Roberts, 1996). Protective orders are still one of the most frequently used legal options in family violence cases to protect women and children from further contact and harassment by their abusers. Court advocates became integral members of a team approach with prosecutors to minimize "re-victimization" by the legal system during the court proceedings. With the victims rights movement and advocacy groups' efforts, every state now has a Crime Victims' Bill of Rights, which requires notification and education about the trial and court process, victims compensation programs and funds to assist in meeting their medical and counseling needs, and notification about prisoner release and probation/parole status.

The Violence Against Women Act of 1994, which was just reauthorized in 2005, provided resources and funding to an industry of domestic violence programs in criminal justice, human service, and health care systems improving services to battered women (Shepard, 2005). Funding for domestic violence shelters allowed more effective interventions than just basic needs (shelter, food, and clothing). Education, job training, transportation, child care, counseling services, health and medical care, legal assistance, coordination with law enforcement and the courts, drug and alcohol treatment, minority outreach, prevention and public awareness programs, and school-based intervention programs are some of the many interventions and services commonly found at domestic violence shelters now. With this increase in different intervention strategies and services, we have learned that battered women and their families have multiple needs, that family violence has different dimensions for intervention, and that there is no "cookie-cutter" answer to meeting those multiple needs and dimensions (Mears & Visher, 2005).

However, there is a need for more research to determine the effectiveness of these multiple interventions and services to determine which are more effective with the different types and dimensions of family violence. There is a small body of research that indicates that these types of advocacy and social support services are successful strategies impacting on family violence (Goodman & Epstein, 2005; Mears & Visher, 2005). There is also some evidence that women who receive such services and material aid are twice as likely to follow through with the prosecution and criminal process compared to those who did not have these services available to them (Bennett, Goodman, & Dutton, 1999).

COMMUNITY RESPONSE MODELS

The most important accomplishment from the past 25 years is that these comprehensive institutional reforms have been successful in changing how our communities and systems respond to battered women and their families. Coordinated community responses (CCRs) that provide support services and advocacy can be successful strategies that make a difference (Goodman & Epstein, 2005; Shepard, 2005). According to Gray (1985), there are five stages of growth for community collaboration:

- Coexistence: awareness of other community organizations.
- Communication: informal communication with each other to learn more about other community organizations.
- Cooperation: formal relationships among community organizations.
- Coordination: formal working relationships to prevent redundancy and increase effectiveness.
- Collaboration: involves long-term strategies to formalize a system designed to engender coordination (Townsend, Hunt, & Rhodes, 2005).

One of the most well-known CCRs adopted by many domestic violence shelters and communities is modeled after the Domestic Abuse Intervention Project (DAIP) in Duluth, Minnesota, which advocates reforming the criminal justice system response by developing a coordinated community response (Pence & Shepard, 1999; Shepard, 2005). Components of this model include pro-arrest or mandatory arrest policies, follow-up support and advocacy for victims/survivors, aggressive and prompt prosecution, monitoring of offender compliance with probation conditions, court-mandated batterers counseling programs, and monitoring of the systemwide response to domestic violence cases (Shepard, 2005). The Duluth Model is a macro-level model that focuses on changing social institutions, improving communication and coordination between providers and professionals, and monitoring and evaluating institutional reforms and services/programs (Shepard, 2005). The Women's Shelter of South Texas in Corpus Christi follows this model by providing multiple interventions and services at both the micro- and macro-levels of practice to battered women and their children, as well as services and counseling for batterers at a separate location. The agency also coordinates with other community providers, law enforcement, and the court system in a multidisciplinary approach.

A collaborative community response that developed in the drug and alcohol field of practice is the "one-stop shopping" model. This type of community collaboration model provides comprehensive services onsite, rather than coordinate services among different community providers. The Parent and Child Enrichment Demonstration Project (PACE) that began in 1990 was a pioneer study in assessing the effectiveness of the one-stop shopping model for women who used crack cocaine. Onsite services included medical and physical care; pediatric care; group and individual counseling; nutritional assessments; enrollment for supplemental services and emergency services, such as Women, Infants, and Children (WIC) food supplements, emergency shelter, Medicaid, and so forth; psychosocial assessments; parenting education; GED classes; vocational counseling; and legal assistance (McMurtrie, Rosenberg, Kerker, Kan, & Graham, 1999).

This model increased opportunities for the women to work collaboratively and openly with multiple professionals and provided a coordinated care plan that increased the likelihood that the women would use a wider range of services. Some of the lessons learned from this project included the following findings and recommendations:

- The importance of a female model of drug treatment because women come into and stay in drug treatment for different reasons and have different needs than men.
- The need for program flexibility was crucial because of the different dynamics and needs of the women and their children.
- That comprehensive care in one location decreased barriers to treatment, allowed women to establish trusting relationships with a consistent team of providers, enabled staff to get to know clients well, and allowed women to feel comfortable disclosing sensitive information to providers.
- Many of the women lacked good role models for parenting, were not prepared for being parents, and had neglected or abandoned their children during their drug-using years.
- Many PACE clients experienced abuse, both as children and adults, which had not been disclosed. Positive urine toxicologies were often related to abusive incidents, and drug use

was a common form of self-medication during these difficult
times.

- Many women enter drug treatment programs because they have
  lost custody of their children, and it is important to establish good
  working relationships with Child Protective Services (McMurtrie,
  Rosenberg, Kerker, Kan, & Graham, 1999).

Another study that compared outcomes between a case management outpatient drug treatment program (where clients were referred to other community providers) and a one-stop shopping
model (where multiple services were provided onsite) found the
women who attended the one-stop shopping model had higher retention and lower drug use at the 12-month followup (Sun, 2006;
Volpicelli, Markham, Monterosso, Filing, & O'Brien, 2000). Although
there are only a few empirical studies of the one-stop shopping model,
it appears to be effective in both retention of clients in drug treatment and provision of multiple services that impacted positively on
progress in treatment.

The connections and similarities between the PACE clients and
battered women are apparent, with these findings being consistent
with what we have learned about domestic violence. Many of these
dynamics and factors (multiple needs, substance abuse, poor parenting, childhood abuse, obstacles to treatment, etc.) are also associated with child protective services clients. The Children and Domestic Violence Services (CADVS) study is a project that examined
the organization and relationship of child welfare services for children and domestic violence services for women (Smith et al., 2005).
The co-occurrence of domestic violence and child abuse is well documented, with studies indicating that 30% to 40% of child welfare
caseloads involve families who have also experienced domestic violence (Appel & Holden, 1998; Edleson, 1999). Research also indicates that the frequency and severity of domestic violence directed
to mothers is positively correlated with both mothers' and fathers'
physical aggression toward children (Ross, 1996). The CADVS study
concluded that the high rate of co-occurring domestic violence and
child maltreatment is a serious problem that requires systematic research on a national level about the types of assessment tools to
identify these families and the coordination of services for these
families.

Another study that used data from the National Survey of Child
and Adolescent Well-Being (as did the CADVS study) examined the

identification of domestic violence by Child Protective Services (CPS) workers during investigations. It found that CPS workers indicated that domestic violence was present in only 12% of families investigated for child abuse, whereas 31% of caregivers reported domestic violence victimization (Kohl, Barth, Hazen, & Landsverk, 2005). The study also found that substance abuse by the primary caregiver was a strong predictor of underidentification by CPS workers, and that only half of the caregivers who were identified with active domestic violence received any domestic violence services over the 18 months following the investigation (Kohl, Barth, Hazen, & Landsverk, 2005). The recommendations concluded that the barriers between multiple systems that address domestic violence and child maltreatment must be overcome to increase the availability of appropriate services to caregivers of abused children who have experienced domestic violence (Kohl, Barth, Hazen, & Landsverk, 2005).

Because CPS and law enforcement have been required by the majority of states to work together when investigating criminal cases of child abuse, Child Advocacy Centers (CACs) developed as a community collaboration model for a multidisciplinary team approach (Newman, Dannenfelser, & Pendleton, 2005). The purpose of these centers is to provide a comprehensive, multidisciplinary team response that includes CPS and law enforcement investigations, forensic interviews, medical evaluation, crisis intervention, specialized therapeutic services, advocacy, and case review and monitoring. The one-stop shopping model used by CACs provides more advantages than coordination models such as more resources, a visible identity, facilities and equipment for conducting child-friendly interviews, more accessible investigative team members, and greater expertise among trained child interview specialists (Newman, Dannenfelser, & Pendleton, 2005).

Child Advocacy Centers are usually located in a more child-friendly environment, such as a large house renovated to meet the various service and client needs, than police departments or CPS offices. They are user-friendly in that children and families can go to one location, which minimizes transportation problems and time considerations that occur when agencies are in multiple locations. Collaborative investigations with CPS, law enforcement, and prosecutors decrease the number of times a child has to be interviewed, which can impact negatively on both the child and a successful prosecution. Lessons learned through collaboration among child abuse professionals are now being applied to domestic violence.

The initiative began in 1986 when City of San Diego District Attorney Casey Guinn evaluated the formula for Children's Advocacy Centers and envisioned a "one-stop shop" for victims of domestic violence. San Diego's Family Justice Center was established in 2002, and is one of the most comprehensive one-stop-shop facilities in the nation for battered women and their children. The center's 25 participating agencies housed under one roof provide onsite services where victims can get a restraining order, talk to police and prosecutors, develop a safety plan, receive medical assistance, get transportation to a safe place, obtain nutrition or pregnancy services, receive crisis counseling, and receive comprehensive advocacy services (www.sandiegofamilyjusticecenter.org).

The President's Family Justice Center Initiative (PFJCI) was established in 2003 as a pilot program for planning and implementing comprehensive, collaborative domestic violence services, and in 2004, $20 million dollars was awarded to 15 communities to develop family justice centers that provide comprehensive services, including medical care, counseling, law enforcement assistance, faith-based services, social services, employment assistance, and housing assistance. The San Diego Family Justice Center Foundation provides training and technical assistance to the President's FJC Initiative, under supervision by the Office of Violence Against Women, and facilitates the National Family Justice Center Alliance, which is a coalition of FJCs that are developing close working relationship, sharing training and technical assistance, and coordinating funding assistance (www.sandiegofamilyjusticecenter.org/info/national-alliance).

In July 2004, San Antonio was awarded over $1.2 million dollars, and was the only Texas city to be a grant recipient. With the guidance and leadership of Susan Reed, the Bexar County District Attorney, the Bexar County Family Justice Center opened in August 2005. Over 30 public and nonprofit agencies were involved in the planning and development of the FJC, which is housed in over 10,000 square feet in a secure setting on the second floor of the University Health Systems Downtown Clinic. The goals of the Bexar County FJC are to:

- Improve access to services for domestic violence victims/survivors.
- Integrate information systems and data collection.
- Develop culturally competent education and prevention strategies.

- Break the cycle of domestic violence with children who witness it.
- Create a Bexar County Domestic Violence Council and 501(c)(3) foundation (Townsend, Hunt, & Rhodes, 2005).

There are 21 community partner agencies represented onsite. No appointment is necessary, with people being served on a first-come, first-served basis. An advocate interviewer assists with the intake application and protective order process, and interpreters are available onsite. Agencies providing legal services onsite are San Antonio City Attorney's Office, the San Antonio Police Department, the Texas Department of Family and Protective Services (CPS & APS), and the U.S. Department of Defense because of the large military population at San Antonio's Air Force and Army bases. Protective orders can be obtained onsite at no charge. Information about the criminal justice system and judicial process is available and is explained during the intake process. Texas Rio Grande Legal Aid also provides free legal services to indigent residents and migrant and seasonal farm workers throughout Texas and six other Southern states.

The intake application also obtains information about other possible sources of assistance, such as crisis counseling, employment and educational assistance, family services, housing, substance abuse counseling, individual, family and child counseling, health care needs, military services, parent training, financial needs, and basic needs. On the application under each of these sections are several questions to gather information and a list of agencies that can assist in meeting those needs through the FJC. Child care is provided onsite for clients to use and is staffed by the Foster Grandparent program of Catholic Charities.

Other onsite services provided by community agencies include counseling services, assisted living, vocational training, sexual assault counseling, and substance abuse services, from the Baptist Child & Family Services, the Alamo Area Resource Center, the Family Service Association of San Antonio, the Rape Crisis Center for Children and Adults, the Family Violence Prevention Services (battered women's shelter), and the Diversity Center, which provides a nonpolitical, nonjudgmental venue for gay, lesbian, bisexual, and transsexual clients. The Center for Health Care Services ensures that clients with mental health and disability needs receive quality services. The City of San Antonio Department of Community Initiatives coordinates numerous social service programs onsite for emergency assistance services, and the San Antonio Metropolitan Ministry provides emergency shelter, transitional housing services, and services to the homeless. Public health services are provided by Christus Santa Rosa Hospital and the University Health Systems Center.

There are also 18 off-site partners who accept referrals from the Bexar County FJC and the other partner agencies. These agencies include the Alamo Children's Advocacy Center, and ChildSafe, which is a program that provides services to child and adolescent victims of sexual abuse. The Children's Shelter of San Antonio provides emergency shelter and foster care. The Rape Crisis Center Hotline answers the center's phone calls after hours and on weekends to provide information, referral, and support. The U.S. Department of Health and Human Services supports Project WATCH (What About the Children), which is a 2-year planning initiative to develop a coordinated response and provide early intervention to children exposed to domestic violence. Alamo Workforce Development provides employment and training opportunities. Other legal services and referrals are provided by the Bexar County Commissioners Court & District Judges, the Bexar County Department of Criminal Justice Planning and Coordination, Bexar County Juvenile Probation, Bexar County Sheriff's Office, and the Center for Legal & Social Justice at St. Mary's University.

In the first 5 months of operation, the Bexar County Family Justice Center has served over 2,700 families, and approximately 50% of the families received services from three or more providers at the FJC. Over 51% applied for protective orders, and more than 50% of the families specifically requested follow-up contacts from the FJC. Also, the center has trained over 350 individuals on issues relating to domestic violence (McCormick, 2006). Evaluation services are being provided locally by the Violence Prevention Center at the University of Texas Health Services Center School of Nursing.

Evaluation of the 15 pilot programs is being done by Abt Associates, which was awarded a contract by the National Institute of Justice and the Office of Violence Against Women. The plan is to have a two-part evaluation of sites with a process component covering the steps in establishing the FJCs, barriers and successes, cost utilizations, community cooperation, and history. The second evaluation component examines the impacts of this model through simple counts of clients served, numbers of successful prosecutions, numbers of services utilized by the clients, and so forth (Townsend, Hunt, & Rhodes, 2005).

CASE SCENARIOS: APPLICATION OF THE COLLABORATION COMMUNITY RESPONSE MODEL

Case 1. Angela

The victim services counselor provides crisis intervention services on the scene, while the police officer arrests and transports her boyfriend to jail. Angela learns about the Family Justice Center's services from the victim services counselor, who offers to transport Angela and the children to the agency. When they arrive, the FJC advocate interviewer makes sure that the children are comfortable in the child-care room, while she and Angela proceed with the intake application. Angela is informed about her legal rights and options at this time, and decides to apply for a protective order, which she and the advocate interviewer complete during the interview.

Angela also wants information about the counseling and health services offered through the FJC, so the advocate interviewer takes her to meet with the representatives from those agencies after completing the intake application and protective order. Angela applies for the WIC Program and makes an appointment with the health center for both her and the children. After talking to the counselor from the battered women's shelter, Angela decides to attend a support group at the shelter next week. Transportation needs are now a problem since she depended on her boyfriend and his car, so she receives a bus pass for future needs. She and the children are transported home after she completes her applications and interviews. Before leaving, the advocate interviewer informs Angela about the next legal steps, and arranges for a follow-up visit when she returns for her medical appointment the next day. Angela expresses her appreciation for the assistance, and states she had no idea so many services were available.

Case 2. Estelle

The APS investigator goes to meet with Estelle at the hospital after the police finish the investigation on the scene, and arrest her son for

Injury to an Elderly Person. While at the hospital, the APS investigator lets Estelle know about the Family Justice Center, and encourages her to follow up with the agency after her release from the hospital. The hospital social worker is familiar with the Center's services, and also follows up on referrals to appropriate agencies before Estelle's discharge.

Her daughter arrives at the hospital from her home in another state to help out temporarily, but will not be able to stay very long. After talking to the hospital social worker, her daughter decides to go to the Family Justice Center to find out what is going to happen legally with her brother, and if there are other services to assist her mother. During the intake interview and application process, the daughter speaks to representatives from APS and the police about the legal status of the case and receives information about a protective order for her mother. Estelle's daughter is concerned about her brother's power of attorney and her mother's financial situation, and receives legal assistance from the county court representative about guardianship services for her mother. Before leaving, she talks to the agency representative from the medical center, who assists her in arranging for home health services when her mother is discharged from the hospital.

Case 3. Mary

Mary knows about the Family Justice Center through the local newspaper articles about its opening last summer. She decides to look up the Center's Web site to find out what type of services are offered. She learns that both legal and counseling services are available and decides to go the FJC to check out her options about divorcing her husband. When she arrives at the FJC, the advocate interviewer informs her about the legal services available and protective orders. She meets with the Legal Aid representative to learn about the divorce process. Mary also meets with a counselor from the battered women's shelter to find out about individual counseling and support groups offered there. She decides that the first step for her is to start counseling, because she is unsure of what direction she wants to go legally, and how divorce might impact her and her children.

Case 4. Lauren

Lauren knows about the Family Justice Center because brochures are available on campus to inform students about the agency's services. She feels more comfortable going to the Center than calling the police because she is still not sure she wants to take any legal action, especially because she can't remember if anything sexual happened on their last date and she feels guilty for getting so drunk. During the intake with the advocate interviewer, she starts crying and says she is really bothered about what happened that night, and she decides to make an appointment at the health center to take a pregnancy test and be tested for STDs. She also learns about her legal options and steps if the medical exam shows evidence that a rape occurred. She agrees to talk to the victim services counselor from the police department who is housed at the Center and receives crisis counseling. The victim services counselor also introduces her to the rape crisis representative, who provides her with information on counseling/support groups, date rape and stalking, and offers to accompany her to the medical exam. Lauren is relieved to have someone go with her and feels she made the right decision to go to the FJC for help.

CONCLUSION AND RECOMMENDATIONS

These case scenarios illustrate the flexibility and multiple services offered by the one-stop shopping model of Family Justice Centers to meet the needs of victims and survivors of family violence. Although many of the FJCs are still not in full operation, there are already some concerns and suggestions on how to improve service delivery. First, the Family Justice Centers are primarily open only from 8 a.m. to 5 p.m., which is an obstacle for some clients to access services in the evening or on weekends. There is also concern that the centers may not be able to meet the needs of all victims, especially immigrant and minority populations who may be distrustful of government and police involvement.

Concerns about privacy and confidentiality arise when criminal justice and counseling agencies are co-locating, and may discourage some clients from accessing services at the FJCs (Townsend, Hunt, & Rhodes, 2005). If the criminal justice presence and philosophy is too prominent at the FJC, it may endanger the feminist perspective of advocacy organizations by minimizing and micromanaging the client's right to make her own choices and decisions. There is also a need for cross-training and open dialogue among agency representatives about philosophical differences to ensure the quality and consistency of services.

Sustainment of the Family Justice Centers is another major concern, especially when federal dollars are not available, and other funds and agency commitments are needed for the future of the FJCs. There may be some difficulties maintaining the level of services and staff needed, as well as problems with territorial issues that may occur with funding needs and priorities. Also, most of the FJCs are located in urban areas so there is concern about rural areas and how those communities and residents could access comparable services.

The need for systematic research is apparent to measure the effectiveness of this model, and it is encouraging that the local FJCs are participating in local evaluation efforts, along with the federal evaluation procedures mandated by the grants. It is recommended that program evaluation research be both quantitative and qualitative in nature to examine the impact on the clients and their families, not just counting the numbers receiving services. The use of focus groups to evaluate the services provided and the staff at the FTCs is valuable to those providing direct services to determine which interventions and services are most effective and more frequently accessed by the clients.

Although the future looks promising for the Family Justice Center Initiative, we will have to wait and see whether the hopes and dreams of those involved in this effort will be realized. Innovative community response models such as these are in the beginning stages for most communities, and it is a challenging yet exciting time to be involved as professionals in domestic violence.

REFERENCES

Appel, A. E., & Holden, G. W. (1998). The co-occurrence of spouse and physical child abuse: A review and appraisal. *Journal of Family Psychology*, *12*(4), 578–599.

Bennett, L., Goodman, L., & Dutton, M. A. (1999). Systemic obstacles to the criminal prosecution of a battering partner. *Journal of Interpersonal Violence*, *14*(7), 761–772.

Edleson, J. L. (1999). The overlap between child maltreatment and women battering. *Violence Against Women*, *5*(2), 134–154.

Goodman, L., & Epstein, D. (2005). Refocusing on women: A new direction for policy and research on intimate partner violence. *Journal of Interpersonal Violence*, *20*(4), 479–487.

Gray, B. (1985). Conditions facilitating inter-organizational collaboration. *Human Relations, 38*, 91–936.

Knox, K. S., & Roberts, A R. (2002). Police social work. In G. Greene & A. R. Roberts (Eds.), *Social workers' desk reference* (pp. 668–672). New York: Oxford University Press.

Kohl, P. L., Barth, R. P., Hazen, A. L., & Landsverk, J. A. (2005). Child welfare as a gateway to domestic violence services. *Children and Youth Services Review, 27*(11), 1203–1221.

McCormick, B. (2006). Where are we after 21 weeks of service and where are we going? *Bexar County Family Justice Center Newsletter, 2*(2). Retrieved June 25, 2006, from www.bexarcountyfjc,org.

McMurtrie, C., Rosenberg, K. D., Kerker, B. D., Kan, J., & Graham, E. H. (1999). A unique drug treatment program for pregnant and postpartum substance-using women in new york city: Results of a pilot project, 1990–1995. *American Journal of Drug & Alcohol Abuse, 25*(4), 701–713.

Mears, D. P., & Visher, C. A. (2005). Trends in understanding and addressing domestic violence. *Journal of Interpersonal Violence, 20*(2), 204–211.

Newman, B. S., Dannenfelser, P. L., & Pendleton, D. (2005). Child abuse investigations: Reasons for using child advocacy centers and suggestions for improvement. *Child and Adolescent Social Work Journal, 22*(2), 165–181.

Pence, E., & Shepard, M. (1999). Developing a coordinated community response: An introduction. In M. Shepard & E. Pence (Eds.), *Coordinating community responses to domestic violence: Lessons from the Duluth Model* (pp. 3–23). Thousand Oaks, CA: Sage.

Roberts, A. R. (1996). Police responses to battered women. In A. R. Roberts (Ed.), *Helping battered women: New perspectives and remedies* (pp. 85–95). New York: Oxford University Press.

Roberts, A., & Fisher, P. (1997). Service roles in victim/witness assistance programs. In A. McNeece & A. R. Roberts (Eds.), *Policy and practice in the justice system* (pp. 127–142). Chicago: Nelson-Hall Publishers.

Roberts, A. R., & Roberts, B. S. (2005). A comprehensive model for crisis intervention with battered women and their children. In A. R. Roberts (Ed.), *Crisis intervention handbook: Assessment, treatment, and research* (pp. 441–482). New York: Oxford University Press.

Ross, S. (1996). Risk of physical abuse to children of spouse abusing parents. *Child Abuse & Neglect, 20*(7), 589–598.

Shepard, M. (2005). Twenty years of progress in addressing domestic violence: An agenda for the next 10. *Journal of Interpersonal Violence, 20*(4), 436–441.

Smith, K. C., Kelleher, K. J., Barth, R. P., Coben, J. H., Hazen, A L., Connelly, C. D., et al. (2005). Overview of the children and domestic services study. *Children and Youth Services Review, 27*(11), 1243–1258.

Sun, A. (2006). Program factors related to women's substance abuse treatment retention and other outcomes: A review and critique. *Journal of Substance Abuse Treatment, 30*(1), 1–20.

Townsend, M., Hunt, D., & Rhodes, W. (2005). *Analytic support program contract: Evaluability assessment of the President's Family Justice Center Initiative.* Cambridge, MA: Abt Associates, Inc.

Volpicelli, J. R., Markham, I., Monterosso, J., Filing, J., & O'Brien, C. P. (2000). Psychologically enhanced treatment for cocaine-dependent mothers: Evidence of efficacy. *Journal of Substance Abuse Treatment, 18*(1), 41–49.

Children and Adolescents From Violent Homes

Complex Trauma and Crisis Intervention With Children in Shelters for Battered Women

Peter Lehmann and Emily Spence

Children exposed to the emotional, physical, or sexual violence of their female caretakers by their partners continues to be a serious social problem. Current estimates (McDonald et al., 2006a) suggest that approximately 15.5 million children live in homes where violence against a female caretaker occurred at least once in the last year. The same study found that 7 million children had also experienced severe partner violence. The fact that a sizeable proportion of children are exposed to violence is further illustrated by the large number of shelters for battered women and their children in North America.

At the present time, there are approximately 2,000 shelters with 800 children's programs in the United States (National Coalition Against Domestic Violence, 2006) and 480 shelters in Canada, 31% of which have a children's program (National Clearinghouse on Family Violence, 2004). Shelters often represent the first haven of safety for children and their mothers. This safety net provides a source of protection for those who must cope with the stressful and often traumatic experience of exposure to violence, including children who have survived or witnessed dangerous and/or life-threatening behavior (e.g., seeing, hearing, or direct involvement). Shelters may also be an entry point to help caretakers and children of all ages address the crisis that violence by a partner/caretaker has come to represent. For the purposes of definition, Roberts and Roberts (1990, 2005) have written extensively on what it means to be in crisis. Essentially, four situations are likely to precipitate a crisis state for survivors of violence. First, the survivor experiences a dangerous event that is perceived as threatening to herself and her children. Second, tension and distress intensify, and third, customary attempts at problem solving do not ameliorate the problem. Finally, the event creates unbearable discomfort, creating a sense of imbalance or disequilibrium and a subsequent state of crisis.

The purpose of this chapter is to present a model of crisis intervention with children who may be experiencing complex trauma behaviors and who are residing in shelters for battered women. The underlying assumption of this model is that witnessing partner violence is a frightening, traumatic, and terrifying experience, placing some children under such extreme stress that a crisis is created. The crisis situation may be further exacerbated by contextual factors such as moving from the home (often abruptly), poverty, family separation, and feelings of ambivalence toward the abusive parental figure. These same children may be impacted in many areas of development, and expressions of symptoms can be observed in multiple areas of functioning including school, with peers, and personal functioning. The severity of violence experienced by women is correlated with higher levels of behavioral problems observed in their children (Lemmey et al., 2001). Women utilizing domestic violence shelters often have experienced more severe violence, poverty, and isolation than community samples of domestic violence survivors (Gondolf & Fisher, 1988). Thus, it can be reasoned that children residing in domestic violence shelters represent a particularly vulnerable and symptomatic population. The chapter begins with a brief overview of the crisis intervention literature in shelter settings. Next, the use of the complex trauma perspective (van der Kolk, 2005) is proposed, followed by a model of crisis intervention with child witnesses. Finally, a series of tables illustrates the application of crisis intervention with toddlers, school-age children, and adolescents who may be exhibiting complex trauma behaviors. Two cases are presented to illustrate how a crisis management approach can be used with children in shelter settings.

There is general agreement in the field that the experience of violence in relationships can create a crisis for all those involved.

Typically, the shelter literature has focused on the needs of women and mothers and has supported the usefulness of crisis intervention approaches with women (Andrews, 1990; Dziegielewski & Resnick, 1996; Dziegielewski, Resnick, & Krause, 1996; Roberts, 1984; Roberts & Roberts, 1990, 2003, 2005).

In spite of recognition given to crisis intervention work with women, much less has been written regarding how crisis theory and crisis intervention might be applicable to children who reside in shelters for battered women. Early references (Alessi & Hearn, 1984) focused on identifying feelings, problem solving, love, and termination; whereas others (Rhodes & Zelman, 1986) emphasized the crisis intervention principles of relieving feelings of isolation and alienation and strengthening the relationship between mothers and children. Likewise, Lehmann and Matthews (1998) demonstrated the utility of this approach in shelters using case examples with families. Next, Lehmann and Carlson (1998) used a five-stage model with a focus on trauma symptoms as a way of reducing the crisis experience for children. In spite of these beginnings, current intervention modalities tend to be less oriented toward crisis management, instead focusing on psychoeducational, emotional, and attitudinal changes (Peled & Davis, 1995; Peled & Edleson, 1995). More recently, Rivett, Howarth, and Gordon (2006) reviewed 12 evidence-based programs with children exposed to domestic violence. None of the reviewed programs detailed outcomes of crisis intervention.

CHILD EXPOSURE AND PTSD, COMPLEX TRAUMA, AND DEVELOPMENT

The literature detailing children's exposure to domestic violence along with its impact has been established (e.g., Carlson, 1991, 1996; Jaffe, Wolfe, & Wilson, 1990; Lewis-O'Connor, Sharps, & Humphreys, 2006; Wolfe, 2006). Not surprising, there are short- and long-term consequences (e.g., Lewis-O'Connor, Sharps, & Humphreys, 2006; Wolfe, 2006). At the same time, the professional field has increasingly recognized that in the midst of a child's crisis to exposure some children may exhibit posttraumatic stress disorder (PTSD) symptoms. This section begins by briefly examining the literature regarding children exposed to domestic violence, resulting PTSD symptoms, and a discussion of recent perspectives advocating for a newer trauma overview. To warrant a diagnosis of PTSD, three diagnostic criteria must be met (American Psychiatric Association [APA], 1994). First, there must be exposure to a traumatic stressor that results in a response of fear, helplessness, horror, or, in the case of children, agitated or disorganized behavior. A trauma or traumatic stressor is an experience that involves the threat or perceived threat of death or serious injury. In addition, to receive a PTSD diagnosis, three clusters of symptoms must be experienced for at least 1 month:

1. Reexperiencing of the traumatic event (e.g., repetitive play, upsetting dreams, or psychological and physiological distress in response to reminders of the traumatic event).
2. Avoidance of stimuli associated with the trauma and emotional numbing (e.g., avoiding thoughts or feelings connected with the event, a sense of foreshortened future, or restricted affect).
3. Symptoms of arousal (e.g., angry outbursts, irritability, or trouble sleeping). Acute Stress Disorder can be diagnosed if these responses occur within 1 month of the event (APA, 1994).

Jaffe, Wolfe, Wilson, and Zak (1986) first proposed the view that a subgroup of children exposed to domestic violence could display PTSD. At the present time, a large part of our current understanding of PTSD in children exposed to violence has come from two sources, non-shelter studies of children exposed to violence and studies of children residing in shelters for battered women. First, clinical descriptive accounts have detailed children's PTSD from exposure to domestic violence (e.g., Arroyo & Eth, 1995; Lehmann, Rabenstein, Duff, & Van Meyel, 1994; Pynoos & Eth, 1986; Pynoos & Nader, 1990; Silvern, Karyl, & Landis, 1995) who were not residents in shelters for battered women. Second, the literature has also documented clinical accounts of PTSD (Rossman, 1994; Scheeringa, Zeanah, Drell, & Larrieu, 1995; Silvern & Kaersvang, 1989; Silvern, Karyl, & Landis, 1995) and empirical studies with shelter populations (e.g., Graham Bermann & Levendosky, 1998; Jarvis, Gordon, & Novaco, 2005; Kilpatrick, 1998; Kilpatrick & Williams, 1997; Lehmann, 1997; Lehmann, Spence, & Simmons, in press; Rossman, 1998; Rossman & Ho, 2000).

In spite of the studies looking into the PTSD nomenclature in children, there have been suggestions to broaden the PTSD conceptualization as current criteria may not constitute an exhaustive list (Wolfe & Birt, 1995). For example, some authors have reported other negative coping behaviors such as guilt, shame, fear of recurrence of the event, worry about another person, intervention fantasies, and grief reactions as commonly occurring in the aftermath of exposure to traumatic events (Monahon, 1993; Mowbray, 1988; Nader & Pynoos, 1990). In addition, Terr's (1990, 1991) type II trauma classification scheme includes responses of depression, anger, and dissociation, which are said to be common in children exposed to violent events. Likewise, in a study of traumatized infants, fears and aggressive behaviors not present before the trauma were found (Scheeringa & Zeanah, 1995).

More recently, new advances in the field of child psychiatry and neurodevelopment have questioned the usefulness of a traditional trauma perspective and instead suggested childhood exposure to maltreatment and other traumatic events are multifaceted, complex, and potentially cumulative in terms of disorder over the developmental span of the child (Cook et al., 2005; van der Kolk, 2005).

Van der Kolk (2005) has raised a number of diagnostic issues that must be considered as the responses to children in shelters change. First, a PTSD diagnosis is not child sensitive, in that children who experience one or more traumatic experiences display complex disturbances. Next, he argues this leads to mistakenly seeing children with comorbid symptoms, thus running the risk of losing the complexity of symptom presentation and possibly applying unhelpful treatment conditions. Third, a traditional diagnosis does not capture the multiplicity of symptoms resulting from exposure during developmentally sensitive periods. Finally, the author raises the point that many chronically traumatized children might not qualify for a PTSD diagnosis unless they were exposed to events defined as traumatic even though they might be symptomatic.

Complex Trauma and Development

This chapter not only advocates for an expanded understanding of how exposure to violence includes much of the PTSD nomenclature but also encompasses a broader classification of trauma. Hence, we refer to complex trauma as one possible avenue of understanding a child's response to the crisis of domestic violence. Complex trauma is the experience of chronic exposure to developmentally adverse traumatic events that often begin in the child's caregiving

environment from an early age (Spinazzola et al., 2005). Although
children may continue to exhibit PTSD, additional symptoms extend
beyond the original complaints. For example, Ackerman et al. (1998)
found that PTSD was the fourth most common diagnosis behind that
of separation anxiety and oppositional and conduct disorders in a
sample of sexually and physically abused children. Even in adults
with complex trauma, domains of functioning have extended beyond PTSD (Felitti, Anda, & Nordenberg, 1998; van der Kolk et al.,
1996).

Complex trauma may be seen as one possible way to organize
the traumatic, behavioral, and emotional responses in child witnesses who are in shelters for battered women. An important assumption here is that multiple exposures to interpersonal violence are
complex, with consistent and predictable effects in many areas of
functioning (van der Kolk, 2005). To assist the reader, Table 8.1 highlights the Trauma Developmental Disorder as an alternative diagnosis that articulates the range of a child's suffering (National Child
Traumatic Stress Network–NCTSN, 2003; van der Kolk, 2005). The
disorder is organized around three major issues for children. First,
there is likely to be dysregulation in response to traumatic reminders.
Here, children may respond along a wide continuum ranging from
underreacting to overreacting behaviorally and/or emotionally in response to stimuli (e.g., a loud noise). In this case stimuli might have
little to no effect on nontraumatized children. The second issue includes stimulus generalization or the expectation that the violence
and hurt will continue unabated. The end result may be children who
respond to minor stresses with hyperactivity, aggression, or freezing.
Finally, complex trauma disorder presumes that children organize
their behavior to avoid the impact of the trauma. As a result, children develop relationships around the expectation or prevention of
victimization.

Table 8.2 refers to the potential outcomes of complex trauma that
extend beyond PTSD. In this case, we consider the outcomes to be
responses child witnesses to domestic violence may exhibit given the
chronic nature of their experiences. Table 8.2 (Cook et al., 2005)
highlights a list of each domain along with respective symptoms. The
table and responses have been identified from existing child clinical research literature as well as from the National Child Traumatic
Stress Network expertise (NCTSN, 2003). The domains are intended
to be developmentally sensitive, in that outcome of chronic exposure

TABLE 8.1   Trauma Developmental Disorder

A. Exposure
  • Multiple or chronic exposure to one or more forms of developmentally adverse interpersonal trauma (e.g., abandonment, betrayal, physical/sexual abuse, threats to body integrity, emotional abuse, witnessing violence, and death)
  • Subjective experience (e.g., rage, betrayal, fear, resignation, defeat, shame)
B. Triggered pattern of repeated dysregulation in response to trauma cues. Dysregulation (high or low) in presence of cues. Changes persist and do not return to baseline; not reduced in intensity by conscious awareness.
  • Affective
  • Somatic (e.g., physiological, motoric, medical)
  • Behavioral (e.g., reenactment, cutting)
  • Cognitive (e.g., thinking it may happen again, confusion, dissociation, depersonalization)
  • Relational (e.g., clinging, distrustful, oppositional, compliant)
  • Self-attribution (e.g., self-hate, blame)
C. Persistently altered attributions and expectancies
  • Negative self-attribution
  • Distrust of protective caretaker
  • Loss of expectancy of protection by others
  • Loss of trust in social agencies to protect
  • Lack of access to social justice/retribution
D. Functional impairment
  • Educational
  • Familial
  • Peer
  • Legal
  • Vocational

to violence might be traced from attachment experiences through more cognitive related problems later in adolescence. Table 8.2 also takes into account the growing relationship among neurodevelopment, stress management, and trauma. It should be noted that each of the domains is thought to have a place in the stages of child development and can act as markers for identifying age-appropriate and age-disrupted changes. The correlation between mind and body changes in the domains are thought to develop when an infant or child is exposed to unpredictable and uncontrolled danger because the child's body must allocate survival resources normally reserved for growth and development (NCTSN).

TABLE 8.2   Domains of Complex Trauma: Associated Outcomes

I. Attachment
Uncertainty about the reliability and
  predictability of the world
Problems with boundaries
Distrust and suspiciousness
Social isolation
Interpersonal difficulties
Difficulty attuning to other people's emotional
  states
Difficulty with perspective taking
Difficulty enlisting other people as allies

II. Biology
Sensorimotor developmental problems
Hypersensitivity to physical contact
Analgesia
Problems with coordination, balance, body tone
Difficulties localizing skin contact
Somatization
Increased medical problems across a wide span,
  for example, pelvic pain, asthma, skin
  problems, autoimmune disorders,
  pseudoseizure

III. Affect Regulation
Difficulty with emotional self-regulation
Difficulty describing feelings and internal
  experience
Problems knowing and describing internal
  states
Difficulty communicating wishes and desires

IV. Behavioral Control
Poor modulation of impulses
Self-destructive behavior
Aggression against others
Pathological self-soothing behavior
Sleep disturbance
Eating disorder
Substance abuse
Excessive compliance
Oppositional behavior
Difficulty understanding and complying with
  rules
Communication of traumatic past by
  reenactment in day-to-day behavior or play
  (sexual, aggressive, etc.)

V. Self-Concept
Lack of a continuous,
  predictable sense of self
Poor sense of separateness
Disturbance of body image
Low self-esteem
Shame and guilt

VI. Dissociation
Distinct alteration in states of
  consciousness
Amnesia
Depersonalization and
  derealization
Two or more distinct states of
  consciousness, with impaired
  memory for state-based events

VII. Cognition
Difficulties in attention
  regulation and executive
  functioning
Lack of sustained curiosity
Problems with processing novel
  information
Problems focusing on and
  completing tasks
Problems with object constancy
Difficulty planning and
  anticipating
Problems understanding own
  contribution to what happens
  to them
Learning difficulties
Problems with language
  development
Problems with orientation in
  time and space
Acoustic and visual perceptual
  problems
Impaired comprehension of
  complex visual–spatial
  patterns

CRISIS INTERVENTION: A MODEL FOR WORKING
WITH CHILD WITNESSES

Crisis intervention models have been used effectively with children
and adolescents who have experienced traumatic stressors such as
community violence (Pynoos & Nader, 1988), natural disasters (Haizlip & Corder, 1996; Terr, 1992), homicide and rape (Eth & Pynoos,
1994; Pynoos & Eth, 1986; Pynoos & Nader, 1990, 1993), and school
suicide (Wenckstern & Leenaars, 1993). In each case, addressing
trauma symptoms was considered essential to reducing the stress
of those involved. The section below proposes an adaptation of
Roberts's Crisis Intervention Model (Roberts, 1990, 1996; Roberts
& Roberts, 1990, 2005). These authors have promoted the idea that
knowledge of crisis theory and intervention approaches are essential
to workers in shelter settings.

Roberts's (1991, 1996) model of crisis intervention describes seven
stages of working through crises with adults. These stages include:

1. Assessing lethality and safety needs.
2. Establishing rapport.
3. Identifying major problems.
4. Dealing with feelings and providing support.
5. Exploring alternatives.
6. Formulating an action plan.
7. Follow-up.

Dziegielewski, Resnick, and Krause (1996, p. 129) have characterized this approach as "clearly applicable in the case of intervention
with those involved with domestic violence." As currently formulated,
the model is intended for adults, although Jobes and Berman (1996)
have applied it to suicidal adolescents.

The Roberts model (Roberts, 1990, 1996; Roberts & Roberts, 1990,
2005) takes the position that crisis intervention can be a positive
experience, bringing about balance as well as change. At the heart of
the model is the worker–client relationship, through which support
is offered and expression of feelings and alternative problem solving
are facilitated, thereby providing the context for the client to return
to the state of functioning that existed prior to the crisis.

The following discussion highlights a model of crisis intervention specific to child witnesses for use by child advocates. Roberts's

seven-stage crisis intervention approach has been modified and collapsed into five stages. The model is flexible, in that symptoms and
problems may appear at different stages, and tasks or activities from
earlier stages may be employed in subsequent stages. For example,
although safety should be assessed in the initial stage, child advocates must be mindful of the need to assess safety during the entire
intervention process.

Stage I: Establishing Rapport and Assessing Danger

The safety of all family members must be the first priority. Because
the risk to family members for further harm by the abuser may continue during the shelter stay, it is important to assess lethality during
the initial stage of crisis intervention. Consequently, advocates need
to ask mothers about the extent of risk for current or future harm to
themselves and children as early as possible. Information on factors
such as the severity and frequency of injury, availability or previous
use of weapons, threats of homicide/suicide, personal assaults in public, strangulation behaviors, substance abuse, sexual assault, criminal,
or stalking behavior provides the child advocate with information regarding the level of danger (Campbell et al., 2003). Additional factors
to screen include proximity of children to the violence, relationship
with the perpetrator, parental psychopathology such as mental illness,
chronicity of the violence, external family response, and children's
worries about the safety of significant others (Pynoos & Nader, 1988,
1990, 1993).

Stalking issues are of particular concern for mothers and children fleeing abuse. The presence of stalking behaviors serves as a
significant correlate to lethality (McFarlane, Campbell, & Watson,
2002); thus, mothers must maintain a high level of hypervigilance
to ensure their survival. This survival mode poses challenges to parenting, whether or not the abuser is the parent. In circumstances
where the abuser is not biologically related to the children, the risk
for lethality increases (Campbell et al., 2003). When the abuser is
the biological parent, custody and visitation issues often serve as
pseudo-legitimate means for abusers to manipulate, threaten, and
harass their ex-intimates (Spence-Diehl, 2004). Under these conditions, children are placed at the center of a volatile and dangerous
conflict. Through legal mandates or agreements, they may spend

time or share residence with their abusive parent on a regular basis. During those times, they are expected to maintain parent–child bonds, and may or may not be cognizant of their role as an information source for the abusive parent to manipulate and utilize for ongoing stalking pursuits. Given this complexity, it is critical for advocates to carefully assess these factors and consider the interplay of individual, familial, and community systems. As such, advocates may find it helpful to coordinate the involvement of multiple agency representatives in the assessment and strategizing process (Spence-Diehl).

Establishing rapport forms the basis for developing a relationship among the child witness, the female caretaker, and the child advocate. Rapport building generally begins shortly after families enter the shelter and the advocate is introduced to the child. Children may be upset, appear passive, inhibited, or agitated, demonstrating the initial signs of posttraumatic stress. Providing information, smiles, positive gestures, or touring the shelter can convey a sense of respect, nonintrusiveness, and safety to the child.

Additional methods of establishing rapport can occur via the intake process. Advocates are given an opportunity to interview the child about who they are, what has occurred, what the child may have seen, how the child feels about the violence, and whether the child has been assaulted. This process can create a "window of opportunity" to help establish trust, a sense of safety, and a working relationship with the child. Introduction booklets encourage the child to describe personal strengths, talents, and special interests. Examples of such resources may be found in Peled and Davis (1995), Jaffe, Wolfe and Wilson (1990), and Carlson (1996).

Stage II: Identifying the Presence of Complex Trauma

Some children who enter a shelter may react immediately to the violence, whereas others may seem to show no reaction. Regardless of a child's early response, it is possible for traumatic memories to resurface, sometimes in response to internal or external triggers that are reminiscent of the trauma and at other times seemingly unpredictable. Because children need to make sense of what has happened, their minds can remain active in trying to make sense of the traumatic event (Pynoos & Nader, 1993). With help and over time, painful events can be processed and responded to so that the child can feel some relief.

During Stage II, and over the course of a child's stay in the shelter, advocates need to assess for the presence of behaviors in four domains that originate from Table 8.1 (cited earlier).

Domain 1: Exposure.   Advocates need to assess and get accurate information of the extent of exposure. Here, it is important to determine the extent the child has been a witness to short- or long-term violence. In particular, advocates should be aware of the type of violence and whether there was proximity to the event. It is also important to place all the exposed behavior into a developmental context with the idea that the younger, the longer, the more exposed a child may be, the greater developmental effects are likely to be observed.

Domain 2: Complex Trauma and Dysregulated Symptomatology.   Typically, observations of these responses are associated with much of Table 8.1. Following this table, advocates may be able to identify the dysregulated responses as related to a number of trauma/PTSD responses observed in children entering a shelter. Three main features are identified.

Reexperiencing Responses. A hallmark of this feature is the experience of intrusive memories, coupled with intense physiological reactions. Most children will not have flashbacks (Pynoos & Nader, 1988); instead, their recall will be organized around anchor points. "Anchor points" refer to certain features of the traumatic event that become central and serve as cues for recall (Pynoos, 1996). These anchor points (e.g., remembering a mother's scream, injury, or blood; the fear of being hurt and feeling unsafe; the angry look of the perpetrator) may influence their disclosures and emotional intensity of responses. Upsetting nightmares are another common form of intrusion where children may incorporate direct reenactment of the violence (Pynoos & Nader, 1988). Such dreams can be particularly troublesome due to the fears and anxiety they engender. Traumatic play is yet another reexperiencing symptom. Examples include the re-dramatization of episodes of the event or the repetition during play of traumatic themes (Pynoos, 1996; Pynoos & Nader, 1990, 1993). Observing and responding to traumatic play in shelter children may be critical, particularly in the case of toddlers who may not have the verbal maturity to express themselves. The outcome of traumatic play will be dependent on whether it provides relief for the child or instead only creates more anxiety (Nader & Pynoos, 1990). Impaired learning is thought to be associated with sleep disturbance and intrusive reminders.

Avoidance Responses. The responses in this section have been found inconsistently in children during the aftermath of trauma (Pynoos & Nader, 1988). Avoidance symptoms may appear as a general distancing or withdrawal from the external world. Following the witnessing of a mother's assault, children may exhibit a number of specific avoidance behaviors, including "(1) lessened interest in play or usually other enjoyable activities, (2) feeling more distant from their parents or friends and/or more alone with their feelings, and (3) not wishing to be aware of feelings" (Pynoos & Nader, 1988, pp. 448–449), and (4) a sense of a foreshortened future (Arroyo & Eth, 1995).

Arousal Responses. In their work with children exposed to violent death, Pynoos and Nader (1990) described behaviors typical of this second domain, including prolonged hypervigilance and exaggerated startle reactions, concentration problems at school, and irritability in response to reminders of the traumatic event. For example, child advocates may see children in extended states of physical and mental readiness, as if the violent event could reoccur at any moment. These symptoms may be coupled with the observation of anger directed toward the mother, who may be perceived as having not protected herself or the family, or conversely, breaking up the family.

Domain 3: Complex Trauma and Developmental Harm. The current domain follows from the seven criteria listed in Table 8.2. Here, advocates have a template for observing any number of areas that may be developmentally impacting the child witness. It is also equally important advocates notice areas of the child's behavior/responses that are appropriate and which may speak to their natural coping ability. Furthermore, if the advocate identifies areas where the child appears to be developmentally behind, these should be discussed with the mother to determine whether the behaviors represent a temporary regression or actual delays. For example, a potty trained 5-year-old may regress in a shelter setting and wet or soil himself or herself.

Domain 4: Parental Involvement.   The final domain of Stage II looks to
the role of parental involvement in the aftermath of exposure to violence. The experience of an assault, police involvement, leaving for
the safety of a shelter, and the crisis this entails will understandably be
upsetting to most caretakers. When mothers are in distress and frightened, their ability to nurture their children and maintain routines
and predictability may be compromised as they attempt to cope with
all that has occurred. Mothers may need assistance to understand
the link between the exposure to chronic violence and the extent
of their children's development and complex trauma responses. It is
also helpful for advocates to minimize discussions of the violence with
the mothers in the presence of the children and encourage mothers
to be cognizant of this when they are talking with other parents at
the shelter.

In the aftermath of a traumatic event, parental support appears
to be the key mediator in determining how children adapt to their
situations (NCTSN, 2003). Three key parental responses advocates
can look for in caretakers include believing a child's experience,
tolerating a child's responses, and managing their own responses.
Additionally, for mothers of children showing conduct problems,
the combination of social and instrumental support for the family
and child management and nurturing skills training for the mothers
has been effective in reducing behavioral problems and promoting
children's happiness and well-being (McDonald, Jouriles, & Skopp,
2006b).

The technology for assessing complex trauma has grown and child
advocates have a number of options from which to choose. For very
young children, assessment should include direct observation of behaviors and asking mothers about possible problems or symptoms
(Osofsky & Fenichel, 1994, 1996; Zeanah & Scheeringa, 1994). Additionally, Nader and Pynoos (1991) and Arroyo and Eth (1995) have
identified play and drawing techniques that may be useful with older
children and adolescents. The play and drawing (draw-a-picture, tell-
a-story) exercises allow for "reexamination and giving new meaning
to aspects of the event or for reexperiencing and reworking of the
memory and the emotions" (Nader & Pynoos, p. 378).

If time permits for children in shelters, Arroyo and Eth (1995)
recommend a three-stage evaluation interview that is appropriate
for crisis intervention work. The opening, trauma, and closure
phases of the interviews facilitate exploration of the child's subjective

experience and provide an opportunity to discuss the early emotional and traumatic impact of the witnessed violence. In the opening phase, the child is provided with reassurance that the adult is experienced and knows something about what the child has gone through. The child is then invited to partake in a drawing or clay-modeling exercise of their own choosing. After it is completed, the child is asked to talk about the drawing or figures.

During the trauma phase of the evaluation, the child is asked about references to the trauma that are evident in the drawing or figure. It is essential to proceed slowly, offering support and reassurance throughout. When appropriate, the child is encouraged to describe exactly what happened, as well as his or her feelings and fantasies about what occurred. Wishes for revenge are common, as are wishes for reconciliation. It is helpful to validate for children that these conflicting feelings are common.

During the closure phase, the focus is on ending the interview and separating from the interviewer. The content of the session should be summarized and reviewed. The interview not only identifies the intrusive events but also assists the child in finding the words to talk about their experiences. Because traumatic responses change with development, cognitive distortions regarding rescue, intervention, or revenge can be clarified through play or drawings.

Stage III: Providing Support and Addressing Feelings

Two important components of providing support and facilitating expression of feelings in times of crisis are personal qualities of the child advocate and their relationship-building skills. Myer and Hanna (1996) have listed some worker qualities that may be helpful in shelter settings. Child advocates must be quick-thinking; they must be able to assess the severity of the situation and a child's responses in a brief time period. The ability to maintain a sense of calm in the face of a child's upset is very important and should allow rapport to develop. Appropriate humor is also an important attribute, and patience is essential in working with these families. In addition, child advocates must be creative in responding to stressful situations and able to provide nonjudgmental support and validation to children and mothers (Hughes & Marshall, 1995). Finally, knowledge of normal child development is critically important.

The ability to be supportive in the face of crisis calls for relationship-building skills, and Hughes and Marshall (1995) offer useful guidelines for those who wish to work with child witnesses. Empathy, patience, and flexibility are crucial characteristics. Power struggles should be avoided. Children must be allowed to talk at their own pace, taking into account their age and stage of development. Advocates must also be mindful of the fear, anxiety, and sense of displacement children will experience. They must also be sensitive to the burden of secrecy that children experience about what they have witnessed (Peled, 1996). When they talk to others about what has happened in their family, children may fear retribution from parental figures for violating family rules. Unraveling such secrecy must be done in a noncoercive manner. Children need to know they have permission to talk about such secrets, and mothers can prove helpful by giving children explicit permission to talk about what has happened. At the same time, advocates must carefully and respectfully explain the limits of confidentiality, noting that if children share information that suggests they are being harmed by someone, the advocate may need to speak to other adults. Children must feel empowered to discuss issues freely, but also have the right to withdraw at any stage of the interview.

Similarly, the writings of Pynoos and Nader (1988) offer some specific skills for dealing with support and feelings. They suggest that support should convey acceptance and a willingness to hear everything, regardless of how terrible some events may have been. The integrity of the child can begin to be restored when he or she has permission to speak of the most terrifying experiences. An opportunity is created in a safe and comfortable setting to begin the process of making sense of these frightening events. Being able to discuss the traumatic experience in detail can give the child a sense of mastery and sets them on the road to healthy coping. Dealing with feelings also helps link some of the cognitive understandings to the event as well as to the feelings of helplessness. For example, clarification of revenge fantasies helps to normalize these feelings and prevent a preoccupation with them. The child may also experience a sense of relief from carrying painful secrets. Support and talking about feelings may also assist the child in putting some continuity in their life experiences. Some children may show a marked change in life attitudes or disclose coexisting stresses, and discussion of events and feelings can provide a vehicle for linking events and stressors. Child advocates will find numerous aids to assist in this process in the form of feeling workbooks, storybooks, and videos in the reviews of Peled and Davis (1995) and Carlson (1996).

Stage IV: Exploring Alternatives and Formulating an Action Plan

The traumatic experience of witnessing the violent assault of one's mother and entrance into a shelter can lead to a wide range of changes in the child's life situation (Pynoos & Nader, 1993). Often there is a period of uncertainty as the mother decides whether she will return to the abusive partner or start her life anew. There may be changes in life circumstances and distress related to traumatic symptoms, disrupted peer relations, anger control difficulties, poor school performance, and feelings of incompetence. The child advocate must remain attentive to all these issues, taking an active stance with mothers and school personnel, and be prepared to assist the child with practical and helpful responses.

In Stage IV, two alternatives may face child witnesses. Some children will be returning to the home where the abuse took place. They may have ambivalent feelings about going home and are at continued risk of complex trauma responses due to fears of recurrence. On the other hand, some mothers will be relocating, starting a new life apart from the abusive partner, in a new home. Their children are likely to have mixed reactions, especially if the new home is also in a different neighborhood or community. This may mean the need to adjust to a new set of circumstances with accompanying stressors, such as a new school, having to make new friends, reduced economic circumstances, and so forth. Furthermore, if the abuser is the child's parent, custody and visitation issues may be at the forefront as well. Children will need assistance in preparing for and adjusting to these changes.

Stage V: Follow-Up

After children have left the shelter, there may be opportunities for follow-up activities to monitor their postshelter adjustment. If aftercare services are available, providing an ongoing group experience for children can be helpful.

Because traumatic experiences require time to process, child witnesses are likely to continue to be working on these issues after leaving the shelter. They may continue to encounter reminders of the violence, for instance, when their father gets angry and yells loudly. They are also at risk for developing longer term reactions to the abuse they have witnessed, including mental disorders, such as phobias or conduct disorder. As a result, they may need to be referred to a mental health center or family agency for evaluation by a professional specializing in child mental health. Such reactions are more likely when children have experienced exposure to severe or chronic traumatic events, especially if other stressors are also present (Pynoos, 1996). Referral for a physical examination or evaluation of school-related difficulties may also be appropriate.

APPLICATION OF CRISIS INTERVENTION WITH COMPLEX TRAUMA

Although much has been written with respect to complex trauma and children, the direct application of treatment approaches remains to be developed. In a survey of 118 clinicians who had child trauma caseloads, Spinazzola et al. (2005) concluded that no clear consensus emerged regarding the effectiveness of available modalities (e.g., weekly individual therapy, family therapy, play therapy, and expressive therapy). Consequently, the application of crisis intervention with children exposed to domestic violence who may exhibit complex trauma symptoms should be considered a new, yet exciting field of study. Toward this end, Tables 8.3, 8.4, and 8.5 offer some practical suggestions for addressing complex trauma in young children, school-age children, and adolescents in shelters for battered women. A number of the suggestions have been adapted from the clinical work of Lieberman (2006; young children), Deblinger (2006; school-age children), and Pelcovitz (2006; adolescents). Each 3 × 5 table gives examples of complex trauma/complex trauma relief, child advocate roles/activities, and child advocate aids along the five-stage continuum. These suggestions are not meant to be comprehensive or exhaustive and should be adapted based on the individual case and circumstances. Two case examples illustrate how the suggestions in the tables might be used in shelter settings.

TABLE 8.3 Crisis Intervention With Young Children

	Stage I Establishing rapport and assessing danger	Stage II Identifying symptoms and problem	Stage III Providing support and addressing feelings	Stage IV Exploring alternative action plans	Stage V Follow-up
Complex Trauma/ Complex Trauma Relief	Passivity or withdrawal Helplessness Fear of new environment Confusion Anxious attachment	Re-experiencing symptoms Avoidance symptom Increased arousal/startle responses Affect constriction Decreased concentration Associated Outcome: New Symptoms	Recognizing the stress of mother Support the modeling of acceptable behaviors Child-centered play may help facilitate relief	Support strengths of child/mother Interpretation: linking past and present	Support family decision for follow-up of child's needs Make referrals when necessary Address safety plans
Child advocate roles and activities	Establishing rapport Assessing danger Assessing for maltreatment Assess for coercive or punitive parenting	Assess for complex trauma while providing for comfort and support of all family Pay attention to developmental strengths/disparities	Provide support Facilitate verbal expression of feelings Maintain parental consistency of care and stability	Promote developmental progress through play, physical contact, and language Concrete assistance to caretaker Articulate and support caretaker's plan	Be available for follow-up calls
Child advocate aids	Intake process Introduction booklet Tour of shelter Severity of Violence Matrix	Direct observation Interview mother Evaluation interview	Make use of a variety of toys Help child attach names to feelings Drawing Clay modeling Encourage storytelling Encourage active play to reduce biochemical stress responses	Facilitate play, art work Mother/child engagement in the playroom Reinforce observations of prosocial behaviors	

TABLE 8.4 Crisis Intervention With School-Age Children

	Stage I Establishing rapport and assessing danger	Stage II Identifying symptoms and problem	Stage III Providing support and addressing feelings	Stage IV Exploring alternative action plans	Stage V Follow-up
Complex Trauma/ Complex Trauma Relief	Responsibilty and guilt Fear of new environment Confusion Safety concerns Concern for other, e.g., father	Re-experiencing symptoms Avoidance symptom Arousal symptom Intervention fantasies Associated Outcome: New Symptoms	Individual/group therapy Provide information to mother re: child's needs & development Encourage humor and fun	Help mother respond to child's behavior Support all family members' strengths Deal with missing/absent parent Deal with fear of returning home or unknown future	Support family's wish for referrals Address safety plans
Child advocate roles and activities	Establishing rapport Assessing danger Assessing for maltreatment Assess for coercive or punitive parenting	Assess for complex trauma symptoms Pay attention to developmental strengths/disparities Clarify responsibility for the abuse Assess for perceived threat to death/harm Assess for multiple sources of trauma	Provide support Facilitate verbal expression of feelings Maintain consistency of care and stability Encourage expression of feelings Facilitate school entry	Be available for individual/family work Monitor play Prepare for leaving shelter Prepare for return to home school or new school	Be available for follow-up calls
Child advocate aids	Intake process Introduction booklet Tour of shelter Severity of Violence Matrix	Direct observation Interview mother Interview child re: what they witnessed Use paper/pencil tests	Listen to feelings and help child attach label Drawing Clay modeling Encourage storytelling Encourage exercise and active sports to reduce biochemical stress responses	Use of group curriculums (e.g., Loosley, 2006) Identify and reinforce child's strengths, positive coping strategies, and prosocial behaviors	

TABLE 8.5   Crisis Intervention With Adolescents

	Stage I Establishing rapport and assessing danger	Stage II Identifying symptoms and problem	Stage III Providing support and addressing feelings	Stage IV Exploring alternative action plans	Stage V Follow-up
Complex Trauma/ Complex Trauma Relief	Anger at having to be at the shelter Embarrassment, shame	Re-experiencing symptoms Avoidance symptom Arousal symptom Associated Outcome: New Symptoms Be cognizant of use of substances Physiological response to stress may be high	Individual/group therapy Provide information to mother re: adolescent needs Encourage humor and fun	Look for and support all family strengths Consider career plans Support coping skills in nonviolent ways Help identify family/friends who are nonviolent	Support family's/adolescent's wish for referrals Address safety plans
Child advocate roles and activities	Establishing rapport Normalize embarrassment Assessing danger and safety Assess for coercive or punitive parenting	Assess complex trauma and associated behaviors Assess for suicide/ideation Assess for perceived threat of death/harm Assess for multiple sources of trauma	Provide support Facilitate verbal expression of feelings Maintain consistency of care and stability Encourage expression of fantasies	Be able to address power/control issues Help with school entry Be aware of and deal with developmental issues of autonomy, puberty, sexuality, peers Be prepared to actively engage caretaker	Be available for follow-up calls from mother or adolescent
Child advocate aids	Intake process Introduction booklet Tour of shelter Severity of Violence Matrix	Direct observation Interview mother Interview adolescents re: what they witnessed Evaluation interview (Arroyo & Eth, 1995) Use of paper/pencil tests	Art therapy Use of journal Encourage telling of story Normalize emotions Encourage exercise and supports to minimize biochemical stress response	Use of group curriculums Identify and reinforce positive coping strategies and prosocial behaviors	

CASE SCENARIOS

Case 1

Allison, age 7, entered the shelter with her mother, 9-year-old brother, and 3-year-old sister. Allison appeared frightened and clung to her mother. This was Allison's second stay at the shelter in 2 years. A child advocate completed a children's intake with her mother. Allison had seen her mother hit, pushed, and kicked by her father. She had witnessed this kind of violence for most of her life. The first night Allison and her family came to the shelter, a tour of the shelter was arranged. The child advocate met with Allison the next day to complete a "Get to Know You" form that addressed her favorite food, hobbies, school subjects, and so forth. In addition, Allison was asked if she knew why her family had come to the shelter and she replied, "Dad and Mom are always fighting too much."

The "Get to Know You" form helped to identify symptoms and negative feelings Allison associated with the abuse and coming to the shelter. Allison disclosed that she was scared and worried about the past hitting. The advocate asked Allison to identify three wishes. The first and only wish she had was that her mom and dad would not fight. Children's staff noted other problem areas in Allison that included fighting with her siblings, displaying anger toward her mother, and general defiance. Allison also seemed to be very protective of her mother and showed reluctance to participate in activities with the other children.

Allison's feelings and symptoms were addressed primarily through a shelter support group. The groups emphasized that abuse was not acceptable and that children were not to blame for the violence. During a feelings support group, Allison learned to recognize and label the different feelings associated with family abuse. Subsequent groups helped Allison look at her strengths, coping skills, and friendships. In addition, Allison worked on developing a protection plan and safety skills by practicing calling 911. She wrote on an index card where she would hide and which adult she would talk to about the abuse.

Close to exiting, the child advocate spoke with Allison about what she had learned while in the shelter and addressed continued concerns about safety for the future. . . . Overall, Allison showed an understanding of abuse, said she felt safe, and reported positive feelings about participation in the children's program. Allison's mother was accepted into the transitional living program that includes weekly outreach support groups for children focused on family violence, safety, self-esteem, and anger control.

Case 2

Glen, age 4, and his mother were admitted into the shelter. Both were fleeing the abusive father for the first time. At admission, both were very anxious. To be helpful, the case manager introduced Glen and his mom to the child advocate, who encouraged Glen to pick out a stuffed animal. He smiled and clung to the animal tightly, while his mother completed the intake interview. Glen and his mother were taken on a tour of the shelter, with Glen continuing to hug his stuffed animal, staying close to his mother's side.

Once the family settled, the mother completed the PTSD Semi-structured Interview and Observation Record for Infants and Young Children (Zeanah & Scheeringa, 1994). From the mother's observations, Glen appeared to exhibit symptoms in each of the three domains of reexperiencing, avoidance, and hyperarousal. Glen engaged in traumatic play, had regressed to wetting the bed at night, and was having trouble sleeping. He continued to appear anxious. As their stay continued, staff observed Glen behaving aggressively toward his mother and other children. The child advocate was concerned Glen might be reenacting the violence he had seen his father direct toward his mother.

The child advocate talked to Glen's mother about his aggressive behavior, and both agreed to a time-out plan to be used when Glen behaved aggressively. The advocate helped model appropriate parenting behavior when Glen's mother gave a time out by using eye contact, speaking softly, and validating his feelings of anger or frustration. This approach helped Glen feel safe and understand the limits and rules at the shelter. He was also encouraged to verbalize his feelings, rather than act them out on others. Staff worked with his mother to use praise as positive reinforcement when Glen was able to express his feelings. Although it was difficult for his mother, she was able to remain calm while Glen was crying and angry. She made an effort to talk softly to Glen, and her soothing voice seemed to calm and reassure him. Although still crying, he would hug her as she rocked him back and forth, whispering, "Mommy loves you."

When staff noticed Glen playing at the shelter, they would help him express his feelings. When he engaged in trauma play, he seemed to be acting out revenge behaviors toward his father. The shelter staff would permit such play, in the playroom using behaviors to reflect feelings Glen might have.

With regards to Glen not sleeping, the advocate suggested maintaining a consistent routine at bedtime. She also suggested that the mother ask Glen about his bad dreams, which were based on his fears that his father would come and find them and hurt his mother. She was encouraged to let him describe his nightmares, followed by reassuring him that they were in a safe place now, and allowing him to remain in her bed.

Prior to leaving the shelter, Glen's mother received referrals to agencies that might further help Glen. At the same time, the child advocate and Glen's mother noticed a small change in how Glen responded to his mother. He seemed less anxious and more comfortable with his surroundings.

CONCLUSION

The experience of witnessing domestic violence between one's parents can leave some children vulnerable to exhibiting one or more complex trauma responses. When this occurs, observing for responses can be found in virtually any number of a child's functioning. These reactions create a state of crisis for affected children that may require crisis intervention when children and their mothers enter a shelter for battered women. Consequently, child advocates may have an opportunity to provide some relief to the child.

We have presented a model of crisis intervention for child witnesses with a focus on complex trauma behaviors that may impact children at any stage of development. The intent here has been to present a broader conceptualization of a trauma developmental perspective (van der Kolk, 2005), one that includes PTSD symptoms as well as a host of associated behavior and emotional responses. The model recognizes that children's complex trauma responses are influenced not only by the nature of the violence itself, but also by key issues that can help explain resulting behavior. To begin a process of placing the child's crisis in context, we have adapted Roberts and Roberts's crisis intervention approach for use with children in shelters for battered women. The five stages of the model we proposed include establishing rapport and assessing danger, identifying symptoms and problems, providing support and addressing feelings, exploring and formulating alternative action plans, and follow-up. A 3 × 5 table matrix has been provided with suggestions on how child advocates might intervene with shelter children. Finally, two case studies are presented to illustrate further how the model can be applied in shelter settings.

REFERENCES

Ackerman, P. T., Newton, J. E. O., McPherson, B. W., Jones, J. G., & Dykman, R. A. (1998). Prevalence of post traumatic stress disorder and other psychiatric diagnoses in three groups of abused children (sexual, physical, and both). *Child Abuse and Neglect, 22,* 759–774.

Aguilera, D. C., & Messick, J. M. (1984). *Crisis intervention: Theory and methodology.* St. Louis, MO: Mosby.

Alessi, J. J., & Hearn, K. (1984). Group treatment of children in shelters for battered women. In A. R. Roberts (Ed.), *Battered women and their families* (pp. 49–61). New York: Springer Publishing.

American Psychiatric Association. (1994). *Diagnostic and statistical manual of mental disorders* (DSM–IV) (4th ed.). Washington, DC: American Psychiatric Association.

Andrews, A. B. (1990). Crisis and recovery services for family violence survivors. In A. R. Roberts (Ed.), *Helping crime victims: Policy, practice and research* (pp. 206–232). Newbury Park, CA: Sage.

Arroyo, W., & Eth, S. (1995). Assessment following violence-witnessing trauma. In E. Peled, P. G. Jaffe, & J. L. Edleson (Eds.), *Ending the cycle of violence: Community responses to children of battered women* (pp. 28–42). Thousand Oaks, CA: Sage.

Campbell, J., Webster, D., Koziol-McLain, J., Block, C. Campbell, D., Curry, M. A., et al. (2003). Risk factors for femicide in abusive relationships: Results from a multisite case control study. *American Journal of Public Health, 93*(7), 1089–1097.

Caplan, G. (1964). *Principles of preventive psychiatry.* New York: Basic Books.

Carlson, B. E. (1990). Adolescent observers of marital violence. *Journal of Family Violence, 5,* 285–299.

Carlson, B. E. (1991). Outcomes of physical abuse and observation of marital violence among adolescents in placement. *Journal of Interpersonal Violence, 6,* 526–534.

Carlson, B. E. (1996). Children of battered women: Research, programs, and services. In A. R. Roberts (Ed.), *Helping battered women: New perspective and remedies* (pp. 172–187). New York: Oxford University Press.

Cook, A., Spinazzola, J., Ford, J., Lanktree, C., Blaustein, M., Cloitre, M., et al. (2005). Complex trauma in children and adolescents. *Psychiatric Annals, 35,* 390–398.

Davis, L. V., & Carlson, B. E. (1987). Observation of spouse abuse: What happens to the children? *Journal of Interpersonal Violence, 2,* 278–291.

Deblinger, A. F. (2006). *Trauma's impact in middle childhood.* Available from the National Child Traumatic Stress Network. Retrieved July 1, 2006, from http://www.nctsnet.org.

Domestic Abuse Intervention Project. (1997). *Creating a process of change for men who batter.* Unpublished manuscript.

Dziegielewski, S. F., & Resnick, C. (1996). Crisis assessment and intervention: Abused women in the shelter setting. In A. R. Roberts (Ed.), *Crisis management and brief treatment: Theory, technique, and applications* (pp. 123–141). Chicago: Nelson-Hall.

Dziegieliewski, S. F., Resnick, C., & Krause, N. (1996). Shelter based crisis intervention with abused women. In A. Roberts (Ed.), *Helping battered women: New perspectives* (pp. 159–171). New York: Oxford University Press.

Eth, S., & Pynoos, R. S. (1994). Children who witness the homicide of a parent. *Psychiatry: Interpersonal and Biological Processes, 57,* 288–306.

Felitti, V. J., Anda, R. R., & Nordenberg, D. (1998). Relationship of childhood abuse and household dysfunction to many of the leading causes of death in adults: The adverse childhood experiences (ace). *American Journal of Preventive Medicine, 14,* 245–258.

Gondolf, E., & Fisher, E. (1988). *Battered women as survivors: An alternative to treating learned helplessness.* Lexington, MA: Lexington Books.

Graham Bermann, S. A., & Levendosky, A. A. (1998). Traumatic stress symptoms of children of battered women. *Journal of Interpersonal Violence, 13,* 111–128.

Hadley, S. M. (1992). Working with battered women in the emergency department: A model program. *Journal of Emergency Nursing, 18,* 18–23.

Haizlip, T. M., & Corder, B. F. (1996). Coping with natural disasters. In C. R. Pfeffer (Ed.), *Severe stress and mental disturbance in children* (pp. 131–152). Washington, DC: American Psychiatric Association.

Hughes, H. M., & Marshall, M. (1995). Advocacy for children of battered women. In E. Peled, P. G. Jaffe, & J. L. Edleson (Eds.), *Ending the cycle of violence: Community responses to children of battered women* (pp. 121–144). Thousand Oaks, CA: Sage.

Jaffe, P. G., Sudermann, M., & Reitzel, D. (1992). Working with children and adolescents to end the cycle of violence: A social learning approach to intervention and prevention programs. In R. DeV. Peters, R. J. McMahon, & V. L. Quinsey (Eds.), *Aggression and violence throughout the lifespan* (pp. 83–99). Newbury Park, CA: Sage.

Jaffe, P. G., Sudermann, M., & Reitzel, D. (1993). Child witnesses of marital violence. In R. T. Ammerman & N. W. Hersen (Eds.), *Assessment of family violence: A clinical and legal sourcebook* (pp. 313–331). Newbury Park, CA: Sage.

Jaffe, P. G., Wolfe, D. A., & Wilson, S. K. (1990). *Children of battered women.* Newbury Park, CA: Sage.

Jaffe, P. G., Wolfe, D. A., Wilson, S., & Zak, L. (1986). Similarities in behavioral and social maladjustment among child victims and witnesses to family violence. *American Journal of Orthopsychiatry, 56,* 142–146.

Jarvis, K. L., Gordon, E. E., & Novaco, R. W. (2005). Psychological distress of children and mothers in domestic violence emergency shelters. *Journal of Family Violence, 20,* 389–402.

Jobes, D. A., & Berman, A. L. (1996). Crisis intervention and time limited intervention with high risk suicidal youth. In A. R. Roberts (Ed.), *Crisis management and brief treatment* (pp. 60–82). Chicago: Nelson-Hall.

Kilpatrick, K. L. (1998). Potential mediators of posttraumatic stress disorder in child witnesses to domestic violence. *Child Abuse & Neglect, 22,* 319–331.

Kilpatrick, K. L., & Williams, L. M. (1997). Posttraumatic stress disorder in child witnesses to domestic violence. *American Journal of Orthopsychiatry, 67,* 639–644.

van der Kolk, B. A. (2005). Developmental trauma disorder. *Psychiatric Annals, 35,* 401–408.

Lehmann, P. (1997). The posttraumatic stress disorder responses in a sample of child witnesses to mother-assault. *Journal of Family Violence, 12,* 241–257.

Lehmann, P., & Carlson, B. E. (1998). Crisis intervention with traumatized child witnesses in shelters for battered women. In A. R. Roberts (Ed.), *Battered women and their families: Intervention strategies and treatment programs* (2nd ed., pp. 99–128). New York: Springer Publishing.

Lehmann, P., & Matthews, R. (1998). Crisis intervention with families in shelters for battered women. *Journal of Family Psychotherapy, 10,* 71–75.

Lehmann, P., Rabenstein, S., Duff, J., & Van Meyel, R. (1994). A multidimensional model for treating families who have survived mother-assault. *Contemporary Family Therapy, 16,* 8–25.

Lehmann, P., Spence, E., & Simmons, C. (in press). An exploratory look at a variation of Terr's type I type II trauma classifications with children exposed to domestic violence. *Family Violence and Sexual Assault Bulletin.*

Lemmey, D., Malecha, A., McFarlane, J., Wilson, P., Watson, K., Gist, J. H., et al. (2001). Severity of violence against women correlates with behavioral problems in their children. *Pediatric Nursing, 27*(3), 265–270.

Lewis-O'Connor, A., Sharps, P. W., & Humphreys, J. (2006). In M. M. Freeman & G. B. Silverman (Eds.), *Children exposed to violence* (pp. 3–28). Baltimore, MD: Paul H. Brooks.

Lieberman, A. F. (2006). Child-parent psychotherapy with young children exposed to violence. Available from the National Child Traumatic Stress Network. Retrieved July 1, 2006, from http://www.nctsnet.org.

Loosley, S. (2006). *Group work with children exposed to woman abuse: A concurrent group for children and their mothers, children's program manual.* London, ON: Children's Aid Society of London & Middlesex.

McDonald, R., Jouriles, E. N., Ramisetty-Mikler, S., Caetano, R., & Green, C. E. (2006a). Estimating the number of American children living in partner-violent families. *Journal of Family Psychology, 20*(1), 137–142.

McDonald, R., Jouriles, E. N, & Skopp, N. (2006b). Reducing conduct problems among children brought to women's shelters: Intervention effects following 24 months termination of services. *Journal of Family Psychology, 20*(1), 128–136.

McFarlane, J., Campbell, J. C., & Watson, K. (2002). Intimate partner stalking and femicide: Urgent implications for women's safety. *Behavioral Sciences and the Law, 20,* 51–68.

Monahon, C. (1993). *Children and trauma: A parent's guide to helping children heal.* New York: Lexington.

Mowbray, C. T. (1988). Post-traumatic therapy for children who are victims of violence. In. F. Ochberg (Ed.), *Post-traumatic therapy and victims of violence* (pp. 196–212). New York: Brunner/Mazel.

Myer, R. A., & Hanna, F. J. (1996). Working in hospital emergency departments: Guidelines for crisis intervention workers. In A. R. Roberts (Ed.), *Crisis management and brief treatment: Theory, technique, and applications* (pp. 37–59). Chicago, IL: Nelson–Hall.

Nader, K. (1994). Countertransference in the treatment of acutely traumatized children. In J. P. Wilson & J. D. Lindy (Eds.), *Countertransference in the treatment of PTSD* (pp. 179–205). New York: Guilford.

Nader, K. O. (1997). Assessing traumatic experiences in children. In J. P. Wilson & T. M. Keane (Eds.), *Assessing psychological trauma and PTSD* (pp. 291–348). New York: Guilford.

Nader, K., & Pynoos, R. S. (1991). Drawing and play in the diagnosis and assessment of childhood post-traumatic stress syndromes. In C. Shaeffer, K. Gitlin, & A. Sandgrund (Eds.), *Play, diagnosis and assessment* (pp. 375–389). New York: Wiley.

National Child Traumatic Stress Network. (2003). *Complex trauma in children and adolescents.* Available from the National Child Traumatic Stress Network. Retrieved July 1, 2006, from http://www.nctsnet.org.

National Clearing House on Family Violence. (2004). *Transition houses and shelters for abused women in Canada.* Available from the National Clearing House on Family Violence. Retrieved June 10, 2006, from http://www.phac-aspc.org.gc.ca/ncfv-cnivf/familyviolence/pdfs/2004women/_e.pdf.

National Clearinghouse on Family Violence, Health Promotion and Programs Branch Health. (1995). *The Transition Home Survey by Statistics Canada.* Ottawa, Canada: Author.

National Coalition Against Domestic Violence. (2006). *About NCADV.*

Available from the National Coalition Against Domestic Violence. Retrieved June 10, 2006, from http://www.ncadv.org/aboutus.php.

Osofsky, J. D., & Fenichel, E. (Eds.). (1994). *Hurt, healing, hope: Caring for infants and toddlers in violent environments.* Washington, DC: Zero to Three Publications.

Osofsky, J. D., & Fenichel, E. (Eds.). (1996). *Islands of safety: Assessing and treating young victims of violence.* Washington, DC: Zero to Three Publications.

Pelcovitz, D. (2006). Adolescents are uniquely vulnerable to the impact of stress. Available from the National Child Traumatic Stress Network. Retrieved July 1, 2006, from http://www.nctsnet.org.

Peled, E. (1996). "Secondary" victims no more: Refocusing intervention with children. In J. L. Edleson & Z. C. Eisikovits (Eds.), *Future interventions with battered women and their families* (pp. 125–153). Thousand Oaks, CA: Sage.

Peled, E., & Davis, D. (1995). *Group work with child witnesses of domestic violence: A practitioner's manual.* Thousand Oaks, CA: Sage.

Peled, E., & Edleson, J. L. (1994). Advocacy for battered women: A national survey. *Journal of Family Violence, 9,* 285–296.

Peled, E., & Edleson, J. L. (1995). Process and outcome in small groups for children of battered women. In E. Peled, P. G. Jaffe, & J. L. Edleson (Eds.), *Ending the cycle of violence: Community responses to children of battered women* (pp. 78–96). Thousand Oaks, CA: Sage.

Pynoos, R. S. (1996). Exposure to catastrophic violence and disaster in childhood. In C. R. Pfeffer (Ed.), *Severe stress and mental disturbance in children* (pp. 181–210). Washington, DC: American Psychiatric Press.

Pynoos, R. S., & Eth, S. (1984). The child as witness to homicide. *Journal of Social Issues, 40,* 88–108.

Pynoos, R. S., & Eth, S. (1985). Children traumatized by witnessing acts of personal violence: Homicide, rape, or suicide behavior. In S. Eth & R. S. Pynoos (Eds.), *Post-traumatic stress disorder in children* (pp. 18–44). Washington, DC: American Psychiatric Press.

Pynoos, R. S., & Eth, S. (1986). Witness to violence: The child interview. *Journal of the American Academy of Child Psychiatry, 25,* 306–319.

Pynoos, R. S., & Nader, K. (1988). Psychological first aid and treatment approach to children exposed to community violence: Research implications. *Journal of Traumatic Stress, 1,* 445–474.

Pynoos, R. S., & Nader, K. (1990). Children's exposure to violence and traumatic death. *Psychiatric Annals, 20,* 334–344.

Pynoos, R. S., & Nader, K. (1993). Issues in the treatment of posttraumatic stress in children and adolescents. In J. P. Wilson & B. Raphael (Eds.), *International handbook of traumatic stress syndromes* (pp. 535–549). New York: Plenum.

Pynoos, R. S., Steinberg, A. M., & Goenjian, A. (1996). Traumatic stress in childhood and adolescence: Recent developments and current controversies. In B. A. van der Kolk, A. C. McFarlane, & L. Weisaeth (Eds.), *Traumatic stress: The effects of overwhelming experience on mind, body, and society* (pp. 331–358). New York: Guilford.

Rhodes, R. M., & Zelman, A. B. (1986). An on-going multi-family group in a women's shelter. *American Journal of Orthopsychiatry, 56,* 120–130.

Rivett, M., Howarth, E., & Gordon, H. (2006). Watching from the stairs: Towards an evidence-based practice in work with child witnesses of domestic violence. *Clinical Child Psychology and Psychiatry, 11,* 103–125.

Roberts, A. R. (1984). Crisis intervention with battered women. In A. R. Roberts (Ed.), *Battered women and their families: Intervention strategies and treatment programs* (1st ed., pp. 65–83). New York: Springer Publishing.

Roberts, A. R. (Ed.). (1990). *Crisis intervention handbook: Assessment, treatment, and research.* Belmont, CA: Wadsworth.

Roberts, A. R. (1991). *Contemporary perspectives on crisis intervention and prevention.* Englewood Cliffs, NJ: Prentice-Hall.

Roberts, A. R. (Ed.). (1996). *Crisis management and brief treatment.* Chicago: Nelson-Hall.

Roberts, A. R. (2000). An overview of crisis theory and crisis intervention. In A. R. Roberts (Ed.), *Crisis intervention handbook: Assessment, treatment, and research* (pp. 3–30). New York: Oxford University Press.

Roberts, A. R., & Roberts Schenkman, B. (1990). A model for crisis intervention with battered women and their children. In A. R. Roberts (Ed.), *Helping crime victims: Research, policy, and practice* (pp. 186–204). Newbury Park, CA: Sage.

Roberts, A. R., & Roberts, B. (2005). A comprehensive model for crisis intervention with battered women and their children. In A. R. Roberts (Ed.), *Crisis intervention handbook: Assessment, treatment and research* (3rd ed., pp. 441–482). New York: Oxford University Press.

Rossman, B. B. (1994). Children in violent families: Current diagnostic and treatment considerations. *Family Violence and Sexual Assault Bulletin, 10,* 29–34.

Rossman, B. B. (1998). Descartes's error and posttraumatic stress disorder: Cognition and emotion in children who are exposed to marital violence. In G. W. Holden, R. Geffner, & E. N. Jouriles (Eds.), *Children exposed to marital violence: Theory, research and applied issues* (pp. 223–256). Washington, DC: American Psychological Association.

Rossman, B. B. R., & Ho, J. (2000). Posttraumatic response and children exposed to domestic violence. In R. A. Geffner, P. G. Jaffe, & M. Suderman (Eds.), *Children exposed to domestic violence: Current issues in research, intervention, prevention, and policy development* (pp. 85–106). New York: Haworth.

Scheeringa, M. S., & Zeanah, C. H. (1995). Symptom expression and trauma variables in children under 48 months of age. *Infant Mental Health Journal, 16,* 259–270.

Silvern, L., & Kaersvang, L. (1989). The traumatized children of violent marriages. *Child Welfare, 68,* 421–436.

Silvern, L., Karyl, J., & Landis, T. Y (1995). Individual psychotherapy for the traumatized children of abused women. In E. Peled, P. G. Jaffe, & J. L. Edleson (Eds.), *Ending the cycle of violence: Community responses to children of battered women* (pp. 43–76). Thousand Oaks, CA: Sage.

Spence-Diehl, E. (2004). Intensive case management for victims of stalking: A pilot test evaluation. *Brief Treatment and Crisis Intervention, 4*(4), 323–341.

Spinazzola, J., Ford, J. D., Zucker, M., van der Kolk, B., Silva, S., Smith, S. F., et al. (2005). Survey evaluates complex trauma exposure, outcome and intervention among children and adolescents. *Psychiatric Annals, 35,* 433–439.

Terr, L. (1990). *Too scared to cry: Psychic trauma in childhood.* New York: Harper & Row.

Terr, L. (1991). Child traumas: An outline and overview. *American Journal of Psychiatry, 148,* 10–20.

Terr, L. (1992). Mini-marathon groups: Psychological "first aid" following disasters. *Bulletin of the Menninger Clinic, 56,* 76–86.

Wenckstern, S., & Leenaars, A. A. (1993). Trauma and suicide in our schools. *Death Studies, 17,* 151–171.

Wolfe, D. A. (2006). Preventing violence in relationships: Psychological science addressing complex issues. *Canadian Psychology, 47,* 44–50.

Wolfe, D. A., & Jaffe, P. G. (1991). Child abuse and family violence as determinants of child psychopathology. *Canadian Journal of Behavioral Science, 23,* 282–299.

Wolfe, D. A., Jaffe, P. G., Wilson, S. K., & Zak, L. (1985). Children of battered women: The relation of child behavior to family violence and maternal stress. *Journal of Consulting and Clinical Psychology, 14,* 95–104.

Wolfe, D. A., Jaffe, P. G., Wilson, S. K., & Zak, L. (1988). A multivariate investigation of children's adjustment to family violence. In G. Hotaling, D. Finkelhor, J. Kirkpatrick, & M. Straus (Eds.), *Family abuse and its consequences: New directions in research* (pp. 228–243). Newbury Park, CA: Sage.

Wolfe, D. A., Zak, L., Wilson, S. K., & Jaffe, P. G. (1986). Child witnesses to violence between parents: Critical issues in behavioral and social adjustment. *Journal of Abnormal Child Psychology, 14,* 95–104.

Wolfe, V. V., & Birt, J. Z. (1995). The psychological sequelae of child sexual abuse. *Advances in Clinical Child Psychology, 17,* 1–25.

Zeanah, C., & Scheeringa, M. (1994). *The PTSD Semi-Structured Interview and Observational Record for Infants and Young Children.* Unpublished assessment instrument, Louisiana State University, Department of Psychiatry.

CHAPTER 9

Double Jeopardy:
Risk Assessment in the Context of Child Maltreatment and Domestic Violence

Aron Shlonsky and Colleen Friend

Molly is an ongoing caseworker for a Citiville Children's Protective/Protection Services (CPS) agency. One of her ongoing family reunification cases involves the Smith family. The family initially came to the attention of CPS because of concerns of neglect (involving mother's and father's substance abuse of crack cocaine) and domestic violence (DV; father had been charged with assault). The three children—Tom, age 13; Cara, age 7; and Marie, age 3—were all placed with kin. Now, 1 year later, mother has been in recovery and is seeking the return of the children. Father was briefly jailed but managed to hold on to his job. After about 6 months of a traditional batterers' intervention treatment program, he claims to have cleaned up and is supposedly not living in the home. The children come home on a 30-day trial visit. The CPS worker receives a cross-report called in to the child abuse hotline that describes a "domestic violence" incident involving both parents, where father was allegedly "high" and the now 14-year-old son, Tom, was seen chasing Mr. Smith out of the home with a baseball bat. The CPS

The authors gratefully acknowledge the substantial contributions made to this chapter by Raelene Freitag (Children's Research Center), Linda Mills (NYU), and Dennis Wagner (Children's Research Center).

worker checks with the police and learns that the father was slightly injured and was arrested.

First: Assess CPS risk

- What will happen if I do nothing (weighing the risks of any course of action or inaction)?
- Considering safety as the most important goal, how should I proceed?
- How does domestic violence interact with neglect to increase risk?
- Is the risk here low, medium, or high?
- How often do I need to reevaluate the risk?

Second: Assess DV risk

- What is my role when domestic violence is involved?
- Are all DV cases dangerous to kids?
- How are the kids affected psychologically?
- Are there any physical injuries? Do any injuries require emergency room treatment?
- How dangerous is this situation?
- What are the limitations of predictions about this family?
- Is the risk here low, medium, or high?
- How is the substantiation decision shaped by the DV incident?

Third: Assess context

- What are the family dynamics? Is there substance abuse involved?
- Are there social supports and strengths to build on?
- What is the family's perception of the situation?
- How will I attend to some of the risk factors to reduce the likelihood that Mrs. Smith, the children, or Mr. Smith will be harmed or killed?
- How do domestic violence and CPS interact in terms of understanding the family? Must I find a way to treat or prevent both?
- What available services would be most effective?

Responding to child maltreatment is far more complicated than keeping children safe or protected from their own parents. The twin goals of safety and permanence imply that caseworkers must consider both the safety and ultimate well-being of the child. That is, at each decision point, caseworkers must weigh the potential for harm if nothing is done (i.e., leaving the child in a potentially abusive home) with the risk that intrusive actions aimed at child protection will ultimately prove to be harmful (i.e., unnecessarily separating a child from his or her parent). This is no simple equation, and the stakes are high. Yet the combination of severe consequences, the inherent difficulty of making accurate assessments, and differences in skill levels among Children's Protective/Protection Services (CPS) workers is a setup for unreliable case decision making (Shlonsky & Wagner, 2005).

CPS agencies have begun to deal with this complicated decision-making context by using various assessment tools (Rycus & Hughes, 2003; Shlonsky & Wagner, 2005). These include one or more of the following:

1. Safety assessments: consensus-based lists of factors thought to be related to the likelihood of immediate harm
2. Actuarial risk assessments: empirically derived estimations of the likelihood of maltreatment recurrence over time
3. Structured contextual assessments: detailed appraisals of individual and family functioning

The combination of such approaches allows caseworkers to more simply and reliably assess whether children might be safe if left in the home (safety assessment), generates a more reliable and valid prediction of the likelihood of future harm (actuarial risk assessment), and compiles detailed information that can be used to develop an individualized case plan (contextual assessment). Nonetheless, children and families who are reported for maltreatment often present with multiple problems spanning several service systems, each carrying its own risk of harm. Among the most serious of these is domestic violence. Because domestic violence is often included as an item in safety and risk assessments, the intersection of these two threats to children may necessitate an expanded course of action.

This chapter is conceptualized in the context of responding to child maltreatment allegations. That is, it assumes that the entry point for co-occurring child maltreatment and domestic violence cases is a child maltreatment allegation. From this perspective, the literature is reviewed with respect to the prevalence of domestic violence and its link to child maltreatment. Next, we examine the challenges in making predictive assessments in both domestic violence and child protection, positing that a nested or layered risk classification system offers the greatest potential to assist caseworkers in making service decisions. Key to this nested approach is the integration of safety and risk assessment information with a detailed assessment of child and family functioning. This should include consideration of the survivor's perception of risk and the potential for long-term harm that could accompany a range of responses from either a child's placement or removal from the home, as well as the child's remaining in the home. Finally, we suggest that engaging in the process of evidence-based practice (EBP) encompasses the use of these two elements (risk and contextual assessment) and extends to the identification and continued evaluation of services for both child maltreatment and domestic violence. At the outset, we concede that the science of predicting human behavior, especially when it comes to violence, is complex, risky, and not likely to be mastered. Nevertheless, there is a public expectation that vulnerable children and parents will be protected from repeated assault and that state intervention is both necessary and acceptable to prevent such injury (Finkelhor, 1990). Although imperfect, this integrated approach appears to hold promise for minimizing harm and providing effective services.

DOMESTIC VIOLENCE AND CPS:
SCOPE AND CONSEQUENCES

The terms *domestic violence* and *intimate partner violence* can be used interchangeably to represent a pattern of battering or abusive acts in the context of an intimate relationship. Domestic violence spans a continuum of severity and includes physical, sexual, and emotional abuse (Roberts, 2001). In the 1985 U.S. National Family Violence Survey, 16% of American couples (married and cohabitating) reported experiencing at least one episode of physical violence over the course of the relationship (Straus & Gelles, 1986).

Each year in the United States, at least 3 million to 8 million women of all races and classes are battered by an intimate partner (Roberts, 1998; Straus, Gelles, & Steinmetz, 1980). As disconcerting as these figures are, they likely underestimate the true prevalence of single and multiple acts of domestic violence. Such approximations are based on self-report, and survey respondents may be reluctant to disclose events that cause them to harbor feelings of shame or embarrassment. Indeed, Straus and Gelles (1986) estimated that only 14.8% of victims officially report DV incidents. Experts generally agree that women are more likely than men to be seriously physically injured by domestic violence because of men's greater use of force and severity of tactic (Barnett, Miller-Perrin, & Perrin, 1997). Further compounding these gender differences, women are far more likely to experience an injury as a result of assault than men (Straus, 1993).

Although there is still controversy as to whether domestic violence is *bidirectional*, involving aggression by both parties, the issue is relevant to a discussion of domestic violence and child maltreatment for two important reasons: Most reports of child abuse and neglect are made against women (American Association for Protecting Children, 1988; Gelles & Cornell, 1990), and battered women sometimes mistreat their own children (Casanueva, 2005; Ross, 1996). Women's involvement in violence (not merely as responders but as initiators) has been documented in more than 100 studies (Straus, 1999), yet this seemingly intractable finding is at odds with the dominant DV advocacy paradigm, which sees women only as victims (Dutton & Nicholls, 2005). This lack of clarity has caused tension between DV advocates and child protection services, the latter of which operates from the standpoint that the child is always the victim.

Estimates of the number of U.S. children exposed to domestic violence vary greatly and are calculated from data in national surveys. Based on earlier calculations that 3 million U.S. households experienced at least one incident of interpersonal violence in the past year (Straus et al., 1980), Carlson (1998) estimated that 3.3 million children per year are at risk of exposure to parental violence. In their latest (1985) national survey, Straus and Gelles (1990) found that 30% of parents self-reported that their children witnessed at least one incident of physical violence over the course of that marriage. Although this estimate includes incidents that have a wide range of severity, some of which would not be considered by CPS to qualify as child maltreatment, the magnitude of the problem in the general population is of grave concern.

Children exposed to parental violence are frequently the victims of co-occurring maltreatment. This co-occurrence has been investigated in single-site clinical samples and shelter samples of abused women and their physically abused children, with rates of co-occurrence ranging from 30% to 60% (Appel & Holden, 1998; Edleson, 1999). In Canada, where exposure to domestic violence is treated as a maltreatment category, approximately 34% of substantiated cases in 2003 involved exposure to domestic violence,[1] and 28% of indicated maltreatment reports were substantiated primarily for DV exposure, making DV the second most common form of substantiated maltreatment (Trocmé et al., 2005).

Clearly, children are at risk of abuse from both adults in the household. As already discussed, the risk of child maltreatment from battered mothers is an important consideration when discussing risk assessment. It is equally important to note that in households where the male batterer abuses his partner, batterers may also physically abuse the child. Estimates of such co-occurrence range from 47% to 80% (Hart, 1992; O'Keefe, 1995), making it imperative that DV advocates and child protection workers understand and come to terms with both forms of abuse (Mills et al., 2000). Several studies and scholars have identified child protection workers' tendency to hold the mother to a higher standard of responsibility than her partner in protecting her children (Davidson, 1995; Davis, 1995; Magen, 1999; Mills, 2000). DV advocates propose that this is a gender bias, and the differential perception of the role of the battered woman and the batterer has led to friction between the two service systems (Beeman, Hagemeister, & Edleson, 1999; Hartley, 2004; Saunders & Anderson, 2000). Edleson (1999) aptly noted that the CPS system may lack the authority to hold a male batterer accountable if he is not the father of the children. As Hartley (2004) correctly pointed out, not all reported child maltreatment cases in families with DV are inaccurate in their assessment of failure to protect. In some cases, children are also being physically abused or neglected by both parents. Thus, domestic violence and child maltreatment (including neglect) can be two simultaneously occurring events (Hartley, 2004). Having found a surprisingly high level of neglect by mothers in families with severe domestic violence, she argued for a continuing shift from a view of mother's failure to protect to a view that recognizes the need for interventions focusing on the circumstances that endanger both mother and child (Hartley, 2004).

New information about domestic violence in the context of CPS services is also emerging from the National Survey of Children and Adolescent Well-Being. This survey begins with a U.S. national probability sample of children investigated for abuse and neglect between October 1999 and December 2000 and follows them for the next 3 years. Casanueva, Foshee, and Barth (2004) used these data to investigate hospital emergency room (ER) visits by children. Although the survey is limited to the primary caregiver's self-report of domestic violence and only a few caregivers were willing to acknowledge that their child's injury was due to domestic violence, mothers' reports of current, severe domestic violence were positively associated with children's use of the ER. The authors went on to find that maternal depression (a key factor associated with child neglect) and lack of supervision (an element of child neglect) were also associated with children's injuries. They concluded that the identification of current, severe domestic violence in the home and depression among mothers would help prevent future injuries to children. Taken as a whole, Casanueva's (2005) and Hartley's (2004) work supports an earlier finding made by a Los Angeles juvenile court in *In re Heather A.* (1997). Here the Los Angeles Court of Appeals supported the lower court's finding that children's exposure to domestic violence, even if only secondary, constituted neglect on the part of the battering father.

Best practice for families affected by both DV and child maltreatment calls on advocates and child protection workers to "see double," meaning they need to draw from knowledge and understanding of both perspectives (Fleck-Henderson, 2000). But seeing double comes with its own set of impediments, relative to the way these families enter and behave in the two systems. In the DV track, women may self-report and voluntarily remain for services after the violence becomes intolerable. On the other hand, entrance into the CPS system is typically not self-initiated. Services are generally involuntary, and most families fear the child's removal.

Children who witness domestic violence can experience a broad range of harmful responses including behavioral, emotional, or cognitive problems that may follow them into adulthood (Edleson; 1999; Felitti, 1998; Groves, 1999; *Nicholson v. Williams*, 2000). When children both witness and experience abuse, they are more likely to exhibit severe behavior problems than children who only witness domestic violence or children who are not exposed at all (Hughes, 1988), making effective intervention even more important. Despite the increased risk of poor outcomes, some children display remarkable resiliency in the face of exposure to violence. Such resilience may be moderated by the level of violence, degree of exposure, child's exposure to other stresses, and his or her innate coping skills (Edleson, 1999). On the other hand, Groves (1999) attributed this resiliency to children being able to talk about the problem and the presence of another adult who can both mediate the experience and promote coping, which would coincide with the findings of resiliency studies (Werner, 1995; Werner & Smith, 1992). Canadian researchers found that 26% of the children in their school sample could be classified as resilient, despite their exposure to domestic violence (Wolfe, Jaffe, Wilson, & Zak, 1985). Although not immediately obvious, such findings have serious implications for responding to domestic violence in the context of child maltreatment. A U.S. district court judge found these arguments of resiliency to be persuasive when he ordered New York City's Administration for Children's Services to stop removing children solely because they saw their mother being beaten (*Nicholson v. Williams*, 2002). This challenge to a common practice in one of the largest public child welfare agencies in the country put the entire CPS system on notice that decisions about removal had to adequately protect the rights of the nonabusing parent and consider the overall well-being of the child.

THE CHALLENGE OF PREDICTION

The challenges posed in making protective services risk determinations have been detailed elsewhere (Gambrill & Shlonsky, 2001; Wald & Woolverton, 1990), as have risk decisions in DV response (Cattaneo & Goodman, 2005; Dutton & Kropp, 2000). However, few studies have integrated the two areas. DV and child maltreatment assessment share many of the same methodological issues in terms of predicting risk and making subsequent service decisions. Specifically, the discovery of child maltreatment and domestic violence begs the following questions: Will it happen again if nothing is done? What are the consequences if it does recur? How might my actions, as a worker, forestall this eventuality? Who is my client—the child, the battered parent(s), the abusing parents, or all three? At the agency and policy level, what can we do to make sure that we are expending scarce resources only on cases where child maltreatment or domestic violence (or both) are most likely to recur? How can we tell whether services are effective?

Cognitive Biases and Thinking Errors

Clearly in both fields, clinical prediction of risk is marked by cognitive biases and thinking errors, resulting in decisions that tend to have limited predictive validity (Dawes, 1994; Grove & Meehl, 1996). The sheer volume of observed information, the speed in which decisions must be made, and the pressure to get it right can influence a worker's assessment of risk (Shlonsky & Wagner, 2005). Yet there is little evidence that, in the face of such demands, workers can make reliable and valid predictions of future events. In fact, the opposite is likely true, even for those armed with good information and experience (Dawes, 1994; Dawes, Faust, & Meehl, 1989). One of the major reasons for this shortcoming involves the inability of most people to weigh and combine large amounts of disparate and often conflicting information, prompting the worker to select factors for the decision that have no relationship to the behavioral outcome being forecast (Faust, 1984; Shlonsky & Wagner, 2005). For example, in a child maltreatment case, an investigative worker might understandably focus on a parent's combativeness with the caseworker rather than on his or her overall parenting skills. There are situations in which experts can quickly and accurately make judgments (Klein, 1998), but these rarely involve long-term predictions of human behavior.

Fortunately, formal risk assessment measures have been developed in both child protection (Rycus & Hughes, 2003) and DV services (Cattaneo & Goodman, 2005; Dutton & Kropp, 2000) to combat the shortfalls of unassisted clinical judgment. Tools such as the California Family Risk Assessment for child protection and the Spousal Assault Risk Assessment (SARA) for domestic violence are designed to guide decision makers to those characteristics and observed behaviors that best predict the event of interest. Although there is still some debate about whether tools based on a consensus of experts (consensus-based) or that employ statistics to generate an optimal combination of factors that predict the event (actuarial) are more predictive, actuarial instruments tend to perform at least as well as consensus-based tools and almost always outperform unassisted clinical judgment (Dawes, 1994; Grove & Meehl, 1996). Certainly, this is the case in child protection, where the most rigorous of studies testing actuarial and consensus-based tools favor the actuarial approach (Baird & Wagner, 2000; Baird, Wagner, Healy, & Johnson, 1999).[2]

Laying this argument aside, then, what other issues should be considered? Why not merely find an actuarial tool that works for both child maltreatment and domestic violence, implement it, and be done? If only the world were that simple. Although decisions informed by evidence (in this case, validated tools) promise to be better than decisions based on other sources, their predictive capacity is quite limited because of the nearly impossible task of predicting human behavior, as well as the difficulty of accurately predicting events with a low base rate of occurrence (e.g., femicide, child death by maltreatment). In other words, tools can go only so far. In addition, there are several methodological and contextual factors that must be addressed when considering both child maltreatment and DV. Finally, actuarial tools are designed for a very specific purpose: making an optimal classification of risk (e.g., low, medium, or high). They are not inclusive of all risk factors, and there is no guarantee that risk factors are causal for recurrence rather than links in a chain originating elsewhere. That is, the factors contained in a risk assessment instrument cannot be used to develop a comprehensive service plan.

The Tools and Their Capacities

Risk assessment tools for domestic violence have been under development and in use for at least the last decade (Fein, Vossekuil, & Holden, 1995), but there has been somewhat limited success in predicting recidivism (Hilton & Harris, 2005). Two commonly used and validated instruments are the Danger Assessment (DA) and its revision (DA2; Campbell, 1995, 2004) and the SARA (Kropp, Hart, Webster, & Eaves, 1995). The DA and DA2 are measures designed to predict the risk that a woman will be killed (femicide) by her partner. The DA was validated retrospectively on a small sample, calling its properties into question and presenting some interpretive problems (Dutton & Kropp, 2000). Acknowledging these limitations, Campbell (2004) recruited a larger and more diverse multisite sample and revised the instrument based on her findings. All but 1 of the 15 yes–no items were significant predictors of intimate partner femicide, and the nonpredictive item (perpetrator's suicidality) was retained because of its theoretical relationship with femicide. Five items were added, and a few were combined and otherwise modified. The DA2 (see Figure 9.1) contains 20 items and is reported to have acceptable reliability ranging from .74 to .80. Given that the DA2 is predicting lethality, a fairly rare event, there are concerns about its ability to identify simultaneously women who are at risk or not at risk of femicide. That is, as sensitivity (ability to detect women who will be killed) is increased, the specificity (ability to predict women who will not be killed) decreases. For example, in Campbell's (2004) study, a cutoff score of 4 produced a sensitivity of 83.4%, meaning that 83% of

DANGER ASSESSMENT
Jacquelyn C. Campbell, PhD, RN, FAAN
Copyright 2004 Johns Hopkins University, School of Nursing

Several risk factors have been associated with increased risk of homicides (murders) of women and men in violent relationships. We cannot predict what will happen in your case, but we would like you to be aware of the danger of homicide in situations of abuse and for you to see how many of the risk factors apply to your situation.

Using the calendar, please mark the approximate dates during the past year when you were abused by your partner or ex-partner. Write on that date how bad the incident was according to the following scale:

1. Slapping, pushing; no injuries and/or lasting pain
2. Punching, kicking; bruises, cuts, and/or continuing pain
3. "Beating up"; severe contusions, burns, broken bones, miscarriage
4. Threat to use weapon; head injury, internal injury, permanent injury, miscarriage
5. Use of weapon; wounds from weapon

(If **any** of the descriptions for the higher number apply, use the higher number.)

Mark **Yes** or **No** for each of the following.
("He" refers to your husband, partner, ex-husband, ex-partner, or whoever is currently physically hurting you.)

Yes   No

____ ____ 1. Has the physical violence increased in severity or frequency over the past year?
____ ____ 2. Does he own a gun?
____ ____ 3. Have you left him after living together during the past year?
       3a. (If you have *never* lived with him, check here____)
____ ____ 4. Is he unemployed?
____ ____ 5. Has he ever used a weapon against you or threatened you with a lethal weapon?
       5a. (If yes, was the weapon a gun?____)
____ ____ 6. Does he threaten to kill you?
____ ____ 7. Has he avoided being arrested for domestic violence?
____ ____ 8. Do you have a child that is not his?
____ ____ 9. Has he ever forced you to have sex when you did not wish to do so?
____ ____ 10. Does he ever try to choke you?
____ ____ 11. Does he use illegal drugs? By drugs, I mean "uppers" or amphetamines, speed, angel dust, cocaine, "crack," street drugs or mixtures.
____ ____ 12. Is he an alcoholic or problem drinker?
____ ____ 13. Does he control most or all of your daily activities? (For instance, does he tell you who you can be friends with, when you can see your family, how much money you can use, or when you can take the car?)
       (If he tries, but you do not let him, check here: ____)
____ ____ 14. Is he violently and constantly jealous of you?
       (For instance, does he say "If I can't have you, no one can?")
____ ____ 15. Have you ever been beaten by him while you were pregnant?
       (If you have never been pregnant by him, check here: ____)
____ ____ 16. Has he ever threatened or tried to commit suicide?
____ ____ 17. Does he threaten to harm your children?
____ ____ 18. Do you believe he is capable of killing you?
____ ____ 19. Does he follow or spy on you, leave threatening notes or messages on your answering machine, destroy your property, or call you when you don't want him to?
____ ____ 20. Have you ever threatened or tried to commit suicide?
_____ Total "Yes" Answers

Thank you. Please talk to your nurse, advocate or counselor about what the Danger Assessment means in terms of your situation.

FIGURE 9.1   Revised Danger Assessment to assist in prediction of partner femicide.

the women who were killed were correctly identified retrospectively.[3] The trade-off for such a sensitive instrument is a specificity of 39.2%. As a result of this statistical dilemma, the number of false positives (number of women incorrectly predicted to be killed) is very high. This does not mean that the instrument is not valuable or well constructed but, as we discuss subsequently, it does raise philosophical and political questions about where the bar should be set.

Although the DA and DA2 are important factors for intimate partner femicide, this represents a small (albeit important) part of all DV assaults. The most common forms of family violence are so-called minor violent acts, and those acts are performed by both genders (Straus & Gelles, 1990). The SARA, on the other hand, is a consensus-based clinical checklist of 20 factors clustered into five areas. The SARA's original purpose was to structure and enhance professional judgments about risk (Dutton & Kropp, 2000). Similar to actuarial tools in use in child protection (Wagner & Johnson, 2003), the SARA allows for clinical overrides to incorporate some level of clinical judgment into risk decisions (Dutton & Kropp, 2000). Although the SARA's interrater reliability is reported to be high and its internal consistency moderate, evidence of predictive validity (the ability of the tool to predict domestic violence) is modest (Heckert & Gondolf, 2004). In addition, it is unclear whether the SARA's psychometric properties have been tested on a CPS sample. The SARA's 20 factors each have a range of response categories consisting of three items: 0 (*absent*), 1 (*subthreshold*), and 2 (*present*). Each of these items is totaled, and risk of domestic violence is said to increase as the score increases; unlike an actuarial approach, however, there appears to be no preestablished cut-points (measurable points beyond which one can say neglect has occured) to establish low, moderate, or high degree of risk. Unlike the DA, the SARA is completed by a caseworker and, ultimately, yields an estimation of harm rather than lethality. Although they differ in the severity of what they seek to measure, the good news is that both the SARA and the DA2 share certain comments, indicating that there may be reasonable convergence between the two. The measures also appear to have fairly good reliability and are easily completed. Nonetheless, overall predictive validity of both tools remains modest.

The Ontario Domestic Assault Risk Assessment (ODARA) is an actuarial tool developed for use by police officers conducting domestic violence investigations and, in this context, appears to predict recidivism better than the SARA (Hilton et al., 2004). Hilton and Harris (2005) described the tool as a 13-item scale consisting of domestic violence history, general criminal history, threats and confinement during the most recent assault, children in the relationship, substance abuse, and victim barriers to support. Similar to other actuarial tools, each item is binary (0, 1), and the total score is used to generate a probability of recidivism. This tool holds promise for a number of reasons. First, its psychometric properties (Hilton et al., 2004) appear to be similar to other actuarial tools used in different fields. Somewhat related, its simple, easy-to-use structure will likely increase the reliability of domestic violence risk ratings and, by extension, the validity of such predictions. Moreover, the tool was designed for police investigations, and such inquiries have at least some similarity to child maltreatment investigations in terms of their immediacy and inherently coercive nature. Nevertheless, like the DA and SARA, the ODARA has not been normed on a CPS sample.

Child protection safety and risk assessment tools have also been in use for some time (Fluke, Edwards, Bussey, Wells, & Johnson, 2001; Johnson, 1984; McDonald & Marks, 1991; Wald & Woolverton, 1990), although the quality of the measures and the integrity of their application vary. In general, these tools are designed to predict either (a) risk of immediate harm (safety assessment) or (b) risk of maltreatment recurrence over time (risk assessment). The safety assessment is usually completed shortly after the initial contact with the family, and the risk assessment is usually completed toward the end of the investigation period. Unfortunately, most of the early tools lacked sufficient predictive validity to be of much use in the field (Lyons, Doueck, & Wodarski, 1996). More recently, however, safety and risk assessment tools have been successfully used in the field to contend more accurately with unsafe situations and high-risk families (Fluke et al., 2001; Johnson, 2004; Wagner & Johnson, 2003). However, these instruments also suffer from an inability to predict at high levels of accuracy for the same problems detailed previously (i.e., high sensitivity and low specificity). There is some evidence, however, that a well-constructed, easily scored actuarial instrument can be effectively used in the field. Following up on the retrospective validation of the California Family Risk Assessment, a similar tool (Baird & Wagner, 2000), Wagner and Johnson (2003) and Johnson (2004) conducted a prospective validation of the California Family Risk Assessment using a sample of more than 7,000 CPS cases from a variety of California counties. Each tool was completed by trained workers in the field during the course of their investigation. They found that the instrument maintained its psychometric properties, indicating that, with proper training of caseworkers using it, the instrument transfers well to the field.

The Challenge of Measuring and Defining Outcomes

The prediction of child maltreatment is made difficult in the face of vague definitions and outcome measures (Gambrill & Shlonsky, 2000; Wald & Woolverton, 1990), and this likely translates into the DV sphere as well. Arguably, physical and sexual abuse can be more readily defined and classified in terms of severity than other forms of maltreatment. However, child neglect, the most pervasive and common form of maltreatment in the United States (Hines & Malley-Morrison, 2005), is subject to widely ranging definitions and cut-points across studies (Zuravin, 1999). Defining DV itself might be an easier task, but defining when DV becomes child abuse is another matter. Although there are those who would argue that witnessing DV is a form of child maltreatment, and to some extent they may be right, this is not always a viable reason for mandated services and, ultimately, removing a child from his or her family or home (*Nicholson v. Williams*, 2002). At what point does CPS become involved in the response to DV? If we base this on emotional harm to the child, how is this measured? The subtleties involved may make the creation of valid cut-points untenable. The presence of children who appear to be resilient to some of the measurable effects of domestic violence (Edleson, 1999) indicates that children may react differently to similar types of exposure to violence. What is not clear is whether these same children would remain resilient if they were removed from the care of their parents. That is, if resilience is a confluence of personal and situational factors, a change in situation might result in a change in resilience. If resilience involves personal coping strategies, insight capacity, and parental relationship, then removal might compromise or overwhelm the individual's capacity to maintain these so-called traits.

Many risk assessment tools use substantiation or indication (social work finding that maltreatment has occurred) as the sole measure of maltreatment recurrence with the acknowledgment that it is limited to known recurrence. For instance, an unknown number of children are maltreated but are not reported to CPS (English, Marshall, & Orme, 1999). Similarly, there may be a surveillance effect (families receiving CPS services are under increased scrutiny), and such children may be reported more often than would otherwise be expected (Fluke et al., 2001; Lindsey, 1994, 2004). Practically speaking, however, substantiation remains the best measure available for re-abuse. In addition, valid instruments that measure risk re-report, child injury, and foster care placement have been developed and can be used to inform the decision-making process (Johnson, 2004; Wagner & Johnson, 2003). For example, a high-risk rating for a child on the injury scale may inform a service decision differently than a high-risk rating for re-report. DV studies have a similar problem in that they largely rely on subsequent police reports to measure recurrence, although there have been studies that use victim self-report as well (Dutton & Kropp, 2000).

Reliability and validity of the tools is also a challenge. DV and child maltreatment risk assessment tools range in quality, and it is exceedingly important to ascertain a tool's psychometric properties. However, even the best tools have limitations. Risk of domestic violence and child maltreatment is not static. That is, risk likely changes over time in child maltreatment cases (DePanfilis & Zuravin, 1998), and about half of DV incidents are single occurrences (Dutton & Kropp, 2000); thus, we may be observing an escalation or de-escalation at any given moment in time. If escalation is always assumed at the point of risk assessment, the false-positive rate might be very high, whereas if escalation is not assumed, the number of false negatives might be high (Gambrill & Shlonsky, 2000).

In addition, attempts to make simple (yes–no) predictions of whether a child will be reabused are problematic. For instance, the California Family Risk Assessment instrument, although meeting key standards for reliability, is unable to predict maltreatment recurrence at acceptable levels if it is constrained to simply predict whether maltreatment will recur (more detail presented later in this chapter and in Shlonsky & Wagner, 2005). Again, this is due to the near impossibility of trying to predict complex human behavior. Thus, even the best risk assessment tools should not be used as the sole decision-making device, but a good actuarial classification system can be used to reasonably inform service decisions.

Goal and Role Confusion

The co-occurrence of domestic violence and child maltreatment raises some serious questions about the very nature of services involving children and families. Much of the emphasis in child protection is focused on keeping children safe and facilitating a permanent home. Yet a child is less likely to be safe if the parent is not safe. Clearly, the welfare of children depends on the welfare of parents. Likewise, a response to domestic violence that does not consider issues of child maltreatment that go beyond domestic violence (i.e., that the assaulted parent may also be abusive or neglectful) errs in the other direction.

For the purposes of this chapter, we are focusing only on children who are reported for maltreatment. Even with this smaller population, a number of types of risk are present when factoring in the occurrence of domestic violence. These risks generally fall into two categories, risk of harm to the child and risk of harm to the parent, and include the following:

1. Child maltreatment that is not directly DV involved
2. Child maltreatment as a direct result of domestic violence
3. Child emotional harm as a result of observing domestic violence
4. Parent physical harm as a result of domestic violence, potentially limiting the parent's ability to meet the child's needs
5. Parent emotional harm as a result of domestic violence, potentially limiting the parent's ability to meet the child's needs

These overlapping risks pose considerable challenges to both measurement and service response. Actuarial models of risk assessment are statistically derived sets of factors that estimate the likelihood of an event. The items themselves are not necessarily causal. That is, their presence may predict an event without actually causing it. Although it seems logical that domestic violence is both a risk factor and causal for maltreatment recurrence, most tools use overall maltreatment recurrence as a benchmark,[4] rather than recurrence in the context of a DV incident. That is, the presence of the risk factor of domestic violence indicates that some children are probably reabused as a direct result of domestic violence between partners, but this is a subset of the larger group of children who are reabused for other reasons. Thus, predicting maltreatment is not predicting DV, and vice versa.

Additionally, items on child protection risk assessment instruments often ask questions about whether there is currently DV in the home or whether the primary caregiver has a history of DV. What is generally not asked is whether the child was physically or emotionally injured during a DV episode. This is a critical point of inquiry; otherwise, there may not be a child protection issue. The relationships between prior violent acts (presumably including physical abuse of children) as well as battery while pregnant have been established as markers for femicide (Campbell, 1995). Child injury during a DV incident likely indicates a level of severity that should not be ignored. Along these same lines, consideration should be given as to whether a parent was injured as part of the DV issues that brought the family to the attention of CPS.

INTEGRATED ASSESSMENT STRATEGIES: A PROPOSED SOLUTION

Despite the fact that actuarial prediction is likely to produce results that are better than clinical decisions alone, the reality is that we are currently unable to predict either child maltreatment recurrence or DV lethality or injury at sufficient levels to make outright statements about whether either will occur in the future. There are just too many unexplained factors, and the phenomena being predicted occur too infrequently to attain great accuracy. To illustrate this point, Shlonsky and Wagner (2005) combined the four classifications (low, moderate, high, and very high) of the California Family Risk Assessment instrument into two risk classifications forming a simple (yes–no) prediction of whether maltreatment would recur. Although this configuration predicted at levels slightly greater than chance, the rate of false positives (predicting that individuals would reabuse when they, in fact, did not) was exceedingly high. For such a low base rate of recurrence, the best prediction would be that it would not happen. Similarly, the DA2, although clearly reliable in the sense that it predicts lethal domestic violence quite a bit better than chance alone, suffers from the same inability to make an outright (yes–no) prediction (Campbell, 2005; see also www.dangerassessment.com). The limited predictive capacity of high-quality tools means that the best we can do is to develop classification systems that categorize people into varying degrees of risk and tailor the intensity of the response according to these groupings. In other words, we make a statistically informed guess about what will happen in the future and respond accordingly. Given the level of accuracy of risk assessment tools in these fields, a forensic conclusion would never say more than whether a family is at higher risk than most other families for one or both of these outcomes.

With this limitation in mind, actuarial approaches categorize individuals, families, or both into graded levels of risk. Examples of this approach in child protection are the Michigan Actuarial Model, which was validated retrospectively (Baird & Wagner, 2000; Baird et al., 1999), and the California Family Risk Assessment, which has now been validated prospectively (Johnson, 2004; Wagner & Johnson, 2003). These models consist of a short set of questions, mostly binary, that have been found to predict abuse and neglect separately. Again, despite its limitations, this actuarial model clearly differentiates level of risk for resubstantiation, subsequent child placement, and child injury (see Figure 9.2). As level of risk increases, the percentage of children experiencing these outcomes increases. Children classified in the highest risk categories have a higher likelihood of experiencing these events, whereas children classified in the lower risk levels have a lower likelihood. The model does not claim to be right every

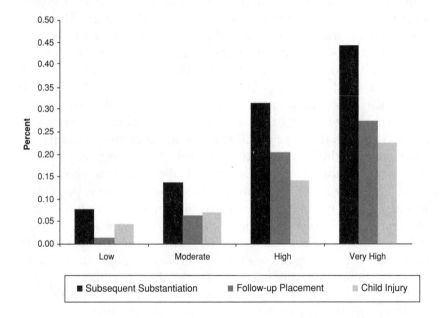

FIGURE 9.2   California Final Family Risk Classification by follow-up substantiation, placement, and injury. Originally reported in Baird and Wagner, 2000.

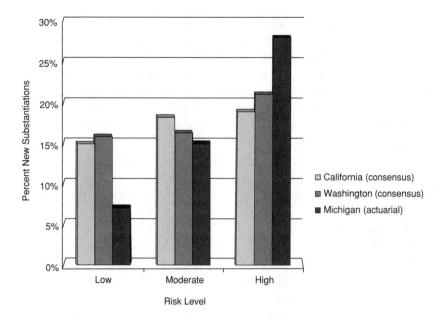

FIGURE 9.3 Actuarial versus consensus-based classification of subsequent substantiations. Originally reported in Baird and Wagner, 2000.

time, nor is it intended to be the sole source for decision making. The risk assessment tool simply assigns a level of risk relative to other cases (Shlonsky & Wagner, 2005). If an instrument cannot adequately distinguish between risk categories, then it cannot serve as a decision aid. That is, if high-risk cases end up recurring as often as moderate-risk cases, the decision maker would not gain any information from the tool. A comparison of this approach (Baird & Wagner, 2000) to two commonly used consensus-based tools found that the actuarial tool differentiated between risk levels, whereas the two expert-driven models struggled to distinguish between risk levels (see Figure 9.3).

Nested Risk Assessment

The presence of related yet separate risk constructs (in this case, maltreatment recurrence and DV recurrence) requires careful consideration with respect to risk instrumentation and application. One of the problems with assessment instruments is their implementation in the field. Instruments that are too long or too difficult to complete are unlikely to be used by practitioners. Clients, too, especially involuntary clients, may not engage with a practitioner who asks them countless questions contained on an endless instrument. Thus, a comprehensive risk assessment instrument that covers all areas of risk would be ill advised. There are statistical as well as practical concerns. How do two instruments interact to alter risk? That is, are all children who are at high risk for DV recurrence also at high risk for child maltreatment? Perhaps so, depending on the definition of maltreatment. But is the converse true? Are all cases at high risk for child maltreatment recurrence also at high risk of DV recurrence? Clearly not. Domestic violence may not have occurred the first time, making an assessment of recurrence somewhat nonsensical. If we are functioning within the CPS realm, it would seem that the primary assessment of risk should be child maltreatment in all its forms.

A nested approach to risk assessment, with risk of child maltreatment recurrence as the first-order assessment, has the potential to optimally employ more than one type of risk assessment instrument. That is, a hierarchy of instruments, beginning with a maltreatment recurrence measure and moving to other assessment instruments as needed, would provide valuable information for making key service decisions. In child protection, one common approach is to screen cases in for investigation, assign a service priority (i.e., immediate or more delayed response), conduct a safety assessment, determine whether the maltreatment occurred (substantiation decision), complete a risk assessment, and decide whether to open a case for services. This is followed by a contextual assessment and the development of a service plan (see, for example, Wagner & Johnson, 2003). This approach can be enhanced by conducting a DV risk assessment at various points along this continuum if there is an indication that domestic violence is a current and ongoing issue for this family (see Figure 9.3): If the original allegation includes issues of DV or if DV is discovered during the safety assessment, a joint assessment for risk of DV might also be conducted focusing specifically on the immediate risk of harm or danger from domestic violence (e.g., DA2). At the end of the investigation period, the original allegations are found to be substantiated or indicated (the maltreatment occurred), unsubstantiated (insufficient evidence), or unfounded (the maltreatment

TABLE 9.1 Service Decisions Based on Risk of Recurrence for Child Maltreatment and Domestic Violence

Recurrence Risk		Child Protection Risk		
		Low	Medium	High
Domestic Violence Risk	Low	Community referral only, no DV referral	Community referral only, no DV referral	High intensity CW services, no DV services
	Medium	Community referral only	Community referral, DV prevention referral	High intensity CW and DV services
	High	Community referral only, DV prevention referral	Community CW referral, high intensity DV prevention services	High intensity CW and DV services

did not occur). At this point, a child protection risk assessment is completed before the decision about whether to open a case for services. The decision is informed by the level of risk as well as caseworker input and agency guidelines. If opened for services (ranging from referral to child placement) and DV has been identified in the child protection risk or contextual assessments as a current family issue, a DV screener for general risk of DV recurrence could be administered and the information used for case planning purposes.

Table 9.1 presents an example of a framework for service decisions based on risk level of both child maltreatment recurrence and domestic violence. These responses are suggestions only. Risk assessment should not dictate service response because of the issues touched on in this chapter and in greater detail elsewhere (Gambrill & Shlonsky, 2000; Shlonsky & Wagner, 2005; Wald & Woolverton, 1990). Especially with mandated services, decisions should be made by carefully weighing risk assessment information and clinical judgment. Because of political considerations and population dynamics, individual agencies may decide on a different set of responses. At the outset, it is acknowledged that most DV instruments have not been extensively tested and, to our knowledge, have not been normed on a CPS sample. This framework is merely a suggestion, and any instruments used in this context should meet basic psychometric standards as well as be rigorously evaluated once implemented.

Beginning with the primary assessment for maltreatment recurrence, low-risk cases would result in referrals to services only. The main function of the CPS system is to keep children safe from maltreatment. Low-risk families, despite the likelihood of having fairly serious problems, should generally not be forced to receive such services. High-risk cases, on the other hand, call for joint evaluations and greater intensity of services. High-intensity services might range from voluntary family preservation services to child placement. If a case is rated as having a high likelihood of maltreatment recurrence but is classified as low risk for DV, then the mix of services would not include DV prevention support. Thus, scarce DV resources would be conserved for families with the highest likelihood of having a subsequent DV incident. As risk for both child maltreatment and DV increases, so too does the intensity of the service mix.

A classification of risk, whether obtained from a consensus or actuarial assessment, estimates the probability that an event will occur among families with similar characteristics. It is not a perfect predictor, nor is it a cookbook for service decisions. Certainly, it is not a substitute for sound professional judgment, and the finding should not be the sole basis for a case decision. Appropriate use in the field requires that workers understand how actuarial risk assessments work, know the limitations of the estimates they make, and receive the training and policy guidance necessary to employ them effectively in the field (Shlonsky & Wagner, 2005). An important component of both the California actuarial tool and the SARA is the presence of an agency and clinical override feature. This option allows caseworkers to upgrade the risk level (generally in consultation with their supervisor) to respond to information that may not be accounted for in the risk assessment instrument. However, this feature should be used sparingly. The very structure of a good actuarial instrument would suggest that, on average, clinical overrides will result in less accuracy. This is not to say that a clinical override used on an individual family will always be the wrong decision. It simply means that, over time, the instrument will be correct more often than the clinical decision maker.

The Integration of Actuarial and Clinical Approaches

Despite the advantages of using actuarial tools (e.g., more reliable and accurate assessment of risk), there are clear limitations, some of which have been detailed here. Perhaps the greatest limitation of the actuarial approach is that its intended use, assessment of risk, tells us nothing about people except how likely they are to act in a certain way. They are not designed to obtain a detailed understanding of family dynamics and functioning, and they are certainly not designed to be the sole basis of a treatment plan (Shlonsky & Wagner, 2005). Actuarial and clinical judgment must be integrated with the client's perception of the situation to make prudent decisions about the type and scope of services offered to children and families. This combination offers the greatest opportunity for improving casework decisions.

A comprehensive, contextualized family assessment identifies and clarifies relevant strengths and needs at the individual, family, community, and societal level (Gambrill, 1997); it explicates the reasons the family came into contact with the CPS system; and provides insight into the type and scope of services that might be necessary to prevent maltreatment and DV recurrence. An example of such an integration is the Children's Research Center's Structured Decision-Making approach. As detailed in Shlonsky and Wagner (2005) and in various state reports (see http://www.nccd-crc.org), the actuarial risk assessment tool is used to help agencies establish the intensity of services. However, case planning relies on a structured assessment of Family Strengths and Needs that is completed after the risk assessment and is used to organize clinical assessment findings. This consensus-based assessment is sometimes completed as part of a case or family group decision-making conference, allowing families the opportunity to participate more fully in the assessment and case planning process, and includes such elements as substance abuse, mental health, domestic violence, physical health, family relationships, housing, and social support. Standardization makes worker assessments more reliable, furnishes a brief format for documenting case notes, supplies additional criteria for classifying cases based on prioritized service or treatment needs, and provides useful information for constructing fundamental progress indicators (see Figure 9.4).

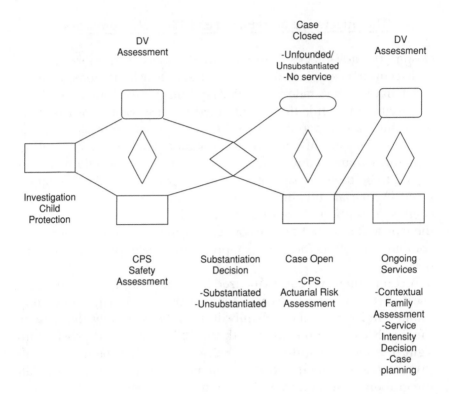

FIGURE 9.4 **Process of assessing family strengths and needs.**

THE LINK TO EVIDENCE-BASED PRACTICE AS A PROCESS

This integrated approach to risk assessment can be seen as the beginning of the full-scale implementation of the process of EBP (Shlonsky & Gibbs, 2004) in CPS (Wagner & Shlonsky, 2005). As outlined for evidence-based medicine (EBM) by Sackett, Richardson, Rosenberg, and Haynes (1997) and adapted for the helping professions by Gibbs (2003), EBP is the integration of current best evidence, clinical expertise, and client state and preferences. This integration is achieved through the process of posing an answerable question, querying a database to find current best evidence, evaluating evidence found, and applying it to client and clinical context (Sackett, Straus, Richardson, Rosenberg, & Haynes, 2000). Thus, EBP is more than simply the application of an intervention that has some evidence of effectiveness. Rather, it is a *process* that allows agencies and practitioners truly to take account of what is known about both the clients and the challenges they face.

The nested risk assessment approach described in this chapter fits within the EBP conceptual model when the model is conceptualized as a recursive *cycle* rather than a single event. Using a more recent conception of the EBM model by Haynes, Devereaux, and Guyatt (2002), risk assessment can be seen as an entry point, targeting scarce resources to clients at highest risk (see Figure 9.5). Moving counterclockwise around the circle, a search is conducted for current best safety and risk assessment instruments for use in child protection. Relevant data sources on current best evidence include the Cochrane and Campbell Collaborations, MEDLINE, PsycINFO, CINAHL, Social Services Abstracts, Social Work Abstracts, and others. Next, the contextual assessment uses clinical expertise to elicit key strengths and needs as well as client preferences as movement is made toward service provision. If, during the investigation process, current DV or a history of DV is discovered, current best evidence is again sought

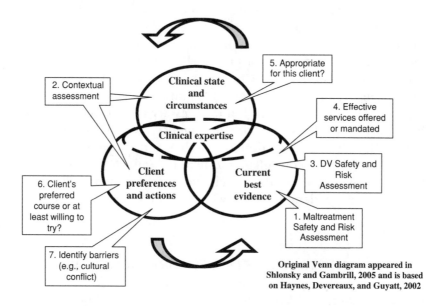

FIGURE 9.5 The cycle of EBP. Original Venn diagram appeared in Haynes, Devereaux, and Guyatt, 2002.

with respect to DV assessment tools (this process would work equally well if other problems such as depression or child behavior problems were discovered). At this stage, service decisions are made with consideration of risk level on both tools (perhaps using a predefined matrix similar to Table 9.1), family circumstances and preferences, and agency mandates. This stage should include a search of the literature for the current best evidence given the family's specific problems. Again, rather than simply throwing services at unwilling clients, consideration of the family's individual and group functioning, their preferences for providers or service type, and any barriers to service that might exist should be carefully weighed and, to the extent possible, used to modify services provided.

There is some debate as to whether conducting a detailed search with every client is realistic given the time constraints faced by caseworkers in the field (Mullen, Shlonsky, Bledsoe, & Bellamy, 2005). Initial searches by caseworkers will be more time-consuming but will amount to updates as problems faced by families are encountered for a second time. There may also be ways for the agency to anticipate the challenges its clients face, conduct specific searches for current best evidence with respect to risk assessment tools and effective services, and begin obtaining or developing such resources for use by caseworkers. Some large CPS agencies have already formed in-house special research units to assist line workers and policy makers (for example, Administration for Children's Services (ACS) in New York City and Department of Children and Family Services (DCFS) in Los Angeles). These could provide the necessary infrastructure for an EBP approach at the site or broader agency level. This would not preclude the need for continued searches and revisions of the assessment and service constellation due to the quickly changing state of evidence. Nonetheless, the anticipation of assessment and service provides a solid evidence base on which to guide service decisions.

RECOMMENDATIONS FOR FUTURE DIRECTIONS

Our examination of risk assessment in the context of child maltreatment and domestic violence has led us to see a number of pressing needs. First, there should be more cross-disciplinary work. To their credit, states such as Massachusetts have pioneered joint CPS and DV case assessments (Aron & Olson, 1997), but far more needs to be done. DV risk assessment instruments must be normed on CPS populations to use these instruments with greater confidence or modify them. For instance, although the SARA is not necessarily a predictive instrument (Dutton & Kropp, 2000), it does contain sets of risk factors that can be developed into an actuarial instrument built upon CPS cases.

Good assessment tools and the skills to use them are meaningless if services are not effective at ameliorating the problems that bring families to the attention of the CPS system. After evaluating multiple batterers' treatment programs, the most recent national analysis called for improved program evaluations and concluded that it was too early to abandon the concept and too early to believe we have all the answers (Jackson et al., 2003). Similarly, the literature is clear in recommending group treatment and various components for battered women's counseling, but program evaluations have been scarce to nonexistent (Lipshik, Sirles, & Yubicki, 1997). In other words, we are not sure what works for whom and at what point. Critics of the current service approaches for domestic violence argue that Western feminist ideology has been the driving force behind the menu of services offered battered women but that this has been done without adequate evaluation that these approaches lead to enhanced safety (Mills, 2003). Regarding children, Cunningham and Baker (2004) have identified only 11 evaluations of children's treatment programs for DV exposure in the published literature, none addressing treatment effectiveness. Thus, we have a small set of DV-specific services that consist largely of shelter care, none have been adequately evaluated, and, where viable programs for families who decide to remain intact exist, they need to be better publicized. These shortcomings must be addressed by moving beyond standard DV service provision, perhaps toward a harm reduction approach.

Given that risk assessments tend to be abuser focused, Cavanaugh and Gelles's (2005) review of the literature found that most male offenders in the low to moderate category do not escalate over time. They make a case for matching these typologies with treatment interventions, much like the stages of change approach (Prochaska, DiClemente, & Norcross, 1992). Batterers appear to be a heterogeneous population as opposed to the homogeneous, ever-escalating group typified by current approaches to treatment and intervention. Thus, we need to find specific strategies that are effective with particular risk groups. The danger of mismatching a batterer to treatment services, according to Cavanaugh and Gelles (2005), is that it is possible, and perhaps likely, that a batterer may complete a program without having his needs addressed. At its worst, a homogenous approach could undermine the victim's future safety.

Understanding that battered women are (for the most part) keenly and uniquely aware of their own danger, we need to study how their knowledge can enhance the performance of risk assessment instruments. Perhaps alternative treatment approaches such as the work of Penell and Burford (2002) in Family Group Decision Making and the experiment in restorative justice approaches for batterers proposed and underway by Mills (2005) hold promise for improving prediction and reducing recurrence by engaging the extended family and community members to monitor and provide acceptable resources for at-risk families.

CONCLUSION

Having explored the connection between child maltreatment and domestic violence, as well as the challenges in making predictive assessments, we are advocating a nested risk assessment that considers child maltreatment recurrence first and then proceeds with a DV risk assessment. Both of these then lead to a comprehensive and contextual family assessment that is the basis of connecting the family with appropriate services. Further, anchoring this within an EBP framework will help workers understand the limits as well as the strengths of risk assessment instruments, the proper use of contextual assessment measures, and the range of effective treatment options available to children and families. Integral to this approach, we recommend the following:

- Child protection workers need more specific focused training in understanding risk assessment. They need to understand the terms discussed in this chapter (i.e., reliability, validity, sensitivity, specificity), as well as the current state of what Cash (2001) called the art and science of risk assessment. Similarly, managers and policy makers must understand that there is no way to eliminate risk; there is only the minimization of harm through risk management (Gambrill & Shlonsky, 2001).
- In addition, child protection workers need more training in determining where and when to intervene and how to conduct

interviews that are sensitive to the issues surrounding domestic violence. Beyond prediction, the workers' goal is to prevent recurrence of harm. On the whole, good risk assessment instruments outperform clinical judgment with respect to prediction, but there is a role for the worker in assessing the dynamic context of child maltreatment and domestic violence. In particular, this will aid in the selection of appropriate treatment. Because instruments such as the DA rely so heavily on victim self-report, workers also need training in engendering a battered woman's trust because she may accurately perceive that honesty may put her at risk of losing her children.

- Reliably placing families into graded levels of risk can be readily accomplished with instruments such as the DA and the California Family Risk Assessment tool. As identified earlier, these gradations may be useful in matching typologies to treatment.
- More research is needed to discover how DV and child maltreatment might interact to alter risk levels. For instance, they may have shared pathways that converge in child neglect. We are just beginning to understand how such markers as children's use of the ER, maternal depression, and severe DV are linked. Because we know that both child maltreatment (Lindsey, 1994) and domestic violence (Edleson, 1999) correlate with poverty, the role of unemployment needs to be excavated fully with respect to both risk assessment and prevention of recurrence.
- Effective services must be identified and made available for locally prevalent problems (Shlonsky & Wagner, 2005). Each agency should identify a core set of commonly needed services for the treatment and prevention of DV, child maltreatment, and their related problems. Where such services do not exist or cannot be found, old services should be evaluated and innovations sought using the EBP methods discussed here. In any case, the current state of knowledge (or lack thereof) should be acknowledged rather than ignored.

CPS workers face the monumental and often impossible task of trying to prevent maltreatment while keeping families together. The presence of another unpredictable and harmful family problem, domestic violence, raises the stakes even higher. Risk assessment tools, despite their ability to predict future harm, are only the beginning of what is needed to prevent harm. Such tools must be integrated with a structured assessment of family functioning and a set of effective, individualized services geared toward addressing both concerns.

NOTES

1. A child has directly or indirectly (e.g., observed physical injuries or overheard the violence) witnessed violence occurring between a caregiver and his or her partner (Trocmé et al., 2005).
2. One recent study testing actuarial versus clinical approaches (Baumann, Law, Sheets, Reid, & Graham, 2005) favored clinical approaches in certain instances. However, serious methodological issues have been raised that call these findings into question (Johnson, 2005).
3. Because Campbell was investigating lethality, her informants were often mothers, sisters, and friends of the decedent.
4. The California Family Risk Assessment tool and other Children's Research Center measures do distinguish between physical abuse and neglect as outcomes.

RESOURCES AND REFERENCES

American Association for Protecting Children. (1988). *Highlights of official child neglect and abuse reporting.* Denver, CO: American Humane Association.

Appel, A. E., & Holden, G. W. (1998). The co-occurrence of spouse and physical child abuse: A review and appraisal. *Journal of Family Psychology, 12*(4), 578–599.

Aron, L., & Olson, K. (1997). Efforts by child welfare agencies to address domestic violence. *Public Welfare, 55*(3), 4–13.

Baird, C., & Wagner, D. (2000). The relative validity of actuarial and consensus-based risk assessment systems. *Children and Youth Services Review, 22*(11/12), 839–871.

Baird, C., Wagner, D., Healy, T., & Johnson, K. (1999). Risk assessment in Children's Protective/Protection Services: Consensus and actuarial model reliability. *Child Welfare, 78*(6), 723–748.

Barnett, O., Miller-Perrin, C., & Perrin, R. (1997). *Family violence across the lifespan: An introduction.* Thousand Oaks, CA: Sage.

Baumann, D. J., Law, J., Sheets, J., Reid, G., & Graham, J. (2005). Evaluating the effectiveness of actuarial risk assessment models. *Children and Youth Services Review, 27*(5), 465–490.

Beeman, S., Hagemeister, A., & Edleson, J. L. (1999). Child protection and battered women's services: From conflict to collaboration. *Child Maltreatment, 4*(2), 116–126.

Campbell, J. (2004, September). *Lethality and risk of re-assault: An overview with new data and practical techniques.* Paper presented at the International Conference on Family Violence, San Diego, CA.

Campbell, J. (Ed.). (1995). *Assessing dangerousness: Violence by sexual offenders, batterers, and child abusers.* Thousand Oaks, CA: Sage.

Carlson, B. (1998). Children's observations of interpersonal violence. In A. R. Roberts (Ed.), *Battered women and their families: Intervention strategies and treatment programs* (pp. 147–167). New York: Springer Publishing.

Casanueva, C. (2005, December). *Child abuse and neglect and its relevance among intimate partner violence victims involved with child protective services.* Paper presented at the American Public Health Association, Philadelphia, PA.

Casanueva, D., Foshee, V., & Barth, R. P. (2005). Intimate partner violence as a risk factor for children's use of the emergency room and injuries. *Children and Youth Services Review, 27*(11), 1223–1242.

Cash, S. (2001). Risk assessment in child welfare: The art and science. *Children and Youth Services Review, 23*, 811–830.

Cattaneo, L. B., & Goodman, L. A. (2005). Risk factors for reabuse in intimate partner violence: A cross-disciplinary critical review. *Trauma, Violence, & Abuse, 6*(2), 141–175.

Cavanaugh, M., & Gelles, R. (2005). The utility of male domestic violence offender typologies: Directions for research, policy, and practice. *Journal of Interpersonal Violence, 20*(2), 155–166.

Cunningham, A., & Baker, L. (2004). *What about me.* Retrieved Sept. 21, 2005, from www.lfcc.on.ca/what_about_me.html.

Davidson, H. A. (1995). Child abuse and domestic violence: Legal connections and controversies. *Family Law Quarterly, 29*, 357–373.

Davis, J. (1995). Failure to protect and its impact on battered mothers. *Courts and Communities Confronting Violence in the Family, 1*, 6–7.

Dawes, R. M. (1994). *House of cards: Psychology and psychotherapy built on myth.* New York: Free Press.

Dawes, R. M., Faust, D., & Meehl, P. E. (1989). Clinical versus actuarial judgment. *Science, 243*, 1668–1674.

DePanfilis, D., & Zuravin, S. J. (1998). Rates, patterns, and frequency of child maltreatment recurrences among families known to CPS. *Child Maltreatment, 3*(1), 27–42.

Dowd, K., Kinsey, S., Wheeless, S., Thisson, R., Richardson, J., Mierzwa, F., et al. (2002). *National survey of child and adolescent well-being: Introduction to wave 1 general and restricted use releases.* Ithaca, NY: National Archive on Child Abuse and Neglect.

Dutton, D. G., & Kropp, P. R. (2000). A review of domestic violence risk instruments. *Trauma, Violence, & Abuse, 1*(2), 171–181.

Dutton, D. G., & Nicholls, T. L. (2005). The gender paradigm in domestic violence research and theory: Part 1—The conflict of theory and data. *Aggression and Violent Behavior, 10*(6), 680–714.

Edleson, J. L. (1999). The overlap between child maltreatment and woman battering. *Violence Against Women, 5*(2), 134–154.

English, D. J., Marshall, D. B., & Orme, M. (1999). Characteristics of repeated referrals to Children's Protective/Protection Services in Washington state. *Child Maltreatment: Journal of the American Professional Society on the Abuse of Children, 4*(4), 297–307.

Faust, D. (1984). *The limits of scientific reasoning.* Minneapolis: University of Minnesota Press.

Fein, R. A., Vossekuil, B., & Holden, G. W. (1995). *Threat assessment: An approach to prevent targeted violence.* Washington, DC: National Institute of Justice.

Felitti, V. J. (1998). *The relationship of adverse childhood experiences to adult health: Turning gold into lead.* Retrieved January 20, 2006, from www.acestudy.org/docs/GoldintoLead.pdf.

Finkelhor, D. (1990, Winter). Is child abuse overreported? *Public Welfare,* 22–29.

Fleck-Henderson, A. (2000). Domestic violence in the child protection system: Seeing double. *Children and Youth Services Review, 22,* 333–354.

Fluke, J., Edwards, M., Bussey, M., Wells, S., & Johnson, W. (2001). Reducing recurrence in Children's Protective/Protection Services: Impact of a targeted safety protocol. *Child Maltreatment: Journal of the American Professional Society on the Abuse of Children, 6*(3), 207–218.

Gambrill, E. (1997). *Social work practice: A critical thinker's guide.* New York: Oxford University Press.

Gambrill, E., & Shlonsky, A. (2000). Risk assessment in context. *Children and Youth Services Review, 22*(5/6), 813–837.

Gambrill, E., & Shlonsky, A. (2001). The need for a comprehensive risk management system in child welfare. *Children and Youth Services Review, 23*(1), 79–107.

Gelles, R. J., & Cornell, C. P. (1990). *Intimate violence in families* (2nd ed.). Newbury Park, CA: Sage.

Gibbs, L. (2003). *Evidence-based practice for the helping professions: A practical guide with integrated multimedia.* Pacific Grove, CA: Brooks/Cole-Thomson Learning.

Grove, W. M., & Meehl, P. E. (1996). Comparative efficiency of informal (subjective, impressionistic) and formal (mechanical, algorithmic) prediction procedures. *Psychology Public Policy and Law, 2*(2), 293–323.

Groves, B. D. (1999). Mental health services for children who witness domestic violence. *The Future of Children, 9*(3), 122–132.

Hart, B. (1992). Battered women and the duty to protect children. In state codes on domestic violence: Analysis, commentary, and recommendations. *Juvenile Family Court Journal, 43*(4), 79–80.

Hartley, C. (2004). Severe DV and child maltreatment: Considering child physical abuse, neglect and failure to protect. *Children and Youth Services Review, 26,* 373–392.

Haynes, R. B., Devereaux, P. J., & Guyatt, G. H. (2002). Clinical expertise in the era of evidence-based medicine and patient choice. *Evidence-Based Medicine, 7,* 36–38.

Hilton, Z. N., & Harris, G. T. (2005). Predicting wife assault: A critical review and implications for policy and practice. *Trauma, Violence, and Abuse, 6*(1), 3–23.

Hilton, Z. N., Harris, G. T., Rice, M. E., Lang, C., Cormier, C. A., & Lines, K. J. (2004). A brief actuarial assessment for the prediction of wife assault recidivism: The Ontario Domestic Assault Risk Assessment. *Psychological Assessment, 16*(3), 267–275.

Hines, D., & Malley-Morrison, K. (2005). *Family violence in the United States: Defining, understanding, and combating abuse.* Thousand Oaks, CA: Sage.

Heckert, D. A., & Gondolf, E. W. (2004). Battered women's perceptions of risk versus risk factors and instruments in predicting repeat reassault. *Journal of Interpersonal Violence, 19*(7), 778–800.

Hughes, H. M. (1988). Psychological and behavior correlates of family violence in child witness and victims. *American Journal of Orthopsychiatry, 58,* 77–90.

In re *Heather A. et al. v. Harold A.,* 52 Cal App 4th 183 (1997).

Jackson, S., Feder, L., Forde, D., Davis, R., Maxwell, C., & Taylor, B. G. (2003). *Batterer intervention programs: Where do we go from here?* Washington, DC: National Institute of Justice.

Johnson, W. (2004). *Effectiveness of California's child welfare structured decision-making (SDM) model: A prospective study of the validity of the California Family Risk Assessment.* Oakland, CA: Alameda County Social Services Agency.

Johnson, W. (2005). The risk assessment wars: A commentary: Response to "Evaluating the effectiveness of actuarial risk assessment models" by Donald Baumann, J. Randolph Law, Janess Sheets, Grant Reid, and J. Christopher Graham, *Children and Youth Services Review, 27*(5), 465–490. *Children and Youth Services Review, 28*(6), 704–714.

Klein, G. (1998). *Sources of power: How people make decisions.* Cambridge, MA: MIT Press.

Kropp, P. R., Hart, S. D., Webster, C. D., & Eaves, D. (1995). *Manual for the spousal assault risk assessment guide* (2nd ed.). Vancouver: British Columbia Institute Against Family Violence.

Lindsey, D. (1994). *The welfare of children.* New York: Oxford University Press.

Lindsey, D. (2004). *The welfare of children* (2nd ed.). New York: Oxford University Press.

Lipchik, E., Sirles, E., & Kubicki, A. (1997). Multifaced approaches in spouse abuse treatment. *Journal of Aggression, Maltreatment, and Trauma 1997, 1,* 131–148.

Lyons, P., Doueck, H. J., & Wodarski, J. S. (1996). Risk assessment for Children's Protective/Protection Services: A review of the empirical literature on instrument performance. *Social Work Research, 20*(3), 143–155.

Magen, R. H. (1999). In the best interests of battered women: Reconceptualizing allegations of failure to protect. *Child Maltreatment, 4,* 127–135.

McDonald, T., & Marks, J. (1991). A review of risk factors assessed in Children's Protective/Protection Services. *Social Service Review, 65,* 112–132.

Mills, L. G. (2000). Woman abuse and child protection: A tumultuous marriage. *Children and Youth Services Review, 22,* 199–205.

Mills, L. G. (2003). *Insult to injury: Rethinking our responses to intimate abuse.* Princeton, NJ: Princeton University Press.

Mills, L. G. (2005). *A comparison study of batterer intervention and restorative justice programs for domestic violence offenders* (National Science Foundation Award #0452933). Unpublished manuscript.

Mills, L. G., Friend, C., Fleck-Henderson, A., Krug, S., Magen, R. H., Thomas, R. L., et al. (2000). Child protection and domestic violence: Training, practice, and policy issues. *Children and Youth Services Review, 22,* 315–332.

Mullen, E., Shlonsky, A., Bledsoe, B., & Bellamy, J. (2005). From concept to implementation: Challenges facing evidence-based social work. *Journal of Evidence and Policy, 1*(1), 61–84.

Nicholson v. Williams, 203 F. Supp. 2nd 153 (E.D.N.Y. 2002).

O'Keefe, M. (1995). Predictions of child abuse in maritally violent families. *Journal of Interpersonal Violence, 10*(1), 3–25.

Penell, J., & Burford, G. (2002). Feminist praxis: Making family group conferencing work. In H. Strang & J. Braithwaite (Eds.), *Restorative justice and family violence* (pp. 108–127). Cambridge, England: Cambridge University Press.

Prochaska, J., DiClemente, C., & Norcross, J. (1992). In search of how people change. *American Psychologist, 47,* 1102–1114.

Roberts, A. R. (1998). *Battered women and their families: Intervention strategies and treatment approaches* (2nd ed.). New York: Springer Publishing.

Roberts, A. R. (2001). Myths and realities regarding battered women. In A.

R. Roberts (Ed.), *Handbook of intervention strategies with domestic violence: Policies, programs and legal remedies* (pp. 3–21). New York: Oxford University Press.

Ross, S. M. (1996). Risk of physical abuse to children of spouse abusing parents. *Child Abuse and Neglect, 17,* 197–212.

Rycus, J. S., & Hughes, R. C. (2003). *Issues in risk assessment in Children's Protective/Protection Services: A policy white paper.* Columbus, OH: North American Resource Center for Child Welfare Center for Child Welfare Policy.

Sackett, D. L., Richardson, W. S., Rosenberg, W., & Haynes, R. B. (1997). *Evidence-based medicine: How to practice and teach EBM.* New York: Churchill Livingstone.

Sackett, D. L., Straus, S. E., Richardson, W. S., Rosenberg, W., & Haynes, R. B. (2000). *Evidence-based medicine: How to practice and teach EBM* (2nd ed.). New York: Churchill Livingstone.

Saunders, D. G., & Anderson, D. (2000). Evaluation of a domestic violence training for child protection workers and supervisors. Initial results. *Children and Youth Services Review, 22,* 373–395.

Shlonsky, A., & Gibbs, L. (2004). Will the real evidence-based practice please step forward: Teaching the process of EBP to the helping professions. *Journal of Brief Therapy and Crisis Intervention, 4*(2), 137–153.

Shlonsky, A., & Wagner, D. (2005). The next step: Integrating actuarial risk assessment and clinical judgment into an evidence-based practice framework in CPS case management. *Children and Youth Services Review, 27*(3), 409–427.

Straus, M. A. (1993). Physical assaults by wives: A major social problem. In R. J. Gelles & D. R. Loseke (Eds.), *Current controversies on family violence* (pp. 67–87). Newbury Park, CA: Sage.

Straus, M. A. (1999). The controversy over domestic violence by women: A methodological, theoretical and sociology of science analysis. In X. Arriaga & S. Oskamp (Eds.), *Violence in intimate relationship* (pp. 17–44). Thousand Oaks, CA: Sage.

Straus, M. A., & Gelles, R. J. (1986). Societal change and family violence from 1975 to 1985 as revealed by two national surveys. *Journal of Marriage and the Family, 48,* 465–479.

Straus, M. A., & Gelles, R. J. (1990). *Physical violence in American families.* New Brunswick, NJ: Transaction.

Straus, M. A., Gelles, R. J., & Steinmetz, S. (1980). *Behind closed doors: Violence in American families.* New Brunswick, NJ: Transaction.

Trocmé, N., Fallon, B., MacLaurin, B., Daciuk, J., Felstiner, C., Black, T., et al. (2005). *Canadian Incidence Study of reported child abuse and neglect— 2003: Major findings.* Ottawa, Canada: Minister of Public Works and Government Services.

Wagner, D., & Johnson, K. (2003). *The California structured decision making (tm) risk revalidation: A prospective study*. Madison, WI: Children's Research Center.

Wald, M. S., & Woolverton, M. (1990). Risk assessment: The emperor's new clothes? *Child Welfare, 69*(6), 483–511.

Walker, L. (1984). *The battered woman syndrome*. New York: Springer Publishing.

Werner, E. E. (1995). Resilience in development. *Current Directions in Psychological Science, 4*(3), 81–85.

Werner, E. E., & Smith, R. S. (1992). *Overcoming the odds: High risk children from birth to adulthood*. Ithaca, NY: Cornell University Press.

Wolfe, D. A., Jaffe, P., Wilson, S. K., & Zak, L. (1985). Children of battered women: The relation of child behavior to family violence and maternal stress. *Journal of Consulting and Clinical Psychology, 53*, 657–665.

Zuravin, S. (1999). Child neglect: A review of definitions and measurement research. In H. Dubowitz (Ed.), *Neglected children: Research, practice, and policy* (pp. 24–46). Thousand Oaks, CA: Sage.

Family Violence Prevention Fund http://endabuse.org	Focuses on public education and contains information on national awareness campaigns. It also posts legislative updates.
Danger Assessment http://www.dangerassessment.com	Centers on Jacqueline Campbell's instrument. It provides access to the instrument, information on its free use and psychometric data, and links to other domestic violence resources.
Child Welfare League of Canada http://www.cwlc.ca/index_e.htm	Provides information advocacy, statistics on abuse and neglect, publications, and membership. There are links to other sites, including the Canadian Incidence Study (2003), whose reports on child abuse and neglect findings can be accessed from this site.
American Profession Society on the Abuse of Children http://apsac.fmhi.usf.edu/	Focuses on all aspects of services for maltreated children and provides links to other resources, membership, their publications, and guidelines.

Child Welfare League of America http://www.cwla.org	Provides information on child advocacy, statistics on abuse and neglect, foster care, child welfare, and membership. Their *Children's Monitor* is a public policy update that can be read free online.
Child Welfare Information Gateway http://www.childwelfare.gov/ 1-800-394-3366	Provides information on statistics, child welfare, child abuse and neglect prevention, and state statutes. Many publications can be viewed free online. There is a section for professionals that addresses a range of topics from promising practices to workforce and training resources, including e-learning training.
Minnesota Center Against Violence and Abuse http://www.mincava.umn.edu	Offers information and resources on violence and various types of abuses. Provides links to related resources, published articles, and other manuscripts; many articles can be downloaded from this site.
Center for Excellence for Child Welfare http://www.cecw-cepb.ca/home.shtml	Fosters research, develops policy, forges networks, and disseminates information. Family violence research can be conducted with the search functions. The Center is part of the Bell Canada Child Welfare Research Unit, located at the University of Toronto.
Canadian Incidence Study http://www.phac-aspc.gc.ca/cm-vee/csca-ecve/index.html	Reports on child abuse and neglect in Canada.

CHAPTER 10

Intervention and Treatment Strategies With Adolescents From Maritally Violent Homes

Maura O'Keefe and Shirley Lebovics

Dad was always really mean. He blamed us whenever anything went wrong at home. He would hit all of us when he was mad, but Mom got most of it. He drank, but hit her when he was sober too. Once he beat her so badly, she could barely get up. We thought he might have killed her. Billy [Susan's brother, age 14] often tried to stop him, but it didn't help. It only made Dad hit Billy too. I tried to stay out of it. I wish I'd been tougher and done something, but I just couldn't get up the nerve.

Dad never let me and Billy have time to be with friends. Billy always had to help Dad with things around the house. I spent a lot of time at home too. I thought helping Mom would be a good idea so there'd be less to make Dad upset. My worst fear right now is that Mom will go back to Dad. I hate him for what he did to Mom, but sometimes I get real mad at Mom too. Billy and me talk about how great it would be for all of us if Dad died. We've been away from home at this shelter for 3 weeks now, and I still hate him. I hope this time Mom never goes back. I don't know what I'll do if she does. (from Susan, age 13)

I is estimated that between 3.3 million and 10 million children in the United States witness physical violence between their parents each year (Carlson, 1984; Straus, 1991). The types of violence children observe may range from overhearing some form of violent behavior from their bedrooms to seeing severe acts of violence such as beatings, chokings, or assaults with guns and knives directed at their mother by their father or father-substitute. In many cases, these children observe repeated acts of violence perpetrated by multiple partners throughout their childhood.

The vast majority of studies documenting the effects of witnessing marital violence on children's functioning have sampled preschool- and latency-age children residing with their mothers at battered women's shelters. However, there is little research on adolescents exposed to marital violence, or on effective treatment interventions to help them cope with the trauma of the violence. This lack of information may be partly due to the fact that adolescents often do not stay with their mothers at shelters. Also, many battered women shelters exclude male children over the age of 13. Further, adolescents, by virtue of their age, physical size, and greater independence, may be viewed as less in need of protection and therefore perhaps less deserving of concern.

The little that is known about the effects of marital violence on adolescents reveals a positive association between witnessing marital violence and aggression toward parents, running away, delinquency, and suicide (Carlson, 1990; Elze, Stiffman, & Dore, 1996; Grusznski, Brink, & Edleson, 1988). Further, there is considerable empirical support for the cycle of violence or intergenerational transmission of violence hypothesis—the notion that children from violent families carry violent and violence-tolerance roles to their adult intimate relationships. Numerous studies have found that witnessing interparental violence places individuals (particularly males) at high risk for perpetrating as well as being the recipient of violence, not only in their dating relationships but also in their marriages as well (Foo & Margolin, 1995; Gwartney-Gibbs, Stockard, & Bohmer, 1987; Kalmus, 1984; O'Keefe & Triester, 1998).

Clearly, the critical nature of the consequences of exposure to interparental violence on adolescents' adjustment underscores the need for accurate assessment of marital violence as well as for effective intervention and treatment. The goals of this chapter are severalfold. First, we discuss common reactions to witnessing marital violence, and some of the ways in which exposure to marital violence may impede adolescent development. Second, we provide guidelines for assessment and intervention with adolescents from maritally violent homes when domestic violence is not disclosed as well as when the presenting problem is wife abuse. Finally, primary violence prevention programs for adolescents are discussed.

ADOLESCENCE

Following are two case vignettes that illustrate some common concerns, issues, and reactions of adolescents who witness marital violence.

CASE SCENARIOS

Case 1

Jimmy, age 13, was the oldest of three children to an intact family. His sisters were ages 9 and 7. His father worked as an accountant and his mother worked as a nurse. Jimmy attended eighth grade at a local public school. Jimmy was referred for treatment by his teacher due to a long-standing history of defiant behavior. His grades included C's and D's and had worsened considerably since seventh grade. Jimmy's acting out involved lying, stealing from peers, and extreme rudeness to all of his teachers. He would often disrupt the classroom with various pranks, or by disturbing other students.

Jimmy was described by his teachers as socially isolated and unpopular due to his aggressive behavior. He spent most of his time alone. His mood was usually sullen and angry. He was also reported to "pick fights" with classmates, which led to physical violence and injuries on the schoolyard. These led the principal to suspend Jimmy on two occasions.

During the intake session with Jimmy and his parents, marital tension was noticeable. Father was dominating and voiced loud and harsh statements about how Jimmy's behavior was not to be tolerated. Father was openly critical of both Jimmy and mother. He blamed his wife for Jimmy's misbehavior because she was "too easy on him." His mother appeared noticeably uncomfortable with her husband's manner and accusations, but said little.

Attempts by the clinician to address any difficulties between the parents were met with resistance by the father. The father insisted he was paying for therapy only to "get Jimmy to shape up." The father refused to participate in future sessions and made no ongoing contact with the therapist. The mother assumed responsibility for bringing Jimmy in and occasionally discussed her difficulties disciplining Jimmy at home.

Jimmy formed a positive relationship with the therapist, who was a male in his mid-30s. Jimmy eventually referred to the terrible shouting matches at home. However, Jimmy voiced high regard for his father and defended his angry outbursts. He continually made excuses for his father, referring to how hard his father worked to support the family, and all the bad breaks he had in life.

Jimmy's love and admiration for his father were the few emotions he voiced with any conviction. He idealized his father, despite his father's physical and verbal abuse of the entire family. Jimmy said little about his feelings about his mother, but regarded her as lazy and as a "bad wife." He blamed his mother for the fights that went on at home, stating she always provoked his father. He wished his parents would divorce so that he could live with his father.

After several months of treatment, Jimmy's mother began seeing the therapist for her own individual sessions. She eventually referred to a disagreement between her and her husband and broke down crying. She finally stated that her husband had hit her, resulting in severe bruises, and that this had happened on numerous occasions throughout their marriage.

Case 2

Lenny, age 16, was one of four sons of a Spanish-speaking mother who was separated from her husband. Siblings were ages 13, 6, and 4. After 17 years of a severely abusive marriage, the mother left home and sought safety at a local shelter with her two younger children. Since adolescents were not admitted there, Lenny and his 13-year-old brother were placed at a crisis youth shelter for children ages 12 through 18. Services between the two sites were coordinated so that family sessions were possible.

Lenny presented as a soft-spoken, sensitive, and gentle young boy. He was engaging, likeable, and communicated well. He maintained a realistic and mature view of people and the world. He never engaged in the power struggles with authority that were typical of many other adolescents at the shelter.

During the intake interview, Lenny relayed examples of the wife abuse he had witnessed. His father would reportedly not only beat his mother but also force her to dress like a prostitute. He would rarely allow her out of the house or to spend time with her family. The threats to harm or even kill his wife were frequently heard by all the children.

Lenny's role at home was that of a parentified child. He took pride in being the protector and caregiver to his mother and siblings. He was consistently focused on offering them reassurance, assistance, or affection. His adoration and high degree of concern for his mother were quite pronounced. One example was his attempt to hide the knife his father used when making threats.

Lenny's protective and caring manner was apparent at the shelter as well. He was often seen holding and kissing his younger brothers. During one incident in which another teenager argued with Lenny's brother, Lenny immediately ran to his brother's defense in an attempt to "rescue" him. He also enjoyed serving as the interpreter for his mother during family counseling sessions.

During another incident at the shelter, Lenny heard screaming from a resident and immediately jumped to offer assistance to staff. He later mentioned in session that whenever he would hear conflict he would respond "automatically." He felt a sense of duty to be helpful by mediating.

In subsequent sessions with his counselor Lenny stated that he loved his father, but felt that his father was "really messed up." He voiced dismay that his mother didn't have the "husband she really deserved." Lenny also expressed his pervasive fear of his father, which did not abate during his shelter stay. He was concerned that despite the protection of the shelter, his father would eventually find and kill them.

ADOLESCENT OBSERVERS OF INTERPARENTAL VIOLENCE

Adolescents vary in their feelings, defense mechanisms, and strategies employed to cope with the trauma of growing up in a maritally violent home. Common reactions to witnessing violence may include feelings of shame, rage, fear, and anxiety. The consequences of the violence, however, may be far-reaching and reverberate throughout many areas of the adolescent's life, including school performance, social relationships, personal safety, self-esteem, and future stability.

Shame

Domestic violence is a family secret. Last night's fight that resulted in mother's black eye is not discussed openly among family members and must never be mentioned outside the family. Adolescents carry these secrets and are often burdened by the responsibility of censoring any remarks about their parents' relationship.

Because adolescents are self-conscious about both their physical and their social appearance, anything that calls attention to themselves as different from peers may be experienced as embarrassing or as a threat to their self-esteem. A home life that includes a father who batters and a mother who shows the physical and emotional consequences of being battered may be a source of great shame. The adolescent may be reluctant to invite friends home due to fear of exposure. The need for secrecy may lead to social isolation at a time when acceptance and support from peers is especially essential to social development.

Maria, a 17-year-old adolescent, who for most of her childhood witnessed her stepfather severely beating her mother, recalled: "I thought violence only occurred at my house. I always felt there was something wrong with me—that I was messed up just like my family. I was good at keeping the secret, but I felt that any minute I would be found out—that somehow I would be exposed and that others would judge me for what my family was like."

Fear and Anxiety

The general climate in homes where domestic violence occurs is often one of apprehension, tension, and a feeling of "walking on eggshells," as evidenced in the vignettes of both Jimmy and Lenny. The family is frequently in a state of disequilibrium, never knowing when the next violent incident may recur. The adolescent may fear being the next target of attack or doing something that will provoke their father to attack their mother. Some adolescents may become paralyzed with feelings of anxiety that may not only permeate the family atmosphere but also affect other areas of the adolescent's life, such as their ability to cope with normative stresses or plan future education or career goals.

Traumatic Reactions

Adolescents may develop symptoms of PTSD as a result of observing repeated or severe interparental violence. This is not surprising, because seeing one's mother being beaten can be a terrifying event at any age. PTSD symptoms identified in children of battered women include a reexperiencing or preoccupation with the traumatic event (e.g., nightmares or distressing recollections of the violence), increased arousal symptoms (e.g., somatic complaints, sleep disturbances, fears, and temper outbursts), and avoidance or psychic numbing (Arroyo & Eth, 1995; Mowbray, 1988; Silvern, Karyl, & Landis, 1995). These symptoms are also found in adolescents and may manifest in ways that are more difficult to discern, particularly if chronic. For example, psychic numbing may present as emotional constriction, flat affect, or withdrawal and disinterest in activities (Jaffe, Wolfe, & Wilson, 1990; Pynoos & Eth, 1984). Other symptoms, for example, running away from home or delinquency, may be expressed in a manner that disguises their origin and etiology (Jaffe, Wolfe, & Wilson, 1990). Because disclosure of family violence is unlikely, there may be little opportunity for resolution of the trauma.

Alliances With the Batterer

It is not uncommon for children of battered women to develop an alliance with the batterer. Some, like Jimmy, may blame their mother for the tension at home and feel angry with her for provoking the abuse. This alliance with the father against the mother may even manifest itself in assaults directed at the mother. These assaults often begin during adolescence, when the child becomes physically stronger than his or her mother. One study of adolescents who were physically abusive toward their parents found that in households where there was wife battering, a high pattern of abuse directed at mothers was reported (Cornell & Gelles, 1982).

A factor that may account for the adolescent's alliance with the batterer is fear. In any fearful situation, a paradoxical attachment and unconscious collusion may develop between victim and aggressor. This phenomenon, originally described by Anna Freud (1974) as "identification with the aggressor," is a process wherein a child may unconsciously identify with the perpetrator as a means of warding off danger. This defense mechanism is never fully effective; even when a strong alliance exists with the father, it is usually accompanied by underlying feelings of ambivalence, confusion, or guilt.

PARENTIFICATION

Adolescents who have grown up in maritally violent homes may feel responsible for maintaining safety and peace in the home. As in the case of Lenny, they may assume a parental role, defending their mother from their father's abuse or providing younger siblings with support and reassurance, particularly during violent episodes.

One of the tasks that adolescents face is individuation from the family system. Due to the dysfunctional nature of a violent family system, however, this becomes a difficult if not impossible task for the adolescent. The parentified adolescent may be concerned about who will take care of the family if he or she leaves. The assumption of a parental role frequently precludes the child from having his or her own dependency needs met and may interfere with the development of a healthy sense of self, as well as the achievement of independence from parents.

Aggression

The relationship between witnessing interparental violence and aggression in children and adolescents has been substantiated by a number of empirical studies (Holden & Ritchie, 1991; Kempton, Thomas, & Forehand, 1998; O'Keefe, 1994; Sternberg et al., 1993). Research also indicates that violent youth are more likely than nonviolent youth to have witnessed or been victims of violence in their homes (Kratcoski, 1985). Modeling has been proposed as one means by which aggression develops (Bandura, 1971). Children from violent homes learn to imitate both the physical expression of anger and the types of problem-solving strategies evidenced by their parents, and thus develop aggressive behaviors and poor conflict resolution skills of their own. Physical aggression is often first directed at siblings and peers and later used in their own family of procreation (Cornell & Gelles, 1982).

Rage

Like their mothers, adolescents from maritally violent homes may be the recipients of physical, sexual, and emotional abuse. A child growing up in such an abusive home may initially use denial to cope with their strong feelings. As the years progress and the violence increases, the feelings of pain and anger may increase in intensity to the point where they cannot be denied effectively. The adolescent may then become overwhelmed by anger and rage.

Since adolescents have a strong need to feel a sense of control over their world, they may experience a deep sense of rage not only about the violence, but also about their powerlessness to remedy the situation. They may also feel rage at their mother for her powerlessness and for her tolerating abuse or staying in the marriage. Like their mother, they may harbor fantasies and wishes that their father would somehow disappear or die. One 15-year-old teen who witnessed his mother's severe abuse spent long hours fantasizing about ways in which he would eventually get even. Another boy, age 13, who was residing at a battered women's shelter with his mother and three younger siblings reported that he and his mother attempted to kill the batterer by poisoning him. This boy reported that after a particularly violent incident, he and his mother bought rat poison, ground it up, and served it to the batterer in his dinner.

Depression

Adolescents from maritally violent homes are at high risk for depression and suicidal behavior (Carlson, 1990; O'Keefe, 1996). Many possible factors contribute to this. The adolescent's experience of wife abuse as a traumatic, uncontrollable, and pervasive stressor may lead to feelings of helplessness, apathy, and despair. Second, chronic or severe battering may result in the mother's psychological unavailability, lack of nurturance, or diminished parenting ability, which leaves the child or adolescent vulnerable to depression (Jaffe, Wolfe, & Wilson, 1990). Third, the adolescent may experience the loss of the idealized and wished-for family, as well as the real loss of one parent, should a divorce take place.

Characteristic symptoms associated with depression in adolescents may include a loss of interest in activities, sluggishness, inability to concentrate, or changes in sleeping and eating patterns. He or she may be unable to set goals, achieve them, or feel a sense of satisfaction when they are achieved. Depression in the adolescent may also be manifested by displays of anger, as it is often the underlying emotion in the adolescent's acting out behaviors (Mishne, 1986).

RUNAWAYS

As children move into adolescence, they may become increasingly unwilling to live with the violence. Some may seek relief by running away from home. One study reported that witnessing marital violence was an important predictor of runaway behaviors among adolescent females (Elze et al., 1996). Another study found that adolescent males in residential placement who had witnessed marital violence were more likely to have run away from home than were males who had not witnessed such violence (Carlson, 1990). Although their unwillingness to live in an unhealthy situation may be viewed as a sign of strength, adolescent runaways are extremely vulnerable to other dangers, such as drug abuse, rape, pregnancy, and sexually transmitted diseases, to name only a few.

Delinquency

As children from violent homes move into adolescence, they may begin to engage in behaviors serious enough to come to the attention of the juvenile justice authorities. These behaviors may include substance abuse, truancy, gang involvement, assaults, robbery, use of weapons, setting fires, or other illegal activity (Gruzsnski, Brink, & Edleson, 1988). Considering the lack of positive role models, it is not surprising to find the adolescent rebelling against authority figures.

Researchers have identified numerous family factors consistently associated with delinquency, including child physical abuse, marital conflict, inconsistent and inappropriate discipline, maternal depression, and criminal behavior of parents (Office of Technology Assessment, 1991). Many of these factors are also present in families in which domestic violence occurs. One researcher noted that delinquent adolescents almost always have another violent member in their family (Kratcoski, 1985).

Dating Violence

There are several unique aspects of adolescence that may make teenagers particularly vulnerable to dating violence. Because they are generally inexperienced in relationships, adolescents may have difficulty managing the complexity of feelings and conflicts that arise in intimate relationships. They may romanticize these relationships and interpret jealousy, possessiveness, and abuse as signs of love. Additionally, peer pressure may require that the adolescent have a boyfriend or girlfriend; the fear of being different or violating peer norms can create enormous stress and rigid conformity to gender-role stereotypes. Finally, due to their struggle for independence or conflicts with parents, many adolescents may not ask for any help from adults to cope with conflict or frightening experiences in their dating relationships (Levy, 1991).

Dating violence has been called a training ground for marriage and a link between witnessing violence in one's family of origin and using it in one's family of procreation (Jorgensen, 1986). A recent study of high school students living in an urban area found alarmingly high rates of dating violence: 42% report they had used physical aggression against their dating partners, and 45% reported that they were victims of that violence (O'Keefe, 1997; O'Keefe & Treister, 1998). Further, adolescents, particularly males, from violent homes have been found to be at increased risk for inflicting violence in dating relationships (DeMaris, 1987; Foo & Margolin, 1995; O'Keefe, 1997). It has been postulated that the intergenerational transmission of violence may be the result of modeling aggressive parental behaviors, learning aggression as a coping or problem-solving strategy, and increased frustration and sensitivity to power imbalances as a result of growing up in a coercive, conflictual, and low-warmth family environment (Langhinrichsen-Rohling & Neidig, 1995).

It should also be noted that whereas witnessing interparental violence may influence the later use of violence in dating relationships, it does not fully explain it. Other factors, such as being the victim of parental abuse, low socioeconomic status, poor self-esteem, acceptance of violence in dating relationships, and exposure to violence in one's community, have been found to differentiate high-risk adolescents who inflicted violence in dating relationship from those who did not (O'Keefe, 1998).

ASSESSMENT AND TREATMENT OF ADOLESCENTS WHO WITNESS SPOUSE ABUSE

Assessment

An adolescent is often referred to treatment by a parent or teacher because of difficulties such as failing grades, acting-out behaviors, or depression. The occurrence of spouse abuse may never be disclosed to the clinician, because both the parents and the adolescent might view the marital violence as having nothing to do with the problem. The clinician's careful attention and screening for spouse abuse therefore becomes critical in conducting an assessment of adolescents and their families, regardless of what the presenting problem appears to be.

The case of Jimmy demonstrated an example of an adolescent referred for treatment due to acting-out behaviors. The clinician in that case did not learn of the violence until several months later. Considering the impact of the home situation on Jimmy's behavior, earlier knowledge of the violence would have been helpful. The following are several guidelines that may assist clinicians with early and effective assessment in similar situations.

Guidelines for Assessment of Spousal Abuse

1. *Assess for Spouse Abuse as a Routine Part of an Evaluation.* Clinicians may be reluctant to approach the subject due to their own fears about how to intervene effectively. Other concerns may be about offending the parents or endangering the mother or adolescent. Failure to address the spousal abuse, however, ignores a significant factor that may be causing, maintaining, or contributing to the adolescent's problem.

2. *Maintain Awareness That Abuse May Not Be Readily Disclosed.* When a family comes in for treatment, they generally do not acknowledge that family violence is a problem. The battered woman may be reluctant to do so because she believes that the violence is her fault. In addition to feeling shame and guilt, she may fear retribution from the batterer. The batterer also may engage in denial and minimization of the severity of the problem and its impact on the children. The adolescent may be hesitant to disclose the violence due to his or her own shame and embarrassment, pressure to keep it a secret, or fear of the consequences.

3. *Watch for Subtle Indicators of Abuse.* During the intake interview with the family, the clinician should be alerted to possible indicators of wife abuse, especially signs of control in the marital relationship. Such signs may include the following:

- Suspicious injuries seen on the mother that are accounted for as accidental.

- The mother's lack of access to money or a car that is not attributable to low income.
- The family's isolation from friends or extended family.
- The mother's references to her partner's temper or fear of getting him angry.
- The mother's reluctance to speak or disagree in the presence of her partner.
- The father's humiliating, insulting, or dominating behavior.
- A history of physical abuse toward the children.

4. *Meet With the Mother Alone.* If wife abuse is suspected, the clinician should ask to interview the parents separately, so that the mother or adolescent is not in danger of an assault when the interview is over. Meeting separately should be explained to the family as a routine procedure; for example, "When I see adolescents I usually get a thorough history from each parent." The clinician's comfort and confidence in making this recommendation will communicate to the family that it is a necessary part of the evaluation process.

The mother is more likely to disclose the violence after she has developed some rapport with the clinician. A technique called "funneling" can be a productive way to ask questions about violence, particularly when it is not the presenting problem. This technique is designed to bring up the subject of abuse gradually, thus diminishing the client's potential defensiveness. The clinician begins by asking clients how conflict is handled in the home, and gradually moves to more specific probes such as: "Is your husband ever jealous of you?" or "Does he ever try to control what you do or where you go?" and "Has your husband ever hit you?"

5. *Explain the Relevance of the Abuse to Her.* If wife abuse is disclosed, it important to ascertain the degree of immediate danger to her and her children. The clinician should inform her that wife battering is a crime, that she is not to blame for his violent behaviors, and that children and adolescents who witness interparental violence are negatively affected by it, even if they are not the direct targets of abuse. The relevance of the violence to the adolescent's problem should be made clear. Additionally, the clinician should provide her with information regarding community resources. The clinician needs to decide whether he or she will work with the battered woman or refer her to another counselor. Follow-up in terms of the intervention for the mother should be offered. In addition, periodic conjoint sessions with the mother and adolescent may be helpful.

Treatment

As noted, adolescents may present for treatment in situations in which the marital violence has not been disclosed, or may be seen in a crisis state when the marital violence is the identified problem, for example, when they accompany their mother to a battered women's shelter. The following section describes a short-term crisis treatment approach that may be used with adolescents in various settings in which wife abuse is identified.

Crisis Intervention

Crisis intervention models emphasize brief, time-limited, focused treatment that is action oriented (Roberts, 1996). Roberts's Seven-Stage Model of Crisis Intervention (1996) has been applied to a broad range of crisis situations, including battered women in crisis, and is clearly applicable to the treatment of adolescents who witness domestic violence. As described by Roberts, the model is a guide to be used flexibly and differentially, as the particular situation requires.

The seven stages of the Crisis Intervention Model are as follows:

1. Make psychological contact and rapidly establish the relationship.
2. Identify the major problems.
3. Encourage expression of feelings and emotions.
4. Explore and assess coping skills.
5. Provide alternatives and specific solutions.
6. Formulate an action plan.
7. Closure and follow-up.

Stage 1: Make Psychological Contact and Rapidly Establish the Relationship. Developing rapport and establishing a therapeutic alliance with adolescents can be challenging. Because they often have mixed feelings about adults in positions of authority, clinicians must make an extra effort to establish themselves as trustworthy and create a safe and therapeutic environment. Adolescents need to feel that the clinician is concerned about them, respects them, and is trying to help them maximize their own potential for growth (Gil, 1996). A supportive, nonjudgmental working relationship is essential to enable adolescents to reveal and begin coping with painful feelings that are often too difficult for them to cope with alone. Most adolescents in crisis will value the opportunity to be heard, understood, and have an ally.

Stages 2 and 3: Identify the Major Problems and Encourage Expression of Feelings and Emotions. It is important to help adolescent witnesses recount the recent episode of violence that precipitated the crisis or brought their family to a battered women's shelter. A recounting of the violence will help them achieve greater psychosocial mastery of the traumatic event. Thus, clinicians should facilitate a full description of the violence, its antecedents, and its aftermath. For example, adolescent witnesses should verbalize what they may have heard or seen, what they were thinking and feeling at the time, what they did, and whom they blame for the violence. It is often helpful to have them discuss the worst moment of the violence for them and how they felt at that time (Arroyo & Eth, 1995).

The clinician should listen closely and ask for clarification or elaboration when needed. Responding empathetically will assist the adolescent to ventilate painful or overwhelming emotions such as fear of harm, a wish for revenge, or intense anger at the batterer or at their mother. It is essential for the therapist to provide emotional support and to normalize the adolescent's feelings by communicating that their emotions are a natural reaction to an extremely distressing situation. The clinician should be particularly attentive to any feelings of guilt or self-reproach the adolescent may have for not being able to prevent or stop the violence. The therapist may help diminish such feelings by providing the adolescent with a more realistic sense of his or her self-efficacy.

If the adolescent is living at a battered women's shelter, it is important for the clinician to inquire what it is like for them to be there, away from their familiar environment, including home and possessions, school, peers, and even pets. For some adolescents, leaving their home and personal possessions to stay at a crowded shelter may be *as* much or more of a crisis *as* the trauma of the violence itself. Problems such as having to attend a new school or deciding what to tell friends may be overwhelming. Some adolescents, with permission from their mother, may elect to stay with relatives or friends. However, this will depend upon a careful assessment of the degree of danger they or their mother might face from the batterer.

Stage 4: Explore and Assess Coping Skills.   As the adolescent's anxiety level lessens, a more comprehensive assessment of major areas of their functioning should be obtained by the clinician. The frequency and intensity of past family violence and previous coping mechanisms should be determined. It is important to obtain a fuller understanding of the roles the adolescent plays in relation to the violence, the meaning they attribute to the violence, and how they have been affected by it.

The nature and quality of the adolescent's relationship with each parent should be explored, as well as whether they have been the target of abuse either directly or indirectly from attempting to intervene in their parents' battles. In addition, the adolescent's characteristic response styles in interactions with parents, teachers, and peers should be determined. The clinician should engage the adolescent in a discussion of how conflicts are handled and how he or she generally copes with anger. Many adolescents from violent homes have poor communication skills, as well as poor problem-solving skills, which interfere with conflict resolution.

The adolescent's relationships with peers and his or her attitudes regarding violence in dating relationships should also be explored. For example, adolescents might be asked whether they believe it is ever justifiable for a boy to hit his girlfriend, or conversely, whether it is ever justifiable for a girl to hit her boyfriend. If they are dating, the clinician should inquire about how problems and conflicts in their dating relationships are handled.

Throughout this process, the clinician should recognize and focus on the client's strengths and positive coping abilities. Adolescents from violent homes often suffer from low self-esteem and self-efficacy as a result of growing up in a violent, nonsupportive home. Consequently, they may need extra help defining areas of strengths, as well as building on these strengths.

Stages 5 and 6: Provide Alternatives and Formulate an Action Plan.   Because adolescents from maritally violent homes present with such a variety of problem behaviors, cognitive behavioral strategies are frequently needed to help them gain new perspectives on their problems, correct faulty cognitions, and increase behavioral competencies (Zarb, 1992). One important component of such treatment is providing the adolescent with information on the prevalence of wife abuse. Simply recognizing that they are not alone and that other families experience the trauma of violence may lessen feelings of shame and isolation.

Another important component of cognitive behavioral treatment is the identification and restructuring of the adolescent's erroneous beliefs regarding family violence. The adolescent may believe that violence is a normal part of relationships, or that violence, intimacy, and love are enmeshed. Another distorted belief may be that someone other than the batterer is responsible for the abuse, that is, their mother or themselves. Interventions that challenge these presumptions should be part of the treatment. It may be useful to explain the dynamics of abuse, power, and control, and the cycle of violence in terms the adolescent can understand.

Cognitive behavioral techniques may also be effective in treating anxiety or phobic responses conditioned during the violence. Those who experience overwhelming anxiety may benefit by relaxation training. The adolescent is instructed to sit in a comfortable position, close his or her eyes, and follow instructions as the clinician guides the client through various steps of the relaxation exercise. The client may then be given a homework assignment of practicing these relaxation skills by listening to a relaxation tape (Zarb, 1992).

The angry or acting-out adolescent may be helped through interventions such as anger-management techniques, which combine relaxation training, cognitive self-instruction, and behavioral rehearsal (Meichenbaum, 1977; Zarb, 1992). First, the client is familiarized with the concept of anger as being maintained by negative self-statements made in situations of provocation. The adolescent's anger pattern is then carefully assessed. The therapist might ask the adolescent to describe specific situations in which he or she got angry and to report accompanying thoughts and somatic affective factors. The therapist then helps the client to analyze the content of these cognitions. Any dysfunctional cognitions and faulty information-processing styles that maintain their aggressive responses are challenged: for example, erroneous attributions leading to anger arousal, such as "The teacher is trying to make me look like a fool," or self-evaluative statements, such as "I have to be tough and prove myself" are pointed out. The client is then helped to consider alternate interpretations of the situation. Additional skills taught might include relaxation skills, humor, or nonhostile responses, such as leaving the scene or agreeing with the other person in a neutral way. Finally, the adolescent is asked to

practice and role-play new behavioral skills during the session, and
then to try out newly learned skills in real-life situations.

Some adolescents are drawn into marital conflicts by one parent
to punish or manipulate the other. In such cases, the adolescent
might be taught to examine dysfunctional family patterns and to
practice techniques for avoiding being drawn into the conflict. In
situations of ongoing marital violence, the goal of therapy may be
analogous to helping the adolescent "be sane in an insane place"
(Jaffe, Wolfe, & Wilson, 1990). In some cases, the only feasible goal
may be to help the adolescent learn not to imitate aggressive acts and
to make educational and vocational plans that will eventually allow
him or her to become independent and successfully move out of the
stressful family home. Meanwhile, they may need help structuring
activities that will get them away from the home situation as much
as possible, such as a part-time job, sports, or other extracurricular
school activities.

As noted, many adolescents from violent homes frequently experience low self-esteem and may view themselves as undesirable and
inadequate. Consequently, they may avoid setting goals or engaging
in constructive pursuits. Treatment should include interventions to
promote self-esteem and increase positive self-statements. The adolescent may be taught to identify self-blaming or self-critical thoughts
and how to replace them with positive counter-thoughts.

Implementing a safety plan is a crucial goal in the treatment of adolescents from violent homes. The adolescent may have strong feelings
of guilt, ambivalence, and conflict about what his/her role ought to
be when the marital violence erupts. One adolescent reported that
she was told by a counselor at a battered women shelter to call 911 during a violent episode. When the mother and daughter returned to the
batterer, however, the mother warned her against taking this action,
fearing that this would only antagonize the batterer. Although the in-
struction to call the police may seem reasonable, this is not a simple
issue. Such an assignment places an inordinate sense of responsibility
and pressure on the adolescent and may endanger the adolescent or
jeopardize his or her relationship with one or both parents.

Each family's safety plan must be individualized to provide the maximum protection to both the mother and children. The plan should
focus on what the adolescent should do during a violent episode
and where he or she can go to get help. The plan should be laid
out in terms of very specific behavior, including which phone she or

he would use, who to call, where to go, and whether the adolescent should call 911.

Stage 7: Closure and Follow-up Measures.   In the final sessions, the clinician and the adolescent might review progress in terms of tasks covered, goals reached, and any unfinished work. An atmosphere that engenders hope and fosters greater independence should be maintained. Treatment has been effective if the adolescent has greater understanding of the dynamics of wife abuse, has greater self-esteem and increased coping skills, and is better able to identify his or her own strengths.

If adolescents reside at a shelter, their concerns and feelings about their mother's decision to leave the abusive relationship or return to the batterer should be discussed. If the mother should decide to return to the abuser, it is helpful to have a conjoint session with the mother and adolescent to review the safety plan. If the mother leaves the abuser, conjoint therapy may also be helpful focusing on defining new roles, rules, or realigning of boundaries as well as planning for the future. A follow-up phone call to discuss how things are going may be helpful if it does not place the adolescent or mother in any danger. The adolescent may be given referrals for individual or group counseling, if warranted.

GROUP INTERVENTION WITH ADOLESCENTS

The most widely recommended intervention for children of battered women is a group counseling program. Most of these, however, are housed in shelters for battered women, and are targeted for latency-age children or younger (Carlson, 1995). As more mental health agencies accurately assess for family violence among their caseloads, more adolescents may be identified and targeted for referrals for group counseling to cope with the trauma related to growing up in a maritally violent home.

There is a growing body of literature on group work with younger children of battered women. The majority of programs involve highly structured sessions, which meet 60 to 90 minutes weekly for approximately 10 weeks. The goals of the program are clearly outlined with specific educational activities designed to achieve these goals. Some of the goals of group treatment include understanding family violence, emotional labeling, increased coping skills and self-esteem, procurement of social support, and safety enhancement (Peled & Edleson, 1995). Clearly, many of these same goals are applicable to treating adolescents. The reader is referred to some excellent children's group programs (Grusznski, Brink, & Edleson, 1988; Peled & Davis, 1995; Wilson, Cameron, Jaffe, & Wolfe, 1986) that can be easily adapted to fit adolescents' needs. An additional component of a program for adolescents should include a discussion of dating violence as well as teaching skills for coping with conflict in dating relationships.

PRIMARY PREVENTION PROGRAMS

Clinicians and researchers in the field of family violence have emphasized the importance of primary prevention programs to change attitudes and behaviors that may sanction or encourage violence in intimate relationships. The problem of violence in intimate relationships is one that concerns high school students. Teen dating violence is almost as widespread and frequent as violence in adult relationships (Girshick, 1993), and this finding becomes more worrisome if one considers dating relationships as the training ground for partners to rehearse future marital roles (Jorgensen, 1986). The extent of violence in intimate relationships and its ensuing mental health problems make prevention a critical priority (Sudermann, Jaffe, & Hastings, 1995).

Several authors have suggested that schools should play a more important role in promoting awareness about violence and teaching alternative forms of conflict resolution in intimate relationships. High schools are uniquely positioned to reach a large proportion of youth and challenge sex-role stereotypes or beliefs that violence in intimate relationships is acceptable or justifiable (Sudermann, Jaffe, & Hastings, 1995). Curricula can be incorporated into high school family life education courses and should include discussion of the normalcy of tension and conflict in relationships, what constitutes violence and sexual assault, how violence can escalate in relationships, and skills for resolving relationship conflict nonviolently. A number of excellent school-based violence prevention programs are currently being offered. Some examples include In Touch With Teens (Aldridge, Friedman, & Guiggans, 1993), Skills for Violence-Free Relationships (Levy, 1984), the Relationship Abuse

Prevention Project (Marin Abused Women's Program, 1986), and the Minnesota Coalition for Battered Women School Curriculum Project (Jones, 1987).

SUMMARY

Little attention has been focused on adolescents who have been exposed to interparental violence. This may be partly due to the fact that adolescents tend not to stay with their mothers at shelters as frequently as do younger children, and are therefore unavailable as research subjects. Yet adolescents may be a particularly vulnerable population, since they may have witnessed severe interparental violence throughout their childhood, and the changes associated with this life stage may further add to their vulnerability.

The present chapter discussed some common reactions of adolescents who witnessed interparental violence. A treatment approach based on careful assessment, crisis intervention, and cognitive behavioral strategies was presented. This approach may be applied to adolescents at shelters or those seen at mental health outpatient settings where domestic violence is not the presenting problem. The need for primary prevention measures with this age group was also discussed.

ACKNOWLEDGMENT

The authors would like to thank Claudia Petrozzi from Klein Bottle Youth Shelter, Santa Barbara, California, for her help.

REFERENCES

Aldridge, L., Friedman, C., & Guiggans, P. O. (1993). *In touch with teens: A relationship violence prevention curriculum for youth ages 12–19.* Los Angeles, CA: The Los Angeles Commission on Assaults Against Women.

Arroyo, W., & Eth, S. (1995). Assessment following violence-witnessing trauma. In E. Peled, P. G. Jaffe, & J. L. Edleson (Eds.), *Ending the cycle of violence: Community responses to children of battered women* (pp. 27–42). Thousand Oaks, CA: Sage.

Bandura, A. (1971). *Social learning theory.* Morristown, NJ: General Learning.

Carlson, B. E. (1984). Children's observation of interparental violence. In A. R. Roberts (Ed.), *Battered women and their families: Intervention strategies and treatment programs* (pp. 147–167). New York: Springer Publishing.

Carlson, B. (1990). Adolescent observers of marital violence. *Journal of Family Violence, 5*, 285–299.

Carlson, B. (1995). Children of battered women: Research, programs, and services. In A. R. Roberts (Ed.), *Helping battered women: New perspectives and remedies* (pp. 172–187). New York: Oxford University Press.

Cornell, C. P., & Gelles, R. J. (1982). Adolescent to parent violence. *The Urban and Social Change Review, 15*, 8–14.

DeMaris, A. (1987). The efficacy of a spouse abuse model in accounting for courtship violence. *Journal of Family Issues, 8*, 291–305.

Elze, D., Stiffman, A. R., & Dore, P. (1996, June). *Family violence as a predictor of runaway behavior among adolescent females.* Paper presented at the First National Conference on Children Exposed to Family Violence, Austin, TX.

Foo, L., & Margolin, G. (1995). A multivariate investigation of dating violence. *Journal of Family Violence, 10*, 351–375.

Freud, A. (1974). *The psychoanalytical treatment of children* (4th ed.). New York: Schocken.

Gil, E. (1996). *Treating abused adolescents.* New York: Guilford.

Girshick, L. B. (1993). Teen dating violence. *Violence Update, 3*, 1–6.

Grusznski, R. J., Brink, J. C., & Edleson, J. L. (1988). Support and education groups for children of battered women. *Child Welfare, 67*, 431–444.

Gwartney-Gibbs, P. A., Stockard, J., & Bohmer, S. (1987). Learning courtship violence: The influence of parents, peers, and personal experiences. *Family Relations, 36*, 276–282.

Holden, G. W., & Ritchie, K. L. (1991). Linking extreme marital discord, child rearing and child behavior problems: Evidence from battered women. *Child Development, 62*, 311–327.

Jaffe, P., Wolfe, D., & Wilson, S. K. (1990). *Children of battered women.* Newbury Park, CA: Sage.

Jones, L. E. (1987). *Dating violence among Minnesota teenagers: A summary of survey results.* St. Paul, MN: Minnesota Coalition for Battered Women.

Jorgensen, S. R. (1986). *Marriage and the family: Development and change.* New York: Macmillan.

Kalmus, D. (1984). The intergenerational transmission of marital aggression. *Journal of Marriage and the Family, 46*, 11–19.

Kempton, T., Thomas, A. M., & Forehand, R. (1988). Dimensions of interparental conflict and adolescent functioning. *Journal of Family Violence, 4*, 297–307.

Kratcoski, P. C. (1985). Youth violence directed toward significant others. *Journal of Adolescence, 8*, 145–157.

Langhinrichsen-Rohling, J., & Neidig, P. (1995). Violent backgrounds of economically disadvantaged youth: Risk factors for perpetrating violence? *Journal of Family Violence, 10*, 379–397.

Levy, B. (1984). *Skills for violence-free relationships.* Long Beach, CA: Southern California Coalition for Battered Women.

Levy, B. (1991). *Dating violence: Young women in danger.* Seattle, WA: Seal.

Marin Abused Women's Services. (1986). Relationship Abuse Prevention Project. San Rafael, CA: Author.

Meichenbaum, D. (1977). *Cognitive behavioral modification: An integrative approach.* New York: Plenum.

Mishne, J. M. (1986). *Clinical work with adolescents.* New York: The Free Press.

Mowbray, C. T. (1988). Post-traumatic therapy for children who are victims of violence. In F. M. Ochberg (Ed.), *Post-traumatic therapy for children who are victims of violence* (pp. 196–212). New York: Brunner/Mazel.

Office of Technology Assessment. (1991). Delinquency: Prevention and services. In D. Dougherty (Ed.), *Adolescent health, Vol. II, Background and the effectiveness of selected prevention and treatment services* (pp. 583–659). Washington, DC: Congress of the United States.

O'Keefe, M. (1994). Adjustment of children from maritally violent homes. *Families in Society, 75,* 403–415.

O'Keefe, M. (1996). The differential effects of family violence on adolescent adjustment. *Child and Adolescent Social Work Journal, 13,* 51–68.

O'Keefe, M. (1997). Predictors of dating violence among high school students. *Journal of Interpersonal Violence, 12,* 546–568.

O'Keefe, M. (1998). Factors mediating the link between witnessing interparental violence and dating violence. *Journal of Family Violence, 13*(1), 39–57.

O'Keefe, M., & Treister, L. (1998). Victims of dating violence among high school students: Are the predictors different for males and females? *Violence Against Women 4*(2), 195–223.

Peled, E., & Davis, D. (1995). *Group work with children of battered women: A practitioner's manual.* Thousand Oaks, CA: Sage.

Peled, E., & Edleson, J. L. (1995). Process and outcome in small groups for children of battered women. In E. Peled, P. G. Jaffe, & J. L. Edleson (Eds.), *Ending the cycle of violence: Community responses to children of battered women* (pp. 77–96). Thousand Oaks, CA: Sage.

Pynoos, R. S., & Eth, S. (1984). The child as witness to homicide. *Journal of Social Issues, 40,* 87–108.

Roberts, A. R. (1996). Epidemiology and definition of acute crisis in American society. In A. R. Roberts (Ed.), *Crisis management and brief treatment: Theory, techniques, and applications* (pp. 16–33). Chicago, IL: Nelson-Hall.

Silvern, L., Karyl, J., & Landis, T. (1995). Individual psychotherapy for the traumatized children of abused women. In E. Peled, P. G. Jaffe, & J. L. Edleson (Eds.), *Ending the cycle of violence: Community responses to children of battered women* (pp. 43–75). Thousand Oaks, CA: Sage.

Sternberg, K. J., Lamb, M. E., Greenbaum, C., Cicchetti, D., Dawud,

S., Cortes, R. M., et al. (1993). Effects of domestic violence on children's behavior problems and depression. *Developmental Psychology, 29,* 44–52.

Straus, M. A. (1991, September). *Children as witness to marital violence: A risk factor for life-long problems among a nationally representative sample of American men and women.* Paper presented at the Ross Roundtable titled "Children and Violence," Washington, DC.

Sudermann, M., Jaffe, P. G., & Hastings, E. (1995). Violence prevention programs in secondary (high) schools. In E. Peled, P. G. Jaffe, & J. L. Edleson (Eds.), *Ending the cycle of violence: Community responses to children of battered women* (pp. 232–254). Thousand Oaks, CA: Sage.

Wilson, S. K., Cameron, S., Jaffe, P. G., & Wolfe, D. (1986). *Manual for a group program for children exposed to wife abuse.* London, Ontario: London Family Court Clinic.

Zarb, J. M. (1992). *Cognitive behavioral assessment and therapy with adolescents.* New York: Brunner/Mazel.

Health Care and Mental Health Policies and Practices With Battered Women

Roles for Health Care Professionals in the United Kingdom and the United States in Addressing the Problem of Domestic Violence

June Keeling and Katherine S. van Wormer

D omestic violence is defined by the British Department of Health (2000) as any violence between current or former partners in an intimate relationship, whether or not they are married or co-habiting. The abuse can include physical violence, sexual violence, emotional abuse, or financial abuse. For an individual to be at risk of experiencing domestic abuse, the single most important risk factor is being a woman (Department of Health, 2000).

According to the American College of Emergency Physicians (ACEP, 2003), domestic violence is the single largest cause of injury to women between the ages of 15 and 44 in the United States—more than muggings, car accidents, and rapes combined. Each year between 2 million and 4 million women are battered, and 2,000 of these battered women will die of their injuries.

Approximately one in four women has experienced domestic abuse at some stage in her lifetime (Bacchus, Mezey, & Bewley, 2004;

Bradley, Long, & O'Dowd, Peckover, 2002). Such abuse accounts for one-quarter of all violent crime in the United Kingdom (Friend, 1998). In the United States, researchers report a disturbingly high figure of nearly 25% of women who report having been raped or physically assaulted (or both) by an intimate partner at some point in their lives (Centers for Disease Control and Prevention [CDC], 2006).

The pandemic problem of domestic abuse, therefore, is well documented in the two countries with which we are concerned. The devastating consequences to the victim are well documented as well (Bacchus et al., 2004; Basile, 2002; Bradley et al., 2002). Such victimization has a known deleterious effect on the psychological and physical health of an individual (Coker, Smith, Bethea, King, & McKeown, 2000) as well as on the emotional health (Dienemann et al., 2000; O'Campo et al., 2006). Universally, the sequelae of domestic abuse has a devastating impact on the lives of the survivors and their families. Often women remain in these violent relationships for years, living in fear. After leaving the abusive partner, many women express regret for their acquiescent approach to the relationship (Fry & Barker, 2001).

THE EXTENT OF THE PROBLEM

In Britain, as elsewhere, a woman is more vulnerable to violence in her home than in public. Diane Dwyer (1995), in a comparative study of the United States and Britain, highlighted the prevalence of domestic assault and the role of the British criminal justice system in processing domestic violence cases. Despite a much lower overall level of violence in British society and despite a much stronger feminist movement, Dwyer found that the prevalence of domestic violence was similar to that in the United States, that the British criminal justice response had been relatively less progressive, and that victims' assistance units were absent from prosecutorial services. Based on her cross-cultural study, Dwyer concluded that woman abuse is gender-based rather than simply a reflection of violence in the wider culture.

In both countries, feminist agitation against domestic violence has ensured that the police, courts, social workers, and health care practitioners handle the issue differently now from how they did in the past; private troubles have come to be addressed as public issues (Dominelli, 2002). In this chapter, we explore the physical and mental health correlates of domestic violence to the female victim of such assault, an assault to both the mind and the body. Research is drawn from the United Kingdom and the United States, where problems are similar as revealed in the statistics but preventive approaches are somewhat different, leaning more toward medical services in the United Kingdom and law enforcement operations in the United States. The chapter concludes with a discussion of treatment innovations related to the health care system.

INCIDENCE OF PHYSICAL INJURY

According to the U.S. Bureau of Justice Statistics (2000), women are significantly more likely to be injured during an intimate partner assault than are men; 39% of female physical assault victims compared with 24.8% of male physical assault victims, reported being injured during their most recent assault. Data from the U.S. National Victimization Survey reveal that women make up 85% of all intimate assault victims (Rennison, 2003). Nevertheless, the belief persists in some quarters that intimate partner violence is practiced equally by men and women, especially as portrayed in media accounts (van Wormer & Bartollas, 2007). Such media accounts conveniently omit the large gender discrepancy in rates of intimate partner murder, rape, and murder–suicide. The CDC (2006), alerts us to the following:

- Forty-four percent of women murdered by their intimate partner had visited an emergency department within 2 years of the homicide. Of these women, 93% had at least one injury visit.
- Previous literature suggests that women who have separated from their abusive partners often remain at risk of violence.
- Between 4% and 8% of pregnant women are abused at least once during the pregnancy.
- In general, victims of repeated violence over time experience more serious consequences than victims of one-time incidents.
- At least 42% of women and 20% of men who were physically assaulted since age 18 sustained injuries during their most recent victimization. Most injuries were minor such as scratches, bruises, and welts.

More severe physical consequences of intimate partner violence may occur depending on severity and frequency of abuse. These include the following:

- Bruises
- Knife wounds
- Pelvic pain
- Headaches
- Back pain
- Broken bones
- Gynecological disorders
- Pregnancy difficulties such as low birth weight babies and perinatal deaths
- Sexually transmitted diseases including HIV/AIDS
- Central nervous system disorders
- Gastrointestinal disorders
- Symptoms of posttraumatic stress disorder (PTSD) including
  - Emotional detachment
  - Sleep disturbances
  - Flashbacks
  - Replaying of assault in mind
- Heart or circulatory conditions

Numerous studies evaluating the association between domestic violence and health outcomes have found that abused women tend to report multiple emotional and nonspecific physical symptoms. In a comprehensive review of the literature, Carlson and McNutt (1998) found that physically abused women also have higher utilization of health care than nonabused women, although not necessarily for injuries. In addition, abused women report more sick days and poorer physical and mental health than nonabused women. These reviewers also researched the fields of family practice, obstetrics and gynecology, internal medicine, gastroenterology, psychiatry pain clinics, and emergency departments and found, confirming their hypothesis, that abused women report more symptoms and poorer health than women who have not experienced abuse.

Roberts and Kim (2005) examined the link between chronic woman battering and head injuries in a sample of 52 battered women. Their research is especially significant in light of the fact that 40% to 70% of abused women are battered on their faces, heads, or neck, as indicated in the article. Traumatic brain injury may result from repeated blows to the head with severe neurological consequences manifested as personality changes or problems with balance and movement. In their examination of interview data of battered women who had received head and neck injuries, they found evidence of flashbacks, insomnia, major depression, and nightmares of the batterer trying to kill them. The results of this study indicate that health and mental health professionals must be careful in diagnosis and screening battered women whose symptoms might be indicative of severe brain injury rather than emotional problems or some other disorder. In locating the true cause of the problem, social workers and psychiatric nurses and others in the emergency rooms and other medical settings will be in the position to facilitate an appropriate intervention.

From their literature review, Carlson and McNutt (1998, p. 234) provided the following list of typical injuries that are presented to physicians and nurses in primary care settings:

HEALTH OUTCOMES ASSOCIATED WITH INTIMATE PARTNER VIOLENCE

Injuries

Bruises
Lacerations and cuts
Fractured and broken bones
Sprains
Hematomas
Black eyes
Detached retinas

Nonspecific symptoms

Problems eating
Loss of appetite
Binging
Purging
Intestinal and urinary problems

Diarrhea
Constipation
Problems passing urine
Gynecology problems
Vaginal discharge
Menstrual problems, endometriosis
Reproductive problems
Sexually transmitted diseases

Pain

Choking sensation
Breast pain
Chest pain
Back pain
Abdominal pain
Pelvic pain
Headaches

Children may become injured during intimate partner incidents between their parents. A large overlap exists between intimate partner violence and child maltreatment.

That physical abuse is responsible for significant health and social disturbances is undeniable. Now we come to a closer look at the direct health consequences of such attacks.

American and Australian studies indicate that domestic violence is common among patients receiving emergency care in the hospital emergency room. With this in mind, Boyle and Todd (2003) conducted more than 250 interviews of patients attending an emergency department at a British hospital. They found that only 1.2% of the patients were victims of domestic violence on that occasion but that lifetime prevalence of domestic violence was around 22% for both men and women. A surprise finding was that many of the women who were victims of partner violence over their lifetimes were seeking treatment for acts of deliberate self-harm. There are several possible interpretations of these findings, but at the least, we could say that health professionals should be alerted to the possibility of wife battering in women receiving aid for self-mutilation.

IMPACT OF ABUSE ON GENERAL HEALTH

Gynecological Problems Related to Forced Intercourse

Previous studies have demonstrated the association between domestic abuse and gynecological complaints. This association has been identified as increasing the likelihood of gynecological morbidity (Campbell, 2002). An abused woman may experience damage to the vagina and rectum, trauma during vaginal examination, and pelvic pain of unknown origin (Campbell & Soeken, 1999). Sexual assault or rape by the partner may lead to health risks related to sexually transmitted disease. Women may find it difficult to be intimately examined by a doctor. The anxiety and fear resulting from their intimate abuse may inhibit the attendance of the cervical screening program (Ussher, 2000). Gynecological symptoms are commonly experienced by abused women, including pelvic pain, dyspareunia, and pelvic inflammatory disease (Friend, 1998; Schei & Bakketeig, 1996). It has also been reported that abused women have more pelvic operations than nonabused women (Drossman, Leserman, & Nachman, 1990).

Women in such abusive relationships are at risk of sexual violence including forced anal, oral, and vaginal intercourse and, in extreme cases, enforced prostitution (Friend, 1998). Sexual assault or forced sex occurs in approximately 40% to 45% of battering relationships (Campbell et al., 2003). This may manifest as sexual dysfunction. Sexual abuse may include rape, forced participation in extreme sexual acts, pornography and prostitution, and the use of a weapon resulting in injuries to the genital tract (Schei & Bakketeig, 1989). The male partner may question the woman's sexual integrity, although he may have other physical relationships. Rape within marriage remains a tolerated phenomenon in many cultures. Indeed, it only became a criminal offense in the United States in 1977 and the United Kingdom in 1992. Despite this legal condemnation, it remains a crime that is difficult to detect or prove. Furthermore, a woman may not conceptualize her experience as rape even though the event itself may meet the legal requirements for such a classification. Rape, particularly marital rape, continues to be underreported and unlikely to result in prosecution, thus being functionally condoned. Rape may result in an unwanted pregnancy. Many women fear this and therefore choose contraception with maximum efficacy. It has been shown that men are reluctant to use contraceptives that might interfere with their sexual desire or pleasure, thus leaving the responsibility for contraception with the woman (Ussher, 2000). Many women may wish to control their own fertility, but for women living with an abusive partner, the choice of contraception and family spacing may not be her own. Abortion remains a difficult issue to discuss. One study demonstrated that 23% of women undergoing termination of pregnancy were doing so because of their partner's desire to end the pregnancy (Torres & Forrest, 1988). Another study demonstrated a direct correlation between rapid repeat pregnancies among adolescents and experiences of abuse in low-income groups (Jacoby, Gorenflo, Black, Wunderlich, & Eyler, 1999).

The deleterious effects of abuse make it a significant contributing factor to women accessing the health care system. Women may present to health professionals complaining of somatic complaints as a direct result of the abuse they have experienced from their intimate partner.

During the first author's work as a domestic violence coordinator, a qualitative study was examining the prevalence and nature of domestic abuse. A comment offered by a woman demonstrates the deleterious effects of domestic abuse:

> My first husband abused me, mainly mentally, sometimes physically. I now have no confidence and feel so insecure. I wish I could talk to someone about all this because it is with me every day, but I wish I could just walk in somewhere without having to be referred by my doctor because wrongly there is a feeling of shame. Good luck in your work towards helping many women—maybe even me!

THE IMPACT OF ABUSE ON PREGNANCY

Pregnancy has been identified as a particularly high-risk period for women, when the physical violence often begins or intensifies (The Confidential Enquiry into Maternal and Child Health, 2004), with prevalence rates cited as being between 2.5%–5.8% (Bacchus, Mezey & Bewley, 2006) and 33.7% (Huth-Bocks, Levendosky, & Bogat, 2002). The nature of the blows are often directed at the women's abdomen and breasts (Bacchus et al., 2004; Berenson, Wiemann, Wilkinson, Jones, & Anderson, 1994). This violence poses a significant threat to the health and well-being of both the woman and her unborn child and may adversely affect the outcome of the pregnancy. It is estimated that up to 30% of the abuse commences in pregnancy (Royal College Obstetricians Gynaecologists, 2001). Many women do not require medical assistance in early pregnancy; therefore, it could be assumed that this percentage is not a true figure. Many will remain at home undetected. Rarely does the abuse diminish. The effects of the abuse can result in long-term psychological and physical morbidity and has a direct impact on the pregnancy. Higher rates of miscarriage have been identified in women who are experiencing domestic abuse (Schei, Samuelson, & Bakketeig, 1991).

Case Study From the First Author's Files

A woman was severely physically assaulted in her first pregnancy, which resulted in the birth of a stillborn baby. The midwife providing care for the woman at this time documented the abuse in the hospital records. The woman requested to meet with me when her second child was 12 months old. She had now decided to leave her abusive partner and wanted information about safe housing and legal support. The catalyst for her decision was that her partner had assaulted her after the baby's birthday party. She now feared for her baby as well as herself. The overriding concern for this woman, however, was the possibility of losing custody of her child because of her medical and psychiatric history. However, the abuse was well documented and resulted in the mother having sole custody of the child.

A recent large-scale study conducted by researchers from Johns Hopkins University similarly reports that infants whose mothers are exposed to domestic violence during pregnancy are more than twice as likely to die in the first weeks of life (Harding, 2006). Actually the research was conducted in northern India, where violence against women is common; results, according to the investigators, should, however, apply to battered women across the world.

Martin, Beaumont, and Kupper (2003) turned up an interesting finding in their research of 85 women at a U.S. prenatal clinic. The researchers examined the relationship between a woman's drinking and drug use in pregnancy and her experience of domestic abuse. Women who had substance abuse problems and were physically and psychologically abused when pregnant increased the level of substance abuse compared with other women with similar substance abuse histories who were not abused.

PSYCHOLOGICAL PROBLEMS STEMMING FROM ABUSE

Women living within a violent relationship suffer from the constant erosion of their self-esteem that undermines their confidence and can lead to self-hatred. Research now clearly shows a direct link between women's experiences of domestic violence and heightened rates of depression, trauma symptoms, and self-harm (Humphreys & Thiara, 2003). Unfortunately, the very social services agencies the victims approached for help compounded the problems in many ways, according to an investigation by British health researchers Cathy Humphreys and Ravi Thiara. Women reported that their contacts within the medical model of mental health were unhelpful in the following ways: lack of recognition of trauma or provision of trauma services; making the abuser invisible by focusing exclusively on the woman's mental health problems; blaming the victim; offering medication rather than counseling; and use of the evidence of mental health problems in later child custody and child protection hearings. In contrast, these women survivors did receive helpful responses from the private sector in responding to the women's special needs and helping in the healing process. The researchers concluded that there must be greater acknowledgment of the link between domestic violence and emotional distress.

An empirically based study of primary care, internal medicine patients had a typical study design and results (McCauley et al., 1995). A total of 1,952 consecutive female patients completed a questionnaire while they were alone in an examination room that asked, "Within the last year, have you been hit, slapped, kicked, or otherwise physically hurt by someone?" An affirmative answer identifying the abuser as a husband, boyfriend, ex-husband, or relative was counted as domestic violence. Compared with women not physically assaulted during the previous year, the 108 (5.5%) physically assaulted women were more than 3 times as likely to experience anxiety, 5 times as likely to be depressed, and more than 6 times as likely to have low self-esteem. Of the 20 nonspecific physical symptoms measured, 15 symptoms were 1.5 to 3.5 times more common for physically assaulted women, including problems with eating, sleeping, breathing, gastrointestinal symptoms, and pain (i.e., chest, abdominal, breast, and headaches). These symptoms are often more common than injuries. All four emotional symptoms and 13 of the 20 physical symptoms were more common than injuries (i.e., frequent or serious bruises) among physically assaulted women (McCauley et al., 1995).

From their review of the literature, Carlson and McNutt (1998) found that the following psychological symptoms were commonly associated with battering in women:

Problems sleeping

Nightmares
Problems falling asleep
Problems breathing
Asthma
Choking sensation

Other nonspecific symptoms

Seizures (epilepsy)
Fatigue
Pain or irritation of eyes
Fainting and passing out

Symptoms of psychological stress or psychiatric disorders

Depression   Substance abuse
Anxiety   Alcohol abuse
Interpersonal sensitivity Illegal drug use (low self-esteem)
Panic attacks   Prescription drug abuse
PTSD   Smoking
Attempted suicide   Suicidal ideation

According to the CDC (2004), the following psychological factors are associated with intimate partner violence:

- Adolescents involved with an abusive partner report increased levels of depressed mood, substance abuse, antisocial behavior, and, in females, suicidal behavior.
- Abused girls and women often experience adverse mental health conditions, such as depression, anxiety, and low self-esteem.
- Women with a history of partner violence are more likely to display behaviors that present further health risks, such as substance abuse, alcoholism, and increased risk of suicide attempts.

The psychological consequences of domestic abuse including PTSD and depression require specialist treatment both during intervention and postintervention to address the specific psychological consequences of domestic abuse (O'Campo et al., 2006). Psychological support and treatment may be necessary for years following the abuse, even after leaving the violent relationship.

PROFESSIONAL ROLES OF HEALTH CARE PROVIDERS

British health visiting by public health nurses who, in the United Kingdom, visit all women before and after delivery of their babies, is a universal offering of the U.K. National Health Services. Feminists view such health visiting as a gendered activity of mothers receiving help by a primarily female workforce. Yet as Peckover (2002) indicated, male-dominated professional discourses have emphasized the public health and educational nature of the visits, giving relatively little attention to the factor of gender. Drawing on interview data from 24 health visitors' accounts, Peckover found that when the topic of domestic violence came up, the health visitors' primary concern was with personal safety and child welfare. Another study by the same researcher examined interview data from 16 survivors of domestic abuse. All of the women reported difficulties in seeking help and concealing the truth from their health visitors out of fear for their own safety, lack of knowledge about what services could be provided, and concerns about losing custody of their children (Peckover, 2003).

Health professional organizations in the United States note that violence against women is a public health epidemic (Bryant & Spencer, 2002). However, despite the endorsement by the American Medical Association that physicians should routinely inquire about domestic abuse with all female patients, research has demonstrated that on average only 10% of physicians do this (Elliott, Nerney, James, & Friedmann, 2002; Rodriguez, Bauer, McLoughlin, & Grumbach, 1999). Reasons for not inquiring were cited as a lack of physicians' self-confidence in providing adequate care for those who disclose, inadequate resources, and fear of offending patients (Elliott et al., 2002).

SCREENING AND EARLY INTERVENTION

Because of the high prevalence of this often hidden problem, and the fact that medical personnel are often the first point of contact for victims of physical assault, the (British) Home Office (2004), the ACEP (2003), and the American College of Obstetricians and Gynecologists (1995) strongly recommend that screening be done of all adult female patients. Critics suggest that the absence of a strategic screening program for women experiencing domestic abuse reduces the opportunities for disclosure (Edin & Hogberg, 2002; Shadigian & Bauer, 2004). Because women are often psychologically not ready to bring up the topic of abuse, health care professionals need to facilitate this process as much as possible so that the victims can get the help they need.

The ACEP (2003) encourages emergency personnel to screen patients for domestic violence and to refer appropriately any of them who indicate domestic violence may be a problem. As stated on the organization's Web site:

> Despite the magnitude of the problem, identifying domestic violence victims is still a complex task. It is difficult to determine whether someone fell or was pushed, and emergency physicians are working to improve the identification of domestic violence when it occurs. ACEP encourages emergency personnel to screen patients for domestic violence and appropriately refer those patients who indicate domestic violence may be a problem in their lives.

The first thing a physician can do is recognize the signs of violence. These vary depending on the type of abuse and the victim's position in the family. Medical findings such as the following should prompt direct questioning about domestic violence (see http://www.acep.org/webportal/PatientConsumers):

- Central pattern of injuries
- Contusions or injuries in the head, neck, or chest
- Injuries that suggest a defensive posture
- Types or extent of injury that are inconsistent with the patient's explanation
- Substantial delay between when the injury occurred and when the patient sought treatment
- Injuries during pregnancy
- Pattern of repeated visits to the emergency department
- Evidence of alcohol or drug abuse
- Arriving in the emergency department as a result of a suicide attempt or rape
- Physicians also can gain clues from observing a patient and his or her partner

For example, a battered patient may seem evasive, embarrassed, or inappropriately unconcerned with his or her injuries, whereas the partner may be overly solicitous and answer questions for the patient. Or a partner of the victim may be openly hostile, defensive, or aggressive, setting up communication barriers.

U.K. residents have a major advantage over people in the United States, as mentioned earlier, in the active role of public health nurses who make periodic visits to all homes where there are children. Public health nurses have a pivotal role in the detection of domestic abuse and the support of the woman and child. They are uniquely able to observe the family dynamics and build a rapport with the woman over several weeks while visiting her in her own home. This encourages earlier detection and intervention of domestic abuse, but personal safety must be paramount. Because of abuser characteristics, women may not have the opportunity to be alone with the nurse, and it may be unsafe for the nurse to question the woman in her own home. In this scenario, the nurse may either arrange to meet the woman in a clinic and plan for an opportune moment of accessing the woman on her own (in the first author's experience, perpetrators can always be removed from their partner, if only for a few minutes, under several pretenses without raising suspicion) or visit the woman without a prior appointment. The majority of public health nurses consider that asking about domestic abuse is within their professional remit, but they are not always sure of how to respond (Dickson & Tutty, 1996).

The growing interface between police and social workers within the context of emergency rooms has resulted in a multidisciplinary approach and rapid response to victims of domestic abuse. However, the access to these services needs to be extended throughout a hospital. Although emergency rooms might be the point of contact, empirical evidence suggests that many women accessing all aspects of health care including oncology, medicine, maternity, and general surgical wards may be experiencing domestic abuse. The use of protocols enables emergency room physicians and nurses to offer appropriate and structured signposting to a survivor of abuse. It informs the physicians and nurses of what questions to ask and how to respond appropriately. Studies have demonstrated that the use of a protocol in emergency rooms increases the identification of domestic abuse (McLeer, Anwar, Herman, & Maquiling, 1989).

The Home Office (2004) recommends routine inquiries of all the female patients in specialized settings such as maternity services and mental health settings but also in primary health care as well. Asking all women, according to the report, has the advantage of not stigmatizing individual women or getting them into trouble with their partners. Studies have shown that although midwives typically hold back for fear of offending patients, after special training, they have been shown to ask women more readily about domestic violence.

Perhaps the most significant deterrent for disclosing domestic abuse may be a deficiency in the health care professional's interpersonal skills because of a lack of knowledge and understanding of the issues surrounding intimate partner abuse; this may result in the professional appearing insincere, ineffectual, or even an unsafe person to whom to disclose sensitive information (Chambliss, Bay, & Jones, 1995; Hathaway, Willis, & Zimmer, 2002). It is generally accepted that the implementation of an educational program specific to the dynamics of domestic abuse is beneficial to health professionals, and it is suggested that these changes would have a positive influence over rates of disclosure (Keeling, 2002; McGuigan, Vuchinich, & Pratt, 2000; Mezey & Bewley, 1997). Other barriers to asking clients about domestic abuse that health care professionals have identified include lack of time in clinical situations, inadequate training, and fear of offending (Hathaway et al., 2002; Keeling, 2002). However, in a recent study in which women were asked anonymously,

"Do you think it is appropriate for staff to ask patients questions about domestic violence?," more than 80% stated that such questions were appropriate (Keeling & Birch, 2004).

The gender of the health professional appeared to make a difference as to whether survivors of abuse disclose, with one study identifying that 16% of women in a study felt it would be easier to disclose to a female health care provider (Hathaway et al., 2002), whereas the heath professional's specialty did not appear to differentiate rates of disclosure (Warshaw, 1989). However, many survivors of abuse have reduced contact with the health service, thereby minimizing their opportunity to disclose (Shadigian & Bauer, 2004).

All experiences of domestic abuse may be affected by recall bias because some experiences are too traumatic to recall, and some women may not consider their experiences as domestic abuse. Some women may minimize their injuries, be in denial, or accept their treatment as a "cultural norm." However, for all abused women contemplating disclosing abuse, a plethora of issues surround the decision. Almost a third of women in a study by Hathaway et al. (2002) were fearful of disclosing abuse. A perceived lack of confidentiality may further affect disclosure adversely. Other factors identified include lack of time or perceived rush to be seen and treated.

This raises a question: Should men accompany women when attending for any intimate female examination? The gradual acceptance of men to accompany their female partner during an intimate examination has denied women the opportunity to disclose abuse and to access the vital support that may be offered by the health care provider. Physical violence is often accompanied by psychological abuse and sexual violence, which tends to intensify over the course of a pregnancy, and therefore the earlier the abuse is detected, the less risk that is posed to the pregnant woman and fetus because the empowerment process can commence earlier.

There appear to be several factors that inhibit a survivor's opportunity and desire to disclose abuse. It is imperative that, as health professionals, we are aware of the implications of abuse and able to offer effective support to those who choose to disclose (Keeling, 2004). Women will rarely volunteer their experiences of abuse without a proactive approach from health professionals. However, the majority of women find it entirely acceptable to be asked, in private, about their experiences of domestic abuse (Stenson, Saarinen, Heimer, &

Sidenvall, 2001). To ensure that all health professionals are skilled at empowering survivors of domestic abuse when they choose to disclose, education of the health care professional should be considered an essential component of any educational health program (Keeling, 2002; McFarlane, Cristoffel, Bateman, Miller, & Bullock, 1991).

Given the unproven effect of implementing routine screening for domestic abuse (Davidson, King, Garcia, & Merchant, 2000; Ramsay, Richardson, Carter, Davidson, & Feder, 2002; Richardson et al., 2002) and the knowledge that women are more likely to disclose abuse if asked (Richardson et al., 2002), a paradox exists. We suggest that by assimilating the factors identified in this chapter and using these skills to increase the knowledge and efficacy of domestic abuse programs within the health service, morbidity and mortality due to the causative effects of abuse may be reduced, and health costs may be reduced as well.

From the comments offered by survivors, we recognize that the experiences of domestic abuse are profound and devastating. As health care professionals, we are responsible for the provision of holistic care. The nature of the health service today and the often ever-present partner can make addressing the issue of domestic abuse extremely difficult. Thus, as care providers we should seriously consider including the provision for all women an opportunity to see a health professional on their own within the acute and community environments.

Leaving a violent relationship is a process that may take a woman months or years to achieve. While working as a domestic violence coordinator in a hospital, the first author encountered many women who chose to disclose for the first time while at the hospital because they perceived it as a safe place. Safety planning is crucial to all survivors of domestic abuse. A hospital is not necessarily safe. Perpetrators can easily gain access to wards and other clinical areas to continue their abuse. Important issues to discuss when the woman discloses are the following:

- Does the perpetrator carry a weapon?
- What has been the nature of the abuse?
- If children are involved, where are they, who are they with, and are they safe? If any concerns arise, then child protection guidelines must be adhered to.

CONCLUSION

The acceptability of being asked about experiences of domestic abuse, coupled with the known deleterious effects of abuse, support the argument for the inclusion of routine questioning of domestic abuse in a woman's life (Keeling & Birch, 2004; Tacket, Beringer, Irvine, & Garfield, 2004). If delivered in conjunction with education, support signposting to appropriate agencies and follow-up care provision, it is suggested that the prevalence rates of domestic abuse can be reduced by 75% (Wist & McFarlane, 1999). The pivotal reason for abuse intervention is to promote the safety of the woman and prevent further injury or loss of life to both the woman and her children. An organized approach to inquiry with a policy and protocol to follow may prevent the disorganized and stereotypical approach that leaves vulnerable women and their children at significant risk to further abuse. All health professionals must be fully aware of the resources available to survivors of abuse and be able to provide effective support as part of the empowerment process for that woman. It is essential that all care providers within the acute and community sectors receive training to recognize and to respond effectively to a woman who chooses to disclose domestic abuse and be able to access multiagency collaboration.

Additionally, this chapter has identified the importance of providing printed information about domestic abuse to raise awareness of these issues. The facts revealed in this review of relevant research have also revealed the significance of the patient–health provider relationship in enhancing the patient's readiness for disclosure and discussed effective ways of asking about domestic abuse (Hathaway et al., 2002; Shadigian & Bauer, 2004).

Common themes emerge when examining the literature regarding intervention strategies within the health service. It appears that although most health care providers are willing to question female patients about domestic abuse, many feel they lack the confidence, knowledge, or skills to undertake this task. Fear of offending a woman has been cited as a negative aspect of questioning even though research has demonstrated that women are not offended by this (Keeling & Birch, 2004; McCauley, Yurk, Jenckes, & Ford, 1998). There is an obvious disparity between professional attitudes and the need for detection of abuse and support for the women involved.

The first author, given her professional experience in working with women in health care and the advantages of her work within a nationalized health care system, recommends that the central government, in conjunction with professional organizations in each county, should consider the development of a training program for all health care providers to achieve consistency in the approach to survivors of abuse. Localized areas of good practice and an essential multidisciplinary approach with statuary and voluntary agencies could be replicated. The second author hopes to see her country, the United States, adopt a universal program of public health visitation to the homes of new mothers not only to detect situations of abuse but also to enhance the lives of the mother and child more generally. Another recommendation would be for the medical providers to order postnatal home nurse visits for patients who are covered under Medicaid and many private insurance policies ("Postpartum Home Nurse Visits," 2004). The availability of these services is little used and not well known.

The detection of domestic abuse is the initial step. This has to be in conjunction with healing programs that should be easily accessible for survivors of abuse and children, social benefit agency, employment advisors, school teachers, legal representatives, and safe housing advocates. If the deviant behavior of perpetrators is not addressed, we are perpetuating the problem because perpetrators will move on to their next victim. Domestic abuse is a major public health issue and should be treated as such; an integral and sustainable policy and protocol should be developed and evaluated in all areas of health care.

REFERENCES

American College of Emergency Physicians. (2003). *Domestic violence.* Retrieved August 2006, from http://www.org/webportal/PatientsConsumers.

American College of Obstetricians and Gynecologists. (1995). Domestic violence (Technical Bulletin No. 209). *International Journal of Gynecology and Obstetrics, 51,* 161–170.

Bacchus, L., Mezey, G., & Bewley, S. (2004). Domestic violence: Prevalence in pregnant women and associations with physical and psychological health. *European Journal of Obstetrics and Gynaecology and Reproductive Biology, 113,* 6–11.

Bacchus, L., Mezey, G., & Bewley, S. (2006). A qualitative exploration of the nature of domestic violence in pregnancy. *Violence Against Women, 12(6),* 588–604.

Basile, C. K. (2002). Prevalence of wife rape and other intimate partner sexual coercion in a nationally representative sample of women. *Violence and Victimology, 17*(5), 511–524.

Berenson, A. B., Wiemann, C. M., Wilkinson, G. S., Jones, W. A., & Anderson, G. D. (1994). Perinatal morbidity associated with violence experienced by pregnant women. *American Journal of Obstetrics and Gynecology, 170,* 1760–1769.

Boyle, A., & Todd, C. (2003). Incidence and prevalence of domestic violence in a UK emergency department. *Emergency Medicine Journal, 20*(5), 438–443.

Bradley, F., Smith, M., Long, J., & O'Dowd, T. (2002). Reported frequency of domestic violence: Cross sectional survey of women attending general practice. *British Medical Journal, 324,* 271–273.

British Department of Health (2000). *Domestic violence: A resource manual for health care professionals.* London: Department of Health. Retrieved October 2006, from www.dh.gov.uk/assetRoot.

Bryant, S. A., & Spencer, G. A. (2002). Domestic violence: What do nurse practitioners think? *Journal of the American Academy of Nurse Practitioners, 14*(9), 421–427.

Campbell, J. (2002). Health consequences of intimate partner violence. *Lancet, 359*(9314), 1331–1336.

Campbell, J., & Soeken, K. (1999). Forced sex and intimate partner violence: Effects on women's risk and women's health. *Violence Against Women, 5*(9), 1017–1035.

Campbell, J., Webster, D., Koziol-McLain, J., Block, C. R., Campbell, D., Curry, M. A., et al. (2003). Assessing risk factors for intimate partner homicide. In Intimate Partner Homicide, *NIJ Journal, 250,* 14–19. Washington, DC: National Institute of Justice, U.S. Department of Justice.

Carlson, B., & McNutt, L. A. (1998). Intimate partner violence: Intervention in primary health care settings. In A. R. Roberts (Ed.), *Battered women and their families: Intervention strategies and treatment programs* (2nd ed., pp. 230–270). New York: Springer Publishing.

The Confidential Enquiry into Maternal and Child Health. (2004). *Why mothers die 2000–2002.* London: Royal College Obstetricians Gynaecologists.

Centers for Disease Control. (2006). Intimate partner violence: Fact sheet. National Center for Injury Prevention and Control. Retrieved September 2006, from http://www.cdc.gov/hcipc/factsheets/ipvfacts.htm.

Chambliss, L. R., Bay, R. C., & Jones, R. F. (1995). Domestic violence: An educational imperative? *American Journal of Obstetrics and Gynecology, 172*(3), 1035–1038.

Coker, A. L., Smith, P. H., Bethea, L., King, M. R., & McKeown, R. E. (2000). Physical health consequences of physical and psychological intimate partner violence. *Archives of Family Medicine, 9*(5), 451–457.

Davidson, L., King, V., Garcia, J., & Merchant, S. (2000). Reducing domestic violence . . . what works? Health services. In *Policing and reducing crime*. London: Home Office Research Development and Statistics Directorate.

Department of Health [United Kingdom]. (2000). *Domestic violence: A resource manual for health care professionals*. London: Author.

Dickson, F., & Tutty, L. M. (1996). The role of public health nurses in responding to abused women. *Public Health Nursing, 13*(4), 263–286.

Dienemann, J., Boyle, E., Baker, D., Resnick, W., Wiederhorn, N., & Campbell, J. (2000). Intimate partner abuse among women diagnosed with depression. *Issues in Mental Health Nursing, 21*, 499–513.

Dominelli, L. (2002). *Feminist social work theory and practice*. Hampshire, England: Palgrave.

Drossman, D., Leserman, J., & Nachman, G. (1990). Sexual and physical abuse in patients with functional or organic gastrointestinal disorders. *Annals of Internal Medicine, 113*, 828–834.

Dwyer, D. (1995). Response to the victims of domestic violence: Analysis and implication of the British experience. *Crime and Delinquency, 41*(4), 527–540.

Edin, K. E., & Hogberg, U. (2002). Violence against pregnant women will remain hidden as long as no direct questions are asked. *Midwifery, 18*(4), 268–278.

Elliott, L., Nerney, M., James, T., & Friedmann, P. (2002). Barriers to screening for domestic violence. *Journal of General Internal Medicine, 17*, 112–116.

Friend, J. R. (1998). Responding to violence against women: A specialist's role. *Hospital Medicine, 59*(9), 678–679.

Fry, P. S., & Barker, L. A. (2001). Female survivors of violence and abuse. Their regrets of action and inaction in coping. *Journal of Interpersonal Violence, 16*(4), 320–342.

Harding, A. (2006, August 17). Domestic violence linked to early infant death. *Medline Plus*. Retrieved from http://www.nlm.nih.gov/medline plus.

Hathaway, J. E., Willis, G., & Zimmer, B. (2002). Listening to survivors' voices. *Violence Against Women, 8*(6), 687–719.

Home Office [United Kingdom]. (2004). *Tackling domestic violence: The role of health professionals* (2nd ed.; Development and Practice Report). London: Author. Retrieved September 2006, from http://www.homeoffice.gov.uk.

Humphreys, C., & Thiara, R. (2003). Mental health and domestic violence: "I call it symptoms of abuse." *British Journal of Social Work, 33*, 209–226.

Huth-Bocks, A. C., Levendosky, A. A., & Bogat, G. A. (2002). The effects of violence during pregnancy on maternal and infant health. *Violence and Victims, 17*, 169–185.

Jacoby, M., Gorenflo, D., Black, E., Wunderlich, C., & Eyler, A. (1999). Rapid repeat pregnancy and experiences of inter-personal violence among low income adolescents. *American Journal of Preventive Medicine, 16*(4), 318–321.

Keeling, J. (2002). Support and education: The role of the domestic violence coordinator. *Nursing Times, 98*(48), 34–35.

Keeling, J. (2004). A community-based perspective on living with domestic violence. *Nursing Times, 100*(11), 28–29.

Keeling, J., & Birch, L. (2004). Asking pregnant women about domestic abuse. *British Journal of Midwifery, 12*(12), 746–749.

Martin, S., Beaumont, J., & Kupper, L. (2003). Substance use before and during pregnancy: Links to intimate partner violence. *American Journal of Drug and Alcohol Abuse, 29*(3), 599–617.

McCauley, J., Kern, D. E., Kolodner, K., Dill, L., Schroeder, A. F., DeChant, H. K., et al. (1995). The "battering syndrome": Prevalence and clinical characteristics of domestic violence in primary care internal medicine practices. *Annals of Internal Medicine, 123*, 737–746.

McCauley, J., Yurk, R. A., Jenckes, M., & Ford, D. E. (1998). Inside "Pandora's box." Abused women's experiences with clinicians and health services. *Journal of General Internal Medicine, 13*, 549–555.

McFarlane, J., Cristoffel, K., Bateman, L., Miller, V., & Bullock, L. (1991). Assessing for abuse: Self-report versus nurse interview. *Public Health Nurse, 8*, 245–250.

McGuigan, W. M., Vuchinich, S., & Pratt, C. C. (2000). Domestic violence, parents' view of their infant and risk for child abuse. *Journal of Family Psychology, 14*(4), 613–624.

McLeer, S. V., Anwar, R. A., Herman, S., & Maquiling, K. (1989). Education is not enough: A systems failure in protecting battered women. *Annals of Emergency Medicine, 18*(6), 651–653.

Mezey, G., & Bewley, S. (1997). Domestic violence and pregnancy. *British Journal of Obstetrics and Gynaecology, 104*, 528–531.

O'Campo, P., Kub, J., Woods, A., Garza, M., Snow-Jones, A., Gielen, A., et al. (2006). Depression, PTSD and co-morbidity related to intimate partner violence in civilian and military women. *Brief Treatment and Crisis Intervention, 6*(2), 99–110.

Peckover, S. (2002). Focusing upon children and men in situations of domestic violence: An analysis of the gendered nature of British health visiting. *Health and Social Care in the Community, 10*(4), 254–261.

Peckover, S. (2003). "I could have just done with a little more help": An analysis of women's help-seeking from health visitors in the context of domestic violence. *Health and Social Care in the Community, 11*(3), 275–283.

Postpartum home nurse visits improve infant health, reduce costs. (2004, October 4). *Medical News Today.* Retrieved September 2006, from http://www.medicalnewstoday.com.

Ramsay, J., Richardson, J., Carter, Y. H., Davidson, L. L., & Feder, G. (2002). Should health professionals screen women for domestic violence? Systematic review. *British Medical Journal, 325,* 314–318.

Rennison, C. M. (2003). *Intimate partner violence 1993–2001.* Washington, DC: Bureau of Justice Statistics, U.S. Department of Justice.

Richardson, J., Coid, J., Petruckevitch, A., Chung, W. S., Moorey, S., & Feder, G. (2002). Identifying domestic violence: Cross sectional study in primary care. *British Medical Journal, 324,* 274–277.

Roberts, A. R., & Kim, J. H. (2005). Exploring the effects of head injuries among battered women: A qualitative study of chronic and severe woman battering. *Journal of Social Service Research, 32*(1), 33–47.

Rodriguez, M. A., Bauer, H. M., McLoughlin, E., & Grumbach, K. (1999). Screening and intervention for intimate partner abuse. Practices and attitude of primary care physicians. *JAMA, 282,* 468–474.

Royal College Obstetricians Gynaecologists. (2001). *The confidential report into maternal deaths in the United Kingdom (1997–1999).* London: Author.

Schei, B., & Bakketeig, L. (1989). Gynaecological impact of sexual and physical abuse by spouse. A study of a random sample of Norwegian women. *British Journal of Obstetrics and Gynaecology, 96,* 1379–1383.

Schei, B., Samuelson, S. O., & Bakketeig, L. S. (1991). Does spousal abuse affect outcome of pregnancy? *Scandinavian Journal of Social Medicine, 19,* 26–31.

Shadigian, E. M., & Bauer, S. T. (2004). Screening for partner violence during pregnancy. *International Journal of Gynaecology and Obstetrics, 84,* 273–280.

Stenson, K., Saarinen, H., Heimer, G., & Sidenvall, B. (2001). Women's attitudes to being asked about exposure to violence. *Midwifery, 17,* 2–10.

Tacket, A., Beringer, A., Irvine, A., & Garfield, S. (2004). *Tackling domestic violence: Exploring the health service contribution.* Retrieved August 28, 2006, from www.homeoffice.gov.uk/rds/pdfs04.

Torres, A., & Forrest, J. D. (1988). Why do women have abortions? *Family Planning Perspectives, 20*(4), 169–176.

U.S. Bureau of Justice Statistics. (2000). *Full report of the prevalence, incidence, and consequences of violence against women: Findings from the national violence against women survey.* Washington, DC: U.S. Department of Justice.

Ussher, J. M. (2000). *Women's health: Contemporary international perspectives.* Leicester, England: British Psychological Society Books.

van Wormer, K. & Bartollas, C. (2007). *Women and the criminal justice system.* Boston: Allyn & Bacon.

Warshaw, C. (1989). Limitations of the medical model in the care of battered women. *Gender and Society, 3,* 506–517.

Wist, W., & McFarlane, J. (1999). The effectiveness of an abuse assessment protocol in public health prenatal clinics. *American Journal of Public Health, 89,* 1217–1221.

CHAPTER 12

Battered Women in the Emergency Room:
Emerging Roles for the Emergency Room Social Worker and Clinical Nurse Specialist

Mary E. Boes

Although many health care organizations in the United States have called for a new response to domestic violence, in view of the staggering numbers of victims and historical lack of medical recognition and response, a determination must be made about whether and in what ways actual health care interventions are changing. National health objectives have called for at least 90% of hospital emergency rooms to have protocols for routinely identifying, treating, and referring victims of spouse abuse. The Joint Commission on Accreditation of Health Care Organizations (JCAHO, 1992) has also recommended that accredited emergency rooms(ERs) have policies, procedures, and education in place to guide staff in the treatment of battered adults. As domestic violence is a public health problem, every woman must be effectively screened for level of risk for abuse in every ER in the United States. A noteworthy comprehensive study on intimate

301

partner femicide identified key markers of battered women's lethal risk. The key factors or red flags were the offender's access to a gun, previous threats with a weapon, physical estrangement or separation, forced sex, having an offender's stepchild in the home, and/or battering the victim while she was pregnant (Campbell et al., 2003). This chapter seeks to profile the efficacy of use of adult-abuse protocols for selected ERs and the emerging roles of the ER social worker and clinical nurse specialist in the implementation and coordination of these initiatives. It is argued that social work and clinical nurse specialist intervention strategies and treatment goals improve the quality of both emergency and ongoing care for this growing and often at-risk population.

STATISTICS AND TRENDS

The most prevalent cause of trauma in women treated in emergency rooms is intimate partner violence. Retrospective chart reviews in hospital ERs indicate that although 30% to 35% of women seen in the ER have symptoms or injuries secondary to battering, the cause of the problem is identified in only 5% of those cases (Randall, 1990). Although it is generally believed that domestic violence is seriously underreported and undiagnosed, within the past year at least 7% of American women (3.9 million) who are married or living with someone as a couple were physically abused, and 37% (20.7 million) were verbally or emotionally abused by their spouse or partner. In the United States, every 9 seconds a woman is physically abused by her husband (The Commonwealth Fund, 1993). The U.S. Department of Justice estimates that 95% of assaults on spouses or ex-spouses are committed by men against women (Douglas, 1991). Domestic violence is the leading cause of injuries to women between the ages of 15 and 44 and is more common than muggings, auto accidents, and cancer deaths combined (U.S. Senate Judiciary Committee, 1992). Sixty percent of all female homicides are due to domestic violence (DelTufo, 1995).

Domestic violence is repetitive in nature: About one in five women victimized by their spouse or ex-spouse reported that they had been a victim of a series of at least three assaults in the last 6 months (Zawitz et al., 1993).

Pregnancy alone is among the highest risk factor for intimate partner violence with annual estimates of 324,000 women experiencing intimate partner violence during pregnancy (Gazmararian, Petersen, Spitz, Goodwin, Saltzman, & Marks, 2000). The level of injury resulting from domestic violence is severe: Of 218 women presenting at a metropolitan emergency department with injuries due to domestic violence, 28% required major medical treatment, and 40% had previously required medical care for abuse (Berrios & Grady, 1991).

A study conducted at Rush Medical Center in Chicago found that the average charge for medical services provided to abused women, children, and older people was $1,633 per person per year. That would amount to a national annual cost of $857.3 million (Meyer, 1992).

Ninety-two percent of women who were physically abused by their partners did not discuss these incidents with their physician; 57% did not discuss the incidents with anyone (The Commonwealth Fund, 1993). Mooney's (1994) study reports that women told friends (46%) and relatives (31%) and only 22% of doctors about domestic violence. "The data suggest that health care settings provide services to many women affected by domestic violence. Unfortunately, many of these settings are unaware of the incidence and prevalence data that make them ideal sites to develop a response" (Edleson & Eisikovits, 1996, p. 56).

The ER is a vital entry point into the health care system, especially for some of the more severely abused women who may be at greatest risk for serious impairment or death (McLeer & Anwar, 1987).

Women who have experienced intimate partner violence are more likely to suffer from depression, alcoholism, substance abuse, and suicidal ideation (Coker, Smith, Bethea, King, & McKeown, 2000). Medical providers are often unaware of the connection of the presenting problem to recurrent domestic abuse (Edleson & Eisikovits, 1996). Albert R. Roberts (1996b) dispels the myth that only a small percentage of battered women who suffer severe beatings for years experience symptoms of posttraumatic stress disorder (PTSD). He details three clinical studies of battered women with PTSD rates ranging from 45% to 84%. Women are frequently misdiagnosed with affective disorders, anxiety disorders, and personality disorders as the primary diagnosis because the trauma that causes the symptoms is unidentified (Keller, 1996).

REASONS VIOLENCE IS MISDIAGNOSED OR UNDIAGNOSED

The reasons violence so often is misdiagnosed—or goes undiagnosed—are multitude. Part of the problem is that physicians are not trained to view violence the way they do bacteria and viruses. Despite its vast medical consequences, domestic abuse is included in only 53% of all U.S. medical school curricula, and most of those devote no more than 90 minutes to the topic. Until the current decade, for the most part, major medical journals ignored it. A study of how ER personnel dehumanize battering victims was reported in *The Journal of the American Medical Association* in 1990 only after it was published in a journal called *Gender and Society*. Early theory-building studies on domestic abuse were prejudiced by the researchers' inability to study batterers. They then turned their attention to "the wife-beater's wife." She would talk to them. Undeterred by having only one side of the story, and the victim's side at that, the researchers found that she had brought on her own suffering because she was masochistic, frigid, and controlling. Someone had to be at fault. More recent research takes a more sympathetic view of the abused woman.

Some hospitals have nothing more than ad hoc protocols. When treating battered women, ER physicians may lose their only chance for early intervention because they have no guidelines for identifying and dealing with abuse victims, nor is it considered their medical obligation.

In many hospitals that do have established procedures for dealing with abuse victims, the medical staff simply does not follow them. Physicians were reported to be less likely to screen if their specialty was emergency medicine, if they thought women would volunteer information without being asked about abuse, or if they perceived such questions might offend or anger patients (Elliott, Nerney, Jones, & Friedmann, 2002). In one study done at a Chicago hospital (Warshaw, 1989), nurses who were supposed to refer abuse victims for social work consultations did so less than 10% of the time. Though their attackers seriously hurt many of their patients, the nurses filed police reports in less than half the cases.

The reluctance of physicians to see and treat intimate violence is explained by tradition. Physical and sexual abuse of women has been regarded as something of a private matter or one better left to the law or the psychiatrists. Many physicians feel it's not part of their job to treat a "social problem."

For various reasons, many physicians simply do not want to see violence. In a study of a New Haven, Connecticut, ER, a team of researchers combing medical records easily identified 340 abuse cases ER personnel had missed. Physicians identified 1 in 35 women they saw as a victim of intimate violence; the researchers found the reality was closer to 1 in 4.

In 1990, researcher Nancy Kathleen Sugg, MD, of the University of Washington in Seattle, asked 38 family-care physicians in a large health maintenance organization why they didn't intervene in cases of domestic violence (Sugg & Inui, 1992). Many told Sugg they were afraid of offending their patients if they broached the subject. Most had never had any training in dealing with domestic violence. The largest majority—71%—told Sugg they were simply too busy. Their greatest fear was that domestic violence would eat up too much of their scarce time.

The extent to which physicians try to distance themselves from victims of violence is clearly detailed in a 1989 study done by Carole Warshaw, MD, at Cook County Hospital in Chicago. Warshaw began her research with the hypothesis that the notations physicians and nurses made on ER charts would reveal the way they thought about their patients. Warshaw read all of the charts for women trauma patients during a 2-week period, identifying those who specifically mentioned being deliberately harmed by someone else. Medical personnel dutifully recorded the extent of the women's injuries, but in only one case was abuse mentioned as a cause (Warshaw, 1989). Warshaw believes the "medical model" contributes to what appears to be callous disregard for the victim. Doctors are taught to remain detached and learn to objectify. Medical school tends to dehumanize doctors, who then dehumanize their patients.

It is not a way for doctors to be better doctors. Physicians may have personal reasons for maintaining a psychological distance from the victim. Many resort to victim-blaming as a form of self-preservation: "If you can discount the victim, you can preserve your belief in your own invulnerability," says Harvard psychiatrist Judith Herman (personal communication, April 4, 1997).

Research by psychologist Diana Russell (1986) found that the risk of rape and battering is double for incest victims. This is frequently misunderstood by physicians and therapists, who are likely to see it as a "character flaw," a propensity for choosing abusive relationships, rather than the result of victims being rendered helpless by repeated traumatization.

Physicians are products of a social milieu in which women are devalued and violence against them is not only tolerated but also is a form of entertainment. Recent studies of male college students found that as many as 30% admit they have committed rape and up to 70% could envision themselves striking a spouse. Several studies have found that female physicians compared with male physicians not only screened more often but also took a more thorough history (Jonassen & Mazor, 2003).

Women have always been on the periphery but not part of the research or theory-building class (Judith Herman, personal communication, April 4, 1997).

> They were allowed to care for victims but not pose the hypotheses or do the research. From initial denial we've come to recognize that yes, battering occurs, but there's still a tendency to see it as unusual and deviant and to not recognize how endemic it is and how pervasive its effects are.

It has taken 20 years of chiding by women's groups to produce even a flicker of medical attention to violence as a public health problem. Although 92% of women surveyed who suffered physical abuse from their partners did not discuss these incidents with their physicians, studies show they would like their health care workers to ask about abuse (Fogarty, 2002). Abused women would also support laws requiring a nurse or physician to screen and report incidents of domestic violence to the police because it would facilitate securing help to end the abuse (Malecha et al., 2000)

PROVISION OF SUPPORT, ASSISTANCE, OR PROTECTION IN ERs

The JCAHO (1992), addressing victims of possible abuse or neglect, states in its "Emergency Services" chapter that the intent of the guideline is to have emergency service personnel be made more alert to the identification and needs of victims of possible abuse or neglect. A plan for educating appropriate staff about criteria for identifying and the procedures for handling child, adult, and elder victims of possible abuse or neglect is required. The JCAHO standards require that procedures for the evaluation of patients who meet the criteria address patient consent, examination, and treatment; the hospital's role in the collection, retention, and safeguarding of specimens, photographs, and other evidentiary material released by the patient; and, as legally required, notification of and release of information to the proper authorities. The standard also requires that a list be maintained in the emergency department/service of private and public community agencies that provide or arrange for evaluation and care for victims of abuse, and referrals are made as appropriate. The items listed in the required characteristic are documented in the medical record. The medical record includes documentation of examinations, treatment given, any referrals made to other care providers and to community agencies, and any required reporting to the proper authorities. JCAHO has mandated a plan for education of appropriate staff about the criteria for identifying and the procedures for handling possible victims of abuse.

GUIDING PRINCIPLES FOR HEALTH CARE CLINICAL INTERVENTION

A set of guiding principles for health care clinical intervention is described by the Family Violence Prevention Fund (Warshaw & Ganley, 1996):

1. Respecting safety of victims and their children as a priority.
2. Respecting the integrity and authority of each battered woman over her own life choices.
3. Holding perpetrators responsible for the abuse and for stopping it.
4. Advocating on behalf of victims of domestic violence and their children.
5. Acknowledging the need to make changes in the health care system to improve the health care response to domestic violence.

Many health care organizations in the United States have called for a response to domestic violence. The American Medical Association has held national meetings calling for a new response to domestic violence and has issued diagnostic and treatment guidelines for physicians. The Nursing Network Against Violence Against Women has also coordinated national conferences and training seminars about domestic violence.

FRAGMENTED CARE IN ER: ORIENTED
TOWARD LIFE AND DEATH

Within emergency rooms alone, at least 16% to 18% of women presenting with trauma have been abused (Boes, 1997; Tilden, 1989). Care in the emergency room is often fragmented and necessarily oriented toward life-and-death situations. Therefore, women are not adequately assessed for prior physical or sexual abuse and so receive little or no emotional support or intervention specific to their needs (Campbell, 1991; Roberts, 1996). It can be surmised that the cost to the health care system is phenomenal, with little or no positive outcome. A cycle persists in which women seek care and receive either no intervention or interventions that are grossly ineffective (Campbell & Sheridan, 1989).

Nursing research has established that at least 8% of women in prenatal and primary care settings are abused by a male partner and approximately 20% of women in emergency departments have a history of abuse (Bullock, McFarlane, Bateman, & Miller, 1989; Goldberg & Tomlanovich, 1984; Helton, McFarlane, & Anderson, 1987; Stark et al., 1981). Other nursing studies indicate that such violence is usually not documented correctly in medical records so that they could be used in court, and that abused women do not feel they have been appropriately assessed and treated (Brendtro & Bowker, 1989; Drake, 1982). However, Tilden and Shepherd (1987) demonstrated that training of emergency room personnel about abuse could significantly increase the accurate identification of abused women.

ASSESSMENT

Assessment for all forms of violence against women should take place for all women entering the health care system, regardless of their point of entry. At each contact, clients should be assessed on the following points: physical safety, legal needs, support needs and options, economic status, feelings of blame, isolation, fear, and responsibility, resources available, community shelters, support groups and counseling, legal options, safety plan, and economic assistance.

Women can be categorized into three groups in terms of abuse: no risk, low risk, or moderate-to-high risk. Women with no signs of current or past abuse are considered at no risk. Women at low risk show no evidence of recent or current abuse. Assessment of moderate-to-high risk status includes evaluation of a woman's fear of both psychological and physical abuse.

Lethality potential should be assessed (Campbell, 1986). Risk factors for homicide in abusive relationships include: physical abuse increasing in frequency or severity; abuser has used a weapon (gun, knife, or baseball bat) against her; abuser has threatened to kill her; abuser chokes or attempts to choke her; gun in the home; she is forced into sex; children abused; abuse during pregnancy; abuser is violent outside of the home; abuser uses crack, amphetamines, "ice," or combination drugs; abuser is drunk every day or almost every day or is a "binge" drinker; abuser is violently and constantly jealous; abuser makes statements such as "If *I* can't have you, no one can"; abuser controls most or all of her daily activities, money, and so on; and either partner has threatened or tried to commit suicide. The determined risk level should also be documented, and any past or present physical evidence of abuse from prior or current assault should be either photographed or shown on a body map as well as described narratively. It is important that the assailant *be* identified in the record, which can be accomplished by the use of quotes from the woman or subjective information. These records can be very important for women in future assault or child custody cases, even if she is not ready to make a police report at the present time.

Indicators of Actual or Potential Abuse

Included in the client's history will be her primary reason for contact, which may include vague information about the cause of the problem, discrepancies between physical findings and the description of the cause, minimizing the injuries, inappropriate delay between time of injury and treatment, and inappropriate family reactions (e.g., lack of concern, overconcern, and threatening demeanor).

Information from a family genogram may reveal family violence in history (child, spouse, elder), history of violence outside of the home, incarcerations, violent deaths in the extended family, and alcoholism or drug abuse in the family history.

The health history may also give an indication of actual or potential abuse. The client may have a history of traumatic injuries, spontaneous abortions, psychiatric hospitalizations, or a history of depression or substance abuse.

Sexual history may note prior sexual abuse, use of force in sexual activities, venereal disease, a child with sexual knowledge beyond that appropriate for his or her age, and promiscuity.

Actual or potential abuse indicators included in the social history may include unwanted or unplanned pregnancy, adolescent pregnancy, social isolation (difficulty naming persons available for help in a crisis), lack of contact with extended family, unrealistic expectations of relationships or age-appropriate behavior, extreme jealousy by spouse or partner, rigid traditional sex-role beliefs, verbal aggression, belief in use of physical punishment, difficulties in school, truancy, and running away.

The psychological history would indicate feelings of helplessness/hopelessness, feeling trapped, difficulty making plans for the future, tearfulness, chronic fatigue, apathy, and suicide attempts.

Included in the financial history as indicators of actual or potential abuse may be poverty, finances rigidly controlled by one family member, unwillingness to spend money on health care or adequate nutrition, complaints about spending money on family members, unemployment, and use of elders' finances for other family members.

Family beliefs and values that may indicate actual or potential abuse may include a belief in the importance of physical discipline, autocratic decision making, intolerance of differing views among members, and mistrust of outsiders.

Finally, family relationships may show a lack of visible affection or nurturing between family members, extreme dependency between family members, autonomy discouraged, numerous arguments, temporary separations, dissatisfaction with family members, lack of enjoyable family activities, extramarital affairs, and role rigidity (inability of members to assume nontraditional roles).

INTERVENTIONS

Immediate care for a woman in a potentially harmful or present abusive situation involves the development of a safety plan. Questions that are important to ask include the following: "How can we help you be safe? Do you have a place to go?" A woman can be assisted to look at the options available to her. Shelter information and access to counseling and legal resources should be discussed. If a woman wants to return to her spouse or partner, she can be helped in the development of plans that can be carried out if the abuse continues or becomes more serious.

When there are no obvious injuries, assessment for abuse is best included with the history about the patient's (both genders) primary intimate attachment relationship. Answers to general questions on the quality of that relationship should be assessed for feelings of being controlled or needing to control. A relationship characterized by excessive jealousy (of possessions, children, jobs, friends, and other family members, as well as potential sexual partners) is more likely to be violent. The patient can be asked about how the couple solves conflicts, for example, if one partner needs to have the final say; frequent and forceful verbal aggression also can be considered a risk factor. Finally, the patient should be asked if arguments ever involve "pushing or shoving." Questions about minor violence within a couple's relationship help to establish the unfortunate normalcy of battering and to lessen the stigma of disclosure. If the patient hesitates, looks away, displays other uncomfortable nonverbal behavior, or reveals risk factors for abuse, she or he can be asked again later in the interview about physical violence.

If abuse is revealed, the professional's first response is critical. It is important that an abused woman realize that she is not alone; important affirmation can be given with a statement about the frequency of spouse/partner abuse.

A COMPARISON OF THE PATERNALISTIC AND EMPOWERMENT MODELS OF INTERVENTION WITH BATTERED WOMEN

Using the paternalistic model, the professional is perceived to be more knowledgeable than the survivor. In contrast, the professional using the empowerment model sees that there is a mutual sharing of knowledge and information. When the paternalistic model is used, responsibility for ending the violence is placed on the survivor. When the empowerment model is used, the professional strategizes with the survivor. Survivors are assisted to recognize societal influences. Using the paternalistic model, advice and sympathy are given rather than respect, whereas using the empowerment model, the survivor's competence and experience are respected.

FOUR STEPS TO SUCCESSFUL INTERVENTION WITH BATTERED WOMEN

These steps build on Roberts's (1996a) Seven-Stage Crisis Intervention Model. The first step according to Roberts is assessment of domestic violence severity, injuries, and lethality. Schecter (1987) in Step 1 focuses on identification.

Identification includes the use of clinical indicators: central injury pattern; patterned injuries (injuries look like the object that caused them); and injury (injuries) inconsistent with patient's or accompanying partner's explanation. The patient may claim to be "accident prone" or "clumsy," or there may be multiple injuries in various stages of healing (pattern of injury), a history of trauma-related injuries, unexplained delay between injury occurrence or severe symptom onset and seeking medical treatment, history of depression, tranquilizer or sedative use, eating disorders, substance abuse, or suicide attempts. The patient may have had multiple visits to the emergency room for anxiety or depression symptoms (Boes, 1997). The patient is accompanied by an overly attentive or aggressive partner and the partner insists on staying with the patient or refuses to leave the patient alone. The patient displays an inappropriate affect, appears fearful of partner; the patient has a flat affect, avoids eye contact, and so forth. The final clinical indicator is that the accompanying partner has injuries to their hands or to other areas such as face or arms.

To facilitate identification, the mental health practitioner can place posters, wallet-sized cards, or brochures on domestic violence in bathrooms, patient-examining areas, or wherever other patient information is displayed. They must interview her alone and out of earshot and eyesight of any accompanying partner. Using nonverbal communication when assessing the patient is also helpful. Ask the patient directly if she is being hurt or threatened by her partner. Show comfort in asking questions about domestic violence. Practice with coworkers.

The second step to successfully intervening with battered women is to validate her experience. Believe what the battered woman tells you. Be prepared to hear information that may shock you or may be painful to listen to. Empathize with her experience and validate her feelings of fear, confusion, love, and hope; reassure her that her feelings are legitimate and normal. Offer positive messages to counter harmful past messages she may have received. The following messages are very simple and powerful: "You are not alone"; "This happens to many women"; "You are not to blame for the things your partner does"; "You are not crazy"; "You do not deserve to be abused"; "You don't deserve to be treated this way"; and "What happened to you is a crime."

Advocating for the woman's safety and expanding her options is the third step to successful intervention with battered women. The woman's safety must be the primary goal of all interventions. Ensure that your actions do not in any way compromise her safety, regardless of any other perceived benefits of those actions. Recognize that she is likely to be the best judge of what is safe for her. Offer information about the formal network of services that may be available. In particular, provide specific information about the local domestic violence services/shelter. Explore informal resources and supports to which she may have access.

Provision of ongoing, unconditional support is the final step. Recognize that you, as a health care professional, may feel frustrated, angry, fearful, or helpless when dealing with battered women. Find support for yourself, and avoid transferring your feelings of frustration onto the victim. Remember: It takes battered women an average of six to eight times of leaving before a final separation occurs, and that ending the relationship doesn't necessarily mean that the violence will end. Recognize that it is a "success" that she is talking about the violence and beginning to explore options. Tell yourself you have done a great job if you have utilized these four steps in your intervention.

AMERICAN MEDICAL ASSOCIATION GUIDELINES FOR INTERVIEWING BATTERED WOMEN

The American Medical Association (AMA; as well as many other professional organizations) recommends routine screening of all women patients in emergency, surgical, primary care, pediatric, prenatal, and mental health settings for domestic violence. The AMA recommends starting with a statement such as, "Because abuse and violence are so common in women's lives, I've begun to screen for it routinely." This kind of statement lets the patient know that you are concerned and knowledgeable about battering. The AMA recommends that health care professionals be aware of the following pitfalls in interviewing. Avoid questions such as: "Are you the victim of domestic violence?" or "Are you being battered?/abused?" Many victims do not identify themselves with those labels. Avoid "why" questions: "Why didn't you call the hotline?" or "Why didn't you call the police?" "Why" questions sound accusatory and tend to be victim-blaming.

MEDICAL DOCUMENTATION FOR VICTIMS OF DOMESTIC VIOLENCE

The medical record is a legal document. Appropriate documentation can provide concrete evidence of violence and abuse and may be critical to the outcome of any legal case. Always write legibly. This can help keep you out of court or provide strong support if you are required to testify. Document the patient's explanation for the injuries. Whenever possible, use the patient's own words in quotes. Ask the patient to be as specific as possible. For example: Documenting "Patient states: My boyfriend, Joseph Smith, hit me with his belt" is better than "Patient has been abused."

When circumstances allow, elicit, and document whether there were any witnesses to the incident, where the incident occurred, and when it occurred. Document any other agency representatives involved. For example, document any prehospital care and transport and police response. If the police are called, document the responding police agency and incident report number and any police action taken.

The author was a medical social worker for 8 years at The Graduate Hospital, an affiliate of the Hospital of the University of Pennsylvania.

The practice regarding confidentiality in Pennsylvania was that health care professionals should call the police only if the patient requests this or exhibits a reportable injury. If you call the police without the request or permission of the adult victim, you are violating patient confidentiality.

MEDICAL PHOTOGRAPHY OF DOMESTIC VIOLENCE VICTIMS

Photographs are an extremely valuable way of documenting intentional injuries. It is helpful to tell the patient, particularly those patients who do not wish to call the police or press charges, that the medical record is a legal document and a confidential record and that it is maintained for a period of 6 years or 3 years past age 18, the age of maturity. Explain that if the patient decides to divorce and/or seek child custody or support, and the abuser denies ever hurting him or her, there will be visual proof of the injuries.

GENERAL EVIDENCE COLLECTION GUIDELINES FOR HEALTH CARE PROFESSIONALS

Based on Virginia Lynch's "Clinical Forensic Nursing: A New Perspective in the Management of Crime Victims From Trauma to Trial" (1995), health care professionals are responsible under the law to maintain physical evidence in all cases of gunshot or stab wounds and injuries serious enough to result in death; however, they are urged to provide appropriate evidence collection for all crime victims. Appropriate evidence collection assists in proving that a crime was committed, that a certain person committed the crime, and how the crime was committed. A solid chain of evidence should be maintained to ensure the integrity of every specimen or piece of evidence collected. Failure to maintain the "chain of custody"—the identity of the individuals having control or custody over evidentiary, potentially evidentiary, or other property—may render potentially important evidence worthless or inadmissible in a court of law.

CLINICAL CLUES OF BATTERING DURING PREGNANCY

Based in part on the March of Dimes's "Abuse During Pregnancy: A Protocol for Prevention and Intervention" (McFarlane & Parker, 1994), in which battering is said to frequently start or escalate during pregnancy, health care professionals who are engaged in the delivery of prenatal care, perinatal care, or childbirth education are told that they have a unique opportunity to identify and assist battered women. Although many of the clinical clues of battering pregnant women are the same as those for battering nonpregnant women, there are additional clues that may occur during pregnancy. Some of these clues may be central injury pattern that includes injuries to the head, neck, pregnant abdomen, breasts, back, buttocks, and genitalia; late entry or no prenatal care; or partner engages in "teasing" behavior with his pregnant partner, calling her "fat," "a cow," or "a blimp."

POLICY ON DOMESTIC VIOLENCE: ST. VINCENT'S HOSPITAL AND MEDICAL CENTER

The purpose of St. Vincent's Hospital and Medical Center's Policy on Domestic Violence is to comply with the New York State Department of Health Regulations and to assist the staff in the treatment of domestic violence victims by following an established protocol. To ensure appropriate treatment referral and support, their protocol states that a referral should be made to the Social Work Department. Staffs are reassured that if the situation has been acknowledged and validated and appropriate referrals have been made, everything has been done to help.

BATTERED WOMEN—IDENTIFICATION, TREATMENT, AND REFERRAL OF: DEPARTMENT OF EMERGENCY SERVICES—RUSH–PRESBYTERIAN–ST. LUKE'S MEDICAL CENTER, CHICAGO, IL

This protocol identifies the person responsible (i.e., physician, R.N., Family Violence Program (FVP) staff, and/or Clinical Coordinator) for each procedure. The Chicago Police Department is notified when a patient presents to Emergency Service with injuries incurred as a victim of crime. It is noted that a battered woman can make a police report without having to sign a criminal complaint and that she will be informed of this right.

RADAR: A DOMESTIC VIOLENCE INTERVENTION OF THE MASSACHUSETTS MEDICAL SOCIETY

RADAR action steps were developed by the Massachusetts Medical Society in 1992.

R = Routinely screen female patients. Although many women who are victims of domestic violence will not volunteer any information, they will discuss it if asked simple, direct questions in a nonjudgmental way and in a confidential setting. Interview the patient alone.

A = Ask direct questions. "Are you in a relationship in which you have been physically hurt or threatened?" If no, "Have you ever been?" "Have you ever been hit, kicked, punched by your partner?" "Do you feel safe at home?" "I notice you have a number of bruises; did someone do this to you?"

D = Document your findings. Use a body map to supplement the written record. Offer to photograph injuries. When a serious injury or sexual abuse is detected, preserve all physical evidence. Document an opinion if the injuries are inconsistent with the patient's explanation.

A = Assess patient safety. Before she leaves the medical setting, find out if she is afraid to go home. Has there been an increase in frequency or severity of violence? Have there been threats to her children?

R = Review options and referrals. If the patient is in imminent danger, find out if there is someone with whom she can stay. Does she need immediate access to a shelter? Offer her the opportunity of a private phone to make a call. If she does not need immediate assistance, offer information about hotlines and resources in the community. Remember that it may be dangerous for the woman to have this information in her possession. Do not insist that she take it, but make a follow-up appointment to see her.

FAMILY SAFETY

The usefulness of couples' counseling or family intervention in the presence of domestic violence is under debate. Attempts to implement family therapy in the presence of ongoing violence may increase the risk of serious harm. The first concern must be for the safety of the patient and any children.

Often, patients are not the only victims at home: Child abuse has been reported to occur in 33% to 54% of families where adult domestic violence occurs. In situations where children are also being abused, coordinated liaisons between advocates for victims of domestic violence and child protective service agents should be used to ensure the safety of both the patient and any children. Otherwise, the reporting and investigation of alleged child abuse might increase the patient's risk of abuse.

CRITICAL/CLINICAL PATHWAYS

Developed by Linda Dyar (personal communication, May 12, 1997) of the Women's Center and Shelter of Montgomery County for Abington Memorial Hospital, Pennsylvania, the critical/clinical pathway clearly outlines social worker and nursing interventions and when they are likely to occur (Figure 12.1). She notes that the patient comes to the ER, is triaged, registers, and is taken to the exam room, at which point family and friends are asked to leave the room. The nurse and doctor then do the screening. If the patient identifies herself as abused, she is referred to the social worker. If she denies abuse and identifying factors exist, she is also referred to the social worker. In the situation where domestic violence is suspected and the patient states that the abuse is occurring, she is placed in a room with a door. The doctor and nurse then obtain the patient's history. The doctor diagnoses and manages the patient's current medical and surgical problems, documents, and then either admits or discharges the patient. The social worker discusses options (safety plan, hotlines, legal advocacy, and shelters) and provides supportive/empowerment counseling and resources/referrals. The social worker will be available to the patient throughout her ER visit, and on admission or discharge there will be patient follow-up.

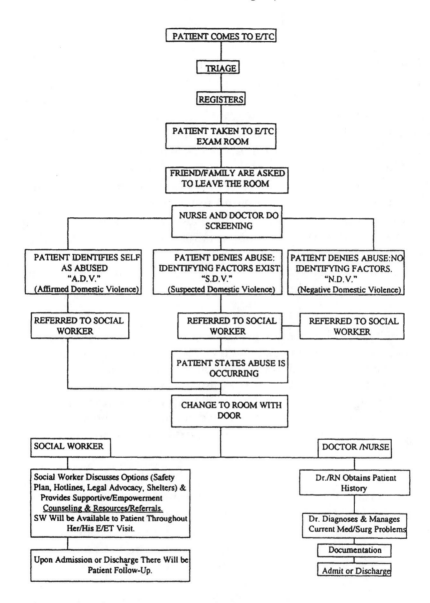

FIGURE 12.1   Critical/clinical pathways.

Source: Linda Dyar, Women's Center and Shelter of Montgomery County Medical Advocacy Project for Abington Memorial Hospital, PA.

CONCLUSION

It should be the role of the ER Social Worker and the main function of the Social Work Department to coordinate and ensure that the ER protocols to identify and treat victims of abuse are effectively utilized.

Paramount to any coordinated initiative is the interdisciplinary education of the entire ER team, which should be initiated by an appointed coordinator from the Social Work Department.

The best programs involve and enlist intercommunity resource cooperation, in which the ER team is a vital link: from paramedics to police, shelters, and other community resources.

Unfortunately, most ERs in the country today are not in compliance with the JCAHO recommendations; only 29% of all California ERs have policies for domestic violence.

St. Vincent's Hospital, New York, New York, includes a note of encouragement to their ER staff:

> Don't judge the success of the intervention by the patient's actions. A person is most at risk of serious injury and even homicide when they attempt to leave an abusive partner and it may take them a long time before they can finally do so. It is frustrating for the treating staff when a patient stays in an abusive situation. Staff should be reassured that if the situation has been acknowledged and validated and appropriate referrals have been made, everything has been done to help. (1996, p. 6)

To intervene effectively, social workers and nurses must understand that abuse is a cumulative process that must be examined as a continuum. During this process, the abuse, the relationship, and a woman's view of her self change, requiring time-specific interventions. It is mandatory that all women be effectively screened for domestic violence in every ER in the United States.

It is critically important that there be immediate referral when necessary to emergency shelter, community mental health center, family service agency, or a community support group. Many of the women are in crisis and transition needs to be developed. Roberts's (1990, 1991, 2005) Seven-Stage Crisis Intervention Model (Figure 12.2) can facilitate early identification of crisis precipitants, problem solving, and effective crisis resolution.

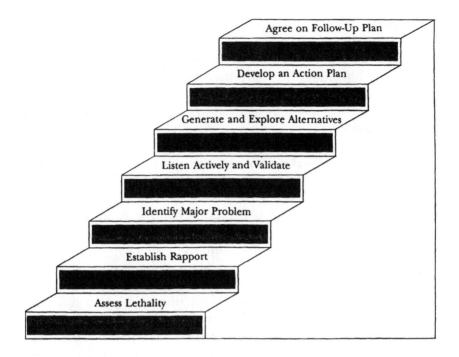

FIGURE 12.2   Roberts's Seven-Stage Crisis Intervention Model.

The seven stages of the crisis intervention model are as follows:

1. *Plan and conduct a thorough assessment* (including lethality, dangerousness to self or others, and immediate psychosocial needs).
2. *Establish rapport* and rapidly establish the relationship (conveying genuine respect and acceptance of the client while also offering reassurance and reinforcement that the client, like hundreds of previous clients, can be helped by the therapist).
3. *Identify major problem(s).* This step includes identifying the "last straw" or precipitating event that led the client to seek help at this time. The clinician should help the client to focus on the most important problem by helping the client to rank order and prioritize several problems and the harmful or potentially threatening aspect of the number one problem. It is important and most productive to help the client to ventilate

about the precipitating event or events; this will lead to problem identification.

4. *Deal with feelings and emotions.* This stage involves active listening, communicating with warmth and reassurance, nonjudgmental statements and validation, and accurate empathetic statements. The person in crisis may well have multiple mood swings throughout the crisis intervention. As a result, nonverbal gestures, such as smiling and nodding, might be distracting and annoying to the person in acute crisis. Therefore, Roberts (2005) suggests the use of verbal counseling skills when helping the client to explore his or her emotions. These verbal responses include reflecting feelings, restating content, using open-ended questions, summarizing, giving advice, reassurance, interpreting statements, confronting, and using silence.

5. *Generate and explore alternatives.* Many clients, especially college graduates, have personal insights and problem-solving skills, as well as the ability to anticipate the outcomes of certain deliberate actions. However, the client is emotionally distressed and consumed by the aftermath of the crisis episode. It is therefore very useful to have an objective and trained clinician assist the client in conceptualizing and discussing adaptive coping responses to the crisis. "In cases where the client has little or no introspection or personal insights, the clinician needs to take the initiative and suggest more adaptive coping methods" (Roberts, 2005, p. 13). During this potentially highly productive stage, the therapist/crisis intervenor and client collaboratively agree on appropriate alternative coping methods.

6. *Develop and formulate an action plan.* Developing and implementing an action plan will ultimately restore cognitive functioning for the client. This active stage may involve the client agreeing to search for an apartment in a low-crime suburban area, for example, or it may involve the client making an appointment with an attorney who specializes in divorce mediation, or agreeing to go to a support group for widows or persons with sexually transmitted diseases (STDs). Many clients have great difficulty mobilizing themselves and following through on an action plan. It is imperative that the client be encouraged and bolstered so that he or she will follow through. Clients in crisis need to hear that you have had other clients who have failed and have been lethargic, yet have made an all-out effort to overcome the obstacle and were successful in resolving the crisis.

7. *Follow-up.* Stage 7 in crisis intervention should involve an informal agreement or formal appointment between the therapist and the client to have another meeting at a designated time, either in person or on the phone, to gauge the client's success in crisis resolution and daily functioning 1 week, 2 weeks, or 1 month later.

REFERENCES

Berrios, D. C., & Grady, D. (1991, August). Domestic violence: Risk factors and outcomes. *Western Journal of Medicine, 155*(2), 133–135.

Boes, M. (1997). A typology for establishing social work staffing patterns. *Crisis Intervention and Time-Limited Treatment, 3*(3), 171–188.

Brendtro, M., & Bowker, L. H. (1989). Battered women: How can nurses help? *Issues in Mental Health Nursing, 10,* 169–180.

Bullock, L., McFarlane, J., Bateman, L., & Miller, V. (1989). Characteristics of battered women in a primary care setting. *Nurse Practitioner, 14,* 47–55.

Campbell, J. C. (1986). Nursing assessment for risk of homicide with battered women. *Advances in Nursing Science, 8,* 36–51.

Campbell, J. C. (1991). Public health conceptions of family abuse. In D. Knudson & J. Miller (Eds.), *Abused and battered* (pp. 35–48). New York: Aldine de Gruyter.

Campbell, J. C., & Sheridan, D. (1989). Emergency nursing with battered women. *Journal of Emergency Nursing, 15,* 12–17.

Campbell, J. , Webster, D., Koziol-McLain, J., Block, C., Campbell, D., Curry, M. A., et al. (2003). Risk factors for femicide in abusive relationships: Results from a multisite case control study. *American Journal of Public Health, 93*(7), 1089–1097.

Coker, A., Smith, P., Bethea, L., King, M., & McKeown, R. (2000). Physical health consequences of physical and psychological intimate partner violence. *Archives of Family Medicine, 9,* 451.

DelTufo, A. (1995). *Domestic violence for beginners* (pp. 525–535). New York: Writers and Readers Publishing.

Douglas, H. (1991, November). Assessing violent couples. *Families in Society, 72*(9), 525–535.

Drake, V. K. (1982). Battered women: A health care problem. *Image, 19,* 40–47.

Edleson, J. L., & Eisikovits, Z. C. (1996). *Future interventions with battered women and their families.* Thousand Oaks, CA: Sage.

Elliott, L., Nerney, M., Jones, T., & Friedmann, P. D. (2002). Barriers to screening for domestic violence. *Journal of Internal Medicine, 17,* 112.

Fogarty, C. T., Burge, S. & McCord, E. C. (2002). Communicating with patients about intimate partner violence: Screening and interviewing approaches. *Family Medicine, 34,* 369–375.

Gazmararian, J. A., Petersen, R., Spitz, A. M., Goodwin, M. M., Saltzman, L. E., & Marks, J. S. (2000). Violence and reproductive health: Current knowledge and future research directions. *Maternal and Child Health Journal, 4,* 79.

Goldberg, W. G., & Tomlanovich, M. C. (1984). Domestic violence victims in the emergency department. *Journal of the American Medical Association, 251,* 3259–3264.

Helton, A., McFarlane, J., & Anderson, E. (1987). Prevention of battering during pregnancy: Focus on behavioral change. *Public Health Nursing, 4,* 166–174.

Joint Commission on Accreditation of Healthcare Organizations. (1992). *Accreditation Manual: 1. Standards.* Oakbrook Terrace, IL: Author.

Jonassen, J. A., & Mazor, K. M. (2003). Identification of physician and patient attributes that influence the likelihood of screening for intimate partner violence. *Academy of Medicine, 78* (Suppl 10), S20.

Keller, L. E. (1996). Invisible victims: Battered women in psychiatric and medical emergency rooms. *Bulletin of the Menninger Clinic, 60,* 1–21.

Lynch, V. A. (1995). Clinical forensic nursing: A new perspective in the management of crime victims from trauma to trial. *Critical Care Nursing Clinics of North America, 7,* 489–507.

Malecha, A. T., Lemmey, D., McFarlane, J., Wilson, P., Fredland, N., Gist, J., et al. (2000). Mandatory reporting of intimate partner violence: Safety or retaliatory abuse for women? *Journal of Women's Health & Gender-Based Medicine, 9*(1), 75–78.

McFarlane, J., & Parker, B. (1994). Nursing Module *Abuse during pregnancy: A protocol for prevention and intervention* (pp. 1–44). White Plains, NY: March of Dimes.

McLeer, S., & Anwar, R. (1987, October). The role of the emergency physician in the prevention of domestic violence. *Annals of Emergency Medicine, 16,* 1155–1161.

Meyer, H. (1992, January). The billion dollar epidemic. *American Medical News,* p. 7.

Mooney, J. (1994). *The hidden figure: Domestic violence in North London.* London: Islington Police and Crime Prevention Unit.

Randall, T. (1990). Domestic violence intervention calls for more than treating injuries. *Journal of the American Medical Association, 264,* 939–940.

Roberts, A. R. (Ed.). (1990). *Crisis intervention handbook: Assessment, treatment and research.* Belmont, CA: Wadsworth.

Roberts, A. R. (Ed.). (1996a). *Crisis management and brief treatment.* Chicago: Nelson-Hall.

Roberts, A. R. (Ed.). (1996b). *Helping battered women.* New York: Oxford University Press.

Roberts, A. R. (2005). Bridging the past to the present for crisis intervention. In A. R. Roberts (ed.), *Crisis intervention handbook: Assessment, treatment and research.* New York: Oxford University Press.

Russell, D. E. H. (1986). *The secret trauma: Incest in the lives of girls and women* (pp. 103–105). New York: Basic Books.

Saint Vincent's Hospital and Medical Center. (1996). *Administrative Manual, Executive Committee of the Medical Staff* (pp. 1–6). Policy No. 248. New York: Saint Vincent's Hospital and Medical Center.

Schechter, S. (1987). *Guidelines for mental health practitioners in domestic violence cases* (p. 9). Washington, DC: The National Coalition Against Domestic Violence.

Sheridan, D. J. (1987). Advocacy with battered women: The role of the emergency room nurse. *Response to the Victimization of Women and Children, 10,* 14–15.

Stark, E., & Flitcraft, A. H. (1991). Spouse abuse. In M. L. Rosenberg & M. A. Fenley (Eds.), *Violence in America: A public health approach* (pp. 138–139). New York: Oxford University Press.

Stark, E., Flitcraft, A., Zuckerman, D., Grey, A., Robison, J., & Frazier, W. (1981). *Wife abuse in the medical setting.* (Domestic Violence Monograph No. 7). Rockville, MD: National Clearinghouse on Domestic Violence.

Sugg, N., & Inui, T. (1992). Primary care physicians' response to domestic violence: Opening Pandora's box. *Journal of the American Medical Association, 267,* 3157–3160.

The Commonwealth Fund. (1983, July 14). *First comprehensive national health survey of American women finds them at significant risk.* New York: Author.

Tilden, V. P. (1989). Response of the health care delivery system to battered women. *Issues in Mental Health Nursing, 10,* 309–320.

Tilden, V. P., & Shepherd, P. (1987). Increasing the rate of identification of battered women in an emergency department: Use of a nursing protocol. *Research in Nursing and Health, 10,* 209–215.

U.S. Senate Judiciary Committee. (1992). *Violence against women.* Washington, DC: Government Printing Office.

Warshaw, C. (1989). Limitations of the medical model in the care of battered women. *Gender and Society, 3,* 506–517.

Warshaw, C., & Ganley, A. (1996). Identification, assessment, and intervention with victims of domestic violence. In *Improving the health care response to domestic violence: A response manual for health care providers* (2nd ed., pp. 49–86). San Francisco: Family Violence Prevention Fund.

Zawitz, M., Klaus, P. A., Bachman, R., Bastian, L. D., De Berry, M., Jr., Rand, M. R., et al. (1993). *Highlights from 20 years of surveying crime victims: The National Crime Victimization Survey, 1973–92.* Washington, DC: U.S. Department of Justice.

CHAPTER 13

Imminent Danger of Failing to Redefine Women Battering as Coercive Control:

Contextualizing an Application of Roberts's Seven-Stage Crisis Intervention Model and the Ecological Nested Model

Cynthia Wilcox Lischick

During the course of their victimization by the batterer, battered women may seek assistance from mental health professionals for crisis resolution (Roberts & Roberts, 2000). Unfortunately, there are inherent dangers for the battered woman when mental health professionals apply the medical model to woman battering, because its underlying assumption regarding a biological basis for the presenting problem suggests that individual pathology is the etiological factor that, if treated, will stop the violence and increase the safety of the victim (Gondolf, 1998; Stark & Flitcraft, 1996; Warshaw, 1989). Sometimes the batterer identifies a crisis wherein he seeks assistance for self-defined anger problems or he may be ordered by the court to complete a mental health evaluation. Sometimes the battered woman is asked or asks to join with the batterer in conjoint therapy (Geller, 1998; Madanes, 1995; O'Hanlon, 2005). When any of these events occur, mental health practitioners schooled in family systems theory and anger management techniques extend their analysis of etiological factors contributing to the "violent relationship" to include the couple's interaction patterns, stress reduction, conflict resolution, and problem-solving inabilities, as well as environmental stressors such as unemployment and poverty. Using this analysis, their intervention is designed with the assumption that if skill-building is offered, the violence will stop and the victim's safety will increase.

Both the medical model and the systems approach often blame the victim by holding her accountable for something over which she has absolutely no control: the batterer's perceptions, feeling states, and actions. At the same time, the presenting problem, domestic violence, is narrowly defined as a unilateral phenomenon devoid of a sociopolitical context and in terms of increasingly violent behaviors occurring episodically *between* the couple rather than a pattern of coercive control strategies, supported and maintained by the patriarchal context, consciously selected by the batterer, and directed at the battered woman to take control over her by isolating, intimidating, degrading, or depriving her of rights and freedoms (Lischick, 1999; Stark & Flitcraft, 1996). When victim-blaming analyses involving narrow definitions are enacted, the practitioner unknowingly colludes with the batterer's denial while causing harm to both the victim and the perpetrator. To avoid this problem, woman battering must be contextualized and evaluated with respect to the larger sociopolitical realm in which it operates, redefined as coercive control, and distinguished from other types of domestic violence (Stark, 1992; Stark & Flitcraft, 1996). In addition, mental health practitioners must seek specialized domestic violence knowledge and training beyond graduate school to be better skilled in treatment of battered women and batterers as well as to address any countertransference issues related to their own gender-role socialization and victimization issues (Walker, 1994). At the same time, they must develop and hone their crisis-intervention skills using models specifically designed for application with domestic violence victims to effectively assist in the crisis resolution with the goal of promoting safety for all involved in the process. This process includes an evaluation of batterers' lethality levels, risk factors, protective factors, options, & safety planning (Roberts, 2005; Roberts & Burman, 1998; Dziegielewski & Resnick, 1996).

Crisis intervention involving battered women and their partners must be informed by a thorough understanding of power differentials between men and women, the patterned use of coercive control strategies, and the contribution by systems' helpers that allow batterers to avoid accountability. The purpose of this chapter is to offer a feminist theory of woman battering redefined as coercive control (Stark, in press; Lischick, 1999, 2000, 2005; Stark & Flitcraft, 1996) to expand the practitioner's ability to consider an alternative theoretical framework for evaluating clinical presentations involving anger and conflict within a family system. Next, a published case study involving the pitfalls and caveats will be offered as an example of the possible danger that clinicians will face when evaluating domestic violence myopically as a unilateral phenomenon via a family systems/conflict resolution lens devoid of context. The case example will be evaluated in terms of the increased danger that a family systems model analysis poses so as to guide the practitioner toward a more effective assessment and intervention plan. Next, the practitioner will be introduced to a contextual analysis of risk and resiliency factors using the Ecological Nested Model (Brofenbrenner, 1977, 1979, 1986; Heise, 1998; Lischick, 1999). Finally, a brief review of Roberts's Seven-Stage Crisis Intervention Model (Roberts, 1991, 2005) will be offered in combination with the Ecological Nested Model analysis in order to extend the mental health practitioner's ability and understanding of the entrapment process while enhancing their ability to provide effective interventions.

REDEFINING WOMAN BATTERING AS COERCIVE CONTROL

Domestic violence is not a unilateral phenomenon defined purely by increasing levels of physical violence between two intimates during an episodic conflict where the female victim gives as good as she gets. Yet mainstream theory and research myopically focuses its attention on an episodic analysis of the dyad's communication, conflict resolution, problem-solving, and anger management skills while neglecting to acknowledge power and resource differentials, patterned coercive control strategies involving isolation, degradation, intimidation, and deprivation of rights and freedoms (Lischick, 2000). Domestic violence does not operate in a vacuum occurring behind closed doors. Instead, battering involves batterer behavior that operates and is maintained by a sociopolitical–cultural context that involves patriarchal hierarchies, gender-role socialization, and male violence against women (Lischick, 2000, 2005). Like other systems', helpers using an episodic conflict analysis that ignores patterned strategies by the batterer and contextual factors that maintain the status quo, mental health providers often respond to the victims by labeling them as mutual combatants while blaming them for their own victimization. This process serves to pathologize victims by focusing on their problematic internalized psychological traits and subsequently assigns various personality disorder diagnoses including self-defeating, histrionic, paranoid, or borderline, as well as various other psychiatric disorders such as schizophrenia (Rosewater, 1988; Stark & Flitcraft, 1996).

Equally problematic is the application of trauma theory that identifies psychiatric sequelae labeled as PTSD or battered women's syndrome. Through the trauma theory lens, the clinician more appropriately assigns causality for observed sequelae to the perpetrator, thus exonerating the victim as culpable. However, as a necessary condition for this diagnosis to be made, extreme episodic physical violence such as rape or attempted murder must be present. The necessity of that condition becomes problematic because all battering is not dependent on a high level of extreme physical violence per se; indeed, many battering victims experience chronic patterns of intimidation, degradation, and various forms of psychological abuse including deprivations of rights and freedoms as well as isolation from support systems (Lischick, 1999; Stark & Flitcraft, 1996). Recently, trauma theorist and practitioner Judith Herman (1992) expanded the definition of the traumatic stressor to include the existence of a chronic pattern of psychological stressors that are equally if not more debilitating than physical violence alone. Yet this too is problematic because the victims' responses are defined via a pathology lens rather than viewed as normal self-protective responses to the pattern of coercive control involving victims' constrained options.

In addition, chronic patterns of coercive control related specifically to physical violence can include a whole host of primary problems such as head injuries, miscarriages, damage to eyes, ears, dental injuries, and fractured bones (Ganley, 1995) as well as secondary psychosocial responses that extend beyond PTSD to include suicidality and addiction (Stark & Flitcraft, 1996). Other secondary health problems exacerbated by the stress of living with their partner's coercive control include asthma, lupus, MS, insomnia, and eating disorders. Consequently, when mental health providers observe and evaluate the victim's responses, they must include the level and extent of the batterer's coercive control patterns over and above the physical violence while acknowledging the influence and constraints that frame the victim's response options occurring internally and externally. The interaction among victim, perpetrator, and environment involves behavioral operations within an external context of sociopolitical and cultural determinants that cannot be ignored. Once the mental health provider expands their understanding to include the complex interaction between these external factors, their understanding of the real-world influences on the victim's resulting compliant or resistant behaviors will be enhanced and pathology labels can be avoided.

For the purpose of distinguishing woman battering from episodic conflict, the batterer's behavior is defined as a malevolent course of coercive conduct wherein one social partner dominates another through the use of violence (abuse), coercion (isolation, intimidation, and emotional abuse), and control (Stark & Flitcraft, 1996). This definition is both research and experience based, extending beyond the limited domestic violence statutes that narrowly focus on discrete acts of physical assaults, threats, and stalking. Domestic violence researchers suggest that battering offers a special case of coercive control involving the manipulation of the woman's options wherein the batterer frames the battered woman's choices so as to make the appearance that the most attractive option available is to conform to his desire (Frye, 1983; Stark, 1992). The pattern of subordination and psychosocial problems that distinguishes woman battering requires something beyond violence; avenues of help and escape are both literally and psychologically closed off and women become entrapped. Battering is not about episodic fights characterized by ineffective methods of conflict resolution; rather it is about an ongoing pattern of subjugation of the battered woman's agency, free will, and efforts to function as an independent and autonomous being involving conflict suppression (Lischick, 1999; Stark & Flitcraft, 1996).

Subjugation of the victim follows directly from the batterer's course of coercive conduct. Such conduct includes but is not limited to: repeated abuse (verbal, emotional, physical, or sexual) of the victim, denied access to earnings, monitoring of daily activities, stalking, capricious enforcement of petty rules that include a deprivation of rights and freedoms such as access to employment or schooling, and intermittent rewards (Pence & Paymar, 1993). The restriction of the battered woman's free movement with its consequent isolation is the key method for imposing coercive control (Okun, 1986). The batterer separates the battered woman from friends and family by his efforts to destroy all competing relationships through isolation, secrecy, and betrayal. Additionally, the batterer's coercion of the battering victim may be achieved through his behaviors directed toward the children, pets, property, or others. The current episode builds on the course of conduct involving past episodes while setting the stage for future episodes, which taken together as a pattern define women's experiences in the battering context (Stark & Flitcraft, 1996).

Woman battering must be distinguished from episodic conflict as a specific type of domestic violence involving a *social phenomenon* occurring "... at three levels simultaneously including the political level of female subordination, the level of interpersonal assault and the level of coercive control at which women's social vulnerability is exploited for personal gain" (Stark, 1996, p. 123). *"Battering, the experience,* arises from the particular ways in which these three levels interrelate in a given relationship over time" (Stark, p. 123). Further, battering is viewed as a form of oppression situated in a particular context that extends to all races and cultures while identifying women as its usual victims (Levinson, 1989).

With respect to the myopic focus on physical hits and shoves between partners in mutual combat, contextual aspects of resources and power differentials can be lost resulting in misinformed conclusions (i.e., mutual combatant and provocateur) about relationship dynamics in the context of violence against women. For example, Kirkwood's (1993) qualitative research with battered women revealed an imbalance in personal resources or those granted from the wider patriarchal culture. Findings suggested that when an imbalance occurred providing additional power to the dominant partner, the additional power was used to establish, maintain, or change an existing power dynamic. Thus, power in a romantic relationship involves the *effect* one individual is able to have over the other in terms of controlling that person and is an important factor in understanding the dynamics of violence. *Power,* as defined by Kirkwood (1993) as the degree of influence the batterer has over the battered woman relative to the amount of influence she has over her own available options. *Control*, in the battering relationship, involves an *outcome* of the amount of power wielded by the dominant partner relative to the subordinate's amount of power to confront and resist the batterer's control in terms of her own agency as an active and free subject. *Entrapment*, "in addition to violence ... entails a pattern of control that extends structural inequities in rights and opportunities to virtually every aspect of a woman's life including money, food, friends, sexuality, friendships, transportation, personal appearances and access to supports including children, extended family members and helping resources" (Stark, 1992, p. 282). Thus, *coercive control* involves a systematic fusion of both social and individual dominance, both together and at once, that undermines the psychological, physical, or political autonomy of even the strongest, most aggressive, and capable woman (Jones & Schechter, 1991, cited in Stark, 1996).

When coercive control is enacted by the batterer, according to Marilyn Frye (1983, cited in Kirkwood, 1993), Western culture is predisposed to define coercion in purely physical terms involving the overpowering of one by another while ignoring both its sociostructural and psychological aspects. Further, capturing coercive control in terms of separate physical altercations suggests that the events are discrete rather than continuous (Smith, Earp, & DeVellis, 1995). This predisposition for a myopic focus on coercion defined in purely physical terms, occurring as discrete episodes completely devoid of context, is apparent in the construction, severity weighting, and widespread use of the Conflict Tactics Scale (CTS: Straus, 1979). However, feminist researchers argue that battering offers a special case of coercive control involving a manipulation of the woman's options wherein the batterer frames the battered woman's choices so as to make the appearance that the most attractive option available to her is to conform to his desire (Frye, 1983; Jones & Schechter, 1991; Stark, 1992).

Unfortunately, the alternative coercive control framework described earlier has not found its way into the analyses of many practitioners trained in family systems. When the presenting problem is defined as skill deficits in anger control, problem-solving, or conflict resolution, clinical errors result. In the next section, case scenario highlights from a popular psychotherapist's trade magazine will be offered to elucidate the way in which battered women may be revictimized and exposed to increased danger by practitioner exclusive use of a family systems analysis viewed through an episodic conflict and anger management lens.

CASE STUDY

A recent article in the *Psychotherapy Networker* (O'Hanlon, March/April 2005), entitled "No Way Out: Sometimes You Just Can't Dance Around the Problem," illustrates the inherent problems and dangers identified when family systems relationship dysfunction is the lens through which mental health interventions are designed. In this case scenario, the client, Ben, identified his presenting problem as panic and big temper issues that come to him out of the blue. During the first session, Ben berated mental health practitioners generally and specifically threatened practitioner Bill O'Hanlon with a shotgun. On hearing the verbal threat of bodily harm, Mr. O'Hanlon was the individual in crisis, yet he appeared confused about the dangerousness level as evidenced in his description involving his choice to avoid humor as a treatment tactic, stating that his knee-jerk reaction would escalate the situation. O'Hanlon clearly sensed a heightened level of danger but he chose to avoid an in-depth exploration. He appears to be operating under the assumption that his behavioral response would in some way control the batterer's future response.

Battered women are often placed in the same predicament when the batterer exhibits various patterns of coercive threat directed toward them. Should they leave or should they stay? Battered women often erroneously believe as did O'Hanlon that their responses are causally connected. Victims are often threatened by the batterer with death if they leave, and they are told by the batterer and others that his abusive behavior is caused by them. Victims may be prodded by family to leave or they may be coerced by child-protective services with the threat of losing their children if they don't take some action to control the batterer's behavior (e.g., obtain a protection order). Unfortunately, the implied causal connection is nonexistent. Batterers make choices constantly to do what they want when they want while blaming others for their problems, boasting their privilege or using their power coercively to deprive the victim of her right to safety, autonomy, and freedom.

Mr. O'Hanlon experienced Ben's verbal gun threat with heightened feelings of terror, which he described in various ways such as mind racing, powerlessness, and efforts at placating the client after acknowledging his lack of graduate school preparation to handle this type of situation. Battered women feel similarly intimidated and terrorized, perhaps more so, but neither they nor Mr. O'Hanlon have a crystal ball to predict future behavior or the power to control the batterer's perceptions, feeling states, or actions, ever. Behavioral control over expressed actions involving coercive strategies and violence resides solely within the batterer, and psychosis or neurological impairment very rarely explains this expression (Ganley, 1995). The batterer functions in response to his perceptions as filtered by his belief system, which authorizes him to make choices to take control over others using coercive strategies including angry displays of rage, demands, threats, and sometimes acts of physical violence. He doesn't lose control over his anger; he uses his anger, rage as well as abusive and threatening behavior to take control over others because he believes he is entitled to do so and because it works. Often it works because there are no meaningful consequences to persuade him otherwise and systems' helpers (i.e., mental health practitioners, courts, police) are often unable to effectively hold him accountable or control his behavior.

In O'Hanlon's case scenario, the batterer begins by coercing the practitioner using threats with the expectation of getting what he wants while avoiding culpability. The batterer believes that if the therapy doesn't succeed, it is the therapist's fault. Although the batterer's behavior involves a situation of no control for the practitioner, O'Hanlon erroneously believed that if he referred the client out and the client escalated, then it was his choice to refer that can be considered cause for escalation. However, the batterer is always choosing his response on his own terms within a context that socializes and affords certain privileges. O'Hanlon's prediction implicitly suggests that the practitioner is responsible for the batterer's response and that the practitioner is able to control the predicted response by avoiding certain choices and selecting an alternative option. This is not only incorrect but also dangerous for both the therapist and the batterer. Interestingly, as a course of normal behavior in response to coercive threat, battered women engage in this type of thinking as a survival oriented form of pseudocontrol. It is a way for victims to believe at some level that they are not totally powerless in the face of this threat and have some sort of control. The batterer reinforces this notion by telling them that his abusive and controlling behavior is their fault, so if they change their behavior then the abuse will stop.

Thus, it appears that the therapist and battered woman are exhibiting a normal, survival-oriented response pattern to a coercive threat where imminent or emergent danger is present. Both believe that the option they choose will cause a particular response pattern in the batterer. Unfortunately, this effectively colludes with the batterer's analysis of himself as an object being acted on (seeing himself as the victim) rather than as a subject purposefully acting on others with a control motive to use specific strategies and patterns of behaviors to carry out personal choices involving control and domination. As long as the batterer cognitively frames his behavior as caused by others, he need not take responsibility for it nor does he have to be accountable for the outcome because it was not in his control. It was his mate, his therapist, or his feelings that made him act this way in the moment and therefore he just couldn't help his controlling, abusive, sometimes physically violent behavior. A family systems analysis applied here supports this notion and labels the victim as provocateur, a poor communicator, or equally culpable, thereby placing the blame on her and shifting accountability off of him. As mental health providers of service to domestic violence families, we must extend this single-factor analysis to include alternative theoretical frameworks in order to live up to our oath to 'Do No Harm.' Victims become entrapped by a single-factor analysis and batterers avoid culpability.

It is important to note, however, that although Mr. O'Hanlon (2005) has more than 30 years of clinical experience and authored numerous intervention and treatment-focused books, it appears that his own life-threatening victimization by this client evoked a survival-oriented response involving a pseudocontrol belief as an effort to take control in a situation of no control similarly identified in responses by battered women (Lischick, 2005; Stark & Flitcraft, 1996). Unfortunately, no clinically formulated lethality assessment of Ben's coercive control history was conducted, yet extensive literature on the topic exists for the treatment of batterers (Dutton, 1995; Gondolf, 1998; Pence & Paymar, 1993). Given this client's presentation where threats of violence with a shotgun, the client's self-disclosed background information about extensive jail experiences, and a decided inability to stay engaged in counseling were revealed, it seems obvious that practitioners without specialized knowledge and experience in treating this type of behavior would offer a referral out. Yet Mr. O'Hanlon quickly passed over this option, deciding against it because he assumed that such a referral would set the client off. O'Hanlon's hypothesis formulation may have minimized the danger he was in because he evaluated his choice to treat Ben as a less dangerous option than referring him out, believing instead that this option would control the predicted escalation of Ben's future violent behavioral response. O'Hanlon (2005) designed his treatment intervention to include attempts to mollify Ben with smiles and affability while ultimately deciding on a resource-oriented therapeutic approach.

Herein lies the fundamental problem: When the practitioner assesses the client's presenting problem as a unilateral phenomenon via an episodic conflict resolution lens involving anger gone awry, clinical errors occur and designed intervention proceeds in an increasingly dangerous direction as the course of treatment carries forward. O'Hanlon saw the described anger gone awry as an uncontrollable emotion related to the client's emotional immaturity. In this case example, the myopic focus on conflict as episodic and resultant explosions of anger defined as a loss of control in relation to victim provocation hampers practitioner efforts to effectively treat the batterer by holding him accountable for his behavioral choices. This is due to the fact that the batterer's belief system of entitlement to coercively control others using various manipulation tactics was never hypothesized to exist. Therefore, it was never assessed or recognized such that the batterer could be effectively and overtly held accountable for his intimidating and controlling behavior.

This problem was exacerbated when Mr. O'Hanlon unknowingly extended the danger to Ben's girlfriend several sessions later when he prompted Ben to invite Margie into couples counseling after Ben described a recent argument so ferocious the neighbors called police. Red flags regarding dangerousness were ever present; however, no lethality (dangerousness) or safety assessment was conducted with either the batterer or the victim, yet extensive literature on the topic exists for lethality (dangerousness) assessment and safety planning (Campbell, 1995; Davies, 1998; Dutton, 1992). As a result, Mr. O'Hanlon (2005, p. 56) was caught off guard three or four sessions later when Ben gave Margie permission to reveal that Ben had retrieved a hidden gun from under the sofa cushion and shoved it in Margie's mouth that week during an argument while calmly telling her, "You know I could blow you away?" At this point, Ben's behavior

Battered Women and Their Families

constituted several indictable crimes including terroristic threats and attempted aggravated assault (personal communication with Essex County NJ, DV Hearing Officer Nancy Kessler, Esq., October 2, 2005). Ben cognitively framed his behavioral choice in the context of uncontrolled anger, which he then causally connected to uncontrollable coercive action. Mr. O'Hanlon colluded with episodic analysis of Ben's "no control"—anger gone awry—assessment and minimization of premeditated violent act because after all, Margie had been nagging him about leaving the bathroom a mess and he accused her of being an "old-lady-neat-freak" (O'Hanlon, p. 56). Margie went on to describe their behavior in "mutual combat" terms where they were yelling at each other like a couple of banshees. However, the mutuality analysis falls completely apart when she recalls that all of a sudden Ben goes real quiet while walking over to pull out the gun. Getting *real quiet* doesn't sound like anger exploding and uncontrollable lashing out, so how did the practitioner arrive at this theoretical understanding of the problem, which then directed the course of treatment? He allowed the patient to define the problem in the first session through a lens that they both shared: panic and anger control problems. He did not consider alternative theoretical explanations and supporting research that extends and contextualizes our understanding of domestic violence beyond the dyad's exchanges of slaps and shoves.

O'Hanlon (2005) continued Margie's exposure to this near-lethal level of danger by allowing the couple to leave that session together without acknowledging the danger or offering a safety plan for either client. Clearly the crisis in which Ben placed Mr. O'Hanlon in the first session now extended to Margie many sessions later. Mr. O'Hanlon appears to lack knowledge about intrafamily homicide statistics, where handguns (40%) and other guns (24%) make up 64% of the means chosen to complete the crime (Stark & Flitcraft, 1996). He further appears to lack knowledge about the important need to evaluate danger at the inception of any intervention with victims (Campbell, 1995) and the necessity of conducting a formal lethality (dangerousness) assessment, particularly when a crisis response involving domestic violence victimization is involved (Dziegielewski & Resnick, 1996; Roberts, 2000; Roberts & Burman, 1998).

Allowing both clients to leave without addressing safety issues is a dangerous practice and may result in harm. The American Psychological Association Presidential Report from the APA Presidential Task Force on Violence and the Family (1996) published extensive guidelines for interventions with batterers and battered women to assist the practitioner with these case types. As a profession of interveners, it is incumbent on all of us to be familiar with the domestic violence intervention literature over and above our ethical duty to warn if we plan to engage this population. To Mr. O'Hanlon's credit, he telephoned Margie at work later that night telling her that while he didn't think Ben intended to kill her, the behavior described in the couples' session was serious enough to warrant taking protective steps, which included his recommendation for Margie to leave Ben immediately and hide where Ben couldn't find her. This intervention was loosely framed as the therapist's ethical duty to focus on Margie's safety, but not as a duty to warn because Mr. O'Hanlon reasoned that she was acutely aware of the danger. Yet batterers and victims are sometimes known to minimize danger, and by all accounts neither Mr. O'Hanlon nor Margie predicted this life-threatening event. Thus, it is incumbent on practitioners in this situation to use interventions that are informed by the extensive literature on dangerousness assessment and safety planning (Campbell, 1995; Davies, 1998; Gondolf, 1998), where the victim is the best one to decide if and when to leave, particularly in light of all that has been learned about separation violence and the increased likelihood of being killed after she leaves the relationship (Wilson & Daly, 1995). Although victims are generally considered to be better predictors of the batterer's behavior, it is important to carefully assist them with considering all of their options while identifying the barriers they will encounter if they leave, so that if and when they leave they can leave for good (Roberts & Roberts, 2005). Practitioners should never tell the battered woman that it is safer for her to leave because this judgment call conveys a false sense of safety and an impression that she is incapable of making safety decisions. It is important to remember that she has been making survival decisions long before she came into contact with the practitioner. Finally, consider what may have happened if O'Hanlon wasn't able to reach Margie later that evening. The opportunity to plan for both individuals' safety by speaking to them during the treatment setting was lost. When the victim's life is at stake, the practitioner may not get a second chance.

Fortunately, Margie was able to escape to a location and a new job unknown to Ben before he could kill her. A simplistic resolution to a complex and dangerous matter, but is that the norm? The overwhelming majority of leave-taking by battered women is much, much more complex than this victim's quick disappearance without a trace to a friend's home and a new job. It also implies that the danger is over now that she has taken the advice of the counselor and left the relationship. This couldn't be further from the truth in most cases involving battered women separating from the batterer, particularly when children are involved.

The case scenario ends with a description of the next scheduled couple's session where Ben arrived alone, agitated, and demanding to know if Mr. O'Hanlon had told Margie to leave. Mr. O'Hanlon saw Ben's enraged face and the shadow of a gun, realizing that he himself was again at risk of imminent harm. Mr. O'Hanlon (2005) revealed to the client that he told Margie to leave and finally informed Ben that his threatening behavior with a gun included consequences. Despite evidence to the contrary, Mr. O'Hanlon continued to frame his entire analysis through a conflict resolution lens of episodic unruly anger involving a rush of sudden flaming emotion wherein Ben's progress toward maturity was almost lost. This analysis ignored clear evidence involving Ben's premeditated acquisition and placement of a gun under the sofa cushion. Ben's acquisition and placement of a lethal weapon was not about a flash of anger. His retrieval of the gun was described in the context of quiet and calm, much like the verbal threat of murder directed toward Mr. O'Hanlon during the first session when Ben initially sought individual treatment. Ben's choice to take control was part and parcel of a coercive control, strategy selected as a course of conduct that had been used before to control and dominate his victims—it was used on the practitioner in the first session, and no sudden flaming emotion of anger was present then. This fact appears to have been completely absent in the practitioner's entire family systems analysis, and that is dangerous for battered women engaging in treatment with the batterer. Batterers are not only overt but also covert in the implementation of coercive strategies. Unless the batterer is specifically queried with the purpose of identifying coercive control, then the practitioner will go forward without full information hypothesizing about a family systems problem where uncontrolled anger yields uncontrolled behavior. This analysis colludes with the batterer while allowing him to avoid culpability.

Margie participated in couples counseling at the practitioner's request where both parties admitted to quick tempers, shrieking matches, and a few broken dishes, but never any blows. For all intents and purposes, the underlying assumption was that Margie was able to give it as good as she gets because it appeared to O'Hanlon that Ben had met his match when assessing Margie at the first conjoint session. At that point, Margie placed her trust in this professional to diagnose and treat the problem while doing no harm. How did the course of treatment go so terribly wrong that Margie was almost killed in this process? If Ben had killed her, he alone would be accountable for his behavioral choice. However, the client sought assistance from a counseling professional who applies an inappropriate and dangerous framework to define the necessary crisis intervention, which actually needed application during the first session when Ben threatened to murder Mr. O'Hanlon with a shotgun. An assessment informed by dynamics of coercive control should have taken place long before Margie was involved as a client in treatment. As a systems helper, Mr. O'Hanlon contributed to Margie's entrapment by allowing the batterer to avoid culpability for his pattern of coercive control because it was unacknowledged. Instead, Mr. O'Hanlon defined the presenting problem as a family systems issue where both appeared equally culpable. As a result, both were instructed on basic conflict management, listening, deep-breathing skills, and time-out strategies, and O'Hanlon was lulled into believing that he was effective in delivering his couples counseling techniques. Fortunately, O'Hanlon (2005) lived to share this experience so that others can learn from it.

EXPANDING THE ANALYSIS OF DOMESTIC VIOLENCE: EVALUATING RISK AND RESILIENCY FACTORS USING THE ECOLOGICAL NESTED MODEL

The traditions of academic and activists alike include efforts to advance single-factor theories about domestic violence while ignoring the " ... full complexity and messiness of real life" and concurrently excluding factors operating on multiple ecological levels (Heise, 1998, p. 262). To expand our understanding of domestic violence, a model that includes a rich array of additional contextual factors is required. Brofenbrenner's (1977, 1979, 1986) Ecological Nested Model of Human Development offers a framework through which to examine multiple, embedded, causal, and maintenance factors at work on different levels operating simultaneously, either interactively or independently (Carlson, 1984). The initial model, incorporating both social and psychological contextual aspects, posits five

levels that influence human behavior both singly and in combination with each other. The levels nested within the model include the
Individual, Microsystem, Exosystem, Macrosystem, and Mesosystems
contextualizing human development and function. The first application of this model in the study of abuse involved an effort to organize
the various theoretical perspectives and related research findings on
child maltreatment wherein Belsky (1980) added an additional level
of analysis to include the individual's history. An application of this
model to the theoretical perspectives and related research findings
on domestic abuse in its attempt to explain observed variability in
both batterers' behavior and battered women's responses has found
some support (Carlson; Dutton, 1992, 1996; Edleson & Tolman, 1992;
Lischick, 1999). However, it has not been utilized to any great extent
in the domestic violence treatment, research, or activist communities
"... despite its potential to accommodate feminist and social science
insights about violence" (Heise, p. 264). Yet at all levels of the model
with respect to the differing factors and dynamics occurring on each
level, both the batterer and the victim will actively make meaning of
their individual experiences as they function and respond over time.

The ecological system situates the levels within a set of concentric
circles (Heise, 1998), the outer encompassing and thereby influencing the next circle, and so on, creating something akin to a crocheted
fabric of threads created separately, yet connected together to make
a whole piece of cloth wherein the integrity and function of the cloth
is bound to all of its threads both within and between the circles. The
individual factors, located in the innermost circle, involve threads
related to the developmental experiences such as a history of witnessing marital violence as a child and can contribute to factors operating on the Microsystem and Exosystem levels. The Microsystem
factors, located in the circle around the Individual Level, involve the
immediate context or situation where the abuse takes place, as well
as the interactions with significant members found therein. The Exosystem factors located in the circle around the Microsystem involve
the social structures in which the situation is couched and, as such,
either determine, delimit, or in some way influence the Microsystem
and Individual system factors. Examples of factors in the Exosystem
include socioeconomic status, employment status, and delinquent
peer associations (Heise, 1998). The Macrosystem factors include a
"... broad set of cultural values and beliefs that permeate and inform the other three layers of social ecology" such as sense of male

entitlement, approval of chastisement of women, rigid gender roles, and the notion of masculinity in its link to dominance, toughness, and honor (Heise, p. 277). Finally, the Mesosystem factors are located as the circle encompassing all others and represents the interplay or linkages between the individual or family as well as all individuals or social institutions with which the couple may come into contact.

Recently, Heise (1998, p. 265) used the ecological framework as a heuristic tool to synthesize the existing international, cross-cultural, and North American domestic violence research including all types of physical and sexual abuse into an "intelligible whole." Based on an extensive review of the literature, Heise organized the following predictive factors of violence against women including rape and marital abuse on the following different levels of ecology:

1. Personal History/Ontogenetic/Individual: witnessing marital violence, being the recipient of maltreatment as a child, having an absent or rejecting father.
2. Microsystem: male dominance in the family, male control of the wealth in the family, use of alcohol, marital/verbal conflict.
3. Exosystem: low socioeconomic status/unemployment, isolation of the woman and family, delinquent peer associates.
4. Macrosystem: male entitlement/ownership of women (as property), cultural definitions of masculinity linked to aggression and dominance.
5. Mesosystem: linkages between the individual's family and their place of work, extended family, or network of peers as well as with social institutions such as police, courts, or social services.

The research findings assigned to the various Ecological levels include only factors shown to be empirically related to differential rates of violence against women and girls (Heise, 1998). Similar to the caveat offered in an early domestic violence application of this model by Carlson (1984), a decade and half later, this framework and application of research findings "... should not be interpreted as definitive because they are based on a tentative and incomplete research base ... [such that] ... critical factors may be missing simply because the research has not been done to test their significance. ... [while] ... others may prove to be correlates rather than true causal factors" (Heise, p. 265). However, this framework does allow for the acknowledgment of the influence of individual, situational, cultural, and societal factors in the etiology of abuse where women are the consistent targets of the most serious violence. Thus, the Ecological Nested Model framework offers a foundation for evaluation of the conflict dynamic that better informs both prevention and treatment efforts aimed at batterers.

Elsewhere, the Ecological Nested Model (ENM) has been applied to the study of understanding battered women's reactions to their partner's coercive behavior to address the lack of contextual analysis in this area of research (Dutton, 1996; Lischick, 1999; Mitchell & Hodson, 1986). In an effort to enhance our understanding of the battered women's efforts in the entrapment process to resist, escape, avoid, and stop the violence, it is not sufficient to simply identify the battered women's responses. Indeed, we must move beyond the exclusive psychological and sociological analysis by examining the varying overlapping systems that include contextual aspects of the battered women's experience. Early coping and social support literature had an extremely limited focus. It linked deficits in coping and social support to individual stress while ignoring the broader social context's contribution to stress, coping, and support processes of battered women.

Thus far, theoretical analyses attempting to explain battered women's strategic responses in terms of Seligman's (1975) concept of learned helplessness have been woefully inadequate in offering any understanding for their concrete and resistant actions to survive or minimize the abuse. In response to the inadequacies of this concept that pathologizes battered women, proponents of survivor theory empirically tested a contextual model involving battered women's responses and found support for a myriad of help-seeking actions that leave her need to escape, avoid, or protect herself and her children from the violence unmet (Gondolf & Fisher, 1988). In addition, results suggested that battered women will increase their help-seeking behaviors as the violence increases and as institutional and social support increases, more active coping strategies will be used. The application of this model to research on women's responses to battering demonstrates the importance of contextual variables, in addition to the violence itself, and has extended our understanding of battered women's coping and corollary help-seeking behaviors while simultaneously depathologizing her responses in the abusive relationship.

Specifically, Dutton's (1996, pp. 111–112) analysis of battered women's strategic responses applied to the Ecological Nested Model involves the following:

1. The *individual battered woman*, her individual personal history, and the meaning she makes of it (i.e., ontogenetic).
2. Family, friendship, workplace, and other *personal networks* in which a battered women interacts, the developmental history of each, and the meaning she makes of them (i.e., Microsystem).
3. The *institutions and social structures* defining the battered woman's social environment, the history of those linkages, and the meaning she makes of them (i.e., Exosystem).
4. The *society and cultural blueprint* defined by the cultural, ethnic group, and social class factors, the historical development of the blueprint, and the meaning she makes of it (i.e., Macrosystem Level).
5. The linkages between *larger community networks* in which the battered woman doesn't interact directly but which, nevertheless, influence her indirectly (i.e., Mesosystem), the developmental history of those networks, and the meaning she makes of them.

Factors operating within each ecological system determine both real and perceived options for responding to the batterer's behavior. In addition, the chronosystem involving the developmental history of each of the Ecological systems is also included in each level to account for the impact of her previous experiences on that level. Finally, the Ecological Nested Model as it pertains to coping, evidenced in the battered woman's strategic choices, illuminates an examination of the factors contributing to the entrapment process.

When evaluating the responses of battered women and their options for safety, vulnerability, and resiliency, mental health practitioners must identify risk and resiliency factors on each level of the model to address treatment planning in terms of that factor's ability to offer support or a barrier to safety. Examples at the Individual Level of the model include the victim's immigration issues, mental health issues, substance abuse issues, children issues, trauma history issues, work and education issues, medical issues, and access to financial resources. All of these factors can be manipulated by the batterer to maintain control over the victim. Examples at the Microsystem Level of the model include the level and extent of the batterer's coercive control strategies, his lethality level, his substance abuse issues, his mental health issues, and his ability to successfully deprive the victim of independence and autonomous functioning as well as her workplace response and the responses of the immediate family and

culturally relevant others. If, for example, the batterer's family continually bailed him out of jail such that he regains access to her, then
this would be evaluated as a risk factor that provides a barrier to her
safety and an increase to her vulnerability. Examples at the Exosystem Level of the model include the response of systems' helpers such
as judges, police, mental health practitioners, medical professionals,
welfare workers, child protection workers, clergy, domestic violence
program workers, crisis response workers, tribal elders, and any other
community system responder that potentially can entrap the victim by
offering erroneous victim-blaming responses that allow the batterer
to avoid culpability and restitution. If, for example, the jailer mails the
batterer's letters to the victim despite an active restraining order, then
this would be evaluated as a risk to the victim's safety because the
victim loses faith in the system. If the mental health practitioner unknowingly colludes with the batterer in a family systems analysis of
mutual combat, then this is viewed as a risk factor to her safety.

Systems' responders are particularly vulnerable to victim-blaming
analyses when (a) they view domestic violence as a unilateral phenomenon through a family systems/conflict resolution framework;
(b) they lack adequate knowledge, training, or supervision related to
the complexities involved in domestic violence victimization occurring in relation to all levels of the Ecological Nested Model; or (c)
they see the victim on repeated occasions and are unable to overcome
their own powerlessness feeling states in relation to the batterer's
continued abusive and coercive strategies. As a result, the batterer's
coercive control is maintained by a lack of effective intervention that
can adequately hold the batterer accountable or effectively constrain
the batterer from continuing to execute those coercive strategies.
When helpers communicate their victim-blaming analysis to the victim, they contribute to her entrapment, and empower the batterer
to maintain control over her options while avoiding culpability. At
the Macrosystem Level of the model, factors involving gender-role
socialization, cultural-role socialization, and religious-role socialization beliefs converge together to form one of the cognitive filters
through which she will evaluate her options. The batterer is often
acutely aware of her belief system, which he will use to his advantage to define her "acceptable, respectable" response options. At
the Mesosystem Level of the model, factors include all of the connections between the other levels from which she will make meaning of her experience. The meaning will include past and present

situation outcomes. Every factor on each level of the model as well as the interactions between factors must be evaluated in terms of the contribution to overall risk and resiliency. The victim only has control over her own behavior. She does not have control over any of the other factors or responders on the various levels of the model. This must be acknowledged by the practitioner, and she must be joined in the analysis of all of these factors in order to identify a comprehensive plan of action designed to address her risk.

APPLYING ROBERTS'S SEVEN-STAGE CRISIS INTERVENTION USING A CULTURAL CONTEXTUAL ANALYSIS OF RISK AND PROTECTIVE FACTORS

To avoid the pitfalls experienced by Mr. O'Hanlon, mental health practitioners require an alternate understanding that redefines woman battering as coercive control and distinguishes it from episodic conflict involving anger gone awry. If all interpartner conflict and anger management issues were first viewed and analyzed through this lens, then the practitioner would be more readily able to identify the coercive pattern of strategies where it exists. Because human lives may be at stake and harm might come to the target of the individual's self-defined anger, the practitioner should evaluate the client and the target through a crisis model because effective intervention and brief treatment will depend on it.

Roberts's Seven-Stage Crisis Intervention Model (2000) is particularly useful when the batterer threatens the practitioner. Once the crisis is identified as such via the coercive control lens, the practitioner can proceed to the first step in the crisis model. The first step is to plan and conduct a thorough assessment of lethality (dangerousness) levels, dangerousness to self, and immediate psychosocial needs. This assessment must include evaluating all of the factors on the various levels of the Ecological Nested Model as described earlier with respect to the batterer and the victim. In the second step, the batterer must acknowledge that he alone is accountable for all of his behavioral expressions. At the same time, the practitioner must establish rapport by conveying genuine respect, acceptance, reassurance, and a nonjudgmental attitude that includes accountability using a self-in-control acting on others coercively to take control analysis.

In step three, the practitioner must assist the client in an examination of all dimensions of the problem as a pattern of behavior including last-straw or precipitating event that brought him into treatment. The practitioner is responsible for reframing the client's victim-blaming responses in terms of the batterer's choice to intimidate and control his partner using coercive behaviors and emotional displays of rage to punish, degrade, or obtain compliance. Any deviation from this self-in-control analysis will collude with the batterer's attempt at viewing himself as out of control, controlled by others, and therefore not culpable or responsible to change. Step four involves encouraging the batterer to explore feelings and emotions surrounding a behavioral assessment using this self-in-control lens. Step five involves encouraging the client to generate, explore, and assess past coping attempts in terms of achieving set goals. The practitioner must assist the client in his evaluation of entitlement thinking and beliefs regarding his rights to deprive his partner from her rights to independence, autonomy, or freedom as her own agent. The outcomes should be evaluated in terms of successes and failures.

In step six the practitioner should assist the client in generating and exploring alternative and specific solutions into the development of an action plan. This step should include information about recidivism rates and the necessity of batterer's intervention group treatment as one of the most effective treatment options if the program is completed. Although the batterer's may not want to hear that information, it is the ethical obligation to provide this information as well as the necessary referral when a pattern of coercive control is identified. To avoid the perils that O'Hanlon (2005) faced, the practitioner must acknowledge both to self and client that couples counseling, anger management, conflict resolution, and problem-solving skill-building interventions in the context of coercive control are contraindicated even when it is the victim requesting this treatment. The safety of the victim should be the first priority. The practitioner may assure the client that this is his opportunity to change the course of his life like others before him who completed such a program. In step seven, the practitioner assists the client in restoring cognitive functioning through implementation of an action plan. If the batterer has additional mental health issues or substance abuse issues, then the practitioner may wish to establish ancillary treatment sessions to address these issues in addition to the client's concurrent participation in the Batterer's Intervention Programming (BIP). The practitioner may also wish to establish a follow-up mechanism with booster sessions 3 or 6 months later. It is recommended that as a condition of any ancillary treatment provided, that the client agree to open communication with the BIP as a condition of treatment.

CONCLUSION

Practitioners should never ignore the 23 warning signs of escalating intimate partner violence identified and discussed by Roberts and Roberts (2005). It is also imperative to understand the potentially lethal dangers of the batterers' threats with a gun and the clear differences between coercive control and episodic fights discussed in this chapter. Woman battering involving a dynamic of coercive control is often misunderstood by mental health practitioners and may lead to clinical errors in diagnosis and treatment of mental health disorders in victims (Stark & Flitcraft, 1996) and batterers (Gondolf, 1990, 1998). Misunderstandings have been linked to several theoretical and systemic issues identified in the literature, which include conceptualization of the problem (Dutton & Goodman, 2005; Lischick, 1999; Stark and Flitcraft; Stark, in press; Walker, 1995) and the lack of standardized models of care (Miller, Veltkamp, & Kraus, 1997), as well as the therapeutic framework, relationship diagnosis, structure of the treatment process, therapeutic relationship, and therapist competence level (Enns, Campbell, & Courtois, 1997). All of these problems are interconnected and bear directly on lack of contextualized assessment design, constricted information gathering, myopic diagnostic formulation, and treatment planning. Graduate psychology programs often do not provide relevant training for identifying, assessing, diagnosing, and treating various forms of trauma including domestic violence (Alpert & Paulson, 1990; Williamson, 2000). Child maltreatment researchers document parallel deficits in graduate training programs involving student preparation for treating child witnesses of domestic violence where exposure is limited and specialization opportunities are rare (Horton, Cruise, Graybill, & Cornett, 1999).

To avoid such errors, it is incumbent on practitioners to stay current with the burgeoning research in the fields of crisis intervention, violence against women, feminist psychology, batterers' treatment, family psychology, child maltreatment, multicultural psychology, and trauma. Battered women are crime victims in crisis, exposed to a coercive pattern of abuse, terror, isolation, and deprivation by the batterer to their basic human right to independence, autonomy, and free will. Their resistance to being coercively controlled is suppressed by factors operating at all levels of the Ecological Nested Model. Victims respond to the batterer's pattern of coercive control strategies in a myriad of ways reflecting both internal and external coping responses that are elicited within a cultural context that includes various systems' helpers (Lischick, 1999). Battered women may seek help in crisis after the batterer has escalated his pattern of coercive strategies to a level wherein their existing coping responses no longer offer a satisfactory resolution as defined by the victim. The batterer may seek help, and couples counseling may be prescribed with various caveats and contraindications (Geller, 1998). However, this prescription may be unsafe because a myopic focus on family systems and a lack of familiarity with the extensive domestic violence and crisis intervention research increase the danger for the victim and her partner as well as the mental health practitioner.

Unfortunately, when well-meaning practitioners with limited training view domestic violence myopically as a unilateral phenomenon through a conflict resolution lens where both parties are seen as equally culpable for an episodic problem, entrapment occurs (Lischick, 1999). Such a decontextualized analysis of woman battering by mental health practitioners simultaneously pathologizes and blames her for her own victimization while inadvertently colluding with the batterer's strategy to avoid accountability. Conjoint interventions that follow this analysis are often designed to improve skills in communication, problem-solving, anger management, and constructive conflict resolution. In contrast, battering defined as a pattern of coercive control involves conflict suppression by the batterer in order to dominate and control his victim.

One might conclude from the case study presented above that mainstream psychology's family systems analysis guided Mr. O'Hanlon's (2005) view of conflict resolution gone awry, thus contributing to hypothesis formulation during assessment, modality selection, and intervention strategies. Although controversy exists over the use of conjoint treatment when domestic violence is present, including 20 states that expressly prohibit it in state standards for batterer's treatment programming, Stith, Rosen, and McCullum (2003) report that conjoint treatment can be at least as effective as traditional treatment for domestic violence when carefully conceptualized and delivered while citing preliminary evidence that suggests that women are not placed at increased risk for injury. What does "carefully conceptualized and delivered" mean exactly? Preliminary evidence for pre- and posttest conjoint treatment studies suggest that the research designs are "plagued" with methodological problems including limited sample size, lack of standardized measurement instruments, outcome reported by only one partner, and one sample design (Stith, Rosen, & McCullum, p. 417). Thus, author conclusions "rest on sparse and often unsophisticated" data involving six experimental studies that use different eligibility criteria, outcome measures, and treatment approaches (Stith, Rosen, & McCullum, p. 424). Perhaps it is true that victims are not at increased risk of injury when comparing gender-specific treatment (e.g., batterers intervention programs) with couples counseling; however, the "evidence" reviewed and the authors' conclusion is not based on any scientific certainty that would allow for generalizing the application of conjoint therapy to the at risk population of battered women. Yet, as the authors point out and the O'Hanlon case scenario shows, ". . . family therapists are already working with violent couples" (Stith, Rosen, & McCollum, p. 422). Clearly, the research on this modality of treatment is in its infancy, and interventions are exploratory and experimental at best. Knowing this fact should cause all practitioners to examine the underlying ethical issues while proceeding with extreme caution that includes the caveats, indications, and contraindications, lest we end up colluding with the batterer to do harm while contributing to the victim's entrapment.

Although skill building in these areas might be helpful to any individual, these treatment approaches do not decrease danger for victims or necessarily empower them toward safety, nor do they involve restructuring the batterer's entitlement belief system used to coerce others to get his needs met. Instead, the playing field is assumed level, and the batterer is viewed as equally victimized by a provocative and powerful opponent in a mutual combat dynamic. The analysis lulls the victim into believing that she has control over the batterer's behavior and that she contributed to her victimization. The responsibility assigned to her by both the treatment provider and the batterer involves changing her "provocative" behavior to avoid being re-victimized, whereas the batterer avoids accountability. Clearly, this approach spelled danger for Margie and Mr. O'Hanlon, as well as Ben, and thankfully none were harmed. As ethical treatment providers, we have a responsibility to all parties in the information-gathering process involving relationship conflict and anger to realize that coercive control, conflict suppression, and privileged thinking may be operating in a complex context of system helpers and lives may be at stake, such that we include specific theoretical analysis and application of crisis intervention in the name of safety. When we fail to rule out alternative theoretical explanations involving coercive control in favor of a myopic focus from our limited education and training experiences, our ignorance and naiveté contribute to harm done. At the same time, we contribute to the victim's continued entrapment while simultaneously viewing the problem from the wrong side of the equation—trying to explain why she stays rather than why he gets to continue to do what he does and how we assist in that process.

REFERENCES

Alpert, J. L., & Paulson, A. (1990). Graduate level education and training in child sexual abuse. *Professional Psychology: Research and Practice, 21*, 366–371.

American Psychological Association Report from the APA Presidential Task Force on Violence and the Family. (1996). Washington, DC: APA.

Belsky, J. (1980). Child maltreatment: An ecological analysis. *American Psychologist, 35*, 320–335.

Brofenbrenner, U. (1977). Toward an experimental ecology of human development. *American Psychologist, 32*, 513–531.

Brofenbrenner, U. (1979). *The ecology of human development: Experiments by nature and design.* Cambridge, MA: Harvard University Press.

Brofenbrenner, U. (1986). Recent advances in research on the ecology of human development. In R. Silbereisen, K. Eyferth, & G. Rudinger (Eds.), *Development as action in context: Problem solving behavior and normal youth development* (pp. 287–308). New York: Springer Publishing.

Campbell, J. (1995). *Assessing dangerousness: Violence by sexual offenders, batterers and child abusers.* Thousand Oaks, CA: Sage.

Carlson, B. (1984). Causes and maintenance of domestic violence: An ecological analysis. *Social Service Review, 58*, 569–587.

Davies, J. (1998). *Safety planning with battered women: Complex lives/difficult choices.* Thousand Oaks, CA: Sage.

Dutton, D. G. (1995). *The batterer: A psychological profile.* New York: Basic Books.

Dutton, M. A. (1992). *Empowering & healing the battered woman.* New York: Springer Publishing.

Dutton, M. (1996). Battered women's strategic response to violence: The role of context. In J. Edleson & Z. Eisikovits (Eds.), *Future interventions with battered women and their families* (pp. 105–124). Thousand Oaks, CA: Sage.

Dutton, M. A., & Goodman, L. A. (2005). Coercion in intimate partner violence: Toward a new conceptualization. *Sex Roles, 52*(11/12), 743–756.

Dziegielewski, S. F., & Resnick, C. (1996). Crisis assessment and intervention: Abused women in the shelter setting. In A. R. Roberts (Ed.), *Crisis management & brief treatment: Theory, technique and applications* (pp. 83–102). Chicago, IL: Nelson Hall Publishers.

Edleson, J., & Tolman, R. (1992). *Intervention for men who batter: An ecological approach*. Newbury Park, CA: Sage.

Enns, C. Z., Campbell, J., & Courtois, C. A. (1997). Recommendations for working with domestic violence survivors, with special attention to memory issues and posttraumatic processes. *Psychotherapy, 34*(4), 459–477.

Frye, M. (1983). *The politics of reality: Essays in feminist theory*. New York: Crossing Press.

Ganley, A. L. (1995). Understanding domestic violence. In C. Warshaw & A. L. Ganley (Eds.), *Improving the health care response to domestic violence: A resource manual for health care providers* (pp. 15–45). San Francisco, CA: Family Violence Prevention Fund.

Geller, J. A. (1998). Conjoint therapy for treatment of partner abuse: Indications and contraindications. In A. R. Roberts (Ed.), *Battered women and their families: Intervention strategies and treatment programs* (pp. 76–96). New York: Springer Publishing.

Gondolf, E. (1988). The effect of batterer counseling on shelter outcome. *Journal of Interpersonal Violence, 3*(3), 275–289.

Gondolf, E. W. (1990). *Psychiatric responses to family violence*. Lexington, MA: Lexington Books.

Gondolf, E. W. (1998). *Assessing woman battering in mental health services*. Thousand Oaks, CA: Sage.

Gondolf, E., & Fisher, E. (1988). *Battered women as survivors: An alternative to treating learned helplessness*. Lexington, MA: Lexington.

Heise, L. (1998). Violence against women: An integrated, ecological framework. *Violence Against Women, 4*(3), 262–290.

Herman, J. (1992). *Trauma and recovery*. New York: Basic Books.

Horton, C. B., Cruise, T. K., Graybill, D., & Cornett, J. Y. (1999). For the children's sake: Training students in the treatment of child witnesses of domestic violence. *Professional Psychology: Research and Practice, 30*(1), 88–91.

Jones, A., & Schechter, S. (1991). *When love goes wrong*. New York: HarperCollins.

Kirkwood, C. (1993). *Leaving abusive partners*. Newbury Park, CA: Sage.

Levinson, D. (1989). *Family violence in a cross-cultural perspective.* Newbury Park, CA: Sage.

Lischick, C. (1999). *Coping and related characteristics delineating battered women's experiences in self-defined, difficult/hurtful dating relationships: A multicultural study.* Unpublished doctoral dissertation, Rutgers University, Newark, NJ.

Lischick, C. (2000). *Dating violence and coercive control theory: New evidence.* Paper presented at the 5th International Conference on Family violence: Advocacy, Assessment, Intervention Research, Prevention and Policy, Family Violence and Sexual Assault Institute. San Diego, CA.

Lischick, C. (2005). *Challenging mainstream gender neutral analysis of heterosexual interpartner violence and mutual combat: Empirical support for the feminist theory of coercive control.* Paper presented at the 2005 Association for Women in Psychology Conference: Feminist Psychology: Future Tense. Tampa, FL.

Madanes, C. (1995). *The violence of men. New techniques for working with abusive families: A therapy for social action.* San Francisco: Josey-Bass.

Miller, T. W., Veltkamp, L. J., & Kraus, R. F. (1997). Clinical pathways for diagnosing and treating victims of domestic violence. *Psychotherapy, 34*(4), 425–432.

Mitchell, R., & Hodson, C. (1986). Coping and social support among battered women. In S. Hobfoll (Ed.), *Stress, social support, and women* (pp. 153–169). New York: Hemisphere Publishing Corp.

O'Hanlon, B. (March/April, 2005). No way out: Sometimes you just can't dance around the problem. *Psychotherapy Networker, 29,* 28–31, 56–57.

Okun, L. (1986). *Woman abuse: Facts replacing myths.* Albany, NY: State University of New York Press.

Pence, E., & Paymar, M. (1993). *Education groups for men who batter: The Duluth model.* New York: Springer Publishing.

Roberts, A. R. (2000). An overview of crisis theory and crisis intervention. In A. R. Roberts (Ed.), *Crisis intervention handbook: Assessment, treatment and research* (pp. 3–30). New York: Oxford University Press.

Roberts, A. R. (2005). Bridging the past and present to the future of crisis intervention and crisis management. In A. R. Roberts (Ed.), *Crisis intervention handbook: Assessment, treatment and research* (pp. 3–34). New York: Oxford University Press.

Roberts, A. R., & Burman, S. (1998). Crisis intervention and cognitive problem-solving therapy with battered women: A national survey and practice model. In A. R. Roberts (Ed.), *Battered women and their families: Intervention strategies and treatment programs* (pp. 76–96). New York: Springer Publishing.

Roberts, A. R., & Roberts, B. S. (2000). A comprehensive model for crisis intervention with battered women and their children. In A. R.

Roberts (Ed.), *Crisis intervention handbook: Assessment, treatment and research* (pp. 177–208). New York: Oxford University Press.

Roberts, A. R., & Roberts, B. S. (2005). *Ending intimate abuse: Practical guidance and survival strategies.* New York: Oxford University Press.

Rosewater, L. B. (1988). Battered or schizophrenic? Psychological tests can't tell. In K. Yllo & M. Bograd (Eds.), *Feminist perspectives on wife abuse* (pp. 200–216). Newbury, CA: Sage.

Seligman, M. (1975). *Helplessness: On depression, development and death.* San Francisco, CA: Freeman.

Smith, P. H., Earp, J., & DeVellis, R. (1995). Measuring battering: Development of the Women's Experiencing with Battering (WEB) Scale. *Women's Health: Research on Gender, Behavior & Policy, 1*(4), 273–288.

Stark, E. (1992). Framing and reframing battered women. In E. Buzawa (Ed.), *Domestic violence: The criminal justice response* (pp. 271–292). Westport, CT: Auburn.

Stark, E. (1996). Mandatory arrest of batterers: A reply to its critics. In E. Buzawa & C. Buzawa (Eds.), *Do arrests and restraining orders work?* (pp. 115–149). Thousand Oaks, CA: Sage.

Stark, E. (In press). *Coercive control.* New York: Oxford University Press.

Stark, E., & Flitcraft, A. (1996). *Women at risk: Domestic violence and women's health.* Thousand Oaks, CA: Sage.

Stith, S. M., Rosen, K. H., and McCollum, E. (2003). Effectiveness of couples treatment for spouse abuse. *Journal of Marital and Family Therapy, 29*(30), 407–426.

Straus, M. (1979). Measuring intrafamily conflict and violence: The Conflict Tactics (CT) Scales. *Journal of Marriage and the Family, 41*, 75–88.

Walker, L. (1994). *Abused women and survivor therapy: A practical guide for psychotherapists.* Washington, DC: American Psychological Association.

Walker, L. (1995). Current perspectives on men who batter women— Implications for intervention and treatment to stop violence against women: Comment on Gottman et al. (1995). *Journal of Family Psychology, 9*(3), 264–271.

Warshaw, C. (1989). Limitations of the medical model in the care of battered women. *Gender & Society, 3*, 506–517.

Williamson, T. (2000). *The relationship between formal education/training and the ability of psychologist and marriage and family therapists to assess and intervene when counseling with female victims of domestic violence.* Unpublished doctoral dissertation, The Claremont University.

Wilson, M., & Daly, M. (1995). An evolutionary psychological perspective on male sexual proprietariness and violence against wives. In B. Ruback & N. Weiner (Eds.), *Interpersonal violent behaviors: Social and cultural aspects* (pp. 109–133). New York: Springer Publishing.

CHAPTER 14

Conjoint Therapy for the Treatment of Partner Abuse:
Indications and Contraindications

Janet A. Geller

This chapter is an updated version of a chapter that first appeared in 1984 in the first edition of this volume (Geller & Wasserstrom, 1984). Although the concept of the efficacy of conjoint treatment for partner abuse is much more widely chosen by practitioners than when I first pioneered it in 1977 (Geller & Walsh, 1977–1978), and often is the treatment of choice, there have been changes in my approach, reflecting 29 more years of professional experience with this modality. In this updated chapter I discuss the changes that have come about through critical application over the years, numerous discussions with my colleagues, teaching, training, and review of the literature. I believe these changes have resulted in a more refined approach to conjoint treatment for helping battered women.

I would like to add that conjoint treatment represents but one method. The treatment model that I have developed, and have written about elsewhere, includes individual treatment with battered women and batterers, group treatment for battered women, group treatment for batterers, and multiple-couples groups (Geller, 1992). Although all battered women have battering in common, not all of their needs are the same (Geller, p. 14). A multimodality approach offers practitioners the opportunity to apply a cadre of techniques and modalities to service a broader range of the needs that battered women present. (For a fuller description of this treatment model, see chapters 1 and 6.) For the purposes of this writing, however, I will focus on the modality of conjoint therapy, with its many caveats. The original chapter first appearing in 1984 will be treated similar to a critiqued process recording, indicating how my thinking has been altered from the time that this chapter was first written. I hope that this approach will prove to be both interesting and informative.

When I first began working with battered women in 1976, the women I saw held traditional values, aspiring to be primary caretakers, with family as the cornerstone of their lives, which was their "gender pride and self-respect" (Goldner, Penn, Steinberg, & Walker, 1990, p. 357). These were not women who needed or wanted to go to shelters for battered women, use legal options against their husbands, or separate and divorce. Simply put, they wanted abuse to cease, but their marriages to remain. There are many women today who still hope for the same dream; as Virginia Satir (1967, p. 1) later stated, the couple "is the axis around which all other family relationships are formed." Often, the most common method for achieving the cessation of abuse has been to see each member of the couple separately: for the woman, either individually or in groups and for the batterer, generally, in group treatment. Although I subscribe to this approach and have both employed and described it myself, another method could be conjoint treatment, which I have successfully used for over 20 years, both alone and with staff whom I have trained.

Researchers have now documented the effectiveness of conjoint treatment (O'Leary, 1996). There are, however, contraindications to using conjoint therapy, as well as certain caveats of which to be aware. Using the case study from the chapter in the first edition, the caveats and contraindications to conjoint therapy will be explicated, as well as the changes I have made in the treatment approach. Following is the story of Tom and Terry, who represented the prototypical case in which this model proved effective.

CASE SCENARIO

Teresa called the agency saying she had heard that we work with women whose husbands hit them. She stated that she was really in need of such help. "You see, this is the second time I married a guy like that." Terry's first husband used to hit her when drunk. She had married young and had two small girls. She didn't know what to do. She finally left the marriage and thought she would never marry again. Then along came Tom. She had been single for about 10 years. As things were going well, when he proposed to her, she accepted. She was devastated when he turned out to be a "wife-beater" too. The worker asked Terry what she had done about this the first time and she replied, "Nothing." Terry said, "I didn't know there was anything I could do other than calling the cops." Terry said she never heard of us before, but now that she knows of our existence, she wants help. The worker asked Terry if she thought about her plans with this husband. Did she want a divorce from him too? Terry stated that what she had to say might sound "crazy," but she loves Tom and when he doesn't hit her he's a very good husband. The worker assured her that this didn't sound crazy to her and that a lot of wives felt as she did. Terry was surprised to hear that and said, "Well, that's a relief. I thought there was something wrong with me." When Terry asked when she could come in, the worker suggested that she bring her husband. Since Terry wanted to stay married, the worker thought it would be better to see him too. Terry told her that Tom would never come. The worker explained that a lot of wives think that, but husbands do come in. Terry told the worker that her husband was Italian and they were very "close-mouthed" about their problems. The worker said that other Italians had come here, and that unless he came for help, the battering would never stop. The worker correlated how our seeing her would not stop Tom from hitting her. The worker directly stated that unless she got him to come in, nothing in the marriage would change. The worker asked Terry if she would like him to come for help, to which she replied, "Of course." Then the worker suggested that she find a way to get him in. She asked the worker what she could do. The worker turned the question back to her, stating that she knew her husband better and that Terry could find a way to get him in. When Terry hesitated, the worker suggested they go through all of her options. Together they figured out that her choices were as follows: She could end the marriage; she could come in alone but the violence wouldn't stop; she could get an Order of Protection; or she could convince him to get help for himself. Terry stated that she didn't want to end the marriage, that an Order of Protection was ineffective as she had gotten one before. She did not think Tom would come in with her, and he surely wouldn't go for help himself. Of the options available, she could see that the best one was to come in with him. She stated she thought she did know a way to get him in. The worker could hear the determination in her voice when she said, "I'll threaten him with an Order of Protection. That will get him to come in! After all, what do I have to lose? If things continue as they are, I'll either be dead or divorced." The worker reinforced her statements. She asked Terry to call her back the next day to tell her what happened, to which Terry agreed.

The next day Terry called to tell the worker that it had worked. She said, "I told him either he comes to you people or I go to court." We made an appointment. Just before we hung up, Terry said that she didn't really know if this was going to work. She asked the worker, "Do you think he'll change?" The worker suggested that Tom and she come in and they would all find out.

DISCUSSION

At the time that the first edition appeared, there was an insistence on my part on seeing the dyad together for conjoint to be successful. This has since been amended in the following ways.

An assessment must occur regarding (a) the severity of abuse, (b) whether conjoint is the woman's choice, and (c) individual contacts between the worker and clients should be mixed with conjoint. There should also be regular phone calls. Allow me to discuss each of these points below.

Assessing Severity of Abuse

Initially, during the first phone contact, the severity of abuse should be briefly assessed. This can be achieved by asking the woman to describe the worst incidence of abuse, which does not have to be the most recent. The worker asks questions expanding and clarifying this incident. These are critical questions for two reasons. First, conjoint should only be offered when the abuse is mild and possibly moderate, which can be determined as defined by the Criminal Justice System (see criminal codes) or by scales measuring levels of abuse, such as

Hudson's (1994). If abuse is severe, the element of danger can be great to the woman who makes statements in the conjoint sessions that anger her abuser; therefore, this becomes an essential assessment criterion. Second, and in some ways more importantly, there may be a need for immediate intervention if abuse is severe.

Was Conjoint the Woman's Choice?

Women may be coerced into conjoint by their partners. It may not be possible to determine this over the phone; therefore, if conjoint is initially assessed as possible based on the abuse being mild or possibly moderate, the next step is for a more in-depth assessment through an individual session for each partner before conjoint treatment has begun. The couple can be interviewed separately back-to-back or on different days, depending on the needs of the case. In the individual session, each partner is asked to describe the worst incidence of abuse in detail and a standardized test to measure level of abuse is administered, such as the Conflict Tactic Scale (CTS), Hudson's Partner Abuse Scale: Physical (1994), and so on. The remainder of the time can be used as needed, but in addition, the woman is questioned concerning her desire for conjoint.

This is the time to discover whether she genuinely is comfortable and desirous of being seen in this modality. "What if's" are discussed; for example: "What if he gets angry at something that you say?" "Could that lead to abuse after the session?" It is also determined whether there are certain topics to stay away from. I have even developed code words with women that signal me to withdraw from certain issues because she knows they are not safe. Some women wish to pursue conjoint even with some prohibitions, as just described, but others may not. In no circumstances should conjoint be offered or advised if the woman does not wish it. Issues of resistance or homeostatis do not apply, as she knows her batterer best, and that is to be honored and respected. Although it is true that the batterer most likely will not stop battering unless he receives help, and she is advised of this, there are other options for helping her as delineated in the multimodal model described in chapters 1 and 6. Further, even if the woman is in favor of conjoint, if the worker assesses it as too dangerous, then it is contraindicated. A compromise position is to treat the couple individually until it is safe for conjoint.

The Use of Individual and Conjoint Therapy

Because of the potential for violence in partner-abuse cases, even once conjoint has been assessed as suitable and safe, individual sessions are regularly held to ensure that conjoint continues to be indicated, as conditions can rapidly shift with partner-abuse cases. This is also the purpose of the phone calls. Individual sessions mixed with conjoint and phone calls between the worker and the woman deviate from traditional systems couples therapy theory, where the worker avoids the potential for coalitions to develop between worker and client, and endeavors to remain neutral. Because of the element of violence, it becomes a necessary and an essential safeguard against abuse to deviate in this way. If antitherapeutic coalitions do develop, they are worked through in the sessions.

FIRST SESSION

Terry and Tom arrived on time. They both appeared very nervous. The Abdellas were a very attractive couple. Tom was a broadly built, six-foot tall, dark-haired, bearded man. Terry was small in contrast, about five feet four inches tall, and a Cheryl Tiegs lookalike. Tom had never been married before. The Abdella household consisted of Tom, Terry, and her two daughters, ages 14 and 16. Tom was a construction worker and Terry a housewife.

Most of the session was spent with Tom and Terry ventilating. Terry talked about how upset she was with Tom's violence, while Tom attempted to defend himself by blaming her for his hitting her; this resulted in her blaming him. When Tom was not defending himself, he was questioning his reasons for being here, saying, "I don't know what I'm doing here. I never thought I'd be in a shrink's office." At one point Tom turned to the worker and said, "This is no use. You're probably on her side anyway."

Before the worker could respond, Tom went on to say that he didn't want to hit her. "I know it's wrong, but she makes me." The worker asked him how. Tom replied, "She just nags and nags." He turned to Terry and said, "If you would just quit your nagging, I wouldn't have to hit you."

Terry's response was to defend herself and then blame him. The only role the worker was able to play in this session was to remain neutral, assuring both parties that she was not on anyone's side. The worker said, "I'm not going to take sides here. This is not a court of law and I'm not interested in finding someone to blame. Anyway, the two of you do that quite well. What I am interested in is finding a way to help the two of you, as I can see that both of you are in pain. Both of you are not happy with things as they are. Maybe we can find a way to make things better for the two of you." The session ended as it began. Another appointment was set for the following week.

DISCUSSION

Treatment begins long before the client enters the office (Haley, 1976). In the waiting room, the worker could sense Tom and Terry's self-consciousness and discomfort. One can guess that were it not for their pressing need, this couple would never think of going for help. For many people, seeking help is alien to their subcultural values and beliefs (Minuchin, 1974). Therefore, care must be taken to facilitate the helping process.

The initial point of entry for the clients is the initial phone call to the agency and then the waiting room. In this agency, the person chosen to greet people as they came in the door was friendly, respectful of others, and warm. Clients were offered tea or coffee to indicate hospitality. The waiting room was attractive, with comfortable chairs and a couch. All of this was deliberately designed to create a therapeutic atmosphere with the intention of relaxing troubled people.

The first session was expected to be used for ventilation with little else occurring. Couples who are violent have little opportunity for arguing in a violence-free atmosphere. At home, the same issues could escalate to violence. Arguing in the therapist's office offers the couple an opportunity to get things off their chests in an environment with safeguards; the therapist can stop them or help modify the atmosphere. Workers who are uncomfortable working with violent couples might tend to suppress anger or prematurely cut off angry expressions. In addition to the safety-valve feature, it is important to permit a free expression of anger so that the worker can, first, monitor patterns of arguing in the couple and, second, convey to the couple that the worker is accepting and tolerant of their arguing. Contrasted to family therapy practice, the couple is encouraged to talk to the worker, not to each other. This allows the worker to monitor both the batterer's anger level and the woman's discomfort level, and keeps control primarily in the worker's hands.

Beginning sessions are also a time for establishment of a therapeutic environment and rapport. By assuring Tom and Terry that the worker was interested in helping to ease their pain, the worker helped to create the necessary atmosphere in which help could take place. The worker's conscious neutrality was a critical factor in helping both members of the dyad. It is unusual today for men to be ignorant that battering is against the law. Were they assaulting anyone but their wives, they could be charged with assault and battery (New York State Law, 1977). Men not cognizant of the law know that they are causing physical harm. As a result, they are sensitive to blame and often expect to be blamed. Further, the couple's pattern focuses on the issue of blame. If the worker were to continue that pattern, he or she would be joining the system rather than offering something different. If the worker did think the husband was to blame, which is different from being solely responsible for abuse, she or he would not be able to help him. One of the basic tenets of therapeutic practice is freedom from judgments (Minuchin, 1974). Without it, a therapeutic alliance between worker and client is not possible. It is no different with partner abuse.

At the end of the session, the worker points out commonalities between Tom and Terry. Couples who live with violence are in enemy camps. Life is war. They do not cooperate, they are not a team, and there is no mutuality. Whatever opportunity presents itself to pull them together must be capitalized on. For change to take place, there must be healthy bonding. The presentation of mutual goals, feelings, and needs will help create a bond between them that will begin to bridge the gulf that divides them.

THIRD SESSION

By the third session the couple was doing much better. For the first time they could openly express mutual love, caring, and commitment. Tom expressed to both his wife and the worker that if Terry continued to act like this he would never have to hit her again. The worker allowed and encouraged the positive expression of feelings. As far as Tom's statements about the batterings were concerned, she addressed Tom concerning his responsibility for his actions. When he protested, saying his wife nags him so much that it "drives him crazy," the worker asked whether Tom thought that other wives were nagging too. Tom stated that his friends also complained about their nagging wives. The worker wondered if those women got beaten because they nagged. When Tom said he didn't know, he did agree that they may not. The worker then wondered, if some women were hit for nagging and others weren't—was the only response to nagging, hitting? Tom could see the logic in this and had to agree that it was his choice to respond by hitting. The worker also asked whether Tom knew what the law stated concerning assault and battery. Tom did. The worker wondered if the law said that assaulting a person was wrong, did that apply to a wife, too. Tom became very defensive and said that he knew everyone thought he was to blame. The worker reiterated that that was not an important issue for her, but rather, it was important to know how he felt about hitting his wife. Tom stated that he already said he didn't want to hit her. Before he could once again blame Terry, the worker stated that she thought he needed to change this for himself because it clearly wasn't making him feel good.

The worker focused on change for him, not for Terry. Finally Tom said that he would like to stop hitting her and it was true that he felt terrible about this. The worker said that she would be available to help him and asked Terry if she would help too. Terry agreed. The worker attempted to move to a plan for doing this, but Tom said he needed to think things over first. They agreed that this would be the focus of the next session.

DISCUSSION

It is not unusual for people in treatment to experience a flight into health (Framo, 1965). Tom and Terry went into what is commonly called "a honeymoon period." Although the worker knew that this was temporary, she capitalized on the positive, as it would lay groundwork for change when a regression occurred. In other words, when things turned for the worse, the worker could remind them of the positive feelings they had experienced as an example of how things could be between them. Further, most therapy time is devoted to the negative. It can be therapeutic to focus on the positive when it occurs. Violent couples are at such extreme odds with one another that emphasis on the positive is healing and continues the bonding response.

The worker used this session to discuss the responsibility for the violence. As things were calm between them and the tone had been set by

the worker in previous sessions concerning the purpose of their meetings, it appeared that this controversial issue could now be discussed.
It is difficult to discuss emotionally charged issues when people are
already feeling emotionally upset, as during crisis. It must be noted
and underscored that an unequivocal stance about who is responsible for the violent behavior must be taken. With couples who live with
abuse, the wife is often targeted as causing the battering. In actuality,
however, the husband externalizes blame, and the most convenient
person to blame is, of course, his wife. In his eyes, he does believe that
she is at fault. Because of her "learned helplessness" (Walker, 1989,
p. 42) and gender development, she accepts the blame.

If there is to be any change in this system, the worker must be
clear and consistent about the batterer's responsibility for violence.
This statement alone is an attempt at changing the homeostasis. This
approach is consistent with therapeutic practice in which people are
helped to assume responsibility for their functioning. A focus on
responsibility for violence must be established early in the therapeutic
process before the patterns that are entrenched at home become
embedded in the therapy sessions as well.

Once Tom and Terry acknowledged that he was responsible for the
violence, a therapeutic contract was established. The couple agreed
to focus on how the battering could stop. Without a therapeutic contract, no help is possible. Asking Terry to be of assistance to Tom was
again an attempt at bringing the couple together with both working
cooperatively. It also changes Terry's role from that of victim to that
of partner. Although Tom was not ready to focus on the "how" of
change, he did admit to the need to change.

DISCUSSION

It was previously my theory that battering was related to an impulse
disorder. I now believe that this reasoning is too linear, as is any one
explanation of causality, such as the power-and-control theory relating to patriarchy. It may be true, and I believe that it is, that some men
batter because of an impulse disorder such as intermittent explosive
disorder (American Psychiatric Association, 1994). Some men may
batter because they can, as those who favor a power-and-control theory believe (Brownmiller, 1975). However, it is now my belief that
men batter for numerous reasons, some of which are amenable to

a counseling approach whereas others are not. I have stated in my book that assessing men for counseling requires taking into account psychobiological disorders, psychiatric disorders, environmental and subcultural issues, and altered states (Geller, 1992). A case-by-case assessment may be an accurate method for determining causality.

Some men batter because of other issues; for example, narcissistic vulnerability with accompanying feelings of vulnerability and betrayal (Siegel, 1992), or gender development and societal acceptance of violence (Straus & Hotaling, 1980). Why battering occurs, in other words, is complex and multicausal, taking into account psychological, psychiatric, biological, sociopolitical, and behavioral and learning theories.

FOURTH SESSION

The day before the fourth session there was a phone call from a crying Terry who said that she and Tom had had a terrible fight, that she had gotten hit, and he was not coming to the session. While the worker expressed sympathy, she cut off a flow of feelings, saying that this was too important to talk about over the phone, and that she would like to hear more about it from both of them in the session. When Terry doubted that Tom would come, the worker reiterated her expectation that they would both be there.

Terry came alone, saying that Tom refused to come. Terry began to vent and question whether Tom would ever change. The worker discussed this a little further in the office, but stated that there could not be a couple session without a couple. She suggested that they call for a new appointment. Terry wanted to be seen alone, but the worker insisted, saying that they had contracted for couple sessions. If there was to be a change in the contract, they would have to come in and discuss it. Since Tom didn't keep the appointment with her, the worker said that she would call him at home.

DISCUSSION

Originally, the couples therapy theory that couples be seen conjointly prevailed in my treatment. I now believe that this should not automatically apply in cases of abuse. The main consideration is for the woman's safety.

When Terry called to say she had been hit again, the focus first needed to be on her injuries, the care they required, and on her safety. Questions concerning both are addressed, as well as suggestions for her care: whether this be a safety plan, discussion of legal options, or fleeing to a safe haven. This may be an appropriate time for an individual session. In Terry's case, her request for an individual session would be honored, with a new assessment made concerning conjoint treatment.

Another abusive episode does not necessarily rule out conjoint treatment, but the batterer must be held fully accountable and responsible for his abusive behavior. In addition to a focus on injuries and safety, there is always an emphasis on batterer responsibility.

Determining if conjoint treatment is continued or not is based on repeating the initial assessment, which, once again, focuses on the woman's willingness and level of abuse. Any form of abuse is unequivocally unacceptable, but as clinicians, we must have an understanding of symptom regression. Because abuse arouses such concern, and rightly so, it appears to be the only time treatment resorts to a "cut-it-out" school of therapy, with regression not tolerated. The danger is that a case that may be salvageable could be lost to the therapeutic process altogether. I am reminded of certain colleagues' work wherein a contract is made: If there is a resumption of abuse while conjoint is used, the therapy terminates, or "You're not going to do it and she's not going to take it." This is a trap for the worker, putting the worker in a self-made bind as described by Bograd (1986). I believe that a more therapeutic approach would be to focus the session on the batterer, holding him accountable for his regressive behavior, reinforcing the contract representing alternatives to violence and subsequently described in this chapter, and imposing a stiff consequence for his abusive behavior that is meaningful to him. For example, one consequence may be to fine the batterer an amount of money significant to him and given to her; another, to exclude him from the home for a certain length of time. Each decided consequence needs to be case specific.

In the event that a member of the couple absents himself from the session, conveying that message through the other party, as did Tom, it would be important for the worker to call. If the batterer did this, as Tom did, the message to him is for him to cancel directly, with the worker, and not through his wife. In Tom's case, it was difficult for him to continue to avoid coming in the face of a direct confrontation from the worker. Her call caused him to focus on individual responsibility for actions, which was consistent with the discussion in the previous session.

This phone call was one of several outreach calls. Often, men who batter will refuse to come in after a regression. The worker must be prepared to reach out and reestablish the therapeutic contract, as men need reminding of long-range goals (a cessation of violence) when they are disappointed in their ability to be nonviolent. If the woman cancels, sending the message through her partner, calling her directly also provides the opportunity to check on her safety and continued willingness for conjoint.

FIFTH SESSION

Most of this session was a recapitulation of the first session. The couple had regressed and said change was futile. The worker focused on Tom, reminding him of his desire to change for himself. She got him to focus on how unhappy he was feeling, and she confirmed that he looked miserable. Feebly, he said that Terry wanted to get hit. The worker didn't think that was so, but felt it was beside the point. She again focused on his own motivation for change, regardless of what it would do for his wife. He needed to feel better, to which Tom agreed. Tom then reiterated his desire to improve the marriage. Dialogue around this issue occurred with both partners. The worker stated that she was glad to hear this and thought that maybe they were ready to figure out how to accomplish this. When Tom and Terry agreed, the worker asked Tom how he thought he could accomplish this; he didn't know. The worker asked for a description of what happens when he becomes violent. He talked about his inability to stop his anger once it starts, and the only way it stops is as a result of an explosion. He could not think of what he could do to control this, which was to be the following week's discussion.

DISCUSSION

It was natural for the couple to regress. However, this time, the worker did not encourage a venting session. She already knew the couple's arguing pattern, and she had already demonstrated her acceptance of their anger. Because the regression was a direct result of their attempt to change, staying with the arguing would have been counterproductive in that it would have fed into their unconscious resistance to change, and would have been an avoidance of the pain that they were both experiencing as a result of the violence.

It was clear to the worker that with the couple so divided, attempting to have Tom change for the sake of the relationship probably would have failed. At that moment, neither of them felt positive about the other or hopeful that the marriage would succeed. Each partner was preoccupied with his or her own sense of disappointment and hurt. Therefore, the only possible leverage the worker had was in appealing to Tom's sense of internal discomfort surrounding his disappointment in himself for resorting to violence. Batterers often feel victimized by their wives, as evidenced by Tom's consistent statements that Terry "made him hit her." Although some of the literature indicates that externalizing blame is a defensive maneuver, others feel that batterers do feel victimized (S. Shapiro, personal communications, 1980–1982). Telling Tom that he needs to change for himself serves more than one purpose; it makes clear that change is up to him, and that no one can absolve him of responsibility or make him behave in any particular way. Tom also restated his hopelessness by saying he didn't see any use in coming for help. Workers at times need to shore up clients' strengths and re-motivate them. Outreach and expectation for change is a way of doing this.

The worker moved quickly here in establishing a change-oriented treatment plan; first, because they left off at this point in the last session, before the regression occurred. Had the worker not moved for change (i.e., upset the homeostatis), there could be a resumption of battering for the purpose of maintenance of the homeostatis. When Tom said that he didn't know what he could do to change, the worker acted to facilitate and clarify so that all three of them might understand the pattern of violence. The suggestions for how to change had to come from Tom. It would reinforce his responsibility for change; but also, only he would know what would be helpful for him. Although certain personality types can be classified as violence-prone (Fromm, 1973), and a batterer's profile can be developed, the ingredients needed to change must be tailored to the individual and to his unique circumstances. Further, when a batterer develops his own ideas for change, he can claim it as his own plan, and the chances for internalization are greater.

The contract for change is developed as early as possible, prefer-
ably no later than the second session. Because it is a tangible tool,
couples find comfort in having a specific plan to use. More important, this is a method for dealing with the violence, which is employed
as early as possible for obvious reasons.

Although Tom was able to develop a treatment plan himself for
rechanneling his violence, I usually develop such a plan in the
session with the abuser, formalizing and ritualizing it as "the contract," and drawing on cognitive/behavioral techniques for alternatives to abusive behavior. For a fuller explanation of how to develop a
contract, as well as a sample contract, see Geller (1992). It should
be noted that no discussion concerning the details of the violence
ensued; this would have been counterproductive. It was clear that the
couple felt badly about the fight. To recount the details might have
reactivated angry feelings, preventing a positive movement (development of a change plan). There are occasions in which dwelling on
the details of the fight might be necessary. One such occasion would
be the need to gain greater clarity of the dynamics. There are times
that dwelling on the details helps to convey the seriousness of the
situation. Sometimes one or another of the dyad has not internalized
this, and the worker can dramatize the destructiveness of violence
through recapitulation.

In the following session, Tom did come in with a treatment plan
for rechanneling his violence. The couple began to feel more comfortable with one another. Due to the noncritical nature of the subsequent sessions, the worker was able to gather background information on the couple and to focus on improving communication and
enhancing interaction.

With couples who are desperate—as partner-abusing couples are—
it is better to attempt the gathering of background information after the crisis subsides. When these couples come for help, they are
bursting with feelings. Psychosocial material gathering at that time
impedes their ability to unburden their troubles, and can be a source
of frustration to them. After the crisis subsides, there is time for information gathering, and it may even be helpful in making the transition
from crisis orientation to conjoint therapy.

A word about ethnicity seems appropriate here. Tom would regularly declare that people in his family did not go for help but kept their
problems to themselves. He would question his coming for help. However, he continued to attend sessions and put to use in his life what
was discussed. In Tom's close-knit Italian American community, it was

not common to seek help. The same was true among his coworkers and friends. References to psychology were made only at someone's expense or if someone was crazy. The worker interpreted Tom's objections not as resistance to treatment, but as an ethnic consideration that was supported and deserving of respect.

SIXTH SESSION

After about 10 sessions of conjoint therapy, another crisis occurred. Once again Tom refused to attend the session, and Terry was left to convey this information to the worker. She stated that they had had a very bad fight the previous night. The worker reiterated the importance of both parties coming in. She gave Terry the choice of convincing Tom herself, or of enlisting the aid of the worker. Terry chose the latter. When the worker called Tom, after his initial declaration that he did not take his problems "outside," he said to the worker, "Well, I guess I just better come in because you're going to try and convince me of that anyway, right?" Tom and Terry came in, once again depressed and dejected. The major difference, however, was that there had been no violence. Tom said that Terry tried to defend herself with a chair, which stopped him "dead in his tracks." He turned to the worker and said that there was "no way" she could have stopped him had he wanted to "get her." He went on to say, when he saw Terry "so defenseless with only that chair to protect her," he just couldn't hit her. He looked at Terry and then at the worker and said that he didn't want to hurt Terry; he loved her. The couple seemed set to focus on the hopelessness of their situation. The worker thought that the argument was a success as there was no violence. The worker told the couple that fighting between couples was normal. Up until that time they had been having abnormal fights, but this time they had just had a fight like all other couples.

This session marked a turning point in Tom and Terry's relationship. For the first time, Tom was able to see beyond his own feelings and empathize with Terry's position. Once that occurred, the desire to hit her dissipated. Stephen Shapiro of Volunteer Counseling Service of Rockland County, in a personal communication, stated that one characteristic of the batterer is lack of empathy. He has noted that one way to help batterers control their violence is to teach the abuser to develop such empathy.

In the same light, observations made while working with acting-out adolescents showed how their anger could escalate without direct provocation (Geller & Walsh, 1977–1978). During what they perceived as confrontation, these young people appeared to go into a daze; their eyes became glassy; they weren't able to focus on anyone in particular and they rhythmically stated over and over again their intention to harm (Fadely & Hasler, 1979). Such behavior can be likened to a sports coach giving his team a pep talk. Perhaps something similar occurs to people (like batterers) who inflict violence without premeditation.

After this breakthrough session, the violence did not recur. Tom and Terry were seen for another year and a half. Other family problems were uncovered. For that reason, and to ensure that the gains made in treating battering were sustained, there was a continuation of weekly sessions, but with a change to family therapy. Terry's two daughters were brought into the sessions because of the emotional difficulty they had suffered from witnessing the violence, as well as the upheaval they underwent in their adjustment to having a father. Communication between Tom and Terry's daughters were poor, and they were not getting along as a family. Tom became the strongest advocate for family sessions. The daughters were resistant and rebellious, making the sessions very difficult. However, Tom and Terry joined together in ensuring their continuation, and eventually they began to prove successful.

Eliminating the patterns of abuse among couples choosing to stay together is a laborious process. There are many pressures on the couple that may impede the process, as was shown in this case, not the least of which are the roots of violence that remain deep within the fabric of our society (Straus, 1976). Cultural background, ethnic identity, and certain personality features may keep the couple from seeking treatment. Nonetheless, the model presented here has been successful in reversing the cycle of violence. The case presentation format was attempted in order to shed light on the mechanics of adopting this model. It is hoped that it could be useful to practitioners interested in using these techniques with partner-abuse cases.

Working with the dyad, as opposed to with the entire family, is preferred initially because it is a method of isolating the behavior and not diluting it with the many other relevant family issues. In addition, there is an awareness that other family members are affected by the violence that occurs between the partners, and that they too need an opportunity for working through being in a violent household. A basic premise of family therapy relates to the way in which the entire system is affected by a problem in one of its members (Haley, 1976). Family therapists would then choose to treat the entire family constellation, rather than only certain of its members.

In the case of Tom and Terry, the children were brought in at a certain point, and this proved helpful. Many of the children of other couples in treatment participated in peer-group therapy. The question arises as to whether it would have been more expeditious to start with the whole family, rather than with just the couple. In this model, the choice was to work solely with the couple. This arose from a consideration for the family therapy theory, which proposes that if patterns are changed between partners, thereby changing the homeostasis, benefits will filter down to the entire family (Satir, 1967), and also because of the focus on the need to ameliorate the violence.

This model has been successfully used with well over 250 couples. However, model design can be studied further. Conjoint treatment for couples with the presenting problem of partner abuse, when delivered responsibly, has proven to be one viable and therapeutic option; but the use of family therapy, a combination of couple and family therapy, or couple and children's groups combined with violence-eliminating techniques is open to further exploration.

There has been a prohibition in certain circles against any treatment where the couple is seen together. This is informed more by a sociopolitical context than by a clinical context. Dogmatically dictating how treatment should be conducted parallels what it is that we are addressing in the first place with partner abuse: control exerted over one party by another. We should not repeat what it is that we are opposed to, but more importantly, to close ourselves to any modality that is useful for some is a disservice to ourselves and to those battered women whom we are dedicated to helping.

REFERENCES

American Psychiatric Association. (1994). *Diagnostic and statistical manual of mental disorders* (4th ed.). Washington, DC: American Psychiatric Press.

Bograd, J. (1986, May–June). Holding the line: Confronting the abusive partner. *Family Therapy Networker*, 44–47.

Brownmiller, S. (1975). *Against our will.* New York: Simon and Schuster.

Fadley, J. T., & Hasler, V. (1979). *Confrontation in adolescence.* St. Louis: Mosby.

Framo, J. L. (1965). Rationale and techniques of intensive family therapy. In I. Boazormeny-Nagy & J. Framo (Eds.), *Internal family therapy* (pp. 177–182). New York: Harper & Row.

Fromm, E. (1973). *The anatomy of human destructiveness.* New York: Holt, Rinehart & Winston.

Geller, J. (1992). *Breaking destructive patterns: Multiple strategies for treating partner abuse.* New York: Free Press.

Geller, J., & Walsh, J. C. (1977–1978). A treatment model for the abused spouse. *Victimology, 1*(1), 627–632.

Geller, J., & Wasserstrom, J. (1984). Conjoint therapy for the treatment of domestic violence. In A. Roberts (Ed.), *Battered women and their families* (pp. 33–48). New York: Springer Publishing.

Goldner, V., Penn, L., Steinberg, M., & Walker, G. (1990). Love and violence: Gender paradoxes in volatile attachments. *Family Process, 29*(4), 357.

Haley, J. (1976). *Problem-solving therapy.* San Francisco: Jossey-Bass.

Hudson, W. (1994). Partner Abuse Scale: Physical (PASPH). In J. Fischer & K. Corcoran (Eds.), *Measures for clinical practice* (pp. 461–462). New York: Free Press.

Minuchin, S. (1974). *Families and family therapy.* Cambridge, MA: Harvard University Press.

O'Leary, K. D. (1996, September). Physical aggression in intimate relationships can be treated within a marital context under certain circumstances. *Journal of Interpersonal Violence,* 450–455.

Satir, V. (1967). *Conjoint family therapy.* Palo Alto, CA: Science & Behavior Books.

Siegel, J. (1992). *Repairing intimacy.* Northvale, NJ: Aronson.

Straus, M. (1976). Social perspective on the causes of family violence. In M. R. Greene (Ed.), *Violence in the family* (pp. 7–31). Boulder, CO: Westview Press.

Straus, M., & Hotaling, G. (1980). *The social causes of husband/wife violence.* Duluth, MN: University of Minnesota Press.

Walker, L. (1989). *Terrifying love: Why battered women kill and how society responds.* New York: Harper & Row.

CHAPTER 15

Domestic Violence Against Women With Mental Retardation

Leone Murphy and Nancy J. Razza

W omen who are mentally retarded are frequently victimized and sexually or physically abused. The incidence of abuse is much higher in this population because of their vulnerability, low self-esteem, and lack of assertiveness. The Arc of Monmouth County has developed a unique and comprehensive model of identification of victims of abuse, therapeutic intervention, and treatment. The victim in the following case vignette typifies many of the women seen in the program.

CASE SCENARIO

Maryann is a 26-year-old woman who has mild mental retardation and lives in a small apartment with her 5-year-old son and her boyfriend. Her boyfriend is not the child's father and her son has developmental disabilities. She was referred to the Arc clinic for counseling by her job coach because of ongoing problems at her fast food placement. Issues of concern were unexplained absences, tardiness, and symptoms of depression. After

*several weeks of counseling, Maryann confided that her boyfriend was
verbally abusive to her but denied physical abuse. On more than one
occasion she appeared at the clinic with bruises, but continued to deny
any physical abuse.*

*Since Maryann's family lived out of state and she was without friends
and other support services, a referral was initiated for social work services at the Arc's Program Support Unit. The social worker was able to
arrange for a summer day camp program, including transportation, for
Maryann's son. This was a tremendous benefit for the mother, since she
had previously relied on her boyfriend for babysitting while she worked.
The boyfriend had not been reliable and frequently let the little boy wander
around the apartment complex by himself. Maryann confided that her
boyfriend would often threaten her as she was leaving for work, saying
that he was not going to watch her son. Her son had a speech impedi-
ment, and Maryann said that her boyfriend would often ridicule and
mock her son's behavior.*

*Finally, after many months of group therapy, Maryann trusted the
women in the therapy group enough to admit to being physically abused by
her boyfriend. She was supported by these other women and then she was
able to initiate changes to improve her situation. She was hesitant to go
to a women's shelter because she felt they would not be able to manage her
son's disabilities and the problems associated with her own disability such
as being unable to read, having no means of transportation, and having
difficulties communicating. The Arc's social worker assisted Maryann in
obtaining a restraining order against her boyfriend and the Arc provided
access to services such as day care, budgeting assistance, meal planning,
and parenting skills.*

ASSESSMENT AND DETECTION OF ABUSE

A growing concern for advocates of women who are mentally retarded is the sexual and physical abuse of this population. No exact
figures have been kept on the incidence of abuse of women with
mental retardation who live in the community, but leading advocates
estimate the incidence to be 4 to 10 times that of the general population. It is widely believed by developmental disability experts that
90% of women who are mentally retarded will be sexually or physically victimized in their lifetime (Sgroi, 1989). The actual reporting of abuse and violence is low, because many of the women have

difficulties communicating or can become easily confused about times, places, and details.

In addition to the visible signs of physical or sexual abuse, the victim often may have sleep problems, depression, increased aggression, or self-injurious behaviors. Our initial health assessment is comprehensive and includes a family history, an extensive medical history, records of any hospitalization or surgeries, and a medication profile. It is sometimes difficult to obtain this information, because many women who are mentally retarded were placed in institutions early in their lives and they may not know of their families. With the current movement to close large institutions and relocate the residents back into the community, medical records and information are often missing. The woman herself, because of her cognitive limitations, may give conflicting information. For example, she may know that she had a surgical procedure, but may not understand what surgery was done.

Factors such as unemployment, alcohol or drug abuse, and social isolation are carefully screened for, because they contribute to abusive situations. Most of the referrals we receive are from day-program or group home staff who suspect that the woman may be being abused. It is in everyone's best interest to proceed slowly and collect as much evidence as possible. In the past when staff has moved too quickly, there have been situations where the person doing the abuse has taken the victim out of the Arc's programs and even moved her to another state.

A medical file is slowly and carefully documented. Interviews with staff, caregivers, and family members are conducted cautiously. Guardianship of the woman is also of concern, because the state or a family member may have been previously declared the woman's legal guardian. The victim does not usually admit to being abused. Any bruises, lacerations, or injuries are carefully documented and photographed. We try to have two staff present for the examinations and interviews to corroborate the evidence. We frequently need to build a trusting relationship with the victim before she will admit to being abused. It then takes more effort, and cultivation of more trust, before the victim will allow staff to help her alter the situation.

The Arc's model of care integrates staff from a variety of disciplines. A clinical nurse specialist and a family practice physician carefully examine and document the medical and physical evidence of abuse. The Arc's psychologist and the clinical nurse specialist then conduct carefully selected interviews to verify the abusive situation. The findings are shared with the Arc's social worker, who completes the victim's team of health care professionals. This team then develops a plan for intervention, therapy, and support services.

SCOPE OF PROBLEM AND INTERVENTION APPROACHES

Although no data have been collected as of this writing on the prevalence rates of domestic violence against individuals with mental retardation, Carlson (1997) states that experts in the field estimate that women with mental retardation are believed to be at even greater risk for domestic violence than are women from the general population. This thinking is consistent with preliminary studies that show that women with mental retardation are more frequently victimized by sexual abuse than are women in the general population (Furey, 1994). For example, from data collected by the Wisconsin Council on Developmental Disabilities (1991), it is estimated that up to 83% of women and 32% of men with developmental disabilities suffer sexual abuse at some point in their lives. Additionally, in a survey of 162 individuals with disabilities who experienced sexual abuse, Sobsey and Doe (1991) found that 81.7% were women, and that the majority of these women had intellectual impairments as their disability.

It is important to consider that women with mental retardation often live in dependent situations, not just with a husband or boyfriend, but with nuclear or extended family or in government or agency-sponsored homes (described later in greater detail). As a result, there is a greater range of experiences that may be considered domestic abuse. For example, we worked with one woman who was repeatedly the target of physical battering by one of her fellow group home residents. She very much displayed the complex of behaviors seen in battered women. As might be imagined, intervention at the systems level is paramount in such a case.

Carlson (1997) describes a three-tiered approach to work with domestic violence victims who have developmental disabilities. Her approach reflects the importance of assessing the unique characteristics, abilities, and history of the individual, as well as the immediate social/familial context in which the violence takes place.

Finally, Carlson addresses the need for looking at the larger cultural and societal systems that impact on the individual in question. She makes recommendations for intervening in each of these three areas.

Models of clinical work support this multilevel approach with non-handicapped domestic violence victims as well. Pioneering work done by Almeida (Wylie, 1996) involves the concerned parties in individual and group sessions, including groups for both the offending and the victimized partner. Police, the court system, and extended family members are also involved. In keeping with McGoldrick's focus on the individual along with his or her social/cultural context, Almeida's work "widens the lens" through which the problem is viewed and addressed in marked contrast to more traditional models of psychopathology with an intraindividual focus. Importantly, Almeida's work has yielded a measure of success not often found in domestic violence treatment.

Work with individuals who have mental retardation is often approached in a similar fashion. That is, individual issues are addressed while at the same time interventions are being made within the individual's surrounding system. This is fairly common practice within agencies that provide services to persons with mental retardation for all manner of needs and problems. The nature of the disability is such that the individual's dependency on the surrounding network is more apparent (although, arguably no more—or less—significant than that of nonhandicapped persons). Experts in the treatment of mentally retarded persons with concomitant psychological disturbances have advocated for interventions that include the individual along with their natural family and professional caregivers (Petronko, Harris, & Kormann, 1994). These authors note that such interventions not only are beneficial to the individual, but also have resulted in increased leisure time and satisfaction and decreased stress and depressive moods in family members and caregivers.

In considering how to approach the problem of domestic violence as it affects persons with mental retardation, then, there appears to be good support for the idea that a multilevel approach is essential. We will begin with a look at assessing the individual victim of domestic violence, followed by a discussion of the assessment process as it pertains to the familial and social systems that encompass the individual's life.

INDIVIDUAL ASSESSMENT

Performing clinical evaluations of individuals who have mental retardation poses certain challenges for mental health professionals.
Nezu, Nezu, and Gill-Weiss (1992) specify potential obstacles, such
as limited capacity for verbal expression, concrete thinking, stereo-
typic motor behaviors, and a poor understanding of time (e.g., an
inability to be clear as to when events took place). Moreover, accurate assessment of mental disorder rests on the clinician's ability to
differentiate between psychologically significant symptoms and predictable behaviors or deficits that are solely a function of the individual's level of cognitive development. An additional complicating
factor is that with some individuals who have mental retardation,
particularly those at the lower ends of the range, psychological symptoms are sometimes displayed in unexpected ways. For example, we
treated a woman with mental retardation who also suffered from posttraumatic stress disorder (PTSD). She would spontaneously act out
traumatizing events she had experienced. These displays appeared
to be essentially like those described in the *DSM–IV* criteria for children with this disorder, in which they are referred to as "trauma-
specific reenactments." However, such displays—dramatic, sudden,
and unexplained—would make the woman appear "crazy" to those
around her, scaring involved staff members into thinking she was
more unbalanced than she truly was. In addition, staff often got the
impression that the traumatic abuses were currently taking place. It
took a great deal of observation to put together the posttraumatic
nature of this particular symptom.

A set of guidelines have been described by Nezu, Nezu, and
Gill-Weiss (1992) that provide a helpful overview when making
clinical assessments of individuals with mental retardation. Their
recommendations outline a multifaceted assessment including the
following:

A clinical interview, in which the clinician questions and observes
the individual with an eye toward his or her mental status, in
much the same way as would be done with a nonhandicapped
patient.
An observational analysis, in which the clinician observes the individual in his or her environment.

A caregiver interview, with a focus on gaining information about the individual as well as on assessing the quality of the caregiving relationship.

Psychological testing, along with the procurement of a neuromedical assessment to rule out possible neurological or physiological causes of symptoms.

In cases of suspected or known abuse, such symptoms may also represent the effects of abuse. The issue of neurological assessment is of particular importance, and can be complicated to assess in persons with mental retardation who may have been battered. In many cases, there is likely to be an intelligence test available in the individual's records, since documentation of impaired intellectual functioning is required for the individual to receive services. A prior neuropsychological battery is less commonly available. As trauma specialist Lenore Walker (1994) points out in discussing assessment of battered, non-handicapped women, exposure to battering in the form of blows to the head may result in organic brain damage. Prolonged exposure to such battering may result in progressive deterioration in key areas of functioning, including feelings of disorientation, sensorimotor difficulties, language difficulties, and coordination problems. Care must be taken to determine if the individual's functioning has been compromised due to exposure to abuse; the individual's condition may not be solely the function of their mental retardation.

For clinicians unfamiliar with individuals who have mental retardation, it is important to be aware that the majority of these individuals have only mild mental retardation. Intelligence test scores, though not the sole criterion for determining mental retardation, tend to cluster around the average score of 100 for the population as a whole. Deviations from this average, both higher and lower, tend to fall close to the average range. Thus, profoundly retarded individuals are as rare as truly brilliant ones. Recent estimates of retardation in countries with advanced medical care put the prevalence rates of severe retardation at 2.5 to 5.0 per 1,000, and that of mild retardation at 2.5 to 40.0 per 1,000 (Durkin & Stein, 1996). This is important because individuals with mild mental retardation generally have verbal abilities that, although limited, are sufficient for the purposes of psychotherapy. Individuals with moderate mental retardation are also often capable of sufficient verbal exchange to make therapeutic dialogue possible. It is not responsible to exclude a person from a therapeutic service simply because the diagnosis of mental retardation comes with them. Individual assessment is needed to determine that person's capacity for self-expression. For those with a greater degree of impairment, assessing and intervening with key figures in the individual's environment takes on essential significance.

ASSESSMENT OF THE SOCIAL/FAMILIAL ENVIRONMENT

The next level of assessment, evaluating the individual's social/familial context, can be extremely challenging or relatively uncomplicated, depending on the clinician's access to reliable informants and on whether or not the clinician is able to observe the individual in his or her environment.

Due to the nature of their disability, individuals with mental retardation often live in situations in which they are, to varying degrees, dependent on others. The living arrangement may be one in which the family takes primary responsibility (living with parents, adult siblings, or, less commonly, their own apartment with assistance in daily living responsibilities), or in which the state or a state-supported agency takes primary responsibility (institution, group home, apartment with staff nearby who provide assistance, or with a family which the state pays to provide shelter and care for the individual, similar to a foster family). In each of these cases, it is important to make contact with one or more of the individuals who have some responsibility for the individual's care, being mindful that the caregiver could be the abuser. The other party's perspective can offer valuable insights.

It is important, however, to keep in mind that even well-meaning caregivers can be a part of the individual's problem. For example, we worked with one woman who had moderate mental retardation and who was generally characterized by a sweet demeanor and was well liked. She displayed sudden and intense self-biting and tantrum-like behavior under certain conditions of frustration, such as being teased. Staff would respond to this behavior by rushing to her aid and encouraging her to talk, thinking she was upset about her father who had recently died. The woman would engage in talks with them about her feelings, and the episode would end. Additionally, the staff brought her to a therapist who, though unfamiliar with individuals with mental retardation, helped her talk further about her feelings. The self-abusive episodes continued to increase in frequency, however. When staff agreed to try actively withdrawing their attention from her following these self-abusive episodes, and engaging her in nurturing, supportive discussions on a regular basis during periods of nonabusive behavior, the episodes eventually made a significant decrease. The staff had unintentionally been "reinforcing" her episodes of self-injurious behavior by their increased attentiveness at such times. Thus, when the staff made the effort to supply her with their attention when she was peaceful, the instances of self-abuse decreased. This intervention was carried out along with the introduction of individual and, later, group, therapy in which the focus was directed toward helping the woman become aware of the types of situations that triggered her self-abusive behavior, and of adaptive alternatives she could employ. We often treat women who are aggressive toward themselves rather than toward others.

It is often very helpful to obtain information from more than one source. Most people spend the majority of their time in two distinct environments, residential and vocational. For example, staff who work with an individual in a vocational training program may refer her because they suspect she is being abused or battered in her home environment. If the clinician feels that the individual cannot provide clear information concerning her experiences, it is important that an effort be made to observe and assess the dynamics in both environments.

CASE MANAGEMENT AND DELIVERY SERVICES

Ideally, interventions in the lives of women with mental retardation who experience domestic violence are the product of a team effort, and affect the individual woman, as well as the immediate and extended systems of which she is a part. Following a comprehensive assessment of the individual and her situation, an effort should be made to connect with the various parties involved with the individual for the purposes of planning and executing a strategy to address the particular woman's needs.

Individuals with mental retardation in New Jersey are entitled to services through the Division of Developmental Disabilities. The Division assigns them a case manager who is responsible for seeing that the full gamut of the individual's needs are met, for example, for appropriate housing, medical concerns, vocational preparation, and so on. This case manager is involved with staff members from various agencies who provide such services. Traditionally agencies, such as the many Arcs (formerly Association for Retarded Citizens) across the country, have supplied primarily vocational and residential support, while medical services were generally sought on a case-by-case basis from clinics and individual practitioners. This has been and continues to be an arduous task, as many practitioners do not welcome patients with mental retardation, and because only those practitioners who accept Medicaid can usually even be considered. (Most adults with mental retardation have only Medicaid for their insurance coverage.) Our work in providing medical and mental health treatment to people with mental retardation has occurred in the context of an innovative project in the State of New Jersey.

Meeting with the individual's case manager is a key step toward intervention, as this person is in a position to convene the other important figures in the person's life for a planning meeting. For example, with respect to the woman who was being battered by a fellow group home resident, a multilevel intervention was developed and then carried out with the help of various parties. The woman and her father advocated for her to be moved, and the agency was able to find a home for her in which she was safe from abuse. (They had previously worked quite hard to prevent the violence from occurring in the home, but proved unable to stop it entirely.) Also, the woman was evaluated for psychological services, and proved to be quite symptomatic, with an anxiety disorder that predated the battering experience, and was, of course, exacerbated by it. (Unfortunately, her agitated expressions of anxiety seemed to trigger the battering resident's attacks.) The woman's father was able to engage a private psychiatrist who prescribed medication that helped with her anxiety, and finally, the project of which we are a part was able to provide the woman with individual and then group psychotherapy. This woman, who has moderate mental retardation, has been able to receive support through the therapy not only to manage her anxiety but also to re-develop her sense of herself, that is, to begin to see herself as being able to make good decisions for herself and take action for herself. Her sense of self-efficacy had been extremely damaged because of her lifelong experience of shame as she saw herself failing at school, being made fun of by peers, and unable to do the growing number of things her sisters could do. Added to this, her experience of victimization in her group home made her feel even more that there was little she could do for herself. Much of her treatment has been, and continues to be, aimed at helping her to see that she has done much to help herself (e.g., complaining when she was unhappy, repeatedly asking to be moved until she was listened to). Even steps she takes to lessen her experience of anxiety, which often sound eccentric to us, are acknowledged and affirmed because they build her sense of self-efficacy. Her growing sense of herself as an effective person, even though she knows she has limitations, seems to hold the most promise for her to function optimally and enjoy her life. It is apparent in even this one case that the intervention effort must involve the individual in a process of her own recovery, as well as systems-level change.

Another woman with whom we still work has always managed to live in apartments of her own and functions with a fair degree of independence. She manages her social security income (SSI) and utilizes local medical clinics for her health care. She makes use of food stamps and will seek assistance as she feels the need.

She was referred to us for treatment of depression. At the time she was living alone and reported that her son, then age 4, had been taken by Department of Youth and Family Services (DYFS) and placed with her sister. She continued to have contact with him via visits, but was very unhappy. As we uncovered the details of her life, we eventually learned that she had been living with her boyfriend (not the child's father), and that they had gotten into such raucous fights that neighbors had called the police, who in turn called DYFS. We also learned that the boyfriend would become abusive to her at times, and that these fights occurred in the context of her efforts to protect herself.

The woman became less depressed with the help of therapy and was assisted by our project in connecting with a social worker at the Arc to help her in her efforts to regain custody of her son, or at least increase visitation to include weekends at her home. Soon after, the woman began seeing the boyfriend again. She was very happy about this, and was starting to believe that he would help her to get custody of the son. During this time he treated her quite well. Although we were unable to evaluate him ourselves, we got the impression that he had some type of mental health problems, as the woman told us that he went for regular monthly appointments at a mental health clinic and was taking medication. She eventually decided to marry him, stating she thought this would certainly help her to get back her son. Those of us involved with her reminded her that this man had been instrumental in her losing custody of the child, but to no avail. Her husband, perhaps with good intentions, would talk to her about how he would help her get the boy back, and the woman reported that her son had gotten quite attached to him, and that he was good to the boy.

Eventually the woman's husband stopped taking his medication. He began behaving in what sounded like a psychotic fashion, and became abusive and threatening to her at times. On one occasion, he began to choke her, but she was able to get away. After this incident, she was able to end the relationship with him. Since that time, she has been somewhat more amenable to accepting support services again for her custody issues. She remains in therapy and has begun a relationship with another man who appears to be nonabusive. We focus our efforts in the therapy on affirming her actions on her own behalf, which gives her a sense of herself that buffers her against the depression. It seems that when she is depressed she is particularly vulnerable to engaging in a relationship with a man in an effort to make herself feel better, even if that man is periodically hurtful to her.

A BRIEF HISTORY OF MENTAL HEALTH TREATMENT

Within recent years there has been increasing recognition that individuals with mental retardation both need and deserve mental health services (Hurley, Pfadt, Tomasulo, & Gardner, 1996; Nezu, Nezu, & Gill-Weiss, 1992; Petronko, Harris, & Kormann, 1994). During the 1980s, significant advances were made in promoting the use of psychotherapeutic techniques with persons who have mental retardation, and in assessing their utility (Hurley & Hurley, 1986). The literature reflects a growing interest in the provision of specialized mental health treatment for individuals with this disability. Moreover, preliminary outcome research suggests that individuals with mental retardation are able to benefit from certain therapeutic experiences. For example, Tomasulo, Keller, and Pfadt (1995) report on a study that provides the first wave of outcome research on the development of therapeutic factors in groups being run with individuals having mental retardation (Keller, 1995). Raters familiar with group psychotherapy procedures and processes observed videotapes of selected sessions without knowledge of whether they were viewing initial or advanced sessions. They were able to identify the presence of eight distinct therapeutic factors in the advanced groups, supporting the idea that groups with persons who have mental retardation are able to make the same types of therapeutic gains as are found in groups with nonhandicapped members.

The success of such therapeutic endeavors is particularly important in that it has been established in recent years that the mental health needs of individuals with mental retardation are considerable. With reference again to the extensive volume by Nezu, Nezu, and Gill-Weiss (1992), their comprehensive review of the existing literature makes clear that persons with mental retardation experience the full spectrum of psychiatric disorders, and in very similar ways as nonretarded individuals. Importantly, these authors have found that psychiatric disorders are, in fact, even more prevalent among persons with mental retardation than in the general population.

It is clear that mental health treatment for individuals with mental retardation is a field that is still quite young. It is not surprising, then, that the literature reveals a lack of published work on the treatment of domestic violence issues in the lives of persons with mental retardation.

We will now turn to some of the broader policy areas that bear on the issues of abuse and domestic violence in the lives of people with mental retardation, and we will briefly discuss the role of our project in this context.

POLICY

Most research and educational efforts regarding people with developmental disabilities have been directed at those who live in institutional settings. In 1962, President Kennedy's Committee on Mental Retardation initiated the shift to mainstreaming people into the community. Advocacy efforts have continued for inclusion into schools and "person-centered" planning. Many state institutions have closed, and there is a long-range plan to return as many individuals as possible to the community. The survival of these people depends on the strength of the support services in the community (Furey, 1994).

The New Jersey Division of Developmental Disabilities (NJ-DDD, 1994) has a policy designed to protect the rights of those they serve and to ensure that people who have a developmental disability are not exploited, or abused physically or sexually (Division Circular # 4). However, NJ-DDD has not specifically addressed the problem of domestic violence. The return of many individuals to the community from state institutions will no doubt create a need for such a policy to be drafted.

Paul Stavis's (1991) landmark position paper advocates for the right of people with a developmental disability to express their sexuality but still be protected from harm. This progressive philosophy is new to those who work in the field of developmental disabilities, and one that many families find difficult to accept. People who have a developmental disability have the right to develop intimate relationships, but need education on the process. Families, staff, and other caregivers also need education in this area. Marchetti and McCartney (1990) explain that inadequate staff training, poor administrative practices, and inadequate supervision of staff and clients contribute to the lack of reporting of abuse of people who have a developmental disability.

People who have lived in institutions are more vulnerable than those who have been exposed to others in the community. They are easily coerced and preyed upon by abusers and batterers (Marchetti & McCartney, 1990). Many of them were abused in the institution, and this makes them more easily victimized in the community. Many may have a lower cognitive level that makes them less assertive and less informed of their rights. Women who have a developmental disability are usually not familiar with community resources, and often do not know how to seek assistance. Many of them are dependent on others for financial support and this dependency creates more opportunities for abuse. Their credibility is easily attacked, because they can be confused about facts such as dates and times. They often believe they deserve the abuse and feel powerless against their attackers. Carlson (1997) describes the learned helplessness that may cause the victim to give up because her actions appear ineffective.

It is our policy at the Arc that if a woman reports that she has been sexually or physically abused in any way, she is supported totally and provided with every available resource to address the situation. Many women with mental retardation have poor or nonexistent relationships with their families and find it impossible to extricate themselves from abusive relationships without this tremendous support by our staff. Many women have been conditioned to accept abuse, and it is only when the abuse reaches beyond themselves to their children that they find the strength to remedy the situation. Conditions that they have been able to tolerate for many years become suddenly intolerable when one of their children is abused. McFarlane and Parker (1994) have done extensive research on the frequency of abuse in pregnant women. Their abuse assessment screen focuses on three key areas: physical abuse, physical abuse during pregnancy, and sexual abuse. Abuse during pregnancy may also act as an impetus to cause the victim to seek assistance.

In a recent case we were treating, the woman became pregnant and her boyfriend would not believe the child was his. We often see the male partners deny that they are responsible and they then accuse the woman of seeing other men. The abusive situations escalate and the woman may decide to terminate the pregnancy.

TREATMENT ISSUES

The Arc of Monmouth provides a comprehensive array of services that includes educational, vocational, residential, recreational, supported employment, and health care programs. Approximately 1,000 adults who have a developmental disability and live in the community receive these services. For the past 6 years, The Arc of Monmouth's Ambulatory Care Center has provided primary health care and mental health services to men and women who have mental retardation and other disabilities.

A team of dedicated health care professionals with expertise in meeting the needs of this population has developed an integrated model of care that includes the disciplines of medicine, psychiatry, psychology, nursing, and social work. Care coordination is a key component of this model of care and exceeds the limitations of the well-known concept of case management. Care coordination is a more involved form of case management that is needed because of the individual's complex needs. It is not unusual to coordinate care for a person who is mentally retarded, has seizures, a cardiac condition, and needs psychotropic medications.

Initially, in providing medical care to men and women with developmental disabilities, the growing incidence of sexual abuse of this population became apparent. Women who have a developmental disability are viewed by perpetrators as easily preyed upon due to the very nature of their disability (Furey, 1994). These women have difficulty communicating, have low self-esteem, are easily confused, and are desperately seeking affection. Many of them have spent years in state developmental centers and other institutions where they were taught to be obedient and compliant. These behaviors contribute to their sense of helplessness and vulnerability. They may never have had someone in their lives who was able to protect and advocate for them. They are frequently abused by those who are closest to them, and they are often unable to develop trust. Many of the situations we are involved with include incest with brothers and fathers, sexual abuse by stepfathers or their mothers' boyfriends, and sexual abuse by staff members or peers. Physical abuse or assault is also a problem because of crowded day programs and the congregate living situations in which many of these women must live on a permanent basis. The decision of where and with whom they will live is made for them, and is often developed out of what living situation is available at the time it is needed. Residential options include group homes, skilled sponsor homes, boarding homes, supervised apartments, and living with their parents or other relative. Men and women usually live together in residential service settings. Also of concern is the fact that few agencies have guidelines for regulating intimacy between two individuals with developmental disabilities. Residents of these living arrangements tend to get little, if any, education on the topic of sexuality. They may also get mixed messages from staff who approve and those who disapprove of sexual contact between two adults with developmental disabilities. This lack of education about sexuality and intimacy contributes to this population's being unprepared to deal with life experience issues such as sexual abuse (Furey).

Women in the Arc's vocational programs are often referred by staff for sexuality education and sexual abuse prevention training prior to their referral for community job placements. Families voice concerns that the woman will be easily coerced into sexual activity, and the families feel unprepared to deal with the issues themselves.

Women who have a developmental disability and have been abused find it difficult to locate health care professionals who will be willing and comfortable in providing therapy. Professionals, because of the woman's mental retardation and lack of assertiveness, often dismiss their need for therapy. Available, accessible, and appropriate services to address violence and abuse are seriously limited. Services are practically nonexistent, if the woman's limitations and specialized needs have to be accommodated. Many victims who have mental retardation need accommodations that acknowledge their disability (Carlson, 1997).

The Arc of Monmouth's Ambulatory Care Center has addressed this unmet need and provides individual and/or group counseling for these women. Our psychologist first evaluates the woman and a treatment plan is developed. Frequently, these women need individual therapy before they are ready to benefit from group therapy. Assertiveness training is an integral part of the therapy, and the woman is empowered to assert herself in abusive situations. The Arc of Monmouth has a rich array of services that the woman is taught to access to improve her situation. For example, she may need a job coach to assist her to explore better employment and financial opportunities. The Program Support Unit with its social workers is available to help her obtain a restraining order, find day care for her children, or search for a new living arrangement. Staff supports the woman in every effort she makes to alter the current abusive situation. Medical care and psychiatric services are readily available if indicated.

Treatment issues that often need to be addressed are guardianship, financial resources, transportation, and insurance coverage. Most of the women we see do not drive and rely on public transportation. So even a factor as simple as transportation can require coordination by our professionals to ensure that the woman can access therapy, work, and child care. A major goal of therapy is empowerment of the victim. Areas to be developed with the client include self-esteem, independence, coping skills, and decision making. The woman who is mentally retarded needs to develop a self-protection plan for when the abuse occurs. One of the best options for women in domestic violence situations is a women's or family shelter. However, staff at these shelters are not usually trained to meet the needs of women with mental retardation (Carlson, 1997). It is necessary to advocate for this training and to ensure that the needs of these women can be met.

The Arc of Monmouth Ambulatory Care Center currently provides group therapy sessions for four different groups of approximately 40 individuals. The groups meet every week. One group is for women only; two groups are exclusively for men; and one group is mixed equally with men and women. All of the participants are initially screened and evaluated by the Arc's lead psychologist. The psychologist determines the major treatment issues and develops the treatment plan. If psychiatric care with medication monitoring is needed, that is scheduled. In some cases, individual therapy may be indicated before the person will benefit from the group process.

Women who have been abused participate in two of the ongoing groups. The women are at different stages in the treatment process, and the progress at times may seem slow. The women receive tremendous support from others in the group, and sometimes continue a friendship with other group members outside of the group relationship. They exchange telephone numbers and call each other in between the group sessions. They are able to learn from each other's experiences and develop a sense of empowerment from the knowledge that someone else was able to leave the abusive situation. The women are challenged by each other to set goals for themselves, and they receive feedback each week on what they did or did not accomplish. A psychologist and a clinical nurse specialist facilitate the groups, but the majority of the feedback comes from the group members themselves.

EDUCATING PROFESSIONALS

It is imperative that physicians, nurses, psychologists, and social workers be educated in meeting the needs of victims of physical and sexual abuse who have a developmental disability. Many professionals voice concerns over managing the complexities of the person's situation. This unfamiliarity with the population, coupled with the low reimbursement rate offered by Medicaid, discourages most professionals from developing expertise in this area. The national movement toward managed health care will integrate those with developmental disabilities into generic service providers such as community mental health clinics. Carlson (1997) advocates for co-leaders in group therapy models, where one leader is experienced in developmental disabilities and the other has expertise in domestic violence. It must also be impressed upon generic service providers that progress for those with a developmental disability is slow and that more therapy sessions need to be allocated for this population.

Graduate schools need to include information about people with developmental disabilities in the curricula and offer clinical training sites that provide experiences with this population. Graduate students in nursing and psychology spend time in the Arc's Ambulatory Care Center learning from skilled clinicians, and actually participate in the care of people with developmental disabilities. Medical students elect to do their community clinical rotation at the Ambulatory

Care Center and often select a second semester of studies at the center. The students enjoy the experience and develop a comfort level working with this population. It is hoped that this improved comfort level will encourage the students to provide treatment to people with developmental disabilities when they open their own practices.

Several of our staff have positions as professors or adjunct faculty at area colleges and universities, and introduce the concepts surrounding care for individuals who have a developmental disability. Areas currently being taught include primary health care, women's health care, sexual abuse prevention, and mental health care. It is our staff's belief that these educational efforts will result in more professionals being trained to provide quality services to men and women who have a developmental disability. It is imperative that the needs of this vulnerable population be addressed and that community providers be prepared to treat them.

REFERENCES

Carlson, B. (1997). Mental retardation and domestic violence: An ecological approach to intervention. *Social Work, 42,* 70–89.

Durkin, M. S., & Stein, Z. A. (1996). Classification of mental retardation. In J. W. Jacobson & J. A. Mulick (Eds.), *Manual of diagnosis and professional practice in mental retardation* (pp. 67–73). Washington, DC: American Psychological Association.

Furey, E. (1994). Sexual abuse of adults with mental retardation: Who and where. *Mental Retardation, 32,* 173–180.

Hurley, A. D., & Hurley, F. J. (1986). Counseling and psychotherapy with mentally retarded clients: The initial interview. *PAMR Review, 5,* 22–26.

Hurley, A. D., Pfadt, A., Tomasulo, D., & Gardner, W. (1996). Counseling and psychotherapy. In J. W. Jacobson & J. A. Mulick (Eds.), *Manual of diagnosis and professional practice in mental retardation* (pp. 371–378). Washington, DC: American Psychological Association.

Keller, E. (1995). *Process and outcomes in interactive-behavioral groups with adults who have both mental illness and mental retardation.* Unpublished doctoral dissertation, Long Island University, Glen Head, NY.

Marchetti, A. G., & McCartney, J. R. (1990). Abuse of persons with mental retardation. *Mental Retardation, 28,* 367–371.

McFarlane, J., & Parker, B. (1994). *Abuse during pregnancy: A protocol for prevention and intervention* (March of Dimes Nursing Monograph). White Plains, NY: March of Dimes.

Nezu, A., Nezu, C., & Gill-Weiss, M. J. (1992). *Psychopathology in persons with mental retardation*. Champaign, IL: Research Press.

Petronko, M., Harris, S. L., & Kormann, R. (1994). Community-based behavioral training approaches for people with mental retardation and mental illness. *Journal of Consulting and Clinical Psychology, 62*, 49–54.

Sgroi, S. (1989). *Vulnerable populations*. Lexington, MA: Lexington Books.

Sobsey, D., & Doe, T. (1991). Patterns of sexual abuse and assault. *Sex Disability, 9*, 243–259.

State of New Jersey, Department of Human Services, Division of Developmental Disabilities. (1994). *Manual for case management*. Division Circular #4.

Stavis, P. (1991). Harmonizing the right to sexual expressions. *Sexuality and Disability, 9*, 131–141.

Tomasulo, D., Keller, E., & Pfadt, A. (1995). The healing crowd: Process, content, and technique issues in group counseling for people with mental retardation. *The Habilitative Mental HealthCare Newsletter, 14*, 43–50.

Walker, L. E. A. (1994). *Abused women and survivor therapy*. Washington, DC: American Psychological Association.

Wisconsin Council on Developmental Disabilities. (1991). *Greater risk: Legal issues in sexual abuse of adults with developmental disabilities (A training guide for caregivers)*. Madison, WI: Author.

Wylie, M. S. (1996, March/April). It's a community affair. *Family Therapy Networker,* 58–96.

High-Risk Groups and Vulnerable Populations

CHAPTER 16

Domestic Violence and Substance Abuse:
An Integrated Approach

Katherine S. van Wormer

V ery often, when family members are beaten, alcohol or some other drug is involved. *Cherchez la drogue,* as the French might say. The abuser may be arming himself with 40-proof courage in preparation for an attack; the victim may be drowning her anguish with tranquilizers or alcohol. Moreover, the children may grow up to have problems with substance abuse or violence. All of these interconnections we know. What we don't know is the exact nature of the substance abuse/violence configuration: Does drinking cause violence, or does the urge to be violent lead to drinking? How does the victim's drinking come into play? Are such patterns of abuse/victimization intergenerational?

The previous edition of this volume noted the absence of clearcut research findings in the substance abuse literature concerning the substance abuse/partner abuse connection. Since that time, this situation has changed. A number of articles have probed the intersection of substance use and domestic violence, both from a victimization and from a substance abuse standpoint. The former literature, however, has been much more abundant than the latter with the major focus being on the use of alcohol and other drugs by the perpetrator of violence, as noted by Rogers, McGee, et al. (2003) and Stuart, Moore, et al. (2004). The real world of substance abuse treatment, meanwhile, continues to be strong on ideology and soft on substance (pun unintended). And whether by design or tradition, the particular ideologues concerning substance abuse and domestic violence sharply demarcate the boundaries between them. The good news is that new trends in substance abuse treatment are opening the doors to more flexible approaches. The traditional one-size-fits all model is slowly but surely becoming a thing of the past.

On the whole, nevertheless, substance abuse and domestic violence programs view the relationship between substance abuse and partner violence narrowly: the former, through the lens of addiction and co-addiction; the latter, through the lens of feminism. The absence of a coordination of efforts further impedes the growth of knowledge. As a feminist and former member of both a domestic violence women's advocacy board and a substance abuse treatment center board, and with over 4 years experience as an alcoholism counselor, I am constantly made aware of the potential and necessity for a holistic, coordinated approach to fighting the twin evils of substance abuse and domestic violence.

Recently (May, 2006), I requested permission to reprint the well-known figure, the power and control wheel, in a book I was writing. The two spokeswomen at the Duluth Domestic Abuse Intervention Project requested to read relevant portions of the book; they then held a meeting to decide if my writings were consistent with their ideology. To my surprise, permission was denied. (My attempts to rewrite the passage were to no avail.) Their reasoning, as explained in telephone conversations and an e-mail communication, was their belief that there is only one reason for domestic violence, and that is the reinforcement that these batterers get from the patriarchal culture in which we live. My holistic approach to male-on-female violence was not acceptable. Since this Minnesota establishment at Duluth is the foremost center in the world for the prevention of domestic violence, and since their office conducts workshop trainings nationwide on batterer education and treatment, I believe this event was of no little significance. Based on my encounter with the Duluth Model representatives, I must conclude that the rift in the fields of substance abuse treatment and domestic violence still exists.

With this understanding in mind, my purpose in writing the present chapter is to make the case for a coordinated approach to the treatment of perpetrators and victims of such violence. In exploring the links between substance abuse and partner violence, the first task will be to summarize pertinent research findings. From this abundant scholarship that is now available, perhaps we can identify central themes and filter out competing explanatory models that concern the relationship between intoxication and domestic violence. We will want to consider the substance abuse counselor's *addictions* explanatory model and contrast that with the domestic violence program's feminist conceptualization. For a more complete understanding of substance-related domestic violence, we will briefly consider biopsychosocial factors that come into play. Our attention will be drawn to the role of substance abuse in gay-lesbian partner violence as well as in both male-on-female and female-on-male assault. The final portion of the chapter is devoted to implications for substance abuse counselors and domestic violence workers who need to work together on these problems and overlapping areas.

THE CORRELATION BETWEEN SUBSTANCE ABUSE AND PARTNER ABUSE

Violence against women and girls is a major health and human rights concern in every country in the world; reports are between 10% and 50% of women are abused in their lifetime (World Health Organization, 2000). Violence against women is a leading cause of injury for American women between the ages of 15 and 54 (U.S. Department of Health and Human Services, 2005). Despite more hotlines and shelters and substance abuse treatment for wife abusers, the number of assaults against women has not declined. A high risk factor reported by virtually all the experts is alcohol and drug abuse. Persons who are prone to violence are likely to abuse drugs—especially alcohol, crack cocaine, and methamphetamines—and those who abuse these drugs are prone to assault. Although recognizing that many alcoholics are never violent and many aggressors are sober, research findings reveal the following:

• Approximately one-half of clinically treated spouse-batterers have significant alcohol problems (Bennett & Williams, 2003).

- One-half to two-thirds of married male alcoholics are physically aggressive toward their partners during the year before alcoholism treatment (Gondolf & Foster, 1991; Stuart, Moore, et al., 2004).
- In men, the combination of blue-collar status, drinking, and approval of violence is significantly associated with a high rate of wife abuse (Associated Press, 1996).
- Binge drinkers, as opposed to daily drinkers, have an inordinately high rate of reported assault (Humphreys, Regan, et al., 2005; Murphy & O'Farrell, 1997).
- The female victims of abuse often also have substance abuse problems (Bennett & Williams, 2003; Humphreys et al., 2005).
- Sixty percent of female substance abusers were victims of partner assault, according to estimates by treatment providers (Humphreys et al., 2005).
- Over one-third of substance abuse patients in a V.A. program survey reported assaulting their wives in the previous year (Gondolf & Foster).
- More than 50% of men in batterer programs are evaluated as substance abusers (Bennett & Williams, 2003).
- Cocaine, methamphetamine, and alcohol in high doses are all associated with hyperactivity and violence. Marijuana and heroin have not been proven to be associated with violence (van Wormer & Davis, 2003).
- A study of alcohol consumption in the army revealed that soldiers who drink heavily are likely to abuse their partners both when they drink and when they don't, compared to moderate drinking soldiers (Bell et al., 2004).
- A study of men in treatment for domestic violence showed that severe physical aggression was 11 times higher on days when the male partners were intoxicated than on other days (Fals-Stewart, 2003).
- Women in methadone treatment who reported frequent crack cocaine use or frequent marijuana use were likely to be victimized over the next 6 months; women who were physically assaulted were more likely than other women to indicate frequent heroin use over the next 6 months (El-Bassel et al., 2005).

Of the close correlation between substance abuse and partner violence, therefore, there can be no doubt. The only doubt is over the interpretation of this relationship. What all researchers and treatment personnel agree on is the crying need to put a stop to the violence and the high-risk substance abuse. The relationship between substance abuse and domestic violence programs is complex. At the core of the problem is the tendency to dichotomize problems and to treat various components of antisocial behavior as separate entities. The differences arise not only from differing worldviews—disease model versus feminist approach—but also from a parallel tendency to view reality in terms of linear causation.

THEORETICAL MODEL: INTERACTIONISM

The central guiding social work principle of today is the ecosystems conceptualization. This multidimensional approach views the human organism in its full biopsychosocial context. The ecological framework or metaphor is interactionist; it does not view the person and the environment as separate entities; rather, it looks at the intersection between them. In sharp contrast to linear or simple cause-and-effect thinking, wherein a cause (such as mental illness) precedes an effect (abusive drinking), ecological causality occurs in a circular loop (van Wormer, 2007).

An event or pattern such as violence may be viewed, accordingly, as at once both the cause and effect of substance abuse. Individuals joined in a system are impacted to the degree that they are reciprocally linked to the disturbed group or family member. The stress of substance abuse or violence has a synergistic or multiplying effect throughout the family system and related environmental network. From the practitioner's standpoint, what we are talking about is the need to perceive the *total* picture of the client's situation, the need to understand problematic behavior multidimensionally. Narrow specialization by discipline encourages a perception of reality as partial, incomplete, and ideological. Child welfare workers, for example, in their unidimensional focus on abuse of the child, very often overlook the dynamics of family violence in which wife assault as well as, perhaps, substance abuse, plays a vital role in the gestalt of family crisis.

One often finds that seemingly diverse worldviews, which seem to say opposite things, actually provide crucial information and are understandable when seen in terms of an integrative new theory.

OPPOSING MODELS

Persons trained in the highly influential disease model of substance abuse are subject to criticism for their failure to address the multidimensional nature of substance addiction (see van Wormer & Bartollas, 2007). Under this formulation, the substance (usually alcohol) is seen as the primary cause of any and all antisocial behavior. The treatment effort is geared overwhelmingly to acceptance of Step One of the AA (Alcoholics Anonymous) creed of admission that one is powerless over alcohol (or other substance or relationship).

Previously, I came across a pamphlet from Al-Anon (the 12-step group for families of alcoholics) entitled "Domestic Violence" (Al-Anon, 1994). The personal story presented marks a positive step by this self-help group to address the dangers facing many of their members who are being abused by alcoholic family members. Some of the wording, however, would raise eyebrows among women's crisis line counselors. For instance:

> It was his violence that brought me to Al-Anon, where I learned I was dealing with a very sick person, and I too was ill. . . .
> Arguments are useless against sickness, and in this case, abuse is a symptom of the disease of alcoholism. (p. 2)

Labeling the endangered woman as "sick" and then having her see the abuse as secondary to the alcoholism are examples of forcing the facts to fit the dogma of the disease model. For the sake of clarification (if the reader will forgive a little oversimplification), I will summarize the substance abuse treatment ethos as follows. Generalizations are drawn from my personal experience as an alcoholism counselor and from the literature on addictions work. Substance abuse counselors tend to:

- Work primarily with men in a program developed by White males in the 1930s.
- Perceive violence as a symptom of alcoholism and other substance abuse.
- Blame alcoholic women in their care for their tendency to get involved with violence-prone, alcoholic men.
- Assume that bad behavior (such as battering) will cease with sobriety.

- Subscribe to disinhibition theory, which states that intoxication lowers inhibitions and accounts for any bad behavior that might ensue.
- View the family as a system and the victim as playing a role (as chief enabler, codependent) in perpetuating the disease.
- Focus on abstinence and recovery.

The addictions focus in the substance abuse treatment field is matched by the male culture determinism of the domestic violence field. Let me simplify the basic precepts of the feminist model of wife/partner abuse in order again to clearly enunciate its differences. Workers in domestic violence programs have no less firm and sincere a commitment to their clients than do substance abuse counselors to theirs. And just as their counterparts in addictions work tend to be recovering addicts/alcoholics, many of those who counsel battered women have themselves been abused. Characteristically, however, women's shelter workers tend to:

- Work predominantly with women in a program founded by and for women who have been abused by their spouses/partners, but also by the system.
- Resist the disease model of addictions and stress individual/cultural culpability for antisocial behavior.
- Resist even more strongly the victim-blaming notions inherent in the codependency formulation so bandied about in the addictions literature.
- Oppose the primacy given to drug use in dysfunctional behavior.
- View drug usage as an excuse for deliberate acts of aggression, commonly called the disavowal position (Bennett & Williams, 2003; Silva & Howard, 1991).
- See partner assault as reflecting perpetrators' underlying need for power and control.
- Subscribe to a feminist model of violence as primary.
- Focus on safety rather than on recovery and on social change at the societal level.

With such disparate treatment ideologies, it is no wonder that in my counseling work I often heard animosity expressed by practitioners and recovering alcoholics toward the women's shelter staff. "They just don't understand," it was said. Similarly, today I hear among volunteers working with battered women strong reservations expressed about some of the belief systems of substance abuse treatment providers. Again I hear the complaint, "They don't understand."

So how, oh how, will these competing, contradictory models ever be brought together, subsumed under one theory? And how will workers suspicious of one another's creeds and ideologies come to trust and respect each other for their mutual interests, including the protection of victims from further abuse?

As a background for transcending the addictions/feminist split, let us first consider the facts concerning the co-occurrence of substance abuse and violence.

COMMONALITIES BETWEEN SUBSTANCE ABUSE AND VIOLENCE

Basically, we are looking here at facts that emerge from the research and which are not in dispute; facts pertaining to the biological, psychological, and social aspects of drug-related aggression. We can say at the outset that substance abuse and violence are behaviors that are learned, reinforced, cultural, and characterized by denial. And the similarities go far beyond these, spanning the biopsychosocial continuum.

BIOLOGICAL FACTORS PERTAINING TO ALCOHOL

Included in this category are findings from alcohol–violence studies that investigate alcohol-induced aggression, the role of serotonin in substance abuse and aggression, the background of brain injuries among perpetrators, and research on violence in relation to a variety of drugs, both legal and illegal.

Violence, impulsiveness, and early-onset alcoholism in young males are highly correlated (Cloninger et al., 1989). This type of alcoholism, defined by Cloninger and his associates after extensive studies of adopted sons of alcoholics, is highly hereditary, develops in late childhood, and is characterized by high risk-taking and antisocial behavior. Murphy and O'Farrell (1997) speculate that marital aggression among alcoholics may be linked to an underlying predisposition as revealed in the Cloninger team's adoption studies.

"I'm Dr. Jekyll and Mr. Hyde." This is how many of my male clients, in both Washington State and Norway, described their love affair with alcohol. To objectively test alcohol's reputed role in aggression, Taylor (1993) set up an experimental, pseudoshock design. Under highly controlled conditions of the experiment, alcohol was observed to have potent effects on aggression toward others. In other words, intoxicated subjects were more likely to administer shocks to others than were nonintoxicated subjects. Chemicals in the drink can actually create a rage in the brain that was not present before because of the interaction between a person's limbic chemistry and the drug's properties (Johnson, 2004). A point worth noting in reference to such laboratory studies is that aggression is much more evident when distilled spirits are used as opposed to wine and beer, even at comparable blood alcohol levels (Lang, 1992). In any case, the results of this experiment, according to the author, seem to indicate that one's behavior when drunk is more than a result of social expectations. Although subjects receiving placebo manipulations did not respond aggressively to the stimuli, those whose intoxication was real, typically did so. Some verification is found in monkey studies, where intoxication is associated with attacking behavior in high-ranking, male-dominant monkeys although not in nondominant monkeys (Miczek, Weerts, & DeBold, 1992). Other studies, however, do indicate that when human subjects believe they are drinking alcohol—even when they are actually not doing so—they are apt to react with heightened aggressiveness to stimuli (Bennett & Williams, 2003). One may infer from these results that in cultures where people are expected to get violent when drunk, they will do so. This does not preclude, of course, a biochemical, aggression-inducing response to alcohol as well.

Research into deficiencies in levels of serotonin (the neurotransmitter responsible for a sense of well-being) in the brain reveals that aggression in monkeys is associated with reduced levels of this natural chemical (Pihl & Peterson, 1993). Impaired behavioral control induced by decreased brain serotonin may affect a person's ability to resist drinking alcohol once started. Thus, alcohol, serotonin levels, and aggression may be interconnected in predictably destructive ways. Consistent with this finding is the discovery of White, Hansell, and Brick (1993) that alcohol use and aggressive behavior during early adolescence is associated with subsequent alcohol-related violence.

Use of medication, of Prozac-style antidepressants, may be help-ful in curbing men's aggressiveness just as it is in curbing obsessive-compulsive behavior, bulimia, and so forth (Marano, 1993). Some studies have already demonstrated, as Johnson (2004) suggests, that impulsivity and aggression can be attenuated with selective serotonin reuptake inhibitors (SSRIs) such as Paxil and Prozac. Research is cur-rently underway at the University of Washington where the effects of SSRIs on battering men are being studied.

In summary, alcohol's role in producing violence may be in asso-ciation with other variables stemming from personality traits, or as an indirect factor in violence in that alcohol impairs the drinker's social judgment. Disruptive effects of the drug on the cognitive pro-cesses in the brain presumably limit the intoxicated person's abil-ity to process information rationally. Any bartender can attest to changes in behavior associated with heavy drinking, bellicosity be-ing one pattern especially disturbing in its consequences. As Her-man Melville (1856/1943) warned us through his hero in *Moby Dick*, "Better sleep with a sober cannibal than a drunken Christian" (p. 20).

EFFECTS OF OTHER DRUGS ON INTERPERSONAL VIOLENCE

How about the effects of other drugs on aggression? Marijuana, LSD, and heroin do not appear to cause users to become violent (Gelles, 1993; van Wormer & Davis, 2003). Cocaine, however, like alcohol, is associated with hyperactivity and violence in high doses (Goldberg, 1997). Cocaine acts at the brain's synapses to affect the release of dopamine (see Ginsberg, Nackerud, & Larrison, 2004; National In-stitute on Drug Abuse [NIDA], 2005). PCP's (the horse tranquilizer) association with dangerous forms of violence is legendary. Its calcu-lated use by gang members in preparation for a fight is reported by Fagan (1989).

Widely used in the 1960s and 1970s in both amateur and profes-sional sports, amphetamines are widely implicated in the occurrence of violent and aggressive outbursts (McNeece & DiNitto, 2005). Be-cause amphetamines (such as speed) increase the adrenaline flow, they may produce impulsive behavior that is violent, although Gelles (1993) argues that underlying personality attributes determine the exact nature of the outcome. Amphetamine psychosis is a condition marked by aggressiveness, paranoia, disordered thinking, and mania, and often accompanied by violent behavior. The psychotic-like behaviors, however, may be caused by sleep deprivation rather than by the chemical effect of the drug itself (Goldberg, 1997). The currently popular drug, methamphetamine (or crank), is especially problematic. Anecdotal reports provided to me by counselors in the field tell of bizarre sexual behavior that is associated with use of this drug.

Psychological Aspects

Due to the interconnectedness of the physiological and psychological aspects of behavior, it is often difficult to separate one from the other. Antisocial personality disorder is a case in point. Studies on jail and prison populations reveal a strong correlation among three elements—a diagnosis of antisocial personality disorder (defined in terms of impulsiveness, high risk-taking, and a tendency to externalize blame), substance abuse, and arrest for violent crimes. For subjects with alcohol problems, according to a tightly controlled empirical investigation by Abram, Teplin, and McClelland (1993), the probability of re-arrest for violent crime was high, but only if an antisocial disorder was also present.

Also related to biological predispositions is a tendency toward obsessiveness, possessiveness, and jealousy stemming from insecurity. Marano (1993) provides a portrait of abusive men in which disturbances at the biological level seem to be linked to disturbances in the cognitive realm and a tendency to overreact. Exposure to violence in childhood is a related pattern. (Interestingly, these same qualities are found among persons with a tendency toward addiction.) Star (1980), similarly, likened violent spouses to alcohol users in such characteristics as extreme jealousy, external blame, sexual dysfunction, and severe mood shifts. Often, offenders, tending to be antisocial and to shirk responsibility for their acts, attribute their destructive behavior to drugs consumed. We can term this response *deviance disavowal* (Bennett & Williams, 2003). Often, also, persons bent on a violent course including assault and rape will bolster their "courage" through the use of chemicals. This sort of premeditation is characteristic of the antisocial personality.

Social Factors

Subsumed under social factors are cultural variables, such as oppression of women, and situational stressors, such as poverty. We are concerned here with the *context* of partner violence associated with substance abuse.

Sociocultural attitudes concerning the treatment of women and the resolution of conflict are salient dimensions in partner violence. In fact, Kantor and Straus (1989), in an analysis of data from a national family violence survey, found that cultural approval of violence emerged as the strongest correlate of family violence, and was even more significant than the level of drinking itself. Alcohol-linked violent socialization undoubtedly plays a crucial role in intergenerational wife battering. Blue-collar men, argued Kantor and Straus, are especially prone to tolerate male aggression, and consequently to beat their wives more often than white-collar men. Economic stresses at this level, including circumstances of poverty, exacerbate the likelihood of violence. All in all, according to these researchers, husband's drug use, low family income, and a history of violence in the wife's family of origin were consistently associated with violence against the wife. And once violence is an established norm within the family, it will occur even under conditions of total abstinence. Abusive men with alcohol and other drug problems are apt to be violent both when intoxicated and when sober (Bennett & Williams, 2003).

It is theorized, as Humphreys et al. indicate (2005), that attitudes to drinking and masculinity are significant, that some see drinking as a defining aspect of masculinity. In this sense, the use of alcohol becomes another strategy for domination and control. Gondolf (1995) argues effectively that the key to the link between alcohol abuse and wife assault is in man's craving for power and control, a craving fostered by distortions of masculinity rooted in social upbringing. Underscoring this argument is the finding from sex-role studies that wife-assaulters in clinical samples score low on masculinity measures and femininity measures also. Gondolf bolsters this finding with research pointing to verbal deficits and poor communication skills among physically aggressive men. Drinking to gain a sense of power, therefore, comes naturally to such men, especially when they are under stress. The effect of the drug alcohol, in turn, contributes to a misreading of social cues through cognitive impairment, and violence may provide some sense of immediate gratification. Alcohol use and wife assault, according to this argument, are not causally related, but are both underlying manifestations of a bid for power and control.

A related factor is the belief that the alcohol or other drug is disinhibiting can serve as an "excuse" and allow the individual to feel freed from norms for acceptable behavior (Humphreys et al.). In this connection, perpetrators who wish to be violent can get themselves drunk or high in order to be violent.

A few words should be said about *psychological* abuse. As Chang (1996) makes clear, psychological, like physical abuse, can be explained as an extension of the patriarchal pattern of maintaining dominance and control over a vulnerable partner. Physical abuse does not exist apart from psychological abuse, and it is often the psychological pain that endures long after the physical wounds have healed.

Putting it all together, we can concur with Bennett and Williams, (2003) in viewing substance abuse and relationship violence as two sides of the same coin. Trying to answer the question whether men are violent because they drink or whether they drink because they are violent may be an exercise in futility. Instead, violence must be viewed interactively within a context of individual, situational, and social factors. This review of contemporary research reinforces the need for a multidimensional understanding of the dynamics of partner violence.

ROLE OF SUBSTANCE ABUSE IN FEMALE VIOLENCE AND VICTIMIZATION

Measures of self-reported partner violence reveal that women readily engage in slapping and hitting their partners, behaviors they often initiate (Morse, 1995). Nevertheless, women are far more likely than men to fear injury and, indeed, to sustain it. Data from the National Victimization Survey reveal that women make up 85% of all intimate assault victims (Rennison, 2003). There is extensive evidence in the empirical literature that women who report regular heavy drinking are several times more likely to be abused by their intimate partners than are other women, and such victimization most often occurs on the days that these women were drinking (Stuart et al., 2004). Following victimization, research shows that women who drink are highly likely to drink heavily as a means of self-medication. There is a distinct possibility, moreover, that victimization of women leads to the development of alcoholism in women. To test this hypothesis, Downs and Miller (1997) studied both alcoholic and nonalcoholic women at 18-month intervals. For women with lifetime alcohol dependence, experiences of partner abuse at the earlier time is associated with more severe alcohol problems at the later time interval.

My interpretation of these findings is that highly addictive women are more psychologically vulnerable to experiences of victimization and more apt to use alcohol to escape from the pain of abuse than are nonalcoholic women. Downs and Miller (1997) propose a trauma hypothesis to explain alcoholic women's susceptibility: The cumulative effects of a lifetime of traumatic abuse characteristic of such women, argue Downs and Miller, heighten her ability to be retraumatized by recent partner abuse. This theory linking trauma and a later liability to cope with psychological stress is consistent with recent neurological evidence of brain chemistry changes that result from early trauma (Basham & Miehls, 2004). These findings have important implications for substance abuse treatment counselors. Recovering women who are involved with abusing men are at primary risk of relapse.

Studies of women committing acts of violence while under the influence of alcohol or other drugs are scarce. For example, the extensive government research report, *Alcohol and Interpersonal Violence* (Martin, 1993), focused almost exclusively on male partner violence. According to Leonard (1993), writing in the same volume, only two studies had specifically examined the possibility that husband-and-wife drinking patterns might interact to predict marital aggression. In Leonard's own research, the wife's excessive drinking was associated with the husband's aggression. The focus was on *victimization,* not victimizing by the wife, however. Kantor (1993) also referred to the lack of attention in the literature to women's alcohol-related aggression. Alcohol-abusing women, she suggested, are more at risk of victimization because they are violating gender-role expectations by the very fact of being intoxicated. Moreover, alcoholic women's stigmatization as being "sexually loose" may set them up for maltreatment. And if such women become verbally or physically aggressive, the violence in their partners may escalate. Kantor's observation (1993) that it is extremely rare for sober husbands to remain with their addictive wives perhaps explains the shortage of studies on hard-drinking, battering women.

More recent research on women with addiction problems continues to focus on violence against women rather than violence by women. The new book published by the National Center on Addiction and Substance Abuse at Columbia University (2006), *Women Under the Influence*, for example, devotes attention to the victimization of women "under the influence" but only mentions violence by such women in one place referring to girls who binge drink being more likely than other girls to get into a physical fight.

Studies of alcoholic women in treatment (Miller, Downs, Testa, & Keil, 1991) reveal that such women are more likely to initiate violence against partners than are battered women in shelters or women without alcohol problems. Chermack, Walton, et al. (2001) studied women in substance abuse treatment programs and found that over half had perpetrated violence toward a partner in the past year, much of it having been severe violence. Stuart et al. (2004) recruited a sample of 35 women arrested for domestic violence and found that approximately one-third had an alcohol-related diagnosis. In a later study of over 100 such women, these researchers found that hazardous drinkers both perpetrated and received more violence than did a comparison group of non-hazardous drinkers. The results suggest the importance of substance abuse assessment and the offering of integrated alcohol treatment in programs for women arrested for battering.

Domestic violence ending in homicide is an area, due to the magnitude of the crime, where hard data are relatively easy to come by. Nationwide, about one-third of the women in prison for homicide have killed a partner. Whereas men kill partners as the violence escalates, women do so as a means of escape. It is clear that substance use is implicated in many of these domestic situations as we know that the degree of injury increases in conjunction with the level of intoxication (Humphreys et al., 2005).

Al Roberts (1996) confirmed, in his in-depth interviews with incarcerated battered women who had killed their partners, that such women had acted following a history of death threats and beatings. In sharp contrast to the community sample of battered women, the battered women in the prison sample frequently had a history of drug use. Other relevant factors that emerged in the study were the batterer's extreme jealousy, emotional dependency, and drunkenness.

The role of substance abuse in homicide has been substantiated in a study by the National Institute of Justice (Zahn, 2003). Men who murder their partners are more likely to be drunk every day or use drugs than those who abuse but don't kill their partners. This makes substance use a clear risk factor for partner homicide.

SAME-SEX PARTNER VIOLENCE

A high consumption rate of alcohol and other drugs is characteristic of gay and lesbian social life (van Wormer & Davis, 2003). A review of the literature on same-sex partner abuse reveals the use of alcohol or drugs to be prevalent. The use of crystal meth, which is closely associated with sexually risky and violent behavior, is widely used by gay men (Shernoff, 2006). A review of the literature on same-sex battering reveals that over half of the batterers were under the influence of alcohol or other drugs at the time of the assault (Renzetti, 1997). In one survey of 39 lesbians in abusive relationships, 64% reported use of alcohol or drugs by both partners prior to the incidents of abuse (Schilit, Lie, & Montagne, 1990). Significantly well over a third of the lesbian sample has experienced physically abusive relationships. With such a small sample, however, one cannot draw any definitive conclusions.

In probing the substance abuse/violence link, researchers on gay and lesbian relationships tend to perceive the use of chemicals as an excuse to allow batterers to escape responsibility for their acts (Island & Letellier, 1991; Renzetti, 1997). Extreme emotional dependency is viewed as a likely determinant of the violence (Renzetti). Island and Letellier argue that the batterers drink as a premeditated strategy before they beat their partners. They view the substance-abuse problems as separate from the "battering disorder." I would again argue for a holistic rather than a monocausal approach. Yet, in the absence of solid research data on same-sex domestic violence, generalizations are hard to make. We can all agree on the need for further research and for greater openness by service providers to meet the needs of battered lesbians and gay men. Although most women's shelters would never provide counseling for heterosexual males who are battered, they do sometimes counsel lesbians and gay men as well as battered women.

TREATMENT ISSUES

Batterers who are court ordered to treatment for battering need to be screened for substance use problems, and substance abusers in substance abuse treatment should be screened for battering. The focus of substance abuse agencies, as Bennett and Williams suggest, has been more on violence in the family of origin than to ongoing family violence.

The barriers to cooperation between the addictions providers and feminist crisis intervention workers are formidable. As mentioned earlier, the frameworks are contradictory and ideological, and opportunities for cross-fertilization of research are few. The differences are not irreconcilable, however. The barriers to cooperation could be lifted through the following moves: the adoption of a holistic, biopsychosocial framework for a common understanding of the addictions/violence/victimization configuration; by a repudiation of all victim-blaming terminology and orientations; and participation in joint training workshops in the dynamics of substance and partner abuse.

An illustration of a positive development that may set an example for other communities has taken place in Waterloo, Iowa. Pathways Behavioral Services, a substance abuse agency, and Seeds of Hope, a grassroots crisis service for battered women, have joined forces in obtaining a grant for mutual training programs. As a starting point, counselors from Seeds of Hope provide workshops on the dynamics of domestic violence.

To what extent incompatible worldviews, however, will impede networking remains to be seen. Counselors at Pathways, as is typical of the addiction field, are steeped in a codependency model, which they apply to spouses and partners of substance abusers. Codependency implies shared responsibility in a spouse's problems; women are often faulted or declared to be sick for "enabling" the alcoholic to behave irresponsibly. Where there is partner abuse, the role of male violence in subduing women is apt to be overlooked. Couples counseling, often a part of substance abuse treatment, can be especially dangerous to the battered woman and is contraindicated. Practitioners at women's shelters, for their part, tend to overlook the significance of substance abuse and addiction in destroying families, destroying lives, and the fact that indeed, for some individuals, involvement in a 12-step program can be a godsend.

FROM BIFURCATION TO INTEGRATION

As long as their worldviews are so vastly different, as long as ideology rather than research shapes practice, domestic violence and substance abuse programs will continue to go their separate ways, and lives will continue to be lost unnecessarily. Substance abuse treatment alone will not address the physical abuse adequately, and supportive counseling and advocacy for battered women will not end addiction problems that may exist.

A biopsychosocial understanding bolstered by empirical research concerning biological (e.g., the link between serotonin depletion and aggression/addiction), psychological (e.g., insecurity/jealousy components), and social (e.g., cultural supports for male drunken aggression) dimensions offers a holistic approach to the violence/substance abuse link. Such an approach effectively unites what we know about the potency of addiction—and the extensive treatment plan required to help addicts/alcoholics find healthy ways to cope with feelings, pain, and resolving conflict—with an awareness from gender-based research of how violence toward women is related to power-and-control issues in a patriarchal society. Alcoholic battered women need to see how involvement in high-risk situations jeopardizes their sobriety.

In substance abuse treatment agencies, moreover, safety must be given priority. A "sobriety first" approach with women who face ongoing abuse and danger and who may rely on alcohol or tranquilizers as coping devices is almost destined to fail (Zubretsky & Digirolamo, 1996). Male batterers with substance-related problems first of all need extensive substance abuse treatment. According to the World Health Organization, there is a significant reduction in mutual violence following substance abuse treatment of an offending male as measured 12 months following treatment. Alcoholic batterers need work in the areas of empathy, stress management, social skills training, and acceptance of the feminine sides of their personalities. *All* clients need to know how alcohol and other substance abuse contribute to cognitive dysfunction and to a dangerous misreading of cues that may precipitate overreaction and violence.

Harm reduction principles informed by motivational enhancement strategies can offer an effective bridge between substance abuse and domestic violence programming. Motivational interviewing has been found to be a highly effective way of prompting individuals to change destructive behavior patterns through the use of sophisticated techniques borrowed from social psychology (see Miller & Rollnick, 2002; van Wormer & Davis, 2003). This approach conceptualizes concrete stages that both client and therapist can identify to understand exactly where the client is in terms of readiness to change and shapes interventions accordingly (Shernoff, 2006). This model teaches principles of indirect rather than direct persuasion that are of proven effectiveness (Miller & Rollnick, 2002).

How can this approach apply to both batterers and substance abusers? Keeping in mind that the tendency toward antisocial, risk-taking, and impulsive behavior likely plays a role in the development of both substance abuse problems and violence, as does cultural tolerance for violent outbursts in certain pro-masculine, anti-woman circles, we can conclude that a harm reduction approach geared to tackle these interconnected problems might be indicated. Such an integrated approach can be applied at either substance abuse treatment centers or in batterer educational programs because it targets cognitive impairment. In other words, irrational thought patterns, the kind associated with extreme and impulsive behavior, can be tackled through skills of motivational counseling. Such skills are easily mastered, especially by social workers familiar with the strengths approach for reinforcing the positive in a client's behavior. Teaching empathy and rolling with resistance are fundamentals of harm reduction.

For women survivors of violence, harm reduction provides her with a safety plan, and techniques to ensure her safety even if she chooses to return to an unsafe situation. Choice is the key word here. Motivational techniques are used to help her in that choice and to prepare the way for her to move through the stages of contemplation of change to preparation for change to decisive action. For female batterers, the same principles of harm reduction are relevant as these women are often in precarious situations as well, and substance abuse commonly figures in the picture.

The move from theory bifurcation to integration is central, as we have seen, to a coming together of treatment forces. Building on similarities in approaches that already exist can enhance such integration. As Gondolf (1995) indicates, both substance abuse treatment and domestic violence programs confront denial and minimization of destructive behaviors. Both address distortions and rationalizations, work on communication skills, and promote personal change. Conjoint substance abuse/violence treatment is only possible, however, when a holistic framework *is* employed. Under the rubric of integrated theory, substance abuse and aggression would not be viewed as either/or—cause-and-effect terms—but as *both/and* multidimensional constructs. Thus, both disorders—harmful use of substances and abuse of people—are seen as manifestations of the same biopsychosocial forces. Interventions guided by this unifying theory should go far toward addressing the needs of victims and perpetrators alike. Interventions based on myths and narrow ideology, on the other hand, can have a devastating effect on victims and their families and indirectly, on their treatment providers.

CONCLUSION

Much remains to be learned about the exact nature of the substance abuse/aggression link. In this chapter, the attempt has been made to get beyond simplistic ideology and to single out from the contemporary, available literature the findings on the incidence of domestic violence (as influenced by gender, intoxicating substances, and cultural norms). To replace the narrow, unidimensional approaches of rival programs, a multidimensional, harm reduction approach has been proposed, an approach that accurately reflects truths as revealed in much of the groundbreaking research currently being done. The current state of the knowledge suggests that the close relationship of substance abuse and violence in men results primarily from (a) a biochemical susceptibility to react to stress through aggression and chemical use, (b) a substance-induced or psychologically induced cognitive impairment, (c) cultural definitions conducive to intoxicated aggression in men, and (d) a resented emotional dependency on one's partner. An approach geared only to one aspect of the violence problem—the cultural dimension—may be politically correct but ineffective in motivating these men for change. Of substance-abusing, battered women we know (a) a history of past abuse trauma is common; (b) self-esteem is extremely low; (c) psychoactive drugs may be used as a way of coping with the terrors of violence; and (d) traditional, male-oriented addictions treatment programs may actually compound the problem.

Yet the parallels between the stages of deciding to leave a battering relationship and deciding to refrain from unhealthy addictive patterns are obvious. Safety is the key concern of the harm reduction bridging approach.

The present situation of dichotomizing problems that are not in reality separable is counterproductive. This discussion has shown, hopefully, how differences in language and assumptions can be reconciled through a basic reconceptualization for a broader, more comprehensive approach. The links between substance use and violence make harm reduction a logical concept to embrace to meet the needs of men and women affected by both issues. Organizations are only now beginning to explore ways of tailoring services accordingly. Encouraging developments in networking across disciplinary lines are currently underway. Such collaborations are essential to meet the common good of preventing and curbing the violence even as the substance abuse is curbed.

REFERENCES

Abram, K., Teplin, L., & McClelland, M. (1993). The effects of co-occurring disorders on the relationship between alcoholism and violent crime: A 3-year follow-up of male jail detainees. In S. Martin (Ed.), *Alcohol and interpersonal violence: Fostering multidisciplinary perspectives* (pp. 237–252). Rockville, MD: U.S. Department of Health and Human Services.

Al-Anon. (1994). Domestic violence. In *In all our affairs: Making crises work for you* [Brochure, pp. 1–4]. New York: Author.

Associated Press. (1996, September 23). Violence research brings startling results. *Waterloo/Cedar Falls Courier,* p. A6.

Basham, K., & Miehls, D. (2004). *Transforming the legacy: Couple therapy with survivors of childhood trauma.* New York: Columbia University Press.

Bell, N., Hartford, T., McCarroll, J., & Senier, L. (2004). Drinking and spouse abuse among U.S. army soldiers. *Alcoholism: Clinical and Experimental Research, 28*(12), 1890–1897.

Bennett, L., & Williams, O. J. (2003). Substance abuse and men who batter. *Violence Against Women, 9*(5), 558–575.

Chang, V. N. (1996). *I just lost myself: Psychological abuse of women in marriage.* Westport, CT: Praeger.

Chermack, S., Walton, M., Fuller, B., & Blow, F. (2001). Correlates of expressed and received violence across relationship types among men and women substance abusers. *Psychology of Addictive Behaviors, 15,* 140–151.

Cloninger, C. R., Sigvardsson, S., Gilligan, S., De Knorring, A. L., Reich, T., & Bohman, M. (1989). Genetic homogeneity and the classification of alcoholism. *Advances in Alcohol and Substance Abuse, 7,* 3–16.

Cohen, J., Dickow, A., Horner, K., Zweben, J., Balabis, J., Vandersloot, D., et al. (2003). Abuse and violence history of men and women in treatment for methamphetamine dependence. *American Journal on Addictions, 12*(5), 377–385.

Downs, W. R., & Miller, B. A. (1997). *The longitudinal association between experiences of partner-to-woman abuse and alcohol problems for women.* Unpublished manuscript.

El-Bassel, N., Gilbert, L., Wu, E., Go, H., & Hill, J. (2005, March). Relationship between drug abuse and intimate partner violence. *Affilia, 13*(4), 411–434.

Fagan, J. (1989). The social organization of drug use and drug dealing among urban gangs. *Criminology, 27,* 633–667.

Fals-Stewart, W. (2003). The occurrence of partner physical aggression on days of alcohol consumption: A longitudinal diary study. *Journal of Consulting and Clinical Psychology, 71,* 41–52.

Gelles, R. J. (1993). Alcohol and other drugs are associated with violence: They are not its cause. In R. J. Gelles & D. R. Loseke (Eds.), *Current controversies on family violence* (pp. 182–196). Newbury Park, CA: Sage.

Ginsberg, L., Nackerud, L., & Larrison, C. (2004). *Human biology for social workers.* Boston: Allyn & Bacon.

Goldberg, R. (1997). *Drugs across the spectrum.* Englewood, CO: Morton.

Gondolf, E. W. (1995). Alcohol abuse, wife assault, and power needs. *Social Service Review, 69,* 274–284.

Gondolf, E. W., & Foster, R. A. (1991). Wife assault among V.A. alcohol rehabilitation patients. *Hospital and Community Psychiatry, 42,* 74–79.

Humphreys, C., Regan, L., River, D., & Thiara, R. (2005). Domestic violence and substance use: Tackling complexity. *British Journal of Social Work, 35,* 1303–1320.

Ingrassia, M., & Beck, M. (1994, July 4). Patterns of abuse. *Newsweek,* pp. 26–33.

Island, D., & Letellier, P. (1991). *Men who beat the men who love them.* New York: Harrington Park Press.

Johnson, H. C. (2004). *Psyche, synapse, and substance: The role of neurobiology in emotions, behavior, thinking, and addiction for nonscientists* (2nd ed.). Greenfield, MA: Deerfield Valley.

Kantor, G. (1993). Refining the brushstrokes in portraits of alcohol and wife assaults. In S. Martin (Ed.), *Alcohol and interpersonal violence: Fostering multidisciplinary perspectives* (pp. 281–290). Rockville, MD: U.S. Department of Health and Human Services.

Kantor, G., & Straus, M. A. (1989). Substance abuse as a precipitant of wife abuse victimization. *American Journal of Drug and Alcohol Abuse, 15,* 173–189.

Lang, A. (1992). Psychological perspectives. In S. Martin (Ed.), *Alcohol and interpersonal violence: Fostering multidisciplinary perspectives* (pp. 121–147). Rockville, MD: U.S. Department of Health and Human Services.

Leonard, K. (1993). Drinking patterns and intoxication in marital violence: Review, critique, and future directives for research. In S. Martin (Ed.), *Alcohol and interpersonal violence: Fostering multidisciplinary perspectives* (pp. 253–280). Rockville, MD: U.S. Department of Health and Human Services.

Marano, H. (1993). Inside the heart of marital violence. *Psychology Today, 26,* 50–53,76–78, 91.

Martin, S. (Ed.). (1993). *Alcohol and interpersonal violence: Fostering multidisciplinary perspectives.* Rockville, MD: National Institutes of Health.

McNeece, C. A., & DiNitto, D. M. (2005). *Chemical dependency: A systems approach.* Boston: Allyn & Bacon.

Melville, H. (1943). *Moby-Dick or the whale.* New York: Heritage Press. (Original work published 1856).

Miczek, K., Weerts, E., & De Bold, J. (1992). Alcohol, aggression, and violence: Biobehavioral determinants. In S. Martin (Ed.), *Alcohol and interpersonal violence: Fostering multidisciplinary perspectives* (pp. 83–120). Rockville, MD: U.S. Department of Health and Human Services.

Miller, B. A., Downs, W. R., Testa, M., & Keil, A. (1991, November). *Thematic analyses of severe spousal violence incidents: Women's perceptions of their victimization.* Paper presented at the annual meeting of the American Society of Criminology, San Francisco, CA.

Miller, W., & Rollnick, S. (2002). *Motivational interviewing: Preparing people for change* (2nd ed.) New York: Guilford Press.

Morse, B. (1995). Beyond the conflict tactics scale: Assessing gender differences in partner violence. *Violence and Victims, 10,* 251–272.

Murphy, C. M., & O'Farrell, T. J. (1997). Couple communication patterns of maritally aggressive and nonaggressive male alcoholics. *Journal of Studies on Alcohol, 15,* 83–90.

National Center on Addiction and Substance Abuse at Columbia University. (2006). *Women under the influence.* New York: Columbia University Press.

National Institute on Drug Abuse (NIDA). (2005). *Mind over matter.* Retrieved June 2006, from http://teens.drugabuse.gov.

Pihl, R., & Peterson, J. (1993). Alcohol and aggression: Three potential mechanisms of the drug effect. In S. Martin (Ed.), *Alcohol and interpersonal violence: Fostering multidisciplinary perspectives* (pp. 149–159). Rockville, MD: U.S. Department of Health and Human Services.

Rennison, C. M. (2003). *Intimate partner violence 1993–2001.* Bureau of Justice Statistics (BJS). Washington, DC: U.S. Department of Justice.

Renzetti, C. (1997). Violence and abuse among same-sex couples. In A. Cardarelli (Ed.), *Violence between intimate partners: Patterns, causes and effects* (pp. 70–89). Needham Heights, MA: Allyn & Bacon.

Roberts, A. (1996). Battered women who kill: A comparative study of incarcerated participants with community sample of battered women. *Journal of Family Violence, 11*, 291–304.

Rogers, B., McGee, G., Vann, A., Thompson, N., & Williams, O. (2003). Substance abuse and domestic violence: Stories of practitioners that address the co-occurrence among battered women. *Violence Against Women, 9*(5), 590–598.

Schilit, R., Lie, G., & Montagne, M. (1990). Substance use as a correlate of violence in intimate lesbian relationships. *Journal of Homosexuality, 19*, 51–65.

Shernoff, M. (2006). Condomless sex: Gay men, barebacking, and harm reduction. *Social Work, 51*(2), 107–113.

Silva, N., & Howard, M. (1991). Woman battering: The forgotten problem in alcohol abuse treatment. *Family Dynamics Addictions Quarterly, 1*, 8–19.

Star, B. (1980). Patterns in family violence. In M. Elbow (Ed.), *Social casework reprint services* (pp. 5–12). Ann Arbor, MI: Books on Demand.

Stuart, G., Moore, T., Ramsey, S., & Kahler, C. (2004, January). Hazardous drinking and relationship violence perpetration and victimization in women arrested for domestic violence. *Journal of Studies on Alcohol, 65*(1), 46–54.

Taylor, S. (1993). Experimental investigation of alcohol-induced aggression in humans. *Alcohol Health and Research World, 17*, 93–100.

Tolman, R. M., & Bennett, L. W. (1990). A review of quantitative research on men who batter. *Journal of Interpersonal Violence, 5*, 87–118.

U.S. Department of Health and Human Services. (2005, September). *Violence against women.* Retrieved August 2006, from www.womenshealth.gov.

van Wormer, K. (2007). *Human behavior and the social environment, micro level: Individuals and families.* New York: Oxford University Press.

van Wormer, K., & Bartollas, C. (2007). *Women and the criminal justice system.* (2nd ed.) Boston: Allyn & Bacon.

van Wormer, K., & Davis, D., R. (2003). *Addiction treatment: A strengths perspective.* Belmont, CA: Wadsworth.

Vines, G. (1999, November 29). The gene in the bottle. *New Scientist,* 29–43.

White, H., Hansell, S., & Brick, J. (1993). Alcohol use and aggression among youth. *Alcohol Health and Research World, 17*, 144–150.

World Health Organization. (2006). Intimate partner violence and alcohol fact sheet. Retrieved September 2006, from www.who.int/entity/violence.

Zahn, M. (2003, November). Intimate partner homicide. *Institute of Justice Journal,* issue 250. Retrieved September 2006, from www.ncjrs.gov/pdffiles1.

Zubretsky, T. M., & Digirolamo, K. (1996). In A. Roberts (Ed.), *Helping battered women: New perspectives and remedies* (pp. 222–228). New York: Oxford University Press.

CHAPTER 17

Poverty, Women, Welfare, Work, and Domestic Violence

Diane L. Green and Patricia Brownell

> My husband wouldn't allow me to work. I had an interview and he went with me into the interview to sabotage it. He wouldn't allow me out of his sight. I thought he was gone for a while one day, so I went to an interview. When I got home, everything was broken, he had beaten my son and swore he would do more the next time.

According to the National Organization for Women (NOW, 2004), it is estimated that 60% of women on welfare have experienced domestic violence at some point in their lives and 30% have experienced it within the past year. Women experiencing intimate partner abuse and are welfare recipients face numerous barriers to employment, including, but not limited to, mental and physical health problems, lack of transportation, substance abuse, lack of child care, and partners that will not allow them to work, such as the vignette above. Lyon (2002) found that there was an 80% to 83% rate of lifetime abuse for welfare recipients. Most battered women work or want to work *if they can do so safely*. Many women use welfare and work as a way to escape an abusive relationship.

Abusive partners often sabotage women's efforts to become more financially self-sufficient by preventing women from working, attending interviews, or studying. By starting fights or inflicting visible injuries before key events, abusers also may prevent women from attending job interviews or going to work. Abusers may also threaten to kidnap the children or fail to provide promised child care or transportation. Some abusive partners may try to stop women from working by calling them frequently during the day or coming to their place of work unannounced as can be seen in the chapter by Green and Viani (this volume). Roughly 50% of battered women who are employed are harassed at work by their abusive partners (Family Violence Prevention Fund, 2006). Economic dependency is a barrier to safely leaving an abusive relationship. Welfare is one tool many battered women use as temporary assistance to become independent of their abusers. With the federal welfare reform in the last few years, domestic violence advocates have been concerned that new restrictions on welfare may hinder the efforts of survivors of domestic violence to get valuable resources.

On June 29, 2006, the Department of Health and Human Services (HHS) issued regulations regarding the Temporary Assistance for Needy Families (TANF) program. George W. Bush proposed adding the marriage promotion initiative to TANF. The National Organization for Women (NOW, 2004) find several critical flaws with this program. They state that it "is fiscally irresponsible to divert already-tight funds from TANF supports that have been proven effective for the purpose of financing an unproven social experiment. They further claim that there is no evidence that marriage helps lift people out of poverty. In the House and Senate plans, at least $1.4 billion would be spent on untested marriage promotion plans over the next 5 years. They also indicate that 60% of female TANF recipients are the victims of domestic violence at some point during their life; pushing these at-risk women into marriage as a way to get them out of poverty and off welfare further endangers their already-precarious situation. They conclude that encouraging couples to get married brings with it the very real possibility of stigmatizing and encouraging discrimination against single parents and unmarried couples" (NOW). This chapter provides an overview of the past, present, and future of welfare and battered women.

PAST

Aid to Dependent Children, as it was then known, was enacted as an entitlement program for all families who met categorical and financial criteria defined by federal and state law. It afforded a minimum level of financial security to primarily poor women and children deprived of a male breadwinner, by virtue of death, illness, or abandonment. By the 1970s, in the wake of the great civil rights and women's movements, it had also become an important source of support for women and children made destitute through fleeing domestic violence situations.

Domestic violence (also known as intimate partner abuse or intrafamilial violence) refers to any assault, sexual assault, or other crime that results in the personal injury or death of one or more family or household member(s) by another who is or was residing in the same dwelling (Bartol & Bartol, 2004). Since domestic violence was defined as a significant social problem in the 1970s, startling statistics have emerged about its impact on domestic life in the United States. In 2001, women accounted for 85% of the victims of intimate partner violence (588,490 total), and men accounted for approximately 15% of the victims (103,220 total; Bureau of Justice Statistics, 2003).

Around the world, at least one woman in every three has been beaten, coerced into sex, or otherwise abused in her lifetime. Most often the abuser is a member of her own family. Physical violence is estimated to occur in 4 million to 8 million intimate relationships each year in the United States. Nearly one in every three adult women experiences at least one physical assault by a partner during adulthood. Approximately 4 million American women experience a serious assault by an intimate partner during a 12-month period (Newton, 2001). Approximately one-fourth of American women will be abused in their lifetime. Up to 35% of women and 22% of men presenting to the emergency department have experienced domestic violence (Newton).

State statistics also demonstrate the impact of domestic violence on children. Seventy percent of men who batter their partners also abuse their children. Children in homes where domestic violence occurs are physically abused or seriously neglected at a rate 1,500% higher than the national average in the general population.

WELFARE AND DOMESTIC VIOLENCE

During the past 10 years, so-called welfare reform policies such as the Personal Responsibility and Work Opportunity Reconciliation Act (PRA/PRWORA or Public Law 104-193) eliminated entitlements and denied benefits to the most needy and vulnerable groups such as unwed teenage mothers, non-English-speaking immigrants with young children who are not able to work at least 30 hours per week, and domestic violence victims who divorce their abusive husbands. Research indicates that immigrants and limited English speakers still make up a significant share of those on the welfare rolls. Immigrants compose around one-third of the TANF caseload in California and New York and nearly one-fifth in Texas. Many of these immigrants have significant barriers to obtaining decent-paying jobs due to their lower education levels and less work history than natives. Immigrants on TANF are less likely to be working than natives and more likely to be working in occupations that provide little opportunity for speaking English, gaining skills, and achieving self-sufficiency. PRWORA's strict work requirements limit opportunities for states to deliver education and training programs to welfare recipients, including language training to limited English speakers. Many job-training programs have English-language requirements, which limit access for immigrants who do not speak English well. Proposed TANF reforms increasing the number of required hours of work and limiting the types of activities that count as work will make it even more difficult for immigrant and limited-English-speaking welfare recipients to receive language or vocational training (Tumlin & Zimmerman, 2003).

REAUTHORIZATION OF PERSONAL RESPONSIBILITY ACT

The reauthorization measure was H.R. 240, the PRA/PRWORA of 2005. Not surprisingly, it includes punitive provisions similar to those adopted by the House in the last Congress—higher work participation rates for states, increased work hours for benefit recipients (up to 40 per week, from the current 30), and reduced flexibility for states in determining what counts as work. As in the current TANF program, the provisions for child care are completely inadequate to meet the current need, despite the requirement for increased work hours. In the hope of gaining the support of key members of the Senate, Herger's bill also includes "marriage promotion" provisions.

This bill reauthorized TANF. It also specifies the mandatory funding part of the Child Care and Development Block Grant. This bill is essentially the same as the 108th Congress (2003–2004) bill, H.R. 4. The bill makes the following changes on important issues:

Work Requirements

H.R. 240 requires parents with children under 6 to work 40 hours a week, rather than the 20 hours they are required to work under current law. The bill requires parents with children over age 6 to work 40 hours a week, rather than the 30 hours a week they are required under current law; 24 of those 40 hours must be in "work activities," which may include employment, community service, or on-the-job training. This requirement would prevent welfare recipients from engaging in education and training, which is the best path to self-sufficiency. The bill also increases work participation rates (the percentage of the caseload a state is required to have in work activities) from 50% to 70%.

Marriage Promotion

H.R. 240 mandates that every state TANF program set numerical performance objectives for promoting marriage, and allocates $1.8 billion dollars over 6 years to fund marriage-promotion programs. TANF marriage promotion diverts welfare funds from basic economic supports to activities of unproven effectiveness, which may have the effect of encouraging battered women to remain with their abusive partner.

Child Care

H.R. 240 includes only a $1 billion increase in child care funding over 5 years, an increase that does not even keep up with inflation, let alone provide enough funds to help cash-strapped states meet growing child-care needs.

The reauthorization bill came to an end with the passage of S. 1932, the *Deficit Reduction Act of 2005*. The bill was signed into law by

President George W. Bush on February 8, 2006, and contained 10 distinct Titles. Included as Title VIII, TANF, is legislation from the House *Committee on Ways and Means, the Work, Marriage, and Family Promotion Reconciliation Act of 2005*. This section of Public Law 109-171, the *Deficit Reduction Act of 2005*, reauthorizes the PRWORA of 1996, the law that created a new TANF program. Recently passed TANF legislation reauthorizes the program through the year 2010. The following is an overview provided by Communication Workers of America (CWA, 2006):

Basic Grants

The basic TANF block grant remains capped at $16 billion. State contingency grants continue at $2 billion per year through 2010. Supplemental grants are reauthorized at $319 million per year. The new ceiling on transfers of TANF funds to the Childcare Development Grant is now 50%. Transfers of TANF funds to Title XX Social Security Block grants are increased from 4.25% to 10%.

Work Hours and Participation Rates

Changes in work hours are not directly addressed. However, the measure does require the Secretary to publish a list that specifies which activities will count as federally accepted work activities. Work participation rates now increase in 5% increments. Starting with 50% in 2006, the increase follows as 55% in 2007, 60% in 2008, 65% in 2009, and 70% in year 2010.

Child-Care and Child-Support Enforcement

Under Subtitle B of the Act, entitlement funding for child care is set at $2 billion for each of the fiscal years 2006 through 2010. States must review and adjust child-support orders in TANF cases every 3 years. Families that have never been on TANF must pay a $25 annual user fee "when child support enforcement efforts yield $500 or more. ..." Noncustodial parents whose child support payments are in arrearages that exceed $2,500 may have their passports denied, revoked, or restricted. States may not intercept tax returns to cover uncollected child support.

Marriage Promotion

The Out-of-Wedlock Birth bonus is eliminated and replaced by the Healthy Marriage Promotion and Responsible Fatherhood Program. Under this provision, TANF grant funds may be used by states to fund Marriage Promotion Grants. States may use their own funds to match the federal grant. Also under this program, the Secretary may offer competitive grants to public and private entities to use TANF funds to promote the following activities:

Public advertising campaigns on the value of marriage.
High school classes.
Marriage education and marriage skills classes for nonmarried parents.
Premarital education.
Marriage enhancement courses for married couples.
Divorce reduction education.
Marriage mentoring programs.

Several studies cited at the beginning of this chapter demonstrated a strong relationship between domestic violence and Aid to Families with Dependent Children (AFDC). A national symposium sponsored by the University of Utah Graduate School of Social Work in May 1996 identified at least four types of linkages between family violence and the use of welfare (Brandwein, 1996).

First, many battered women are forced to turn to public assistance to extricate themselves from a violent relationship. The choice such women may face is to return to the batterer and a style of life to which they may have become accustomed—even if subjected to repeated violence and psychological abuse—or leave and enter a life of poverty, at least temporarily.

Second, many women are coerced by their partners (husbands or boyfriends) not to attend education or job programs, or not to show up at jobs. Some studies have suggested that abusive partners fear loss of control and are threatened by their partner becoming independent of them.

Third, child abuse, particularly child sexual abuse, provides another pathway to welfare. In cases of child sexual abuse or incest, the nonoffending parent—usually the mother—is required to protect the child from the family offender—often the boyfriend, stepfather, or father. If losing the financial support of the offender means destitution for her and her family, a mother may be forced to turn to welfare.

Fourth, the route to welfare may stretch over a longer period of time. Girls who have been sexually abused are more likely to act out sexually, which can result in pregnancy during adolescence (Navarro, 1996). In one shelter for unwed mothers in New York State, social worker interns found that every girl there had been previously sexually abused. Although only about 12% of welfare recipients at any one point in time are teenage mothers, a large proportion of welfare recipients had their first child when teenagers (Brandwein, 1996).

ELIMINATION OF THE FEDERAL GUARANTEE TO ASSISTANCE FOR POOR FAMILIES WITH CHILDREN

The AFDC program was eliminated by President Bill Clinton on August 22, 1996, when he signed into law the PRA/PRWORA (the PRA or Public Law 104-193). This ended the 60-year federal guarantee of a minimum level of social assistance for poor families with dependent children, established by Title IV of the Social Security Act in 1935. The PRA changed Aid to Families with Dependent Children from an entitlement program to a block grant, renamed Temporary Assistance to Needy Families (TANF). A primary purpose of TANF was to move heads of AFDC households into the workforce. Basically, the federal Act gave the states the legislative foundation to transform the welfare program from an entitlement program to a work program focused on assisting families in attaining self-sufficiency and transitioning from welfare to work.

The PRA denies benefits to teen unwed mothers until they turn 18, based on the belief that this will serve as a warning to other young girls not to become pregnant or to marry if they do (Gillespie & Schellhas, 1994). Two drug-related provisions of the PRA include terminating access to TANF for life for anyone convicted of a drug-related felony (including women of child-bearing age or with dependent children), unless state legislatures pass affirmative legislation to the contrary. A second—a state option—permits mandatory drug testing of TANF applicants and recipients. The PRA also eliminates access to federally funded public benefits including TANF for immigrant women with dependent children.

The 1996 PRA welfare reform grants ran out in 2003, and the reauthorization debate involved impractical minimum 40-hour/week work requirements on TANF parents, cutoffs even for those working 20 to 30 hours a week, and an increase in state work participation targets to unrealistic levels—particularly without aggressive economic expansion. Future federal devolution help is uncertain.

PERSONAL RESPONSIBILITY PUBLIC POLICY IN HISTORICAL CONTEXT

The term *personal responsibility* as a social welfare concept suggests a value shift away from social responsibility (Uchitelle, 1997). To talk about welfare and domestic violence in this era of defining welfare reform as "personal responsibility" is a contradiction. It harkens back to an earlier time in U.S. history—to the Colonial era, when members of the agrarian European settlements spoke of values such as "pulling oneself up by one's bootstraps" because that was all the social support that existed. This was a time when it was legal for a husband to beat his wife with a stick no thicker than a thumb.

Reform eras in United States social welfare history have served to focus public attention on social injustices and domestic ills beyond the control of the individual. During the Progressive era of the late 19th century to World War I, social reformers such as Charles Loring Brace (1872), a worker for the charity organization movement and founder of the Children's Aid Society, and Jane Addams (1911), a founder of the settlement house movement in the United States, documented spouse abuse and domestic violence in the communities they served. Brace, a leader of the early child-saving movement, and Addams, a Progressive-era maternalist who believed that women's primary role was in raising children and maintaining family life, not only documented incidences of family violence but also advocated for policies to protect women and children against abuse by male household heads (Gordon, 1988).

Although not an explicit purpose of the Social Security Act of 1935, Perkins and others envisioned the Aid to Dependent Children program as a new form of "outdoor relief"—based on the concept of government entitlement, and not charity—that could sustain mothers with dependent children in the community without the support of a male breadwinner if necessary. The Great Depression served to underscore the belief that poverty was not necessarily the result of individual deficiencies and moral failings of the afflicted, but could result from systemic forces outside the control of the individual.

Wife-beating was redefined as domestic violence and a significant social problem during the 1960s and 1970s in the wake of the civil rights movement (Pleck, 1987). Domestic violence, like institutionalized racial discrimination, was framed in communitarian terms as a social issue of concern to everyone in society. Feminists framed the issue of domestic violence as one that affected women of all social classes. This reflected a conscious strategy designed to ensure that it was not perceived as a problem specific to the poor and communities of color, and—as a result—marginalized.

In 1969, President Nixon proposed abolishing AFDC and replacing it with a guaranteed annual income for poor families with children under 18 called Family Assistance Program (FAP). The guaranteed income would take the form of a negative income tax (NIT). A recipient could increase family income through additional work. However, this bill was never reported outside the Senate Finance Committee, and the Senate defeated a substantially revised proposal in 1972.

On March 24, 1995, the House of Representatives passed the PRA. H.R. 4 is an omnibus welfare bill that would make sweeping changes in cash welfare, food aid, and services, ending unlimited federal funding for cash and food aid to eligible needy families with children. The bill would repeal the 60-year-old program of AFDC and its corollary JOBS program. The passage of the PRA, ending AFDC as an entitlement program, has focused new attention on the relationship between domestic violence and public welfare. The block grant replacing AFDC by the PRA is named Temporary Assistance to Needy Families or TANF to emphasize the transitory nature of the program. In addition, the federal requirement is eliminated that all families who meet the categorical and financial requirements must receive assistance. Available funds can be used for other purposes in addition to cash assistance, including the reduction of state budget deficits.

TANF AND WORK REQUIREMENTS

Requirements that women receiving AFDC participate in work or work-related activities as a condition of continuing eligibility for assistance is not new. The Work Incentive Program, legislated during the Nixon Administration, was one of the first such welfare-to-work programs. Most recently, the Family Support Act of 1988 required states and localities to enroll AFDC heads of households in work-related programs, ranging from remedial literacy and training to job clubs to college programs. Ensuring adequate day care and transitional benefits such as Medicaid were the responsibility of the state. The federal safety net remained for those AFDC heads of households who were unable to attach or sustain attachment to the job market (U.S. House of Representatives, 1991, 1992).

Under the new TANF legislation, women must comply with rigid work or workfare requirements to maintain benefits for themselves and their children (U.S. House of Representatives, 1996). Missing time from workfare or job training can result in loss or reduction of benefits, even if this was due to a battering incident in the home, the need to seek medical attention for domestic violence related injuries, or obtaining an order of protection. The burden of making child-care arrangements is transferred under TANF from the state to the head of the household receiving assistance. By establishing a maximum 5-year lifetime cap on federal TANF benefits per family, the PRA has effectively eliminated the federal safety net for poor women and children.

This has important implications for a battered woman's access to needed emergency services for herself and her children. For example, many domestic violence shelters are funded through emergency assistance to families (EAF), now part of the TANF block grant, or the Social Services Block Grant (SSBG or Title XX of the Social Security Act), the funding for which has been cut as well. If in a domestic violence shelter, a TANF recipient may be required by shelter protocols to stop work. These protocols are intended to ensure that the batterer does not discover the location of the shelter by following the victim home from work. However, she could risk being found out of compliance with work regulations, or experience loss or reduction of benefits by not reporting to a mandated work assignment.

If the family is receiving federally funded child-care assistance in addition to TANF cash benefits and is not disabled or caring for a disabled child, both parents must meet TANF work requirements. At least one parent must work the required 35 hours per week, whereas the second parent can work 20 hours per week in employment, work experience, on-the-job training, or community service activities. Because states can define what constitutes work, anything from parent training to mandatory volunteering may be used to fulfill work requirements. Some states (e.g., Maryland) already consider follow-up with drug treatment referrals as meeting work requirements for those who need such services in order to find and keep a job. Following through with counseling in family violence cases is also considered as meeting work requirements.

WOMEN, WELFARE, WORK, AND ABUSE

In terms of "welfare reform," what we need to do is look at domestic violence victims as individuals, and the welfare system actually has to be flexible and responsive to the needs of individual women. Instead of asking "Why doesn't she leave?," we have to reframe the issue to "What does she need to leave and become self-sufficient?"

Roberts and Roberts (2005) identified several important reasons why women stay in abusive relationships, including that they are dependent on the husband's income, and they want their children to be able to maintain their current lifestyle, including remaining in the same school district with their current friends. Even public assistance programs, although traditionally an important safety net program for women who are victims of domestic violence and their children, do not raise families out of poverty (U.S. House of Representatives, 1996). For welfare recipients to successfully make the transition from welfare to work, they may require a continuum of supportive services flexible enough to meet individual needs, as well as access to an array of educational opportunities that allow them to secure long-term, stable jobs that provide family health benefits as well (Brandwein, 1997).

STUDIES ON DOMESTIC VIOLENCE AND JOB TRAINING PROGRAMS

One factor associated with success in permanently ending an abusive relationship for a woman with dependent children is education and training leading to stable employment, self-sufficiency, and a sense of personal efficacy. However, studies on domestic violence and welfare-to-work programs conducted by the Taylor Institute in Chicago, the National Organization of Women Legal Defense and Education Fund in New York City, the Center for Urban Affairs and Policy Research at Northwestern University, and the Washington State University for Policy Research have identified significant barriers to achieving the goal of self-sufficiency through employment for women on public assistance involved in abusive relationships (Kenney & Brown, 1996; Raphael, 1995, 1996). The NOW (2006) cite a study conducted in 2003 by Lovell, which highlighted three main findings of her most recent research. The NOW states that Lowell found that a 40-hour-a-week, year-round work requirement, would be significantly higher than the current level of mothers' employment activity. Although most mothers do work for pay, half of those are employed either part-time or part of the year, or both.

In 1995, the Taylor Institute, a public policy research and advocacy organization in Chicago, published a groundbreaking study examining welfare-to-work public policies and found them to be based on a number of misconceptions (Raphael, 1995). Cited as primary among them was a misconception that women on welfare did not have relationships with men. Furthermore, it was the male in the picture who frequently sabotaged the woman's efforts to become self-sufficient.

A 2-year demonstration project by the Taylor Institute, Self-Sufficiency and Safety: The Case for Onsite Domestic Violence Services at Employment Services Agencies (Center for Impact Research, 2002), provided domestic violence services to participants in programs at employment services agencies, highlighted the challenges, service needs, and outcomes of low-income domestic violence survivors as they struggle to keep themselves and their children safe, become and remain employed, and attain self-sufficiency. The findings indicated that domestic violence interferes with employment efforts in many ways: It can involve explicit acts of violence and sabotage or more subtle forms of psychological and emotional manipulation.

The Taylor Institute study, Domestic Violence: Telling the Untold Welfare-to-Work Study (Raphael, 1995), was based on a nationwide telephone survey of grassroots welfare-to-work programs to determine the extent of this problem as noted by program case managers and administrators. Anecdotal evidence reported by those surveyed included sabotaging ploys of male partners, such as hiding or ripping work clothing; failing to appear as promised to care for children; revealing jealous fantasies about men at work sites; behaving seductively toward program participants; inflicting visible bruises, including black eyes, broken teeth, and cigarette burns; and picking fights prior to examinations and critical job interviews. Respondents stated that they believed that estimates of such incidents were low, as the women involved were often reluctant to report them.

Findings from the Taylor Institute study are corroborated by studies by other welfare-to-work programs. The Manpower Demonstration Research Corporation (MDRC), at the forefront of welfare-to-work demonstrations in the country, in 1991 reported on a study of 617 young women (ages 16–22) participating in the New Chance program designed for recipients at high risk of long-term welfare dependency. Of these, 16% of participants across the program sites reported being battered by boyfriends while in the program; 15% reported being actively discouraged from attending by a boyfriend; and another 15% reported being abused or discouraged from attending by other family members (Raphael, 1995). Estimates from other programs were higher. The Women's Employment Network in Kansas City, Missouri, estimated that 70% to 80% of welfare-to-work program participants self-reported domestic violence during program participation. The Family Support and Education Center in Maryland reported that at least 20% of its participants were affected by this problem. A study of 824 respondents in Chicago (Loyd, 1997) found "if respondents reported having experienced aggression, they also reported lower personal income and greater receipt of public assistance. Those who reported being controlled, harassed, or threatened (or experiencing other symbolic aggression) in the past 12 months reported incomes $215 lower than those who did not. Those who reported being pushed, shoved, or grabbed (or other physical aggression) reported incomes $211 lower than those who didn't, and those who had experienced being beaten or raped (or other severe aggression) reported incomes $997 lower than those who had not experienced severe aggression. Not surprisingly then, women who were the target of physical or severe aggression, either in the past 12 months or ever in life, were also significantly more likely to have received Aid to Families with Dependent Children, food stamps, and Medicaid."

Another report by the Taylor Institute, Prisoners of Abuse: Domestic Violence and Welfare Receipt: A Second Report of the Women,

Welfare and Abuse Project (Zorza, 1996), continues to emphasize the barriers domestic violence poses for women transitioning from welfare to work. In addition to continuing to document male partners' efforts to sabotage women's efforts to achieve self-sufficiency through education and job training, this report also documents the risks women face in cooperating with child support enforcement efforts (Raphael, 1996).

The extreme dangers posed by child support collections from violent noncustodial fathers are notorious. In the early 1990s, several government workers in the Watkins Glen, New York, Child Support Enforcement Office were murdered by an irate father ordered to pay back child support. In New York City, bulletproof Plexiglas and a buzzer system prevent casual access to the Child Support Enforcement Office workforce. The 1996 PRA mandates cooperation with child support enforcement for TANF recipients as another condition of their continued eligibility for assistance (U.S. House of Representatives, 1996).

The NOW Legal Defense and Education Fund published a study, Report from the Front Lines: The Impact of Violence on Poor Women, based on interviews with New York City direct service staff, including job training and job placement program coordinators, vocational counselors, and job developers (Kenney & Brown, 1996). This survey "involved interviewing knowledgeable informants to determine the scope and extent of the problem of domestic violence for women in welfare-to-work programs" in New York City (p. 6).

Like the Taylor Institute studies, the NOW Legal Defense and Education Fund study found that high proportions of women in welfare-to-work programs are being abused by partners, as cited earlier in this chapter. Reported estimates ranged from 30% to 75% (Kenney & Brown, 1996). Respondents reported that the abuse took many forms (including physical and emotional abuse, stalking, and harassment), and it appeared intended to undermine women's efforts to develop employment-related skills. Unfortunately, it was successful in a number of cases. Study respondents reported that women in training programs who were being abused were more likely to drop out prior to completion of programs than those who did not report abuse (Kenney & Brown).

The NOW report points out that under the enriched job training and educational opportunities provided through the Family Support Act of 1988, battered women may have been advantaged by the availability of case management services that improved detection and intervention for domestic violence as a barrier to participant self-sufficiency. Under TANF, the low-cost "jobs-first" strategy that emphasizes movement into entry-level jobs and workfare over training and education for recipients could place women at greater risk of abuse or—alternatively—increase the sanctions for lateness and absenteeism that penalize the TANF heads of household as well as their children.

The "welfare reform" social experiment initiated by the 1996 PRA is being closely tracked by conservative and liberal "think tanks," journalists, academics, and advocates (Harwood, 1997). Three indicators that would suggest failure of the PRA as a public policy include increased homelessness among families, increased numbers of children entering the foster care system, and increased mortality of women and their children at the hands of their abusers.

Wife-battering has already been cited as a major cause of homelessness among poor families (Zorza, 1991). Ninety-two percent of homeless women have experienced severe physical and/or sexual assault at some point in their lives (Brown, 1998). Domestic violence victims have trouble finding apartments because they may have poor credit, rental, and employment histories as a result of their abuse. In one study, sexual abuse before leaving home was reported by 61% of homeless girls and 19% of homeless boys (Estes & Weiner, 2001).

In 1987, the New York State Office for the Prevention of Domestic Violence found that battered women and their children comprised 40% of the state's homeless shelter residents. HUD has reported that one-half of adult clients in U.S. shelters that serve families with children have experienced domestic violence (U.S. Department of Housing and Urban Development, 1988). More recently, advocates in Milwaukee, Wisconsin, have reported an off-season increase in use of family homeless shelters among welfare recipients affected by the Wisconsin new highly touted "welfare reform" program. Public child welfare systems have been bracing for over a year for the impact of "welfare reform" on child abuse and neglect reports, as well as foster care caseloads (Kilborn, 1996). Concerns have been raised on the part of public child welfare officials about the availability of foster care families—including kin—if TANF work requirements are not relaxed or waived for foster care parents, who may be receiving public assistance in order to remain home to care for dependent children. Although the PRA permits states to exempt up to 20% of the TANF caseload from the work requirements without penalty, a number of recipient categories far exceeding the 20% allotted cap are competing for exemption (Swarns, 1997).

A recent study on women murdered during the past 5 years in New York City was conducted by New York City Department of Health epidemiologist Dr. Susan Wilt. Wilt found that more women are killed by their husbands and boyfriends than in robberies, disputes, attacks, or any other crime in cases where the relationship between victim and murderer is known (Belluck, 1997). When they were killed by their husbands, one-third of the time the women appeared to be trying to end the relationship. Also, in one-fourth of the cases where husbands or boyfriends were the killers, children were killed, injured, were onlookers, or found their mothers' bodies.

Challenging the often-cited belief that domestic violence affects women of all economic classes and ethnicities equally, two-thirds of the domestic violence killings were in the poorest boroughs—the Bronx and Brooklyn—and three-fourths of the women killed by husbands or boyfriends were Black or Hispanic. Dr. Jeff Fagan, director of the Center for Violence, Research and Prevention at Columbia University's School of Public Health, was quoted in the article as noting that domestic violence is a problem of poverty, associated with other characteristics like high unemployment (Belluck, 1997).

The correlation between poverty and domestic violence comes as no surprise to advocates such as Brandwein (Brandwein, 1996; Raphael, 1995, 1996; Women Fighting Poverty, 1996). Although domestic violence has been cited as a primary reason that women with children enter public assistance programs, it has also been documented as a significant barrier to leaving public assistance for stable, long-term employment. Although among the general population about 22% of women have experienced domestic violence in their adult lives, this figure doubles when applied to women on welfare. Most studies of women on welfare find lifetime prevalence of domestic violence ranging from 34% to 65%, with most rates in the 50% to 60% range. Rates of recent or current physical violence generally range from 8% to 33%. There is a growing body of evidence indicating a higher prevalence of domestic violence among the welfare population. This suggests that poverty may increase women's vulnerability to abuse. In this context, welfare becomes an important economic resource for women seeking to escape abuse (Lawrence, 2002).

For those battered women fortunate enough to find a job, there is no guarantee that they will sustain it in the face of a determined batterer. A 1988 study revealed that close to 75% of battered women are harassed by their abusers at work, causing 20% to lose their jobs (Brandwein, 1996). The danger that battered women face on the job after leaving violent partners was underscored in 1996 by the deaths of Falina Komar and Helen Coppola, both murdered in their place of work by their abusers (Gonnerman, 1997a; Krauss, 1996).

Domestic violence in the workplace is an issue of growing concern to corporations, government, and policymakers (Brownell, 1996). Although some corporations and agencies are making workplace security for domestic violence victims a priority (Hardeman, 1995), women in low-wage service sector jobs remain vulnerable to assault (U.S. Department of Labor, 1996). Public policies that force a population known to be at risk of domestic violence—women with dependent children on public assistance—into unprotected community service and entry-level service jobs are courting disaster for those families.

TANF AND THE 5-YEAR LIFETIME CAP ON BENEFITS

With the passage of the PRA and the 5-year maximum lifetime cap on benefits, the stakes have been raised considerably on ensuring the employment—as well as the employability—of poor women with dependent children currently receiving welfare benefits. In addition to those women with active or past histories of domestic violence including incest and child abuse, another vulnerable group of public assistance recipients is the population with active substance abuse problems.

Many domestic violence victims and substance abusers have been found to experience long-term chronic or episodic periods of need for support and treatment (see chapters 1 and 2 in this book for further details on chronically battered women and intervention strategies). Batterers, for example, may not be so considerate as to confine themselves to a 5-year lifetime limit of domestic abuse per victim. Relapse among substance abusers is generally viewed as an integral part of the recovery and healing process.

WOMEN, WELFARE, AND SUBSTANCE ABUSE

According to Joseph Califano, President of the National Center on Addiction and Substance Abuse at Columbia University in New York City and former Secretary of Health, Education and Welfare in the Carter Administration, "Substance abuse and addiction have changed the nature of poverty in America. But the welfare reform legislation that . . . President Clinton signed . . . ignores this grim truth" (Califano, 1996, p. A23). Califano states that at least 20% of women on welfare—or as many as 1 million mothers—have drug or alcohol problems that are severe enough to require treatment. However, far from mandating that states provide treatment, the PRA permits—at state and county discretion—mandatory drug testing of TANF applicants and recipients. This may serve as a deterrent to eligible heads of households from seeking needed benefits. It also stipulates that unless state legislatures pass affirmative legislation to the contrary, anyone convicted of drug-related felonies after August 22,1996, can be denied TANF benefits for life. This includes women of childbearing age or with dependent children.

Studies by the National Center on Addiction and Substance Abuse (CASA) have demonstrated that, like women who are victims of domestic violence, substance-abusing women are largely victims of their own poverty. Although low-income women are less likely to try an illegal drug than high-income women, the low-income women are four times more likely to become addicted when they do (National Center on Addiction and Substance Abuse, 1996). However, the PRA does not require states to finance substance abuse treatment for TANF recipients.

The link between women's alcohol consumption and domestic violence has been well documented. A study by Miller, Downs, and Gondoli (1989) on spousal abuse among alcoholic and nonalcoholic women found that alcoholic women were nine times more likely to be slapped by their husbands, five times more likely to be kicked or hit, five times more likely to be beaten, and four times more likely to have their lives threatened (National Center on Addiction and Substance Abuse, 1996, p. 51).

Although most research has focused on the link between domestic abuse and alcoholism, violence is most lethal when linked to illegal drug use by women. For example, 70% of drug-addicted, low-income pregnant women in methadone treatment programs have been beaten—86% of them by husbands or partners, many of whom are also drug users (National Center on Addiction and Substance Abuse, 1996).

The National Center for Addiction and Substance Abuse designed several projects as a follow-up to its 1994 study, Substance Abuse and Women on Welfare. There are at least three follow-up studies in various stages of planning and implementation. One is intended to study the relationships among the frequency with which a woman cycles on and off welfare, the cumulative length a woman is on welfare, and her patterns of drug and alcohol abuse. The second is a demonstration program to provide welfare recipients with substance abuse, health, employment, and other services through community-based organizations, with the goal of enabling recipients to remain drug free and off welfare. The third is a study of the ways in which states intend to meet the treatment, job training, and health care needs of substance-abusing welfare recipients with dependent children (National Center on Addiction and Substance Abuse, 1995). Incorporated into planned demonstration project models are social work interventions intended to address domestic violence experienced by participants (M. Nakashian, personal communication, March 4, 1997).

New York State Senator Catherine Abate has identified a relationship between domestic violence and drug-related felony convictions for women. She cites surveys of the prison population that found some women convicted on drug-related charges are coerced into drug dealing by abusive partners (G. Sharwin, personal communication, August 13, 1997). As noted, the PRA eliminates access to TANF benefits and food stamps for life for anyone with a drug-related felony conviction, unless states pass affirmative legislation to the contrary.

IMMIGRANTS, WELFARE, AND DOMESTIC VIOLENCE

The federal welfare reform act of 1996 (PRWORA) dramatically revamped the welfare system, turning it into a block grant program run by the states, imposing new, stricter work requirements and setting a 5-year lifetime limit on benefit receipt. For immigrants, the law did all that and much more. In a major departure from previous policy, the law sharply curtailed noncitizens' eligibility for welfare and other major federal benefits.

The PRA eliminates access to TANF, food stamps, and Medicaid for many legal immigrants. Battered immigrant women—both legal and nondocumented—face all the problems that citizen victims of domestic violence face, and more besides. In addition to the loss of home and income, they may also face ostracism and stigmatization from families and communities when they attempt to leave battering spouses. However, not to leave is to risk losing their children to the child welfare system if the children are found to be at risk due to the domestic violence in the household. Some states, such as New Jersey, have restored some benefits to the legal immigrant community using state tax levy funds. This remains an important advocacy issue in states that have not yet submitted their state plans for use of the TANF block grant.

Tumlin and Zimmerman's (2003) key findings include the following:

- Despite declining use of welfare nationally, immigrants and limited English speakers still make up a significant share of those on the welfare rolls. Immigrants compose around one-third of the TANF caseload in California and New York and nearly one-fifth in Texas.
- Many immigrants remaining on the rolls have significant barriers to work, including lower education levels and less work history than natives.
- Immigrants on TANF are less likely to be working than natives and more likely to be working in occupations that provide little opportunity for speaking English, gaining skills, and achieving self-sufficiency.
- PRWORA's strict work requirements limited opportunities for states to provide education and training to welfare recipients, including language training to limited English speakers. In addition, the work-first norm embodied in welfare reform and embraced by the states meant that states did not use the opportunities that remained available to provide language and other training programs.
- Many job-training programs have English-language requirements, which limit access for immigrants who do not speak English well.
- Proposed TANF reforms increasing the number of required hours of work and limiting the types of activities that count as

work will make it even more difficult for immigrant and limited-English-speaking welfare recipients to receive language or vocational training.

- Combining an emphasis on employment with opportunities for developing skills—a strategy supported by recent research on all welfare recipients—could be an especially effective model for limited English speakers, who could combine part-time work with language training. Proposed increases to work participation requirements would make it more difficult for states to pursue these types of strategies.

SUMMARY

Most studies of families who left welfare in the 1990s found that a majority of welfare leavers found jobs. More recent research shows a decline in the share of welfare leavers with jobs and an increase in "disconnected" leavers who do not have income from work or welfare.

- **Recent studies show that families that left welfare recently (2000 or later) are less likely to be working than families that left welfare in the 1990s.** A recent Urban Institute report shows that the proportion of families that leave welfare and are not employed rose from 50% in 1999 to 58% in 2002 (Loprest, 2003). Similarly, a recent study of welfare leavers in Cuyahoga County, Ohio (Cleveland), found that employment rates for families leaving welfare were relatively constant between 1998 and 2000 but have fallen steadily since 2001 (Colton, Bania, Martin, & Lalich, 2003). In New York City, the job placement rate of public assistance recipients has declined markedly between 2000 and 2003, even though the city continues to engage a very high percentage of welfare recipients in welfare-to-work activities (New York City Human Resources Administration, 2004).
- **The share of families that leave welfare and are not working and do not have another stable source of support has increased.** A recent study by the Urban Institute shows that the share of leavers who were "disconnected"—leavers who were not working, did not have a working spouse, and were not receiving TANF or SSI—rose from 9.8% in 1999 to 13.8% in 2002 (Loprest, 2003).

- **"Disconnected" welfare leavers faced significant barriers to employment and difficulty making ends meet.** Disconnected leavers are significantly more likely to have health problems, less likely to have completed high school, and more likely to have been jobless in the past 3 years (Loprest, 2003). Nearly two-thirds of disconnected leavers reported running out of money to buy food.
- **A New Jersey study of TANF leavers who do not have jobs found that about 40% of these jobless leavers have not worked recently, do not receive SSI or unemployment benefits, and do not live with an employed spouse or parent.** Almost one in five of these "least stable" leavers experienced hunger in the past year, and two-thirds say that they are "barely making it from day to day" (Wood & Rangarajan, 2003).
- **The overall unemployment rate of low-income single mothers increased from 9.8% in 2000 to 12.3% in 2002.** After decreasing at a faster rate than the unemployment rate for the overall population in the last half of the 1990s, low-income single mothers' unemployment rate *increased at a faster rate* between 2000 and 2002 than the national unemployment rate (Chapman & Bernstein, 2003).

IMPLICATIONS FOR SOCIAL WORK PRACTICE

The interest and involvement of the National Association of Social Workers (NASW) in welfare reform is very much rooted in the mission and core values of the social work profession. These core values, which include social justice and belief in the dignity and worth of each person, have been embraced by social workers throughout the profession's history and are the foundation of social work's purpose and perspective. (NASW, November 30, 2001, Cynthia Woodside, Senior Government Relations Associate, Government Relations and Political Action)

With the passage of the new National Association of Social Workers Code of Ethics in 1996 (NASW, 1996), the mandate for social workers to advocate for policies that benefit clients is significantly strengthened. Social workers, who are experts in the interactions between people and their environments, are more attuned than most to the implications of irresponsible public policies such as the Personal Responsibility and Work Opportunity Reconciliation Act of 1996.

Clinicians who work with battered women and their families, victims of incest and child abuse, substance abusers struggling with feelings of powerlessness, and families without homes or dependable sources of income know the toll these social pressures take on the health and mental health of family members and their ability to remain together in the community. As noted by Belle (1990, p. 388): "Poverty is a complex phenomenon, with wide-ranging implications for the well-being of individuals. Future research [and practice] must build connections to therapies and public policies designed for poor women. The tragically increasing prevalence of poverty among women [and children] gives these issues particular urgency."

Women and children receiving public assistance are by definition poor. Public policy that mandates work for TANF recipients without consideration of circumstances that may limit achieving this goal—such as domestic violence—can only doom large numbers of women and children to a Hobson's choice of life-threatening abuse or life-threatening destitution.

There is another alternative. A coherent national family policy to include social supports like adequate housing, child care, job training and development, and guaranteed jobs, as well as workplace security and effective intervention programs for domestic violence victims and batterers, could go a long way to breaking the link between poverty and domestic abuse. Finally, more practice research is needed into the dynamics of domestic violence—including interventions that prove successful and the time and supports needed to ensure their success. Social workers have the expertise, as well as the ethical obligation, to inform and shape enlightened public policy that severs, not tightens, the link between family abuse and poverty.

REFERENCES

Addams, J. (1911). *Twenty years at Hull House.* New York: Macmillan.
Addams, J. (1995). *The social work dictionary* (3rd ed.). Washington, DC: NASW Press.
Bartol, C. R., & Bartol, A. M. (2004). *Introduction to forensic psychology.* Thousand Oaks, CA: Sage.

Belle, D. (1990). Poverty and women's mental health. *American Psychologist,* *45,* 385–388.

Belluck, P. (1997, March 31). Women's killers are very often their partners, a study finds. *The New York Times,* p. B1.

Bowker, L. B. (n.d.). *Domestic violence: The shameful facts.* Trenton, NJ: State of New Jersey, Department of Community Affairs, New Jersey Division on Women.

Brace, C. L. (1872). *The dangerous classes of New Yom and twenty years' work among them.* New York: Wynkoop & Hallenbeck. Reprinted by NASW Classic Series.

Brandwein, R. (1996, May). *Family violence and welfare reform: What are the links?* Proceedings from the National Invitational Symposium Sponsored by the University of Utah Graduate School of Social Work, Salt Lake City, UT.

Brandwein, R. (1997, January 23). *Statement Presented to New York State Assembly Standing Committee on Ways and Means, Assembly Standing Committee on Social Services and Assembly Standing Committee on Children and Families on Behalf of NASW New York State Chapter.*

Browne, A. (1998). Responding to the needs of low income and homeless women who are survivors of family violence. *Journal of American Medical Women's Association, 53*(2), 57–64.

Brownell, P. (1996). Domestic violence in the workplace: An emergent issue. *Crisis Intervention, 3,* 129–141.

Bureau of Justice Statistics Crime Data Brief. (2003). *Intimate partner violence,* 1993–2001, February.

Burgess, A. W., & Roberts, A. R. (1996). Family violence against women and children: Prevalence of assaults and fatalities, family dynamics, and interventions. *Crisis Intervention, 3,* 65–80.

Califano, J. A. (1996, August 24). Welfare's drug connection. *The New York Times,* p. A23.

Center for Impact Research. (2002). Retrieved on July 14, 2006, from http://www.impactresearch.org/.

Chapman, J., & Bernstein, J. (2003). *Falling through the safety net: Low-income single mothers in the jobless recovery.* Washington, DC: Economic Policy Institute.

Colton, C., Bania, N., Martin, T., & Lalich, M (2003). *How are they managing? A retrospective of Cuyahoga County families leaving welfare.* Center on Urban Poverty and Social Change, Case Western Reserve University.

Communication Workers of America. (2006). Retrieved July 21, 2006, from http://www.cwa-legislative.org/ and http://www.cwa-governmentaffairs.org/.

Estess, C. L., & Weiner, J. M. (2001). *Social policy and aging: A critical perspective.* Thousand Oaks, CA: Sage.

Family Violence Prevention Fund. (2006). Retrieved July 21, 2006, from http://endabuse.org.

Gillespie, E., & Schellhas, B. (Eds.). (1994). *Contract with America.* New York: Times Books.

Gonnerman, J. (1997a, January 28). The judge of abuse. *Village Voice,* p. 28.

Gonnerman, J. (1997b, March 10). Welfare's domestic violence. *The Nation,* pp. 21–23.

Gordon, L. (1988). What does welfare regulate? *Social Research, 55*(4), 609–630.

Hardeman, J. (1995, October). *Domestic violence in the workplace.* Conference sponsored by the Human Resources Administration, New York.

Harwood, J. (1997, January 30). Think tanks battle to judge the impact of welfare overhaul. *The Wall Street Journal,* p. A1.

Horn, P. (1994). Creating a just economy will reduce violence against women. In K. L. Swisher & C. Wekisser (Eds.), *Violence against women* (pp. 182–188). San Diego, CA: Greenhaven.

Jensen, R. H. (1995, July/August). *Welfare.* Unpublished manuscript, p. 56.

Kenney, C. T., & Brown, K. R. (1996). *Report from the front lines: The impact of violence on poor women.* New York: NOW Legal and Educational Defense Fund.

Kilborn, P. T. (1996, November 30). Shrinking safety net cradles hearts and hopes of children. *The New York Times,* p. A1.

Krauss, C. (1996, November 2). Man fatally shoots his wife in her Manhattan office. *The New York Times,* p. 27.

Lawrence, S. (2002). Domestic violence and welfare policy. Columbia University, Mailman School of Public Health. Retrieved July 5, 2002, from http://72.14.209.104/search?q=cache:ZrPco1-JPaUJ:www.researchforum.org/media/DomVio.pdf+correlation+between+poverty+and+domestic+violenc e&hl=en&gl=us&ct=clnk&cd=8.

Loprest, P. (2003). *Disconnected welfare leavers face serious risks.* Washington, DC: Urban Institute.

Loyd, S. (1997). Retrieved July 16, 2006, from http://www.northwestern.edu/ipr/publications/nupr/nuprv03n1/lloyd.html.

Lyon, E. (2000). Welfare, poverty and abused women: New research and its implications. Policy and Practice Paper #10. *Building Comprehensive Solutions to Domestic Violence.* National Resource Center on Domestic Violence. Harrisburg, PA. Retrieved July 21, 2006, from http://www.vawnet.org/DomesticViolence/Research/VAWnetDocs/AR_Welfare2.php.

Miller, B. A., Downs, W. R., & Gondoli, D. M. (1989). Spousal violence among alcoholic women as compared to a random household sample of women. *Journal of Studies on Alcohol, 50,* 533–540.

National Association of Social Workers. (1996). *NASW code of ethics.* Washington, DC: Author.

National Association of Social Workers. (1997a). States eye domestic abuse welfare option. *NASW News, 42,* 3.

National Association of Social Workers, New York State Chapter. (1997b). *Testimony to the New York State Assembly from NASW Welfare Reform Response Network by Dr. Ruth Brandwein, Chair,* January 23, 1997.

National Center on Addiction and Substance Abuse at Columbia University. (1994). *Substance abuse and women on welfare.* New York: Columbia University.

National Center on Addiction and Substance Abuse. (1995). *Annual report.* New York: Columbia University.

National Center on Addiction and Substance Abuse. (1996). *Substance abuse and the American woman.* New York: Columbia University.

National Organization for Women. (2004). *Truth-telling about welfare: As Senate votes to temporarily extend TANF, expert panel advises lawmakers to address challenges that face low-income women and children.* Retrieved July 23, 2006, from http://www.now.org/issues/economic/welfare/072604tanf.html.

Navarro, M. (1996, October 31). Teen-age mothers viewed as abused prey of older men. *The New York Times,* p. A1.

New York City Human Resources Administration, Office of Program Reporting, Analysis, and Accountability. Job Placements (FA & SNA): Trend; % Change from Previous Month; % Change from Previous Year. January 2004.

Newton, C. J. (2001, February). *Domestic violence: An overview.* TherapistFinder.net Mental Health Journal. Retrieved July 3, 2006, from (http://www.therapistfinder.net/journal/)

Pleck, E. (1987). *Domestic tyranny: The making of American social policy against family violence from colonial times to the present.* New York: Oxford University Press.

Quadagno, J. (1990). Race, class, and gender in the US welfare state: Nixon's failed Family Assistance Plan. *American Sociological Review, 55,* 11.

Raphael, J. (1995). *Domestic violence: Telling the untold welfare to work story.* Chicago: Taylor Institute.

Raphael, J. (1996). *Prisoners of abuse: Domestic violence and welfare receipt.* Chicago: Taylor Institute.

Roberts, A. R., & Roberts, B. (2005). *Ending intimate abuse: Practical guidance and survival strategies.* New York: Oxford University Press.

Schechter, S. (1982). *Women and male violence: The visions and struggles of the battered women's movement.* Boston: South End Press.

Shepard, M., & Pence, E. (1988). The effect of battering on the employment status of women. *Affilia, 3,* 55–61.

Swarns, R. (1997, March 29). Welfare family advocates, once allies, become rivals. *The New York Times,* p. AI.

Tumlin, K., & Zimmerman, W. (2003). *A look at immigrant welfare recipients in three cities.* Retrieved July 6, 2006, from http://www.urban.org/publications/310874.html.

Uchitelle, L. (1997, January 5). The shift toward self-reliance in the welfare system. *The New York Times,* p. A15.

U.S. Department of Housing and Urban Development, Division of Policy Studies. (1988). *Report on the 1988 National Survey of Shelters for the Homeless.* Washington, DC: Author.

U.S. Department of Labor. (1996). *Guidelines for preventing workplace violence for health care and social service workers-OSHA* 3148–199. Washington, DC: Occupational Safety and Health Administration.

U.S. House of Representatives, Committee on Ways and Means. (1991). *Green book.* Washington, DC: U.S. Government Printing Office.

U.S. House of Representatives, Committee on Ways and Means. (1992). *Green book.* Washington, DC: U.S. Government Printing Office.

U.S. House of Representatives, Committee on Ways and Means. (1996). *Green book.* Washington, DC: U.S. Government Printing Office.

van De Bergh, N. (1991). *Feminist perspectives on addictions.* New York: Springer.

Weinstein, H. E. (1997, February 10). Weinstein calls on governor to protect domestic violence victims from potentially dangerous welfare requirements and urges full adoption of Wellstone/Murray. *News from Assemblywoman Helene E. Weinstein,* pp. 1–2.

Women Fighting Poverty. (1996, March 16). *Organizing for economic justice* (Miriam Friedlander, Chair). New York.

Wood, Robert, & Anu Rangarajan. (2003). *What's happening to TANF leavers who are not employed? Trends in welfare-to-work.* Mathematica Policy Research, Issue Brief # 6. Retrieved from http://www.mathematica-mpr.com/publications/PDFs/tanfleave.pdf.

Zorza, J. (1991). Women battering: A major cause of homelessness. *Clearing House Review, 25,* 421–429.

CHAPTER 18

Same-Sex Domestic Violence:
Myths, Facts, Correlates, Treatment, and Prevention Strategies

Nicky Ali Jackson

Same-sex domestic violence is a relatively new area of study. In general, there has been ongoing silence among researchers, victims, and society about gay and lesbian intimate violence. This silence has led to ignorance and misunderstanding within academic and social circles. Historically, domestic violence research focused on traditional heterosexual relationships. Public interest in domestic violence is apparent as the media showcases these incidents, particularly those cases that also involve infidelity. As expected, sex and murder are key ingredients in drawing the public's attention. Nevertheless, little attention has been given to homosexual battering. The extremely limited amount of research on same-sex domestic violence has focused "on one segment of the population, such as lesbians, rather than on the entire gay community" (Kuehnle & Sullivan, 2003, p. 87). Part of the reluctance to examine same-sex domestic violence is related not only to heterosexual ignorance but also to the homosexual community. Gay and lesbian leaders were

451

afraid that recognition of same-sex battering would be used by a homophobic society to further condemn homosexuality (Sullivan and Kuehnle, in press). It is difficult, if not impossible, for many gays and lesbians to recognize abuse taking place within their own relationships (Island & Letellier, 1991). Due to fear of retaliation, gays and lesbians may live very secretive lives. This makes it difficult to assess the true incidence and prevalence of same-sex battering. Obtaining accurate statistics on same-sex domestic violence is also problematic, in that domestic violence, in general, is highly underreported. Victims may not want to report the abuse or may not even recognize that abuse is occurring. Researchers and the media have focused more heavily on "gay bashing" than on gay and lesbian intimate partner violence. As with their heterosexual counterparts, gays and lesbians are more likely to be injured by someone they know than by a stranger. Although difficult to assess accurate domestic violence statistics, it is estimated that the rate of intimate assault among homosexual couples is the same as their heterosexual counterparts (NCAVP, 2003). Studies are continuously in debate over whether domestic violence is equally perpetrated by males and females. Through the National Coalition on Anti-Violence Programs (NCAVP) report, it appears that domestic violence is not a gender-specific problem, even though society continues to perceive women as passive and men as aggressive. In a recent study by Seelau and Seelau (2005), undergraduate participants reported that domestic violence perpetrated by women was less serious than those assaults perpetrated by males. Moreover, they found that respondents believed that assaults against males were less serious than assaults against females. Their study reveals the traditional images of males as aggressive and females as submissive. Same-sex battering injures gays and lesbians alike. The victim's gender does not lessen the severity of the injuries, nor does the perpetrator's gender increase the severity of the injuries. Tjaden and Thoennes (2000) reported a difference in gender perpetration in that males are more likely to assault their partners, whether in a same-sex or straight relationship. Their study, consistent with the Seelau and Seelau's findings, continue to support the ideology that males are more aggressive than females. Regardless of whether one gender is more prone than the other to committing violence, research must continue to explore all facets of same-sex battering in order to assist all victims of homosexual battering.

WHAT IS SAME-SEX DOMESTIC VIOLENCE?

To address same-sex domestic violence, defining the term *same-sex* is essential. Same-sex is synonymous with homosexual. This chapter recognizes two forms of homosexual relationships: gay and lesbian. *Homosexuality* is defined as a sexual attraction to a member of one's own sex. *Homosexual* refers to someone who practices homosexuality. *Gay* refers to a homosexual male and *lesbian* refers to a homosexual female. Although these definitions are fairly simplistic, their interpretations are debatable. Members of the homosexual community often do not share similar definitions of these terms. Nonetheless, these definitions, although broad, are widely accepted. As noted earlier, the terms domestic violence and intimate violence are often used interchangeably. A more recent term utilized by researchers is *intimate partner violence* (IPV). There is no one single definition of domestic violence, particularly addressing same-sex domestic violence. Nonetheless, the following is an appropriate working definition of homosexual domestic violence: Any unwanted physical, psychological/emotional, verbal, sexual, or material damage inflicted by one person against his or her intimate partner.

Physical, psychological, verbal, or material abuse may occur simultaneously or independently. According to the forefathers in family violence research, Murray Straus and Richard Gelles (1990, p. 76), "[v]iolence is defined as an act carried out with the intention, or perceived intention, of causing physical pain or injury to another person." Drawing from their Conflict Tactics Scale (CTS), behaviors that are considered physically abusive include: (a) throwing something; (b) pushing or grabbing; (c) slapping; (d) kicking, biting, or hitting; (e) beating; (f) choking; and (g) using a knife or gun. Psychological abuse is also referred to as emotional abuse. This type of abuse may not leave physical scars, yet its effects are just as damaging as physical abuse. There is shared belief by victims and perpetrators that the initial acts of aggression are "soft forms" of abuse in that there is no real danger. All forms of abuse are equally potent. It has been suggested that emotional injury will occur once physical battering has been perpetrated upon the victim (Walker, 1979). Clearly, emotional abuse is present with the onset of physical battering. Nevertheless, they may exist independently. Emotional abuse is more difficult to identify than physical abuse. As a result, it appears to be "noninjurious" to the victim. Furthermore, due to its lack of visibility,

victims, offenders, and criminal justice agencies are often unaware
of the existing damage.

Emotional abuse is defined as any form of mistreatment, including (a) neglect, (b) threats, (c) withholding love and affection, (d)
staying away from her lover for any unanticipated time, (e) humiliation, and (f) manipulation. A common type of emotional abuse
is seen in forms of threatening behavior. These include threats to
(a) leave her, (b) hit her, (c) cut off her funds, and (d) kill her.
One unique form of psychological abuse experienced by same-sex
couples but not by heterosexual couples is the threat of "outing."
Outing is the nonconsensual disclosing of one's sexual orientation.
Another form of psychological abuse is when the batterer threatens
to harm the victim's children or other family members. The goal is
to keep the victim in a passive, frightened position leaving the batterer in control. Verbal abuse also results in psychological harm. Insults, name-calling, screaming, and swearing aim at hurting someone.
These verbally assaultive behaviors result in psychological injury. The
aggressive partner uses these techniques as a method of control and
intimidation.

Sexual abuse is the "most understudied topic in same-sex domestic violence" (Elliott, in Renzetti & Miley, 1996, p. 4). One explanation for this is the sensitivity of the subject matter. It is difficult
enough for heterosexual women and even more difficult for heterosexual males to disclose sexual victimization, so imagine the fear
lesbians and gay males face sharing similar personal information
to a homophobic society or their own community in denial. Sexual abuse occurs in many forms. An individual forcing his or her
partner into unwanted sexual activity (i.e., oral sex, fondling, or
penetration) is in fact engaging in deviant sexual conduct. Unfortunately, most states do not recognize same-sex rape. Other types
of sexual abuse include withholding sex as a form of punishment,
making negative comments about his or her partner's physical appearance or sexual performance, and forcing his or her partner
to watch or engage in pornographic materials. Another form of
psychological terror occurs in the form of material abuse. *Material abuse* is destroying the victim's property or keeping the victim
away from financial or other resources. Whether the injurious act
is physical, emotional/verbal, sexual, or material, its roots are the
same—power. The perpetrator hungers for power over his or her
victim.

SAME-SEX DOMESTIC VIOLENCE MYTHS

The heterosexual world has given little consideration to gays and lesbians. Although there is greater publicity surrounding gay and lesbian couples, particularly the issue of legal marriage and adoption, there remains little understanding about homosexual relationships. Lack of knowledge results in misperceptions and continued ignorance, as well as perpetuating homophobia. The following are some of the most prevalent myths about same-sex domestic violence:

Myth: Violence between two men or two women is a fight between equals.

Fact: Domestic violence is not a consensual fight; it is about control and power. Irrespective of gender, the abuser has the control/power and the victim remains powerless.

Myth: Battering only occurs against heterosexual women by men.

Fact: Battering may occur against any person, regardless of race, gender, or socioeconomic status. Violence knows no boundaries. Perpetration and victimization cannot be determined by one's gender. Males and females can be victimized as well as be abusive.

Myth: If a victim fights back, then it's not abuse.

Fact: Fighting back may be a safety precaution. It is not equivalent to "mutual battering." For the victim to be safe, he or she may have to use force to defend himself/herself.

Myth: Victims exaggerate the abuse. If the abuse was that bad, they'd leave!

Fact: There are many reasons victims do not exit a violent relationship. This does not minimize the abuse or suggest the acceptance of the abuse. Leaving isn't always the answer to solving the abuse.

Myth: It is easier for gays and lesbians to exit a violent relationship.

Fact: It is just as difficult, if not more difficult, for homosexual victims to exit an abusive relationship as it is for straight victims. Oftentimes, gays and lesbians feel it is their fault for the abuse because they may consider themselves "abnormal." This attitude creates guilt and self-blame for their victimization. In addition, gay and lesbian couples may have children, which makes it extremely difficult to leave the relationship. Their recourse is more limited than for heterosexual couples, resulting in greater difficulty in breaking off the relationship.

Myth: Homosexual sexual violence is a form of sadomasochism (S & M).

Fact: Sexual violence is not a joke. Victims do not enjoy the assault. Rather, they are left confused and abused. One's sexual orientation does not dictate sexual domination. Simply put, being gay or lesbian does not suggest that he/she enjoys sexual domination/submission.

Myth: Abusers are physically superior to their victims.

Fact: Size does not cause abuse nor does it determine who the abuser is. Abusers come in all shapes and sizes. Domestic violence is not about physical strength; it is about power and control. Therefore, when there is unequal distribution of power, the partner with the greatest level of control is more likely to be abusive.

CORRELATES/THEORETICAL PERSPECTIVES OF ABUSE

The correlates of same-sex domestic violence are similar to those of their heterosexual counterparts. So, what influences a gay or lesbian to batter his or her lover? It is important to understand that there is no one single factor that causes an individual to batter. Rather, there are factors that may influence one's behavior. Social scientists agree that an individual cannot cause certain behavior nor can any factor cause someone to behave violently. Rather, there may be a relationship between or among two or more variables working together that increases the probability of perpetration and victimization. Theoretical perspectives attempt to help explain a particular behavior such as intimate partner violence.

Intergenerational Transfer/Transmission

Researchers often turn to the possibility that violence is learned by children through watching their parents. This is referred to as *intergenerational transfer* or *intergenerational transmission*. This theory argues that living in a violent home increases the probability that an individual will grow up to be violent toward future family members or more likely to fall victim at the hands of his or her partner. The family may actually serve as a breeding ground for violent behavior. The teaching of violence occurs mostly without such an intention. Children learn many lessons in relation to physical violence. Straus (1979) outlines several unintentional lessons learned:

1. Those who love you the most are also those who hit you.
2. Violence can be and should be used to secure positive ends: This reinforces the moral rightness of violence.
3. Violence is permissible when other things don't work.

Thus, people learn to associate love with violence and to believe that, at times, violence may be necessary. Violence is not innate; it is learned through socialization. "Aggressive behavior is learned and is acquired through direct experience (trial and error), by observing the behavior of others (modeling) or in both ways" (Straus & Gelles, 1990, p. 441). Regardless of sexual orientation, children who grew up in violent homes are more vulnerable to engaging in violence in their intimate relationships. Homosexuals are not immune from learning aggressive behavior. They too observe that violence is rewarded and are more likely to be abusive if they grew up in violent households. Research has also suggested that a "double-whammy" effect occurs among those who have witnessed and experienced domestic violence during childhood. Children who have experienced *and* witnessed domestic violence were more likely to be victims and/or perpetrators of violence in their future relationships than those who either witnessed *or* experienced domestic violence.

Substance Abuse

There appears to be a very strong relationship between alcohol/drugs and domestic violence. Do not confuse this with the argument that someone's alcoholism or drug addiction caused the violence. Rather, alcohol and drug usage may stimulate an already-volatile temper. It is imperative to note that domestic violence and substance abuse are two serious independent health matters requiring much needed attention. Drinking and using drugs reduces one's inhibitions, which may trigger a violent episode. This does not suggest that alcoholics or substance abusers are batterers, nor does it suggest that batterers are alcoholics or drug abusers. Studies have shown that there are batterers who are not drunk or high at the time of the assault. Thus, substance abuse may increase the probability for a violent outburst; however, it does not cause the violence. Substance abuse is a leading health problem among gay males. It is also prevalent among lesbians. This can best be explained by first looking at gay and lesbian communities. It is common to have bars and other late-night establishments within homosexual neighborhoods. The readily available alcohol increases the likelihood for abuse. In addition, gays and lesbians are often isolated from others, leading to alcohol serving as a social substitute.

Animal Abuse

Violence against animals has been linked to domestic violence. Evidence suggests that when a batterer mutilates or injures a pet, he is more likely to kill his partner (Meuer, Seymour, & Wallace, 2002). Children who commit violent acts against animals are more likely to engage in adult violence. Cruelty to animals is often a strong warning sign that violence will escalate.

Dependency

There appears to be a codependent relationship among abusers and intimate violence victims. This is exacerbated in homosexual relationships due to their separation from mainstream society. When individuals are separated from society, resentment and anger are directed toward the cause of their isolation: being a homosexual in a homophobic society. This isolation creates greater dependency among one's partner, resulting in a potentially dangerous situation.

The Cycle Theory of Violence

Research suggests that a cyclical pattern of abuse occurs in domestic violence relationships. Lenore Walker formulated the cycle theory of violence to help explain the patterns of a violent relationship. Walker's theory, although primarily design to explain heterosexual domestic violence, may be applied to same-sex domestic violence.

The cycle of violence has three stages or phases: the tension-building stage, the acute battering stage, and the honeymoon stage. The first phase is referred to as the *tension-building* stage. During this phase, certain events may occur that increase tension within the relationship. Examples of such events include loss of a job, demotion at a job, loss of a loved one, perception of infidelity, and so forth. At this stage, there may be some minor battering of the victim at which time the victim may simply try to avoid contact with the batterer in hopes of avoiding conflict. The second phase is called the *acute battering* or *explosive stage*. During this stage, the abuser loses control, and the assault takes place. The assault is not like what may have occurred in the tension-building phase. Rather, it is severe and explosive. After the attack, both victim and abuser are left in shock and disbelief. This leads to the third phase of the cycle theory of violence: the *honeymoon stage*. During the honeymoon stage, the abuser attempts to demonstrate loving and kind behavior toward the victim. Flowers may be sent, and forgiveness is begged with the promise that this will never happen again. These unrealistic promises and acts eventually subside, leading back to the first phase.

The Culture of Violence Theory

This theory argues that there is widespread acceptance of violence within society. Violence is not only acceptable within society; it is a legitimate means to solve disputes among individuals. This holds particularly true within familial relationships. The culture of violence perpetuates the belief that it is reasonable to use violence to settle arguments among couples and legitimizes the idea that violence is a part of normal conflict resolution.

Deterrence Theory

The major proponents of deterrence is that swift, certain, and severe punishments will scare a potential offender from committing violence. This theory argues that an individual will refrain from criminal activity due to fear of sanctions. When sanctions are minimal and uncertain, individuals have little fear of getting caught. For homosexual couples, this theory is logical in explaining same-sex domestic violence. Specifically, domestic violence laws are designed to protect heterosexual couples while often ignoring homosexual relationships. Policymakers have yet to create specific laws to protect gays and lesbians in violent relationships. As such, police are reluctant to "get involved" in these types of domestic disputes. It is, therefore, obvious that when laws are nonexistent or minimally set, that abusers will have free reign to terrorize their victims.

PROFILING OFFENDERS AND VICTIMS

There are certain characteristics a person possesses that increase his or her likelihood of perpetration and victimization. Profiling serves as a guideline; it is not definitive. Offenders and victims may share all or none of the identifiable traits. However, recognizing certain traits related to lesbian battering enables us to understand vulnerability as well as prevention. So, who are the offenders and their victims?

Abuse cuts across all racial, ethnic, socioeconomic, religious, age, and gender groups. However, certain individuals are more vulnerable than others. The following serves as an outline of offender characteristics:

1. Those with greater economic, social, and personal power. They ultimately have the ability to control their victim through threats of denying resources.
2. Those who display severe bouts of jealousy and possessiveness. The abuser, out of fear of loss of control, attempts to isolate his or her lover from his or her family and friends. A narcissist, the abuser craves full attention from his or her partner.
3. Those who experience or observe childhood victimization. They learned in order to gain compliance, physical and emotional injury may be necessary.
4. Those who suffer low self-esteem. Individuals who feel a sense of powerlessness and failure may project their own inward anger and frustration onto those they care for the most—their lovers.
5. Those who suffer a job loss or other stressful event. Stress does not cause the actual acute battering incident; rather it stimulates it. A major loss in one's life may result in anger and a sense of futility. Hopelessness may lead to atypical behavior. The abuser

wants his or her partner to suffer as he or she is; this results in a temporary feeling of control.

6. Those who overconsume alcohol or drugs. Recall, substance abuse does not cause violence. It acts as an appropriate defense against inappropriate behavior. People engage, all too often, in fantasy rather than reality. They use the alcohol and drugs as a method of escaping culpability.

Just as batterers share certain qualities, victims also possess characteristics that place them at risk. Profiling victim characteristics does not suggest victims are to blame for their own victimization; it only serves as a method of better understanding who is in potential danger. The following are traits that increase the likelihood of same-sex victimization:

1. Those who feel a sense of powerlessness. They believe they have no control over their lives.
2. Those who experienced or observed childhood victimization. Childhood exposures to violence teach children it is acceptable for the dominant members of the household to utilize physical and emotional sanctions in order to gain compliance.
3. Those who suffer from low self-esteem. They believe that they deserve to be punished; if they had some value then there would be no reason for bad things to happen to them.
4. Those who are economically and socially dependent on their partners. These victims rely heavily on their lovers to provide resources and companionship. Often, this leads to isolation and despair.

Victimization is a process. Where there is physical violence, there are events leading to the actual battering incident. In situations of emotional abuse, there is a pattern of inappropriate behavior. For example, a lover who calls his or her partner "stupid" will repeatedly demean and humiliate the victim. It is not an isolated occurrence. Gay and lesbian victims, as with their heterosexual counterparts, suffer greatly from physical, emotional and sexual abuse. "[B]attered lesbians experience nightmares, brief dissassociative episodes, and excessive fear in situations that trigger an association to the abuse" (Hammond, in Rothblum & Cole, 1989, p. 91). Victims also suffer from shame, helplessness, guilt, social withdrawal, sleep disorders, eating disorders, and anxiety.

Physical and psychological injury lasts for years, often a lifetime. The long-term effects can be devastating. If a victim does escape the abusive relationship, it will be extremely difficult to learn to trust again, damaging potential future intimate relationships. For this reason, it is essential that the victim receives assistance to cope with his or her victimization. In addition, the abuser must seek out help to understand and recognize abusive behavior.

WHY DO *VICTIMS* REMAIN IN THESE *ABUSIVE RELATIONSHIPS*?

It is difficult to understand why a domestic violence victim would stay with his or her partner. By staying in a violent relationship, it is wrongly assumed that the abuse is imaginary or overexaggerated. At times, it is also believed that the victim must "enjoy" the abuse. These misperceptions need to be corrected, and the reasons victims stay in violent relationships must be addressed. There are many reasons why gays and lesbians remain in abusive relationships: (a) Not recognizing abuse—victims may not be cognizant that certain behaviors are abusive. For example, a victim may believe that screaming and threatening is a normal part of a relationship. They may believe that only physical injuries that require medical attention are abusive. (b) Denial—victims may pretend that the abuse didn't occur or that it "wasn't a big deal." (c) Victim-blaming—victims may buy into the argument that it was his or her fault for the abuse. Oftentimes, the batterer will state that if the victim hadn't provoked the abuser, the abuse would not have occurred, leaving the victim feeling guilty for provoking such an attack. (d) Fear of future abuse—victims may stay in abusive relationships because they fear that the batterer will find them and the "punishment" will be far worse. (e) Loyalty—some victims believe that as a partner they must "stand by their mate" even when times are tough. (f) Fear of loneliness—victims are often told that "no one else will want you" by the abuser. This form of emotional abuse leaves the victim with continued low self-esteem and the belief that no other person would want them. Therefore, they stay in the relationship due to fear of being alone. (g) Belief that the batterer will change—victims may believe that when things get better (i.e., increased financial security, improved health) the abuse will stop. It is necessary to understand that hardships do not cause the abuse; rather they may help stimulate it. (h) Financial dependency—there remains some controversy regarding financial dependence as an explanation for remaining in a gay or lesbian relationship. Some believe that gay and lesbian relationships are similar to their heterosexual counterparts, in that whoever "brings home the bacon" is the breadwinner and the person with the greatest control in the relationship. Others believe that gay men have greater financial independence because men are more likely to earn a higher salary than females and, more importantly, males are more likely to be employed than females. Moreover, gay males are less likely to have children than heterosexual or lesbian couples; therefore, they have greater financial freedom than couples with children. Regardless of which argument appears attractive, victims may stay in an abusive relationship out of fear of losing economic stability. (i) Physical attraction—victims may find their partner to be so physically and sexually attractive that they stay in the abusive relationship. This attraction is not to be confused with love. (j) Love—it is difficult to believe that one could love the person who hurts them. Victims do love their partners. They fell in love with their partner for certain reasons, and abuse doesn't change those reasons. Perpetrators are not abusive all of the time; thus, the victim focuses on the tender moments rather than the volatile times. (k) Gender socialization—men are taught to be "tough" and "take it like a man." For gay males, this machismo attitude discourages them from leaving violent relationships. They have been taught throughout their lives to be tough and handle situations "as a man." (l) HIV/AIDS—victims may feel that if they do not stay with their infected partner, the abuser may withhold necessary medication, resulting in casualty. In addition, victims may not want to abandon their partners during this time. Infected victims may have a fear of dying alone so they stay with their abuser. They would rather remain in the abusive relationship than face their illness alone. (m) Lack of support—same-sex victims do not have the same resources available to them as their heterosexual counterparts. Shelters have traditionally been reserved for heterosexual battered women. Although rare, some shelters do allow lesbian victims into the facility. Most shelters cannot accommodate male victims of abuse. Few shelters offer limited external housing, that is, motel or apartment;

but for the most part, male victims have extremely limited resources available. In addition, same-sex victims may not know where to turn for help. Typically, gay and lesbian communities do not want to recognize abuse is taking place within their own communities; therefore, they do not develop safe houses for same-sex domestic violence victims. (n) Legal obstacles—many states narrowly define domestic violence and therefore deny legal protection to homosexual victims. Most states define relationships in terms of heterosexual and not homosexual couples. For this reason, victims may feel helpless forcing them to remain in this unwanted relationship. (o) Outing—abusers may threaten to "out" their partner to family, friends, and/or coworkers. Outing refers to the nonconsensual disclosure of one's sexual orientation. Abusers may tell their partners that if they leave the relationship, they will tell others that the victim is homosexual. Gays and lesbians often are forced to live secretive lives as they encounter a homophobic society. Fear of straight people learning about their homosexuality is frightening enough to keep them in abusive relationships.

PREVENTION AND TREATMENT

In attempts to reduce gay and lesbian battering, it is essential to study homosexuality. To prevent same-sex battering, scholars must focus on the homosexual population. Part of understanding homosexuality is exploring homophobia. How can we know how to prevent and treat same-sex domestic violence when we do not understand the population? The most vital tool in assisting homosexual victims is to recognize their cultural needs and practices. The United States encourages freedom and equality to its members. However, somehow lost in this philosophy are gay and lesbian communities. Americans fear homosexuality. If we let our children play with children of gay parents, surely our children will learn to accept homosexuality, maybe even become gay. These irrational fears stem from misunderstanding and lack of education.

Gay males and lesbians also must take part in helping others understand their culture. Their world is not vastly different from the heterosexual culture; this is what both communities must realize. Gay individuals need to interact with heterosexual men and women. Isolation results in anger and indignation. More importantly, alienation feeds into homophobia. Currently, many gays and lesbians live in areas primarily occupied by other homosexuals. Those who do live and work in heterosexual communities often fear disclosure. It is essential that these individuals feel comfortable in a heterosexual society. Each population must be tolerant and accepting of their differences. Assimilation is necessary in a healthy society. One group should not dominate over another. Ethnocentrism should not be tolerated by either community.

Currently, society has provided greater preventive and treatment programs for women. Although it is essential to have these programs available, males should be granted equal availability of resources. Programs for heterosexual and homosexual male victims lag significantly behind those of females. The rationale for this has been the ideology that women are more likely to be victimized by males. The scholarly debate for this argument continues. Some argue that women are abused at significantly higher rates than males, whereas others argue that men and women are equally abused by their partners. Regardless of which argument is supported, the fact remains that programs must exist for all victims of domestic violence—straight, gay, lesbian, poor, rich, White, Black, male, female, and so forth. Shelters need to be established servicing male clientele with competent counselors. Professionals must be trained in gay and lesbian domestic violence issues. Unfortunately, many social service agencies are trained to focus solely on battered heterosexual women. Gay and lesbian victims are often left to fend for themselves without adequate support. Police departments need sensitivity training and better understanding of homosexual issues. All too often gay male victims report that officers dismissed the abuse took place following the myth that when two boys fight, it's mutual battering. Gay and lesbians are fearful of law enforcement due to perceived homophobia among police officers. They are reluctant to call the police for help when needed for fear of retaliation, humiliation, or nonperformance (failing to act when there is a duty to act).

Same-sex domestic violence victims must turn to an outsider for help. Whomever the victim seeks out for support, whether it is a therapist, psychologist, or clergy, Hammond (1989) outlines nine issues to be addressed during therapy:

1. During intake, ask clients about the abuse. However, do not directly ask them whether they've been abused. Rather, ask questions such as, "Have you ever been afraid of your lover?" This type of question is not perceived as threatening.

2. Assess the extent and severity of abuse. Distinguish between battering and self-defense.
3. Assess violent or abusive incidents carefully if there is a question of mutual battering. Identify the batterer and the victim.
4. Distinguish, to your clients, between abuse and appropriate assertive behavior.
5. Help develop protection plans with clients who face future endangerment.
6. "Offer free or minimal cost support or networking groups for victims." Victims need to interact with other victims.
7. Prior to offering couples counseling, determine the safety of the victim.
8. Be patient and nonjudgmental.
9. Clearly reassure the victim he or she is not to blame for the abuse (in Rothblum and Cole, 1989, pp. 101–103).

Heterosexual therapists must be able to determine any prejudgment they have toward gays and lesbians. Their attitudes impact the process as well as outcome of treatment. Homosexual therapists also carry stereotypes about violence in the gay and lesbian community. They may unintentionally deny the nature and extent of the problem, failing to provide adequate support.

Similar to battered wives, lesbian victims need to seek out shelter when placed in danger. Unfortunately, it is not a simple task to receive assistance from shelters. Traditionally, shelters housed solely heterosexual women. This remains the case in many shelters. Feminists have struggled to receive support from the community and they fear their work will be undermined in recognizing females as perpetrators of violence. Moreover, in accepting lesbians into shelters, homophobic staff and residents are ill-equipped to cope with these clients. In addition, staff and residents are placed in danger of outside attacks from gay bashers. Another problem shelters face is funding. Staff fear that resources will be reduced, if not cut off completely, if it is known to house lesbian victims.

For these reasons, it has been suggested that lesbians develop their own safety networks. The primary problem in obtaining lesbian shelters is funding. Finances are minimal and staffs are limited, such that it is virtually impossible to legitimately operate shelters for lesbian victims. The first step in allocating resources and locating qualified staff is to change society's attitudes toward homosexuality. Lesbians must feel comfortable in seeking support from battered women's shelters. Staff and volunteers must be trained to better understand the needs of lesbian victims. Porat argues that it "is not the role of abused lesbians to educate domestic violence programs about their plight, but rather the responsibility of the movement to establish consistent programs which meet the special needs of *all* women" (in Lobel, 1986, p. 82). As noted earlier, it is also imperative that shelters be developed to serve the male population. There needs to be greater awareness and education regarding male domestic violence, straight or gay, for there to be adequate treatment and prevention programs for these understudied victims.

LEGAL ISSUES AND FUTURE TRENDS

Battered lesbians face great resistance in receiving assistance from the legal system. "An examination of the domestic violence laws of all 50 states reveals that battered lesbians and gay men are often afforded less protection than their heterosexual counterparts, or in some states, no protection at all" (Fray-Witzer, 1999, p. 20). Although laws may exist, they continue to be weak or unclear, leaving same-sex victims extremely vulnerable. In addition, many criminal justice personnel suffer from homophobia and thus do not take their cases as serious or even legitimate. It has been a long struggle for heterosexual battered women to achieve recognition, and unfortunately, they still do not receive adequate support from the criminal justice system. Law enforcement officers do not take these calls as seriously as they do other offenses. Part of the problem lies with victims themselves. All too often police are familiar with these households; they go to the scene and are now treated as the "enemy" rather than as the supporter. They are then placed in an adversarial position rather than viewed as supportive. Police may also hold sexist views on marriage, supporting punishment when necessary. In cases of lesbian battering, these women have increased opposition in turning to police for help. At times, police have harassed members of the gay community, leaving little reason to trust them.

Other agencies have also done little to help gay victims. "[A] number of states have recently revised their domestic violence statutes by substituting a term such as household member for the term spouse" (Renzetti, 1992, p. 91). Although some states have made available temporary restraining orders regardless of sex, lesbians are often denied protection from their abusers. "Judges who are otherwise sympathetic to battered women may tend to see all abuse in lesbian relationships as mutual, or may actually provide the batterer with legal protection or legal sanctions over the victim" (Hammond, in Lobel, 1989, p. 96).

CONCLUSION

Little attention has been given to same-sex domestic violence. Scholars and practitioners alike must study gay and lesbian domestic violence to better serve this unique population. For victims to feel safe, they must be provided with adequate resources and be comfortable in contacting law enforcement for assistance. It is easy to put blame on the heterosexual community for the lack of understanding about same-sex battering, but blame also lies with the homosexual community. Their resistance to recognize gay and lesbian domestic violence serves only to minimize the problem. It is much simpler to continue to believe that domestic violence is a heterosexual problem rather than one in their own communities. This belief suggests that homosexuals are not as deviant as their heterosexual counterparts are. This imaginary perception leaves gay males and lesbians who are victimized by their partners with little recourse and support. Gay or straight, society must come to the aid of all its victims.

REFERENCES

Bologna, M. J., Waterman, C. K., & Dawson, L. J. (1987). *Violence in gay male and lesbian relationships: Implications for practitioners and policy makers.* Paper presented at the Third National Conference for Family Violence Researchers, Durham, NH.
Cecere, D. J. (1986). The second closet: Battered lesbians. In K. Lobel (Ed.), *Naming the violence: Speaking out about lesbian battering* (pp. 21–31). Seattle: Seal Press.
Clunis, D. M., & Green, G. D. (1993). *Lesbian couples: Creating healthy relationships for the '90s.* Seattle: Seal Press.
Coleman, V. E. (1990). *Violence between lesbian couples: A between groups*

comparison. Unpublished doctoral dissertation: University Microfilms International, 9109022.

Elliott, P. (1996). Shattering illusions: Same-sex domestic violence. In C. M. Renzetti & C. H. Miley (Eds.), *Violence in gay and lesbian domestic partnerships* (pp. 1–8). Newbury Park: Sage.

Fray-Witzer, E. (1999). Twice abused: Same-sex domestic violence and the law. In B. Leventhal & S. E. Lundy (Eds.), *Same-sex domestic violence: Strategies for change* (pp. 19–42). London: Sage.

Gosselin, D. K. (2005). *Heavy hands: An introduction to the crimes of family.* Upper Saddle River, NJ: Prentice Hall.

Hammond, N. (1986). Lesbian victims and the reluctance to identify abuse. In K. Lobel (Ed.), *Naming the violence: Speaking out about lesbian battering* (pp. 190–198). Seattle: Seal Press.

Hammond, N. (1989). Lesbian victims of relationship violence. In E. D. Rothblum & E. Cole (Eds.), *Lesbianism: Affirming nontraditional roles* (pp. 89–106). New York: File Haworth Press.

Island, D., & Letellier, P. (1991). *Men who beat the men who love them.* New York: Harrington Park Press.

Jackson, N. A. (Ed.). (in press). *The encyclopedia of domestic violence.* New York: Routledge.

Kelly, E. E., & Warshafsky, L. (1987). *Partner abuse in gay male and lesbian couples.* Paper presented at the Third National Conference for Family Violence Researchers. Durham, NH.

Kuehnle, K., & Sullivan, A. (2003). Gay and lesbian victimization: Reporting factors in domestic violence and bias incidents. *Criminal Justice and Behavior, 30,* 85–96.

Kurst-Swanger, K., & Petcosky, J. L. (2003). *Violence in the home: Multidisciplinary perspectives.* New York: Oxford University Press.

Lobel, K. (Ed.). (1986). *Naming the violence: Speaking out about lesbian battering.* Seattle: Seal Press.

Meuer, T., Seymour, A., & Wallace, H. (2002). *Domestic violence.* National Victims Assistance Academy Textbook. Washington, DC: Office for Victims of Crime.

NCAVP. (2003). *National report on lesbian, gay, bisexual, and transgender domestic violence in 2002.* New York: National Coalition of Anti-Violence Programs.

Porat, N. (1986). Support groups for battered lesbians. In K. Lobel (Ed.), *Naming the violence: Speaking out about lesbian battering* (pp. 80–87). Seattle: Seal Press.

Renzetti, C. M. (1988). Violence in lesbian relationships: A preliminary analysis of causal factors. *Journal of Interpersonal Violence, 3,* 381–399.

Renzetti, C. M. (1992). *Violent betrayal: Partner abuse in lesbian relationships.* Newbury Park: Sage.

Renzetti, C. M., & Miley, C. H. (Eds.). (1996). *Violence in gay and lesbian domestic partnerships.* Newbury Park: Sage.

Rothblum, F. D., & Cole, E. (Eds.). (1989). *Lesbianism: Affirming nontraditional roles.* New York: File Haworth Press.

Seelau, S. M., & Seelau, E. P. (2005). Gender-role stereotypes and perceptions of heterosexual, gay and lesbian domestic violence. *Journal of Family Violence, 20,* 363–371.

Straus, M. A. (1979). Measuring intrafamily conflict and violence: The Conflict Tactics Scale. *Journal of Marriage and the Family, 41,* 75–88.

Straus, M. A., & Gelles, R. J. (Eds.). (1990). *Physical violence in American families.* New Brunswick: Transaction.

Sullivan, A., & Kuehnle, K. (in press). Lesbian battering. In N. A. Jackson (Ed.), *The encyclopedia of domestic violence.* New York: Routledge.

Tjaden, P., & Thoennes, N. (2000). Extent, nature, and consequences of intimate partner violence. (Publication No. NCJ 181867). Retrieved from National Institute of Justice Web site: www.ojp.usdo.gov/nij.

Walker, L. E. (1979). *The battered woman.* New York: Harper & Row.

CHAPTER 19

Global Issues in Elder Abuse and Mistreatment:
Policy, Research, and Practice

Patricia Brownell

CASE SCENARIOS

Case 1: Adult Children

Mrs. A., a 93-year-old widow with severe dementia living in Japan, is dependent for her total care from her daughter-in-law, who is 75 years old. Although Mrs. A.'s care needs exceed the daughter-in-law's caregiving capacity, the daughter-in-law believes it is her duty to personally provide all of Mrs. A.'s care. To manage this, she uses restraints and other behavioral control methods that cause bruising of Mrs. A.'s skin and extreme discomfort (Shibusawa, Kodaka, Iwano, & Kaizu, 2005).

Case 2: Formal Caregiving

Mrs. H., an 80-year-old widow with dementia, developed HIV, even though she lived alone and was cared for by a home aide from a local agency in a Caribbean island community. On further investigation, it was discovered that she was raped by an HIV-positive 43-year-old man in her home. Her door had been left unsecured by her home aide (Baboolal, Konings, & Maharajh, 2005).

Case 3: Spouse/Partners

Mr. S., a 78-year-old retired businessman, lives with his partner of 5 years, a 45-year-old male who is a former house painter. Mr. S.'s partner has been caring for Mr. S. since he became incapacitated through suffering a series of strokes 2 years ago. Both Mr. S. and his partner have been living on Mr. S.'s savings, and recently Mr. S. was sent a notice by his bank that his account was overdrawn, even though there were significant savings still in the account as recently as a year ago. Mr. S.'s partner took over the management of Mr. S.'s finances since Mr. S. suffered his first stroke (Kosberg, 1998).

PURPOSE OF CHAPTER

The purpose of this chapter is to provide an overview of elder abuse and neglect from a global perspective. Although the mistreatment of older people is not new, elder abuse as a recognized social problem in developed countries only dates back to the 1970s (Wolf, 1988). Since then, the primary focus of research has been on defining elder abuse, learning more about characteristics of victims and perpetrators, and measuring incidence and prevalence.

Unlike domestic violence, professionals in gerontology have defined elder abuse, and evaluations of elder abuse interventions have been largely descriptive (Wolf, 2000). Internationally elder abuse is still evolving as a social issue of concern to nations, practitioners, and older adults themselves (Wolf, Daichman, & Bennett, 2002).

This presents both challenges and opportunities for the international community. United Nations' social demographers project 2050 as the year in which, for the first time in human history, there will be more people 60 years of age and older than those under 18 years living on the planet (United Nations Department of Economic and Social Affairs, 2002).

Existing prevalence studies and other estimates (Pillemer & Finkelhor, 1988; Podnieks, 1992a) have found that between 3% and 10% of older adults may experience abuse and mistreatment in old age.

However, in many countries around the world, elder abuse is not identified as a significant social problem. In addition, little is known about how different countries and cultures define elder abuse, establish policies to prevent it, and implement practice models to address it (Brownell & Podnieks, 2005).

By the second half of the century, the older American population of 84.5 million will be dwarfed by the projected 331 million older people in China (who will nearly equal the total projected populations of all ages in the United States). Canada is graying as well. Although smaller than the United States (33.8 million people, compared with the United States' 283 million), in 2000, people 65+ represented a slightly larger proportion of its population (16.7% compared with 16.5% in the United States), and by 2050, Canada is expected to have 30.5% of its population 65+, compared with the United States, as 26.9%, according to the United Nations Department of Economic and Social Affairs (2002).

As more people live longer, some studies estimate that an increasing proportion of the older population will experience debilitating disorders like Alzheimer's disease and be more vulnerable to family and institutional abuse and mistreatment. The fact remains that most older adults live independent and productive lives into advanced old age. However, if current senior abuse prevalence data continue to hold, larger numbers of older people can mean increased cases of senior abuse, unless vigorous efforts are mounted to address ageism in all its forms and prevent senior abuse through education, policies, and programs that have been empirically tested as effective.

The Second World Assembly on Ageing, held in Madrid, Spain, in April 2002, took this on as a challenge, and included a section on elder abuse and neglect as part of the Madrid 2002 International Plan of Action on Ageing (Brownell, 2003). Included in this implementation plan is the issue of neglect, abuse, and violence against older people (United Nations Department of Public Information, 2003). It states: "Neglect, abuse and violence against older persons takes many forms—physical, psychological, financial—and occurs in every social, economic, ethnic, and geographic sphere."

The section on elder abuse of this document, also known as the Madrid 2002 International Plan of Action on Ageing (MIPAA), reflects the understanding that the process of aging brings with it declining ability to heal, so that older victims of abuse may never fully recover physically or emotionally from trauma. The impact of trauma may be worsened because shame and fear cause reluctance to seek help. Nations and communities, including older citizens themselves, must work together to prevent abuse, consumer fraud, and crimes against older persons. Professionals need to recognize the risk of potential abuse or violence by formal or informal caregivers both in the home and in community and institutional settings (United Nations Department of Public Information, 2003, p. 38).

The International Network for the Prevention of Elder Abuse (INPEA) has accepted the challenge to collaborate with other non-governmental organizations (NGOs) and governments in promoting an awareness of elder abuse internationally, and encouraging "further research into the causes, nature, extent, seriousness, and consequences of all forms of violence against older women and men, and widely disseminate findings of research and studies" (United Nations Department of Public Information, 2003, p. 39). INPEA is a NGO recognized by the United Nations with special consultative status, and is also a standing committee of the International Association of Gerontology and Geriatrics (IAGG).

INPEA was founded in 1997 in Adelaide, Australia, by the late Dr. Rosalie Wolf, a leading expert in elder abuse research, and a group of scholars, practitioners, and government officials committed to recognizing and responding to the mistreatment of older people, so their later years will be free of abuse, neglect, and exploitation (www.inpea.net). Its objectives are to increase public awareness and knowledge of this issue; to promote education and training of professionals and paraprofessionals in identification, treatment, and prevention of elder abuse; to further advocacy on behalf of abused and neglected elders; and to stimulate research into the causes, consequences, prevalence, treatment, and prevention of elder abuse and neglect (www.inpea.net).

INPEA members have conducted studies, presented at conferences, published chapters and articles in scholarly journals, and edited special issues of journals that focus on elder abuse and neglect from an international perspective.

Three English-language international journals with special issues or sections on elder abuse edited by INPEA members include *Brief Treatment and Crisis Intervention, Journal of Elder Abuse and Neglect,* and *Journal of Gerontological Social Work.* INPEA also collaborates with other

NGOs recognized by the United Nations with consultative status to encourage cooperation among governments and civil society in addressing elder abuse.

The literature review and discussion presented in this chapter provides an overview of selected articles and book chapters that present information and findings on elder abuse from a global perspective on policies, research, and practice models. The policies, research findings, and practice models discussed here reflect perspectives grounded in the cultures of nations around the world, and can inform thinking on how to address the prevention and treatment of elder abuse in the United States.

The literature drawn on here is from English-language sources, which is a limitation. However, it is also intended to provide a framework within which to develop an international exchange of ideas and information as the review and appraisal of the MIPAA implementation moves forward (United Nations Commission for Social Development, 2005).

POLICY ISSUES FROM A GLOBAL PERSPECTIVE

MIPAA provides a comprehensive set of guidelines for nations to consider in reviewing their policies to empower, support, and protect their older adult populations (Brownell, 2003). MIPAA (in Section C. Priority direction III: Ensuring enabling and supportive environments, Issue 3. Neglect abuse and violence) defines elder abuse or mistreatment as physical, emotional, and financial. It emphasizes the special risk faced by women due to social attitudes and practices that result in discrimination, poverty, and sexual abuse. Under Issue 3, Objective 1, MIPAA encourages governments to enact legislation and strengthen legal efforts to stop elder abuse.

Ageism and lack of respect for older adults is identified in MIPAA as a key area of concern and is addressed through Issue 4: Images of ageing. This section notes that a positive view of aging is an integral part of the MIPAA (United Nations Department of Public Information, 2003). Ageism is defined as the denial of basic human rights of older persons and is considered one of the most pervasive prejudices across human society, in spite of professed worship and valuing of older adults in many societies (International Longevity Center, 2006).

Although combating ageism is of paramount importance in ensuring the human rights of older adults, Dr. Robert Butler—who coined the word ageism in 1968—notes that it still thrives in cultures and societies. Podnieks (2006) focuses on a key policy objective of MIPAA: addressing elder abuse and neglect by ensuring complete social inclusion of older adults in society.

Researchers around the world have begun to address the gap in our knowledge about elder abuse and neglect from a global perspective, and culturally specific strategies for addressing this problem. In the future, INPEA hopes to support and encourage more research that will result in empirically tested brief treatment and crisis intervention models, to be adopted by the global community as the implementation of MIPAA unfolds (Brownell & Podnieks, 2005).

Societal conditions like social isolation and changes in marital status were found to be key risk factors in elder abuse and mistreatment, according to an analysis of the 1999 General Social Survey in Canada (Brozowski & Hall, 2004). Elder abuse is identified as an escalating problem in Africa, according to Ferreira (2004). However, lack of understanding of this social problem, including the failure of governments to frame it as a human rights issue, and lack of resources to address it are cited as the reasons for the failure of violent forms of elder abuse to be contained.

In contrast, government is identified as being proactive in addressing elder abuse in Israel (Doron, Alon, & Offir, 2004). However, recognition of the problem is not sufficient for governments to formulate and implement effective policies to prevent and intervene in elder abuse situations. Four stages of policy development are highlighted: paternalistic, punitive, protection and treatment-oriented, and promotion of education and information and expertise as part of a prevention strategy.

Although feminists have been instrumental in drawing attention to domestic violence against women in nations around the world, there has been less success in bringing a feminist perspective to the problem of abuse of older women (Jönson & Åkerströn, 2004). However, one unintended consequence of framing elder abuse from a feminist perspective is that policy makers may overlook service needs of older abused men (Kosberg, 1998).

RESEARCH FINDINGS FROM A GLOBAL PERSPECTIVE

Although there have been a few prevalence and incidence studies conducted during the past 25 years, all have methodological problems such as differing definitions of elder abuse, different sampling techniques, and other problems. To date, prevalence studies have identified from 3% to 10% of the older adult population as having experienced abuse at some time in their later years (Pillemer & Finkelhor, 1988; National Center on Elder Abuse, 2006). The aging of the world's population has been identified as cause for concern. A life course perspective has guided qualitative inquiry into the phenomenon of aging and elder abuse (Podnieks, 1992b).

More recently smaller studies examined incidence and prevalence of elderly mistreatment in communities around the globe. In India, one prevalence study found a 14% prevalence rate of mistreatment, the most common of which was chronic verbal abuse, followed by financial abuse (Chokkanathan & Lee, 2005). Anme, McCall, and Tatara (2005) used an exploratory research method to examine the presence and form of elder abuse and associated risk factors among frail older adults in a Japanese village. The findings indicated that 17% of those studied were categorized as abused. The most common forms of abuse were psychological, neglect, and financial. This study expands our understanding of older adults in rural and village setting, unlike many studies that focus on urban elderly populations.

A pilot incidence study conducted in Israel found 120 new cases of elder abuse within a 1-year period, out of an elder population of 24,800 residents (or 0.5%). Mental abuse was the most prevalent form of mistreatment and was usually combined with other forms of abuse and neglect. Family conflicts were found to be the most common cause of those forms of abuse identified, with caregiving responsibilities for a dependent relative found as the least common cause (Iecovich, Lankri, & Drori, 2004).

Kosberg, Lowenstein, Garcia, and Biggs (2003) examined methodological and other challenges in conducting cross-national studies in elder abuse. The study conducted in Sweden by Erlingsson, Saveman, and Berg (2005) was intended to explore the perceptions of elder abuse held by older people in Sweden. It also examined coping strategies of victims, which ranged from changes in individual life decision making to efforts to engage in social change.

Although the focus of this study was on the perceptions of older adults about elder abuse, the study identifies the importance of professionals in the health care field becoming aware of what older people believe is the cause of elder abuse and what they consider abusive. The researchers make recommendations about incorporating these findings in interview and assessment techniques and training manuals. This addresses the recommendation in the MIPAA to include handling of elder abuse in the training of the caring professions.

Podnieks and Wilson (2003) present findings from studies focusing on faith communities and their responsiveness or lack of responsiveness to elder abuse among congregation members. Spirituality and religiosity are dimensions of faith-based interventions considered to be significant for practice with older adults and their families, and these articles provide a timely examination of the readiness of faith communities to address this significant social issue among their own members.

Laypersons' attitudes toward elder abuse were examined, using vignettes about older adults with Alzheimer's disease or osteoporosis. Findings suggested that responses from lay subjects were mixed: Some identified the vignettes as representing elder abuse, and some did not. However, respondents were moved by the vignettes, which elicited emotional reactions and expressed desires to help perceived victims (Werner, Eisikovits, & Buchbinder, 2005).

Researchers focused on elder abuse are challenged by definitional problems, ethical and methodological considerations, and the difficulties of gaining access to vulnerable subjects who may wish to conceal their mistreatment by loved ones and con artists. Beaulieu and Leclerc (2006) present the findings of a qualitative study intended to learn from practitioners more about issues and ethical dilemmas in work with elder abuse clients. Issues of informed consent to services on the part of victims as well as abusers, particularly if family members, are among key ethical issues that must be addressed by the professional community in serving clients and their families when abuse and exploitation are factors.

Powerlessness was identified as a risk factor for elder abuse and neglect by Nahmiash (2002), who examined the interaction between the environmental context of caregiving and the mistreatment of older care-dependent adults in Quebec, Canada. This includes changing family patterns and demographics that influence how societies plan for and support caregiving systems at all levels of society:

macro-, meso-, and microsystems. Findings suggest that violence against older care-dependent adults is caused by interacting macro-, meso-, and microsystems, and significant events that can result in feelings of powerlessness on the part of both caregivers and care-dependent older adults receiving care.

Another perspective on elder abuse and caregiving in South Korea is provided by Lee and Kolomer (2005), who examined characteristics that could increase risk of abuse by caregivers of older Korean adults with dementia. For the population studied, risk of abuse was significantly increased by caregiver burden, mental impairment, level of care needs of the older adult receiving care, and formal service utilization. Hightower, Smith, and Hightower (2006) examine domestic violence of older women. Using a qualitative methodological approach, they explore the experiences of women age 50 years and older who have been abused by spouses and partners, comparing these experiences with those of younger battered women. Each of these studies applies different methodologies and research questions to diverse populations of elder abuse victims and their situations. In doing so, they expand our understanding of elder abuse and neglect in all its complexity, and strengthen the foundation on which effective policies and practice models and modalities can be developed.

Categories and definitions of elder abuse have been created by professionals and policymakers without seeking significant input from older adults, including victims of elder abuse. Researchers are seeking to address this gap through qualitative studies using interview and focus group methodology. Buchbinder and Winterstein (2003) examine the perceptions and feelings of older women victims of abuse in Israel, and identify themes that have universal application for what they identified as abusive family behavior and the impact on their emotional, psychological, and financial well-being.

INPEA has also collaborated with the World Health Organization (WHO) Ageing and Life Course unit on a study of eight countries: Argentina, Austria, Brazil, Canada, India, Kenya, Lebanon, and Sweden. The study used a focus group methodology to examine the meanings of elder abuse and neglect for older people in their communities and primary health care workers (WHO/INPEA, 2002). Analysis of major themes that emerged from the study identified similarities across older adults from participating countries as to their perception of abuse.

Three major areas included neglect (isolation, abandonment, and social exclusion), violation (of human, legal, and medical rights), and deprivation (of choices, decisions, status, finances, and respect). Recommendations that emerged from the study included the dissemination of research findings through scientific journals, developing a global inventory of good practice, and "mobilizing civil society through raising awareness of the widespread magnitude of elder abuse" (WHO/INPEA, 2002, p. IV).

Missing Voices

"Missing Voices: Views of Older Persons on Elder Abuse" identified a number of prevention and intervention strategies that both developed and developing nations can implement to address the global problem of elder abuse. These include promoting education and awareness of the general population, ending social isolation of older adults through promotion of intergenerational relationships, training of professionals, empowering older adults, and supporting more research and the dissemination of research findings on elder abuse. The full text of the Missing Voices report can be found on the Web site of the WHO (www.who.org).

INPEA is currently mounting an ambitious new project to promote "World Elder Abuse Awareness Day": The first annual observation occurred beginning June 15, 2006, in collaboration with the International Association of Gerontology (IAG), WHO, the International Federation of Ageing (IFA), HelpAge International, the Subcommittee on Elder Abuse of the NGO Committee on Ageing, the American Association of Retired Persons (AARP), The International Longevity Center, (ILC—USA), The Ontario Network for the Prevention of Elder Abuse (CNPEA), the National Network for the Prevention of Elder Abuse (NNPEA), the Ontario Seniors/Secretariat/Government of Ontario, and other NGOs. The day focused on efforts across the globe to raise awareness of elder abuse in a coordinated fashion for the first time. As the project progresses, participating organizations, localities, and nations will continue annually to plan activities recognizing World Elder Abuse Awareness Day, including educational activities to raise awareness of this social problem.

A second project undertaken by INPEA is the launch of its research agenda in New York City in 2003: A World View on Elder Abuse.

Phase one of this project is an environmental scan. This project is being undertaken in collaboration with the WHO to examine the studies, programs, projects, laws, and policies related to elder abuse and neglect globally (www.inpea.net).

Many of the studies discussed here, including those conducted in Japan and Sweden, reflect a qualitative approach to understanding elder abuse and neglect from a cultural perspective taken by the WHO in collaboration with INPEA. The underlying assumption of these studies is that it is essential to understand elder abuse from the perspectives of older people and their health care providers in order to plan, implement, and evaluate culturally appropriate crisis intervention and longer term prevention and treatment strategies.

The studies referenced here add to our understanding of elder abuse, its meaning for older adults and their families, and how it can be identified and addressed by health and service professionals. Although the studies raise concerns about the vulnerability of care-dependent older adults, in fact, most older adults are healthy and active contributors to their families, communities, and societies. Care-dependent elders may be vulnerable to abuse by formal and informal caregivers, but frailty is not necessarily a risk factor, according to some studies: In fact, abuser characteristics may be more predictive of abuse than those of older victims (Wolf, Daichman, & Bennett, 2002).

Practice Issues From a Global Perspective

Crisis intervention strategies for elder abuse and neglect reflect a focus on individual and family levels and debates about their application inevitably revolve around issues of autonomy versus paternalism. Developed countries have instituted legal underpinnings for interventions that may involve involuntary action on the part of health and service providers to address elder abuse and neglect emergencies. For developing countries that are only beginning to acknowledge that elder abuse is a social problem, more research is needed to understand the problem of elder abuse and neglect within specific cultural contexts, and develop culturally appropriate and feasible interventions (Brownell & Podnieks, 2005).

We know that older women move into old age less advantaged financially than older men, and single women of color are the least advantaged. In the United States the most economically disadvantaged cohorts of older people are Latino older women who are single and living alone or with non-family household members. Gender biases in the family have historically made women more vulnerable to domestic violence, and many studies have suggested that this continues into old age, with adult sons as well as older spouses and partners abusing older women (Hightower, 2004). The vulnerability of older men is finally being examined in the elder abuse literature as well (Kosberg, 1998).

Shibusawa, Kodaka, Iwano, and Kaizu (2005) examine crisis intervention strategies that are implemented by social workers at Japanese home-care support centers when encountering abuse of frail elders by their families. Although at the present time there is no formal notification system for elder abuse in Japan, there is an extensive formal system of in-home care for older adults to supplement or supplant care by family members. This reflects a policy decision by the national government of Japan to mandate local governments to establish home-care support centers to assist families in caring for elderly members.

As noted in the MIPAA, victims of elder abuse may not seek help to address abuse or neglect by family members because of shame or fear. The in-home service program in Japan employs social workers as well as nurses to visit homes of older adults receiving government-mandated services to ensure their well-being. This also provides opportunities to identify mistreatment when it occurs and take action on behalf of the elderly victim. The case examples presented by Shibusawa, Kodaka, Iwano, and Kaizu (2005) illustrate the health and social situations encountered by health and service professionals in Japan, and the strategies they have developed for addressing them.

Penhale (2003) discusses the importance of considering the links among older women, elder abuse, and domestic violence. Using a feminist framework, she advocates for practitioners and researchers to incorporate a consciousness of power inequities in society as they may affect older women, as well as younger ones. Erlingsson, Carlson, and Saveman (2003) present findings of a survey on screening questions and risk assessments intended to identify potential elder abuse victims in primary health care settings.

A key concern of practitioners is strengthening the practice response to elder abuse and neglect. From a professional practitioner's perspective, this can be challenging, as interdisciplinary collaboration is often essential to successfully prevent or address this tragic social issue. Brownell and Heiser (2006) discuss a community-based psychoeducational support group model for victims of elder abuse that is adapted from a shelter program model developed by NOVA House, an elder abuse shelter in Manitoba, Canada.

Cohen (2006) addresses the widespread problem of financial abuse of older adults, including consumer fraud. Financial abuse is considered the most common form of elder abuse, and Cohen presents an overview of some successful initiatives developed to educate and protect older adults against this form of abuse. Intergenerational learning opportunities are addressed in another section of MIPAA Priority direction A.: Older persons and development, Issue 5: Intergenerational solidarity (UN, 2003). Neiking (2005) presents an intergenerational model for teaching about elder abuse. This is an example of a preventive service strategy that educates several generations about elder abuse, both to recognize it and to prevent it from happening.

Example of International Promotion of Public Policy to Address Elder Abuse

The MIPAA (Elder Abuse and Mistreatment section) establishes objectives and action steps to promote public policies and programs in nations around the world. This plan emerged from the Second World Assembly on Ageing, held in Madrid, Spain, in April 2002, 20 years after the First World Assembly on Ageing was held in Vienna, Austria. MIPAA (Priority direction III: Ensuring enabling and supportive environments—Issue 3: Neglect, abuse and violence) includes the following objectives:

- Objective 1: Elimination of all forms of neglect, abuse, and violence of older persons.
- Objective 2: Creation of support services to address elder abuse (Brownell, 2003).

The Plan can be found on the Internet at http://daccessdds.un.org/doc/UNDOC/GEN/NO2/397/51/PDF/NO239751.pdf?OpenElement (retrieved on October 22, 2006).

Currently the United Nations plans to monitor the implementation of the Madrid Plan, in a process named Madrid Plus Five (or, 5 years after the promulgation of the plan of action in 2002). This will be a grassroots "bottom-up" review, with the assumption of the availability of "top-down" support. Governments can decide what part(s) of MIPAA to monitor; however, NGOs must advocate with governments on what part(s) of MIPAA to include in their monitoring plan. First, NGOs and older adults must advocate with governments to participate in the review; and second, they must advocate for governments to include the elder abuse objectives as part of their review. The Secretary General (UN Bureaucracy) will support and provide technical assistance through two offices: the Department of Economic and Social Affairs (DESA) and the Department of Public Information (DPI).

The General Assembly representing governments will oversee the hearings on Madrid Plus Five through the Commission on Social Development (CSD). The Commission on Social Development will oversee the Madrid Plus Five monitoring plan and implementation, based on the following timetable:

- 2006: Nations that signed onto MIPAA must decide what sections to include in their monitoring plan.
- February 2007: At CSD, member nations will be requested to report on laws passed, programs established, and so forth, since MIPAA (without outcome analyses), and on what aspects of MIPAA they have decided to review.
- During 2007, "bottom-up" action review appraisal will begin on those aspects of MIPAA selected for monitoring (review).
- February 2008: At CSD, governments will present their responses to what they have found about:
  - Impact of policies, programs, and other initiatives
  - Outcomes for older adults
  - Direction of future social welfare policies

There is an important role for elder abuse advocates, NGOs, and academic institutions in determining what constitutes "good" and "bad" laws; how are older persons' rights balanced against intrusive "protection"; and what good is a law without adequate funding to implement it?

To date, draft recommendations on the review methodology have been distributed to the member nations by the United Nations Department of Economic and Social Affairs (DESA). The United Nations Commission for Social Development (CSD) has approved the modality for the first review and appraisal; endorsed calendar to start global review in 2007 and report back in 2008; CSD has established theme for first review at global level: "Addressing the Challenges and Opportunities of Ageing"; and CSD has recommended format for 2008 review: plenary debates, series of panel discussions, and events.

The WHO, the NGO Committee on Ageing, and the INPEA are taking the lead in promoting global awareness of elder abuse through educational programs and the United Nations World Elder Abuse Awareness Day project, to be held on June 15 of every year starting 2006. The NGO Committee on Ageing, which is an umbrella NGO for over 45 NGOs with an aging focus, supports education and awareness about elder abuse.

CONCLUSION

Elder abuse is a complex phenomenon, and any actual or suspected case of elder abuse must be assessed before an intervention strategy is formulated and initiated. Ensuring that health and social service providers are aware of elder abuse and strategies for addressing it in situations involving care-dependent older victims are essential. Interventions for older adults have been guided by global principles reflecting dignity, choice, freedom, safety, and least intrusive and disruptive choices (Wolf, Bennett, & Daichman, 2003). Levels of intervention include social policies, community efforts, neighborhood networks, and family and individual interventions.

Researchers around the world have begun to address the gap in our knowledge about elder abuse and neglect from a global perspective, and culturally specific strategies for addressing this problem. In the future, INPEA hopes to support and encourage more research that will result in empirically tested brief treatment and crisis intervention models, to be adopted by the global community as the implementation of the MIPAA unfolds (Brownell & Podnieks, 2005).

REFERENCES

Anme, T., McCall, M., & Tatara, T. (2005). An exploratory study of abuse among frail elders using services in a small village in Japan. *Journal of Elder Abuse and Neglect, 17*(2), 1–20.
Baboolal, N. S., Konings, M., & Maharajh, H. D. (2005). Sexual abuse

resulting in HIV positive in a patient with Alzheimer's disease: A case report from Trinidad and Tobago. *Journal of Elder Abuse and Neglect, 17*(2), 77–82.

Beaulieu, M., & Leclerc, N. (2006). Ethical and psychosocial issues raised by the practice in cases of mistreatment of older adults. *Journal of Gerontological Social Work, 46*(3/4), 161–186.

Brownell, P. (2003). Madrid 2002: Global ageing and violence against older persons post 9/11. *New Global Development, 19*(1), 15–25.

Brownell, P., & Heiser, D. (2006). Psycho-educational support groups for older women victims of family mistreatment: A pilot study. *Journal of Gerontological Social Work, 46*(3–4), 145–160.

Brownell, P., & Podnieks, E. (2005). Long-overdue recognition for the critical issues of elder abuse and neglect: A global policy and practice perspective. *Brief Treatment and Crisis Intervention, 5*(2), 187–191.

Brozowski, K., & Hall, D. (2004). Growing old in a risk society. *Journal of Elder Abuse and Neglect, 16*(3), 65–81.

Buchbinder, E., & Winterstein, T. (2003). "Like a wounded bird": Older battered women's experiences with intimate abuse. *Journal of Elder Abuse and Neglect, 15* (2), 23–44.

Chokkanathan, S., & Lee, A. E. Y. (2005). Elder mistreatment in urban India: A community based study. *Journal of Elder Abuse and Neglect, 17*(2), 45–61.

Cohen, C. A. (2006). Consumer fraud and the elderly: A review of Canadian challenges and initiatives.. *Journal of Gerontological Social Work, 46*(3/4) 137–144.

Doron, I., Alon, S., & Offir, N. (2004). Time for policy: Legislative response to elder abuse and neglect in Israel. *Journal of Elder Abuse and Neglect, 16*(4), 63–82.

Erlingsson, C. L., Carlson, S. L., & Saveman, B. (2003). Elder abuse risk indicators and screening questions: Results from a literature search and panel of experts from developed and developing countries. *Journal of Elder Abuse and Neglect, 15*(3/4), 185–203.

Erlingsson, C., Saveman, B., & Berg, A. (2005). Perceptions of elder abuse in Sweden: Voices of older persons. *Brief Treatment and Crisis Intervention, 5*(2), 213–227.

Ferreira, M. (2004). Elder abuse in Africa: What policy and legal provisions are there to address the violence? *Journal of Elder Abuse and Neglect, 16*(2), 17–32.

Hightower, J. (2004). Age, gender and violence: Abuse against older women. *Geriatrics & Aging, 7*(3), 60–63.

Hightower, J., Smith, M. J., & Hightower, H. C. (2006). Hearing the voices of abused older women. *Journal of Gerontological Social Work, 46*(3/4), 205–227.

Iecovich, E., Lankri, M., & Drori, D. (2004). Elder abuse and neglect—A pilot incidence study in Israel. *Journal of Elder Abuse and Neglect, 16*(3), 45–63.

International Longevity Center. (2006). *Ageism in America: The status reports.* New York: International Longevity Center, The Anti-Ageism Taskforce.

Jönson, H., & Åkerströn, M. (2004). Neglect of elderly women in feminist studies of violence—A case of ageism? *Journal of Elder Abuse and Neglect, 16*(1), 47–63.

Kosberg, J. (1998). The abuse of older men. *Journal of Elder Abuse and Neglect, 9*(3), 69–88.

Kosberg, J. I., Lowenstein, A., Garcia, J. L., & Biggs, S. (2003). Study of elder abuse within diverse cultures. *Journal of Elder Abuse and Neglect, 15*(3/4), 71–89.

Lee, M., & Kolomer, S. (2005). Caregiver burden, dementia, and elder abuse in South Korea. *Journal of Elder Abuse and Neglect, 1*(1), 61–74.

Nahmiash, D. (2002). Powerlessness and abuse and neglect of older adults. *Journal of Elder Abuse and Neglect, 14*(1), 21–47.

National Center on Elder Abuse—NCEA. (2006). *Fact sheet.* Retrieved August 5, 2006, from www.elderabusecenter.org.

Neikung, S. (2004). Creating an intergenerational learning community for the study of elder abuse. *Journal of Elder Abuse and Neglect, 16*(2), 33–49.

Penhale, B. (2003). Older women, domestic violence, and elder abuse: A review of commonalities, differences, and shared approaches. *Journal of Elder Abuse and Neglect, 15*(3/4), 71–89.

Pillemer, K., & Finkelhor, D. (1988). The prevalence of elder abuse: A random sample survey. *Gerontologist, 28*(1), 51–57.

Podnieks, E. (1992a). Emerging themes from a follow-up study of Canadian victims of elder abuse. *Journal of Elder Abuse and Neglect, 4*(1/2), 59–111.

Podnieks, E. (1992b). National survey on abuse of the elderly in Canada. *Journal of Elder Abuse and Neglect, 4*(1/2), 5–58.

Podnieks, E. (2006). Social exclusion: An interplay of the determinants of health—new insights into elder abuse. *Journal of Gerontological Social Work, 46*(3/4), 57–79.

Podnieks, E., & Wilson, S. (2003). Elder abuse awareness in faith communities: Findings from a Canadian pilot study. *Journal of Elder Abuse and Neglect, 15*(3/4), 71–89.

Reingold, D. A. (2006). An elder abuse shelter program: Build it and they will come, a long-term care based program to address elder abuse in the community. *Journal of Gerontological Social Work, 46*(3/4), 123–135.

Shibusawa, T., Kodaka, M., Iwano, S., & Kaizu, K. (2005). Interventions for elder abuse and neglect with frail elders in Japan. *Brief Treatment and Crisis Intervention, 5*(2), 203–211.

United Nations Commission for Social Development. (2005). *Modalities for*

the review and appraisal of the Madrid International Plan of Action on Ageing.
New York: United Nations E/CN.5/2006/2.

United Nations Department of Economic and Social Affairs. (2002). *World population ageing 1950–2050.* New York: DESA Population Division, UN.

United Nations Department of Public Information. (2003). *Second world assembly on ageing political declaration and Madrid 2002 international plan of action on ageing.* New York: United Nations Publications DPI/2271—February 2003—20M.

Weeks, L., Richards, J. L., Nilsson, T., Kozma, A., & Bryanton, O. (2004). A gendered analysis of the abuse of older adults: Evidence from the professionals. *Journal of Elder Abuse and Neglect, 16*(2), 1–15.

Werner, P., Eisikovits, Z., & Buchbinder, E. (2005). Lay persons' emotional reactions toward an abused elderly person. *Journal of Elder Abuse and Neglect, 17*(2), 63–75.

WHO/INPEA. (2002). *Missing voices: Views of older persons on elder abuse.* Geneva: World Health Organization. Retrieved from http://www.who.int/ageing/projects/elder_abuse/missing_voices/en/index.html.

Wolf, R. S. (1988). Elder abuse: Ten years later. *Journal of the American Geriatrics Society, 36,* 758–762.

Wolf, R. S. (2000). Elders as victims of crime, abuse, neglect and exploitation. In M. B. Rothman, B. D. Dunlop, & P. Entzel (Eds.), *Elders, crime, and the criminal justice system: Myth, perceptions, and reality in the 21st Century* (pp. 19–42). New York: Springer Publishing.

Wolf, R. S., Daichman, L. & Bennett, G. (2002). Abuse of the elderly. In E. E. Krug, L. L. Dahlberg, J. A. Mercy, A. B. Zwi, & R. Lozano (Eds.), *World Report on Violence and Health.* Geneva: World Health Organization, 125–145.

AUTHOR'S NOTE

Patricia Brownell, PhD, is Associate Professor at the Fordham University Graduate School of Social Service, New York City, and is Representative for the International Network for the Prevention of Elder Abuse and Co-Chair of the Sub-Committee on Elder Abuse for the Non-governmental Organization (NGO) on Ageing to the United Nations.

The author thanks Susan B. Somers, Esq., the Secretary-General of the International Network for the Prevention of Elder Abuse, for technical comments and editorial suggestions on the final draft of this chapter.

Cross-Cultural Issues, Policies, and Practices With Battered Women

The Use of the Culturagram in Understanding Immigrant Women Affected by Domestic Violence

Elaine P. Congress and Patricia Brownell

Du004ring the 21st century, social workers and other family service providers in the United States are challenged by the globalization of social issues and the immigration of families from cultures significantly different from the dominant European American cultural background. The number of first-generation immigrants has increased markedly both in rural as well as in urban areas, with 11.5% of those living in the United States being foreign born (Schmidley, 2003). It is estimated that 8 million to 9 million immigrants are undocumented (Brownell & Ko, 2005). In large urban areas like New York City, as many as 33% are foreign born, with another third of residents being children of immigrants (*The newest New Yorkers,* 2004). Immigrants are now more likely to come as families in contrast to earlier immigration periods that consisted primarily of single men (Foner, 2005). No matter in what setting or location social workers are employed, they are likely to work with immigrant families.

Domestic violence can occur across all ethnicities, genders, religions, sexual orientations, ages, and socioeconomic status (Kwong, 2002). Yet immigrants because of lack of financial and social supports, stresses related to immigration, as well as language and cultural barriers may experience additional challenges when domestic violence occurs within families (Brownell & Ko, 2005).

To effectively work with immigrant families facing domestic violence, clinicians must be sensitive to the cultural differences of families and communities and learn to provide culturally competent services.

While in the beginning of the 20th century, most immigrants came from Western Europe, now immigrants are more likely to come from Africa, East and South Asia, Eastern Europe, Mexico, and Central and South America (Schindley, 2003). Social workers need to be prepared to work with situations of domestic violence within many different immigrant populations.

The following examples demonstrate the variety of immigrant groups, as well as the range of types of domestic abuse:

- Mr. and Mrs. T. are Orthodox Jews who recently emigrated from Russia. Mrs. T. was able to find work in a cleaners, whereas Mr. T. still is unemployed. He is very depressed because of his unemployment and has become verbally and physically abusive to his wife.
- Mrs. H. is a Chinese woman who has been physically and emotionally abused by her husband, especially when he has large gambling debts.
- Mrs. S. is a woman from the Dominican Republic living in New York City. Recently she has been abused by her husband, especially around the holidays.
- Ms. M. is an undocumented Mexican woman living with Mr. G., an American citizen, and their three children (also American citizens). He abuses her and threatens to report her to immigration so that she will be deported and lose custody of her children, who can remain here.
- Mr. and Mrs. D. are a college educated couple who emigrated from India 2 years ago. Mr. D. is physically abusive to his wife, as he says she is too independent and does not respect his role as head of the household. He was particularly angry because of her recent interest in attending graduate school.

Each of the families is experiencing domestic violence, although this may not be the presenting problem when they first visit a social service agency. Even practitioners experienced in family work with American families may find it challenging to identify and work with immigrant families affected by domestic violence (Brownell & Congress, 1997; Brownell & Ko, 2005).

Domestic violence has been defined as a social problem in which the victim's physical, emotional, and spiritual health, as well as property, is threatened or harmed because of the behavior of a spouse, partner, family member, or significant other (Barker, 1995). Brownell and Congress (1997) defined domestic violence as both a social issue and a woman's issue. There is some evidence that domestic violence is more prevalent among immigrant women than native-born women (Orloff & Little, 1999). Types of domestic violence that affect immigrant women include emotional abuse, economic abuse, sexual abuse, use of coercion and threats involving children, using citizenship or residency privilege, intimidation, isolation and minimizing, blaming, and denial of abusive behavior (Brownell & Ko, 2005).

Undocumented immigrant women are particularly at risk, especially if abusive spouses threaten to have undocumented spouses deported and separated from their children if they attempt to terminate the abusive relationship (Kwong, 2002; Orloff, 2001, 2003). Immigration status is often used as a mechanism to control and maintain undocumented women in abusive relationships (Romkens, 2001; Sitowski, 2001).

EXAMPLES OF DOMESTIC VIOLENCE AMONG DIVERSE IMMIGRANT GROUPS

Domestic Violence Within the Immigrant Russian-Jewish Community

Families bring with them their own beliefs about the appropriate roles for men and women. Men are used to being providers in Russian society. As new immigrants, Russian men may have difficulty finding work, especially of similar status and income to their previous employment (Chazin & Ushakova, 2005). This may lead to anger, resentment, and domestic violence, especially in families where the wife becomes the principal provider. The loss of status and position of Mr. T. as breadwinner contributed to domestic violence in the family.

Case 1: Mr. and Mrs. T.

Mr. and Mrs. T. and their three children immigrated to the United States because as Jews they felt that they did not have the religious freedom they wanted. Mr. T. had had a high-level computer job in Russia, but in the United States with his limited English skills he had not been able to find employment. His wife had initially been hired to work in a Russian restaurant in New York. She recently had been asked to manage the store and received a raise. Mr. T., who was unemployed, increasingly spent his days drinking and had become physically abusive toward Mrs. T. when she returned home from work.

Domestic Violence in the Chinese American Community

Social isolation and deferential behavior to one's husband often characterize first-generation Chinese American women. The following example demonstrates how domestic violence affects a Chinese family.

Case 2: Mr. and Mrs. Cheng

The Chengs have lived in the United States for 20 years. They both work in a Chinatown restaurant. Mr. Cheng expects his wife to always demonstrate obedient behavior toward him, and in fact he has spoken negatively to her about a young female cousin who has forgotten traditional ways. In the last few years he has begun to gamble excessively, and often there is not enough money to pay the rent on time. When Mrs. Cheng has expressed concern about this, he has become physically and emotionally abusive.

DOMESTIC VIOLENCE IN THE LATINO IMMIGRANT COMMUNITY

Families from different Latin American countries are very diverse (Congress & Kang, 2005), but because of poverty and the stress of immigration they may experience similar problems with domestic violence. The following example illustrates the multidimensional issues associated with domestic violence in a Latino immigrant family.

Case 3: Latino Immigrant Family

Mrs. S. had come to the United States from Columbia as a live-in childcare worker. After she had saved some money, she sent for her 11-year-old son Jesus, whom she had left behind with an elderly aunt. Here in the United States she had met Mr. R., who was also from Columbia, and they had moved in together. Mr. R. had much difficulty finding a job and was able to secure only occasional day work. Her son Jesus did not respect his stepfather, saying that he was not his real father and he did not have to listen to him. Recently Mr. R. had struck Jesus, and when Mrs. S. had tried to intervene, Mr. R. struck her giving her a black eye. Another fight had ensued recently when Mrs. S. requested that Mr. R. use a condom. She had seen a sign in Spanish about AIDS and practicing safe sex and she was not certain about Mr. R.'s fidelity. He had erupted saying that he was a man and would make decisions about this.

Even though there were reoccurring instances of violent behavior, Mrs. S. had never gone for help. She was very embarrassed and did not want others to know about her family problems. Often immigrants come to the United States at different times and this produces much stress for families. Children often question why they have been separated from their parents, while siblings were chosen to accompany their parents.

Women may have an easier time securing work. Gender changes and disparities in employment may contribute to domestic violence. Another factor is the challenge of adolescents in blended families (Congress, 2002). Finally, AIDS is rapidly increasing among Latino women. Yet traditional machismo beliefs may affect Latino women's ability to advocate for safe sexual practices.

DOMESTIC VIOLENCE WHEN ONE PARTNER IS UNDOCUMENTED

Power and control issues have been identified as positively correlated with domestic violence (Brownell & Ko, 2005), and this issue is certainly related to legal status. The current and future presence of undocumented people in the United States is a subject of much social and political debate. It is important to note that families rarely consist of all documented or undocumented members. A more typical pattern is to have one or more members undocumented and other members who are American citizens, as this example illustrates:

Case 4: Mr. B. and Ms. C.

Twenty-five-year-old Mr. B. came from Puerto Rico with his family when he was teenager. At a party he had met Ms. C., who had recently emigrated with her sister from Mexico. Very shortly afterwards they began to live together, and in less than a year they had a son and then 2 years later a daughter. Mr. B. had been injured on a construction job last year and thus was not able to work. He had begun to spend his days drinking with his friends at a local social club. When Ms. C. complained about his drinking, Mr. B. threatened to call immigration services and have Ms. C. deported. He also vowed to take her children who were American citizens and have them raised by his sister, who lived on the next block.

DOMESTIC VIOLENCE WITH A HOMOSEXUAL COUPLE

Domestic violence occurs in homosexual, as well as in heterosexual relationships. Gay immigrant couples may face additional challenges in acknowledging and seeking services for domestic violence because of the stigma in other countries, as well as in the United States, associated with homosexuality (Mallon, 2005). The following example illustrates how a homosexual immigrant couple experienced domestic violence in the United States.

Case 5: Mr. S. and Mr. T.

Mr. S. and Mr. T. are a gay couple who legally emigrated from Singapore 5 years ago on work permits. They wanted to come to the United States because their homosexual relationship was not accepted in Singapore. Rather than finding the happiness they thought they would have in a country and city where their homosexual relationship was more accepted, they had begun to fight more. Mr. S. was so pleased that his relationship was so accepted here that he wanted to tell his family. Mr. T., on the other hand, still felt that they had to keep there relationship secret as their family would never accept them. In fact, when Mr. T.'s family visited recently, Mr. S. had been forced to check into a Y during the visit. This had resulted in a major physical fight that resulted in Mr. S. receiving a broken arm.

Domestic Violence in the Indian/South Asian Community

Although domestic violence may be fueled by unemployment and poverty, domestic violence affects families from all socioeconomic classes as the following example illustrates.

Case 6: Mr. and Mrs. D.

Mr. and Mrs. D. emigrated from New Delhi 3 years ago. From a professional family in India, Mr. D. has a high-level job in a software company. Their conflict began when she started to pursue graduate studies. Sometimes she was not home at dinner time at night because she was taking an evening course or studying at the library. Mr. D. had become increasingly verbally and sometimes even physically violent, saying she had become too Americanized and no longer was respectful of his position as head of the household.

This example depicts value differences in appropriate roles for men and women that lead to domestic violence. Beliefs that women should be submissive and subjugate themselves to their husband's wishes in the Indian community that are challenged in the more egalitarian American society may lead to domestic violence (Gupta, 1992).

APPLICATION OF THE CULTURAGRAM TO THE IDENTIFICATION AND ASSESSMENT OF DOMESTIC VIOLENCE

The culturagram has been used as part of a professional assessment of an immigrant family. Using the culturagram has helped the practitioner incorporate cultural values, beliefs, and experiences into the assessment process; identify more clearly problem areas; and plan more effectively for culturally sensitive and competent interventions.

Although it is one of the most dangerous and deadly of social problems, domestic violence may be difficult to identify even for the most skilled practitioner. Both victims and perpetrators often strive to keep domestic violence secret within the family. Even in cases of serious abuse, victims may choose to remain in potentially life-threatening situations. Identifying and addressing domestic violence may be particularly challenging with immigrant families. Using the culturagram is most helpful to the practitioner in detecting domestic violence and planning for culturally sensitive interventions.

Although the increasing amount of literature on cross-cultural approaches in working with families (Congress & Gonzalez, 2005) helps understanding of immigrant families from diverse backgrounds, there are few specific instruments that can be specifically applied in practice with immigrant families. Two widely used family-assessment tools, the ecomap and the genogram, do not focus specifically on culturally diverse families. The ecomap looks at the family's relationship to outside resources (Hartman and Laird, 1983), although the genogram (McGoldrick, Gerson, & Schallenberg, 1999) focuses on intergenerational relationships. Culture did not seem to be a major component, yet understanding the influence of a family's cultural background seemed crucial in clinical work with family from different backgrounds.

To provide a culturally based tool to help clinicians' understanding of families from diverse backgrounds, the culturagam was first developed in 1994 and modified in 2002 (Congress, 1994, 1997, 2002; Congress & Kang, 2005). The purpose of completing a culturagram is to engage, assess, and plan individualized interventions with families from diverse backgrounds. Since its original development, the culturagram has been applied to work with people of color (Lum, 2004), children (Webb, 1996), older people (Brownell, 1997), people with health problems (Congress, 2004b), immigrant families (Congress, 2004a), and domestic violence (Brownell & Congress, 1997).

The culturagram helps practitioners avoid stereotyping and generalizations about immigrant families. In her practice experience, one author became increasingly aware of how different families were. For example, a family with many undocumented members who recently emigrated from Mexico and a Puerto Rican family who has lived in New York for many years presented differing values and issues. One can call both families Latino/Hispanic, but there were many differences between them. Even families from the same ethnic and national group might be very different. The culturagram helps the practitioner individualize families from different cultural backgrounds as well as from within the same culture by looking at the family from 10 different aspects of culture. These categories are reasons for immigration; legal status; time in the United States; language spoken at home and in the community; health beliefs; contact with cultural and religious institutions; holidays and special events; impact of crisis events; values concerning education and work; and values regarding families such as power, gender relationships, rules, and family myths. These 10 aspects are perceived as the most important in individualizing each family and very important in understanding domestic violence and immigrant families. These 10 aspects of the culturagram are discussed in relationship to domestic violence.

Reasons for Immigration

The main focus with immigrant families is their current situation with minimal attention to the premigration or transit stage for these families. Yet as Pine and Drachman (2005) indicate, it is crucial to have an understanding of the three stages—premigration, transit, and current status. The reasons for immigration relate to the premigration stage. Many families have experienced much stress before emigrating and make decisions to come to the United States because of economic, political, or religious oppression in their homelands. Often families come not as a unit, but individually. Family separation can contribute to domestic violence when families are reunited. Immigrant men may believe that their economic problems will be easily resolved in the United States. Yet when they are not able to secure work easily, this leads to role reversal in families and subsequently to domestic violence.

Length of Time in the Community

Knowing the length of time family members have lived in the United States may be helpful to practitioners in detecting family violence. New arrivals from countries with strong patriarchal traditions may be unaware of laws prohibiting domestic violence (Reichert, 2003).

Even families who have lived in the United States for a long time within closely knit immigrant communities may still adhere to cultural beliefs from their country of origin. They may also believe that no one should know their personal family issues and be reluctant to seek help outside the home for incidents of domestic violence. Sometimes second-generation immigrants become more aware of domestic violence as a social and legal problem and are more likely to insist that their parents who are threatened by domestic violence seek help (Brownell & Congress, 1997).

Legal or Undocumented Status

An unequal power dynamic exists in families in which one spouse is a citizen or legal resident and the other is nondocumented. If nondocumented, the victim may be reluctant to seek help for abuse because she fears deportation and separation from her children. If both partners are undocumented, they may be fearful of the intervention of law enforcement or social service providers. The Personal Responsibility and Work Opportunity Reconciliation Act of 1996 (PRA; PL. 104-193, August 22, 1996) unfortunately prevented many legal and undocumented immigrants from securing needed social services. The Violence Against Women Act of 1994 (VAWA; PL 103-322, September 13, 1994) and PRA did offer emergency and other social services to immigrant women who are victims of domestic violence. Yet immigrant women may not be aware of these possibilities and furthermore may not be able to access them if they remain with the perpetrators.

Although immigrant undocumented women in large cities may be able to avail themselves of needed social services, such services may not be available to undocumented women in smaller towns. Often health care workers and school social workers are the first and possibly the only practitioners to provide services to undocumented victims of domestic violence (Brownell & Congress, 1997).

Language Spoken at Home and in the Community

Immigrant families who speak only the language of their country of origin are much less likely to know about American laws and policies about domestic violence. Often bilingual members do not share information about available resources as a way to keep monolingual members isolated and powerless. The lack of interpreters or the use of family interpreters may also serve to prevent abused immigrant women from seeking assistance.

Health Beliefs

Some cultures may support the somatization of emotional distress, which can lead to victims denying the impact of domestic abuse. Immigrants may seek out native healers who may not view domestic violence from the same cultural and legal perspective as do American-trained health and social service providers. Some immigrant advocacy groups are reaching out to native healers and nontraditional health care providers with information about domestic violence

Contact With Cultural and Religious Institutions

Cultural and religious institutions may strongly reinforce hierarchical roles within the family, including the right of the husband to exert authority over other family members, even if this involves verbal and physical abuse. The cultural and religiously supported role of the male as head of household and the belief that women are responsible for keeping the household together even in the face of extreme difficulties may perpetuate domestic violence in immigrant families. Educating religious leaders in the community about domestic violence may raise awareness of this problem in religious institutions that immigrant families often frequent.

Holidays and Special Events

Holidays and special events may be associated with heavy alcohol consumption. There is some evidence that many immigrant men faced with unemployment and loss of status in their family may turn to alcohol (Hanson & Sealy, 2005), and often alcohol abuse has been seen to be linked to domestic violence.

Even when alcohol is not an issue in immigrant celebrations, holidays and special events may be a time of stress and sadness for immigrants, especially for immigrants who have recently immigrated and lost previous support systems. This increased stress may leave immigrant families at higher risk for domestic violence. Practitioners working with immigrant families can use the culturagram to learn more about holidays and special events for families and the impact of this on domestic violence within the family

Impact of Crisis Events

The meaning of crisis events to immigrant family can be explored. For example, if a wife from a traditional immigrant community is raped, she may be blamed not only by her spouse but also by others in the immigrant community for having invited the rape. She may not seek needed medical care because of feelings of shame and guilt. Her husband may use the rape as a reason for continued verbal and physical abuse. The culturagram helps the practitioner learn what unique crisis events the immigrant family has experienced and what has been their reactions. The relationship among crisis events, the meaning of these events, and domestic violence can be explored.

Values About Education and Work

In cultures that support a hierarchical family structure with a dominant male breadwinner, deviation from cultural norms may lead to family violence. Husbands may become angry when they perceive their wives as seeking more education than they have had or that they think is appropriate. If the husband is unemployed (a risk factor for domestic violence in American culture), he may become abusive, even if the wife is working and supporting the family. She may also seek to protect him by denying or minimizing the abuse, in order to support his dominance in the family.

Women working outside the home may be a source of discomfort to males from some cultures, because they are in contact with male coworkers. Older parents and other community members may reinforce the idea that daughters and daughter-in-laws should be submissive to their husbands.

Values About Family—Structure, Roles, Myths, and Rules

In working with immigrant families, the clinician may discover that the family has a hierarchical structure in which the male has the greatest power. Women's roles are seen as caring for the house and children and never questioning her husband. There may be a rigid difference among children of different genders, with the expectation that girl children should be submissive and protected as their mother, whereas boy children are permitted much more freedom. Often these rigidly defined gender roles can lead to conflict, especially when children reach adolescence. After influence from the more egalitarian structured families, immigrant women and adolescent girls may question these rigidly assigned roles. The result may be increased risk for domestic violence.

Even if risk factors are present, this does not mean that domestic violence is occurring or will occur in families. However, they can be noted as predisposing factors to be looked at more closely during the assessment process. If abuse is detected, it may be denied or rejected unless detection and interventions are framed in a culturally sensitive manner. Often a referral to a provider who is culturally and linguistically similar to the immigrant family may be helpful. Some families, however, may be embarrassed to see a provider from the same community and may prefer an Anglo practitioner.

USE OF THE CULTURAGRAM IN DEVELOPING AND IMPLEMENTING EFFECTIVE INTERVENTION STRATEGIES

Not only is the culturagram useful in engaging and assessing immigrant families that have been affected by domestic violence, but the culturagram can also be used to plan for interventions with families.

Russian-Jewish Immigrant Families

With the case of the Russian-Jewish family previously discussed, immigrant advocacy organizations such as the New York Association for New Americans (NYANA) can be helpful. They provide employment services, mentoring programs, and culturally sensitive counseling programs that are compatible with the values and needs of diverse immigrant groups. There needs to be an expansion of opportunities for Orthodox women who do choose to leave their abusive spouses, as the lack of kosher kitchens can be a barrier (Cramer, 1990).

Chinese Immigrant Families

Isolation of an immigrant victim of domestic violence by the abuser or other family and community members may prevent a victim from knowing about options. Increasingly, immigrant communities are developing culturally specific domestic violence services for their members (Lee & Au, 1998). However, older women like Mrs. Cheng in Case 2 may not feel comfortable in choosing service systems that are primarily geared toward younger abused women and their children.

The Chinese culture emphasizes respect and fear of authority (Kwong, 2002). Knowing this, the use of law enforcement strategies may be a useful intervention strategy for some victims. Often, the Chinese community does not want involvement with law enforcement agents, and might therefore pressure the abuser to stop the abuse in order to avoid contact with the law.

Latino Immigrant Families

It is most important for practitioners to understand that there are major differences among Latino groups depending on their country of origin as this can affect differing access to service.

Puerto Rican Families

Families who have Puerto Rico as their country of origin have more service possibilities than those who come from other Latin American countries. Puerto Rican nationals have access to all government benefits and services in the United States, assuming that other eligibility requirements are met. There may be family pressure, however, to keep the family together and respect the father despite the abuse (Brownell and Ko, 2005). Understanding the concept of "machismo" is helpful in working with Puerto Rican families (Mayo, 1997). Bilingual staff in domestic violence shelter facilities is helpful in working with Latino victims of domestic violence.

Nondocumented Latino Family Members

Nondocumented victims of family violence, like Ms. C. in Case 4, may be especially vulnerable, particularly if they are living with or married to citizens who take advantage of their undocumented status to threaten her with deportation and separation from her children. If there is a language barrier with the victim speaking no English and the perpetrator being bilingual, then exploitation can be exacerbated. The VAWA can protect undocumented victims of domestic violence from deportation and separation from their children. Education about legal options can be most helpful in working with nondocumented women.

Indian/South Asian Immigrant Families

The Indian family described previously indicates that domestic violence does occur in all classes. Although one would think that because of their educational level, they would have an understanding of domestic violence, this might not be the case. As India does not have a concept of spouse abuse or laws prohibiting it, the behavior of Mr. T. toward his wife may seem perfectly acceptable.

Providing information to the husband about the illegality of his behavior in this country, and the possible consequences to him and his work if this continues, may serve as a disincentive for him, as well as important information for his wife. Social stigma and pressure from the extended family to maintain the marriage may prevent the abused Indian woman from seeking help (Gupta, 1992). Because of family traditions of maintaining marriage, the family may be particularly disposed to couple counseling rather than feminist-oriented domestic violence service that might work toward separating the couple (Lipchik, 1994).

CONCLUSION

The interest and concern about culturally sensitive and competent practice with families has grown in recent years (Congress & Gonzalez, 2005). This coupled with increased knowledge about domestic violence in immigrant communities points to a need within the domestic violent service community to develop effective ways of working with immigrant families affected by domestic violence.

Detecting and developing culturally sensitive interventions, however, continues to be a challenge. The culturagram is a culturally sensitive assessment instrument that practitioners can use in understanding and improving services to domestic violence victims and their families from immigrant communities.

The culturagram can also serve as a tool for research on assessment and detection of domestic violence, as well as intervention choices, among victims from ethnically diverse families. Effective practice models and the incidence and prevalence of domestic violence in immigrant families are increasingly important areas for future research.

REFERENCES

Barker, R. (1995). *The social work dictionary* (4th ed.). Silver Spring, MD: National Association of Social Workers.

Brownell, P., & Congress, E. (1997). Application of the culturagram to empower culturally and ethnically diverse battered women. In A. Roberts (Ed.), *Battered women and their families: Intervention strategies and treatment programs* (pp. 387–404). New York: Springer Publishing.

Brownell, P., & Ko, E. J. (2005). Multicultural social work practice with immigrant victims of domestic violence. In E. Congress & M. Gonzalez (Eds.), *Multicultural perspectives in working with families* (2nd ed., pp. 377–409). New York: Springer Publishing.

Chazin, R., & Ushakova, T. (2005). Working with Russian speaking immigrants. In E. Congress & M. Gonzalez (Eds.), *Multicultural perspectives in working with families* (2nd ed., pp. 167–198). New York: Springer Publishing.

Congress, E. (1994). The use of culturagrams to assess and empower culturally diverse families. *Families in Society, 75*(9), 531–540.

Congress, E. (Ed.). (1997). *Multicultural perspectives in working with families.* New York: Springer Publishing.

Congress, E. (2002). Using culturagrams with culturally diverse families. In A. Roberts & G. Greene (Eds.), *Social work desk reference* (pp. 57–61). New York: Oxford University Press.

Congress, E. (2004a). Crisis intervention and diversity: Emphasis on a Mexican immigrant family's acculturation conflicts. In P. Meyer (Ed.), *Paradigms of clinical social work, Volume 3, Emphasis on diversity* (pp 125–144). New York: Brunner-Routledge.

Congress, E. (2004b). Cultural and ethnic issues in working with culturally diverse patients and their families: Use of the culturagram to promote cultural competency in health care settings. *Social Work in Health Care, 39* (3/4), 249–262.

Congress, E., & Gonzalez, M. (2005). *Multicultural perspectives in working with families.* New York: Springer Publishing.

Congress, E., & Kung, W. (2005). Using the culturagram to assess and empower culturally diverse families. In E. Congress & M. Gonzalez (Eds.), *Multicultural perspectives in working with families* (2nd ed., pp. 3–21). New York: Springer Publishing.

Cramer, L. (1990). Recommendations for working with Jewish battered women. National Coalition Against Domestic Violence (NCADV), Fall, 4–5.

Foner, N. (2005). *In a new land: A comparative view of immigration.* New York: New York University Press.

Gupta, V. (1992, June). The weakest link: Domestic violence in our community. *The Indian-American,* 42–44.

Hanson, M., & Sealy, V. (2005). Evidence–based marriage and family treatment with problem drinkers: A multicultural approach. In E. Congress & M. Gonzalez (Eds.), *Multicultural perspectives in working with families* (2nd ed., pp. 339–355). New York: Springer Publishing.

Hartman, A., & Laird, J. (1983). *Family oriented social work practice.* New York: Free Press.

The newest New Yorkers. (2000). Briefing book–Immigrant New York in the new millennium. New York: Department of City Planning.

Kwong, D. (2002). Removing barriers for battered immigrant women: A comparison of immigrant protections under VAWA I & II. *Berkeley Women's Law Journal, 17,* 137–152.

Lee, M., & Au, P. (1998). Chinese battered women in North America: Their experience and treatment. In A. R. Roberts (Ed.), *Battered women and their families: Intervention strategies and treatment programs* (2nd ed., pp. 448–482). New York: Springer Publishing.

Lipchik, E. (1994). Therapy for couples can reduce domestic violence. In K. Swisher & C. Wejesser (Eds.), *Violence against women* (pp. 154–163). San Diego, CA: Greenhaven.

Lum, D. (2004). *Social work practice and people of color* (5th ed.) Belmont, CA: Brooks Cole Thomson.

Mallon, G. (2005). Practice with families where sexual orientation is an issue: Lesbian and gay individuals and their families. In E. Congress & M. Gonzalez (Eds.), *Multicultural perspectives in working with families* (2nd ed., pp. 199–227). New York: Springer Publishing.

Mayo, Y. (1997). Machismo, manhood, and men in Latino families. In E. Congress, *Multicultural perspectives in working with families* (pp. 181–197). New York: Springer Publishing.

McGoldrick, M., Gerson, J., & Schallenberg, J. (1999). *Genograms: Assessment and intervention.* New York: Norton.

Orloff, L. (2001). Lifesaving welfare safety net access for battered immigrant women and children. *William & Mary Journal of Women and Law, 7*(3), 597–657.

Orloff, L. (2003). *Concerning New York City executive order.* Federal Clearing House Congressional Testimony. Retrieved April 3, 2003, from http://80-web.lexix.com.avoserv.library.fordham.edu/universe/doc.

Orloff, L., & Little, R. (1999). Public benefits access for battered immigrant women and children. In L. E. Orloff (Ed.), *Somewhere to turn: Making domestic violence services accessible to battered immigrant women.* Retrieved from http://www.vawnet.org/vnl/library/general/BIW99.cll.html.

Pine, B., & Drachman, D. (2005). Effective child welfare practice with immigrant and refugee children and their families. *Child Welfare, 84*(5), 537–562.

Reichert, E. (2003). *Social work and human rights: A foundation for policy and practice.* New York: Columbia University Press.

Romkens, R. (2001). Law as a Trojan horse: Unintended consequences of rights-based interventions to support battered women. *Yale Journal of Law and Feminism, 13*(2), 265–290.

Schmidley, D. (2003). The foreign-born population in the United States: March 2002. Current Population Reports, P20–539, U.S. Census Bureau, Washington, DC.

Sitowski, L. (2001). Congress giveth, congress taketh away, congress fixith its mistake? Assessing the potential impact of the Battered Immigrant Women Protection Act of 2000. *Law and Inequality Journal, 19*(2), 269–305.

Webb, N. (1996). *Social work practice with children.* New York: Guilford Press.

CHAPTER 21

Venezuelan American Abusive Relationships:
Assessment and Treatment

Diane L. Green and Mary W. Viani

Inthe United States every year, about 1.5 million women and more than 800,000 men are raped or physically assaulted by an intimate partner. This translates into about 47 intimate partner violence (IPV) assaults per 1,000 women and 32 assaults per 1,000 men (Tjaden & Thoennes, 2000). Nearly 5.3 million incidents of IPV occur each year among U.S. women ages 18 and older, and 3.2 million occur among men. IPV results in nearly 2 million injuries and 1,300 deaths nationwide every year (Centers for Disease Control and Prevention [CDC], 2003). Estimates indicate more than 1 million women and 371,000 men are stalked by intimate partners each year (Tjaden & Thoennes, 2000). IPV accounted for 20% of nonfatal violence against women in 2001 and 3% against men (Rennison, 2003). From 1976 to 2002, about 11% of homicide victims were killed by an intimate partner (Fox & Zawitz, 2004). In 2002, 76% of IPV homicide victims were female; 24% were male. The number of intimate partner homicides decreased 14% overall for men and women in the span of about 20 years, with a 67% decrease for men (from 1,357 to 388) versus 25% for women (from 1,600 to 1,202). One study found that 44% of women murdered by their intimate partner had visited an emergency department within 2 years of the homicide. Of these women, 93% had at least one injury visit (Crandall, Nathens, Kernic, Holt, & Rivara, 2004). Previous literature suggests that women who have separated from their abusive partners often remain at risk of violence (Campbell et al., 2002; Fleury, Sullivan, & Bybee, 2000). Firearms were the major weapon type used in intimate partner homicides from 1981 to 1998 (Paulozzi et al., 2001). A national study found that 29% of women and 22% of men had experienced physical, sexual, or psychological IPV during their lifetime (Coker et al., 2002). Between 4% and 8% of pregnant women are abused at least once during the pregnancy (Gazmararian et al., 2000). The National Crime Victimization Survey found that 85% of IPV victims were women (Rennison, 2003). Prevalence of IPV varies among race. Among the ethnic groups most at risk are American Indian/Alaskan Native women and men, African American women, and Hispanic women (Tjaden & Thoennes, 2000). Young women and those below the poverty line are disproportionately victims of IPV (Tjaden & Thoennes, 2000). Intimate partner abuse knows no cultural boundaries.

The United States is not the only industrialized nation with intimate partner abuse and with laws prohibiting such violence. Venezuela is a constitutional democracy with a population of approximately 25 million people. The law prohibits domestic violence, and violators face penalties of 6 to 18 months in prison. Violence against women continues to be a problem, and women face substantial institutional and societal prejudice with respect to rape and domestic violence. The Center for Women's Studies reported that in 2004 there were 3,900 cases of domestic violence reported, and that 1 woman in Caracas died every 10 days from domestic violence. The most prominent types of abuse are psychological (42.75%), followed by physical (37.61%) and verbal (15.25%). The majority (89%) of the women abused have not completed high school, which seems to indicate that there is a corollary between lack of education and abuse. Thirty-six percent of the abusers are conjugal and 43% are cohabitants. The law requires police to report domestic violence and obligates hospital personnel to notify the authorities when they admit patients who are victims of domestic abuse. Police generally are reluctant to intervene to prevent domestic violence, and the courts rarely prosecute those accused of such abuse. Women generally were unaware of legal remedies and had little access to them. The government sought to combat domestic violence through a public awareness campaign and a national victim assistance hotline. The law prohibits rape, including spousal rape, but it remained a problem. Rape is punishable with prison terms of 8 to 14 years, although cases often were not reported to the police. An adult man guilty of raping an adult female acquaintance may avoid punishment if he marries the victim before sentencing (http://www.state.gov/g/drl/rls/hrrpt/2005/61745.htm).

The right to life is a basic prerequisite to definitions of the right to live a healthy life. However, because of violence against women and various other stringent challenges to their daily lives, neither women's health nor their daily lives are fully secure. The National Institute for Women recently celebrated its fifth birthday in which it presented the National Plan for Equality for Women 2004 to 2009, which is designed to prevent and eradicate violence against women, ensure women's rights and access to justice, strengthen the participation of women in politics and society, and to develop and execute a plan for equal economic rights for women.

Venezuela is one of the few Latin American countries that acknowledge violence and discrimination against women as impeding the evolution of a truly democratic society based on equality. However, despite this and despite the Labor Law (1997), the Law of Violence Against Women (1998), the Law for Equal Opportunities for Women (1999), and the Law of Micro Financial System (2001), while Venezuela has taken significant steps to eradicate discrimination legally, these problems continue to persist in society. "We are amidst a profound social transformation in which discrimination, prejudices, and the injustices against women are coming to the forefront. This revolution has recognized women as human beings. But we still are unable to say that we have eradicated discrimination against women in society or even in the minds of women. Discrimination is a phenomenon that has existed for centuries and it is impossible to eradicate within 5 years. Our values do not change overnight. However, Venezuelan women now know that this revolution is for them too and they are beginning to wake up," says Nora Casteñeda, the president of the Woman's Bank.

Under the government of Hugo Chávez, women have been instrumental in initiating legal and institutional reforms, have helped to draft a Constitution that creates the framework for a society based on social justice, have made significant and rapid progress in creating nongovernmental organizations (NGOs), have increased their representation in politics, and have defended their democracy. In the participatory democracy of the Bolivarian Revolution, in which the rights of citizens are not defined as purely political but instead embark on encompassing social justice and gender equality, women have the potential to construct a new humane society that could not only change their reality but also set an example for the world in terms of gender equality. Although the laws in place to protect women in Venezuela are extremely favorable and far reaching, the culture of the country is deeply entrenched in the patriarchal system.

When a man and woman are married, the husband has complete autonomy over her. Even if she is subject to abuse, her family members will not intervene because no one interferes between a man and wife. This practice also holds true for couples who live together. The husband or man is the undisputed head of the family and the family honor is dependent on the reputation of the wife, so the man will control every aspect of her behavior. A man who has other relationships is not viewed in a negative connotation, but the rules are very different for women. The divorce rate is rising gradually because of the global influences, but in the areas outside the big city, men are still very much in charge and the double standard is alive and well. The woman is the moral compass by which the family navigates through society. She can give class to a man who has none if she is above reproach. The family is only as good as the wife and mother. This may also explain why the social programs are lacking. Women are required to attend to home and family and unable to become involved in other causes.

In the remainder of this chapter, we explore an intimate partner abuse experience through the eyes of Christy, a victim, and her relationship with a Venezuelan man, her eventual husband. We will then discuss how to get help for domestic violence or domestic abuse between spouses and intimate partners from different cultures. The first question Christy has is "Why are many women attracted to Latinos?" What we find in her story is that, often, he pursues her with passion. It seems as though his whole world revolves around her. He wants to be part of every aspect of her life. He takes an interest in her appearance, her work, her feelings, her family, her ideas, and her philosophy. It appears that he truly cares about her and who she is. She has never had someone be involved in the little details of her daily routine. He is romantic and takes the time to court her. It does not appear that he wants anything from her but to be with her. He paints a beautiful picture of them together and she is in the center. He erodes her sense of logic and can see that she is affected by his attention and that she responds. He sees her vulnerability and her need for this attention. All of these statements by Christy reflect stages in intimate partner abuse as described later in this chapter. The following case illustrates techniques for the diagnosis and management of women experiencing interpersonal violence.

Case 1: Christy, 1992 to 2006

We were introduced by a mutual acquaintance where I was employed. I was 28 and married to another man; Carlos was 21. He was born and raised in Venezuela and began living in the United States at the age of 13. His education was poor, and he advanced by getting girls and American friends to help him. He was charming and very attentive at first and asked me to meet him several times. I did arrange to meet him and began to deceive my husband, who did not suspect anything. Carlos never promised me anything, but I found him irresistible. After 2 weeks of seeing each other, he was suddenly called home to be with his family. His sister had died of a gunshot wound—some said accident; some said suicide. He returned after 1 month away and I was as smitten as before. I left my husband to be with him. He was completely involved with me and I with him. I walked away from my very nice upwardly mobile life to spend every moment with him. I thought he cared about me. I was college educated and 7 years older than him, and he seemed to need me for advice about everything. I helped him in school and with his finances and just about every aspect of his life. The physical attraction was intense and constant. About 2 months after I moved in with him, we had an argument about how long I was gone for a hair appointment. He thought I was lying. I got angry and he got angrier. I thought he was going to hit me. He did not, but I knew he was capable of it and eventually he did on a regular basis. He scared me. He went wherever he wanted to go, but I could not go anywhere by myself. If I asked him about where he went or what he did, he did not tell me. I became very insecure about his feelings for me. He said an honorable woman never went anywhere by herself. I learned many things about what his mother had endured in her life. His father was a womanizer and he seemed proud of that fact. Five months into the relationship we went to Miami, and he left me in the hotel room for the evening. I ordered several drinks through room service and confronted him when he returned, and he became angry. I tried to slap his face, and he blocked me and slapped me very hard across the face. He was very angry and accused me of flirting with the room service person. I had a bruised face, but it went much deeper than that. He told me many negative things about myself and said that I had a lot of work to do to be the right woman for him. That made me want to be perfect so he would love me. He rewarded me by taking me to Orlando for the day. I felt fabulous. My husband filed for divorce and it was granted. I asked for nothing because I had left him. I went to Venezuela to be with Carlos for Christmas, and his mother died December 26. Shortly after Christmas I thought about leaving him and told him. He was very quiet and actually cried, so I decided to stay because I felt so sorry for him. He had lost his sister and his mother within 6 months of each other. Our relationship affected all aspects of my life. I was very isolated and really had no friends at all. We decided to move to south Florida, and I rented an apartment. I had to interview for a teaching position, and he went to all of the interviews and sat in on them with me. It was very awkward, but that is how he wanted it. At this point he was extremely possessive and controlling. I did get a job in the public school system, and he was out of the country much of the time. I lived a very simple life and did not socialize at all. He came back and began to come to school to check up on me, and I resigned instead of being fired. Several times he asked me to leave so I packed up and moved to be with my parents. I let him control my life even when he was in one city and I was in another. We broke up again at the end of the third year, and I went to visit my ex-husband and found that I did not have feelings for him at all. I went to visit relatives for the holidays, and there was a Christmas card from him waiting for me when I returned. I called him and it started all over again. I went to see him and he said he wanted to have a child with me. I did not object. He and I saw each other regularly until he asked me to move back down. I got a job in the area and immediately became pregnant. He was gone when I discovered I was pregnant and did not call me when he returned. He still monitored me and controlled my life. He did hit me on several occasions during my pregnancy. He did stay around for the birth of our daughter. I changed my name to have it appear that we were married. He saw that she was much like he was. He adored her. I became invisible. We were very poor. His son from another relationship came to live with us, so I had the responsibility of two children. We had a son almost 3 years later. Carlos moved to Venezuela to work. There was no relationship, no respect. We saw him every 3 months. The jealousy and insecurity were constant. He once took all my makeup away for 3 weeks and forbade me from wearing any makeup during that time. I thought that if I did what he said he would accept me and approve of me. It never happened. We did get married in 1988. I was happy for a time. I resented him when he was home and really began to want him out of my life. He forced me to have sex over and over again. He began to spend more time at home between 1991 and 1995. He would stay up all night and sleep all day. I had a full-time job from the time our daughter was 3 years old until the present. Sometimes I had a part-time job to pay for the family. He did not participate financially in the family. He did not participate on a regular basis with the children. He did what he wanted to when he wanted to. One evening he asked me for money to take the children to the mall for dinner. Apparently what he ordered was more than I had given him. He came home with the food and in front of the children threw the food at me and then beat me for embarrassing him in public. The children saw this behavior consistently, and my son took on some of his father's behavior, in one instance yelling at me and throwing a table over because I was "stupid." My son has ended up in numerous altercations with the criminal justice system as a result of his behavior. Carlos continued to hold me responsible for what was wrong with the relationship or the children. He showed rage at me and his son from time to time. His daughter was his pride and joy. People were aware that he played favorites. He spent a great deal of time working with her and said it was my job to get his son ready for him to work with and I never did it well. I asked for a divorce, and he immediately thought I was having an affair. He had me followed as well as having my friends followed. He threatened to kill one of my friends. He refused to accept any responsibility for any aspect of the marriage. It took the help of friends and family to procure the divorce as he knew to be careful when coming to the United States to avoid having papers served. As long as he could not be served, I was his. Eventually he came to the United States and took all of my belongings and went to a hotel. When he returned, the police arrested him and fortunately held him long enough for the papers to be served. After many months of severe threats to me and my friends, the divorce began. The trial lasted 1 hour and the judge awarded all assets to me. The funny thing is that regardless of what the judge awarded me, because Carlos is not a U.S. citizen, I get nothing.

Carlos was secretive, demanding, negative, critical, angry, and controlling. Any problem could be traced to something I had done wrong. I was long-suffering, patient, invisible, responsible, guilt-ridden, insecure, totally lacking in self-confidence and self-worth.

As a child I perceived that we have worth based on what we do, not who we are. My father may have loved me, but he expected his children to be a reflection of himself; therefore he had very high standards. Only a 95, not a 100? My mother and brother also contributed to the perception that men must be obeyed and are in charge. Pleasing them was admirable. I was molested by my brother. I did make an attempt to balk and rebel as a teenager, but my father was relentless in always being right. Feelings did not matter—actions were important. He had no idea that he was cementing the behaviors I would exhibit as an adult. He was charming and fun-loving with those outside the nuclear family, but I do not remember much of that in our home. My mother always put him first, and I carried that philosophy with me to my marriages. I had trouble expressing what I wanted and how I felt.

I did have great success as a professional educator, but did not have the confidence to go for a graduate degree or enter law school. I was not comfortable going to the next level. Fear of failure.

Christy is a classic example of an individual living with sporadic long-term abuse. Roberts and Roberts (2005) identified three reasons that women stay in these abusive marriages: (a) they want to believe that, because the battering is so infrequent, it will not reoccur; (b) they want their children to grow up in an intact family; and (c) they are dependent on the husband's income, and they want their children to be able to maintain their current lifestyle, including remaining in the same school district with their current friends. They further indicate that these women were often abused by one or both of their parents or at the very least had very unhappy childhoods with controlling parental figures. Christy also rationalized that her spouse's brutality was a result of his stress, and his apologies seemed sincere.

Roberts and Roberts (2005) discuss several components typical of long-term abuse that we can see in Christy's recounting: (a) critical incident(s) in childhood, (b) an overwhelming love for the man they marry, (c) an initial incident, and (d) escalation of abuse and eventual isolation. Roberts and Roberts suggest looking at critical incidents in the victim's childhood. Some incidents may be outwardly violent, whereas others, like Christy's, displayed the nuances of emotional abuse. The impact of Christy's childhood abuse is clear in her explanation of why she remained in the abusive relationship.

Let us first take a look at Christy's case from the typical development of an IPV relationship. Meuer et al. (2002) outline a typical sequence that is characteristic and identify nine stages. During the first stage, the relationship seems strong, powerful, and overall wonderful.

Christy's husband demonstrated an interest in everything Christy did and everywhere she went. Christy, like many victims, mistakenly sees these obsessive and very controlling behaviors as affection and dedication rather than as abusive. These behaviors continue and go further with her husband wanting to know where she is at all times; stage 2. At this point he begins to make decisions for her and requires her demonstrated loyalty. From this point on he will make the decisions, be in charge, and make the "rules." He further expects Christy to attend to all of his needs. In stage 3 Christy adjusts to his controlling behaviors and jealousies. She convinces herself that she will be happier with him than anyone else because he cares so much. Stage 4 is the beginning of the psychological and emotional abuse. He no longer only controls the little things, but now he controls every aspect of her life. This can be seen when Christy had an interview and he went to the interview to be sure of her loyalty. This stage also is marked by his controlling her makeup and dress. He punishes her behavior by taking her makeup away so that no one could find her attractive. Meuer et al. identify stage 5 as being characterized by the first physical abuse. Christy, as many women do, thought that her behavior must have provoked him and that it was a one time incident. He apologizes for hitting her and she is convinced it won't happen again. Stage 6 marks the co-occurrence of physical and psychological abuse. When Christy would ask why he was behaving in an abusive way, he was quick to point out that it was all her fault, and she is the sole reason that he was "set" off. He further assures her that it won't happen again if she behaves properly. Meuer et al. place stage 7 occurring at the same time as stage 6. This is where the isolation begins. Christy's husband wanted to know her whereabouts at all times. On one occasion when her husband was in Venezuela, he thought he was losing control of her. He was very angry that she was spending time with her girlfriend, who was staying with her for a visit. He told Christy to make her friend leave. With much reluctance, Christy asked her friend to leave. However, once Christy's husband knew that Christy had done what he asked, he then gave her "permission" to ask her friend to come back. Typical of this stage, her husband did not want her to spend time with anyone that she had a good time with, so eventually she stops seeing people of whom he disapproves, further isolating her. During stage 8, the abuser consistently blames the victim, who is unsure of what is wrong. The final stage, 9, is characterized by the abuser using the psychological and physical threats to maintain dominance and control. He may eventually threaten her if she leaves and thus many women stay in the relationship. Often the threats and outbursts are followed by apologies. In all abuse situations there are identifiable power and control issues that know no cultural boundaries. Table 21.1 depicts many abuse factors. This may be a helpful tool in assisting the victim with her personal assessment of the relationship.

As people deal with being victimized, workers can identify common reactions. These reactions are normal, but may still mean that the victim requires help to deal with being overwhelmed. Table 21.2 lists some common reactions to crime victimization in general.

Additionally, we need to look at the severity of the victim's reaction to develop ideas of how to best help victims rebuild their lives. Some victims may benefit the most from relatively minor interventions, for example, sharing information. Others with more severe reactions might require more intensive support that might be provided in a peer group. Finally, there are those clients experiencing severe reactions that may require a referral to mental health counseling or even hospitalization. It would not make sense to only give information to someone experiencing severe distress, nor would it make sense to require a person coping well to enter therapy. Table 21.3 describes a proposed model to help workers think about these issues. The key element to understand is that crime victims are a diverse group with diverse needs. This diversity requires workers to adapt to the victim in providing those services that best meet the victim's needs.

One thing to keep in mind is that leaving the abuser is not always the best initial approach and may actually place the victim in more danger. "Many batterers continue to harass, stalk and harm the woman long after she has left him, sometimes resulting in death" (Walker, 1999, p. 25). The first thing that should be done is a complete risk assessment: Is the victim safe? One instrument used for risk assessment is the Spousal Assault Risk Assessment (Kropp, Hart, Webster, & Eaves, 1999). Jacquelyn Campbell developed the Danger Assessment, which determines the severity and frequency of battering. The Historical/Clincial/Risk Management Scale includes items based on personal background, attitudes or mental disorders, and external factors (Webster, Harris, Rice, Cormier, & Quinsey, 1994). The Iterative Classification Tree (Monahan, Bonnie, et al., 2001) is a flowchart that considers clinical observations associated with the prediction of violence.

TABLE 21.1 Power and Control Issues

Physical abuse	
Tripping	Twisting
Kicking	Using a weapon
Throwing partner down	Choking
Hitting	Pushing
Punching	Grabbing
Beating	Pulling hair
Slapping	Shoving
Biting	

Power and control

Threats
- Making or carrying out threats to do something to hurt partner emotionally
- Threatening to commit suicide
- Threatening to take away the children
- Threatening to report partner to a government agency, or betraying other important secrets

Emotional abuse
- Putting partner down
- Making the partner think she or he is crazy
- Making the partner feel bad about self
- Playing "mind games"

Using male privilege
- Treating partner like a servant
- Acting like the "master of the castle"
- Making all the big decisions

Isolation
- Controlling what partner does
- Controlling who partner talks to
- Controlling who partner sees
- Controlling where partner goes

Sexual abuse
- Making partner do sexual things against his or her will
- Physically attacking the sexual parts of partner's body
- Treating partner like a sex object

Using the children
- Making partner feel guilty about the children
- Using visitation as a way to harass partner
- Using the children to give messages

Economic abuse
- Trying to keep partner from getting a job
- Taking partner's money
- Making partner ask for money
- Giving partner an "allowance"

Intimidation—putting partner in fear, by
- Looks, actions, gestures, and a loud voice
- Destroying partner's property
- Smashing things
- Killing, hurting, or threatening pets

Eyler & Cohen (1999).

TABLE 21.2   Common Reactions to Crime Victimization

Mood/Emotions	Social	Thinking/Memories	Physical
Fear/phobias[a,c,d,e]	Changes in	Intrusive memories[b]	Nausea[a]
Anger/hostility[a–d,g]	relating to	Lower self-efficacy[b]	Stomach
Embarrassment[a]	people[b,f]	Vigilance[b]	problems[a]
Anxiety[b,e,g]	Avoidance[e,g]	Flashbacks[e]	Muscle tension[a]
Depression[b,d,f]	Alienation[e]	Confusion/poor	Sleep problems[b]
Grief[a,b,d]		concentration[d,e]	
Guilt/shame[d–f]		Dissociation[d]	
Difficulty			
controlling			
emotions[d]			
Apathy[e]			
Lower self-esteem[g]			

[a]Casarez-Levison (1992).
[b]Everly et al. (2000).
[c]Greenberg and Ruback (1992).
[d]Leahy, Pretty, and Tenenbaum (2003).
[e]Mezy (1988).
[f]Nishith, Resick, and Griffin (2002).
[g]Norris et al. (1997).

STRATEGIES FOR INTERVENTIONS

Victims of intimate partner abuse are at increased risk of suffering from physical and mental health problems. To minimize these negative effects, service providers should follow several basic steps. First, a core needs assessment must be conducted. Second, care must be taken not to retraumatize the victim by the criminal justice system or by recounting their story. Third, the psychological, social, and health effects of trauma identified in the needs assessment must be addressed. Fourth, for those in need, scientifically supported multi-session interventions should be implemented.

Crisis Intervention

Crisis intervention is a model of treatment of acute states of psychological decompensation. In addition to crisis resolution, the intervention maximizes the related potential for psychic growth and maturation. Crisis intervention provides the conceptual framework

TABLE 21.3   Severity by Service Type: A Proposed Model

Needs level	Description	Possible service options
Low	They are coping well with few symptoms, easily managed through natural coping skills and social support. They may not have experienced a severe crime or may have many ways to cope.	Minimal services: information sharing, provide written material, brochures of available supports, and education about signs of deeper problems. These services would also be useful for those who do not feel they have any problems, but are trying to hide their suffering.
Moderate	Experiencing some symptoms and need to expand coping skills or need a place to deal with overwhelming emotions. Generally they cope well but are overwhelmed by being victimized.	Peer-run support groups, paraprofessional and volunteer support. Some professional support may be needed but only on a short-term basis.
High	Experiencing many symptoms and display poor coping behaviors. Overwhelmed by being victimized and with few effective supports. Severe trauma may have occurred. Likely evidence of multiple problems and multiple victimizations.	Need for professional treatment. This may include long-term individual or group therapy or even hospitalization to help the person stabilize.

Note. http://www.canada.justice.gc.ca/en/ps/voc/publications/hill/contact.html.

for an increasing number of community-based multidisciplinary services. Crisis intervention with battered women must be approached with empathy, sensitivity, and caution. Stress management techniques can build on the battered woman's inner strengths and potential for positive growth.

The following is a description of the application of the seven stages in Roberts's Crisis Intervention Model. First, it is important to be aware that stages 1 and 2 often take place simultaneously.

STAGE 1—Plan and Conduct a Crisis Assessment.   The therapeutic goal of the intervention during the initial crisis assessment is for the crisis worker to facilitate the restoration of equilibrium in favor of living. The profoundly depressed person will find it easy to find reasons for staying but may need help in identifying reasons for living.

- Assess lethality.
- Was there a trigger?
- Obtain background information quickly.
- Assess the presence of suicidal thoughts or homicidal thoughts, substance abuse history and preexisting mental disorders.
- It is important to ask about the frequency of thoughts about suicide, the method and the plan for carrying it out, whether any preparations have been made, and whether the client has talked to others about suicidal thoughts.
- Investigate social support and follow through with procedures to ensure safety (e.g., removal of medications or potentially dangerous items referred to in the suicide plan).
- Listen for unexpected pieces of the client's story and reflect these parts back.
- Assess sense of helplessness and hopelessness.

STAGE 2—Establish Rapport.   It is very important to introduce yourself and speak in a calm and neutral manner. The crisis worker should do their best to make a psychological connection in a precrisis or acute crisis situation. Part of establishing rapport and putting the person at ease involves being nonjudgmental, listening actively, and demonstrating empathy.

- Establish a bridge, bond, or connection by asking the client what sports or music he likes.
- "Are you playing in any sport now?"
- "Do you have a favorite team?"
- "Do you have a favorite recording artist?"
- Don't lecture, preach, or moralize. Make concise statements, be caring, display keen interest, and do not make disparaging or insulting statements of any kind.

Stages 3 and 4 sometimes take place simultaneously.

STAGE 3—Identify the Major Problem, Including Crisis Precipitants or Triggering Incidents.

- Ask questions to determine the final straw or precipitating event that led to the current situation.

- Focus on problem or problems, and prioritize and focus on the worst problem.
- Listen carefully for symptoms and clues of suicidal thoughts and intent.
- Make a direct inquiry about suicidal plans and nonverbal gestures or communication (e.g., diaries, poems, journals, school essays, paintings, or drawings).

STAGE 4—Deal With Feelings and Emotions, and Provide Support.

- Deal with the client's immediate feelings or fears.
- Allow client to tell his or her story and why he or she seems to be feeling so bad.
- Tune in and provide preliminary empathy to the impact of the assault.
- Active listening skills (i.e., paraphrasing, reflection of feelings, summarizing, reassurance, compliments, advice giving, reframing, and probes).
- Normalize client's experiences.
- Validate and identify emotions.
- Examine past coping methods.
- Encourage ventilation of mental and physical feelings.

STAGE 5—Exploring Possible Alternatives.

- First reestablish balance and homeostasis, also known as *equilibrium.*
  a. Ask what has helped in the past: For example, what has he or she done to cope in earlier situations. By assessing inner resources, the discovery develops as a collaborative experience and looking at pros and cons of perceived helpless and hopeless situation. When the client is able to view the situation logically, his or her sense of hopelessness decreases.
  b. Integrate solution-based therapy (e.g., full or partial miracle question).
  c. Ask about hobbies, birthday celebrations, sport successes, academic successes, and vacations.
  d. Mutually explore and suggest new coping options and alternatives.
  e. It is important for the crisis worker to jog the client's memories so he/she can verbalize the last time everything seemed to be

going well, and he/she was in a good mood. Help the client to find untapped resources.

- Provide client(s) with a specific phone number of a therapist and plan to follow. The therapist needs to be someone who is willing and able to work with challenging and difficult clients in crisis.

STAGE 6—Restore Cognitive Functioning Through Implementation of an Action Plan. Clients must feel a sense of ownership in the action plan so that they can increase their level of autonomy and ensure that they are not dependent on other supportive persons or agency staff. Obtaining a commitment from the client to follow through with the action plan and any referrals to community-based agencies and therapists can be maximized by using a mutual and collaborative process of intervention planning. Termination and closure of crisis intervention should begin soon after the client has achieved the goals of the action plan or has been referred to another social service or mental health center.

STAGE 7—Follow-up Phone Call, in-Person Appointment for Booster Session, or Home Visit. Let her know that she can call you, and give her your beeper number. Let her know that the beeper is for an emergency. In addition, depending on the crisis worker's assessment when leaving the home, it would be useful to schedule a follow-up with the therapist who Christy is being referred to, so that there is a team approach. Follow-up may include a booster session with the crisis worker scheduled for 1 week or 30 days later.

Meaning Reconstruction: Reconciling Shattered Assumptions Through Narrative Therapy

Christy's recollection of her relationship highlights the struggle individuals experience when core assumptions about oneself and the world have been shattered. Janoff-Bulman (1992, p. 5) posited that "our fundamental assumptions are the bedrock of our conceptual system; they are the assumptions that we are least aware of and least likely to challenge." She further stated that one's core assumptions (the world is benevolent, the world is meaningful, and the self is worthy) are shattered by traumatic stress. Pearlman and Saakvitne

(1995) claim that one's frame of reference (which includes one's worldview, one's identity, and one's spirituality) is disrupted through trauma. Christy provides evidence that supports both of these theories of the traumatic impact on one's assumptive world. How are we to understand and help victims understand the process of meaning reconstruction in the wake of their experiences and losses? Narratives can often be used as a dynamic process to understand not only the victim's story but also how the victim recounts the experience, which sheds light on the recovery process. Cognitive therapists listen to narratives to identify and point out logical errors to the client. The client's telling of the story is a necessary precursor for therapy, or as an initial intake interview, from which a treatment plan is derived.

SUMMARY AND CONCLUSION

It is estimated that between 1.8 million and 4 million women are assaulted in their home by an intimate partner every year, and that women suffer 10 times as many incidents of domestic violence as do men. Intimate abuse is a leading cause of mortality and morbidity. Practitioners must be prepared to work with clients who are victims that have been hesitant to seek help from a variety of cultures. In all cultures, remember, the danger is real. If you are controlling or have a controlling partner, don't ignore these behaviors. They are not the result of stress, anger, drugs, or alcohol. They are learned behaviors that one person uses to dominate, intimidate, and manipulate. They are destructive and dangerous. If the abuse continues without outside help, the abusing partner may risk being arrested, going to jail, or losing the relationship. Domestic violence hurts all family members. When a person is abusive, he or she eventually loses the trust and respect of his or her partner. Abused partners are afraid to communicate their feelings and needs. Everyone has the right to feel safe in a relationship. With help, people who are abusive can learn to be nonviolent. Remember that disagreements develop from time to time in relationships. Domestic violence is not a disagreement. It is a whole pattern of behaviors used by one partner to establish and maintain power and control over the other. These behaviors can become more frequent and intense over time. The abusive person is responsible for these behaviors. That person is the only one who can change them. Don't wait until someone gets hurt.

In summary, abuse in a relationship is any act used to gain power and control over another person. Women who are abused physically are often isolated. Their partners tend to control their lives to a great extent as well as verbally degrade them. Why do women, such as this one, stay in an abusive relationship? There is a plethora of research on why women stay in abusive relationships, and these cross all cultural lines.

- Lowered self-esteem and lack of confidence in their own perceptions of reality.
- Lack of conviction that the relationship is bad enough to leave.
- Fear of being alone; emotional dependence.
- A fear that they will not find a better relationship elsewhere.
- Belief that the children need their father in the household.
- Fear of losing their children.
- A focus on the good times, rather than on the abusive times.
- "Love" for the abuser, which is often really love based on dependence, attachment, or gratitude.
- A belief that they are to blame, that they need to work harder to make a better marriage or partnership, that they deserve no better.
- Fear of retaliation by the very person whom they wish to leave.
- Lack of financial resources to survive on their own or to take care of their children. Women are traditionally more tied to a marriage than a man and cannot leave as easily.
- Lack of institutional support to leave the relationship (lack of support from police, clergy, counselors, the courts, or social services). Society sometimes lacks sympathy toward the victim of domestic violence, particularly when the victim is within a marital or permanent domestic partnership. People often believe that the abuse must have been provoked, and therefore it is appropriate.
- Lack of support from friends and family to leave an emotionally abusive relationship. Friends and family are often more sympathetic to the impact of physical abuse than they are to verbal or nonverbal emotional abuse.

Women stay because of fear, isolation, some form of love, or a combination of these, which Christy's story exemplified.

REFERENCES

Calvert, P., & Palmer, C. (2003). Application of the cognitive therapy model to initial crisis assessment. *International Journal of Mental Health, 12,* 30–38.

Campbell, J., Jones, A., Dienemann, J., Kub, J., Schollenberger, J., & O'Campo, P. (2002). Intimate partner violence and physical health consequences. *Internal Medicine, 162*(10), 1157–1163.

Centers for Disease Control and Prevention. (2003). *Costs of intimate partner violence against women in the United States.* Atlanta, GA: CDC, National Center for Injury Prevention and Control. Retrieved May 15, 2006, from www.cdc.gov/ncipc/pub-res/ipv_cost/ipv.htm.

Coker, A. L., Davis, K. E, Arias, I., Desai, S., Sanderson, M., & Brandt, H. M. (2002). Physical and mental health effects of intimate partner violence for men and women. *American Journal of Preventive Medicine, 2*(4), 260–268.

Coker, A. L., Smith, P. H., Thompson, M. P., McKeown, R. E., Bethea, L., & Davis, K. E. (2002). Social support protects against the negative effects of partner violence on mental health. *Journal of Women's Health and Gender-Based Medicine, 11*(5), 465–476.

Crandall, M., Nathens, A. B., Kernic, M. A., Holt, V. L., & Rivara, F. P. (2004). Predicting future injury among women in abusive relationships. *Journal of Trauma: Injury, Infection, and Critical Care, 56*(4), 906–912.

Eyler, A. E., & Cohen, M. (1999). Case studies in partner violence. *American Academy of Family Physicians.* Retrieved June 3, 2006, from http://aafp.org/afp/991201ap/2569.html.

Fleury, R.E., Sullivan, C. M., & Bybee, D. I. (2000). When ending the relationship does not end the violence. Women's experiences of violence by former partners. *Violence Against Women, 6,* 1363–1383.

Fox, J. A., & Zawitz, M. W. (2004). *Homicide trends in the United States.* Washington, DC: U.S. Department of Justice. Retrieved May 30, 2006, from www.ojp.usdoj.gov/bjs/homicide/homtrnd.htm.

Gazmararian, J. A., Petersen, R., Spitz, A. M., Goodwin, M. M., Saltzman, L. E., & Marks, J. S. (2000). Violence and reproductive health: Current knowledge and future research directions. *Maternal and Child Health Journal, 4*(2), 79–84.

Heise, L., & Garcia-Moreno, C. (2002). Violence by intimate partners. In E. Krug, L. L. Dahlberg, J. A. Mercy, et al. (Eds.), *World report on violence and health* (pp. 87–121). Geneva, Switzerland: World Health Organization.

Janoff-Bulman, R. (1992). *Shattered assumptions.* New York: The Free Press.

Kropp. P., Hart, S., Webster, C., & Eaves, D. (1999). *Spousal assault risk assessment guide user's manual.* Toronto, Canada: Multi-Health Systems, Inc. and B.C. Institute Against Family Violence.

Meuer, T., Seymour, A., & Wallace, H. (2002). Domestic violence. In J. Monahan, R. Bonnie, P. Appelbaum, P. Hyde, H. Steadman, &

M. Swartz. (2001) Mandated community treatment: Beyond outpatient commitment. *Psychiatric Services, 52,* 1198–1205.

Parkinson, G. W., Adams, R. C., & Emerling, F. G. (2001) Maternal domestic violence screening in an office-based pediatric practice. *Pediatrics, 108*(3), 43–45.

Paulozzi, L. J., Saltzman, L. E., Thompson, M. P., & Holmgreen, P. (2001). *Surveillance for homicide among intimate partners-United States, 1981–1998.* CDC Surveillance Summaries, *50*(SS-3), 1–16.

Pearlman, L. A., & Saakvitne, K. W. (1995). *Trauma and the therapist: Countertransference and vicarious traumatization in psychotherapy with incest survivors.* New York: W.W. Norton & Co.

Plichta, S. B. (2004). Intimate partner violence and physical health consequences: Policy and practice implications. *Journal of Interpersonal Violence, 19*(11), 1296–1323.

Rennison, C. (2003). *Intimate partner violence, 1993–2001.* Washington, DC: Bureau of Justice Statistics, U.S. Department of Justice, Publication No. NCJ197838.

Roberts, A. (2005). *Crisis intervention handbook* (3rd ed.). New York: Oxford University Press.

Roberts, A., & Burgess, A. (1998). *Battered women and their families* (2nd ed.). New York: Springer Publishing.

Roberts, A., & Roberts, B. (2005). *Ending intimate partner abuse.* New York: Oxford University Press.

Seymour, A., Murray, M., Sigmon, J., Hook, M., Edmunds, C., Gaboury, M., et al. (Eds.), *National Victim Assistance Academy textbook.* Washington, DC: U.S. Department of Justice, Office for Victims of Crime.

Tjaden, P., & Thoennes, N. (2000). *Full report of the prevalence, incidence, and consequences of violence against women: Findings from the National Violence Against Women Survey.* Washington, DC: U.S. Department of Justice, Publication No. NCJ183781. Retrieved May 30, 2006, from www.ncjrs.org/txtfiles1/nij/183781.txt.

Walker, L. E. (1999). Psychology and domestic violence around the world. *American Psychologist, 54,* 21–29.

Webster, C. D., Harris, G. T., Rice, M., Cormier, C., & Quinsey, V. L. (1994). *The violence prediction scheme: Assessing dangerousness in high risk men.* Toronto, Canada: Center of Criminology, the University of Toronto.

CHAPTER 22

Chinese Battered Women in North America:
Their Experiences and Treatment

Mo-Yee Lee and Patrick Au

Affter more than 30 years of work by feminist activists, scholars, and practitioners who have been the force behind the battered women's movement, the issue of domestic violence has gained enough public prominence that it now can be considered mainstream in North America. In addressing the issue of domestic violence, grassroots activists and concerned professionals have set up more than 2,500 shelters for battered women in the United States and Canada; established hundreds of programs and services available to victims, offenders, and children; reformed protection order legislation and arrest policies; expanded safeguards for women seeking custody of their children; and offered community education of domestic violence to both laypersons and professionals (Roberts & Kurst Swanger, 2002; Schechter, 1996). The number of available shelters for abused women in Canada increased from 18 in 1975 to 524 in 2002 (Johnson, 2005). The proliferation of our collective knowledge and understanding of violence against women and its treatment in North America has, however, largely neglected the experience of women from diverse ethnoracial backgrounds (Lee &

Law, 2001; Lum, 1998; Yoshihama, 1999). The impact of race and ethnicity on one's experience of battering has been poorly documented or studied. The conceptualization of gender as the primary foundation of battering as a social problem mitigated consideration of race or other factors as significant in understanding the phenomenon of domestic violence (Kanuha, 1996). Such a conceptualization, however, may have served a purpose for the early battered women's movement. Instead of portraying a battered woman as "the bad woman" who is poor, or a racial/ethnic minority, or drug-addicted, it is easier to gain public sympathy by portraying her as a victim who does not know how to fight back and is morally deserving of protection (Loseke, 1992; Mahoney, 1994)—an image fitting a collective interpretation of Everywoman that is often equivalent to a white, middle-class, moral, "good" woman (Kanuha).

The abandonment of women from diverse ethnoracial backgrounds in defining the image of battered women in the battered women's movement, however, shortchanges our understanding of their experiences as well as our provision of culturally competent and culturally sensitive interventions for this population. In addition, such neglect reproduces the existing racism in society. Our lack of knowledge about woman victims from diverse ethnoracial backgrounds is well matched by our ignorance of the experiences of men who batter. Gondolf (1997), in reviewing existing batterer programs, called for an expanded effort to understand the experience of minority men because they often perceive, interpret, and justify their abuse differently, and their experiences with the criminal justice system and social services are oftentimes different from those of other men. To better understand domestic violence and provide effective intervention to stop violence in intimate relationships, it is important to produce additional images of domestic violence that capture the experience of *many* men, women, and children.

The purpose of this chapter is to describe the experience of Chinese battered women in North America and appraise existing services available to them. Because there is a lack of established literature in this area, the discussion is based on interviews with prominent Chinese or Asian professionals and activists working with Chinese battered women, and documents provided by them. The informants come from seven major cities in North America that have a large Chinese population: San Francisco, Santa Clara, Los Angeles, New York, Toronto, Montreal, and Vancouver (see Table 22.1). All

TABLE 22.1   Informants of the Study: Personal Communications Conducted in May–June, 1997

Name	Agency	Location	Nature
Au, Patrick, Executive Director	Chinese Family Life Services of Metro Toronto	Toronto, Ontario, Canada	Ethno-Specific Chinese Family Service Agency
Cheung, Rhoda, Counselor	Support Network for Battered Women	Santa Clara County, California, US	Mainstream Women's Shelter Founded in 1978
Eng, Patricia, Executive Director	New York Asian Women's Center	New York, New York, US	Asian Women's Shelter Founded in 1982
Hsieh, Stephanie, Program Director/Counselor	Center for the Pacific-Asian Family	Los Angeles, California, US	Asian Women's Shelter Founded in 1981
Lam, Cynthia, Executive Director	Chinese Family Service of Greater Montreal	Montreal, Quebec, Canada	Ethno-Specific Chinese Family Service Agency
Masaki, Beckie, Executive Director	Asian Women's Shelter	San Francisco, California, US	Asian Women's Shelter Founded in 1988
Ng, Kelly, Program Director, Family and Youth Counseling	United Chinese Community Enrichment Services Society	Vancouver, British Columbia, Canada	Ethno-Specific Chinese Family Service Agency
Shum, Tina, Program Director/Counselor	Department of Social Services of Donaldina Cameron House	San Francisco, California, US	Ethno-Specific Chinese Family Service Agency
Yee, Jo Ann, Family Service Manager	Asian Women Home, Asian Americans for Community Involvement	Santa Clara County, California, US	Asian Women's Shelter Founded in 1994
Yung, Vanda, Counselor	Chinatown Service Center	Los Angeles, California, US	Ethno-Specific Chinese Family Service Agency

informants come from agencies and shelters providing ethnospecific and bilingual services to Chinese battered women.

Apparently, many Chinese in North America are native-born. Their experiences and challenges would be very different from that of the first-generation Chinese, and more likely to resemble the mainstream experiences of battering. The focus of the discussion in this chapter is on Chinese battered women who utilize ethnospecific services. Many of them are foreign-born Chinese who are more likely to be influenced by traditional Chinese values and beliefs. Even so, traditional Chinese values have undergone tremendous challenges in the past several decades as a result of political and socioeconomic changes. It is, therefore, important to notice the process of continuity and the process of change that underlies the evolving value systems affecting the Chinese people.

THE PHENOMENON

Prevalence of Spouse Abuse in the Chinese Community

In the United States, domestic violence is estimated to occur annually in one out of every six households. Nearly one-third of all married women report having experienced at least one incident of physical violence during the course of their marriage (Straus & Gelles, 1986). Based on the report "Intimate Partner Violence" published by the U.S. Department of Justice, Bureau of Justice Statistics, the rate of intimate violence was 7.7 per 1,000 women in 1998 with women ages 16 to 24 experiencing the highest per capita rates of intimate violence (19.6 per 1,000 women) (U.S. Department of Justice, May 2000). In actual terms, women experienced about 900,000 violent offenses at the hands of an intimate partner. In addition, intimate partner violence made up 22% of violent crime against women between 1993 and 1998. On the other hand, there was a trend of decrease in intimate violence from 1993 to 1997 where the rate of intimate partner violence fell from 9.8 to 7.5 per 1,000 women. The data included in this report was based on the National Crime Victimization Survey and on data from the FBI (homicide data). Such data only included violent crimes of lethal (homicide) and non-lethal (rape, sexual assault, robbery, aggravated assault, and simple assault) offenses and did not include emotional and verbal abuse. In Canada, it is estimated that

25% of all Canadian women age 16 and over have been abused by their current or previous partner. In the case of married or previously married women, the figure goes up to 29%. Further, 20% of these cases were serious enough to have caused physical injuries (Statistics Canada, 1995, p. 105). The 1999 General Social Survey of Victimization provides more current estimates of the level of partner violence. Based on GSSV, 8% of women were victims of partner violence in the previous five years and 3% were victims of partner violence in the previous year (Family Violence in Canada, Statistics Canada, 2001).

Prevalence studies for the Chinese population in North America regarding domestic violence are unavailable. Official statistics in both the United States and Canada do not include Chinese (nor Asians) as a separate category in their analyses. The Consultancy Study commissioned by the Hong Kong Social Welfare Department, however, reported that 13.9% of adult respondents were battered by their spouse (Chan, Chiu, & Chiu, 2005; HKSAR Women's Commission, 2006). Professionals and activists working with Chinese battered women in North America, on the other hand, unanimously cited the following observations regarding prevalence of wife assault in the Chinese community.

It is an unfounded myth that domestic violence does not occur in the Chinese community, because Chinese women rarely utilize services provided by women's shelters (Chan, 1989; Ho, 1990). Domestic violence certainly exists in the Chinese community. However, there is a problem of underreporting and low utilization of social services, especially services offered by mainstream women's shelters, as a result of cultural and/or language barriers—reasons that have been repeatedly cited by many other researchers examining the low utilization rate of social services by Chinese in North America (e.g., Matsuoka, Breaux, & Ryujin, 1997; Sue, Fujino, Hu, & Takeuchi, 1991).

Spouse abuse in the Chinese community happens across all socioeconomic strata regardless of an individual's immigration status. For instance, R. Cheung (personal communication, May 9, 1997) noted that the husbands of some Chinese women who contacted the Support Network for Battered Women (a women's shelter in Santa Clara County, California) are accomplished engineers working for big companies in Silicon Valley, California. Likewise, P. Au (personal communication, May 20, 1997) estimated that 40% of women seeking services from the Chinese Family Life Services of Metro Toronto in 1996 came from middle-class, professional families. A study conducted by the same agency in 1989 on 54 wife-assault cases (Chan, 1989) indicated that 26% of the abusers were either entrepreneurs or professionals. Further, 46% of the batterers had attained postsecondary education and 24% were university graduates. Regarding the length of residency, 80% of the abusers and 61% of the victims had been in Canada for more than 6 years. The myth that only poor, uneducated, or new immigrants abuse their spouses is not true in the Chinese community. Those who stay at the women's shelters are, however, predominantly from the lower classes or are new immigrants who do not have alternative, outside resources (New York Asian Women's Center, 1992; J. A. Yee, personal communication, May 9, 1997).

The Faces of Chinese Battered Women

The Chinese community in North America consists of many peoples from different regions who come to stay in this land for various reasons. Many of them come to North America for a better future, but some arrive here as refugees. They come from different socioeconomic and educational backgrounds. They all speak Chinese, although they may not be able to communicate between themselves because of the different dialects. They share similar traditional Chinese values about family, although they also express unique ways of thinking because of their different sociohistorical contexts. Each group carries its own heritage as well as historical burdens. They are the people from Cambodia, Hong Kong, Malaysia, Mainland China, Lao, Singapore, Taiwan, Vietnam, and other Southeast Asian countries. They are people with many faces.

CASE SCENARIOS

Case 1

The Chan couple had come to San Francisco from Taishan in Mainland China 30 years ago. Mr. Chan was in his 60s and Mrs. Chan was 8 years younger. They were married for almost 30 years and had three children who were all married. Mr. Chan owned a small restaurant in Chinatown and Mrs. Chan helped him. Both of them had their life built around Chinatown and they spoke little English. Mr. Chan was a traditional man who considered himself the head of the household and deserving of absolute respect and obedience from his wife and children. He was hot-tempered and quick to criticize, especially after he lost money in gambling. He would then pick on minor things to degrade and demean Mrs. Chan. Sometimes, he would slap, push, and shove her. Mr. Chan treated her badly for many years and Mrs. Chan just endured his "rough behavior." Given their cultural values, divorce or separation was just unthinkable, because it would bring shame to the family.

Case 2

The Wong couple came to Toronto from Hong Kong 3 years ago. Mr. and Mrs. Wong were in their early 40s and they had a 12-year-old daughter. Both were elementary school teachers in Hong Kong, but because their credentials were not recognized in Canada, Mr. and Mrs. Wong had great difficulty in finding good jobs. Mrs. Wong finally got a receptionist's job at a Chinese dental office. Mr. Wong, however, could not find any jobs other than working in restaurants or factories. Although both suffered a downward shift in their occupation, Mr. Wong found such a change extremely degrading and unacceptable. Further, Mr. Wong resented the fact that Mrs. Wong had a higher salary than him. All along, Mr. Wong believed that a man should be the breadwinner of the family.

Initially, Mr. Wong became easily irritable and agitated after a "bad" day at work. He would become verbally aggressive and would call her names. Mrs. Wong sometimes cried and sobbed quietly. She did not argue with him because she "understood" where his frustration came from. She believed that the situation would improve if she treated him better. Lately, Mr. Wong started accusing Mrs. Wong of flirting with patients at the dental office. The couple got into big fights because Mrs. Wong could not tolerate being degraded as "flirting around with men." Mr. Wong hit her the first time. Mrs. Wong found the situation extremely frustrating and she wrote to her mother who was still in Hong Kong. Her mother wrote back asking her to endure the situation. "You are married to him. Maybe that's fate."

Case 3

Jimmy came from a wealthy family, and he was an accomplished businessman in Taiwan; he was in his early 50s. He married Mimi more than 20 years ago and Mimi was 10 years younger than him. Jimmy and Mimi had three children. The family moved to Vancouver 5 years ago. Jimmy still maintained a business, and he flew back and forth between Taiwan and Vancouver. Both Jimmy and Mimi were educated. Mimi had never worked after she was married. The abuse started in Taiwan soon after the birth of the second son. At that time, Mimi suspected that Jimmy was having affairs. When she confronted Jimmy, the latter got very agitated and exploded at her. "Even if I have affairs, so what? Remember, I provide you with everything you need. I'm the man of the house. If you don't like it that way, you can leave and see how you can survive." Mimi got very upset, although she did not have the means to support herself and her children. Further, in Taiwan, she will lose the custody of her children if she files for divorce [this law was changed in 1995]. She got so depressed and angry that she refused to have sex with Jimmy. It was at that point that Jimmy started to hit her and forced her to have sex with him. The abuse continued after the family moved to Vancouver. Mimi decided to stay in the marriage mainly for economic reasons and for fear of "losing face." Her in-laws and parents also knew about their "conflict." They all "persuaded" her to stay in the marriage. After all, children need a father, a moral, "good" woman only marries once in her life, and the family name should be protected at all cost.

Case 4

L. was a construction worker in his late 30s. L. had a schizophrenic breakdown in his early 20s but currently was in remission. He was the only son and still lived with his parents in Los Angeles. Three years ago, his mother was concerned about L. being single since that meant the family would have no male heir. Through a go-between, the parents assisted him in going back to China to marry S., who was a young woman in her early 20s. The couple only met briefly before they were married in China. The L. family paid good money to S.'s parents for the marriage. L. then sponsored S. to come to the United States.

Under the Marriage Fraud Act, S. was granted a 2-year conditional entry. At the end of the 2-year period, L. will sponsor her to apply for the "Green Card" (Permanent Residency). It will take at least 7 years for her to formally become a U.S. citizen. S. found L. and his parents very controlling. L. did not allow S. to enroll in ESL (English as a Second Language) classes or to learn how to drive. They found a job for S. in a factory operated by a Chinese owner. However, the L. family took away her salary and gave her a meager weekly allowance. The L. family was afraid that S. would leave L. once she became independent.

The worst experience for S. was that L. would literally wake her up in the middle of the night and demand to have sex with her. Because S. came from rural China and sex education was almost unheard of, she was literally traumatized by the experience. When she did attempt to say no, he beat her. Her in-laws knew about the situation, although they did nothing to help her. S. knew nothing about wife abuse or sexual assault. She thought that L. might have the right to have sex with her; after all, "he is my husband." S. found Los Angeles a totally strange and foreign place. She was totally isolated and could neither speak nor understand English. She felt bad about the situation, although she did not know whom to seek help from. She thought that the situation might improve if she were able to give birth to a son for the L. family. Meanwhile, the only thing that she could do was to endure the situation.

As exemplified by the different cases, the faces of Chinese battered women are as varied as the dynamics of spouse abuse. There is no one Chinese vision of spouse abuse. The dynamics involved are multifaceted and multilayered, influenced by culture-specific, contextual, interactional, as well as individual factors (see Figure 22.1). Despite the fact that Mrs. Chan, Mrs. Wong, Mimi, and S. come from different countries and socioeconomic backgrounds and have

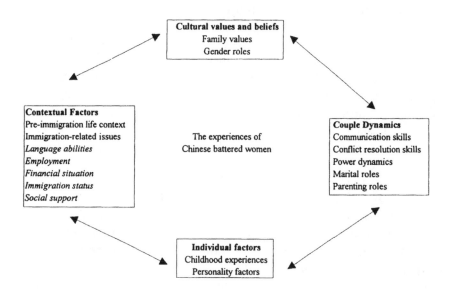

FIGURE 22.1 Factors influencing the experiences of Chinese battered women.

experienced different life circumstances surrounding the abuse, there are two common themes regarding their responses to the abusive situation: (a) they tried to endure the situation, and (b) they did not consider divorce/separation a viable solution (at least at the beginning). Their decisions were also supported and reinforced by their relatives and friends. A closer look at the culture-specific factors may help us better understand their experiences of and responses to the abusive situations.

CULTURE-SPECIFIC INFLUENCES

Feminist social critics focus on how cultural beliefs about sex roles and the resulting institutional arrangements contribute to and maintain gender inequality and the oppression of women by men (Gondolf & Fisher, 1988; Martin, 1976; Warrior, 1976). For the Chinese, such a dynamic is maintained by cultural beliefs and values around family and gender roles that profoundly influence one's definition of self.

As suggested by Chu (1985), the traditional Chinese self as rooted in Confucianism exists primarily in relationship to significant others (Chu). In the past, the self–other relationships among Chinese were built on the traditional collectivity of extended family/kinship networks. Such a collectivity extends even beyond the living relatives to include their ancestors. Thus, a male Chinese would consider himself a son, a brother, a husband, a father, an heir to the family lineage, but hardly *himself.* Likewise, a Chinese woman is a daughter, a sister, a wife, and a mother, but not an independent woman striving for self-actualization. It seems as if outside the relational context of the significant others, there is very little independent self left for the Chinese (Chu).

Another major characteristic in understanding Chinese self is that individual self-worth is not measured by what one has personally achieved for *oneself,* but by the extent to which one has lived up to the behavioral expectations of the significant others, as defined by predominant cultural ideas. In a family situation, these behavioral expectations are circumscribed by the well-defined roles within a hierarchical structure. Power is distributed based on one's age, generation, and gender (Chan, 1989). Based on a patriarchal family structure, Chinese men are legitimate heirs to continue their family lineage and, therefore, are endowed with a strong sense of importance and entitlement. In the past, the social institutions have reinforced such an arrangement by providing men with educational and occupational opportunities, but not women. With a culturally endowed sense of importance and socially viable means to accumulate resources and wealth, men are naturally given permission to exercise authority over women and children.

At the other end of the continuum, women internalize values and beliefs about endurance, perseverance, and submission to men as ultimate virtues for any moral, good woman. The "three obediences" are widely accepted codes of behavior for moral, good women: Before marriage, a woman follows and obeys her father; after marriage, she follows and obeys her husband; after the death of her husband, she follows and obeys her son (Chu, 1985; Lum, 1988). The three obediences establish cultural ideas of unquestionable submission of women to men. If the situation demands the shortchanging of individual well-being to fulfill the ideals, the virtues of endurance and perseverance are used to regulate the discomfort involved. After all, "repeated endurance produces precious gold."

Such a cultural definition of self as influenced by cultural beliefs around family helps us better understand the responses of Chinese battered women to spouse abuse, and the dynamic of abuse.

Responses of Chinese Battered Women to Spouse Abuse and Cultural Influences

Chinese battered women face tremendous pressures in trying to break through the abusive cycle within their cultural milieu. As mentioned by most informants of this study who work closely with Chinese battered women, the first problem is the issue of nonrecognition of abuse as a problem. Because Chinese cultural values support male supremacy and dominance over women, male violence against women in the forms of physical, emotional, and sexual abuse can be justified differently based on culturally acceptable "reasons." For instance, some Chinese (e.g., Vietnamese Chinese) tend to accept hitting as a legitimate way to discipline or educate women (J. A. Yee, personal communication, May 9, 1997). The Chinese Family Service of Greater Montreal conducted a study on Chinese attitudes and beliefs pertaining to domestic violence (Ming-Jyh, Li, Zhang, & Yao, 1994). Forty-one percent of male respondents in the Montreal study agreed that in a Chinese family, if a man beats his wife or girlfriend, a probable reason is to educate her (Ming-Jyh, Li, Zhang, & Yao). Fourteen percent of female respondents were also in agreement with such an assertion. It is, therefore, not surprising that some victims may believe that they deserve the beating because they have indeed done something wrong. The cultural beliefs offer a gracious "excuse" for the abuser, because he is doing it to fulfill his duty as the head of the house.

Emotional abuse in the form of verbal abuse and financial restraint is accepted under the premise that "He is the man, he knows better than I do about *whatever.*" Sexual abuse is the most grossly underreported form of abuse. Many Chinese women do not recognize sexual abuse as a form of abuse, especially those with little education. In fact, only 64% of the female respondents who had elementary education agreed that "forcing the other party to have sex" could be considered domestic violence, whereas 91% of the same group agreed that "hitting with fist and kicking" and "verbal intimidation or assault" are domestic violence (Ming-Jyh, Li, Zhang, & Yao, 1994). Many victims believe that marriage is a license for the man to have sex with them in whatever forms, at whatever time, and under whatever circumstances. In addition, it is considered taboo for a woman to talk about sex and, therefore, it is difficult for many Chinese battered women to talk about sexual abuse with their social workers, shelter workers, or doctors. J. A. Yee (personal communication, May 9, 1997) mentioned a situation whereby a former medical doctor was abused by her husband. She mentioned both physical and emotional abuse, although she never talked about sexual abuse, despite the fact that she had to take medication for pain control after forced sexual relations with her husband. She believed that it was her duty to have sex with her husband.

Because the family name has to be protected at all cost and because individual well-being should be subordinated to family well-being, it is difficult for Chinese women or Chinese families to admit to the occurrence of abuse. First, such an admission will bring shame to the family. Second, such an act may lead to divorce or separation. For many Chinese, marriage is for life. As a result, many women, and even supportive relatives, may go through a massive denial of the abuse. Many women are in fact under pressure from the extended family to either cover up or tolerate the abuse (P. Au, personal communication, May 20, 1997; R. Cheung, personal communication, May 9, 1997; K. Ng, personal communication, May 13, 1997). In the study conducted by the Chinese Family Life Services of Metro Toronto on Chinese battered women (Chan, 1989), 50% of the women respondents did not find their relative, family, or friends helpful to their situation. Twelve percent of those who had a supportive social network found their supporters to be either too pushy, or too timid in advising them in ways to deal with the abuse.

In many circumstances, some women and their families may give a different label to the problem, such as the man is hot-tempered, or he just lost money gambling (see Case 1), or he is just frustrated with his work situation (see Case 2). In fact, over half of the female respondents (53%) of the Montreal study (Ming-Jyh, Li, Zhang, & Yao, 1994) agreed that a probable reason for a man to beat his wife or girlfriend was "he's in a bad mood." Giving abuse another label, however, is not a helpful solution, because it prevents the man from taking responsibility for his violent behavior and finding solutions to the problem. As a result, the woman still shoulders the responsibility to find a solution for the man's problem, which is always an impossible task.

The dilemma faced by many Chinese women has to be understood within a cultural context. For Chinese women influenced by traditional values, leaving the abuser is not just a demonstration of self-assertiveness or saying no to the abuse. Such an act also means exposing family weakness to outsiders (or at least to the helping professionals involved), shaming the family name, violating the virtues of perseverance and endurance, and causing divorce or separation to the family. So, instead of developing a "victim mentality" (that I am a victim of abuse, it is not my fault, and I deserve to be helped) as commonly understood from a feminist perspective, the woman may instead develop an "instigator mentality" (that I am the bad person who brings shame to the family or causes family breakdown because I expose the abuse or leave my husband). The Chinese community clearly reinforces the "instigator mentality" by viewing the woman as the troublemaker. It is not uncommon for the community to shift its sympathy and support from the battered wife to the batterer, once the abuse is made known to the police or any outside agencies (R. Cheung, personal communication, May 9, 1997; T. Shum, personal communication, May 14, May 21, 1997). A common scenario is for the in-laws or elders in the family to beg the wife to drop charges on the husband. Individual suffering is no longer important once the family name and losing face are involved.

Not subordinating individual interests to family well-being has far-reaching, negative, repercussions on the woman herself. In leaving the abusive relationship, the woman also divorces the network of social support offered by her role as a wife. The more a woman builds her life around the role of mother and wife, the greater is her sacrifice in not giving in to the abuse. Knowing these cultural issues help us better understand the passivity, ambivalence, guilty feelings, and shame characteristics of many Chinese women's responses to spouse abuse.

Dynamics of Spouse Abuse and Cultural Influences

Similar to a feminist understanding of domestic violence, the core dynamic of spouse abuse in the Chinese community in North America is about male dominance and the quest for control and power in intimate relationships. The ways for those power dynamics to be manifested are, however, uniquely influenced by cultural factors. The following characteristics of the dynamics of spouse abuse in Chinese couples elucidate the possible influences of culture on spouse-battering.

In defining who is the abuser, mainstream understanding based on a feminist perspective focuses on male violence against women in intimate relationships. Gender is the fundamental defining concept in woman battering. Because of the patriarchal nature of Chinese families, violence against wives, however, may be instigated by female relatives on the male side, especially from the in-laws (R. Cheung, personal communication, May 9, 1997; B. Masaki, personal communication, May 12, 1997; Ming-Jyh, Li, Zhang, & Yao, 1994). In Chan's study (1989), 20% of the abused wives lived with in-laws. Among those abused women, 64% were also physically and emotionally abused by the parents of their husband. For all battered women, 39% perceived in-law issues as factors precipitating violence. Even though the data are limited and not representative of all Chinese, such findings did suggest that for Chinese, wife assault may not be confined to male violence against women. Women, especially mothers-in-law, can derive power from their association with the male figures in the family, and induce violent acts against other women. Of course, complex family dynamics such as triangulation (Minuchin & Fishman, 1981) are commonly involved in such a situation. Still, such a phenomenon poses new challenges to the predominant conceptualization of gender as the primary foundation of wife-battering.

Another observation concerns the cycle of violence. Lenore Walker (1984, 1994) described the cycle of violence as involving four stages. A period of tranquility is followed by a stage where tension builds up and finally accumulates in a violent episode. Following the violent episode is often the "honeymoon" period, whereby the abuser becomes remorseful and asks for forgiveness. Rather than having a honeymoon period after the abusive incident in which the abusers seek reparation, the Chinese version of the honeymoon period for many battered women is at best a period of relative calm (P. Au, personal communication, May 20, 1997; V. Yung, personal communication, May 22, 1997). The cultural beliefs operate in such a way that the man may not feel guilty about the abuse and, therefore, sees no need to seek reparation. Most women will just endure the situation and stay in the relationship. As such, there is no pragmatic need for the man to do anything to keep the woman in the relationship. In this way, cultural factors influence how the abusive cycle is manifested in Chinese intimate relationships.

The final observation is about the involvement of gambling versus alcohol in domestic violence. Alcohol involvement is a widely recognized factor related to spouse abuse, even though not of a causal nature (Zubretsky & Digirotama, 1996). It is part of a routine procedure to assess the influence of alcohol on domestic violence and its treatment (Dziegielewski, Resnick, & Krause, 1996). All informants of the current study, however, raised questions about the role played by alcohol in spouse abuse. T. Shum (personal communication, May 14, 21, 1997) has provided counseling to Chinese battered women in San Francisco for 15 years. Based on her work experience, only two abuse cases were alcohol-related, and none were drug-related. Instead, one-third of all cases she worked with involved gambling. The detrimental impact of gambling, a favorite pastime for many Chinese, has been well documented (Chinese Family Life Services of Metro Toronto, 1996). Although the relationship between gambling and wife abuse is anecdotal and has yet to be empirically determined, many informants of the study support such an observation.

Apparently, the universal, underlying dynamic of spouse abuse is essentially one of control and dominance. Its manifestation, however, can be influenced by culture-specific and contextual factors. An understanding of those issues will have important implications for assessment and treatment of Chinese battered women.

Pure traditional Chinese values have undergone tremendous challenges in the past several decades. A process of discontinuity in terms of traditional values and beliefs is obvious in both the motherlands of many Chinese (e.g., Mainland China and Hong Kong) and of Chinese who reside in North America. On the other hand, underlying this process of discontinuity is also a thread of continuity that is distinctive of a particular culture (Chu, 1985). It is important to recognize both the patterns of continuity and the pattern of change within a cultural milieu in order to understand any phenomena.

The complex issue of cultural continuity and change is obviously beyond the scope of our discussion. However, the study conducted by the Chinese Family Service of Greater Montreal (Ming-Jyh, Li, Zhang, & Yao, 1994) on Chinese attitudes and beliefs pertaining to domestic violence is illustrative of some of the issues raised by the present discussion of traditional values and beliefs around family. The findings of the study indicated that the process of change was more obvious regarding the superiority of men. Among the 281 respondents, only 6% of females and 12% of males still believed that "Men are superior to women and a wife belongs to her husband." On the other hand, 35% of male respondents and 19% of female respondents agreed that a woman should accept the "three obediences and four virtues" as the standard for a moral, good woman. Regarding the issue of saving face and protecting the family name, 44% of male respondents and 21% of female respondents still agreed that "No family scandal should be made public." Apparently, despite changes in the society, values around gender roles and the family name are still important for many Chinese in North America. Men seem to be the guardians of traditional values more than women.

CONTEXTUAL FACTORS—IMMIGRATION-RELATED ISSUES

Mary Dutton (1996) warned against a single vision of the experiences of battered women and argued for a contextual analysis of battered women's experience that includes the woman's unique individual and social context. In the same manner, it is dangerous as well as doing a disservice to Chinese battered women if one adopts a single vision of their experiences solely based on an understanding of cultural factors. The experience and strategic responses of Chinese battered women are multifaceted and multilayered, influenced by cultural, contextual, and individual factors. Although individual factors do not lend themselves to meaningful discussion because of their extreme heterogeneity, one contextual factor that profoundly influences an individual woman's experience is her immigration experience in North America.

Many Chinese batterers have used immigration status as a "weapon" to psychologically threaten the woman and to keep her in an abusive relationship despite physical, psychological, and sexual sufferings (P. Au, personal communication, May 20, 1997; R. Cheung, personal communication, May 9, 1997; K. Ng, personal communication, May 13, 1997). The experience of S. (see Case 4) clearly illustrates this dynamic. These women belong to the more vulnerable group, because they are new immigrants who usually have little social and financial resources, minimal language skills, and little knowledge about North American culture. Many of them are socially isolated and are still struggling to understand and adjust to the new environment.

Immigration-related stress may have a negative impact on couple relationships, triggering or exacerbating violent behaviors in intimate relationships. Except for those Chinese who immigrate to North America on a refugee status (e.g., Vietnamese Chinese), most immigration is voluntary, planned, and welcomed by the families. Still, leaving the familiar country of origin and venturing into a new culture involves drastic change and disruption in one's life. The degree of cumulative stress experienced by an individual and the discrepancy between his or her expectation and the actual quality of life in North America influences how well an individual adjusts to the life and culture of the receiving country (Drachman, 1992). One common phenomenon affecting some couples is spousal role reversal. Some wives have found employment more easily than their husbands because they tend to accept lower paying jobs; for instance, garment work. In addition, it is not uncommon for professional men to lose their status because of unrecognized credentials, working experiences, or limited language skills (Ming-Jyh, Li, Zhang, & Yao, 1994). To most male immigrants, underemployment, downward occupational changes, and redistribution of power in the family are ego-shattering realities that directly threaten their concept of manhood and husbandhood (Chan, 1989). In an attempt to regain a sense of power and to reduce their pain, some men unfortunately resort to spouse and child abuse, gambling, or chemical abuse to deal with the adverse situation (Drachman & Ryan, 1991). Immigration-related stress cannot be an "excuse" for abuse. Further, many abuses in fact happen prior to the immigration (Chan, 1989; T. Shum, personal communication, May 14, 21, 1997). Immigration-related stress, however, can be perceived as another layer of stress factors that exacerbate the dysfunctional couple dynamics, which are, at the core, still an issue of dominance and control.

Immigration-related experiences, on the other hand, significantly influence a woman's help-seeking responses to her battering experiences. Oftentimes, the seeming passivity of many Chinese battered women is not just a result of cultural values. Their passivity can be a reaction to their immediate life circumstances in North America. One major issue is social isolation. In the Montreal study (Ming-Jyh, Li, Zhang, & Yao, 1994), when respondents were asked for the reasons for tolerating domestic violence, the two mostly cited reasons, regardless of educational level, were: "Nowhere to seek help because of isolation" and "To tolerate the abuse for the future of the children." Apparently, "Nowhere to seek help because of isolation" is more related to contextual factor than to cultural influences.

Because of social isolation, many women do not have information about available services. Not having the language abilities, many Chinese women cannot utilize mainstream shelters' services. The most often cited reasons by both clients and helping professionals for the low utilization of shelter services by Chinese women are language barriers, food choices, cultural dissimilarities, fear of fights among children, and stigma of women's shelters (Chan, 1989; R. Cheung, personal communication, May 9, 1997). In the Toronto study (Chan), only 6 out of 50 abused women who received counseling services used shelter services, and only 2 women were able to adapt to shelter living without much difficulty.

Sometimes, not being able to speak fluent English becomes an insurmountable barrier, even when the woman actively seeks outside help such as calling the police or going to the emergency room at the hospital. R. Cheung (personal communication, May 9, 1997) mentioned situations whereby the police used various members of the household as translators, or even only talked to the batterer to gather information because "he is the only one who speaks English." Language is clearly a formidable barrier to the help-seeking efforts of many immigrant women.

In understanding and assessing the experience of Chinese battered women and their strategic responses to their plight, one needs to consider cultural and contextual as well as individual factors, including couple dynamics. Each battering situation constitutes a unique configuration of the interaction of those factors. Each factor may take on varying importance in an individual's experience. Neglecting any one dimension, however, is likely to result in a biased understanding of the situations of Chinese battered women.

RESPONSES OF THE CRIMINAL JUSTICE SYSTEM

The criminalization of spouse abuse can be considered a significant victory for those working diligently to end violence against women in intimate relationships. Currently, all states and provinces in the United States and Canada have passed civil or criminal statutes to protect battered women (Roberts, 1996b). Many police departments have also responded with a pro-arrest policy and provide immediate protection to battered women (Roberts, 1996b). The five cities surveyed in this study all have pro-arrest polices or even mandatory arrest laws/zero-tolerance policies to prevent batterers from intimidating and pressuring victims to drop charges or restraining orders. In those situations, the police will prosecute the abuser regardless of the victim's decision, if there are visible injuries (K. Ng, personal communication, May 13, 1997; Roberts, 1996a).

The responses of criminal justice systems to spouse abuse have positively affected the Chinese community. A Chinese battered woman has expressed the advantages of being in North America as follows:

> Wife beating is really common in China. No laws deal with this problem. . . . [In North America] domestic violence is illegal and the social welfare system protects women victims, which, in turn, encourages women to seek help. (Ming-Jyh, Li, Zhang, & Yao, 1994, p. 12)

The implementation of mandatory arrest laws further assists victims to receive the needed help who might otherwise choose to "endure" the situation. Before the advent of such a policy, many Chinese battered women would not prosecute their abusers for both cultural and contextual reasons. They are also under tremendous pressure from their extended families and communities to "give a second chance" to the abuser. In fact, many abuse cases are being reported by neighbors and friends, and not by the victim herself (R. Cheung, personal communication, May 9, 1997; J. A. Yee, personal communication, May

9, 1997). Many Chinese offenders, further, are ignorant of the legal consequences of wife-battering in North America (V. Yung, personal communication, May 22, 1997).

The responses of the criminal justice systems to spouse abuse have forced the Chinese community to face the issue that will otherwise remain hidden. Informants from the Chinatown Service Center at Los Angeles, Chinese Family Life Services of Metro Toronto, and United Chinese Community Enrichment Services Society in Vancouver mentioned the pressure of increased referral of male batterers from the courts to receive group or individual treatment after the advent of pro-arrest or mandatory arrest policies. The involvement of the court system is a strong deterrence against men's violence toward women in the Chinese community. In traditional Chinese society, government is perceived as an oppressive authoritarian apparatus with which anybody in his or her right mind should avoid having any contact. The old saying: "Never go to court when alive and never go to hell after death" clearly illustrates the fear of government in many Chinese. Further, many Chinese men feel degraded and shamed by the procedure of being body-searched when arrested (T. Shum, personal communication, May 14, 21, 1997). K. Ng (personal communication, May 13, 1997) mentioned that there is not one re-offense in all the male offenders whom he has treated in the past 5 years. All of them are afraid of the legal penalty.

As a result, court involvement by itself can be a very effective deterrent in stopping visible abuse in the Chinese community. The question is whether such intervention can alter the power dynamics in couple relationships. The man may learn how not to abuse his wife in a way that will cause him trouble with the court system. It does not mean, however, the cessation of violence in intimate relationships. Edleson and Syers (1991) found that many men who received group treatment still used threats despite a decrease in violent behavior. The impact of court involvement on the dynamics of spouse abuse in Chinese couples needs to be further investigated.

Despite the overall positive impact of the criminal justice system in preventing and stopping spouse abuse in the Chinese community, language and cultural barriers still exist. When victims and the police or judge do not share a similar language, the latter have to rely on translators. The problems of using translators and cultural biases of an individual police officer or judge are considerable.

In situations where translators are unavailable, police may rely on information provided by the husband or other family members who may, intentionally or not, distort the situation.

Lacking any coordinated or planned efforts to deal with the issue of cultural and language barriers in the criminal justice system, many agencies serving the Chinese community take the initiative to develop beneficial and positive working relationships with their respective police departments and courts. Oftentimes, such individual outreach efforts involve doing consultation and training related to cultural issues. The success of these efforts, however, depends very much on the openness and flexibility of individual police departments and courts that vary from place to place.

TREATMENT PROGRAMS FOR CHINESE BATTERED WOMEN

Chinese battered women in North America face tremendous pressure and many obstacles in confronting and escaping abuse. The criminalization of spouse abuse and the corresponding responses of the court system serve important and irreplaceable social control functions. On the other hand, individual men and women still need to find solutions to attain a life that does not contain violence in intimate relationships. Because cultural values influence a person's problem perception, perceived problem resolution, and help-seeking behaviors (Lee, 1996), treatment for Chinese battered women needs to be sensitive to those culturally based dynamics. Grassroots efforts initiated by the Chinese community have established various culturally and linguistically sensitive services to assist Chinese men and women. These organizations provide invaluable and irreplaceable services for those who cannot effectively utilize mainstream services because of cultural and language barriers.

Women's shelters for Asians and family services agencies for Chinese are the two major types of organizations that provide services for Chinese battered women and their families in North America. Their inception mostly involves the efforts of concerned Chinese/Asian grassroots activists and professionals who recognize the insurmountable barriers faced by Chinese women in seeking help from mainstream agencies.

Women's Shelters

The Center for the Pacific-Asian Family at Los Angeles, founded in 1981, was the first Asian women's shelter established in the United States (Hsieh, 1997). In 1982, the New York Asian Women's Center was opened on the East Coast by formerly battered women, sexual assault survivors, and other concerned women to combat the problem of battering and sexual assault in the Asian communities (New York Asian Women's Center, 1992). In San Francisco, the Asian Women's Shelter was opened in 1988 as the third shelter in North America to serve the Asian population. Likewise, in 1994, Asian Americans for Community Involvement opened the Asian Women Home in Santa Clara, California. Similar to other shelters, these Asian women's shelters provide crisis intervention, hotline services, residential services, legal services, referral services, counseling, support groups and activities, advocacy, accompaniment services (the staff/volunteers accompany the battered woman in accomplishing various tasks), and community education. The distinctive aspect of these shelters, however, is their attempts to provide culturally and linguistically sensitive services to their clients. These shelters have developed innovative programs specifically for Asian women.

Language Access. To overcome language barriers faced by Asian women seeking help from mainstream shelters, many Asian women's shelters provide 24-hour Asian multilingual hotline services (e.g., New York Asian Women's Center, Asian Women's Shelter in San Francisco, Center for the Pacific-Asian Family). All shelters, further, provide a language match between the shelter staff and battered women as best they can. Still, Asia encompasses many different groups. Even Chinese have many diverse dialects. Some shelters have developed innovative programs to deal with such an issue. A good example is the Multi-Lingual Access Model developed by the Asian Women's Shelter in San Francisco since 1988 (B. Masaki, personal communication, May 12, 1997). In this model, the shelter provides 58 hours of training for bilingual domestic violence advocates who also function as translators. These people are language advocates who are also equipped with knowledge about domestic violence. Their names are placed in an on-call "language bank" that can be accessed at all times to provide language services for all Asian battered women. Masaki mentioned that this model has been such a success that it will be expanded on a citywide base in 1998, with six additional agencies in San Francisco offering such services to their clients. As expressed by many Chinese battered women, being able to speak in their own language makes it easier for them to seek outside, professional help. They feel understood and acknowledged by the shelter staff and are more comfortable at expressing themselves (R. Cheung, personal communication, May 9, 1997).

Culturally Sensitive Shelter Environment. Besides providing a language match, most Asian women's shelters strive to provide a culturally sensitive shelter environment (New York Asian Women's Center, 1992). Several informants have mentioned food as a major concern for their clients. Some Asian women's shelters (e.g., Asian Women Home) allow women to prepare food for themselves and their children. Such a minor modification, however, assists many Chinese women and their children to better adjust to their life at shelters (J. A. Yee, personal communication, May 9, 1997). Because isolation is a widely used strategy by Chinese male batterers in controlling their spouse, and many Chinese women also lack language skills to access useful information, educating women about their rights and service available to them becomes an important part of the empowering process (S. Hsieh, personal communication, June 11, 1997). Sharing similar cultural values, many shelter staff members recognize the cultural dilemma for a Chinese woman in leaving the abusive relationship. While not replicating the dynamics of abuse, in which the women were told what to do or what was best for them, the shelter staff members fully respect the women's decision while at the same time providing the required assistance.

Similar to mainstream philosophy, the ultimate goal of shelter services is to empower Asian/Chinese women. Through the empowering process that fosters an internal locus of control and a positive sense of self in Chinese battered women, they will become more aware of their needs and resources. Consequently, there is a greater likelihood for them to develop solutions that are appropriate to their needs and viable in their unique cultural milieu. From this perspective, services at the shelters are provided in a way that respects the client's culture and supports self-determination. These empowering efforts have been successful in helping many battered women to leave the abusive relationships. For instance, only 30% of Asian women who stayed at the New York Asian Women's Center between 1982 and

1992 returned to the batterers (New York Asian Women's Center, 1992).

Besides Asian women's shelters that specifically serve Asian women, including Chinese, some mainstream shelters attempt to provide culturally sensitive services by including Chinese-speaking staff. Such a situation is more prevalent in Canada because there are no ethno-specific women's shelters. Culturally and linguistically sensitive services are provided mainly through the Chinese-speaking staff in shelters and the use of translators.

Ethno-Specific Family Services

Because of the cultural dilemma created by leaving one's marriage and the pragmatic, economic concerns of many Chinese battered women, many of them prefer to seek help from a family service agency. Although some Chinese women know that a shelter provides a safe place for them, many of them still choose not to use the service because they attach a feeling of homelessness to a shelter, and/or perceive that their marriages will dissolve once they leave home (Chan, 1989). Counseling services provided by ethno-specific family agencies allow them to talk to someone about their problems without having to leave their homes.

The development of ethno-specific agencies in the different parts of North America is neither coordinated nor planned. Each agency has their own distinctive history, although all represent grassroots efforts to provide needed services for ethnic Chinese. Many agencies, not by coincidence, have made domestic violence a priority of their services to the Chinese community. Such a phenomenon probably reflects the need of the Chinese community for services to assist both battered women and their husbands. For instance, over 20% of all family cases served by the Chinese Family Life Services of Metro Toronto in 1996 were spouse abuse cases (P. Au, personal communication, May 20, 1997). The United Chinese Community Enrichment Services Society in Vancouver recently launched a 3-year Family Violence Prevention and Intervention Project to deal with the increasing reports of spouse abuse cases (K. Ng, personal communication, May 13, 1997). Similar services are provided by ethno-specific agencies in the United States. For instance, Donaldina Cameron House in San Francisco started domestic violence assistance services

15 years ago. The Chinatown Service Center at Los Angeles has provided services for domestic violence victims and offenders since 1991.

Services for Battered Women. An array of services is provided for battered women, including counseling services, legal assistance, referral services, and support groups. The actual services provided by each agency vary depending on the resources available. All agencies, however, provide counseling services. Besides being linguistically sensitive, the helping professionals also provide therapy in a manner that takes into consideration culture-specific issues.

Because Chinese tend to be more reserved, and disclosing family problems is almost equivalent to shaming the family name or losing face, talking about family abuse to an outsider is very difficult for most women. In addition, many of them do not have prior experience with therapy. As such, it is necessary for the staff to carefully explain to them about the therapy process and respect their reserved attitude. The pacing of therapy becomes a very important part in enjoining and engaging the clients. Clients are given time and space to slowly open up at their own pace and in a way that they feel comfortable. Lack of direct eye contact will not be misinterpreted as a symptom of avoidance or anxiety, because it may be a sign of respect in the more traditional Chinese. Being silent or reserved does not necessarily mean resistance or unwillingness to seek help; it may be just a matter of the client's needing more time to open up herself.

Because "no family scandal should be made public" and because of the strong fear of shaming the family name and losing face, issues of confidentiality should be communicated clearly and unambiguously to Chinese clients. Case management services, including escort services, may be prominent because of the usual lack of resources and language skills of many Chinese battered women.

Some agencies also provide "telephone therapy" because of the relative privacy, flexibility, and feeling of anonymity afforded by such a mode (Shepard, 1987). Such a form of therapy can be more readily accepted by those women who otherwise will not seek help because of the strong fear of losing face, both for her and the family. Further, many Chinese battered women may not have the means of transportation to attend sessions. Telephone therapy makes it easier, at least at the beginning stages, for the helping professionals to reach out to those battered women who might otherwise not be able to utilize the much-needed services.

Services for Offenders.   The vast majority of mainstream treatment programs for offenders are characterized as group-based, psychoeducational approaches (Rosenfeld, 1992). Because of the lack of resources and training, very few treatment groups are offered to Chinese-speaking offenders. The Chinatown Service Center at Los Angeles has run batterer groups since 1991. In 1997, Chinese Family Life Association of Metro Toronto also began offering group treatment to offenders. The first one is a 52-week, 2-hour, open group using the Duluth Model as the basic guide. The second one is a 16-week treatment group focusing on anger management, marital relationships, and relational skills. The difference in the length of the two groups is a reflection of the different policies adopted by the state/province regarding the ideal length of treatment for batterers. Both groups, however, focus on culture-specific issues, including traditional values and beliefs around gender roles, family relationships, and communication; in-law relationships; conflict resolution; parenting issues; immigration and its impact on couple relationships; and cultural aspects of adjustment to life in North America.

The dynamics exemplified by these Chinese batterers' groups resemble the mainstream experiences, but are not limited to them. The beginning stage is characterized by group members' immense anger, resistance, and blaming. It may be the first time that their manhood as a Chinese man is being openly challenged in a way that they cannot neglect or avoid. Speaking from her several years of experience running Chinese batterers' groups, V. Yung (personal communication, May 22, 1997) mentions the very difficult group dynamics at the beginning stage because all members reinforce and fuel each other's anger and blaming. Currently, a model of open group is adopted instead because members at different stages of their development can assist each other to understand the problem of dominance and control. These men progress slowly to be less blaming and more able to be confronted about power-and-control issues, and recognize their contribution to the marital problems. The group process is oftentimes slow and frustrating for the leaders. However, it yields useful outcomes at the end, when the member requests additional counseling services or mentions his new but difficult learning through participating in the group (P. Au, personal communication, May 20, 1997; V. Yung, personal communication, May 22, 1997).

Individual counseling for male batterers is also offered by some agencies. For instance, the United Chinese Community Enrichment Services Society in Vancouver provides an eight-session individual counseling service using a cognitive-behavioral approach and focusing on stress and anger management. Culturally relevant metaphors have been found to be useful in assisting Chinese men to learn new, adaptive behaviors in relating to their spouses (K. Ng, personal communication, May 13, 1997).

Culturally sensitive treatment is readily received by Chinese offenders, despite their initial suspicion and resistance (P. Au, personal communication, May 20, 1997; K. Ng, personal communication, May 13, 1997). T. Shum (personal communication, May 14, 21, 1997) mentioned that she would sometimes receive complaints from the husbands of their clients: that Cameron House is unfair in the sense that the agency only provides services for battered women but not for the men. However, due to the absence of federal or state financial support and the inability or unwillingness of many Chinese batterers to pay for services, services for men have been developed on a sporadic and fragmented manner, despite great demand from the community.

Couple Therapy. Couple therapy, despite being practiced and supported by some professionals (Lipchik & Kubicki, 1996), has been cautioned against by most feminist therapists because of the issue of power imbalance in relationships. On the other hand, informants from these family service agencies suggest that couple therapy is, oftentimes, being requested by both Chinese men and women, and is an appropriate form of treatment in the Chinese community. Strongly influenced by the ideals of "marriage for life" and family togetherness despite adversities, it is estimated that between 80% and 90% of those women who seek help from a Chinese family services agency choose to stay in the marriage (P. Au, personal communication, May 20, 1997; K. Ng, personal communication, May 13, 1997; V. Yung, personal communication, May 22, 1997). In such a situation, the best thing for a therapist to do is to advocate for a violence-free relationship. Couple therapy becomes a viable choice of treatment under the following conditions: The woman requests couple treatment; there is a cessation of violence in the relationship; and the man is willing to take responsibility for the abuse (P. Au, personal communication, May 20, 1997; K. Ng, personal communication, May 13, 1997).

Community Education. Both Asian women's shelters and ethno-specific agencies perceive community education as serving significant preventive and remedial purposes with respect to ending spousal violence in the Chinese community. Consistent with their beliefs, all agencies launch extensive efforts regarding community education of domestic violence. The targets include victims, offenders, and the general public and involve mainstream helping professionals.

Oftentimes, Chinese battered women do not seek help because they are ignorant of available services. Many of them do not even label their suffering as abuse as a result of ignorance or denial. Thus, effective dissemination of information about spouse abuse and services available to Chinese battered women is the necessary first step in reaching out to this population. Effective ways that have been used by various agencies include: pamphlets printed in Chinese about domestic violence and services offered by an individual organization; informational brochures (e.g., "A Resource Manual and Divorce Information for Battered Women and Abused Children in the Bay Area," prepared by the Cameron House); advertisements or educational programs in Chinese newspapers; radio-broadcasting services; and multicultural television channels of the respective cities.

Community education, to Chinese men, serves a very important preventive function. As mentioned before, some Chinese men believe it is their right and duty to educate and discipline their spouse through corporal punishment. The mere knowledge of spouse abuse as a criminal act with legal consequences can be an important first step in deterring them from using violence toward their spouses. Educating the Chinese community about detrimental consequences of abuse for an individual and his or her children will, in the long run, reduce the community pressure being put on battered women to yield to the abuse. Such a change in attitude will reduce the negative social consequences for the woman when she decides to leave the abusive relationship. Such education is even more important for the younger generation. The best way to stop a man's violence against a woman is to educate children early on about gender equality and mutual respect. To this end, some agencies have launched large-scale, citywide campaigns to raise the community awareness of the issue (e.g., Domestic Violence Campaign for Chinese in San Francisco, 1996; British Columbia Family Violence Day in Vancouver).

Another target for community education is the various professionals involved in providing services to Chinese battered women. Some effective ways that have been used are: providing consultations or training/seminars around cultural issues to mainstream organizations; conducting studies on Chinese battered women (e.g., Toronto, Montreal); and organizing conferences around issues of Asian/Chinese battered women (e.g., Voices Heard: Taking Steps Past Domestic Violence in Asian Communities in Ohio, May 30, 1997; Gathering Strengths: Coming Together to End Domestic Violence in Our Asian and Pacific Islander Communities, June 20–21, 1997, San Francisco).

Lacking state or provincial financial support for community education, many ethno-specific organizations rely on private fundraising to launch educational campaigns for various target populations. According to Shum (T. Shum, personal communication, May 14, 21, 1997), "patch-up" work is inadequate to stop violence in intimate relationships. The Chinese community needs to be educated about domestic violence and available services for dealing with it.

THE FUTURE

The services available to Chinese battered women can best be described as innovative efforts initiated and provided by the local Asian/Chinese community to best serve their people. The roles of ethno-specific social services in a multicultural society are always controversial because of the fear of fragmentation of social services as a result of the existence of so many diverse groups in society (Lee, 1993). In addition, there is the pragmatic concern of financial consequences for the government. Nevertheless, being culturally and linguistically similar, these ethno-specific agencies successfully provide culturally sensitive, direct services to many Chinese battered women and their families. In other situations, they serve as mediators or "brokers" between their clients and mainstream organizations (Lee). Despite inadequate financial support and the lack of trained professionals in many situations, these organizations maintain a safety net for many Chinese in North America, who otherwise have immense difficulties utilizing mainstream services as a result of cultural and language barriers.

In appraising the services provided by these ethnic organizations, many informants mentioned the need for more extensive community education, improved networking, and coordination with the mainstream organizations, and more treatment groups for Chinese male batterers. There is also a lack of treatment programs for children who are often the forgotten victims of domestic violence. Currently, New York Asian Women's Center is one of the few organizations that provide regular programs and services for children who witness parental violence. In addition, there are virtually no services for gay and lesbian Chinese couples—another silent group in the Chinese community. Expanded effort to provide services for these neglected groups is necessary.

The most critical issue, however, is how supportive is society in assisting those battered women and their children to lead an independent life in situations when they decide to leave the abusive relationship. The problems of housing, employment, and child care are common to all battered women, even though Chinese battered women face additional barriers because of language and cultural factors that may be further compounded by racism in society. The continuing advocacy work by activists and helping professionals to ensure the exemption of battered women from the recent welfare reforms (which aims to eliminate welfare benefits for immigrants) and to allow battered women to self-petition for their immigration status are certainly hopeful signs that they are not a totally neglected group.

CONCLUSION

Chinese battered women are both similar to and different from other battered women in North America. They are similar to all other abused women in the sense that they are victims of male dominance and control. Their battering experience can also be different, however, as a result of the additional burdens imposed by traditional Chinese cultural beliefs and values, their immigration experience, or racism in the society. Oftentimes, they are locked in a vicious cycle that makes it extremely hard for them to escape violence in intimate relationships. Besides embattling the traditional values, they have to choose between "being exploited by their husbands if they stay in the abusive relationship, or being exploited by the socioeconomic system if they leave the abusive relationship" (B. Masaki, personal communication, May 12, 1997).

Being in North America renders Chinese women legal protection from spouse abuse, although many Chinese battered women have not been able to benefit from such protection because of cultural and language barriers. The ethno-specific organizations, including both shelters and family services agencies, have provided a safety net for many first-generation Chinese-Americans or Chinese-Canadians. These community-initiated programs work diligently to serve their local Chinese communities, despite inadequate financial support in many situations. The effectiveness of their work, however, depends on how well the legal, criminal, and mainstream social service systems coordinate with each other to serve in the best interest of battered women of all colors.

REFERENCES

Bachman, R., & Saltzman, L. E. (1995, August). *Violence against women: Estimates from the redesigned survey, Special Report NCJ-154348, National Crime Victimization Survey*. Washington, DC: U.S. Department of Justice, Bureau of Justice Statistics.

Bureau of Justice Statistics. (August, 1995). *Violence against women: Estimates from the redesigned survey* (Special report NCJ-154348, National Crime Victimization Survey).

Chan, K. L., Chiu, M. C, & Chiu, M. S. (2005). *Peace at home: Report on the review of social and legal measures in the prevention and intervention of domestic violence in Hong Kong* (A Consultancy Study commissioned by The Social Welfare Department of HKSAR). Hong Kong: Department of Social Work and Social Administration, University of Hong Kong.

Chan, S. L. L. (1989). *Wife assault: The Chinese Family Life Services experience*. Toronto: Chinese Family Life Services of Metro Toronto.

Chinese Family Life Services of Metro Toronto. (1996). *Working with gambling problems in the Chinese community, development of an intervention model*. Toronto: Author.

Chu, G. (1985). The changing concept of self in contemporary China. In A. J. Marsella, G. DeVos, & F. L. K. Hsu (Eds.), *Culture and self: Asian and Western perspectives* (pp. 252–277). New York: Tavistock Publications.

Davidson, B. P., & Jenkins, P. J. (1989). Class diversity in shelter life. *Social Work, 34*, 491–495.

Drachman, D. (1992). A stage-of-migration framework for service to immigrant populations. *Social Work, 37*, 68–72.

Drachman, D., & Ryan, A. S. (1991). Immigrants and refugees. In

A. Gitterman (Ed.), *Handbook of social work practice with vulnerable populations* (pp. 618–646). New York: Columbia University Press.

Dutton, M. A. (1996). Battered women's strategic response to violence: The role of context. In J. L. Edleson & Z. C. Eisikovits (Eds.), *Future interventions with battered women and their families* (pp. 105–124). Thousand Oaks, CA: Sage.

Dziegielewski, S. F., Resnick, C., & Krause, N. B. (1996). Shelter-based crisis intervention with battered women. In A. R. Roberts (Ed.), *Helping battered women: New perspectives and remedies* (pp. 159–171). New York: Oxford University Press.

Edleson, J., & Syers, M. (1991). The effects of group treatment for men who batter: An 18-month follow-up study. *Research on Social Work Practice, 1,* 227–243.

Gondolf, E., & Fisher, E. (1988). *Battered women as survivors.* Lexington, MA: Lexington Books.

Gondolf, E. W. (1997). Batterer programs: What we know and need to know. *Journal of Interpersonal Violence, 12,* 83–98.

HKSAR Women's Commission (2006). *Women's safety in Hong Kong: Eliminating domestic violence.* Hong Kong Special Administration Region: The Women's Commission.

Ho, C. K. (1990). An analysis of domestic violence in Asian American communities: A multicultural approach to counseling. In L. Brown & M. P. P. Roots (Eds.), *Diversity and complexity in feminist therapy* (pp. 129–150). New York: Haworth.

Hsu, J. (1985). The Chinese family: Relations, problems and therapy. In W. S. Tseng & D. Y. H. Wu (Eds.), *Chinese culture and mental health* (pp. 95–112). Orlando: Academic Press.

Johnson, H. (April 2005). *Assessing the prevalence of violence against women in Canada.* Paper presented at expert group meeting "Violence against women: A statistical overview, challenge and gaps in data collection and methodology and approaches to overcome them," organized by the UN Division for the Advancement of Women, in collaboration with ECE and WHO, April 11–14, 2005, Geneva, Switzeland.

Kanuha, V. (1996). Domestic violence, racism, and the battered women's movement in the United States. In J. L. Edleson & Z. C. Eisikovits (Eds.), *Future interventions with battered women and their families* (pp. 34–50). Thousand Oaks, CA: Sage.

Lee, M. Y. (1993, June). *Canadian multiculturalism policy and the development of ethnic specific mental health services: The case of Hong Fook Community Mental Health.* Paper presented at the Sixth Biennial Conference on Social Welfare Policy, St. John's, Newfoundland.

Lee, M. Y. (1996). A constructivist approach to the help-seeking process of clients: A response to cultural diversity. *Clinical Social Work Journal, 24,* 187–202.

Lee, M. Y., & Law, P. F. M. (2001). Perception of sexual violence against women in Asian American communities. *Journal of Ethnic and Cultural Diversity in Social Work, 10,* 3–25.

Lipchik, E., & Kubicki, A. D. (1996). Solution-focused domestic violence views: Bridges toward a new reality in couples therapy. In S. D. Miller, M. A. Hubble, & B. L. Duncan (Eds.), *Handbook of solution-focused brief therapy* (pp. 65–98). San Francisco: Jossey-Bass.

Loseke, D. R. (1992). *The battered women and shelters: The social construction of wife abuse.* Albany: State University of New York Press.

Lum, J. (1998). Family violence. In L. C. Lee, & N. W. S. Zane (Eds.), *Handbook of Asian American psychology* (pp. 505–525). Thousand Oaks, CA: Sage.

Lum, J. (1988). Battered Asian women. *Rice, 2,* 50–52.

Mahoney, M. R. (1994). Victimization or oppression? Women's lives, violence and agency. In M. A. Fineman & B. Mykitiuk (Eds.), *The public nature of private violence* (pp. 59–92). New York: Routledge.

Martin, D. (1976). *Battered wives.* San Francisco: Glide.

Matsuoka, J., Breaux, C., & Ryujin, D. (1997). National utilization of mental health services by Asian Americans and Pacific Islanders. *Journal of Community Psychology, 25,* 141–145.

Ming-Jyh, S., Li, N., Zhang, W. M., & Yao, K. (1994). *Research on conjugal violence in Chinese families of Montreal.* Montreal: Chinese Family Service of Greater Montreal.

Minuchin, S., & Fishman, H. C. (1981). *Family therapy techniques.* Cambridge, MA: Harvard University Press.

New York Asian Women's Center. (1992). *New York Asian Women's Center: Tenth anniversary report 1982–1992.* New York: Author.

Roberts, A. R. (1996a). Court responses to battered women. In A. R. Roberts (Ed.), *Helping battered women: New perspectives and remedies* (pp. 96–101). New York: Oxford University Press.

Roberts, A. R. (1996b). Police responses to battered women: Past, present, and future. In A. R. Roberts (Ed.), *Helping battered women: New perspectives and remedies* (pp. 85–95). New York: Oxford University Press.

Roberts, A. R., & Kurst Swanger, K. (2002). Court responses to battered women and their children. In A. R. Roberts (Ed.), *Handbook of domestic violence intervention strategies: Policies, programs, and legal remedies* (pp. 127–146). New York: Oxford University Press.

Rosenfeld, B. (1992). Court-ordered treatment of spouse abuse. *Clinical Psychology Review, 12,* 205–226.

Schechter, S. (1996). The battered women's movement in the United States: New directions for institutional reform. In J. L. Edleson & Z. C. Eisikovits

(Eds.), *Future interventions with battered women and their families* (pp. 53–66). Thousand Oaks, CA: Sage.

Shepard, P. (1987). Telephone therapy: An alternative to isolation. *Clinical Social Work Journal, 15,* 56–65.

Statistics Canada (2001). *Family violence in Canada: A statistical profile 2001, catalogue no. 85-224-XIE.* Ottawa: Canadian Centre for Justice Statistics, Statistics Canada.

Statistics Canada. (1995). *Women in Canada: A statistical report* (3rd ed.). Ottawa: Ministry of Industry.

Straus, M. A., & Gelles, R. J. (1986). Societal change and change in family violence from 1975–1985 as revealed by two national surveys. *Journal of Marriage and the Family, 48,* 465–479.

Sue, S., Fujino, D. C., Hu, L. T., & Takeuchi, D. T. (1991). Community mental health services for ethnic minority groups: A test of the cultural responsiveness hypothesis. *Journal of Consulting and Clinical Psychology, 59,* 533–540.

U.S. Department of Justice (May 2000). *Intimate partner violence, May 2000, NCJ 178247.* Washington, DC: U.S. Department of Justice, Office of Justice Programs, Bureau of Justice Statistics.

Walker, L. (1984). *The battered woman syndrome.* New York: Springer Publishing.

Walker, L. (1994). *Abused women and survivor therapy: A practical guide for the psychotherapist.* Washington, DC: American Psychological Association.

Warrior, B. (1976). *Wifebeating.* Somerville, MA: New England Free Press.

Yoshihama, M. (1999). Domestic violence against women of Japanese descent in Los Angeles: Two methods of estimating prevalence. *Violence Against Women, 5,* 896–897.

CHAPTER 23

Validating Coping Strategies and Empowering Latino Battered Women in Puerto Rico

Diana Valle Ferrer

Violence in the family has been a part of family life throughout recorded history. The actual extent of family violence is not known; estimates of child abuse, wife abuse, and elder abuse vary depending on the source. Estimates of the incidence of wife abuse also vary considerably. For example, on the basis of a nationally representative study of 2,143 U.S. families, researchers estimated that violence (behavior legally considered assault if it were to occur between two unrelated adults) occurs each year in at least one out of six couples that live together, married or unmarried (Straus & Gelles, 1995). Puerto Rico Police Department (1995) statistics reveal that 19,411 cases of spouse abuse were reported in 1995. In 92% of these cases, the victim was a woman; the most frequent type of wife abuse reported was aggravated assault (e.g., use of weapons, committed in front of children), which was perpetrated in 56% of the cases. Forty percent of the 625 women murdered in Puerto Rico between 1987 and 1994 were victims of domestic violence.

Domestic violence statistics, argues Abbott (1996), may well be underestimates. We agree with Abbott when she asserts that "only the most severe cases are reported in the crime statistics, and shame and fear tend to restrict the victims' reports of abuse" (Abbott, 1996, p. 236). However, although the figures vary, and wife assault is likely to be underreported behavior, it may be that between 33% (Rivera Ramos, 1991) and 60% (Preamble Law 54 for the Prevention of and Intervention with Domestic Violence, 1989) of all adult women in relationships have been or will be abused by their partners in Puerto Rico.

Historically, in Puerto Rico, and as has been evidenced in many other countries, Silva Bonilla, Rodriguez, Caceres, Martinez, and Torres (1990) assert that violence against women in the family has been supported by two main ideas: first, that women are the property of men, and second, that the home is a private or domestic sphere where strangers should not interfere. Socioeconomic constraints, derived from the sexual hierarchy through which women are made economically dependent on men, place women in a subordinate position within society (Silva Bonilla, 1985). Silva Bonilla explains that social and economic factors are mediated in each person by their personal history (e.g., their socioeconomic class), the ideology that they support or question, and their accumulation of concrete social experiences. In a more recent publication on wife abuse, Silva Bonilla, Rodriguez, Caceres, Martinez, and Torres elaborate on the notion that women have been ideologically conditioned to feel and think of themselves as the property of men (father, husband, boyfriend, and lover) and "responsible" by their "nature" to produce and maintain "good," loving marital and family relationships. Women assume the responsibility of maintaining the integrity of the family and the marriage. When the marriage "fails," the woman feels guilty for its "failure." She feels that she might be responsible for the abuse. Furthermore, Silva Bonilla argues that even though many women subscribe to these ideological premises, they actually participate in a historical questioning of them. Women in their praxis, in their daily lives, actively question and resist the ideas that many times are kept intact in their affective and emotional sphere.

COPING WITH ABUSE

How does a woman cope with battering in an intimate relationship? How does she appraise the situation? What cognitive, emotional, and behavioral efforts does she make to manage the battering situation? How does previous exposure to violence and current battering influence her coping strategies? How does she cope, survive, and resist in a hierarchical structure where she has unequal power?

Ramona, a 37-year-old Puerto Rican woman, the mother of three children, is a victim/survivor of 18 years of physical and psychological abuse in her marriage. She is also a victim/survivor of child abuse perpetrated by her father and a witness of abuse perpetrated by her father against her mother. Ramona described the variety of coping strategies that she used to deal with a battering incident, explaining:

> Our daughter went to our next door neighbor's house and found my husband kissing our neighbor on the mouth. At that point I would have liked to be dead. . . . When he came back home I told him "your daughter saw you kissing that woman." He said that it was not true, that our daughter was inventing things. When I insisted that our daughter was not a liar, he shouted and insulted me and locked himself in our bedroom. That night I slept in my daughter's bedroom. Next day, I called a lawyer friend of ours to ask for his advice and he told me that after so many years of marriage I should not get a divorce nor ask for a protective order under Law 54. He said that I should talk to my husband and appeal to his feelings, because he knows that he loves me and men are "like that." So I tried to talk to him, I cooked breakfast for him and took it to our bedroom, I told him "We have to talk." He answered that he didn't have anything to talk to me about. I told him that I couldn't continue like this, that the situation was intolerable, that I needed time to think about it and I asked him to leave our home. He said that I was crazy and that they would have to kill him before he would leave the house. I said O.K., but I'm going to put a chain and lock on the door so the neighbor cannot come in, "She has to respect me, this is my home." Then he said, "If you do that I'll kill you" and he took a knife from the kitchen and tried to stab me. I pleaded with him not to hurt me and I promised that I would not do it, "I won't put a chain and lock on the door." He went back to the bedroom, I don't know what for, and then I ran like crazy, I took my children and left. I went to my sister's home, I was away for a week and I requested a

Protective Order. .... I felt so hurt, so humiliated , it was not the first
time that he had cheated on me or beaten me . . ., she was my friend
. . . I never thought he would go so far, that's why I decided that he
had to leave before he destroyed me and my children.

Although the literature on the incidence, dynamics, and psychological impact of wife abuse is extensive, researchers, practitioners,
and policy analysts have paid less systematic attention to the range
of ways women cope with, resist, and survive wife abuse. Battered
women have been viewed as either masochistic, frigid, provocative,
or nagging (Gayford, 1977; Gelles & Straus, 1988; Roberts, 1996) or
passive, helpless, and apathetic (Bowker, 1993; Walker, 1979, 1984).
These profiles emerge from different psychological and sociological
theoretical perspectives; however, by concentrating on the characteristics of the female "victim," they contribute to blaming the woman
and perpetuating the violence directed at her. Even discussing family,
social structural, and sociocultural levels, many researchers fail to recognize the woman as an active social agent, the unequal distribution
of power in the family and in the society, and the socially structured
and culturally maintained patterns of male/female relations.

Moreover, the work of feminist theoreticians and researchers like
Gordon (1988), Davis (1987), Hoff (1990), Kelly (1988), Bowker
(1993), and Emerson and Russell Dobash (1988) challenge definitions of battered women as victims or provocateurs, arguing instead
that these women might be better understood as survivors. In their
historical, social, and psychological research these theoreticians have
clearly demonstrated that women who are battered are not passive in
confronting the violent situations in which they live. However, only
a few studies have integrated the psychological literature on coping
with the research on wife abuse. Mitchell and Hodson (1986) have
studied women's coping responses to wife abuse; nonetheless, they
have not integrated feminist perspectives and ideas. On the other
hand, feminist researchers Hoff (1990) and Kelly (1988) have carried
out important qualitative studies focusing on women's coping, resistance, and survival strategies in battering situations. Nevertheless, in
their groundbreaking studies, they have not integrated the accumu-
lated theoretical and empirical knowledge on stress, appraisal, and
coping.

By "coping," we refer to the effort that people exert to manage
specific external or internal demands that are appraised as taxing or

exceeding the resources of the person (Lazarus & Folkman, 1984). At the very heart of this concept is the fundamental assumption that people are actually responsive to forces that impinge upon them (Pearlin & Schooler, 1978). Because many of these forces are social and relational, the understanding of coping is necessary for understanding the impact exerted on people by institutions like the patriarchal family and society in general, and how people respond to them. Yet, we know relatively little of the coping strategies that women use in response to such a prevalent and taxing experience as wife abuse, which we define as the use of physical and nonphysical force by a man against his intimate cohabiting partner. Wife abuse is conceptualized as part of a continuum of violence against women in patriarchal social and familial structures.

The purpose of my study is to examine the ways Puerto Rican women cope with wife-abuse situations and to ascertain what aspects of women's lives, personal and contextual, influence their coping responses to battering. More specifically, I sought answers to the following questions:

1. How do women's coping responses to battering vary as a function of the frequency and severity of the battering?
2. How does previous exposure to violence relate to the coping strategies used by women in response to battering?
3. How do the primary and secondary appraisals of the battering situation influence the coping strategies used by women?

For the purpose of this study, the term *wife abuse* is used to define a broad category of abuse against women in intimate relationships, even though the intimate partners may not be legally married. Battering is theoretically defined as the use of coercive behavior (physical, sexual, or psychological) by a man against his intimate cohabiting partner, to force her to do what he wants her to do, regardless of her own needs, desires, rights, or best interests.

THEORETICAL FRAMEWORK

In this study, multiple theoretical and research perspectives from the psychological literature on stress, appraisal, and coping (Lazarus & Folkman, 1984) and feminist theories and research on violence in the family, specifically wife abuse, are used. Wife abuse is understood as part of a continuum of violence against women in patriarchal social and familial structures. The research is guided by feminist theory supplemented by Gramsci's (1971) concept of ideological hegemony and Foucault's (1981) concepts of power and resistance.

It is argued that violence against women does not happen in a vacuum: It occurs in the sociohistorical context of the patriarchal society. Violence against women in intimate relationships takes place in the context of the patriarchal family, which is one of the basic units of the patriarchal organization. In a similar fashion, coping and resisting violence in intimate relationships exists in the patriarchal context, and women use the coping strategies that they perceive as available to them at that moment. Women think, feel, and act to manage the internal and external demands that they appraise as taxing.

In the patriarchal family and social institutions of male dominance over women and children, women's interests are subordinated to the interests of men (Frye, 1983; hooks, 1984; Lerner, 1986; Weedon, 1989). In the relations of power existing within the family, specifically in intimate relationships, battering is used as a tool for social control to maintain and perpetuate the interests of men over those of women (Martin, 1983; Pagelow, 1981; Roberts, 1996; Schechter, 1982). The childhood exposure to violence (emotional abuse, sexual abuse, physical abuse, and neglect) that women experience in their families of origin is another tool in the continuum of violence against women that men use to control and "teach" women who has the power (Kelly, 1988).

Many women, because of the ideological hegemony of domesticity (Barrett, 1988; Gramsci, 1971) enforced in patriarchal societies, might feel and think that the interests of their partners (husband, cohabiting partner) or men in general are their interests. However, hegemony is not total, and power is not absolute, and wherever there is power there is resistance to that power (Foucault, 1981). The family, the home, the "homeplace" is the site of oppression and also the site of resistance (hooks, 1990).

COPING THEORIES

The application of coping theory to understand and explain how women deal with abusive episodes is a way to explicate and clarify their efforts to manage these encounters. As mentioned earlier, the concept of coping has been applied to wife abuse in an unsystematic, informal way, or by implication (Hoff, 1990; Kelly, 1988; Silva Bonilla, Rodriguez, Caceres, Martinez, & Torres, 1990). In addition, those researchers who have applied coping theory to battering situations have not used a feminist perspective. Richard Lazarus and Susan Folkman's theory of stress, appraisal, and coping (1984) was selected as the conceptual framework to guide the analysis of women's coping responses to wife abuse.

Lazarus and Folkman's theory is transactional; the person and the environment are viewed as being in a dynamic, mutually reciprocal, bidirectional relationship. Stress is conceptualized as a "relationship between the person and the environment that is appraised by the person as taxing or exceeding his or her resources and endangering his or her well-being" (Lazarus & Folkman, 1984, p. 19). The theory identifies cognitive appraisal and coping as two processes that mediate between the stressful person–environment encounter and the immediate and long-term outcome.

Cognitive appraisal is a "process through which the person evaluates whether a particular encounter with the environment is relevant to his or her well-being and, if so, in what way" (Lazarus & Folkman, 1984, p. 31). There are two kinds of cognitive appraisal: primary and secondary. In primary appraisal, the person evaluates whether he or she has anything at stake in this encounter. In secondary appraisal, the person evaluates what, if anything, can be done to overcome or prevent harm or improve the prospects for benefit.

In this theory, coping is defined as "constantly changing cognitive and behavioral efforts to manage specific external and/or internal demands that are appraised as taxing or exceeding the resources of the person" (Lazarus & Folkman, 1984, p. 141). According to Lazarus and Folkman, this definition addresses limitations of traditional approaches to coping. First, it views coping as process-oriented, rather than trait-oriented. Second, it views coping as contextual, that is, influenced by the person's appraisal of the actual demands in the encounter and the resources for managing them. Finally, the authors make no a priori assumptions about what constitutes good or bad coping, since their definition recognizes the efforts the person makes to manage the environment without taking into account whether the efforts are successful.

In this theory, coping has two major functions: First, problem-focused coping deals with the problem that is causing the distress by altering the troubled person–environment situation. Emotion-focused coping regulates the stressful emotions. Lazarus and Folkman (1984) have identified several forms of problem-focused and emotion-focused coping. For example, problem-focused forms of coping include aggressive interpersonal efforts to alter the situation, as well as cool, rational, deliberate efforts at problem solving. Emotion-focused forms of coping include distancing, self-controlling, seeking social support, escape/avoidance, accepting responsibility or blame, and positive reappraisal.

Lazarus and Folkman's (1984) Stress, Appraisal and Coping Transactional Model views coping as process-oriented rather than trait-oriented and does not judge coping strategies as "good" or "bad." Wife-abuse literature points to contextual factors, such as frequency and severity, influencing the ways women cope with battering. Guided by these and by a feminist perspective, which proposes that there is a continuum of violence against women in patriarchal societies, the following relationships were hypothesized:

1. The number of women's coping responses to battering will vary as a function of the frequency of the current battering.
2. The number of women's coping responses to battering will vary as a function of the severity of the current battering.
3. There is a difference in the use of coping strategies between the women who experienced or witnessed abuse in their families of origin and the ones who did not experience or witness abuse.
4. The women who experienced or witnessed abuse in their families of origin will use more emotion-focused coping strategies than the ones who did not experience or witness abuse in childhood.
5. The women who experienced or witnessed abuse in their families of origin will use less problem-focused strategies than the ones who did not experience or witness abuse in childhood.
6. The greater the stakes in the intimate relationship, the higher the rate of emotion-focused coping responses.
7. The women who appraise that they are in control of the battering situation will use more problem-focused coping strategies than the ones who perceive they are not in control.

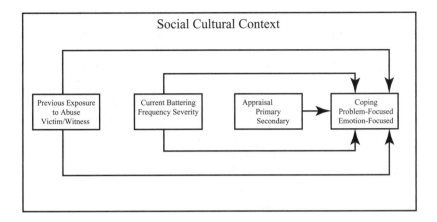

FIGURE 23.1   Conceptual framework: A model of women's ways of coping with battering in intimate relationships.

Source: Adapted from Mitchell and Hodson's conceptual framework (1983).

8. The women who perceive that they are in control of the battering situation will use less emotion-focused coping strategies than the ones who perceive they are not in control.

The diagram in Figure 23.1 outlines the hypothesized relationships between previous exposure to violence, severity and frequency of battering, and primary and secondary appraisal and coping strategies, both emotion and problem-focused. The diagram suggests pathways through which battering, child abuse, and appraisal may influence coping. This model draws upon previous work that has examined similar factors influencing women's reactions and responses to wife abuse (Blackman, 1989; Browne, 1987; Kelly, 1988; Mitchell & Hodson, 1983, 1986; Walker, 1984) and adjustment and coping with stressful events (Folkman, 1984; Folkman, Lazarus, Gruen, & DeLongis, 1986; Folkman & Lazarus, 1988; Lazarus & Folkman, 1984; Pearlin & Schooler, 1978).

METHODOLOGY

The research sample in my study consisted of 76 women who had sought assistance from one of three agencies in San Juan, Puerto

Rico, which offered counseling, legal services, or shelter to women victims/survivors of battering. To be included in the study, a woman must have been battered (physically, sexually, or psychologically) at least twice in the last year by a man with whom she has or had an intimate relationship.

The 76 participants were screened by agency workers when they telephoned or attended the agency's offices to request or continue psychosocial counseling or legal orientation. They were interviewed by the researcher in the offices, the shelter, or in their homes between the months of January and July of 1994. The data were gathered with a structured interview schedule used on the entire sample and a semistructured in-depth interview, with open-ended questions on a subsample of participants. Embedded in the interview schedule were several scales, such as a modified version of the Conflict Tactic Scales (CTS; Straus, 1979) and the 66 Ways of Coping Questionnaire (Folkman & Lazarus, 1988).

The computer program Statistical Analysis System (S.A.S.) was used to conduct data analysis. Frequency and descriptive statistics were used to describe the data. T tests, analysis of variance, and measures of association were used to test for differences and associations between the variables.

The mean age of the women was 34.4 years; 93.4% identified themselves as Puerto Rican, 20% were married or living with the batterer, and 80% were separated or divorced, 62% of them for less than a year. The majority (68%) of the women had been in a relationship with their partner for less than 10 years, and in 62% of the cases the battering had begun before the first year of marriage was over (in 12%, before getting married). In terms of education, 30% had completed high school, 36% had some college education, and 14% were college graduates and postgraduates. The majority of women had few independent financial resources (only 38% were employed, and of these 52% earned less than $10,000 a year); however, their family income (when living with or separated from the husband) was more substantial, with only 46% making less than $10,000 a year and 29% earning $20,000 or more a year. The mean number of children was 2.5. At the time of the interview, a mean of 2.0 children lived in the homes of the women. Five women had no children living with them at that point.

All the women participants manifested having been victims/ survivors of psychological abuse in their current intimate relationship. Sixty-six percent were victims/survivors of physical abuse, 43%

of sexual abuse, and 42% of economic abuse. Forty-three percent of the women had been victims of child abuse in their families of origin, and 61% had witnessed abuse in their families of origin. In 65% of these cases, the father was the aggressor, and in 11% the perpetrator was the stepfather. In 76% of the cases, the participant's mother was the victim of abuse.

LIMITATIONS OF THE STUDY

The major limitations of the present study are shared by research using nonexperimental, cross-sectional, retrospective designs. First, the cross-sectional design allows for alternative explanations of the findings. For example, severity of the current psychological abuse or previous exposure to childhood abuse may influence coping, and coping may influence the woman's appraisal or reappraisal of the current or previous abuse.

Similarly, it is possible that in addition to primary and secondary appraisal influencing coping, coping may influence the women's appraisal of what is at stake and what control they have over their situation. Thus, although the pathways in the model presented earlier are unidirectional, we recognize that these processes are likely to be bidirectional and reciprocal.

Second, the self-selected nature and small size of the sample make it difficult to assess the generalizability of the findings. For example, are women who seek assistance from agencies that serve women victims/survivors of abuse more likely to have identified abuse as a social or common problem for women, thus using more problem-solving coping strategies to try to change or alter the abusive situation? Are the coping strategies used by women who have made a decision to seek help different from those used by women who have not? Nevertheless, these women can provide useful and vital information, especially if the study is considered exploratory in nature and followed by larger, more representative samples of women in Puerto Rico.

FINDINGS

This study's findings are placed in the context of the conceptual framework that we proposed to help us understand how personal, social-cultural, and contextual factors are related to the ways women cope with battering in intimate relationships. The model (see Figure 23.1) suggests potential paths through which previous exposure to violence, frequency and severity of current battering, and the primary and secondary appraisals of the worst battering incident in the year of the study influenced women's coping strategies in a social context of structural oppression and discrimination and a situational context of abuse.

In general, the results of the study suggest that women victims/ survivors of battering used both emotion-focused (e.g., seeking social support and escape avoidance) and problem-focused (problem-solving, confrontive) forms of coping to deal with the worst battering incident during the study year. Furthermore, the relative proportions of each form of coping vary according to how the battering encounter is appraised (e.g., amenable or not amenable to control; the magnitude of the stakes) and if the woman was or was not a victim/or witness of child abuse in her family of origin. The quantity or number of coping strategies used during the encounter vary according to the severity of the current psychological abuse (verbal aggression) and if the woman was or was not a victim/survivor of child abuse. Previous exposure to abuse in the family of origin influenced the proportion of emotion-focused and problem-focused forms of coping, as well as the total number of coping strategies women use.

The findings in the present study suggest that the women participants who were victims of abuse in childhood, who appraised that the stakes (e.g., risk to the integrity of the marriage and the family, women's health security and physical welfare) in the battering situation were high, and who perceived that they were in control during the battering incident used more problem-focused coping strategies as a response to the worst battering incident during the year of the study. In addition, the women who were abused in their families of origin used significantly more coping strategies, both problem-focused and emotion-focused, to deal with the battering situation than did nonvictims. Moreover, in the current study, only the severity of psychological abuse (verbal aggression) in the marriage, rather than physical or sexual abuse, was positively related to the use of more coping strategies in the worst battering situation.

Women's appraisal of the battering situation psychologically mediates the women with the environment. Their appraisal of the immediate battering situation is individual and contextual at the same time that it is influenced by social–cultural variables, such as the hegemonic ideology of family and marriage and the social structure that oppresses and discriminates against women.

It can be observed how the "macro" level of cultural and social structural variables influences the "micro" level of the individual woman's actual life context and her response to it. The view of women as both influenced and influencing the social structure and culture is imperative, and recognizes that coping involves changing the environment as well as one's self (Lazarus & Folkman, 1984). Women appraise and cope in the battering relationship responding to personal history, cultural, and social structural variables (both "concrete" and "perceived") and in the process they change the immediate situation, themselves, and their environment.

The important message that we can draw from these findings is that we have to view the women victims/survivors of battering as actively coping in the battering situation; appraising harm, threat, and control of the immediate situation; drawing strength from their past history and their present resources; and evaluating the constraints in the environment. Women as individual, active agents are firmly embedded within the social–cultural, political, and economic context in which they live. However, cultural and social structural variables interact with women's commitments and beliefs that shape cognitive appraisals in every situation, as well *as* with the demands, constraints, and resources of the immediate battering situation. The women's personal history of abuse, the demands of the current psychological abuse, and their appraisal of the battering situation help us understand women's ways of coping with battering in intimate relationships.

IMPLICATIONS FOR SOCIAL WORK

Implication for Social Policy

In the United States and in Puerto Rico, social policy has long been dominated by the medical or psychological treatment model that view any problem as existing entirely within the individual. Only unidirectional, static, antecedent-consequent causality is addressed. The individual or psychological focus adopted from the medical model is also evident in public policy development around the issue of violence against women. Romany (1994) argues: "The Puerto Rican experience shows how deeply ingrained dysfunctional characterizations of woman battering are, and the significant role the helping professions have played in maintaining them" (p. 289). Even though the feminist and battered women's movements in Puerto Rico were at the forefront in bringing violence against women into public discussion, and were fundamental in the establishment of the first shelter for battered women in 1979 and the approval of Law 54 for the Prevention of and Intervention in Domestic Violence in 1989, the helping professions' discourse dominates in the implementation of the law and the provision of services to women victims/survivors of domestic violence.

Law 54 clearly recognizes the political nature of violence against women and its patriarchal foundations; conservative and liberal ideologies of familialism and domesticity, which are at the core of the idea of preserving the violent family and the status quo, however, permeate social policy and social work in Puerto Rico. Social work and the other helping professions operate within a sociocultural, political context that takes as "natural" the nuclear heterosexual family. On the other hand, social policy focuses on individual "victims" (women and children) and on "why are families so violent?," which obliterates the gender perspective of violence against women. So-called "liberal" policies place the violent family at the top of the ladder of social institutions to be preserved (Romany, 1994). The social organization of the family that makes it "violent prone" (Gelles & Cornell, 1990) and the dysfunctional, helpless woman with her helpless, depressed, anxious, and aggressive children (Gibson & Gutierrez, 1991) are at the center of the issue and in need of being "rehabilitated" and "treated." Institutional, social work and other helping professions' discourse privilege the dysfunctional and pathological over the sociocultural, political, and gender dimensions of violence against women in intimate relationships.

For example, women survivors of violence are seen as suffering from learned helplessness and the "battered woman syndrome" (Walker, 1979, 1984), which is meant to explain why women do not leave their violent partners; though many of its adherents also think it explains why women become victims of violence (Dobash & Dobash, 1992). Like most psychologically or individually oriented approaches, it identifies the primary roots of victimization in the background of the victim, and not in the aggressor or the social structure. Dobash and Dobash (1992) argue: "It is not clear from these accounts whether a majority or small proportion of women who are abused by their male partners suffer from learned helplessness" (p. 225). Most of this literature implies or explicitly states: "all battered women, possibly all women, suffer from learned helplessness." However, as stated before, the results of the study, as well as other research on the reactions and responses of women who endure, resist, cope, and survive abuse, reveal that they do not remain helpless or passive, but rather seek help from a wide variety of formal and informal sources, while they make the decision to "save," change, or end the intimate relationship.

"Women's lives-in-violence, their stories of survival and resistance" asserts Romany (1994, p. 296), "are filtered through the lens of expert categorizations—a logical consequence in a society compartmentalized by expert knowledge, giving preeminence to the scientific, objective and primarily male ways of knowing (Harding, 1986; Keller, 1985; Smith, 1990)." Moreover, social policy, programs, and services regarding violence against women continue to try to solve social, structural problems by using individual counseling and therapeutically oriented solutions.

In recent years, social policy and social work dealing with violence against women has moved from the gender perspective of the earlier battered women's movement to the "professionally" and therapeutically oriented perspective that focuses on the family as a unit and on the children of battered women, and not on women's needs and rights in the context of the structural oppression where they live. As the shelters for battered women, originally developed through the efforts of grassroots feminist organizations, have been institutionalized and managed by the helping professions, the focus has shifted to family- and children-oriented work, once again making women's voices and experiences silent and invisible. As pointed out by Gibson and Gutierrez (1991), programs focused originally on providing services to battered women "quickly understood" the necessity of developing programs for children. Because many of these programs are run with a protective services focus on children and the family as a unit, it is not surprising that researchers (Gibson & Gutierrez) have identified as limitations of these programs the fact that women "focused most of their attention on support and counseling for themselves and arrangements for independent living" (p. 561).

Recognizing that women's focus is on "realistic concrete needs," they recommended that workers use this focus to develop supportive and trusting relationships with women. Gibson and Gutierrez go on to advise workers: "Willingness to provide concrete services and be an advocate with community agencies can be an effective *entry work* on emotional issues" (p. 561).

Clearly, in Puerto Rico as well as in the United States, the focus has changed from women to children and from advocacy and community work to psychologically oriented work. Women's experiences of gender-based violence and its consequences are again made invisible or hidden beneath the violence that plagues the family unit (Romany, 1994). Restructuring the family system, building new ways of interacting, and looking into the emotional and psychological "deficits" of women and children seem to have taken the place of using a gender perspective with a vision of transforming the position of women in society. The need to confront structural violence, poverty, sexism, racism, and other persistent inequalities has once again been erased as a central issue for social policy, programs, and services.

Without oversimplifying the complexities of women's ways of coping with abuse, the present study provides a view of women actively coping in the battering context; appraising harm, threat, and control over their immediate situation and drawing strength from their past history, their present resources, and evaluating the constraints of their environment. This snapshot view of women confronting abuse makes imperative a social policy that takes into account women's experiences, appraisals, and concrete needs and rights in their path of transforming themselves, their families, and their social–cultural context.

Social policy should validate and facilitate women's coping and resistance to abuse, instead of silencing and erasing their contextual experiences. Can social policy, programs, and services for women survivors of abuse in Puerto Rico move away from a victim-blaming, deficit-focused agenda to a more complex vision of women's coping, resisting, and surviving in a gendered, violent, unequal society? Social work and social workers face a challenge to collaborate with feminist scholars, researchers, and activists to develop, examine, and provide critiques of legislation and social policy affecting women such as equal pay and opportunities, housing, child care, marriage, divorce, custody, welfare benefits, and job and training opportunities.

IMPLICATIONS FOR DIRECT SERVICES

The importance of knowledge of women's ways of coping with abuse in intimate relationships must not be overlooked in the provision of direct services to women. While helping practitioners are not likely to be surprised by the fact that personal history, the severity of verbal aggression, and the appraisal of the abusive situation influence how women cope with abuse, such findings help to remind us of their importance. In working with women survivors of domestic violence, one may overlook the complexity of the association and relationship of individual, contextual, and sociocultural variables in the response to abuse. The determination of what efforts a particular woman victim/survivor of abuse has made to protect, avoid, confront, or escape the abuse, in addition to the variables that influence her ways of coping, are important components of a comprehensive assessment of her situation.

Assessing women's situations and facilitating women's decision-making, problem-solving, and healing processes is more effective if the helping professional analyzes battering within the context of the dynamics of oppression, based on gender, race, ethnicity, class, and age among other factors, and in a framework of male power and dominance over women. In this way, women's ways of coping with abuse are viewed as a process, and contextualized in the battering situation and the patriarchal society in which it occurs.

The findings of the present study illustrate the complexity of women participants' experience: the types, frequencies, and severities of the abuse they experienced in childhood and in intimate relationships, the resources (or lack of resources) in the community, and the constraints of the battering situation; the way they thought, felt, and acted during incidents of severe battering; how their appraisal of the battering situation was circumscribed by an ideology of domesticity that encourages women to try to save their marriages at all costs and feel responsible for its "success" or "failure," and the enormous strength and determination it takes to cope with abuse. This section explores the ways that social workers might use to understand, assess, and facilitate women's processes of protection, self-defense, decision making, problem solving, healing, and social action. To support women, social and psychological intervention should involve the following elements.

Validating Women's Experiences

When battered women seek help, social workers need to listen and believe what they say. The reported abuse must always be taken seriously. The woman needs to tell her history in her own way, without being interrupted or pressured to make immediate decisions. This involves a genuine sense that the social worker has truly heard what she is saying and can validate her experience by an appropriate response. Questions, comments, and interpretations from the social worker that may seem "appropriate" may feel distancing, judgmental, or even damaging if they serve as barriers between the social worker and the woman's own experience (Dutton, 1992).

A woman participant in our study expressed pain, anger, and disbelief when she remembered the night she arrived at a women's shelter. After going through an ordeal of abuse where, among other violent actions, her husband had threatened to kill her with a gun while playing Russian Roulette, she was asked during the intake interview if she was on drugs. She had escaped from her husband's aggression, leaving her children in her sister's home, where they had been visiting. When she arrived at the shelter she was scared, disheveled, and feeling guilty for having left her children behind. Apparently, the social worker misunderstood her reaction to the abusive incident as evidence of drug use. The participant felt hurt, damaged, and revictimized by the social worker who was supposed to help her. The participant stayed overnight in the shelter and left early next day. She went back to get her children at her sister's home. Her husband found out about it and went to pick her up to take her back "home" to continue the abuse.

Nonjudgmental acceptance and understanding was mentioned by many of the women participants as helpful in their process of identifying the abuse, asking for help, and decision making.

Understanding Women's Feelings Toward the Abuse and the Abuser

Women participants in the study expressed feelings of humiliation, anger, grief, sadness, fear, impotence, guilt, insecurity, and loneliness among others, during the abusive incidents. It is important that the social worker identify, accept, and validate women's sometimes contradictory feelings toward the abuse and the abuser. Anger, for example, was one of the most common reactions to the experience of abuse of the women in the study. Facilitating the acknowledgment and safe expression of anger is the essential task of rage expression (Dutton, 1992). Overt expressions of anger are generally considered to be unacceptable for women (Jaggar, 1988; Lorde, 1984) and thus are distrusted and experienced negatively by both battered women and helping professionals. Women who are viewed as passive and helpless are not expected to feel or demonstrate anger and rage; therefore, one of the first tasks in working with women's anger is for the woman herself to identify, name, and accept the feeling, and for the professional to accept it. Anger and rage can be used positively, and turned into positive, active, powerful action. Free-floating anger has to be channeled in a manner that is not destructive or converted into anxiety and depression. Lorde argues that women should learn to "cherish, respect our feelings, respect the hidden sources of power" (p. 133).

Learning to trust our perceptions and using our emotions positively can have a surprisingly powerful effect. However, the social worker needs to be careful not to condone violent acts, and yet support the women's right to feel angry and use that anger creatively (Dutton, 1992; Lorde, 1984). The emotional and physical energy accompanying feelings of anger can be directed toward expression in a variety of ways, including journal-keeping, creative writing, and other expressions of art; self-protection, empowerment, and social and political activism (Dutton).

Feelings of anger and humiliation led a woman participant in the study into action:

> I told myself, wait, I have the enemy in my home and I have to kick him out, completely, because he is destroying me, destroying the values I have taught my daughters and I don't want them to learn that they have to allow any man to act with them the way their father has acted with me.

The importance of expressing our feelings was manifested by another participant:

> I think one should not be silent, should not take it. You can't, because that's like dying, you are killing yourself slowly, you are killing who you are. . . . It does not matter how evil . . . you have to express it because that is the only way you can be free.

Other feelings, like loneliness and grief, have to be explored, named, and accepted. Many women in our study talked about their feelings of loneliness, both while still living with the abuser and afterwards, if they had left him. Some of them remarked:

> My greatest worry is my loneliness. . . . I told my daughter that I was looking for help, that if something happened to me she should know that it was him who did it, I asked her not to forget me, please come visit once in a while because I feel very lonely . . . he even criticizes me because no one visits. . . .
>
> I decided that this is the moment for me to leave, get a divorce, because I have a man at my side but he doesn't support me, I don't have anything, what am I doing here?
>
> I don't have any one, I have someone, and I don't have any one. . . . I don't want to forget about myself. . . .
>
> People can't see both parts of me, that I'm not that strong, that I have my moments of vulnerability, that I need support sometimes, someone to hold me and tell me that everything is going to be all right.

Sometimes it is hard for helping professionals to accept, and even to listen to battered women express their feelings of love for their abusers. Sometimes women are reluctant to disclose these feelings because they might feel embarrassed or ashamed and fear judgmental reactions from the social worker. A social worker reluctant to hear contradictory feelings fails to provide the context where healing is possible. The emotions surrounding the loss of a relationship and loss of love can be shattering. Dutton (1992) argues that "it is not the loss of the abusive aspect of a relationship that battered women grieve, but the loss of the real or hoped for loving, caring relationship" (p. 138). If helping professionals are reluctant to listen nonjudgmentally to battered women's feelings of anger, rage, sadness, grief, love, humiliation, and shame, the message is that their experiences and their feelings must remain invisible and silent.

Supporting and Advocating for Self-Protection and Safety Planning

All the women participants in the study used coping strategies directed at protecting themselves and their children. They sought psychological and medical treatment; they called the police; sought support from family, friends, social workers, and counselors; and went to hospitals or to shelters. During the most severe battering incident occurring in the year of the interview, the participants (in descending order of frequency) cried, shouted back, and insulted the batterer; they left the house; responded to the aggression physically; called the police; listened; locked themselves in their rooms; and pretended to be asleep. All of these strategies were carried out to protect themselves psychologically, physically, and sexually. As social workers, we have to support women's ways of coping to protect themselves, which may include a wide range of emotion- and problem-focused strategies. The social worker must recognize the woman's strategies and her ability to defend herself.

Safety planning should also be discussed with the women, whether their immediate decision is to separate from or to remain with the abuser. Informing about and building options toward safety acknowledges the battered woman's central role of choice (Browne, 1988; Dutton, 1992). Many of the women interviewed in the present study shared stories of using plans and information they had discussed previously with family, friends, neighbors, and social workers/counselors. One of the participants narrated that she had the local battered women's shelter telephone number hidden inside a Bible she had next to her bed. She had it hidden there for months, and immediately after the most severe incident of battering had ended, she called the shelter and made arrangements to go there. It is of the utmost importance that we trust the woman's appraisal of danger, risks, and control over the battering situation, as well as share with her the options available to her and be available when she needs us.

Sharing Educational Material About Violence and Abuse

It is useful to share, in conversation or in writing, articles, books, movies, and statistics about violence against women in your country and other countries around the world. Talking and reading about the roots of violence and oppression against women, as well as women's ways of coping, resisting, and survival, can be a very powerful experience. Many women participants in the study talked about how magazine articles, TV programs, movies, and educational material given to them by counselors or friends had helped them to understand abuse and identify themselves as victims/survivors of abuse; other radio and television shows had offered them information about service programs and shelters in their community. Universalizing as well as contexualizing their experiences was very helpful in their process of consciousness-raising and realization that the root of battering was not in themselves, but in the sociocultural context where they live.

Recognizing and Building on Women's History, Experiences, Coping Strategies, and Strengths

Women's experiences with abuse, and sharing those experiences with understanding family members, friends, and professionals, made them aware of inner strengths that many were unaware they possessed. Many women participants expressed that they felt stronger after having been through the battering experiences. Some of them used positive reappraisal coping strategies to find strength in their history of abuse. After the worst battering incident of abuse in the year they were interviewed and in response to the 66 Ways of Coping Questionnaire, 84% of the women expressed that they had rediscovered what was important in life, and 76% said that they came out of the experience better than when they went in. Some of their comments were:

> I feel valor and strength to confront the situation.
>   I did not value myself, now I learned to love myself ... I learned by myself as a consequence of the abuse.
>   I did not value myself ... now I know my body is important, I am important.

One woman narrated how she had stopped using crack—she started using it after being coerced by the abuser—by looking at herself in the mirror. She would stand in front of the mirror and tell herself, "I'm not filth, I'm a worthy person."

This acknowledgment of personal strength and determination was reflected in many of the women's responses to the structured interview. Although most women stressed the support they received from others, especially mothers, parents, and sisters, it was their own strength and determination that was the crucial factor in their reappraisal of the battering situation and how it had helped them survive and become stronger. Many of the women recognized their own strengths in retrospect, demonstrating how important it is for social workers and helping professionals to support and build on women's strengths, instead of pathologizing, underestimating, or disbelieving their recollection of their past.

The use of other coping strategies, such as distancing, self-controlling, and escape-avoidance, is often necessary to resist and survive the abuse. Viewed as a process, not as a trait, and as valid efforts to cope with the abuse or its after-effects, these coping strategies are recognized for their survival and resistance value. Viewed in the context of the abusive situation and the structural oppression of women, all coping strategies are recognized as valid efforts to deal with the environment and to exercise power and resistance.

Understanding That Violence Against Women Is Rooted in the Hierarchical Structure of Power Relations in the Family and in Society

Viewing violence against women and women's responses within the cultural, racial, ethnic, political, and economic contexts within which the woman and her family live is essential in working with women who are battered. Understanding women's appraisal of and coping with abuse in a context of women's oppression and paying attention to the interplay of sexism, racism, and economic inequality are crucial in working with battered women.

Women's choices of coping strategies are influenced by their appraisal of the stakes and control over the abusive situation, as well as of their personal and family histories. Appraisal of the abusive situation and a personal history of child abuse is at the same time influenced by a patriarchal culture and a hegemonic ideology of familialism, domesticity, and maternity where women are adjudicated responsibility for the "success" or "failure" of family life and simultaneously seen as a "property" of the man who is seen as the head of the household/family. Contradictory demands are made upon women to be "strong," "passive," "vulnerable," "weak," and "responsible." Listening to, understanding, and analyzing these contradictory demands upon women can be empowering and revealing. When asked about the influence of culture and family ideology on their ways of coping with abuse, some of the women participants in the study answered as follows.

You hear that when people get married, the husband works, that his obligation is to be a good provider. That you have to do what he says, he is the one who gives the orders . . . it's like a rule, and it has to be that way.

The man is the one that thinks, he knows how to do it.

It's like I want to be good, I want to please everybody, I want to support everybody, I want to help everybody, but when I get home I feel depressed and I ask myself, who is going to give to me? Whom could I rely on? Who is going to provide a shoulder for me to cry on?

You have to be submissive, have patience, tolerance . . . give in. What he says is the way it has to be. One gets used to that type of upbringing, and you accept it.

Another woman spoke about the crevices of the dominant ideology.

Because I was told that women have to endure, tolerate, suffer and the man? well, happy all the time and I always say no to this.

One woman explained the process of internalizing the hegemonic family ideology as well as the questioning of it:

It's like when you have a pair of shoes that hurt you, and you grow a callus and after some time they don't hurt you anymore. When you find options . . . you study them. . . .

Listening to women, recognizing their ways of resistance, accepting their questioning of the dominant ideology, and sharing options is an empowering experience. To recognize and share the experiences of women, social workers must recognize and contest the dominant ideology of familialism, domesticity, and maternity, and ensure space for women to get away from caring and obligations to men. Moreover, we must recognize and discuss with women the power imbalances and unequal treatment that women receive in our society.

CONCLUSION

In summary, my study found first that the women participants in the present study who had been victims or witnesses of abuse in childhood used significantly more coping strategies, both problem-solving-focused and emotion-focused, to deal with the worst battering incident of the last year, than the women who were not victims or witnesses of childhood abuse. Second, the women who were more frequently abused in childhood were more likely to use emotion- and problem-solving-focused strategies to deal with the worst battering incident during the year of the study. Third, the severity of psychological abuse (verbal aggression) during the marriage is associated with the use of more coping strategies to deal with the worst incident of abuse during the year of the study. Fourth, the higher the stakes during the worst battering incident, the more likely were the women participants to use problem-focused strategies to deal with the incident. Fifth, the women participants who felt in control of the situation during the worst battering incident used more problem-focused strategies than the women who felt they had no control during the worst battering incident of the past year.

These findings suggest, first, that women participants in the study were behaviorally and emotionally engaged in managing efforts to protect, defend, avoid, escape, confront, plan, and problem solve to deal with the worst incident of battering in the past year. Second, the experience of abuse in their families of origin did not render the women passive or helpless in coping with current abuse. Third, when appraising high stakes and feeling in control over the situation during battering incidents, women are more likely to use problem-solving strategies to deal with abuse. Finally, psychological more than physical abuse is related to the use of more coping strategies to deal with it.

These findings exhort us to change the way we think about women victims/survivors of abuse in intimate relationships. Rather than viewing them as helpless, deficient, passive women, we must comprehend the complexity and multidimensionality of abuse in intimate relationships and all the factors—personal, familial, social, cultural—that impinge on women's feelings, thoughts, and actions in coping with, resisting, and surviving abuse. When women face abuse, they are confronting their inner thoughts and feelings about womanhood, mothering, about who they are and what they stand for, in a society where women are seen as subordinate and inferior to men. Women confront not only the abusive actions of "the man she loves and who loves her" but also society's ideas about how he and she should feel, think, and behave. When women confront abuse they confront economic hardships, loss of a home, loss of love, loss of friends, loss of their children, loss of self-esteem and self-respect, and loss of their lives. They confront their society, their community, their family, their children, and most of all they confront themselves. Coping under extreme circumstances of duress, women victims/survivors of abuse face up to the formidable task of appraising their circumstances and making decisions about their lives and the lives of their children. We must not underestimate, simplicize, or trivialize their situation with reductionist explanations or interpretations that they are "masochists," or suffer from "problem-solving deficits," or from "learned helplessness." The women participants in this study demonstrated high-level emotional and cognitive coping under the most difficult circumstances of abuse from their spouse, in a context of economic, political, and social oppression.

REFERENCES

Abbott, A. (1996). Epilogue: Helping battered women. In A. R. Roberts (Ed.), *Helping battered women: New perspectives and remedies* (pp. 235–237). New York: Oxford University Press.

Barrett, M. (1988). *Women's oppression today: The Marxist/feminist encounter.* London: Verso.

Blackman, J. (1989). *Intimate violence: A study of injustice.* New York: Columbia University Press.

Bowker, L. H. (1993). A battered woman's problems are social, not psychological. In R. J. Gelles & D. R. Loseke (Eds.), *Current controversies on family violence* (pp. 154–165). Newbury Park, CA: Sage.

Browne, A. (1987). *When battered women kill.* New York: Free Press.

Davis, L. V. (1987). Battered women and the transformation of a social problem. *Social Work, 32,* 306–311.

Dobash, R. E., & Dobash, R. (1992). *Women, violence, and social change.* London: Routledge.

Dobash, R. E., & Dobash, R. (1988). Research as social action: The struggle for battered women. In K. Yllo & M. Bograd (Eds.), *Feminist perspectives on wife abuse* (pp. 51–74). Beverly Hills: Sage.

Dutton, M. A. (1992). *Empowering and healing the battered woman: A model for assessment and intervention.* New York: Springer Publishing.

Folkman, S., & Lazarus, R. E. (1988). The relationship between coping and emotion: Implications for theory and research. *Social Science Medicine, 26,* 309–317.

Folkman, S., Lazarus, R., Gruen, R. J., & DeLongis, A. (1986). Appraisal, coping, health status, and psychological symptom. *Journal of Personality and Social Psychology, 50,* 517–549.

Foucault, M. (1981). *The history of sexuality: Vol. I: An introduction.* Harmondsworth, England: Pelican.

Frye, M. (1993). *The politics of reality: Essays in feminist theory.* Freedom, CA: Crossing Press.

Gayford, J. J. (1975). Wife battering: A preliminary survey of 100 cases. *British Medical Journal, 25,* 194–197.

Gelles, R., & Cornell, C. P. (1990). *Intimate violence in families.* Newbury Park, CA: Sage.

Gelles, R. J., & Straus, M. A. (1988). *Intimate violence.* New York: Simon and Schuster.

Gibson, J. W., & Gutierrez, L. (1991). A service program for safe-home children. *Journal of Contemporary Human Services, 72,* 554–561.

Gordon, L. (1988). *Heroes of their own lives: The politics and history of family violence.* New York: Penguin.

Gramsci, A. (1971). *Selections from the prison notebooks.* London: Lawrence and Wishart.

Harding, S. (1986). *The science question in feminism.* Ithaca, NY: Cornell University Press.

Hoff, L. A. (1990). *Battered women as survivors.* London: Routledge.

hooks, b. (1984). *Feminist theory: From margin into center.* Boston: South End Press.

hooks, b. (1990). *Yearning: Race, gender and cultural politics.* Boston: South End Press.

Jaggar, A. M. (1988). *Feminist politics and human nature.* Totowa, NJ: Ronman and Litlefield.

Keller, E. (1985). *Reflections on gender and science.* New Haven, CT: Yale University Press.

Kelly, L. (1988). How women define their experiences of violence. In K. Yllo & M. Bograd (Eds.), *Feminist perspectives on abuse* (pp. 114–132). Newbury Park, CA: Sage.

Komter, A. (1989). Hidden power in marriage. *Gender and Society, 3,* 187–216.

Lazarus, R. S., & Folkman, S. (1984). *Stress appraisal and coping.* New York: Springer Publishing.

Lerner, G. (1986). *The creation of patriarchy.* New York: Oxford University Press.

Lorde, A. (1984). *Sister outsider.* Trumansburg, NY: Crossing Press.

Martin, D. (1983). *Battered wives.* New York: Pocket Books.

Mitchell, R. E., & Hodson, C. A. (1983). Coping with domestic violence:

Social support and psychological health among battered women. *American Journal of Community Psychology, 11*, 629–654.

Mitchell, R. E., & Hodson, C. A. (1986). Coping and social support among battered women. In S. E. Hobfall (Ed.), *Stress, social support and women* (pp. 153–169). Washington, DC: Hemisphere.

Pearlin, L. I., & Schooler, C. (1978). The structure of coping. *Journal of Health and Social Behavior, 19*, 2–21.

Preamble Law 54 for the Prevention of and Intervention with Domestic Violence. (1989, August 15). Rio Piedras: Women's Affairs Commission, Office of the Governor of Puerto Rico.

Rivera Ramos, A. N. (1991). *The Puerto Rican woman: Psychosocial research.* Rio Piedras: Editorial Edil.MB1.

Roberts, A. (1996). Myths and realities regarding battered women. In A. Roberts (Ed.), *Helping battered women: New perspectives and remedies* (pp. 3–12). New York: Oxford University Press.

Romany, C. (1994). Killing the angel in the house: Digging for the political vortex of male violence against women. In M. Albertson Fineman & R. Mykitiuk (Eds.), *The public nature of private violence* (pp. 285–302). New York: Routledge.

Schechter, S. (1982). *Women and male violence: The visions and struggles of the battered women's movement.* Boston: South End.

Silva Bonilla, R. (1985). *El marco social de la violencia contra las mujeres en la vida conyugal.* Rio Piedras: Publicaciones Centro de Investigaciones Sociales, Universidad de P.R.

Silva Bonilla, R. M., Rodriguez, J., Caceres, V., Martinez, L., & Torres, N. (1990). *Hay amores que matan: La violencia contra las mujeres en la vida conyugal.* Rio Piedras: Ediciones Huracan.

Smith, D. E. (1990). The conceptual practices of power, public wrongs, and the responsibility of states. *Fordham International Law Journal, 13*(1).

Straus, M. A. (1979). Measuring intra-family conflict and violence: The conflict tactics (CT) scales. *Journal of Marriage and the Family, 41*, 75–88.

Straus, M. A., & Gelles, R. J. (1995). *Physical violence in American families: Risk factors and adaptations to violence in 8,145 families.* New Brunswick: Transaction Books.

Walker, L. E. A. (1979). *The battered woman.* New York: Harper & Row.

Walker, L. E. A. (1984). *The battered woman syndrome.* New York: Springer Publishing.

Walker, L. E. A. (1993). The battered woman syndrome is a psychological consequence of abuse. In R. J. Gelles & D. R. Loseke (Eds.), *Current controversies in family violence* (pp. 133–153). Newbury Park, CA: Sage.

Weedon, C. (1991). *Feminist practice and poststructuralist theory.* Oxford: Basil Blackwell.

Author Index

De Berry, M., Jr., 302, 325
Deblinger, A. F., 198, 205
De Bold, J., 407, 421
DeChant, H. K., 286, 287, 298
De Jong, P., 91, 92, 106
De Knorring, A. L., 406, 419
DeLongis, A., 571, 589
DelTufo, A., 302, 323
DeMaris, A., 261, 272
Denison, J. A., 36, 59
DePanfilis, D., 227, 243
DePaola, L. M., 260, 272
Derogatis, L., 72, 86
Desai, S., 527
de Shazer, S., 92, 94, 95, 96, 101, 103, 106
DeVellis, R., 333, 355
Devereaux, P. J., 237, 245
Dickow, A., 419
Dickson, F., 290, 297
DiClemente, C. C., 35, 37, 38, 39, 60, 239, 246
Dienemann, J., 277, 297, 510, 527
Digirolamo, K., 416, 422, 544
Dill, L., 286, 287, 298
DiNitto, D. M., 408, 421
Dobash, R., 566, 576, 577, 588
Dobash, R. E., 566, 576, 577, 588
Doe, T., 380, 396
Dolan, Y. M., 90, 106
Dominelli, L., 279, 297
Dore, P., 252, 260, 272
Doron, I., 476, 486
Doueck, H. J., 225, 245
Douglas, H., 302, 323
Downs, W. R., 412, 413, 420, 421, 441, 448
Drachman, D., 499, 508, 546, 560
Drake, V. K., 308, 323
Drell, M. J., 184
Drori, D., 477, 486
Drossman, D., 283, 297
Duff, J., 184, 207
Durkin, M. S., 383, 395
Dutton, D. G., 74, 86, 91, 106, 217, 220, 221, 222, 224, 226, 227, 239, 243, 244, 336, 352

Dutton, M. A., 40, 41, 43, 54, 59, 89, 91, 93, 104, 106, 165, 176, 337, 342, 344, 349, 352, 353, 545, 560, 580, 581, 582, 583, 588
Dwyer, D., 278, 297
Dyar, L., 318, 319
Dye, E., 159
Dziegielewski, S. F., 64, 86, 98, 104, 106, 107, 134, 157, 183, 189, 205, 206, 329, 338, 353, 544, 560

E

Earp, J., 333, 355
Eaves, D., 222, 245, 518
Eckhardt, C. I., 36, 59
Edbril, S. D., 149, 156
Edelson, J. A., 40, 60
Edin, K. E., 289, 297
Edleson, J. L., 168, 176, 183, 209, 217, 218, 219, 226, 241, 243, 244, 252, 260, 270, 272, 273, 303, 323, 342, 353, 548, 560
Edwards, M., 225, 226, 244
Eisikovits, Z. C., 93, 94, 106, 303, 323, 478, 488
El-Bassel, N., 402, 420
Elliot, D. M., 72, 86
Elliott, L., 289, 297, 304, 323
Elliott, P., 454, 469
Elze, D., 252, 260, 272
Emerling, F. G., 528
English, D. J., 226, 244
Enns, C. Z., 349, 353
Epstein, D., 163, 165, 166, 176
Erlingsson, C. L., 477, 482, 486
Estess, C. L., 438, 447
Eth, S., 184, 189, 193, 194, 205, 206, 209, 257, 265, 271, 274
Everstine, D., 145, 148, 152, 157
Everstine, L., 145, 148, 152, 157
Eyler, A. E., 284, 298, 519, 520, 527

F

Fadley, J. T., 373, 375
Fagan, J., 408, 420
Fallon, B., 217, 242, 247
Fals-Stewart, W., 402, 420

Subject Index

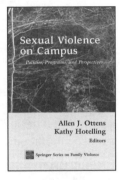

SPRINGER PUBLISHING COMPANY

Handbook of Forensic Mental Health With Victims and Offenders

Assessment, Treatment, and Research

David W. Springer, PhD, LCSW
Albert R. Roberts, PhD, DABFE, Editors

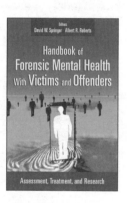

Together for the first time: all your forensic social work best practice needs in one volume. From expert testimony advice to treating HIV-positive incarcerated women, this handbook contains the most current research and tested field practices for child welfare through adulthood in the civil and criminal system.

Encompassing a wide range of treatments, roles, specialized practices, research, and diagnoses, the *Handbook of Forensic Mental Health* will guide practicing professionals through the forensic social work issues they encounter on a daily basis, such as:

- Prevention of prisoner sudden deaths
- Expert witness testimony in child welfare and women battering
- Treating dually diagnosed adolescents
- The overrepresentation of African Americans for juvenile delinquency
- Jail mental health services for adults
- Drug courts and PTSD in inmates with substance abuse histories
- Recidivism prevention
- Basic tasks in post-trauma intervention with victims and offenders
- Culture and gender considerations in restorative justice

Edited by renowned psychologist Dr. Albert R. Roberts and social worker Dr. David W. Springer, with contributions by leaders in the field, this handbook should top the list of must-haves for all forensic social workers.

February 2007 · 650pp · hardcover · 0-8261-1514-4

11 West 42nd Street, New York, NY 10036-8002 • Fax: 212-941-7842
Order Toll-Free: 877-687-7476 • Order On-line: www.springerpub.com

From the Family Violence Series

Gender-Inclusive Treatment of Intimate Partner Abuse

A Comprehensive Approach

John Hamel, LCSW
Foreword by Donald Dutton

This breakthrough handbook for mental health professionals and educators concerned with domestic violence offers practical, hands-on materials for conducting assessments and providing treatments that take the entire family system into account. Rich with research that shows women are abusive within relationships at rates comparable to men, the book eschews the field's reliance on traditional domestic violence theory and treatment, which favor violence intervention for men and victim services for women and ignore the dynamics of the majority of violent relationships.

Gender Inclusive Treatment of Intimate Partner Abuse
A Comprehensive Approach

John Hamel
foreword by Donald Dutton

Partial Contents

Part I: Assessments • Domestic Violence Today • Issues and Problems in DV Assessment • Conducting DV Assessments • Special Considerations in DV Assessments

Part II: Treatment General Features • The Treatment Plan • Group Work • Family Interventions

Part III: Appendices • Appendix A: Assessment Forms • Appendix B: Victim Safety Plan • Appendix C: Client Workbook Introduction, Group Guidelines and Exercises • Appendix D: Resources and Program Agreements for Court-Ordered Clients • Appendix E: Client Exercises for High Conflict Family Violence Parent Group

2005 · 328pp · softcover · 0-8261-1873-9

11 West 42nd Street, New York, NY 10036-8002 • **Fax: 212-941-7842**
Order Toll-Free: 877-687-7476 • **Order On-line: www.springerpub.com**

The Battered Woman Syndrome
2nd Edition

Lenore E. A. Walker, EdD

In this new edition of her groundbreaking book, Dr. Lenore Walker has provided a thorough update to her original findings in the field of domestic abuse. Each chapter has been expanded to include new research. The volume contains the latest on the impact of exposure to violence on children, marital rape, child abuse, personality characteristics of different types of batterers, new psychotherapy models for batterers and their victims, and more. Walker also speaks out on her handling of the O.J. Simpson trial and how he does not fit the empirical data known for domestic violence. This volume should be required reading for all professionals in the field of domestic abuse.

Lenore E. A. Walker

THE BATTERED WOMAN SYNDROME

2ND EDITION

Partial Contents
- The Battered Women Syndrome Study
- Psychosocial Characteristics of Battered Women, Batterers, and Nonbatterers
- Behavioral Description of Violence
- Sexual Issues for Battered Women
- Impact of Violence in the Home on Children
- Violence, Alchohol and Drug Use
- Personality Characteristics and the Battered Woman Syndrome
- Learned Helplessness and Battered Women
- Walker Cycle Theory of Violence
- Future Directions for Research
- Psychotherapeutic Responses to Changing Violent Relationships
- Legal Responses to Changing Violent Behavior

1999 · 352pp · hardcover · 0-8261-4322-9

11 West 42nd Street, New York, NY 10036-8002 • **Fax: 212-941-7842**
Order Toll-Free: 877-687-7476 • **Order On-line: www.springerpub.com**